Teacher Wraparound Edition

Teen Health

Course 1

Mary H. Bronson, Ph.D.
Michael J. Cleary, Ed.D.
Betty M. Hubbard, Ed.D., C.H.E.S.

Contributing Author
Dinah Zike, M.Ed.

New York, New York   Columbus, Ohio   Chicago, Illinois   Peoria, Illinois   Woodland Hills, California

Glencoe

The **McGraw-Hill** Companies

Send all inquiries to:
Glencoe/McGraw-Hill
21600 Oxnard Street
Suite 500
Woodland Hills, California 91367

ISBN: 0-07-861095-8 (Student Edition)
ISBN: 0-07-861096-6 (Teacher Wraparound Edition)

Printed in the United States of America.

1 2 3 4 5 6 7 8 9   071/043   09 08 07 06 05 04

Contributors/Consultants

Michael Rulon
State of Wyoming SCASS Trainer
Health Educator
Johnson Junior High
Adjunct Faculty
Laramie County Community College
Cheyenne, Wyoming

Kristin Danielson Fink
Executive Director
Community of Caring
Washington, DC

Margo Harris
School and Community Health Specialist
Western Washington University
Antioch University, Seattle
Seattle, Washington

Inclusion Specialist
Patricia Sullivan, M.S., Special Education
Chair, Department of Language Arts
Meade Middle School
Fort Meade, Maryland

Reading Specialist
Christine A. Hayashi, M.A.Ed., J.D.
Attorney at Law, Special Education Law
Adjunct Faculty, Educational Leadership
   and Policy Studies Development
California State University, Northridge
Northridge, California

Teacher Reviewers

Debbie Baker
High School Counselor
Searcy High School
Searcy, Arkansas

Victoria E. Biscorca, C.H.E.S.
Health Instructor
California State University, Long Beach
Long Beach, California

Kim S. Bradford
Health Educator
Brawley Middle School
Mooresville, North Carolina

Debra C. Harris, Ph.D.
Department Chair
Health and Physical Education Instructor
West Linn High School
West Linn, Oregon

Cheryl Miller Page, C.H.E.S.
Health Educator
Judson Middle School
Salem, Oregon

C. Edward Pemberton
Consultant and President
Pemberton and Associates, Inc.
Health Teacher, Retired
Knox County Schools, Tennessee

Joan Stear
Health and Physical Education Educator
Andover Central Middle School
Andover, Kansas

Contents

Glencoe/McGraw-Hill's health and fitness program provides a comprehensive health curriculum for students in grades 6 through 12. *Teen Health*, the three-volume series for students in grades 6 through 8, combines scientifically accurate, age-appropriate health content with extensive instruction, practice, and application of the skills necessary to achieve optimal health and wellness. This solid foundation is built upon in *Glencoe Health*, the trusted high-school program. In addition to accurate health content and health-skill practice, high-school students are given additional opportunities to apply their knowledge and skills to real-world situations. *Foundations of Personal Fitness* expands upon the physical activity and fitness content presented in the health program. It contains up-to-date information on developing and assessing every aspect of fitness, and includes detailed instruction on eating for peak performance and maintaining a healthy body weight.

Teen Health

Middle School

Chapter	Course 1 (6th grade)	Course 2 (7th grade)	Course 3 (8th grade)
1	Living a Healthy Life	Learning About Your Health	Understanding Your Health
2	Mental and Emotional Health	Taking Responsibility for Your Health	Health Skills: The Foundation
3	Social Health	Physical Activity and Fitness	Being a Health Consumer
4	Personal Health	Food and Nutrition	Mental and Emotional Health
5	Nutrition and Physical Activity	Personal Health and Consumer Choices	Promoting Social Health
6	Growth and Development	Growth and Development	Relationships: The Teen Years
7	Preventing Diseases	Mental and Emotional Health	Conflict Resolution
8	Tobacco	Social Health: Family and Friends	Nutrition for Health
9	Alcohol and Other Drugs	Resolving Conflicts and Preventing Violence	Physical Activity and Fitness
10	Safety and the Environment	Tobacco	Your Body Image
11		Drugs and Alcohol	Medicines and Drugs
12		Understanding Communicable Diseases	Tobacco
13		Noncommunicable Diseases	Alcohol
14		Personal Safety and Injury Prevention	Personal Care
15		The Environment and Your Health	Your Body Systems
16			Growth and Development
17			Communicable Diseases
18			Noncommunicable Diseases
19			Safety and Emergencies
20			Environmental Health

Health and Fitness Program

Glencoe Health and Foundations of Personal Fitness

High School

Chapter	Glencoe Health	Foundations of Personal Fitness
1	Living a Healthy Life	Physical Activity and Personal Fitness
2	Building Health Skills and Character	Safety and Injury Prevention
3	Being a Health-Literate Consumer	Designing a Personal Fitness Program
4	Physical Activity for Life	Nutrition and Your Personal Fitness
5	Nutrition and Your Health	Your Body Composition
6	Managing Weight and Body Composition	Maintaining a Healthy Body Weight
7	Achieving Good Mental Health	Basics of Cardiorespiratory Endurance
8	Managing Stress and Anxiety	Developing Cardiorespiratory Endurance
9	Mental and Emotional Problems	Basics of Resistance Training
10	Skills for Healthy Relationships	Developing Muscular Fitness
11	Family Relationships	Basics of Flexibility
12	Peer Relationships	Personal Fitness Throughout Life
13	Violence Prevention	
14	Personal Care and Healthy Behaviors	
15	Skeletal, Muscular, and Nervous Systems	
16	Cardiovascular and Respiratory Systems	
17	Digestive and Urinary Systems	
18	Endocrine and Reproductive Systems	
19	Prenatal Development and Birth	
20	Adolescence and the Life Cycle	
21	Tobacco	
22	Alcohol	
23	Medicines and Drugs	
24	Communicable Diseases	
25	Sexually Transmitted Infections and HIV/AIDS	
26	Noncommunicable Diseases and Disabilities	
27	Injury Prevention and Safe Behaviors	
28	First Aid and Emergencies	
29	Environmental Health	

The Student Edition at a Glance

The *Teen Health* Student Edition is organized around ten chapters, each containing independent lessons. The content introduces students to a comprehensive, skills-based health program with an emphasis on abstinence from high-risk behaviors. By laying the foundation for building lifelong health skills, the Student Edition helps students make positive health choices.

Chapter Opener

Each chapter opens with two introductory, motivational activities.

The **Health Online** feature incorporates technology and invites students to take an online health inventory to evaluate their current health knowledge and behaviors.

The **Foldables** activity provides students with step-by-step instructions and illustrations for creating an innovative hands-on study tool.

Teaching Health Skills

With the increasing attention given to skill development, students learn and practice ways to make healthy choices. Each chapter includes opportunities for students to apply, practice, and assess the skills they need to enhance their own and others' health.

Health Skills Activities help students learn to choose the behaviors that protect, promote, and maintain health and to avoid high-risk behaviors. Each activity provides students with an opportunity to practice skill development.

Communicating with Others

The next group of skills involves the way you communicate with other people. Communication is the clear exchange of ideas and information. That means telling others how you feel and listening to and understanding how they feel.

- **Refusal Skills.** Sometimes, you have to say no to others. For example, people you know may try to pressure you into doing something that you think is wrong. Refusal skills help you say no in an effective way without feeling uncomfortable. This is a method of practicing self-control, and a strategy for coping with potentially unsafe situations.
- **Conflict Resolution.** When you have conflicts, or disagreements, with others, it's best to settle them in a way that satisfies everyone. Conflict resolution usually requires talking matters over calmly and reasonably. Everyone must work together to find a solution to the problem.

HEALTH SKILLS ACTIVITY

COMMUNICATION SKILLS

When Friends Change

Tia and Carlos have been friends since second grade. Lately, though, Tia has noticed a change in Carlos. The two friends used to meet at their lockers after school and talk about what happened that day. Twice in the last week, Carlos told Tia he would be there, but then he didn't show up. The last time it happened, Tia had something important to tell Carlos. The next day, she heard from another friend that Carlos had told people that Tia was boring. What should Tia do?

What Would You Do?

Write a dialogue between Tia and Carlos. Have Tia tell Carlos how she feels about his behavior. Then have Carlos explain why he is acting that way. Use the speaking skills shown below.

- Use clear, simple statements.
- State your thoughts and feelings honestly.
- Make eye contact, and use appropriate body language.

Your friendships also become very important to you. In early adolescence, you may be strongly influenced by your friends. You may be part of a group that does everything together. Later on, you may break away from the group and form closer friendships with one or two individuals.

As you mature, you will worry less about your friends' approval and rely more on your own standards. By the end of your teens, you will be able to function on your own. You will have formed your own ideas about who you are and how you fit into the world. In short, you will be independent.

Hands-On Health are science-based health activities and hands-on experiments that require little or no scientific equipment. These activities give students a chance to learn through action while personalizing the concepts presented in the chapters.

Hands-On Health

LOOKING AHEAD

Every day, you show in many ways how you are growing into a healthy, mature adult. This activity will help you recognize some of these changes in yourself.

WHAT YOU WILL NEED
- a pencil or pen
- a sheet of paper

WHAT YOU WILL DO
1. Number the paper 1–10.
2. Read through the list below. It describes many kinds of mature behavior. For each numbered item in the list, try to think of an example from your life.
3. Write down each of your examples on the line with the same number as the statement. Don't worry if you can't think of an example for every statement—just fill in as many as you can.

BECOMING AN ADULT
1. I think about the consequences before I act.
2. I do what I think is right even when it is hard.
3. I feel comfortable with who I am; I don't try to be something I'm not.

4. I respect other people's ideas even when they are different from mine.
5. I think about how my actions affect other people.
6. My parents and I show respect when we talk to one another.
7. I take time to listen to other people's problems.
8. I try to see situations from the viewpoint of my parents and other adults.
9. I think about how the choices I make now will affect my future.
10. I have a good idea of the kind of adult I would like to be.

IN CONCLUSION
1. Discuss your answers as a class. You do not have to share all of your answers unless you choose to.
2. With your classmates, brainstorm more examples of mature and responsible behavior.

TIME Health

TIME Health features are fun, educational articles developed for a middle-school audience by *TIME* magazine. Appearing at the end of each chapter, these colorful two-page spread features will engage student interest and increase familiarity with a journalistic writing style. Each feature is tailored to fit the content of a particular chapter and contains an activity to help students apply what they have learned. Many contain infographics and diagrams, giving students the opportunity to practice reading charts and graphs.

Article text
Contains up-to-date information on a specific health topic, written in a way that will appeal to teens and help them hone their media literacy and critical-thinking skills.

Diagrams, charts, and graphs
Present key health information in a high-interest format to enhance recall of facts and give students practice in evaluating information that is presented visually.

Time to Think...
Helps students develop reading comprehension skills by giving them the opportunity to apply what they have learned to a relevant activity.

Building Health Skills

At the end of every chapter, there is a Building Health Skills activity feature that addresses a skill identified in the National Health Education Standards. Created with teens in mind, they include colorful, lively designs intended to grab students' attention. These two-page features reinforce chapter content. A performance task is included at the end of each feature. The task measures the extent to which individual skills have been achieved. Building Health Skills can also be taught independently as hands-on skills lessons.

Practice
Students are given opportunities to practice the skill.

BUILDING HEALTH SKILLS — PRACTICING HEALTHFUL BEHAVIORS

KEEPING BODY SYSTEMS HEALTHY

Model
Terry is a teen athlete. He knows that he needs to keep his body systems healthy to be able to stay in shape for his sports activities. This year, he is playing basketball and running track. Because these activities require strong lungs, he takes good care of his respiratory system. He always sits in the nonsmoking section of restaurants, and his parents do not allow guests to smoke in their house. He plans his outdoor activities for times when the air quality is good. Whenever he has a cough or cold, Terry rests and drinks plenty of fluids until he is well. These behaviors help him play better and also improve his total health.

Practice
Form small groups. Choose one of the body systems you have learned about in this chapter. Write the name of that body system at the top of a sheet of paper. Then divide the paper into two columns labeled *Healthful Habits* and *Harmful Habits*. Use the first column to identify habits that can benefit your chosen body system. Use the second column to list habits that can harm that body system. At the bottom of the page, write a statement explaining why it is important to care for this body system.

Apply/Assess
Working with your group, create a news report about how to keep your body systems healthy. Your report should be three to five minutes long and should be in a style similar to a television news broadcast. In your report, describe at least three ways to care for all of your body systems. Include an explanation of how these three behaviors can benefit specific body systems. Present your report to the class.

STAY ACTIVE

AVOID HARMFUL SUBSTANCES

EAT HEALTHY FOODS

TAKE CARE OF ILLNESS

MANAGE STRESS

176 CHAPTER 6: GROWTH AND DEVELOPMENT

Model
Students are presented with positive role-modeling of the featured skill.

Apply/Assess
Finally, students perform the skill on their own and evaluate their performance.

Developing Good Character
Highlights core character traits to promote the integration of values into the health curriculum.

Developing Good Character

Respect
All people want respect and are likely to respond well when they receive it. Everyday courtesy and good manners are a show of respect. Practicing them can help you avoid conflicts. *With your classmates, discuss how common gestures of courtesy might help prevent conflict.*

MEDIA WATCH

WATCHING FOR CHARACTER
Many television programs feature teens or children. Some of these young people have positive character traits such as responsibility and trustworthiness. Others act irresponsibly or dishonestly. *How do your favorite TV programs show young people?*

Media Watch
Raises students' awareness about the media's impact on their lives and health.

CONNECT TO

Social Studies

WHAT'S YOUR ANTI-DRUG? In 2000, the National Youth Anti-Drug Media Campaign asked young people between the ages of 10 and 17 to tell what stood between them and drugs. Thousands responded with essays, poems, videos, paintings, music, and even single-word answers. From friends and family to singing and sports, these kids showed that most young people don't use drugs. *How would you respond?*

Connect to...
Provides cross-curriculum activities to help students see how health is related to other curriculum areas such as science, mathematics, language arts, and social studies.

Support for the Health Teacher

The Teacher Wraparound Edition provides complete lesson plans, teaching suggestions, supplemental information, cross-references, lesson and chapter review answers, and more—all conveniently "wrapped" around every page of the reduced Student Edition. Teachers will discover that the consistent, easy-to-follow lesson plan format gives a variety of teaching strategies to motivate students; to introduce, teach, and reinforce concepts; and to provide alternative teaching strategies for adapting the program to meet the individual needs of students.

Chapter Opener includes the following:
- Chapter at a Glance
- Health Skills
- Chapter Introduction
- Health Online
- Glencoe Technology
- TIME Health
- Foldables

Hands-On Activity Every chapter jump-starts with a motivational hands-on activity intended to make students active participants in their health education.

Organized with the Teacher in Mind

Lesson Plans

The teaching material follows a consistent, easy-to-use pattern. The complete lesson cycle—1. FOCUS, 2. TEACH, 3. ASSESS, and 4. CLOSE—make it easy for you to plan a lesson. Included in the lesson plan you will find:

1 FOCUS

- A list of student objectives
- Motivator activities—select from a Quick Write, which corresponds to the Student Edition, or a Bellringer activity
- A Vocabulary activity to help students build vocabulary skills

2 TEACH

Various activities related to the lesson's content have been identified by one of four codes (**L1** **L2** **L3** **INCL**) to give you an idea of their suitability for students of varying learning styles and abilities.

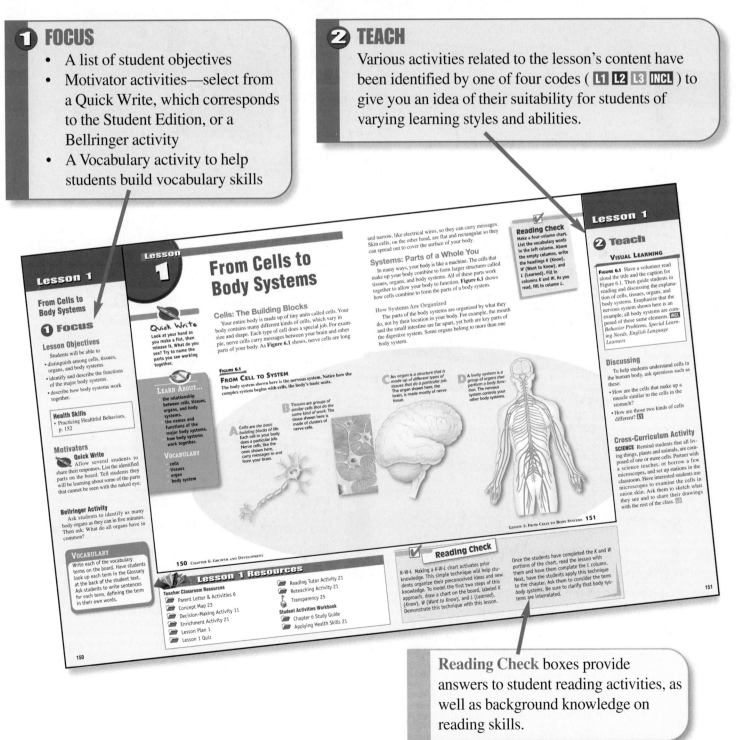

Reading Check boxes provide answers to student reading activities, as well as background knowledge on reading skills.

Teacher Wraparound Edition

❸ ASSESS

- Assessment techniques including strategies for reteaching students who have difficulty mastering the important lesson concepts
- Enrichment activities designed for students who are able to explore the content further

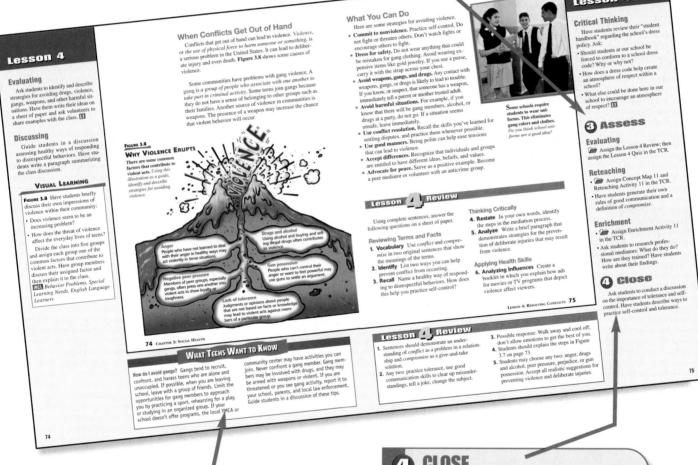

Lesson 4

Evaluating

Ask students to identify and describe strategies for avoiding drugs, violence, gangs, weapons, and other harmful situations. Have them write their ideas on a sheet of paper and ask volunteers to share examples with the class. **L1**

Discussing

Guide students in a discussion assessing healthy ways of responding to disrespectful behaviors. Have students write a paragraph summarizing the class discussion.

VISUAL LEARNING

FIGURE 3.8 Have students briefly discuss their own impressions of violence within their community:

- Does violence seem to be an increasing problem?
- How does the threat of violence affect the everyday lives of teens?

Divide the class into five groups and assign each group one of the common factors that contribute to violent acts. Have group members discuss their assigned factor and then explain it to the class. **INCL** *Behavior Problems, Special Learning Needs, English Language Learners*

When Conflicts Get Out of Hand

Conflicts that get out of hand can lead to violence. Violence, or *the use of physical force to harm someone or something,* is a serious problem in the United States. It can lead to deliberate injury and even death. **Figure 3.8** shows some causes of violence.

Some communities have problems with gang violence. A gang is *a group of people who associate with one another to take part in criminal activity.* Some teens join gangs because they do not have a sense of belonging to other groups such as their families. Another source of violence in communities is weapons. The presence of a weapon may increase the chance that violent behavior will occur.

FIGURE 3.8

WHY VIOLENCE ERUPTS
There are some common factors that contribute to violent acts. *Using this illustration as a guide, identify and describe strategies for avoiding violence.*

Anger People who have not learned to deal with their anger in healthy ways may act violently in tense situations.

Negative peer pressure Members of peer groups, especially gangs, often press one another into violent acts to show loyalty or toughness.

Drugs and alcohol Using alcohol and buying and selling illegal drugs often contributes to violence.

Gun possession People who can't control their anger or want to feel powerful may use guns to settle an argument.

Lack of tolerance Judgments or opinions about people that are not based on facts or knowledge may lead to violent acts against members of a particular group.

74 CHAPTER 3: Social Health

What You Can Do

Here are some strategies for avoiding violence.

- **Commit to nonviolence.** Practice self-control. Do not fight or threaten others. Don't watch fights or encourage others to fight.
- **Dress for safety.** Do not wear anything that could be mistaken for gang clothing. Avoid wearing expensive items like gold jewelry. If you use a purse, carry it with the strap across your chest.
- **Avoid weapons, gangs, and drugs.** Any contact with weapons, gangs, or drugs is likely to lead to trouble. If you know, or suspect, that someone has a weapon, immediately tell a parent or another trusted adult.
- **Avoid harmful situations.** For example, if you know that there will be gang members, alcohol, or drugs at a party, do not go. If a situation seems unsafe, leave immediately.
- **Use conflict resolution.** Recall the skills you've learned for settling disputes, and practice them whenever possible.
- **Use good manners.** Being polite can help ease tensions that can lead to violence.
- **Accept differences.** Recognize that individuals and groups are entitled to have different ideas, beliefs, and values.
- **Advocate for peace.** Serve as a positive example. Become a peer mediator or volunteer with an anticrime group.

Some schools require students to wear uniforms. This eliminates gang colors and clothes. *Do you think school uniforms are a good idea?*

Lesson 4 Review

Using complete sentences, answer the following questions on a sheet of paper.

Reviewing Terms and Facts

1. **Vocabulary** Use *conflict* and *compromise* in two original sentences that show the meanings of the terms.
2. **Identify** List two ways you can help prevent conflict from occurring.
3. **Recall** Name a healthy way of responding to disrespectful behaviors. How does this help you practice self-control?

Thinking Critically

4. **Restate** In your own words, identify the steps in the mediation process.
5. **Analyze** Write a brief paragraph that demonstrates strategies for the prevention of deliberate injuries that may result from violence.

Applying Health Skills

6. **Analyzing Influences** Create a booklet in which you explain how ads for movies or TV programs that depict violence affect viewers.

LESSON 4: RESOLVING CONFLICTS 75

Lesson 4

Critical Thinking

Have students review their "student handbook" regarding the school's dress policy. Ask:

- Should students at our school be forced to conform to a school dress code? Why or why not?
- How does a dress code help create an atmosphere of respect within a school?
- What else could be done here in our school to encourage an atmosphere of respect? **L1**

❸ Assess

Evaluating

📁 Assign the Lesson 4 Review; then assign the Lesson 4 Quiz in the TCR.

Reteaching

- 📁 Assign Concept Map 11 and Reteaching Activity 11 in the TCR.
- Have students generate their own rules of good communication and a definition of *compromise.*

Enrichment

- 📁 Assign Enrichment Activity 11 in the TCR.
- Ask students to research professional mediators: What do they do? How are they trained? Have students write about their findings.

❹ Close

Ask students to conduct a discussion on the importance of tolerance and self-control. Have students describe ways to practice self-control and tolerance.

WHAT TEENS WANT TO KNOW

How do I avoid gangs? Gangs tend to recruit, confront, and harass teens who are alone and unoccupied. If possible, when you are leaving school, leave with a group of friends. Limit the opportunities for gang members to approach you by practicing a sport, rehearsing for a play, or studying in an organized group. If your school doesn't offer programs, the local YMCA or community center may have activities you can join. Never confront a gang member. Gang members may be involved with drugs, and they may be armed with weapons or violent. If you are threatened or you see gang activity, report it to your school, parents, and local law enforcement. Guide students in a discussion of these tips.

Lesson 4 Review

1. Sentences should demonstrate an understanding of *conflict* as a problem in a relationship and *compromise* as a give-and-take solution.
2. Any two: practice tolerance, use good communication skills to clear up misunderstandings, tell a joke, change the subject.
3. Possible response: Walk away and cool off; don't allow emotions to get the best of you.
4. Students should explain the steps in Figure 3.7 on page 73.
5. Students may choose any two: anger, drugs and alcohol, peer pressure, prejudice, or gun possession. Accept all realistic suggestions for preventing violence and deliberate injuries.

❹ CLOSE

An activity that brings closure to the lesson and recaps important concepts from the lesson.

What Teens Want to Know are Q & A features that explore teen-oriented issues. Use these features to respond to student questions and concerns with reliable answers.

Developing Good Character
These features offer teachers character education support and activity ideas.

Developing Good Character ★

Responsibility
As an extension to the activity in the student text, have students take a piece of paper and fold it in half, and then in fourths. On each fourth, have them write headings for different areas of responsibility they have in their lives. Examples might include: responsibility to family, to friends, to school, to self. Ask if they hold any other areas of responsibility. Have students make a list of ways they will be responsible in each area.

Health Online
Each Health Online box offers ways for teachers to access and make use of Glencoe's Health Web site. Students are encouraged to explore Web Links to complete a hands-on activity specifically related to the health content of a lesson.

HEALTH Online
By visiting the Web Links for this chapter at **health.glencoe.com**, students will discover how to resist negative peer pressure. Encourage them to read the article and then complete the activity.

Health Skills Activity
These boxes provide step-by-step reinforcement for student skills-based activities.

HEALTH SKILLS ACTIVITY

ACCESSING INFORMATION
Let volunteers describe the two containers of liquid soap pictured here. Ask students which they would like to buy. Why?

Help students read and discuss the activity introduction. Have students work independently to write their answers to the On Your Own questions; then have students compare and discuss their responses.

Note: This skill is introduced in Chapter 1 on page 9.

Bottom Column Annotations
Boxes at the bottom of the page give you additional information related to the content of the Student Edition. This information supplements the core lesson plan by focusing on various areas of interest. The categories include:

- Inclusion Strategies
- Cultural Perspectives
- Hands-On Activity
- Reading Check
- What Teens Want to Know
- More About. . .
- Health Literacy
- Beyond the Classroom
- Cooperative Learning Activity
- Dealing with Sensitive Issues
- Promoting Coordinated School Health
- Answers to Lesson Review

Health Literacy
Health Influences Psychoneuroimmunology (PNI) is the science that describes the brain's ability to send signals to immune-system produces many substances that enhance health. Feelings of optimism about health and positive expectations can boost naturally occurring substances in the body, such as endorphins, to relieve pain, support the and fight viral and bacterial tes know that positive atti- tations affect performance utcome of an athlete's game.

Beyond the Classroom
Community Divide the class into two research committees. One of the committees is to compile a list of people and places within the community that students can turn to when feeling stress. The list, which is to include phone numbers and, when relevant, addresses, may include outreach centers, neighborhood clubs with gym facilities that welcome young people, counselors in free clinics, and laypeople and members of the clergy. The other committee is to put together a list of original relaxation strategies that also make use of community resources, including playgrounds and interesting locations where people can hike, climb, or simply relax amid peaceful surroundings.

INCLUSION S
Emotionally Disturbed, Special Learning Needs Often, students with attention deficit/hyperactivity disorder, emotional disturbances, or learning disabilities have poor communication skills, which leads to difficulty with both peer and teacher relationships. These students will need good modeling and extra practice with pitch, voice tone, and rate of speaking.

Ra
su
students the choice to role-play the dialogue. This modification of the assignment will support students who have difficulty writing and will allow students to practice much-needed social skills.

Activities

Building Health Skills Activities further reinforce skill development with Reproducible Masters and Transparency Masters that correspond to the activities at the end of every chapter and on the Web site. Guide students in applying health skills with step-by-step teaching suggestions.

Concept-Mapping Activities provide a developmental approach for students to practice concept mapping. They can be used to preview or review a lesson's content by visually reinforcing main ideas and clarifying relationships.

Cross-Curriculum Activities give students an opportunity to relate health information to the content of other subject areas including math, social studies, language arts, science, and the arts.

Decision-Making Activities give students an opportunity to practice the decision-making process as they consider a variety of hypothetical situations.

Enrichment Activities allow students the opportunity to explore lesson concepts further. Answers for the teacher are provided at the back of the booklet.

Health Labs give students experience with making observations and hypotheses, collecting and recording data, and forming conclusions based on analysis and interpretations of experimental results. Teacher pages provide help and answers to questions.

Guide to Using the Internet provides strategies for integrating Internet activities in the health classroom.

Reading Tutor helps students develop their reading skills. It outlines the essential information in each lesson of *Teen Health* and contains all vocabulary terms and definitions. The accompanying study guides can be used to review chapter content.

Reteaching Activities allow students who are having difficulty with mastering the major concepts of a lesson to review the concepts from a different perspective.

The Student Activities Workbook contains a Study Guide and Health Inventory for each chapter and an Applying Health Skills activity for each lesson. A Teacher Annotated Edition is available.

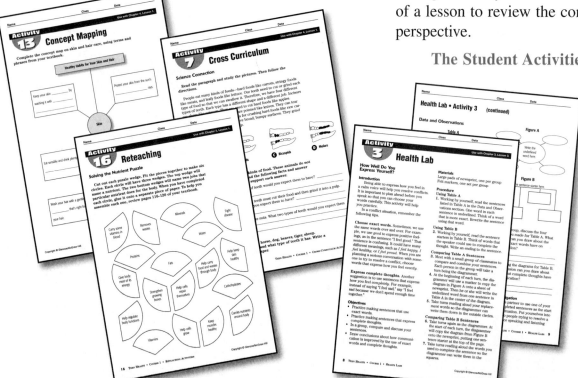

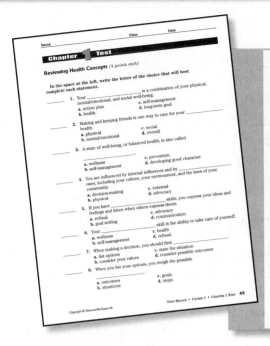

Assessment

Lesson Quizzes provide a one-page quiz for each lesson in *Teen Health*. Answers for the teacher are provided at the back of the booklet.

Chapter Tests provide two forms of tests, A and B. Either or both forms may be used as alternative or makeup tests. Answers for the teacher are provided at the back of the booklet.

Performance Assessment Activities assess learning in ways that require a student to manipulate information in flexible and creative ways.

Teaching Resources

Inclusion Strategies present detailed instructions for addressing the needs of students with different learning styles and ability levels. Specific strategies for each chapter of *Teen Health* are provided.

Reproducible Lesson Plans are provided for each lesson in Teen Health. The lesson plans include references to all resources available with *Teen Health*.

The Teaching Transparencies Binder includes 48 transparencies plus an activity booklet complete with teaching strategies for use with the transparencies.

Parent Letters and Activities include introductory teacher material about how to use these letters and how to inform parents or guardians of the instructional program and assessment techniques to be employed. This material appears in English and Spanish.

Summaries, Quizzes, and Activities include brief summaries of each of the ten chapters of Teen Health. The summaries are followed by quizzes and activities that help students grasp the chapter content and assess their knowledge. Answers for the teacher are provided at the back of the booklet. Both English and Spanish versions are available. (Accompanied by audio summaries.)

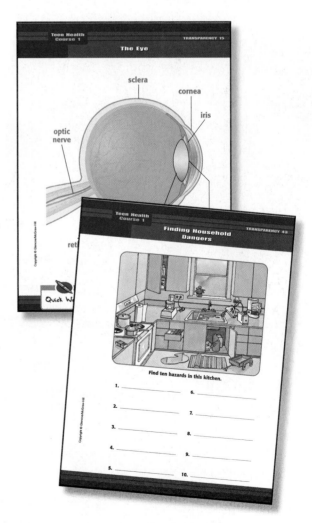

Student Edition

La Salud de los Jóvenes is a complete Spanish translation of the English student edition. It will provide your Spanish-speaking students with the comprehensive health information and instruction in skill development they need for maximum wellness. The attractive photo and illustration program, engaging infographics, and fun hands-on activities will appeal to and motivate your Spanish-speaking students.

Video and DVD Series

Complete translations of each English segment in the three-volume series provide valuable information for today's teens. The content is presented in the following formats to maintain student interest: dramatizations and panel discussions, informative teen talk shows, and informal peer-group discussions.

Summaries, Quizzes, and Activities

Summaries, quizzes, and activities give Spanish-speaking students additional practice in comprehending and applying the main points of each chapter. Answer keys are provided at the back of the booklet. (Accompanied by audio summaries)

Vocabulary PuzzleMaker

Create custom crossword and word-search puzzles completely in Spanish to help your Spanish-speaking students learn important health vocabulary terms.

Parent Letters and Activities

These letters and activities allow you to keep Spanish-speaking parents informed about course content and encourage them to participate in their child's health education.

Media and Technology Resources

Teen Health MindJogger Videoquiz

Teen Health **MindJogger Videoquiz** presents chapter quizzes in a fun, video-gameshow format. Available on both videocassettes and DVDs, the videoquizzes may be used for self-assessment or as an opportunity to preview or review chapter content.

Teen Health Video and DVD Series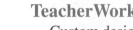

Enliven classroom discussions with this three-volume series. Dramatizations and panel discussions, informative teen talk shows, and peer-group discussions are featured on a variety of topics relevant in the lives of today's teens. Both English and Spanish versions are available.

Nutrition and Physical Activity: On Your Own Explorations

Take students on an interactive journey through a typical Friday and Saturday in a teen's life with this multimedia CD-ROM program. Students will make critical decisions about food intake and physical activity and evaluate these choices to make sure that they are the most healthful ones.

Vocabulary PuzzleMaker

Build vocabulary skills with custom-designed puzzles. Create word searches and crossword puzzles using vocabulary words from each lesson in the text. Both English and Spanish versions are included on one CD-ROM.

Teen Health at health.glencoe.com

The *Teen Health* homepage at health.glencoe.com provides up-to-date resources and activities to complement Glencoe's comprehensive health program. The site includes fun and interactive online games and study tools for students, as well as links to informative health Web sites. Teachers can access a wealth of additional activities to enhance the student text, along with correlations to standards and professional articles.

Interactive Online Student Edition

Now students and teachers can access the entire text of *Teen Health* Course 1 from our Web site at

health.glencoe.com—every chapter and lesson, including all Health Inventories, activities, and Web links! Navigate from the table of contents directly to the lesson you need. Find every Lesson Review and Chapter Assessment for homework, review, and study convenience.

TeacherWorks™

Custom design your lesson plan with this easy-to-use CD-ROM. The electronic format allows teachers to select a pre-set plan or to create their own—either way, it offers access to electronic files of all reproducible resources at the click of a button.

Exam*View*® Pro Testmaker

This computer software test bank for Macintosh and IBM-compatible computers provides questions in various formats and the capability to add your own questions.

Audio Summaries (English, Spanish)

The audio CDs contain summaries of chapter content for review, for reteaching, or for use when you do not have time to teach a particular chapter. Each summary is accompanied by a chapter activity and test based on the content of the audio CD. Spanish summaries are also provided.

Teaching Transparencies Binder

This convenient three-ring binder contains 48 full-color transparencies and a *Teaching Strategies and Activities Instructor Guide*.

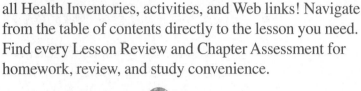

GLENCOE TECHNOLOGY

Teen Health Video and DVD Series
(Each format available in both English and Spanish)

 You may wish to use:

- Tape/DVD 1, Segment 5, "Body Image and Media Influences"
- Tape/DVD 1, Segment 6, "Nutrition and Physical Activity"

MindJogger Videoquiz

 Use MindJogger to preview or review Chapter 5 content.

Inclusion Strategies

How Does *Teen Health* Make Health Accessible for All Students?

The Inclusion Strategies teacher resource booklet offers a variety of activities for every learning style and ability level. In addition, the *Teen Health* program incorporates a wealth of resources specifically designed to help students of every learning style and ability level succeed in achieving health literacy.

ADDRESSING STUDENT NEEDS	STUDENT EDITION	TEACHER WRAPAROUND EDITION (TWE)	TEACHER CLASSROOM RESOURCES (TCR)
Different Learning Styles	**Illustration program** is rich in variety and diversity. **Charts and tables** visually present materials for quick assimilation. **Vocabulary terms** are highlighted in blue. **Clearly marked heads**, subheads, and bulleted lists outline content. **Health Skills Activities** encourage alternative demonstration of health concepts. **Hands-On Health Activities** actively engage students of all learning styles.	**Inclusion Strategies** are specifically written and labeled for different learning styles, including bodily-kinesthetic and visual learners. **Teaching Strategies** are coded Level 1, Level 2, and Level 3 for students of all ability levels. **Quick Demos** capture students' attention with teacher demonstrations. **Assessment Options** include a variety of formats.	Concept-Mapping Activities Cross-Curriculum Activities Decision-Making Activities Enrichment Activities Health Labs Reteaching Activities Audio Summaries Full-Color Transparencies Performance Assessment MindJogger Videoquiz
Physically, Visually, Hearing Impaired	**Quick Write** gets students thinking about the health topics before they begin. **Illustrations** focus on important content.	**Inclusion Strategies** are specifically written and labeled for students with various physical and mental impairments. **Teaching Strategies** coded Level 1 provide options for teacher-directed activities. **Visual Learning** strategies present important concepts in an easily accessible visual format.	Reteaching Activities Concept-Mapping Activities Decision-Making Activities Audio Summaries MindJogger Videoquiz Reading Tutor Vocabulary PuzzleMaker
Gifted Students	**Enrichment Activities** give students an opportunity to extend their knowledge. **Applying Health Skills** activities encourage alternative demonstration of health concepts.	**Inclusion Strategies** are specifically written and labeled for gifted students. **Teaching Strategies** coded L3 are appropriate for independent learners. **Critical Thinking** strategies challenge students with additional questions and situations. **Researching** activities provide further learning opportunities. **Health Literacy** provides expanded ideas and activities for the self-directed learner.	Enrichment Activities Cross-Curriculum Activities Health Labs Student Activity Workbook for independent study Performance Assessment

English Language Learners	**Vocabulary terms** are highlighted in blue. **Vocabulary review** is presented for each lesson. **Spanish Glosario** helps students learn each vocabulary term. *La Salud de los Jóvenes* motivates students and helps them become immersed in the health content.	**Inclusion Strategies** are specifically written and labeled for English Language Learners.	Spanish Audio Summaries Spanish Summaries, Quizzes, and Activities Reading Tutor Spanish Vocabulary PuzzleMaker Parent Letters and Activities (Spanish)
Learning Disabled	**Quick Write** captures student interest and engages them in reading and writing. **Charts and tables** visually present concepts for quick assimilation. **Vocabulary terms** are highlighted in blue. **Clearly marked heads**, subheads, and bulleted lists outline content.	**Vocabulary strategies** are presented for each lesson. **Reteaching strategies** reinforce lesson content before moving on.	Cross-Curriculum Activities Reteaching Activities Concept-Mapping Activities Reading Tutor Health Labs Audio Summaries Vocabulary PuzzleMaker MindJogger Videoquiz
Behavioral Disorders	**Short, focused lessons** hold students' attention. **Clearly marked heads**, subheads, and bulleted lists outline content. **Charts and tables** visually present concepts for quick assimilation. **Illustrations** focus on important content. **Health Skills Activities** and **Building Health Skills** develop important skills that can be practiced and applied to real-life situations. **Hands-On Health** activities actively engage students in health skills practice.	**Inclusion Strategies** are specifically written and labeled for students with behavioral disorders. **Cooperative Learning Activities** foster teamwork and assign specific roles to students who need focus. **Quick Demos** allow teachers to present hands-on demonstrations. **What Teens Want to Know** brings relevance to specific health topics.	Reteaching Activities Concept-Mapping Activities Decision-Making Activities Full-Color Transparencies Audio Summaries MindJogger Videoquiz Vocabulary PuzzleMaker *Professional Series:* Planning a Coordinated School Health Program Dealing with Sensitive Issues
At-Risk Students	**Short, focused lessons** hold students' attention. **Charts and tables** visually present concepts for quick assimilation. **Applying Health Skills** encourage alternative demonstration of health knowledge. **Health Skills Activities** and **Building Health Skills** develop important skills that can be practiced and applied to real-life situations.	**Inclusion Strategies** are specifically written and labeled for at-risk students. **Dealing with Sensitive Issues** provides strategies for at-risk students.	Decision-Making Activities Parent Letters and Activities Reteaching Activities Audio Summaries MindJogger Videoquiz Vocabulary PuzzleMaker

Teen Health Meets the National Health Education Standards

The National Health Education Standards were created with the goal of improving educational achievement for students and improving health in the United States through the promotion of health literacy. The seven Health Standards are each divided into several performance indicators.

Health Education Standard 1:

Students will comprehend concepts related to health promotion and disease prevention.

Performance Indicators:

As a result of health instruction in Grades 5-8, students will:

1.1 Explain the relationship between positive health behaviors and the prevention of injury, illness, disease and premature death.

1.2 Describe the interrelationship of mental, emotional, social and physical health during adolescence.

1.3 Explain how health is influenced by the interaction of body systems.

1.4 Describe how family and peers influence the health of adolescents.

1.5 Analyze how environment and personal health are interrelated.

1.6 Describe ways to reduce risks related to adolescent health problems.

1.7 Explain how appropriate health care can prevent premature death and disability.

1.8 Describe how lifestyle, pathogens, family history, and other risk factors are related to the cause or prevention of disease and other health problems.

Health Education Standard 2:

Students will demonstrate the ability to access valid health information and health-promoting products and services.

Performance Indicators:

As a result of health instruction in Grades 5-8, students will:

2.1 Analyze the validity of health information, products, and services.

2.2 Demonstrate the ability to utilize resources from home, school, and community that provide valid health information.

2.3 Analyze how media influences the selection of health information and products.

2.4 Demonstrate the ability to locate health products and services.

2.5 Compare the costs and validity of health products.

2.6 Describe situations requiring professional health services.

Health Education Standard 3:

Students will demonstrate the ability to practice health-enhancing behaviors and reduce health risks.

Performance Indicators:

As a result of health instruction in Grades 5-8, students will:

3.1 Explain the importance of assuming responsibility for personal health behaviors.

3.2 Analyze a personal health assessment to determine health strengths and risks.

3.3 Distinguish between safe and risky or harmful behaviors in relationships.

3.4 Demonstrate strategies to improve or maintain personal and family health.

3.5 Develop injury prevention and management strategies for personal and family health.

3.6 Demonstrate ways to avoid and reduce threatening situations.

3.7 Demonstrate strategies to manage stress.

Health Education Standard 4:

Students will analyze the influence of culture, media, technology, and other factors on health.

Performance Indicators:

As a result of health instruction in Grades 5-8, students will:

4.1 Describe the influence of cultural beliefs on health behaviors and the use of health services.

4.2 Analyze how messages from media and other sources influence health behaviors.

4.3 Analyze the influence of technology on personal and family health.

4.4 Analyze how information from peers influences health.

Health Education Standard 5:

Students will demonstrate the ability to use interpersonal communication skills to enhance health.

Performance Indicators:

As a result of health instruction in Grades 5-8, students will:

5.1 Demonstrate effective verbal and non-verbal communication skills to enhance health.

5.2 Describe how the behavior of family and peers affects interpersonal communication.

5.3 Demonstrate healthy ways to express needs, wants, and feelings.

5.4 Demonstrate ways to communicate care, consideration, and respect of self and others.

5.5 Demonstrate communication skills to build and maintain healthy relationships.

5.6 Demonstrate refusal and negotiation skills to enhance health.

5.7 Analyze the possible causes of conflict among youth in schools and communities.

5.8 Demonstrate strategies to manage conflict in healthy ways.

Health Education Standard 6:

Students will demonstrate the ability to use goal setting and decision-making skills to enhance health.

Performance Indicators:

As a result of health instruction in Grades 5-8, students will:

6.1 Demonstrate the ability to apply a decision-making process to health issues and problems individually and collaboratively.

6.2 Analyze how health-related decisions are influenced by individuals, family, and community values.

6.3 Predict how decisions regarding health behaviors have consequences for self and others.

6.4 Apply strategies and skills needed to attain personal health goals.

6.5 Describe how personal health goals are influenced by changing information, abilities, priorities, and responsibilities.

6.6 Develop a plan that addresses personal strengths, needs, and health risks.

Health Education Standard 7:

Students will demonstrate the ability to advocate for personal, family, and community health.

Performance Indicators:

As a result of health instruction in Grades 5-8, students will:

7.1 Analyze various communication methods to accurately express health information and ideas.

7.2 Express information and opinions about health issues.

7.3 Identify barriers to effective communication of information, ideas, feelings, and opinions about health issues.

7.4 Demonstrate the ability to influence and support others in making positive health choices.

7.5 Demonstrate the ability to work cooperatively when advocating for healthy individuals, families, and schools.

Correlation of National Health Education Standards

The Chapter Planning Guides in the Teacher Wraparound Edition include a lesson-by-lesson correlation of the *Teen Health* Student Edition to the National Health Education Standards. The health standards addressed are indicated by their specific performance indicator numbers.

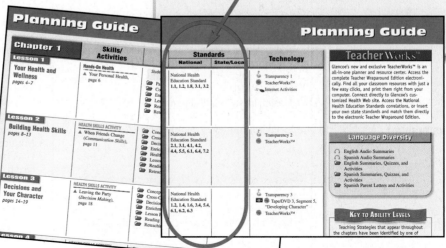

Scope and Sequence

Content Strands	Chapter 1 Living a Healthy Life	Chapter 2 Mental and Emotional Health
Personal Health	• Recognizing health and wellness (1) • Analyzing personal health behaviors (1) • Balancing the health triangle (1) • Managing stress (2) • Practicing refusal skills (2) • Analyzing influences on personal behavior (2) (BHS) • Decision-making skills for good health (2) (3) (BHS) • Risks and benefits of health behaviors (3) • Relationship of character to decision making (3) • Evaluating and adjusting personal health goals (4)	• Understanding self-concept (1) • Developing a positive self-concept (1) • Recognizing benefits of a positive self-concept (1) • Expressing emotions in healthy ways (2) (BHS) • Resisting unhealthy behaviors (2) • Practicing refusal skills (2) • Recognizing positive and negative stress (3) • Identifying stressors and their impact on health (3) • Managing stress in healthful ways (3) • Goal-setting skills to manage stress (3) • Time management skills to manage stress (BHS)
Consumer and Community Health	• Getting regular checkups (2) • Accessing reliable health information (2) • Advocating healthful behaviors and choices (2)	• Seeking health care providers to help deal with emotions (2)
Injury Prevention and Safety	• Wearing protective gear to play sports (2) • Wearing safety belts (2) • Practicing conflict resolution skills (2)	
Tobacco, Alcohol, and Other Drugs	• Avoiding use of tobacco, alcohol, and other drugs (1)	• Describing strategies such as abstinence to refuse engaging in high-risk behaviors (2)
Nutrition and Physical Activity	• Engaging in regular physical activity (1) (2) • Choosing a healthy diet (1) (2)	• Fatigue caused by stress (3) • Reducing body tension through exercise (3) • Managing stress through physical activity (3)
Environmental Health		
Family Living	• Expressing feelings in healthy ways (1) • Maintaining healthy relationships (1) (2) • Seeking input from parents in problem solving (2) • Choosing friends who avoid drugs (2) • Analyzing the influence of family and friends on health (2) (BHS) • Communication skills to express feelings (2)	• Family and friends' influences on self-concept (1) • Supporting others' self-concept through positive communication (1) • Seeking input from trusted adults to deal with emotions (2) • Showing concern for others (2) • Communication skills to deal with emotions (2)
Growth and Development	• Getting adequate rest and sleep (1) (2)	• Recognizing kinds of emotions (2) • Hormones and emotional changes (2) • Understanding interrelationships of emotions to health (2) • Describing stress and its effect on health (3)
Communicable and Noncommunicable Disease	• Handwashing to prevent illness (1) • Recognizing the importance of prevention (2)	• Describing strategies such as abstinence to refuse engaging in high-risk behaviors (2) • Relationship of illness to emotions (2)

KEY: (BHS)=Building Health Skills; (1)=Lesson 1; (2)=Lesson 2; (3)=Lesson 3, etc.

Scope and Sequence

Chapter 3 Social Health	Chapter 4 Personal Health	Chapter 5 Nutrition and Physical Activity
• Recognizing personal values and beliefs (1) • Managing anxiety and grief (1) • Expressing emotions in healthful ways (1) • Decision-making skills to handle responsibilities (1) • Understanding the impact of peer pressure on decision making (2) • Differentiating positive and negative peer pressure (2) • Practicing refusal skills (2)	• Preventing tooth and gum problems (1) • Practicing healthful behaviors for skin care (1) • Proper care of skin, nails, and hair (1) • Caring for healthy eyes and ears (2) • Decision-making skills for health products (3)	• Developing a personal dietary plan (2) • Decision-making skills for healthy eating (3) • Setting goals for healthy eating (3) • Identifying causes and effects of eating disorders (3) • Developing an individualized fitness plan (4) (5) (BHS) • Decision-making skills for physical activity (5) • Goal-setting skills for physical activity (5)
• Finding valid sources to help families with problems (1)	• Regular dental checkups (1) • Recognizing influences on consumer choices (3) • Evaluating health products (3) (BHS) • Identifying and choosing health care providers (4) • Regular physical, vision, and hearing checkups (4) • Health insurance and managed care (4)	• Analyzing food labels (1) • Social/cultural influences on dietary behavior (3) • Influence of the media on dietary behavior (3) • Developing good character by collecting food for food banks (3) • Counseling for eating disorders (3)
• Recognizing types of abuse (1) • Understanding how conflicts develop (4) • Practicing techniques to avoid interpersonal conflicts (4) • Practicing conflict resolution/mediation skills (4) (BHS)	• Protecting eyes from eyestrain (2) • Wearing safety eyewear (2) • Wearing earplugs (2)	• Preventing injury during physical activity (5) • RICE treatment (5) • Following weather safety guidelines during exercise (5)
• Recognizing the influence of drugs and alcohol on violence (4)		
• Benefits of physical activity on social health (2)	• Choosing foods for healthy teeth and skin (1) • Exercising for healthy skin (1)	• Food and energy (1) • Identifying types of nutrients (1) • Using the Food Guide Pyramid (2) • Identifying the five basic food groups (2) • Following the Dietary Guidelines (3) • Balancing food intake and physical activity (3) • Kinds of physical activity (4) • Managing stress through physical activity (4) • Choosing healthy meals and snacks (BHS)
	• Protecting skin from UV rays (1) (BHS) • Protecting eyes from UV rays (2) (BHS) • Protecting hearing from loud noises (2) • Effects of noise levels on hearing (2)	
• Recognizing family types and roles (1) • Supporting and respecting family members (1) • Describing characteristics of healthy families (1) • Coping with unhealthy family behaviors (1) • Identifying qualities of a good friend (2) • Recognizing types of communication (3) • Practicing communication skills (3) (BHS)	• Seeking input from parents on health products (BHS)	• Influence of families on dietary behavior (3)
• Understanding the importance of relationships (2)	• Recognizing long-range effects of dental hygiene (1) • Understanding parts of the skin (1) • Identifying parts of the eye and ear (2) • Describing vision problems (2) • Importance of periodic checkups (4)	• Importance of good nutrition (1) (3) • How nutrients relate to growth and health (1) • Importance of dietary and exercise plans (3) • Physical/psychological benefits of physical activity (4)
	• Formation of tooth decay and gum disease (1) • Avoiding tattoos and piercings (1) • Prevention and treatment of lice infestation (1) • Protecting eyes and ears from infection (2)	• How nutrients prevent disease (1)

Scope and Sequence

Content Strands	Chapter 6 Growth and Development	Chapter 7 Preventing Diseases
Personal Health	• Analyzing role of hormones in personal health (4) • Analyzing level of personal maturity (4) • Role of personal behavior on personality (4) • Planning strategies for healthy body systems (BHS) • Planning strategies for managing stress (BHS)	• Reducing the risk of communicable disease (2) • Practicing abstinence to avoid STDs/HIV (3) (BHS) • Avoiding high-risk behaviors for STDs/HIV (3) • Decreasing the risk of heart disease (4) • Managing stress to decrease risk of heart disease (4) • Goal-setting skills to decrease risk of disease (BHS)
Consumer and Community Health	• Blood typing by health providers (2)	• Promoting positive health behaviors (BHS) • Finding help to deal with STDs (3)
Injury Prevention and Safety	• Protecting the nervous system from injury (3)	• Preventing damage to the reproductive system by avoiding STDs (3)
Tobacco, Alcohol, and Other Drugs	• Avoiding alcohol, tobacco, and other drugs (1) (BHS)	• Relationship of alcohol and drugs to HIV/other STD transmission (3) • Avoiding alcohol or drugs to prevent HIV/other STDs (3) • Avoiding tobacco to prevent heart disease (4) • Avoiding tobacco to prevent cancer (4)
Nutrition and Physical Activity	• Eating healthful foods (1) (BHS) • Drinking adequate amounts of water (1) • Getting regular physical activity (1) • Wearing protective equipment (3) • Accepting/respecting others' body size differences (4)	• Healthy eating to prevent communicable disease (2) • Staying active to prevent communicable disease (2) • Preventing heart disease (4) • Nutrition guidelines to prevent cancer (4) • Maintaining a healthy weight to prevent diabetes (4)
Environmental Health	• Considering air quality when exercising (BHS)	• Protecting skin from the sun to prevent cancer (4) • Effects of environmental factors on asthma (4)
Family Living	• Taking responsibility as a family member (4) • Supporting and respecting family and friends (4) • Family and friends' influences on personality (4)	• Seeking input of parents in dealing with an STD (3) • Family history of cancer (4) • Influencing others to make healthy decisions (BHS)
Growth and Development	• Cells, tissues, organs, and body systems (1) • Structure/functions of skeletal, muscular, circulatory, nervous, digestive, and excretory systems (2) (3) • Structure/functions of endocrine system (4) • Changes in development during puberty (4) • Healthful behaviors for pregnant women (5) • Recognizing stages in the life cycle (5)	• Immune system and general defenses (1)
Communicable and Noncommunicable Disease	• Eating calcium-rich foods to prevent osteoporosis (2) • Testing blood for viruses (2) • Self-care when ill (BHS)	• Identifying types and transmission of pathogens (1) • Common communicable diseases (2) • Vaccines and disease prevention (2) • Identifying STDs, transmission, and treatment (3) • How HIV spreads and attacks the immune system (3) • Causes of noncommunicable diseases (4) • Types of heart disease and treatment (4) • Cancer, allergies, asthma, and diabetes (4)

KEY: (BHS)=Building Health Skills; (1)=Lesson 1; (2)=Lesson 2; (3)=Lesson 3, etc.

Scope and Sequence

Chapter 8 Tobacco	Chapter 9 Alcohol and Other Drugs	Chapter 10 Safety and the Environment
• Effects of tobacco use on personal appearance (1) • Decision-making skills to avoid tobacco use (2) • Resisting peer pressure to use tobacco (2) (BHS) • Refusal skills to avoid tobacco use (2)	• Practicing refusal skills to avoid drug use (3) (4) • Decision-making skills to avoid alcohol or other drug use (4) (BHS) • Resisting peer pressure to use alcohol or other drugs (4) • Goal setting to avoid alcohol or other drug use (BHS)	• Preventing unintentional injuries (1) (3) • Resisting peer pressure that would increase the risk of unintentional injuries (1) • Goal-setting skills to protect oneself from unintentional injuries (1) • Analyzing ways to protect the environment (5)
• Influence of the media on tobacco use (1) (2) • Advocating against tobacco use (1) • Smoking restrictions in public places (1) • Analyzing influence of advertisements on tobacco use (BHS) • Supporting others to prevent tobacco use (BHS)	• Role of FDA in drug safety (2) • Recognizing content of medicine advertisements (2) • Analyzing medicine labels (2) • Media influence on alcohol and drugs (4) • Social influences on drug-taking behaviors (4) • Services for alcohol or other drug use cessation (4)	• Community safeguards against violence (2) • Medical help for frostbite and hypothermia (3) • Influencing others to reduce waste (BHS)
• Understanding the harmful effects of tobacco on the body (1)	• Relationship of alcohol use to accidents (1) • Relationship of illegal drug use to accidents (3)	• Strategies to prevent unintentional injuries (1) • Electrical, fire, and gun safety in the home (2) • Following road and transportation safety rules (2) • Safety rules to protect against violence (2) • Practicing safety rules for outdoor activities (3) • Natural disasters and weather emergencies (3) • First-aid and minor injuries procedures (3) (4)
• Substances in tobacco (1) • Types of dependence on nicotine (1) • Economic consequences of using tobacco (1) (2) • Number of deaths related to tobacco use (1) • Reasons teens smoke (2) • How many young people use tobacco (2) • Reasons to say no to tobacco use (2)	• Effects of alcohol use and abuse (1) (BHS) • Drink equivalents and alcohol content (1) • Addiction and alcoholism (1) • Analyzing the use, misuse, abuse of medicines (2) • Types and effects of illegal drugs (3) • Benefits of not using alcohol and illegal drugs (4) • Choosing alternatives to alcohol and drug use (4)	
• Effects of tobacco on athletic performance (1) • Effects of tobacco on physical activity (2)	• Choosing safe ways to strengthen muscles (3)	• Proper sports equipment to prevent injuries (3) • Adequate food and water for outdoor safety (3) • Warming up and cooling down before and after physical activity (3) • Learning to swim as water safety precaution (3)
• Nonsmokers exposed to secondhand smoke (1) • Smoking restrictions in public places (1)		• Causes of air, water, and land pollution (5) • Effects of pollution on the environment (5) • Developing strategies to decrease pollution (5) • Developing strategies to conserve resources (5)
• Influence of family and peers on tobacco use (2) • Choosing friends who are tobacco free (2)	• Choosing friends who are alcohol and drug free (4) • Coping with family problems through substance abuse organizations (4) • Influencing others to avoid alcohol use (BHS)	• Preventing accidents in the home (2) • Developing strategies to decrease pollution and waste in the home (5) (BHS) • Analyzing trash in the home (BHS)
• How chemicals in tobacco affect the body (1) • Addictive effects of nicotine on the body (1) • Damage to body systems from tobacco use (2)	• Long-term effects of alcohol use on the body (1) • Effects of alcohol on fetus (1) • Physical/psychological effects of illegal drug use (3) (BHS)	
• Health consequences of using tobacco (1) • Heart disease and cancer caused by using tobacco (1) • Health problems caused by secondhand smoke (1)	• Alcohol use and diseases of heart, liver, and stomach (1) • Relationship between injecting drugs and infections (3)	• Health effects of air, water, and land pollution (5)

Skills at a Glance

Teen Health integrates skills throughout the core content. Below is a chart that identifies the skills presented in two skills-related features—Health Skills Activities (found within the lessons of each chapter) and Building Health Skills (found at the end of each chapter).

SKILL	CHAPTERS	TITLES	PAGES
Accessing Information	2	People Who Can Help	39
	4	Understand Unit Pricing	102
	4 (BHS)	Think Before You Buy	110–111
	5	Reading a Food Label	119
	7	Learning More About Noncommunicable and Hereditary Diseases	199
	10	Minor Injury Lookout	277
Practicing Healthful Behaviors	4	Skin Care Strategies	91
	6	Caring for Your Body Systems	152
	6 (BHS)	Keeping Body Systems Healthy	176–177
	10	Dangerous Situations	264
Stress Management	2 (BHS)	Managing Your Time	48–49
	5	Tension Tamers	136
Analyzing Influences	1 (BHS)	Exploring Influences on Your Health	26–27
Communication Skills	1	When Friends Change	11
	2	Reinforcing Your Self-Concept	34
	3	"You" and "I"	72
Conflict Resolution	3 (BHS)	Working Things Out	78–79
Refusal Skills	3	S.T.O.P. the Pressure	64
	8 (BHS)	Stand Firm Against Tobacco	224–225
	9	Say No and Mean It	248
Decision Making	1	Leaving the Party	18
	3	Juggling Responsibilities	57
	5 (BHS)	Fueling Your Body	144–145
	9 (BHS)	How to Avoid Alcohol	252–253
Goal Setting	1	Achieving Health Goals	22
	5	Increasing Your Activity Level	140
	7 (BHS)	Protecting Your Health	204–205
	10	Having Fun and Staying Safe	260
Advocacy	6	The Health of Mother and Child	171
	8	The Dangers of Smoking	216
	10 (BHS)	Reuse to Reduce Waste	286–287

Teen Health

Course 1

Teen Health
Course 1

Mary H. Bronson, Ph.D.

Michael J. Cleary, Ed.D.

Betty M. Hubbard, Ed.D., C.H.E.S.

Contributing Author
Dinah Zike, M.Ed.

Glencoe

New York, New York   Columbus, Ohio   Chicago, Illinois   Peoria, Illinois   Woodland Hills, California

Meet the Authors

Mary H. Bronson, Ph.D., has taught health education in grades K–12, as well as health education methods classes at the undergraduate and graduate levels. As health education specialist for the Dallas School District, Dr. Bronson developed and implemented a district-wide health education program. She has been honored as Texas Health Educator of the Year by the Texas Association of Health, Physical Education, Recreation and Dance and selected Teacher of the Year twice, by her colleagues. Dr. Bronson has assisted school districts throughout the country in developing local health education programs. She is also the co-author of the *Glencoe Health* textbook.

Betty M. Hubbard, Ed.D., C.H.E.S., has taught health education in grades K–12 as well as health education methods classes at the undergraduate and graduate levels. She is a professor at the University of Central Arkansas, teaching classes in curriculum development, mental health, and human sexuality. Dr. Hubbard supervises student teachers and conducts in-service training for health education teachers in school districts throughout Arkansas. Her publications, grants, and presentations focus on research-based, comprehensive health instruction.

Michael J. Cleary, Ed.D., is Professor and School Health Education Coordinator at Slippery Rock University. Dr. Cleary taught at Evanston Township High School in Evanston, Illinois, and later became the Lead Teacher Specialist at the McMillen Center for Health Education in Fort Wayne, Indiana. Dr. Cleary has published and presented widely on curriculum development and portfolio assessment in K–12 health education. Dr. Cleary is the coauthor of *Managing Your Health: Assessment for Action.* He is a Certified Health Education Specialist.

Dinah Zike, M.Ed., is an international curriculum consultant and inventor who has designed and developed educational products and three-dimensional, interactive graphic organizers for over thirty years. As president and founder of Dinah-Might Adventures, L.P., Dinah is the author of over 100 award-winning educational publications. Dinah has a B.S. and an M.S. in educational curriculum and instruction from Texas A & M University. Dinah Zike's *Foldables* are an exclusive feature of McGraw-Hill textbooks.

Send all inquiries to:
Glencoe/McGraw-Hill
21600 Oxnard Street, Suite 500
Woodland Hills, California 91367

ISBN 0-07-861095-8 (Course 1 Student Text)
ISBN 0-07-861096-6 (Course 1 Teacher Wraparound Edition)

Printed in the United States of America.

1 2 3 4 5 6 7 8 9   071/043   08 07 06 05 04

Health Consultants

Christine A. Hayashi, M.A. Ed., J.D.
Attorney at Law, Special Education Law
Adjunct Faculty, Educational Leadership and Policy Studies Development
California State University, Northridge
Northridge, California

Patricia Sullivan, M.S., Special Education
Chair, Department of Language Arts
Meade Middle School
Fort Meade, Maryland

UNIT 1

A Healthy Foundation

Stephanie S. Allen
Senior Lecturer
Baylor University, Louise Herrington School of Nursing
Dallas, Texas

Victoria Bisorca, C.H.E.S.
Lecturer
California State University, Long Beach
Long Beach, California

Howard S. Shapiro, M.D.
Associate Professor
University of Southern California School of Medicine
Los Angeles, California

Linda Stevenson, Ph.D., R.N.
Assistant Professor
Baylor University, Louise Herrington School of Nursing
Dallas, Texas

UNIT 2

Promoting Physical Health

Roberta Larson Duyff, R.D.
Food and Nutrition Consultant/President
Duyff Associates
St. Louis, Missouri

Mark Giese, Ed.D.
Chair, Department of Health, Science, and Kinesiology
Northeastern State University
Tahlequah, Oklahoma

Jan King
Teacher
Neshaminy School District
Langhorne, Pennsylvania

Tinker D. Murray, Ph.D.
Professor and Coordinator of the Exercise and Sports Science Program
Southwest Texas State University
San Marcos, Texas

Alice Pappas, Ph.D., R.N.
Associate Professor/Associate Dean
Baylor University, Louise Herrington School of Nursing
Dallas, Texas

Don Rainey
Instructor, Coordinator of the Physical Fitness and Wellness Program
Southwest Texas State University
San Marcos, Texas

Sherman Sowby, Ph.D., C.H.E.S.
Professor of Health Science
California State University, Fresno
Fresno, California

Catherine Strain, R.D.
Associate Professor
Marian College
Indianapolis, Indiana

UNIT 3

Protecting Your Health

Sally Champlin, C.H.E.S.
Faculty
California State University, Long Beach
Long Beach, California

Jill English, Ph.D., C.H.E.S.
Assistant Professor
California State University, Fullerton
Fullerton, California

Sharon Gonzales, R.N.
Nurse
Thomas Grover Middle School
Princeton Junction, New Jersey

David Sleet, Ph.D.
Associate Director for Science
Division of Unintentional Injury Prevention
Centers for Disease Control and Prevention (CDC)
Atlanta, Georgia

Reviewers

Beverly J. Berkin, C.H.E.S.
Health Education Consultant
Bedford Corners, New York

Donna Breitenstein, Ed.D.
Professor & Coordinator of Health Education
Director of North Carolina School Health
    Training Center
Appalachian State University
Boone, North Carolina

Julie Campbell-Fouch
Health Teacher, Department Chair
Stanford Middle School
Long Beach, California

Pamela R. Connolly
Subject Area Coordinator for Health and
    Physical Education, Diocese of Pittsburgh
Curriculum Coordinator for Health and Physical
    Education, North Catholic High School
Pittsburgh, Pennsylvania

Pat Freedman
Instructional Coordinator for Student Wellness
Humble Independent School District
Humble, Texas

Ginger Lawless, C.H.E.S.
Dyslexia and School Health Education Specialist
Fort Bend Independent School District
Sugar Land, Texas

James Robinson III, Ed.D.
Professor, Assistant Dean for Student Affairs
The Texas A&M University System
Health Science Center
School of Rural Public Health
College Station, Texas

Michael Rulon
Health/Physical Education Teacher
Johnson Junior High School
Adjunct Faculty, Laramie County
    Community College
Cheyenne, Wyoming

Jeanne Title
Coordinator, Prevention Education
Napa County Office of Education and Napa
    Valley Unified School District
Napa, California

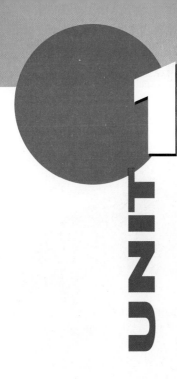

A Healthy Foundation

1

UNIT 2

Promoting Physical Health 82

Hands-On Health

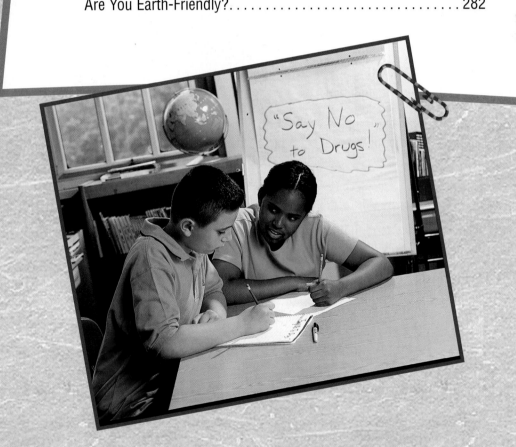

Getting the most out of *Teen* Health

Making healthy and responsible decisions is easy with *Teen Health*. Follow the guidelines below to make the most out of each lesson.

Do the Quick Write

This feature will help you start thinking about the information in a lesson.

Preview the Lesson

Get a preview of what's coming by reading the lesson objectives in the **Learn About....** You can also use this feature to prepare for quizzes and tests.

Review Key Terms

Find each vocabulary term in the text and read its definition. The terms appear in blue so you can locate them easily!

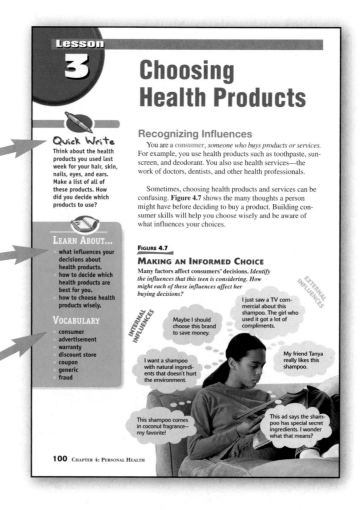

Lesson 3

Choosing Health Products

Recognizing Influences

You are a consumer, *someone who buys products or services.* For example, you use health products such as toothpaste, sunscreen, and deodorant. You also use health services—the work of doctors, dentists, and other health professionals.

Sometimes, choosing health products and services can be confusing. **Figure 4.7** shows the many thoughts a person might have before deciding to buy a product. Building consumer skills will help you choose wisely and be aware of what influences your choices.

FIGURE 4.7

MAKING AN INFORMED CHOICE
Many factors affect consumers' decisions. *Identify the influences that this teen is considering. How might each of these influences affect her buying decisions?*

INTERNAL INFLUENCES

EXTERNAL INFLUENCES

Maybe I should choose this brand to save money.

I just saw a TV commercial about this shampoo. The girl who used it got a lot of compliments.

I want a shampoo with natural ingredients that doesn't hurt the environment.

My friend Tanya really likes this shampoo.

This shampoo comes in coconut fragrance—my favorite!

This ad says the shampoo has special secret ingredients. I wonder what that means?

Quick Write

Think about the health products you used last week for your hair, skin, nails, eyes, and ears. Make a list of all of these products. How did you decide which products to use?

LEARN ABOUT...

- what influences your decisions about health products.
- how to decide which health products are best for you.
- how to choose health products wisely.

VOCABULARY

- consumer
- advertisement
- warranty
- discount store
- coupon
- generic
- fraud

100 Chapter 4: Personal Health

Use Glencoe's Health Web Site to Boost Your Health Smarts!

▶ Rate your health by taking the Health Inventory for each chapter. Jump-start your goals by filling out a Personal Wellness Contract.

▶ Check out Web Link Exercises for fun and interactive games and activities.

▶ Do some detective work on a particular health topic—Health Quests show you how.

▶ Get ready for tests by using the different Online Study Tools to review vocabulary terms and chapter content. E-flashcards, online quizzes, and interactive drag-and-drop games make studying fun!

▶ Building Health Skills features give you another chance to master important skills for wellness.

Comparison Shopping

When evaluating health products, consider these factors.

- **Price.** How much can you afford to spend on the product?
- **Unit Price.** How much does the product cost per ounce or per gram? (See the Health Skills Activity for details.)
- **Benefits.** Does one brand offer more features than another?
- **Reputation.** Do people you know use and like this brand?
- **Warranty.** Does this brand come with a warranty? A **warranty** is *a promise to make repairs or refund money if the product does not work as claimed.*

Saving Money

Smart shoppers know how to save money. For example, they may buy personal products at **discount stores**. These are *stores that offer lower prices but have fewer salespeople and services.* They may also clip and use **coupons,** *slips of paper that save you money on certain brands.* You can often save money by buying store brands or **generic** (juh·NEHR·ik) products, which are *products that imitate name-brand products, and are sold in plain packages.* These cost less because the packaging is cheaper and little money is spent on advertising. However, some generic drugs may not contain all of the same ingredients as name brands; so check with your pharmacist before using them.

HEALTH SKILLS ACTIVITY

ACCESSING INFORMATION

Understand Unit Pricing

To compare the value of two products, you need to compare their unit price, or cost per unit of weight or volume. To do this, follow these steps.

- Find the weight or volume given on each product container. Make sure that both products are measured in the same type of units.
- Divide the price of the product by its weight or volume. The result is the unit price.
- Compare the unit prices.

ON YOUR OWN
Find the unit prices of the two bottles of soap shown here. Which costs less per fluid ounce? Which is the most economical purchase?

102 CHAPTER 4: PERSONAL HEALTH

Try the Health Skills and Hands-On Health Activities

Develop valuable health skills by doing the Health Skills Activities that appear in each chapter. Conduct experiments, create ads, and try the other fun activities in the Hands-On Health features.

Study the Infographics

First, think about the overall message that the infographic is presenting. Then, read each callout carefully and determine what part of the image it is highlighting.

Complete the Lesson Reviews

Completing the lesson reviews can help you see how well you know the material you have just studied. It also gives you a chance to apply what you've learned to different situations, as well as practice a health skill.

FIGURE 4.9

False or Misleading Claims

These product labels make false or misleading claims. *What other false claims have you seen in ads?*

X-treme Tan: Tan Fast with No Sun!

Glisten: Make Your Smile Shine!

Zitex: Makes Pimples Disappear Overnight!

Super Silk: For the Hair You've Always Wanted!

Slimmo: Lose Weight Without Dieting or Exercising!

Mint Mouth: Keeps Breath Fresh All Day!

Spotting False Claims

Consumers need to beware of **fraud,** *deliberate deceit or trickery.* People who practice fraud make false claims about a product or service. **Figure 4.9** shows some examples of false and misleading claims. Health fraud can be especially dangerous. Some products and services falsely claim to cure serious diseases. Use critical thinking skills to research and evaluate health information about products and services. It is unsafe to use any treatment that has not been approved by the U.S. Food and Drug Administration (FDA).

Lesson 3 Review

Using complete sentences, answer the following questions on a sheet of paper.

Reviewing Terms and Facts
1. **Vocabulary** Define the word *consumer.*
2. **Recall** What is the purpose of an advertisement?
3. **List** Give examples of three ways to save money when shopping.

Thinking Critically
4. **Apply** Give two examples of how to evaluate a health product such as a sunblock or an over-the-counter medication.

5. **Synthesize** Give an example of why a less expensive medicine may not be the best purchase. Write a paragraph that examines the concept of cost versus effectiveness of health care products.

Applying Health Skills
6. **Analyzing Influences** Select a personal product that you would recommend to others. Explain to the class why it is worth its cost.

LESSON 3: CHOOSING HEALTH PRODUCTS **103**

A Healthy Foundation

Unit Objectives

Students learn that health and wellness are related to their levels of physical, mental/emotional, and social well-being. They also examine and practice skills related to setting goals, managing stress, and communicating effectively.

Unit Overview

xvi

DEALING WITH SENSITIVE ISSUES

A General Approach As a health teacher, you have the opportunity to help students deal with sensitive issues in several ways. One way is by sharing accurate information and professional resources about the issues with students and doing so in ways that won't embarrass them, make them feel uncomfortable, or jeopardize their self-esteem. Knowledge alone is not enough, however. Experience shows that just conveying information is less effective in changing behaviors than teaching skills. For example, telling students to "just say no" to drugs is a less effective deterrent to drug use than teaching them *how* to say no.

A Healthy Foundation

The same skills you apply to your favorite sport can help you make good decisions, manage stress, and get along well with your friends and family. When you know how to set goals—such as winning a game, doing well on a test, solving a problem, or simply being healthy—you're much more likely to achieve them. Meeting your goals helps you feel good about yourself, and that keeps you on top of your game!

What do working on your bowling score and setting goals have in common?

UNIT 1

Chapter 3
Social Health

Lesson
1 Your Family
2 Your Friends and Peers
3 Communication: More Than Words
4 Resolving Conflicts

Unit Introduction

Ask students to make lists of the first ideas that come to mind when you say the words *health* and *wellness*. Give them enough time to explore all possible associations, and ask them to discuss the interrelationship of *health* and *wellness*. When the allotted time is reached, ask students to share their responses. Discuss how their responses cover a broad range of physical, mental/emotional, and social health issues.

Advise them that wellness is a state of balanced health. Tell students that the chapters in this unit will show them how their personal decisions about health will help them build and maintain a healthy foundation for life.

1

HEALTH in Action

Read the class the question on page 1. Have students consider the relationships between goal setting and physical, mental/emotional, and social health. Then lead the class in the following physical group activity:

Have each student write on a slip of paper one way that goal setting can enhance physical, mental/emotional, or social health. Have students place slips into a basket or bucket. Shake the basket, then have students pass it around the class. Have each student remove a slip, read it aloud, and give an example that relates to that entry. For example, a student whose slip says "goal setting helps people learn things" might relate a story about learning to ski with a friend's help.

Planning Guide

Chapter 1	Skills/ Activities	Reproducible Resources	Assessment
Lesson 1 **Your Health and Wellness** *pages 4–7*	**Hands-On Health** ▲ Your Personal Health, page 6	*Student Activities Workbook available for use with each chapter* 📁 Parent Letter & Activities 1 📁 Concept Map 1 📁 Enrichment Activity 1 📁 Lesson Plan 1 📁 Reading Tutor Activity 1 📁 Reteaching Activity 1	📁 Lesson 1 Quiz
Lesson 2 **Building Health Skills** *pages 8–13*	**HEALTH SKILLS ACTIVITY** ▲ When Friends Change (*Communication Skills*), page 11	📁 Concept Map 2 📁 Cross-Curriculum Activity 1 📁 Decision-Making Activity 1 📁 Enrichment Activity 2 📁 Health Lab 1 📁 Lesson Plan 2 📁 Reading Tutor Activity 2 📁 Reteaching Activity 2	📁 Lesson 2 Quiz
Lesson 3 **Decisions and Your Character** *pages 14–19*	**HEALTH SKILLS ACTIVITY** ▲ Leaving the Party (*Decision Making*), page 18	📁 Concept Map 3 📁 Cross-Curriculum Activity 2 📁 Decision-Making Activity 2 📁 Enrichment Activity 3 📁 Lesson Plan 3 📁 Reading Tutor Activity 3 📁 Reteaching Activity 3	📁 Lesson 3 Quiz
Lesson 4 **Setting Health Goals** *pages 20–23*	**HEALTH SKILLS ACTIVITY** ▲ Achieving Health Goals (*Goal Setting*), page 22	📁 Concept Map 4 📁 Enrichment Activity 4 📁 Lesson Plan 4 📁 Reading Tutor Activity 4 📁 Reteaching Activity 4	📁 Lesson 4 Quiz 📁 Chapter 1 Test 📁 Performance Assessment 1

TIME HEALTH   **Getting the Health Facts Straight** *pages 24–25*

BUILDING HEALTH SKILLS

Exploring Influences on Your Health
(*Analyzing Influences*)
pages 26–27

📁 Building Health Skills Reproducible Master 1

Standards		Technology
National	**State/Local**	
National Health Education Standard **1.1, 1.2, 1.8, 3.1, 3.2**		Transparency 1 TeacherWorks™ Internet Activities
National Health Education Standard **2.1, 3.1, 4.1, 4.2, 4.4, 5.5, 6.1, 6.4, 7.2**		Transparency 2 TeacherWorks™
National Health Education Standard **1.2, 1.4, 1.6, 3.4, 5.4, 6.1, 6.2, 6.3**		Transparency 3 Tape/DVD 3, Segment 5, "Developing Character" TeacherWorks™
National Health Education Standard **3.1, 3.4, 6.4, 6.5**		Transparencies 4 & 5 Tape/DVD 3, Segment 3, "Taking Charge of Your Life" TeacherWorks™ MindJogger Videoquiz **Exam**View® Pro Testmaker
National Health Education Standard **1.4, 4.1, 4.2, 4.4**		Building Health Skills Transparency Master 4

TeacherWorks™

Glencoe's new and exclusive TeacherWorks™ is an all-in-one planner and resource center. Access the complete Teacher Wraparound Edition electronically. Find all your classroom resources with just a few easy clicks, and print them right from your computer. Connect directly to Glencoe's customized Health Web site. Access the National Health Education Standards correlations, or insert your own state standards and match them directly to the electronic Teacher Wraparound Edition.

Language Diversity

- English Audio Summaries
- Spanish Audio Summaries
- English Summaries, Quizzes, and Activities
- Spanish Summaries, Quizzes, and Activities
- Spanish Parent Letters and Activities

KEY TO ABILITY LEVELS

Teaching Strategies that appear throughout the chapters have been identified by one of four codes to give you an idea of their suitability for students of varying learning styles and abilities.

L1 **Level 1** strategies should be within the ability range of all students. Often full class participation is required.

L2 **Level 2** strategies are for average to above-average students or for small groups. Some teacher direction is necessary.

L3 **Level 3** strategies are designed for students able and willing to work independently. Minimal teacher direction is necessary.

INCL Strategies are appropriate for students with particular special needs in a general classroom setting.

Living a Healthy Life

Chapter at a Glance

Lesson 1 defines *health* by using the concept of a health triangle and discusses ways to achieve wellness.

Lesson 2 examines the skills needed to maintain health and prevent illness and injury.

Lesson 3 introduces the decision-making process. It guides students through six steps for making decisions and presents the benefits of making decisions that reflect strong character traits.

Lesson 4 examines what goals are and discusses the steps of goal setting.

Health Skills
- When Friends Change (*Communication Skills*), p. 11
- Leaving the Party (*Decision Making*), p. 18
- Achieving Health Goals (*Goal Setting*), p. 22
- Exploring Influences on Your Health (*Analyzing Influences*), pp. 26–27

HANDS-ON ACTIVITY

Who Am I? Give each student a 3 × 5-inch index card. Have students write their full name in the center of the card. Then tell them to write:

- In the top left corner, their birthplaces.
- In the top right corner, who they admire.
- In the bottom left corner, their favorite foods.
- In the bottom right corner, one goal they would like to reach by the end of the year.

Direct students to draw four lines coming out of their names. Have them write four favorite activities, talents, or personal strengths (e.g., going to the movies, dancing, being a good listener) at the end of each line.

Living a Healthy Life

Chapter Introduction

Use the options below to motivate students and preview chapter content.

HEALTH *Online*

Rate your ability to make healthy decisions. Take the Health Inventory for Chapter 1 at health.glencoe.com.

HEALTH *Online*

Have students take Health Inventory 1 at **health.glencoe.com** to analyze their current health status. For new teaching ideas click on Teaching Today to download helpful tools such as graphic organizers and Webquest activities.

FOLDABLES™ Study Organizer

Before You Read

Make this Foldable to help you organize the main ideas on health and wellness in Lesson 1. Begin with a plain sheet of 8½″ × 11″ paper.

Step 1

Line up one of the short edges of a sheet of paper with one of the long edges to form a triangle. Fold and cut off the leftover rectangle.

Step 2

Fold the triangle in half, then unfold. The folds will form an X dividing four equal sections.

Step 3

Cut up one fold line, and stop at the middle. This forms two triangular flaps. Draw an X on one tab, and label the other three as shown.

Step 4

Fold the X flap under the other flap, and glue together to make a three-sided pyramid.

As You Read

Write the main ideas about the three parts of health on the back of the appropriate side of the pyramid.

3

GLENCOE TECHNOLOGY

Teen Health Video and DVD Series (Each format available in both English and Spanish)

You may wish to use:
- Tape/DVD 3, Segment 3, "Taking Charge of Your Life"
- Tape/DVD 3, Segment 5, "Developing Character"

MindJogger Videoquiz

Use MindJogger to preview or review Chapter 1 content.

TIME HEALTH

Getting the Health Facts Straight
pages 24–25

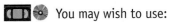

FOLDABLES™ Study Organizer

Dinah Zike Study Fold

Developing Main Ideas Have students use their completed Foldable to organize what they learn about the health triangle. As students read and study the information in Lesson 1, have them write down definitions and main ideas on the back of the appropriate side of the Foldable. To illustrate the concept of balanced health, the pyramid can be made into a mobile. Have students write down or draw examples of each part of health on small cards. Direct them to sort the cards into physical, mental/emotional, and social health and attach the cards in each category to one piece of string. Then have them hang each string from the appropriate side of the Foldable.

Lesson Objectives

Students will be able to

- explain what it means to be healthy.
- describe the relationship between health and wellness.
- explain how to keep their physical, mental/emotional, and social health in balance.

Motivators

Quick Write

Ask several students to share their responses to the Quick Write activity. Have a volunteer write them on the board. Discuss which aspects of health are represented.

Bellringer Activity

Bring in pictures of sports personalities from various magazines. Ask students to describe the physical characteristics of these people. Explain that there is more to health than just being physically healthy. Ask students to name two other components of health. (*social and mental/emotional health*)

VOCABULARY

Write the following words on the board: *health, wellness, habit*. Have students write definitions in their own words. Then have students compare their definitions to the definitions provided in the Glossary at the back of the book.

Lesson 1 — Your Health and Wellness

Quick Write

Describe in a sentence or two what you think it means to lead a healthy life.

LEARN ABOUT...

- the relationship between health and wellness.
- keeping your physical, mental/emotional, and social health in balance.

VOCABULARY

- health
- wellness
- habit

Taking Charge of Your Health

You may have heard the saying "Today is the first day of the rest of your life." Think about the meaning of this statement. What you do today affects you throughout your life. This is especially true where your health is concerned.

Health is *a combination of physical, mental/emotional, and social well-being.* It might help you to think of health as a triangle—see **Figure 1.1**. One part of the triangle is your physical health—the condition of your body. Another part is your mental/emotional health—your thoughts and feelings. The third part of the triangle is your social health—the way you relate to other people.

What other parts of the health triangle are these teens working on?

Playing soccer is one way to improve your physical health.

4 CHAPTER 1: LIVING A HEALTHY LIFE

 Lesson 1 Resources

Teacher Classroom Resources

 Parent Letter & Activities 1
 Concept Map 1
Enrichment Activity 1
Lesson Plan 1
 Lesson 1 Quiz
 Reading Tutor Activity 1

 Reteaching Activity 1
 Transparency 1

Student Activities Workbook

 Chapter 1 Study Guide
Applying Health Skills 1

Maintaining Your Health Balance

Being healthy means keeping your health triangle in balance. Here are some ways to work on all three sides of your health triangle:

- **Physical.** Get regular physical activity, eat nutritious foods, and get enough rest. You will learn about these topics in Chapter 5.
- **Mental/emotional.** Take time to study, to think, and to express your feelings in healthy ways.
- **Social.** Spend time with both family and friends.

Remember that changes you make to one side of your health triangle will also affect the other two sides. For example, if you exercise regularly, your physical health will improve. This will also help you feel better about yourself, benefitting your mental health.

FIGURE 1.1

The Health Triangle

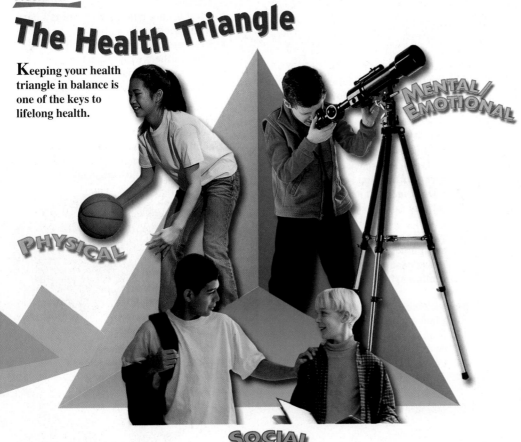

Keeping your health triangle in balance is one of the keys to lifelong health.

LESSON 1: YOUR HEALTH AND WELLNESS **5**

Developing Good Character

Respect

People who respect themselves will take responsibility for their health. Write two or three sentences explaining how avoiding tobacco, alcohol, and other drugs will help you feel good about yourself.

② Teach

VISUAL LEARNING

FIGURE 1.1 Have students look at Figure 1.1 to see examples of each aspect of the health triangle. Ask students to read the caption and lead a class discussion on how the photographs reflect the different sides of the health triangle. **INCL** *English Language Learners*

Developing Good Character

Respect
The important concept here is that feeling good about oneself should come from wanting to develop good character. Have students pair up to discuss the meaning of two character traits, respect and responsibility, and how these traits affect a person's health. Ask: Why is it important to make decisions that show respect for yourself and for the health of others?

Cross-Curriculum Activity

PERFORMING ARTS Divide students into groups of three. Give each group a slip of paper with physical, mental/emotional, or social health written on it. Have each group make up charades for the area of the health triangle that they are assigned. Have the class guess what the charade is and tell which part of the health triangle it represents. **L1 INCL** *Different Learning Styles, English Language Learners*

Health Literacy

Health Behaviors On a piece of drawing paper, have each student draw a triangle and label each side with one of the following terms: *physical, mental/emotional, social.* Tell students that this drawing represents their personal health triangle.

Instruct them to think of ways in which they exhibit good physical, mental/emotional, and social health each day, and to write their ideas next to each side of the triangle. Suggest that students place the triangle in a visible place in their home. Encourage them to add new positive behaviors that they acquire.

Hands-On Health

YOUR PERSONAL HEALTH

Time: 40 minutes

TEACHING THE ACTIVITY

- With students, review the three parts of the health triangle, as shown in Figure 1.1 on page 5.
- Have students work independently to record their responses to the inventory. Then have them use the point system explained in In Conclusion to calculate their inventory scores.
- Have students meet in groups to discuss specific actions to take to improve each side of their personal health triangles. Emphasize that students' responses and scores may be kept confidential.

ASSESSMENT

Have each student answer this question: After completing this health inventory, what changes, if any, will you make to your personal health triangle?

Discussing

Ask students whether they think it is possible for everyone's health triangle to be perfectly balanced at all times. (*No, it is not, but a healthy person is aware of the overall pattern. When one side starts to get out of balance, a change can be made.*) **L1**

Keep in mind that all three sides of your health triangle will not develop at the same rate. This is normal. It's also normal to find your health triangle temporarily out of balance. The important thing is to notice when one side is out of balance and take steps to correct it. This balance is the key to lifelong health and wellness.

Hands-On Health

YOUR PERSONAL HEALTH

Do you have a clear picture of your own health triangle? Take this personal health inventory to identify factors that affect your physical, mental/emotional, and social health.

WHAT YOU WILL NEED
- pencil or pen
- paper

WHAT YOU WILL DO
Number the paper 1–6 for each health area. Think about each of the following statements and respond with *yes* or *no*.

Physical Health
1. I eat at least three well-balanced meals each day, and snack on healthful foods such as fruits and vegetables.
2. I get at least 60 minutes of physical activity daily.
3. I sleep at least nine hours a night.
4. I avoid the use of tobacco, alcohol, and other drugs.
5. I have good personal hygiene habits.
6. I follow safety rules.

Mental/Emotional Health
1. I feel good about who I am.
2. I can name several things that I can do well.
3. I generally keep a positive attitude.
4. I ask for help when I need it.
5. I am able to handle stress.
6. I try to improve myself.

Social Health
1. I relate well to family, friends, and classmates.
2. I try to work out any differences I have with others.
3. I express my feelings in positive ways.
4. I treat others with respect.
5. I can say no to risky behaviors.
6. I communicate well with others.

IN CONCLUSION
Give yourself 1 point for each *yes*. A score of 5–6 in any area reflects good health. If you score 0–2 in any area, try to improve that part of your health triangle.

6 CHAPTER 1: LIVING A HEALTHY LIFE

![checkmark] ## Reading Check

Compound Words Understanding the structure of words and the meanings of their parts will help students decode unknown words and build vocabulary. List the compounds from Lesson 1 (*lifelong* and *yourself*) on the board or chart as students identify them. If they suggest words such as *triangle, maintain, wellness,* or *washing* for the list, point out that, while these contain one part that can stand alone as a word, true compounds contain two or more such parts. Also note that the hyphenated word *well-being* is considered a compound, and add it to the list.

Wellness

Wellness is *a state of well-being, or balanced health.* To maintain wellness, take care of health problems as they come up. You should also try to protect and improve your health.

You can achieve wellness through good health habits. A **habit** is *a pattern of behavior that you follow almost without thinking.* One important habit to develop is getting enough sleep each night. Teens need at least nine hours of sleep each night to be at their best. Developing this healthful habit will enhance your health and wellness now and in the years to come.

Reading Check

Each part in a compound word is a word by itself, as in *notebook.* Find at least three compound words in Lesson 1.

Good health habits help you maintain a high level of wellness. *Explain how this teen's habits protect his health.*

Lesson 1 Review

Using complete sentences, answer the following questions on a sheet of paper.

Reviewing Terms and Facts

1. **Vocabulary** Define *health* and *wellness*.
2. **List** What are the three parts of the health triangle?
3. **Describe** Give an example of good social health.

Thinking Critically

4. **Analyze** Explain how a change to one side of the health triangle can affect the other two sides.

5. **Hypothesize** Do you think it is easier to develop good health habits than to break bad ones? Why or why not?
6. **Apply** Think of two school rules related to health. In a brief sentence or two, describe why these rules benefit health and how you follow them.

Applying Health Skills

7. **Analyzing Influences** Think of one good health habit that you have. Write a paragraph explaining how you first developed the habit. Then describe how the habit contributes to your health and wellness.

LESSON 1: YOUR HEALTH AND WELLNESS **7**

Lesson 1

③ Assess

Evaluating

📁 Assign the Lesson 1 Review; then assign the Lesson 1 Quiz in the TCR.

Reteaching

• 📁 Assign Concept Map 1 or Reteaching Activity 1 in the TCR.
• Direct students to write about someone they know who shows a high degree of wellness. Ask them to explain their choices.

Enrichment

• 📁 Assign and distribute Enrichment Activity 1 in the TCR.
• Have students work in small groups to brainstorm lists of specific habits that support good physical, mental/emotional, and social health.

④ Close

Have students discuss their responses to this question: How has studying this lesson changed your understanding of "a well-balanced life"?

Lesson 1 Review

1. Health is a combination of physical, mental/emotional, and social well-being. Wellness is a state of well-being, or balanced health.
2. Physical health, mental/emotional health, and social health.
3. Examples will vary, but may include spending time with both family and friends.

4. Responses should indicate an understanding of the interrelationships between physical, mental/emotional, and social health.
5. Accept all reasonable responses.
6. Responses will vary, but should accurately link two school rules to health.

Focus

Lesson Objectives

Students will be able to

- identify skills that will help them stay healthy.
- describe ways to promote their health and the health of others.

Health Skills
- Communication Skills, p. 11

Motivators

Quick Write
Have volunteers share their lists of healthful behaviors and the skills associated with each. Continue to have students share until at least one example of each health skill has been provided, if possible. Note skills not addressed.

Bellringer Activity
Discuss how skills are developed for sports and performance activities, such as playing an instrument. Emphasize that learning any new set of skills requires knowledge and practice, and in this lesson students will learn skills to promote their health.

VOCABULARY
Ask students to form small groups and, using a dictionary or the-saurus, to come up with a list of synonyms for the term *prevention*. Make sure students understand synonyms are different words that mean the same thing.

Quick Write

List three things you do to maintain your health. Preview this lesson, and identify the health skills that you are practicing when you do each of these activities.

LEARN ABOUT...

- what skills help you stay healthy.
- how you can promote your health and the health of others.

VOCABULARY

- prevention

Skills for Good Health

One of the keys to wellness is the prevention of illness. **Prevention** is *keeping something from happening.* You can prevent illness and injury in many ways. For example:

- **Physical Health.** Get regular medical and dental checkups, also known as health screenings. Wear protective gear when you play sports. Always wear a safety belt when riding in a vehicle.
- **Mental/Emotional Health.** Talk to your parents or guardians about health-related concerns. Learn to manage stress. Think positively.
- **Social Health.** Try to get along with family and friends. Avoid gossiping and spreading rumors. Choose friends who avoid tobacco, alcohol, and other drugs.

All the examples listed above demonstrate health skills. These are skills that help you become healthy and stay healthy. The health skills that you develop now will have a positive effect throughout your life. **Figure 1.2** shows ten important health skills.

Wearing a safety belt is one way to prevent injury. *What other ways can you think of?*

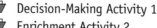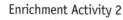

Lesson 2 Resources

Teacher Classroom Resources

- Concept Map 2
- Cross-Curriculum Activity 1
- Decision-Making Activity 1
- Enrichment Activity 2
- Health Lab 1
- Lesson Plan 2
- Lesson 2 Quiz

- Reading Tutor Activity 2
- Reteaching Activity 2
- Transparency 2

Student Activities Workbook

- Chapter 1 Study Guide
- Applying Health Skills 2

FIGURE 1.2

THE HEALTH SKILLS

These ten skills affect your physical, mental/emotional, and social health. These skills can help you, not just during your teen years but throughout your entire life.

Health Skill	What It Means to You
Accessing Information	You know how to find reliable health information and health-promoting products and services.
Practicing Healthful Behaviors	You take action to reduce risks and protect yourself against illness and injury.
Stress Management	You find healthy ways to reduce and manage stress in your life.
Analyzing Influences	You recognize the many factors that influence your health, including culture, media, and technology.
Communication Skills	You express your ideas and feelings and listen when others express theirs.
Refusal Skills	You can say no to risky behaviors.
Conflict Resolution	You work out problems with others in healthy ways.
Decision Making	You think through problems and find healthy solutions.
Goal Setting	You plan for the future and work to make your plans come true.
Advocacy	You take a stand and make a difference in your home, school, and community.

Accessing Information

Knowing how to access, or obtain, reliable health information is an important skill. Sources of information include:

- **Knowledgeable Adults:** parents and guardians, health professionals, teachers, school nurses, and others.
- **Library Resources:** books on health and science topics.
- **Mass Media:** news reports and articles by health professionals, scientists, and others.
- **The Internet:** up-to-the-minute information provided by government agencies and qualified health professionals.
- **Community Resources:** government agencies, hospitals, and health organizations like the American Red Cross.

Always remember to use critical thinking skills to research and evaluate health information. Learning to think critically about health information is a coping strategy that will help you stay healthy throughout life.

LESSON 2: BUILDING HEALTH SKILLS **9**

② Teach

Discussing

Have students identify factors that affect an individual's physical, mental/emotional, and social health. Factors might include school climate and safety measures.

VISUAL LEARNING

FIGURE 1.2 Divide the class into ten small groups (or pairs), and assign each group one of the health skills presented in Figure 1.2. Have group members work together to read about, discuss, and brainstorm examples of their assigned skill. Then let each group present its skill to the rest of the class.
INCL *Behavior Problems, Special Learning Needs, English Language Learners*

Cross-Curriculum Activity

TECHNOLOGY Assign students to work in pairs to select one health practice and one health service available to adults in their community. Have students list ways to evaluate the practice and the service, including utilizing resources on the Web and in computer software. After students have created their lists, they should use critical thinking skills to research and evaluate information about both the practice and the service. Finally, ask students to identify and analyze various media and technologies that influence individual and community health, such as computer software and the World Wide Web.

✔ Reading Check

Suffixes Learning the meanings of common suffixes can help students build vocabulary. List the words *physical, emotional,* and *social* on the chalkboard. Have students identify the common element at the end of each word, the suffix *-al*. Ask volunteers to speculate about its meaning, and to look it up in a dictionary to confirm their ideas. They should conclude that *-al* can be used in adjectives to mean "like," or "referring to," as in the example words listed above. Challenge students to identify other words on pages 8 and 9 containing the suffix and list them on the board. They are *dental, medical, mental, and refusal*.

Lesson 2

Discussing

Guide students in discussing their growing responsibilities for self-management. Ask:

- When you were little, who was responsible for seeing that you had nutritious foods to eat and that you got enough physical activity and sleep?

- To what extent are those people still responsible for helping you maintain positive health habits?

- How has your role in taking care of yourself changed in the past two ·years? How do you expect it to change in the next few years? **L1**

Cross-Curriculum Activity

LANGUAGE ARTS Divide the class into pairs or small groups. Have partners or groups select a TV show that they watch regularly that features teens. Ask students to cite examples of peer pressure in the show and discuss how this pressure impacts the characters' decisions. Then have students write a paragraph explaining the impact of peer pressure on decision making. **L1**

Evaluating

Have students create a chart that compares risks and benefits of various health behaviors, such as choosing not to smoke, eating nutritious meals, exercising regularly, and getting enough sleep.

Talking with a parent, guardian, or other trusted adult is one way to manage stress. *Can you name two other ways to deal with stress?*

Taking Care of Yourself

The next two health skills involve self-management, or taking care of yourself.

- **Practicing Healthful Behaviors.** You can take care of yourself by practicing healthful behaviors, or actions that help maintain good health. These include eating nutritious foods, staying active, and getting enough sleep. When you do not practice these behaviors, you may put your health at risk. For example, not getting enough sleep can cause you to become run-down.
- **Stress Management.** You can also take care of yourself by learning to cope with stress. Stress is part of life. Sometimes you may not be able to control the amount of stress in your life. However, you can control how you react to it. Managing stress means finding a healthy way to deal with it.

Analyzing Influences

Both internal and external factors influence your behavior.

- *Internal* influences come from inside you. For example, your personal likes and desires influence the foods you eat, the activities you choose, and the friends you spend time with.
- *External* influences come from outside sources. People can influence you, including parents, teachers, and friends. TV shows, books, ads, and movies can also influence your behavior. Finally, you are influenced by your culture, your environment, and the laws of your community.

 Beyond the Classroom

Home If your students have access to the Internet at home, their families may wish to share ideas about encouraging teens' use of certain Web sites and restricting their use of others. Suggest that students discuss the use of the Internet with adult family members. Open communication may alleviate many parental concerns. Still, some parents and guardians might be interested to know about blocking devices that can limit the range of options open to teen Web surfers. Encourage these adults to communicate with one another about Internet blocking devices through informal conversations via e-mail, at a scheduled meeting, or through a newsletter.

Communicating with Others

The next group of skills involves the way you communicate with other people. Communication is the clear exchange of ideas and information. That means telling others how you feel and listening to and understanding how they feel.

- **Refusal Skills.** Sometimes, you have to say no to others. For example, people you know may try to pressure you into doing something that you think is wrong. Refusal skills help you say no in an effective way without feeling uncomfortable. This is a method of practicing self-control, and a strategy for coping with potentially unsafe situations.
- **Conflict Resolution.** When you have conflicts, or disagreements, with others, it's best to settle them in a way that satisfies everyone. Conflict resolution usually requires talking matters over calmly and reasonably. Everyone must work together to find a solution to the problem.

FYI

Research conducted by communication specialists indicates that physical appearance, including gestures and facial expressions, accounts for 55 percent of a received message in a typical verbal exchange. Voice, including pitch and rate of speaking, accounts for 38 percent. Content accounts for just 7 percent.

HEALTH SKILLS ACTIVITY

COMMUNICATION SKILLS

When Friends Change

Tia and Carlos have been friends since second grade. Lately, though, Tia has noticed a change in Carlos. The two friends used to meet at their lockers after school and talk about what happened that day. Twice in the last week, Carlos told Tia he would be there, but then he didn't show up. The last time it happened, Tia had something important to tell Carlos. The next day, she heard from another friend that Carlos had told people that Tia was boring. What should Tia do?

What Would You Do?

Write a dialogue between Tia and Carlos. Have Tia tell Carlos how she feels about his behavior. Then have Carlos explain why he is acting that way. Use the speaking skills shown below.

- Use clear, simple statements.
- State your thoughts and feelings honestly.
- Make eye contact, and use appropriate body language.

HEALTH SKILLS ACTIVITY

COMMUNICATION SKILLS

Guide students in reading the explanation of Tia's situation. Ask:
- How does Tia feel?
- What does she want to communicate to Carlos?

Have volunteers explain how the listed speaking skills can help Tia communicate her message to Carlos. Advise students to use "I" messages in their dialogues. (For a discussion of "I" messages see Chapter 3, page 67.) Explain to students that "you" messages tend to place blame on the listener.

LESSON 2: BUILDING HEALTH SKILLS **11**

INCLUSION STRATEGIES

Emotionally Disturbed, Special Learning Needs
Often, students with attention deficit/hyperactivity disorder, emotional disturbances, or learning disabilities have poor communication skills, which leads to difficulty with both peer and teacher relationships. These students will need good modeling and extra practice with pitch, voice tone, and rate of speaking.

Rather than have students write out the dialogue suggested in the Health Skills Activity, offer students the choice to role-play the dialogue. This modification of the assignment will support students who have difficulty writing and will allow students to practice much-needed social skills.

Discussing

To help students understand that many activities involve a whole series of decisions and goals, read aloud the following situations to the class:

Imagine that, after deciding to try out for the track team and setting the goal of running every day for practice, you pull a muscle in your leg.

- What decision would you have to make?
- What new goal would you want to set for yourself?

Now imagine that, after deciding to try out and after fulfilling your goal of running every day, you make the school track team.

- What decisions might you have to make?
- What new goals would you be likely to set for yourself?

Students with behavioral disorders, learning disabilities, or attention deficit disorder often have difficulty making decisions and setting goals. In particular, these students often have difficulty making connections between their actions and the consequences that follow. These students need positive models and may need additional practice and guidance in these skill areas. **L1** **INCL** *Behavior Problems, Special Learning Needs*

HEALTH SKILLS PRACTICE

Accessing Information Bring in copies of a Yellow Pages phone book. Have students do a Yellow Pages scavenger hunt to find organizations that advocate for the health of communities. For extra credit, challenge students to participate in a service learning project.

Martin wants to spend more time on his favorite hobby, swimming. *What specific goals might he set for himself?*

Decision Making and Goal Setting

Decision making and goal setting are related skills. For example, suppose you hear about tryouts for the track team. First, you might make a decision to try out. Then you could set a goal to start running every day for practice. That goal would help you improve your speed so you would be more likely to make the team.

Making decisions and setting goals are step-by-step processes that require careful thought. They are important skills that help you shape your life in a positive way. These skills are also effective strategies for coping with the challenges of life.

Advocacy

To advocate something means to support it or speak out in favor of it. When you advocate for health, you encourage other people to live healthy lives. You can practice advocacy by showing that you feel strongly about healthful behaviors. You can also provide people in your home, school, or community with the information they need to make healthful choices.

12 CHAPTER 1: LIVING A HEALTHY LIFE

WHAT TEENS WANT TO KNOW

I'm young. Why should I care about my health?
Good health allows you to enjoy life. The choices you make today will affect your health later in life. It is harder to break bad habits such as physical inactivity once they are established. Learn to make healthful decisions about the food you eat, the amount of physical activity you participate in, and the amount of sleep you get. Develop healthful behaviors and safe habits when you are young to prevent illnesses and injuries in the future. For example, avoid the use of tobacco, alcohol, and other drugs and always wear a safety belt when riding in a car.

Health Skills and Wellness

Throughout your teen years, you will learn and practice many different skills. For example, you build your skills in reading and math, music and art, and perhaps sports. Like any skill, the ten health skills must be learned and then practiced regularly. Then, as you develop your health skills, you can apply them to everyday activities. Doing so will help you lead a healthy life. Your health skills will also help you keep your health triangle in balance.

Health skills help you maintain a high level of wellness. *What health skill are these two teens practicing?*

 Lesson **2** Review

Using complete sentences, answer the following questions on a sheet of paper.

Reviewing Terms and Facts

1. **Vocabulary** Define the word *prevention.* Use it in an original sentence.
2. **Recall** How do internal influences differ from external influences? Give two examples of each.
3. **Give Examples** Give an example of a situation in which you might need to practice refusal skills.

Thinking Critically

4. **Apply** Think of a decision you made about your health. Name a goal you might set as a result of that decision.
5. **Analyze** Why is advocacy considered a health skill?

Applying Health Skills

6. **Accessing Information** In a paragraph, present ideas on how to use critical thinking skills to research and evaluate health information.

LESSON 2: BUILDING HEALTH SKILLS **13**

Lesson 2

③ Assess

Evaluating

📁 Assign the Lesson 2 Review; then assign the Lesson 2 Quiz in the TCR.

• Present the following situations to students. Ask which health skill a teen in each situation needs to use:

(a) Tyrone has to choose between being on the track team and playing baseball. (*decision making*)

(b) Sarah's friends are urging her to try smoking, but Sarah doesn't want to. (*refusal skills*)

(c) LaToya wants to improve her volleyball skills so she will have a better chance of making the varsity team next year. (*goal setting*)

Enrichment

📁 Assign and distribute Enrichment Activity 2 in the TCR.

④ Close

Have students write a short paragraph (four to six sentences) explaining how they have practiced a specific health skill.

Lesson **2** Review

1. Prevention means keeping something from happening. Sentences will vary.
2. Internal influences come from inside you. External influences come from outside you. Students' examples should show that they understand this distinction.
3. Students should give an example of a situation in which they must say no to a risky or otherwise undesirable behavior.
4. Students should list goals that are clearly related to the health decision they named.
5. Advocacy is a health skill because it promotes the health of others.

13

1 Focus

Lesson Objectives

Students will be able to

- determine the kinds of decisions they make.
- discuss how their decisions reflect their character.
- explain how to make responsible decisions.
- explain how decisions affect their health.

Health Skills
- Decision Making, p. 18

Motivators

Quick Write

If students are comfortable sharing, ask them to form small groups and discuss the decisions they found hardest to make and why. As a class, discuss the types of decisions and reasons that students had in common.

For students desiring privacy, ask them to write independently in their notebooks.

Bellringer Activity

Bring to class a variety of pictures showing professionals. Ask: What kind of decisions did they have to make to get where they are? Explain that in this lesson students will learn about the decision-making process.

VOCABULARY

Write the vocabulary terms on the board. Give a definition of a term and have students identify which one you are defining.

Lesson 3

Decisions and Your Character

Quick Write

List three health-related decisions that you had to make during the past week. Which one was the hardest to make? Why?

LEARN ABOUT...

- how your decisions reflect your character.
- how you can make responsible decisions.
- how your decisions affect your health.

VOCABULARY

- decision
- consequence
- risk
- cumulative risk
- values
- character
- role model

Types of Decisions

Every day you face many decisions. **Decisions** are *choices that you make.* Some decisions are minor, such as picking out clothes to wear. Other decisions can have serious **consequences**, or *results.* During your teen years, you'll have many important decisions to make. For most of these decisions, you will want to seek the input of your parents or other trusted adults. They can help you with problem solving and goal setting as well.

When making decisions, it is important to consider the risk involved. **Risk** is *the chance of harm or loss.* Any decision that involves a risk to your health is an important one and requires careful thought. Here are some examples of decisions that affect your health:

- **Physical Health.** What kinds of foods will I eat? How much physical activity will I get?
- **Mental/Emotional Health.** How much time will I spend studying? Which people can I talk to about my problems?
- **Social Health.** Who will my friends be? What activities will I do in my free time?

Choosing to wear a bike helmet is an important decision for your health. *What other decisions affect your health?*

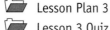 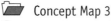   

Lesson 3 Resources

Teacher Classroom Resources

- Concept Map 3
- Cross-Curriculum Activity 2
- Decision-Making Activity 2
- Enrichment Activity 3
- Lesson Plan 3
- Lesson 3 Quiz

- Reading Tutor Activity 3
- Reteaching Activity 3
-   Transparency 3

Student Activities Workbook

- Chapter 1 Study Guide
- Applying Health Skills 3

How to Make Healthy Decisions

For important decisions, you need to take a thoughtful, step-by-step approach. An important decision can seem overwhelming—like a huge mountain you have to climb. You may worry that you'll make the wrong choice. You may even do nothing and hope that you won't have to make any choice at all.

However, making a decision doesn't have to be scary. The "secret" is to view decision making as a *process*—that is, a series of steps. **Figure 1.3** shows several steps you can follow.

FIGURE 1.3

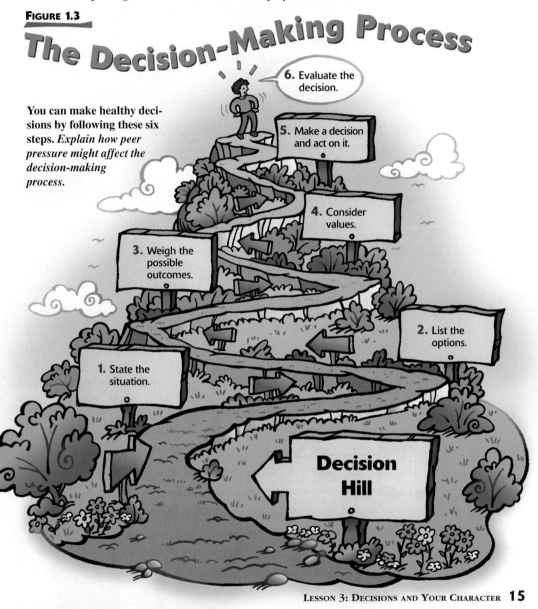

The Decision-Making Process

You can make healthy decisions by following these six steps. *Explain how peer pressure might affect the decision-making process.*

6. Evaluate the decision.

5. Make a decision and act on it.

4. Consider values.

3. Weigh the possible outcomes.

2. List the options.

1. State the situation.

Decision Hill

LESSON 3: DECISIONS AND YOUR CHARACTER **15**

Lesson 3

② Teach

VISUAL LEARNING

FIGURE 1.3 While students look at Figure 1.3, encourage them to discuss the six steps of the decision-making process. In response to the caption question, students should explain that peer pressure can be positive or negative. Negative peer pressure often has a negative effect on decisions. **INCL** *Behavior Problems, Special Learning Needs, English Language Learners*

Discussing

Ask students to suppose there are two movies they are very eager to see, but that they only have enough money to see one. Write the words *State the situation* on the board, and ask a volunteer to come forward and complete that step for the given problem while other students do the same at their desks. Have students share their responses. Make sure all students appreciate that this step in the process is not analytical; rather, it entails simple description. **L1**

MORE ABOUT...

Decisions and Peers The most difficult struggle teens will have regarding their right to make their own decisions will probably be with teens their own age. They want to have friends and be popular with their peer group, but also need to make their opinions and wants known. How to do that can be a real challenge, especially if their friends begin to put pressure on them to act in ways they do not want to act.

- Have the class think of some examples of how other teens may ask them to go along with the crowd and not make their own decisions.

- Have them prepare what they would say to resist negative peer pressure.

15

Lesson 3

Discussing

Write the word *option* on the board. Tell students that an option is one of several available choices. Ask students why it may be a good idea to write down all the options to a problem. (*Writing down the options may help students clarify them.*) Also, parents, teachers, and counselors can help outline options and recommend other perspectives.

Applying

Have each of several groups of students create a fictional character who has a problem. Have the groups state the problem in a "Dear Abby" format. Then have them brainstorm in an effort to isolate all the options available to their character. Allow groups to write a reply to the fictional character. **L2**

Discussing

Ask a volunteer to suggest a situation where a teen must make a decision, such as whether or not to join a friend who wants to skip class. Have the class tell what options are open to the teen. Tell students that options can have both positive and negative outcomes. **L1**

Evaluating

Using material from this chapter, have students discuss and evaluate ways in which they can make healthy choices from among environmental alternatives, such as leaving a smoke-filled room or selecting healthy snacks from vending machines.

Reading Check

Make up a memory device similar to H.E.L.P. to remember the good character traits listed on page 17.

Step 1: State the Situation

To make a healthy decision, first understand the situation. This isn't always simple. You need to consider all the facts and who else is involved.

Step 2: List the Options

Once you have a clear view of the situation, think of your options. Don't limit yourself to just one or two choices. Try to think of all the possibilities. If you can, you may want to ask other people for suggestions too. A family member, teacher, or friend will often come up with ideas you hadn't thought of.

Step 3: Weigh the Possible Outcomes

Consider your options carefully. Use the word *help* to guide your choice.

- **H (Healthful)** What health risks, if any, will this option present?
- **E (Ethical)** Does this choice reflect what you and your family believe to be right?
- **L (Legal)** Does this option violate any local, state, or federal laws?
- **P (Parent Approval)** Would your parents approve of this choice?

Joey set a goal to learn the trumpet. Even though it will be difficult at first, his efforts will make him happier in the long run. *Can you think of a decision that is hard in the short term but desirable in the long term?*

 ## Reading Check

Mnemonics Learning how to design and use memory aids can help students improve their metacognitive abilities as well as their memories. Metacognition is an awareness of how we think and construct meaning and is related to comprehension. Point out that the word *H.E.L.P.* (*Healthy, Ethical, Legal, Parent Approval*) is an acronym—a word formed from the initial letters of a series of words. Other mnemonics can be created using rhymes, melodies, silly sentences, and pictures. You might challenge students to work in small groups to develop mnemonics for the six steps in the decision-making process presented on pages 16–18.

For some decisions, you'll also need to consider **cumulative risk**. Cumulative (KYOO·myuh·luh·tiv) risk is *the addition of one risk factor to another, increasing the chance of harm or loss.* For example, riding your bike without a helmet is one risk factor. Riding in traffic is another. Riding at night is a third. Each of these risk factors is serious and can affect your physical health. When combined, they greatly increase your chances of severe injury.

Step 4: Consider Values

Values are *beliefs you feel strongly about that help guide the way you live.* Your values are based on what's important to you and your family. They're also based on what you believe is right or wrong. If your values are strong, any decision you make should be in agreement with them. If it isn't, you probably won't feel comfortable with the decision.

Values are part of your **character,** or *the way you think, feel, and act.* Examples of good character include:

- **Trustworthiness.** Trustworthy people are reliable and honest. You can count on them to keep their promises.
- **Respect.** Displaying respect means showing regard for other people and for authority.
- **Responsibility.** You show responsibility by being willing to accept the credit or the blame for what you do.
- **Fairness.** Being fair means treating everyone equally and honestly.
- **Caring.** You can show others you care for them by treating them with understanding and consideration. Caring people are kind and try to help others when they can.
- **Citizenship.** Good citizens obey rules and laws. They do what they can to help their school, community, and country.

These character traits influence your decisions in many ways. For example, suppose you saw a friend stealing. As a caring friend, you might want to keep silent to protect your friend. However, your sense of fairness might prompt you to speak out.

Developing Good Character

Decisions and Character

You know that your character affects the decisions you make. You can also use your decisions to help build good character. When you are faced with a decision, ask yourself: *What would a trustworthy person do? A responsible person? A caring person?*

Lesson 3

Developing Good Character

Decisions and Character

Help students learn an important step in making responsible decisions: Put all options through a values filter. Have students brainstorm a decision and several options they could select. Then as a visual aid, have them write those options on pieces of paper and place a values filter (a colored piece of cellophane labeled with a value) over the option. This will symbolically show students how their values color their options. What decision would they make according to that value?

Discussing

Write the word values on the board and have students discuss its meaning. (*beliefs you feel strongly about that help guide the way you live*) Ask students how values play a part in decision making. (*Your values help guide the way you live, therefore, guide your decisions.*) Encourage students to give examples of how values should be considered when making a decision. **L1**

Critical Thinking

Ask students to share their responses to these questions:

- Do you believe most people in your community agree on the definition of good character? Why or why not?
- Do you think people around the world probably agree on that definition? Why or why not? **L1**

DEALING WITH SENSITIVE ISSUES

Discussing Values When discussing values in class, you might find that keeping the discussion in the third person will avoid any unintended judgments or invasion of students' privacy. For example, talk about fictitious people or situations when citing examples.

Values may be especially difficult for at-risk students and students with learning disabilities to understand. Discussing what each value "looks like or sounds like" within a particular context will help these students grasp the concept. For example, you may say: "If you were showing responsibility in the hallway, what behavior would I see to know that you were responsible? What types of things would I hear you say to know that you were being responsible?" **INCL** *Special Learning Needs*

Lesson 3

HEALTH SKILLS ACTIVITY

DECISION MAKING

Use the following suggestions to help students discuss Kim's decision-making process.

1. **Kim is at a party where others are drinking.**

2. **Kim can stay and refuse to drink, which is uncomfortable; Kim can stay and drink, which is illegal and not good for her health; or Kim can go home, which will help her avoid an uncomfortable situation, and shows that she knows not to participate in illegal activity. It also shows she knows the right course of action according to the values she was taught by her parents or guardians.**

3. **Kim values her health and her friendships.**

4. **Students will probably decide Kim should go home.**

5. **Remind students to evaluate both short- and long-term consequences.**

Applying

Name a TV drama that most students watch regularly, and guide them in discussing the characters:

• Which personality in the show most clearly demonstrates good character?

• What actions and attitudes indicate his or her good character? **L1**

WATCHING FOR CHARACTER

Many television programs feature teens or children. Some of these young people have positive character traits such as responsibility and trustworthiness. Others act irresponsibly or dishonestly. *How do your favorite TV programs show young people?*

Step 5: Make a Decision and Act on It

You've thought about and compared the options. You've considered the risks and consequences. Now you're ready to make a decision and act on it. Choose the course of action that seems best and is consistent with your values. You should feel comfortable with your choice even if it isn't a "perfect" solution. If none of your choices satisfy you, go back to Step 2 and look for new options.

Step 6: Evaluate the Decision

After carrying out your decision, evaluate the results. What were the positive results? Were there negative results? Were there any unexpected outcomes? Was there anything you could have done differently? If the action you took was not as successful as you'd hoped, try again. Use the decision-making process to find another way to deal with the situation.

HEALTH SKILLS ACTIVITY

DECISION MAKING

Leaving the Party

Kim and her best friend Bethany are attending a party at a friend's home. After about an hour, Kim notices that several teens have taken beer from the refrigerator and are drinking it. She tells Bethany that she feels uncomfortable and wants to call her dad to take them home. However, Bethany says she wants to stay and might even try a few sips herself. Kim has to decide what to do.

What Would You Do?

Apply the six steps of the decision-making process to Kim's problem. What decision would you make if you were Kim? Write an explanation of your decision.

1. STATE THE SITUATION.
2. LIST THE OPTIONS.
3. WEIGH THE POSSIBLE OUTCOMES.
4. CONSIDER VALUES.
5. MAKE A DECISION AND ACT ON IT.
6. EVALUATE THE DECISION.

COOPERATIVE LEARNING ACTIVITY

Behavior Contract Making a commitment to healthful living includes what is known as the golden rule: "Do unto others as you would have others do unto you." Ask students to work together in groups to discuss what this phrase means. Ask them to brainstorm how they would like to be treated by others. Have the class work cooperatively to create a written contract that would make certain behaviors, such as name-calling and pushing unacceptable. Encourage each student to sign a copy of the contract to be valid for a period of one week. After the week, ask students whether the contracts worked. Did students honor the contract? If not, why not? Have students work in groups to demonstrate ways to have consideration for others.

Good Character, Responsible Decisions

When you think your decisions out carefully, you are more likely to make healthy choices. These decisions can improve your physical, mental/emotional, and social health. They allow you to avoid self-destructive behaviors and help you steer your life the way you want it to go.

Having good character helps you make healthy decisions. For example, if you are responsible, you recognize the consequences of your actions. You think carefully about decisions and avoid health risks.

Responsible decisions also build good character. When you are able to make your own decisions, you become more responsible. You take action and accept the consequences. In this way, you become a positive **role model**, *a person whose success or behavior serves as an example for others.*

Jenny is a good role model. She has made a decision to volunteer at her local library. *How does this decision show good character? How does it help reinforce good character?*

Lesson 3 Review

Using complete sentences, answer the following questions on a sheet of paper.

Reviewing Terms and Facts

1. **Vocabulary** Define the terms *decision* and *consequences*. Write a sentence explaining how the terms are related.
2. **Explain** What should you consider when making decisions?
3. **List** What are the six steps of the decision-making process?
4. **Recall** Why is it important to consider your values when you make a decision?

Thinking Critically

5. **Analyze** How are responsible decisions related to good character?
6. **Select** Choose one of the six steps in the decision-making process, and describe its importance to the process.

Applying Health Skills

7. **Advocacy** Make a colorful poster, or create a puppet show that could help younger children work through the decision-making process. Remember to keep it simple so they can understand and apply the process. Share your work with your class.

③ Assess

Evaluating

📁 Assign the Lesson 3 Review; then assign the Lesson 3 Quiz in the TCR.

Reteaching

📁 Assign Concept Map 3 or Reteaching Activity 3 in the TCR.

Enrichment

• 📁 Assign and distribute Enrichment Activity 3 in the TCR.

• Ask students to write a script or short story in which a teen refers to the decision-making process to make an important choice. Remind students to include each step of the process in their narratives. Let volunteers role-play their scripts or stories aloud to the rest of the class.

④ Close

Discuss the relationship between personal freedom and the additional responsibilities that come as a result of making one's own decisions.

Lesson 3 Review

1. Decisions are choices that you make. Consequences are the results of decisions. Sentences will vary.
2. You should consider the risk involved and your values.
3. See Figure 1.3 on page 15.
4. Your values represent what is important to you and your family. You probably won't feel comfortable with the decision if it does not agree with your values.
5. Good character helps you make decisions that are healthy for you and others. Responsible, healthy decisions reinforce good character.
6. Students should identify a step in the decision-making process that shows their understanding of the process.

Setting Health Goals

1 Focus

Lesson Objectives

Students will be able to
- explain the importance of having goals.
- define the steps in setting goals.
- explain how to reach goals.

Health Skills
- Goal Setting, p. 22

Motivators

Quick Write

Ask volunteers to share the things they would most like to accomplish. Remind students to seek the input of parents and other trusted adults in goal setting.

Bellringer Activity

Show students a maze. Point out that life is similar to a maze, and that in this lesson students will learn how to establish personal goals. Goals provide direction through the maze of life.

VOCABULARY

Have students divide a piece of paper into three columns. Direct them to write one vocabulary term on the top of each column and write the definition under each term. In each column, have students write a sentence using the term as it pertains to them individually.

Setting Health Goals

Quick Write

List three things that you would like to accomplish in the next year. Which of the three is most important to you? Why?

LEARN ABOUT...

- why it is important to have goals.
- how to set goals.
- how to reach your goals.

VOCABULARY

- goal
- short-term goal
- long-term goal

Kinds of Goals

A **goal** is *something that you hope to accomplish*. Some goals are broad, such as wanting to be happy or successful. Others are more specific, such as getting a part in a school play or earning enough money to buy new sports equipment.

Your goals may be short-term or long-term. A **short-term goal** is *one that you plan to accomplish in a short time*. A **long-term goal** is *one that you hope to achieve within a period of months or years*. Short-term goals often lead to long-term goals. For example, to reach the long-term goal of becoming a doctor, a short-term goal would be doing well in science classes. By focusing on the future and setting realistic goals, you take charge of your life. See **Figure 1.4.**

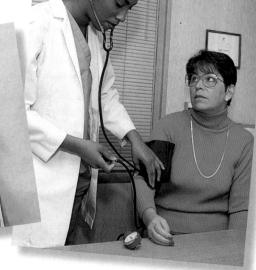

Setting a goal for yourself gives you something to work toward. *What goals have you set for yourself?*

20 CHAPTER 1: LIVING A HEALTHY LIFE

Lesson 4 Resources

Teacher Classroom Resources

 Concept Map 4

 Enrichment Activity 4

 Lesson Plan 4

 Lesson 4 Quiz

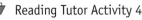 Reading Tutor Activity 4

 Reteaching Activity 4

Transparency 4 & 5

Student Activities Workbook

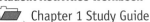 Chapter 1 Study Guide

 Applying Health Skills 4

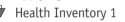 Health Inventory 1

FIGURE 1.4

Why Set Goals?

Achieving your short-term and long-term goals will give you a feeling of accomplishment.

Take control of your life.

Focus your energy.

Give yourself direction.

Shape your life in a positive way.

Improve your health.

Build your self-esteem.

Choosing Your Goals

When you set goals, it's important to consider several factors. First, what are your needs? Everyone has certain basic needs. You need food, clothing, love, and companionship. Second, what are your values? Just as values help you make decisions, they also help you set goals. For example, if your education is important to you, one of your goals may be to get good grades. Third, think about how your goals will affect your health. For example, the long-term goal of eating a balanced diet can improve your health. Career goals can also have long-term effects on health. Choosing a career in which you are helping others can help your own mental/emotional health.

Next, consider your interests, skills, abilities, and knowledge. What do you like? What do you do well? What abilities and knowledge do you need to gain? If you hope to be a writer, one of your goals might be to develop your vocabulary. Keep in mind that your goals should be realistic. If you dream of becoming a great violinist, don't expect to reach your goal in six weeks. You may need more information in order to set a realistic goal. In that case, talk with a parent, teacher, coach, or other trusted adult.

Reading Check

Which term best describes how the information in the Choosing Your Goals section is organized: *sequence, comparison,* or *cause-and-effect*?

LESSON 4: SETTING HEALTH GOALS **21**

Lesson 4

② Teach

Discussing

Present the following goals to students: graduating from college, finishing the first draft of a research report before this weekend, owning a business, getting an A on the science test tomorrow, becoming an auto mechanic.

Have students tell which are long-term goals and which are short-term goals. Have students explain why it is important to seek the input of parents and other trusted adults in setting goals. Then have students suggest other short-term and long-term goals. **L1**

VISUAL LEARNING

FIGURE 1.4 As students look at the characters in the illustration, have volunteers read aloud the six benefits of setting goals. Then ask: Do you think setting goals is beneficial even if something prevents you from achieving your goals? Why or why not? Do you think setting goals can have these benefits even if the goals you set are not appropriate or realistic for you? Why or why not? **INCL** *Behavior Problems, Special Learning Needs, English Language Learners*

Reading Check

Organizing Information Discuss with students that expository text, writing designed to set forth facts and explain ideas, can be organized in several ways. For example, *a sequence of events* tells what happens in order: first, second, and third. A *comparison* tells how things are alike and/or different. Text organized to show *cause-and-effect* explains how factors or events are linked to create an outcome. As students read Choosing Your Goals on page 21, ask them to look for signal words that provide clues to text organization. The words *first* in the first paragraph and *next* in the second paragraph suggest that this passage is organized as a sequence of events.

Analyzing

Divide the class into small groups. Provide each group with a different long-term goal that the members might aspire to attain, such as making the honor roll. Have students list the tasks involved in reaching that goal. Be sure they use each of the steps suggested in Achieving Your Goals. Students should include the importance of seeking the input of parents and other trusted adults in goal setting. Have groups share their lists. **L2**

HEALTH SKILLS ACTIVITY

GOAL SETTING

Ask students to identify personal health goals that they would like to set for themselves. Suggest that students record their goals in their private health journals. Then, as a class, have volunteers give examples of the possible health implications of long-term personal health goals.

At-risk learners and students with disabilities may need additional assistance in breaking goals into short, manageable steps. **INCL** *Special Learning Needs, Physical Disabilities*

CONNECT TO

Language Arts

GOALS IN LITERATURE
Many stories focus on characters who set specific goals and work to achieve them. Read a book or short story about someone who set a goal. Write a paragraph describing the character's goal and what she or he did to reach it. *Was the character successful? If so, why? If not, what could he or she have done differently?*

Achieving Your Goals

To achieve the goals you set, plan carefully, and proceed step by step. Here are some steps that will help you reach your goals:

- **Make your goals specific.** Don't just say "I want to become a better runner." Say "I want to run an eight-minute mile by November 1."
- **List the steps to reach your goal.** Break big goals down into smaller tasks. For example, to improve at baseball, plan to practice hitting, fielding, and throwing.
- **Get help from others.** Identify people who can help you achieve your goals. Seek the input of parents, teachers, and other trusted adults. Also, identify sources of information, such as books and magazine articles.
- **Evaluate your progress.** Check periodically to see how well you're progressing toward your goal. Should you be doing anything differently? Is there a better way to proceed? If necessary, adjust your plan, or seek help.
- **Reward yourself.** Treat yourself in a special way, and celebrate your accomplishments.

HEALTH SKILLS ACTIVITY

GOAL SETTING

Achieving Health Goals

In Lesson 1, you completed a personal health inventory. Review your responses to the inventory. Were some areas of your health weaker than you would like them to be? You can set a goal to improve your physical, mental/emotional, or social health. Remember the guidelines you have learned.

- Consider your needs, values, and interests.
- Consider your skills, abilities, and knowledge.
- Set realistic goals.
- Make your goals specific.
- List the steps to reach your goals.
- Get help from others.
- Evaluate your progress.
- Reward yourself.

ON YOUR OWN
Set two or three short-term health goals based on items for which you answered *no* on the health inventory on page 6. Make a plan for achieving your goals.

PROMOTING COORDINATED SCHOOL HEALTH

The Purpose The primary purpose of a coordinated school health program is to help your community's school tap into a system of health programming already in place. Most schools have health instruction and physical education classes, counselors, nurses, substance-abuse prevention programs, special education programs, and programs linked with state and local health agencies. Because learning is so closely tied to overall health, a student's physical and mental well-being will receive the priority attention it warrants. To help you develop such a program, or to strengthen an existing one, consult *Planning a Coordinated School Health Program* in the TCR.

Changing Your Goals

To achieve your goals, it helps to stay motivated. Being motivated means that you are eager to reach your goal. Remind yourself why you set the goal in the first place. If your needs, values, interests, and abilities have not changed, then you will probably realize that the goal is still important to you.

However, some of your needs, values, interests, and abilities probably will change during your teen years. You will be having new experiences and meeting new people. You'll grow and develop as a person. As a result, you may revise or abandon old goals and add new ones. That's fine. Setting and achieving goals should always be a flexible process.

Goal setting is a skill you will use throughout your life. Don't be afraid to adjust your short-term or long-term goals as you go along. Just remember to follow the guidelines you've learned for choosing and achieving your goals.

This teen set a goal to express his feelings in a healthy way and to disagree without getting angry. *What are your goals?*

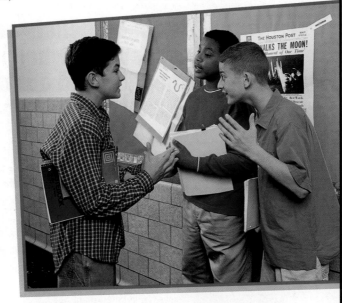

Lesson 4 Review

Using complete sentences, answer the following questions on a sheet of paper.

Reviewing Terms and Facts

1. **Vocabulary** Define *short-term goal* and *long-term goal*. Use the two terms in an original sentence.
2. **Explain** Why is it important to set realistic short-term and long-term goals?
3. **Recall** What factors should you consider when choosing your goals?
4. **Identify** Describe five steps that can help you achieve your goals.

Thinking Critically

5. **Analyze** Explain the meaning of this statement: "Setting and achieving goals should always be a flexible process."
6. **Apply** Give an example of a goal you have now that may change in the future. Explain why.

Applying Health Skills

7. **Goal Setting** Write down one of your long-term goals, and list the steps you will take to reach it. Seek the input of parents and other trusted adults in your goal-setting steps.

LESSON 4: SETTING HEALTH GOALS **23**

Lesson 4

③ Assess

Evaluating

📁 Assign the Lesson 4 Review; then assign the Lesson 4 Quiz in the TCR.

Reteaching

• 📁 Assign Concept Map 4 and Reteaching Activity 4 in the TCR.
• Divide students into eight groups, and assign each group one of the goal-setting guidelines reviewed in the Health Skills Activity on page 22. Have group members work together to draw a picture or cartoon showing how to follow their assigned guideline.

Enrichment

📁 Assign and distribute Enrichment Activity 4 in the TCR.

④ Close

Have students discuss the meaning of the saying, "If at first you don't succeed, try, try again."

Lesson 4 Review

1. A short-term goal is one that you plan to accomplish in a short time. A long-term goal is one that you hope to achieve within a period of months or years. Sentences will vary.
2. Short-term goals often lead to long-term goals. By setting realistic goals, you take charge of your life.
3. Needs, values, interests, skills, abilities, and knowledge.
4. 1) Make your goals specific. 2) List the steps to reach your goal. 3) Get help from others. 4) Evaluate your progress. 5) Reward yourself.
5. Possible response: As you grow and develop as a person, your interests and abilities change. This can affect the goals you set.
6. Responses will vary.

Getting the Health Facts Straight

① Focus

Objectives

Students will be able to
- identify common health sayings.
- access reliable health information about these sayings.
- write their own catchy health saying.

Motivator

Bellringer Activity

Ask students what they do when they get the hiccups. Write their answers on the board. Why do they do this? Who told them to do this? Does it really work?

② Teach

Discussing

Review the five popular health beliefs on this spread with students. Ask, "Is there any risk in believing these common health myths?" Explain that some myths can do more harm than good (skipping meals to lose weight). That's why the ability to access reliable health information is so important.

Direct students to page 9 and the section on "Accessing Information." Review this paragraph with the class. Then, divide the class into five groups. Assign each group one of the popular health beliefs on this spread. Tell each group to
- identify at least four reliable sources of information about this belief.
- briefly describe the type of information each source offers. (How are they different?)
- explain why each is a good source.
- report to the class on the validity of the popular health belief based on these sources.

Getting the Health

Popular beliefs aren't always true, especially when it comes to good health. Find out the facts behind some ideas that have been around for years.

Cracking your knuckles will give you arthritis.

FACT The effects of this "pop"-ular pastime aren't fully understood. We do know that cracking your knuckles might irritate those around you—and your body may not appreciate it either, says Gregg Silverman, M.D., a professor at the University of California at San Diego.

Arthritis occurs when the cartilage that pads your joints wears down and your bones rub against each other, causing the joints to swell and feel stiff. Although there have been no studies proving that one thing leads to another, Dr. Silverman says that cracking your knuckles "causes needless trauma to your joints."

If you swallow gum, it will stay inside your stomach for seven years.

FACT Actually, it takes just a few days for gum to exit the body—not seven years, says Neil Izenberg, M.D., professor of pediatrics at Jefferson Medical College in Philadelphia. However, because gum is made of mostly artificial products, it cannot be fully digested in your stomach. So if you "gum up the works" on a regular basis, you might find yourself in a sticky situation. "There have even been reports of intestinal blockage due to gum swallowing that required surgery," warns Dr. Izenberg.

The best way to stop a nosebleed is to tilt your head back.

FACT Bloody noses are caused by broken blood vessels. Although tilting your head back might stop blood from gushing out of your nose, it won't stop the bleeding itself. In fact, you might end up swallowing lots of blood. Your best bet? Sit upright and lean *forward* while pinching your nostrils shut with your thumb and forefinger. Make sure you hold this position for a full 10 minutes. Use a clean tissue or cloth to catch the blood.

24 CHAPTER 1: LIVING A HEALTHY LIFE

Beyond the Classroom

Community Explain that students are going to test how pervasive common health beliefs are in the community. As a group, brainstorm as many popular health beliefs as you can, including those from this spread. (e.g., "An apple a day keeps the doctor away." "Feed a fever, starve a cold.") Tell students that they are going to conduct an informal survey with eight of their friends and family members. Each student should pick six beliefs and ask, "Is this statement true?" and "Where did you first hear this statement?" Have students record the results and report back to the class.

Facts Straight

Skipping meals helps you lose weight quickly.

FACT There's not an ounce of truth in this advice. Not only will you not lose weight by skipping meals, you may actually *gain* weight, according to Carol Ann Rinzler, author of *Nutrition for Dummies*. Rinzler reasons that missing a meal decreases your metabolism, causing you to burn calories more slowly. This only makes you feel hungrier—and by the time you finally do reach the table, you are more likely to overeat.

Strange as it may seem, studies show that eating several small meals and snacks throughout the day is a more realistic and healthy way to lose unwanted pounds.

You'll cure hiccups if you hold your breath or breathe into a bag.

FACT It could work, but don't hold your breath. Hiccups are caused by a spasm in your diaphragm—the muscle below your lungs and heart that controls your breathing, says Dr. Izenberg. These methods may affect the nerves leading to the diaphragm, which stops the hiccups. However, it's hard to alter your breathing long enough to do the trick, so this won't work every time. ▰

TIME TO THINK...

About Health Tips

List two or three pieces of health advice that you've heard again and again that might be myths. (For example, has anyone ever told you that brushing your hair 100 strokes a day will keep it healthy?) Write down these beliefs and, using the Internet or your school's media center, investigate whether or not they are true. Report your findings to the class.

③ Apply

Time to Think

Ask students, "Why do you think people continue to believe popular, but untrue, ideas about health? How might these beliefs originate?" Direct students to ask an older family member, neighbor, teacher, or coach about popular health tips from an earlier generation that turned out to be false. (For instance, "Cigarette smoking helps you lose weight." or "A suntan is a sign of good health.") Students should ask their interview subjects, "Who started these myths? Did these myths cause people to behave in unhealthful ways? How was the truth eventually discovered?"

VISUAL LEARNING

Ask students to imagine that they are one of the people shown on this spread. Why are they behaving in this way? What might they be thinking? What is the potential outcome of their behavior?

 Health Literacy

Health Facts Tell students that they are going to take a true health fact and write about it in such a way that people are more likely to remember it. (For instance, for physical activity they may write, "Don't just sit to get fit.") Give students the following guidelines:

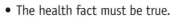

- The health fact must be true.
- Students should identify a key audience for the health fact (teen boys, grown women, and so on).
- The fact should be presented in a catchy, memorable way *for this audience*.

  Ask several volunteers to share their work with the class.

ANALYZING INFLUENCES

Objective

After completing the lesson, students will be able to analyze the internal and external influences that affect the health choices of teens.

Time: 40 minutes

Materials: butcher paper, colored markers, tape or push pins to display work

Teacher Classroom Resources

📁 Building Health Skills Activities

• Transparency Master 4, "Analyzing Influences"

• Reproducible Master 1, "Exploring Influences on Your Health"

---

1. Model

• Remind students that internal influences (*interests, likes/dislikes, fears, curiosity*) and external influences (*family, friends, media, culture*) affect their decisions. (A list of these can be found on Transparency Master 4.) Explain that in this activity they will see how their decisions are affected by these influences.

• Direct students to read or read with a partner how one teen, Thomas, is influenced by friends, family, media, curiosity, and likes and dislikes as he makes an after school snack decision. Students with special learning needs may need help following the decision-making steps.

• Discuss how influences affect the health choices of teens.

EXPLORING INFLUENCES ON YOUR HEALTH

Model

In this chapter, you learned how to make decisions that protect your health. Many internal and external factors influence your decisions. When you understand these influences, you can better understand the health choices you make. Thomas, shown below, is trying to choose an after-school snack. Read about what influences his decision.

FRIENDS
"Ari always has milk and cookies after school."

FAMILY
"Mom is always telling me to eat more vegetables."

MEDIA
"I could try that cereal I saw advertised on TV."

CURIOSITY
"Here are some mangoes— I've never tried those before."

LIKES AND DISLIKES
"I've really got a craving for some crackers and cheese."

26 CHAPTER 1: LIVING A HEALTHY LIFE

📎 **Teaching Tips**

Learning Through Diversity Group work allows students to share their knowledge and their experiences. It also promotes social interaction between students who may not normally associate. Interaction between group members allows students to learn about different ways of living and thinking. Teachers can encourage diverse group membership by assigning members to groups. Here are some factors that create diversity:

• gender
• culture
• social associations at school
• extra-curricular activities

Practice

The chart on this page shows several choices that affect your health. The left side of the chart lists factors that can influence those choices. Copy the chart onto your own paper, and fill it in. For example, if your family influences your choices about the food you eat, put an "X" next to "Family" in the column labeled "Food Choices." You may mark more than one box in each row and in each column. After you have completed the chart, answer these questions:

1. What factors influence you the most? The least?
2. Do internal or external influences affect you more?
3. Why is it important to understand what influences you?

Apply/Assess

In small groups, go over the results of your charts. Make a larger copy of the chart on butcher paper using colored markers. On this chart, record the number of students who checked each influence for each health choice. As a group, present an oral or written report of your findings to the class. In the summary, describe which influences affect your group the most and the least. Identify the influences as internal or external. Then explain why teens should understand the influences on their health.

Coach's Box

Analyzing Influences

Both internal and external influences affect your choices. These influences may include:

Internal
- interests
- likes/dislikes
- fears
- curiosity

External
- family
- friends
- media
- culture

Self-Check

- Did we describe which influences affect our group the most? The least?
- Did we identify whether internal or external factors most affect teens in our group?

Choices

Influences	Food Choices	Physical Activity	Tobacco and Alcohol	Stress	Friendships	Activities
Interests						
Likes and Dislikes						
Fears						
Curiosity						
Total for internal influences						
Family						
Friends						
Media						
Culture						
Total for external influences						

2. Practice

- Have students copy the chart on this page onto their own paper.
- Have students analyze whether internal or external factors have a stronger influence on their choices.
- Ask students to complete the chart and answer the questions.

3. Apply/Assess

- 📁 You may wish to distribute Building Health Skills Reproducible Master 1 to guide students in completing this activity (see Building Health Skills Activities booklet).
- Divide the class into groups of four or five students. Have each student share his or her findings with other group members.
- Have each group compile their findings onto butcher paper and summarize their findings in an oral or written report.
- Remind students to refer to the Self-Check before and after they develop their group reports.

Assessment Scoring

Using a rubric, student work should provide evidence of all criteria to achieve the highest score.

Skills

Student work analyzes
- influences that affect the group most.
- influences that have the least effect.

- whether internal or external influences are most influential.

Concept

Student work provides
- accurate information about the connection between influences and health.

Checking Comprehension

Use the Chapter 1 Assessment to examine the most important ideas presented in Chapter 1.

Answers to Reviewing Vocabulary and Concepts

Lesson 1
1. health
2. physical
3. mental
4. habit
5. wellness

Lesson 2
6. prevention
7. internal
8. communication
9. refusal skills
10. advocacy

Lesson 3
11. false; risk
12. true
13. true
14. false; character
15. true

Lesson 4
16. true
17. false; long-term goal
18. true
19. false; specific
20. false; likely

Thinking Critically

21. Responses should reflect an understanding of long-term goals and the lesson material.
22. Short-term goals may include exercising several times a week, eating a balanced diet, and gradually building the body's endurance.

CHAPTER ASSESSMENT 1

After You Read

Use your completed Foldable to review the information on the three sides of the health triangle.

FOLDABLES™
Study Organizer

Reviewing Vocabulary and Concepts

On a sheet of paper, write the numbers 1–10. After each number, write the term from the list that best completes each sentence.

- advocacy
- communication
- habit
- health
- internal
- mental
- physical
- prevention
- refusal skills
- wellness

Lesson 1

1. The combination of physical, mental/emotional, and social well-being is _____.
2. Eating nutritious foods is an example of good _____ health.
3. _____ health relates to the way you feel about yourself.
4. A(n) _____ is a pattern of behavior that you follow almost without thinking.
5. The achievement of a high level of overall health is _____.

Lesson 2

6. _____ means keeping something from happening.
7. _____ influences are factors that affect your actions and decisions that come from within you.
8. The clear exchange of ideas and information is called _____.

9. _____ help(s) you say no in an effective way without feeling uncomfortable.
10. You can encourage other people to live healthy lives by practicing _____.

On a sheet of paper, write the numbers 11–20. Write *True* or *False* for each statement below. If the statement is false, change the underlined word or phrase to make it true.

Lesson 3

11. The chance of harm or loss is <u>consequence</u>.
12. <u>Decisions</u> are choices that you make.
13. <u>Values</u> are beliefs you feel strongly about that help guide the way you live.
14. The way a person thinks, feels, and acts is called <u>risk</u>.
15. The addition of one risk factor to another, increasing the chance of harm or loss, is <u>cumulative risk</u>.

Lesson 4

16. A <u>goal</u> is something you hope to accomplish.
17. Graduating from high school and going on to college is an example of a <u>short-term goal</u>.
18. When choosing your goals, you should consider your needs, values, and <u>abilities</u>.
19. Making your goals <u>general</u> will help you achieve them.
20. Your goals are <u>unlikely</u> to change during your teen years.

Thinking Critically

Using complete sentences, answer the following questions on a sheet of paper.

21. **Describe** Identify the possible health implications of long-term personal and vocational goals.

INCLUSION STRATEGIES

Special Learning Needs, Behavior Problems, English Language Learners The following suggestions are helpful for students with special learning needs, students with behavior problems, and ELL students:

- Pair these students with more proficient learners who can help summarize the main concepts of the chapter.

- 🎧 Direct these students to listen to the Teen Health Audio Summaries. This component provides an audio and written summary of the chapter in both English and Spanish.

- Use photographs, drawings, or magazine clippings whenever possible to help students visualize the important concepts of the chapter.

22. **Synthesize** Write a plan that breaks down the long-term goal of achieving physical fitness into several short-term goals that can be reached one at a time.
23. **Interpret** How do external influences affect your decisions?
24. **Compare and Contrast** Explain the similarities and differences between a short-term goal and a long-term goal.
25. **Analyze** What does it mean to be a responsible person?

Career Corner

Health Teacher Do you like learning about health? Do you think you have a gift for helping others learn? A career as a health teacher might be for you. This career requires excellent communication skills and the ability to motivate others. You'll also need a four-year teaching degree with courses in health education. One way to prepare for this career is by tutoring others. For more information, visit Career Corner at health.glencoe.com.

Standardized Test Practice

Reading & Writing

Read the paragraphs below and then answer the questions.

You've just come back from an hour's bike ride, a game of basketball, or a long run. Your face is flushed and tingly, your eyes sparkle, and you feel great. What's going on inside your body?

Your breathing and heart rate have increased, bringing more oxygen to cells and removing more carbon dioxide and other waste products. Your body sends more blood to your muscles to deliver the energy and nutrients they need to work efficiently. More blood is also sent to your skin to help maintain body temperature. The rate at which your body uses energy increases, so you burn more calories. The release of energy improves your mood and reduces stress. Over time, your muscles and bones become stronger.

1. What is this passage mainly about?
   - **A** the reasons for being physically active
   - **B** the effects of physical activity
   - **C** how being physically active changes your life
   - **D** the best ways to exercise

2. You can tell from this passage that the author thinks physical activity is
   - **A** dangerous.
   - **B** difficult.
   - **C** enjoyable.
   - **D** beneficial to health.

3. Write a paragraph describing how you feel after participating in some form of physical activity.

 TH05_C1.glencoe.com/quiz

23. Responses will vary. External influences such as television shows and commercials, advice from parents, the opinions of friends, and the laws of the community may be mentioned.
24. Responses should reflect an understanding of the difference between short-term and long-term goals.
25. Responses should reflect that responsible people are willing to be held accountable for their actions.

Test Practice
1. B
2. D
3. Responses should identify a specific physical activity and give details about how the student feels when participating in that activity.

Reteaching
📁 Assign Study Guide 1 in the Student Activities Workbook.

Evaluate
- 📁 💿 Use the reproducible Chapter 1 Test in the TCR, or construct your own test using the **Exam**View® Pro Testmaker.
- 📁 Use Performance Assessment 1 in the TCR.

Assessment

Self-Assessment Direct students to review the activities that are provided throughout the chapter. Encourage each student to select one finished product or activity that demonstrates his or her best work for the chapter. Have students explain what they learned and how the examples they selected show their progress.

Career Corner

Health Teacher After having students review the career profile at health.glencoe.com, talk about how you prepared for a career in teaching. Discuss why you chose this career path.

Have students write a letter to a friend outlining why they might or might not be interested in exploring a career in teaching.

Planning Guide

Chapter 2	Skills/ Activities	Reproducible Resources	Assessment
Lesson 1 **Feeling Good About Yourself** *pages 32–35*	**HEALTH SKILLS ACTIVITY** ▲ Reinforcing Your Self-Concept (*Practicing Healthful Behaviors*), page 34	*Student Activities Workbook available for use with each chapter* 📁 Parent Letter & Activities 2 📁 Concept Map 5 📁 Cross-Curriculum Activity 3 📁 Enrichment Activity 5 📁 Lesson Plan 1 📁 Reading Tutor Activity 5 📁 Reteaching Activity 5	📁 Lesson 1 Quiz
Lesson 2 **Understanding Your Emotions** *pages 36–40*	**HEALTH SKILLS ACTIVITY** ▲ People Who Can Help (*Accessing Information*), page 39	📁 Concept Map 6 📁 Decision-Making Activity 3 📁 Enrichment Activity 6 📁 Lesson Plan 2 📁 Reading Tutor Activity 6 📁 Reteaching Activity 6	📁 Lesson 2 Quiz
Lesson 3 **Managing Stress** *pages 41–45*	**Hands-On Health** ▲ Being a Resilient Teen, page 44	📁 Concept Map 7 📁 Cross-Curriculum Activity 4 📁 Decision-Making Activity 4 📁 Enrichment Activity 7 📁 Health Lab 2 📁 Lesson Plan 3 📁 Reading Tutor Activity 7 📁 Reteaching Activity 7	📁 Lesson 3 Quiz 📁 Chapter 2 Test 📁 Performance Assessment 2
TIME HEALTH **The Stress Test** *pages 46–47*			
BUILDING HEALTH SKILLS **Managing Your Time** (*Stress Management*) *pages 48–49*		📁 Building Health Skills Reproducible Master 2	

Standards		Technology
National	State/Local	
National Health Education Standard **1.4, 3.1, 5.4, 5.5**		Transparency 6 Tape/DVD 3, Segment 2, "Building Confidence" TeacherWorks™
National Health Education Standard **1.2, 1.6, 1.8, 2.1, 5.3, 5.4**		Transparency 7 Tape/DVD 1, Segment 2, "Dealing with Your Emotions" TeacherWorks™
National Health Education Standard **1.1, 1.3, 1.6, 3.1, 3.4, 3.7**		Transparency 8 TeacherWorks™ MindJogger Videoquiz **Exam**View® Pro Testmaker
National Health Education Standard **3.1, 3.4, 3.7**		Building Health Skills Transparency Master 3

TeacherWorks™

Glencoe's new and exclusive TeacherWorks™ is an all-in-one planner and resource center. Access the complete Teacher Wraparound Edition electronically. Find all your classroom resources with just a few easy clicks, and print them right from your computer. Connect directly to Glencoe's customized Health Web site. Access the National Health Education Standards correlations, or insert your own state standards and match them directly to the electronic Teacher Wraparound Edition.

Language Diversity

- English Audio Summaries
- Spanish Audio Summaries
- English Summaries, Quizzes, and Activities
- Spanish Summaries, Quizzes, and Activities
- Spanish Parent Letters and Activities

KEY TO ABILITY LEVELS

Teaching Strategies that appear throughout the chapters have been identified by one of four codes to give you an idea of their suitability for students of varying learning styles and abilities.

L1 **Level 1** strategies should be within the ability range of all students. Often full class participation is required.

L2 **Level 2** strategies are for average to above-average students or for small groups. Some teacher direction is necessary.

L3 **Level 3** strategies are designed for students able and willing to work independently. Minimal teacher direction is necessary.

INCL Strategies are appropriate for students with particular special needs in a general classroom setting.

Mental and Emotional Health

Chapter at a Glance

Lesson 1 examines the meaning of self-concept, who influences one's self-concept, and how to develop a positive self-concept.

Lesson 2 details the various types of emotions, including the role hormones play during adolescence. It emphasizes healthful ways to express emotions, including practicing abstinence from health-risk behaviors.

Lesson 3 addresses the causes and effects of stress. It also provides strategies for coping with stress.

Health Skills

- Reinforcing Your Self-Concept (*Practicing Healthful Behaviors*), p. 34
- People Who Can Help (*Accessing Information*), p. 39
- Managing Your Time (*Stress Management*), pp. 48–49

30

HANDS-ON ACTIVITY

Check the Barometer Draw or paint a life-size barometer to hang in your classroom. Place the numbers one to ten on the barometer (one at the bottom and ten at the top) with equal spacing in between. Make a separate, movable indicator. Encourage your students to rate their emotional state each class day. Ask this question: "On a scale of one to ten, ten being best, how as a class are we feeling today?" Gain consensus from students, and move the indicator to that number. Have students identify what events or situations cause the number to rise or fall. Focus on getting the barometer to rise by making a list of activities that help students feel better and more positive. Record these activities or events on the barometer for students to see and model.

Mental and Emotional Health

Chapter Introduction

Use the options below to motivate students and preview chapter content.

HEALTH *Online*

Visit **health.glencoe.com** and have students complete Health Inventory 2 to rate their mental and emotional health. For other teaching strategies, explore the Lesson Plans and select from Cross-Curriculum, Reading, or Media Literacy activities.

GLENCOE TECHNOLOGY

Teen Health Video and DVD Series
(Each format available in both English and Spanish)

📼 💿 You may wish to use:

- Tape/DVD 1, Segment 2, "Dealing with Your Emotions"
- Tape/DVD 3, Segment 2, "Building Confidence"

MindJogger Videoquiz

📼 💿 Use MindJogger to preview or review Chapter 2 content.

TIME HEALTH

The Stress Test
pages 46–47

HEALTH *Online*

Before you begin Chapter 2, rate your mental and emotional health. Take the Health Inventory at health.glencoe.com.

FOLDABLES™ Study Organizer

Before You Read

Make this Foldable to record what you learn about positive self-concept and high self-esteem in Lesson 1. Begin with a plain sheet of 8½" × 11" paper.

Step 1
Fold a sheet of paper in half along the long axis.

Step 2
Turn the paper and fold it into thirds.

Step 3
Unfold and cut the top layer along both fold lines. This makes three tabs.

Step 4
Draw two overlapping ovals, and label as shown.

As You Read

Under the appropriate tab, take notes on what you learn about positive self-concept and high self-esteem. Under the middle tab, write down what the two have in common.

31

FOLDABLES™ Study Organizer

Dinah Zike Study Fold

Finding Similarities As students read and discuss the chapter, ask them to record what they learn about developing and benefiting from a positive self-concept under the appropriate tab of their Foldable. Guide them as they define self-esteem under the appropriate tab and record things high self-esteem enables a person to do. Under the middle tab, have students describe what a positive self-concept and high self-esteem have in common and explain how together they can help one succeed in life.

Lesson 1

Feeling Good About Yourself

① Focus

Lesson Objectives

Students will be able to
- explain self-concept.
- determine influences of self-concept.
- explain how to build positive self-concept.

Health Skills
- Practicing Healthful Behaviors, p. 34

Motivators

Quick Write
Have students share examples of personal attributes from their lists. Discuss which perceptions seem to be common among classmates.

Bellringer Activity

Tell students that what they think of themselves is called their self-concept. Ask them what their responses to the Quick Write may reveal about their self-concept. Tell them that a healthy view of one's self would incorporate both strengths and weaknesses.

VOCABULARY

Have students familiarize themselves with the terms *self-concept*, *reinforce*, and *self-esteem* by creating a word scramble that incorporates them. Have students exchange puzzles and complete their partner's puzzle.

Feeling Good About Yourself

Quick Write

Make a list of five words or phrases you would use to describe yourself. Briefly explain how each word or phrase fits you.

LEARN ABOUT...

- what your self-concept is.
- what influences your self-concept.
- how you can build a positive self-concept.

VOCABULARY

- self-concept
- reinforce
- self-esteem
- resiliency

Self-Concept and Your Health

The person you see in a mirror is only one part of who you are. There are many other important parts of the total you. Discovering these parts is one of your tasks in growing up. It's an exciting time! You are learning

- about your opinions.
- what matters most to you.
- what you like and don't like.
- whom you like to be with.
- what you do well.
- what you'd like to improve.

Each discovery gives you a clearer picture of who you are. How you think others see you adds still more to the picture. Altogether, your **self-concept** is *the view you have of yourself.* It is also called your self-image.

what I think of myself

Getting to know yourself is an important task during your teen years. *What are some questions you have about yourself?*

32 CHAPTER 2: MENTAL AND EMOTIONAL HEALTH

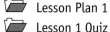

Lesson 1 Resources

Teacher Classroom Resources

📁 Parent Letter & Activities 2
📁 Concept Map 5
📁 Cross-Curriculum Activity 3
📁 Enrichment Activity 5
📁 Lesson Plan 1
📁 Lesson 1 Quiz

📁 Reading Tutor Activity 5
📁 Reteaching Activity 5
🕹 Transparency 6

Student Activities Workbook
📁 Chapter 2 Study Guide
📁 Applying Health Skills 5

Who Influences Your Self-Concept?

Many people influence your self-concept. Your parents or guardians are the first and greatest influence. Messages they send you have a lasting effect. Grandparents, sisters, brothers, and other relatives have an effect too. At school, friends and teachers are yet other influences on your self-concept.

People around you send messages by what they say to you and how they treat you. The messages can be positive or negative. Messages such as "Nice job" will **reinforce**, or *support,* your self-concept. Sending positive messages is a two-way street. You are more likely to support those who have supported you in the past. Notice how positive messages support Jim's self-concept in **Figure 2.1**.

Reading Check
Use context clues. Locate unfamiliar words on these pages. Reread the sentences around them to find their meanings.

FIGURE 2.1

Building a Positive Self-Concept

Positive messages help reinforce a person's self-concept. *What other ways do your relationships with your family and friends affect your health and well-being?*

YOUR DRAWINGS ARE ALWAYS EXCELLENT, JIM.

YOU'RE A TERRIFIC ARTIST, JIM.

YOU CERTAINLY CAN BE PROUD OF YOUR DRAWING, JIM.

---

② Teach

Discussing

Ask students why it is important to have a clear view of themselves. (*will be able to focus on strengths and improve weaknesses, will be able to know what they need to do to stay healthy*) **L1**

Discussing

Ask students to make a list of the people who influence them and the ways students are influenced.

• Speculate why it is important to associate with positive people.

• Differentiate between positive and negative relationships that can affect individual health, such as clubs, gangs, and families.

Share in a small group. Point out that some people become our support systems. **L1**

VISUAL LEARNING

FIGURE 2.1 Students should recognize that positive influences help create a strong self-image. Ask students to describe the attitudes of the teens in the illustrations. Ask: How did each experience contribute to the teen's positive self-concept? Share written answers with the class. **INCL** *Behavior Problems, Special Learning Needs, English Language Learners*

Reading Check

Context Clues Understanding the meanings of words from their context is one of the most powerful comprehension tools available to students. Have students practice figuring out word meanings from context. Model the process for students frequently until using context clues becomes automatic. Stress that students should consult a dictionary only when they can't figure out the meaning of a word from context. Have students explain how context provides clues to the meaning of the word *positive* in the second paragraph on page 33. (*Positive messages must be good because they reinforce, or support, a person's self-concept.*)

Lesson 1

Discussing

Ask students how people demonstrate positive self-concept. Discussion could include

- examples in other teens.
- examples in adults.
- potential problems when friends don't have a positive self-concept.
- the benefits of being around people with a positive self-concept.

Cooperative Learning

Have students form small groups. Ask the members of each group to select a novel, play, or weekly TV drama with which they are all familiar. Then have students discuss what and how the words, actions, and attitudes of the characters reflect the characters' self-concepts. **L1**

HEALTH SKILLS ACTIVITY

PRACTICING HEALTHFUL BEHAVIORS

Use the following suggestions to help students discuss Kim's decision-making process.

Guide students in reading and discussing the suggestions for reinforcing self-concept by developing the positive qualities listed. Let volunteers give examples of each quality.

Then have groups plan and practice their scenes. Let each group present their scene to the rest of the class, and ask students in the audience to provide feedback.

For more about communication skills, see Chapter 3, pages 66–69.

Focusing on what you do well helps you develop a positive self-concept. *What is another way to develop a positive self-concept?*

Developing a Positive Self-Concept

There are several ways to develop a positive self-concept. First of all, recognize your strengths and limitations, and concentrate on what you do well. That gives you the confidence to try new things. Having the courage to try something new also reinforces your self-concept. Some other ways to develop a positive self-concept include:

- Think positive thoughts about yourself and others.
- Say positive things to friends and family members.
- Learn more about yourself and the person you want to be.
- Don't dwell on hurtful remarks you get from others.
- Accept encouragement; use it to recognize your strengths.
- Develop realistic expectations—no one is perfect.
- Build **resiliency**, or *the ability to bounce back from difficulties.* Participating in healthful activities with others, such as being part of a school club, is one way to develop resiliency. Resiliency not only boosts your self-concept, it can also help protect against self-destructive behaviors.

HEALTH SKILLS ACTIVITY

PRACTICING HEALTHFUL BEHAVIORS

Reinforcing Your Self-Concept

To enhance your self-concept and self-confidence, work to develop these positive qualities:

- *Honesty* involves expressing your thoughts and emotions in a way that won't hurt other's feelings.
- *Integrity* means standing by values.
- *Respecting the dignity of others* includes being considerate and accepting people's differences.
- *Critical thinking* and *problem solving* help you make good decisions.

WITH A GROUP
Brainstorm and list ways that a person could demonstrate the qualities listed here. Choose one of the ways you came up with and role-play a situation in which a teen demonstrates this characteristic.

Health Literacy

Influencing Factors On the board write this saying: *Sticks and stones may break my bones, but names can never hurt me.* Discuss what the saying means. Have students conclude that, while name-calling cannot hurt a person physically, it can affect the person's self-concept and adversely influence his or her mental and social health. Point out that the person at whom cruel names or insults are directed may begin to believe that there is something wrong with him or her and become shy or withdrawn. The person may also become insulting and cruel to others. Ask students to imagine that they work for a mental health hot line and have received a call from a person who has been injured by ridicule from others. What advice would they offer?

Benefits of a Positive Self-Concept

Having a positive self-concept helps you build healthy self-esteem. Your **self-esteem** is *the ability to like and respect yourself.* Self-esteem enables you to

- have confidence in yourself.
- feel appreciated, loved, and secure.
- care about yourself and want to look after your health.
- care about others and want to get along with them.
- bounce back after a disappointment.

A positive self-concept helps you appreciate and improve your good points. You will make confident decisions and stand up for what's important to you.

A positive self-concept and high self-esteem will help you achieve what you set out to do. *How does a positive self-concept contribute to success?*

Lesson 1 Review

Using complete sentences, answer the following questions on a sheet of paper.

Reviewing Terms and Facts

1. **Vocabulary** Define the terms *self-concept* and *self-esteem*. Write a sentence that includes both terms.
2. **Identify** Name three people who have had a positive influence on your self-concept.
3. **Give Examples** Name three ways you can develop a positive self-concept.

Thinking Critically

4. **Explain** Why is having a positive self-concept important to your overall health?
5. **Describe** How can recognizing your strengths and limitations benefit your health?

Applying Health Skills

6. **Goal Setting** Make a list of your three best qualities. Write a journal entry describing how you plan to make the most of these strengths over the next few weeks. Follow your plan carefully for a week. Then write another entry describing the results.

❸ Assess

Evaluating

📁 Assign the Lesson 1 Review; then assign the Lesson 1 Quiz in the TCR.

Reteaching

- 📁 Assign Concept Map 5 or Reteaching Activity 5 in the TCR.
- Provide students with sheets of drawing paper large enough to cover their health textbooks. Ask them to design original covers decorated with images—either symbolic or realistic—that emphasize the importance of a positive self-concept.

Enrichment

- 📁 Assign and distribute Enrichment Activity 5 in the TCR.
- Have students write a letter to someone who has influenced or encouraged them in a positive way. Have students bring the address of the person to whom they are writing. With their permission, mail the students' letters from school, or use the faculty mailboxes if students' letters are to teachers or coaches.

❹ Close

Ask students to write their own definitions of *self-concept*.

Lesson 1 Review

1. Self-concept is the view you have of yourself; self-esteem is the ability to like and respect yourself. Sentences will vary.
2. Students may mention parents, guardians, other relatives, friends, or teachers.
3. Students should name any three ways from page 34.
4. A positive self-concept encourages you to care about yourself and to want to look after your health.
5. Responses should reflect a positive self-concept.

Lesson 2

Understanding Your Emotions

① Focus

Lesson Objectives

Students will be able to
- identify different types of emotions.
- describe healthful ways to express strong feelings.
- find help in dealing with emotions.

Health Skills
- Accessing Information, p. 39

Motivators

 Quick Write

Tell students: "Without noise, show me how you look when you are happy." Then have them demonstrate expressions of sadness, worry, fear, concern, and grief.

Students with behavior problems and special learning needs often have difficulty expressing emotion appropriately. Discuss and model appropriate versus inappropriate ways to show emotion. Discuss how impulsive behavior can often lead to negative consequences. **INCL** *Behavior Problems, Special Learning Needs*

Bellringer Activity

Ask students to describe situations that are highly emotional. Discuss what factors tend to elicit strong emotions.

VOCABULARY

Write the vocabulary terms on the board. Instruct students to skim the lesson for the definitions of the terms. Then have them record these important terms and definitions in their notebooks, where they can be referred to as needed.

Quick Write

Make a list of five ways you show that you are happy. Now list five ways you show that you are angry. Do you find one feeling easier to express than the other? What does that mean to you?

LEARN ABOUT...

- the kinds of emotions you experience.
- how you can express strong feelings in healthful ways.
- where you can get help in dealing with your emotions.

VOCABULARY

- emotion
- hormones
- abstinence

Your Emotions

How do you feel right now? Are you happy, sad, or angry? Happiness, sadness, and anger are emotions, or *feelings*. In a single day, you probably experience many different emotions.

Types of Emotions

You may be more comfortable with some emotions than others. Most people like to feel happy, well liked, and appreciated. When you're feeling this way, you enjoy life more. You feel more confident and you respond well to others.

However, emotions such as anger, fear, sadness, and grief are also normal. It's how you express them that makes a difference. For example, being nervous about Friday's math test may drive you to study hard and do well.

Physical activity is one healthy way to release your emotions. *How do you feel after you have been active?*

Lesson 2 Resources

Teacher Classroom Resources

 Concept Map 6
 Decision-Making Activity 3
Enrichment Activity 6
Lesson Plan 2
Lesson 2 Quiz
Reading Tutor Activity 6

 Reteaching Activity 6
 Transparency 7

Student Activities Workbook

 Chapter 2 Study Guide
Applying Health Skills 6

Emotional Changes During Adolescence

Things that happen around you can affect your emotions. Your emotions also have a lot to do with what's happening inside you. This is especially true during your teen years. Teens often experience sudden changes of emotion. Your hormones (HOR·mohnz) are partly responsible for these shifts. **Hormones** are *powerful chemicals, produced by glands, that regulate many body functions.*

During your teen years, hormones cause rapid changes in your body and play an important role in your personal health. They can cause emotional changes too. The results can be confusing. One minute you feel on top of the world, the next minute you're down in the dumps. In short, you're having mood swings—like the teen in **Figure 2.2**.

FIGURE 2.2

Adolescent Mood Swings

Emotional shifts, sometimes called mood swings, are common for teens. Both ends of the swing are normal.

LOVE
HAPPINESS
JOY

ANGER
SADNESS
FEAR

LESSON 2: UNDERSTANDING YOUR EMOTIONS **37**

CONNECT TO

Science

FEELINGS—INSIDE AND OUTSIDE
Emotions can cause physical changes in the body. You may feel lots of energy. Your heart may beat faster, and your muscles may become tense. *How does your body respond to emotions such as anger, nervousness, or excitement?*

Lesson 2

2 Teach

VISUAL LEARNING

FIGURE 2.2 Direct students to study the illustration in Figure 2.2. Ask them to make a list of other emotions they can think of. Allow students to share and compare their lists. Ask which emotions students have experienced. Under what circumstances were these emotions experienced?

Discussing

Help students discuss various ways in which they can express feelings, such as happiness, confidence, and contentment. Ask students:

• Do you think that there are healthy and unhealthy ways to deal with these pleasant emotions? (*An extreme example of an unhealthy expression of joy is the rioting that sometimes breaks out when a local team wins a championship.*)

• What are some healthy ways to deal with them?

• What might cause teens to deal with these pleasant emotions in unhealthy ways? **L1**

Discussing

Point out that mood swings themselves can cause emotional reactions. Ask: How are you likely to feel when your emotions change rapidly, often without clear reasons? How can understanding mood swings make them easier to deal with? **L1**

COOPERATIVE LEARNING ACTIVITY

Examining Emotions Ask groups of students to create a one-act play about a teen who is grappling with his or her emotions. As one possible scenario, the teen might be experiencing a mixture of fear and elation over having been accepted as a member of a school sports team with a citywide reputation for excellence. The play should depict the various emotional stages the student goes through and healthful ways in which he or she vents those emotions. Some students in the class should serve as writers; some as set designers; and some, of course, as actors. When work is complete, students should stage their production, either for the class, for the student body of the school, or for an elementary school.

Listing

Ask: Which emotions are you most likely to hold inside? Why? Have students list at least five factors that make it difficult for them to express certain emotions. Some students may want to discuss their lists; others should feel free to keep their lists confidential. **L1**

Examining the Issues

Write the words *strong emotions* on the board. After eliciting a response, share a personal experience or situation where strong emotions led to positive action. Invite groups of students to brainstorm other examples of strong emotions. Help students through discussion to realize that emotions are complex and often misunderstood. **L2**

VISUAL LEARNING

FIGURE 2.3 Direct students' attention to the illustrations in Figure 2.3 and to the explanations of four healthy ways to deal with strong emotions. Ask: Is one of these methods best for everyone? Why not? What are the advantages to trying out different methods of dealing with strong emotions? Help students identify which emotions require the use of self-control, and methods they might practice when self-control is needed to manage strong emotions, including affection and love. **INCL** *Behavior Problems, Special Learning Needs, English Language Learners*

When you offer support and encouragement, you help a friend express emotions in a healthy way. *What are some other ways to show you care?*

Expressing Your Emotions

As you've learned, emotions are neither good nor bad. It's the way you express them that counts. Holding emotions inside can harm all sides of your health triangle:

- **Physical health**—trouble sleeping, sleeping too much, stomachaches, headaches.
- **Mental/emotional health**—tension, trouble concentrating, anger, being disorganized.
- **Social health**—arguments with friends or family members, sulking, violent behavior.

Figure 2.3 shows some positive ways of dealing with strong emotions. Healthy ways to express affection and love include being respectful to others and helping them.

FIGURE 2.3

Dealing with Your Emotions

Here are four healthy ways to express strong emotions.

Thinking it out can help you understand your emotions and the reasons you are feeling them.

Creating something, such as a poem or a drawing, can help you express your feelings.

Physical activity can help you work out your feelings.

Talking to others— such as friends, siblings, or trusted adults—can help you express your feelings.

38 CHAPTER 2: MENTAL AND EMOTIONAL HEALTH

PROMOTING COORDINATED SCHOOL HEALTH

The Team Under the coordinated school health program, each campus would have a site-based decision-making committee composed of teachers, campus staff, parents, community members, and business representatives. In addition to academic performance objectives, plans related to students' physical and psychological needs also must be addressed. Schools might already have a drop-out prevention committee working together with school/community drug prevention committees. These committees can also focus on the students' academic performance as related to health. For more detailed information about developing such a program, consult *Planning a Coordinated School Health Program* in the TCR.

Practicing Abstinence

Everyone has some basic emotional needs such as the need to be loved and accepted. Unfortunately, some teens try to fill their emotional needs by engaging in risky behavior. These teens may join gangs. Some may use tobacco, alcohol, or illegal drugs. Others may become sexually active. These behaviors, however, do not really meet emotional needs. Dealing with emotions in healthy ways includes resisting these kinds of unhealthy behaviors.

Abstinence (AB·sti·nense) is *not participating in health-risk behaviors.* When you practice abstinence, you are using a strategy for avoiding many harmful situations. This protects your health and the health of others.

Being abstinent communicates your refusal to engage in unsafe behaviors. It's also a way to practice self-control.

Developing Good Character

Caring

Caring is showing concern for yourself and for others. You display acts of caring when you comfort a friend, tutor your peers, share your possessions, or help a classmate who is hurt or upset. Think of times you have shown others that you care for them.

Developing Good Character

Caring

Discuss with students the idea that when you care for someone, you don't do things that would put them at risk or hurt them. Ask them to give examples of ways they have shown caring. Have students describe healthy ways to show love, affection, and caring for others. Students with behavior problems need appropriate modeling of these behaviors. **INCL** *Behavior Problems.*

Cross-Curriculum Activity

LANGUAGE ARTS Have a volunteer use a dictionary to look up and read aloud the definition of *abstain,* the verb from which the noun *abstinence* is formed. (*"to hold oneself back voluntarily, especially from something regarded as improper or unhealthy"*) Ask students: Why is the word *voluntarily* such an important part of this definition? Can someone else choose abstinence for you? Why not? **L1**

HEALTH SKILLS ACTIVITY

ACCESSING INFORMATION

People Who Can Help

Do your emotions get the best of you sometimes? Have you tried several strategies and found that you are still troubled or confused? There are lots of people who can help.

● **TRUSTED ADULTS.** Talking to your parents, guardians, and other relatives can help you understand your emotions. Parents and other trusted adults can help in problem solving. People such as ministers and youth leaders can also provide guidance.

● **TEACHERS, SCHOOL NURSES, AND COUNSELORS.** The people who work at your school are ready to help when you experience troubling emotions or need help with a problem.

● **HEALTH CARE PROVIDERS.** Doctors, nurses, and professional counselors can provide valuable help.

ON YOUR OWN
Think about a time when your emotions troubled you. What did you do? Where did you go for help? What will you do the next time you feel troubled?

HEALTH SKILLS ACTIVITY

ACCESSING INFORMATION

Let students meet in small groups to read and discuss the activity introduction. Ask group members to name specific people who fit each category.

Then have students write journal entries recording their responses to the On Your Own questions.

Health Literacy

Health Influences Psychoneuroimmunology (PNI) is the science that describes the brain's ability to send signals to immune-system cells in the body. Dr. David Felton, a medical doctor with a Ph.D. in neuroanatomy, is credited with discovering the hard evidence confirming the mind-body connection. PNI researchers have demonstrated that the brain produces many substances that enhance health. Feelings of optimism about health and positive expectations can boost naturally occurring substances in the body, such as endorphins, to relieve pain, support the immune system, and fight viral and bacterial infections. Athletes know that positive attitudes and expectations affect performance and often the outcome of an athlete's game.

❸ Assess

Evaluating

📁 Assign the Lesson 2 Review; then assign the Lesson 2 Quiz in the TCR.

Reteaching

• 📁 Assign Concept Map 6 or Reteaching Activity 6 in the TCR.

• Have small groups of students work together to list the health benefits of expressing emotions in positive ways. Remind students to include benefits to physical, mental/emotional, and social health.

Enrichment

• 📁 Assign Enrichment Activity 6 in the TCR.

• Have students work with partners to plan and create original illustrations showing the relationship between abstinence and self-esteem. For example, they could show the mutual effect they have on one another in the following way:

abstinence   self-esteem

❹ Close

Have each student write a one-sentence response to this question: As you studied this lesson, what was the most important thing you learned about your own emotions?

Sometimes, your peers may pressure you to take part in dangerous or unhealthy behaviors. Situations like these really test your emotions. You want to maintain your friendships, but you also want to make healthy decisions. It may help to remember that friends who do dangerous things could get into trouble. Being around them may get you into trouble too. It could also cost you the respect of parents and other people you care about. You could even lose respect for yourself.

Dealing with this pressure will be easier if you practice refusal skills. Refusal skills let you say no to unsafe behaviors and help you stay in emotional control. Chapter 3 tells you more about refusal skills. It also teaches you how to use communication skills. These skills involve strategies for speaking and listening. Both are important as you learn to deal with your emotions.

Caring friends will not pressure you to engage in risky behaviors. *Name some healthy activities you and a variety of friends enjoy doing together.*

Lesson 2 Review

Using complete sentences, answer the following questions on a sheet of paper.

Reviewing Terms and Facts

1. **Vocabulary** Define the word *emotion*, and use it in a sentence.
2. **Explain** Why are mood swings common among teens?
3. **Describe** What are some healthy ways to express affection and love?

Thinking Critically

4. **Analyze** What is the role of hormones as they relate to emotional changes and personal health in teens?

5. **Apply** You are angry because your brother or sister has borrowed your headphones without asking, and you want to use them. How will you deal with your emotions and work out the problem in a way that shows self-control?

Applying Health Skills

6. **Practicing Healthful Behaviors** Describe strategies such as abstinence for communicating refusal to engage in unsafe behaviors.

40 CHAPTER 2: MENTAL AND EMOTIONAL HEALTH

Lesson 2 Review

1. An emotion is a feeling. Sentences will vary.
2. During the teen years, changing hormones cause mood swings, or sudden emotional changes.
3. Possible response: Being respectful to others and helping them.
4. Hormones can trigger emotional changes (mood swings), which can affect attitudes and feelings toward personal health.

5. Steps should include calming down, figuring out exactly why you are angry, talking to others, exercising or doing something creative, and culminate in talking out the problem with the sibling.

Managing Stress

Stress: A Natural Part of Life

Zach is going to be the quarterback this afternoon, but he has played this position only once. His mouth feels dry, and his stomach feels like butterflies are fluttering inside it. Kendall has just found out that she won the part she wanted in the school play. Her heart is pounding. What's going on?

Zach and Kendall feel **stress**. Stress is *your body's response to changes around you*. Ordinary events like forgetting a locker combination or taking a test can cause stress. Big changes—like starting a new school, parents divorcing, or a friend moving away—also create stress. Sometimes, people respond to these types of events with anxiety. Anxiety is feeling uncertain or worried about what may happen. No matter what the situation, try to remember that stress is a natural part of life that can be managed by developing and using effective coping strategies.

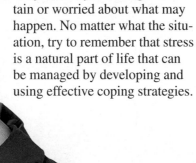

Quick Write

List some situations in which you felt nervous or anxious. Tell what you did to relieve those troubling feelings.

LEARN ABOUT...

- what stress is.
- how your body responds to stress.
- how you can manage stress.

VOCABULARY

- stress
- eustress
- distress
- stressor
- adrenaline
- fatigue

Jerry is feeling stress as he rushes to finish his test. *Define stress. What kinds of situations are stressful for you?*

Lesson 3

Managing Stress

① Focus

Lesson Objectives

Students will be able to
- define stress.
- describe physiological responses to stress.
- identify ways to manage stress.

Motivators

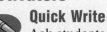

Quick Write

Ask students to share their lists. Ask students to describe the ways they find most effective for coping with anxiety and stress. Ask: What are the effects of stress on individual health and relationships?

Bellringer Activity

Rest each end of a thin sheet of cardboard on a sturdy support. Anchor each end with a heavy object. Place individual items, such as pencils, on the cardboard until it collapses. Ask students to explain how this demonstration might relate to the impact of troubling events on an individual. **INCL** *Special Learning Needs*

VOCABULARY

Point out to students that four of the vocabulary words have a common root: *stress.* Ask students to use a dictionary to analyze the prefixes *eu-* and *dis-* and the suffix *-or* found in the three derived words. Then have them guess at the meanings of the derived words.

Lesson 3 Resources

Teacher Classroom Resources
- 📁 Concept Map 7
- 📁 Cross-Curriculum Activity 4
- 📁 Decision-Making Activity 4
- 📁 Enrichment Activity 7
- 📁 Health Lab 2
- 📁 Lesson Plan 3
- 📁 Lesson 3 Quiz

- 📁 Reading Tutor Activity 7
- 📁 Reteaching Activity 7
- 🔧 Transparency 8

Student Activities Workbook
- 📁 Chapter 2 Study Guide
- 📁 Applying Health Skills 7
- 📁 Health Inventory 2

Lesson 3

② Teach

Comparing

Ask for volunteers who have experienced eustress to share their experiences with the class. After they have shared, ask:

• How are the experiences similar? In what ways are they different?

• How is the stress those individuals experienced different from distress, or negative stress?

VISUAL LEARNING

FIGURE 2.4 Have students examine Figure 2.4 and note the various body parts that play a role in the stress reaction. Divide the class into pairs, and have each pair select one of those body parts. Partners are to use outside resources to investigate the primary function of the organ they have chosen. Have students share their findings. **INCL** *Behavior Problems, Special Learning Needs, English Language Learners*

FYI

The fight-or-flight response was well suited to humans who lived as hunter-gatherers. Their stressors took the form of physical dangers. Today, however, most stressors are primarily psychological rather than physical.

Reading Check

Identify some of the causes of stress. Then define some of the negative and positive effects of stress on individual health and on relationships.

Types of Stress

Stress can be positive or negative. *Positive stress* is called **eustress** (YOO·stres) and can help you accomplish tasks, reach goals, and escape danger. It motivates athletes to work hard during practice. As a result, they perform well in competition. Can you think of an example of positive stress?

Distress, or *negative stress,* gets in your way and holds you back. Personal problems at home or at school produce negative stress. So do natural disasters like storms or floods. Too much negative stress can be unhealthy.

Your Body's Response to Stress

What makes your hands sweat when you worry and your heart jump when you're really happy? It's your body's way of responding to **stressors**, which are *objects, people, places, and events that trigger stress*. A stressor sets off a chain of events called the "fight-or-flight response," shown in **Figure 2.4**.

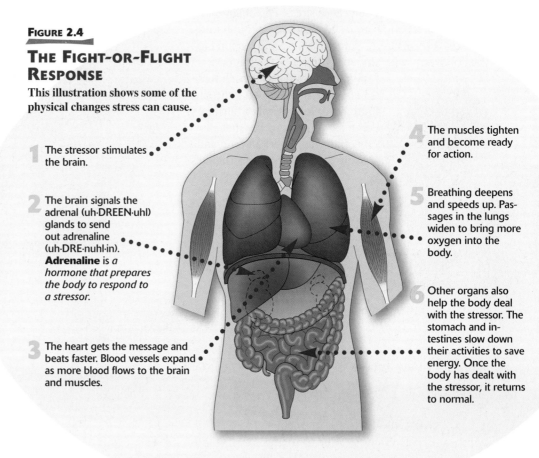

FIGURE 2.4

THE FIGHT-OR-FLIGHT RESPONSE

This illustration shows some of the physical changes stress can cause.

1. The stressor stimulates the brain.

2. The brain signals the adrenal (uh·DREEN·uhl) glands to send out adrenaline (uh·DRE·nuhl·in). **Adrenaline** is *a hormone that prepares the body to respond to a stressor.*

3. The heart gets the message and beats faster. Blood vessels expand as more blood flows to the brain and muscles.

4. The muscles tighten and become ready for action.

5. Breathing deepens and speeds up. Passages in the lungs widen to bring more oxygen into the body.

6. Other organs also help the body deal with the stressor. The stomach and intestines slow down their activities to save energy. Once the body has dealt with the stressor, it returns to normal.

42 CHAPTER 2: MENTAL AND EMOTIONAL HEALTH

Reading Check

Cause-and-Effect Relationships Recognizing causal relationships is critical to comprehension. Students need to understand that events don't simply happen—they have reasons, or causes. Teach students to ask "What happened?" to identify an effect. They should ask, "Why did it happen?" to identify a cause. Explain that a cause may have more than one effect, and an effect may have more than one cause. Point out that *because, so, since, as a result, therefore,* and similar words signal cause-and-effect relationships. Have students identify the causes and effects of stress mentioned on page 42.

Stress and Fatigue

Dealing with too much stress can cause **fatigue** (fuh·TEEG), or *extreme tiredness*. You can deal with the fatigue caused by stress by removing the source of stress, increasing your activity level, or learning ways to manage the stress.

Stress, Health, and Relationships

Stressors can affect both individual and family health. For example, getting behind in your schoolwork may cause you to feel irritable and be disrespectful to others. Knowing how to manage stress can help you avoid its negative effects on relationships.

Ways to Manage Stress

How do you keep negative stress from damaging your health? Sometimes, you can avoid a stressor. For example, if you're often late to school, you can get up earlier. Some stressors, however, are simply part of life. You need to learn to manage them. Some strategies for managing stress and anxiety are listed on pages 44 and 45.

Positive stress can help you accomplish tasks and reach goals. *How can positive stress affect your schoolwork?*

Discussing

Have students read and discuss the definition of *stressors* and *fatigue*. Ask students to indicate by a show of hands whether they have ever experienced fatigue caused by stress.

- Ask volunteers to share the circumstances under which they felt stress-related fatigue and what steps they took to manage this stress.

- Ask students to identify the impact of stressors on the health of the individual and on families. **L1**

HEALTH SKILLS PRACTICE

Stress Management Encourage students to practice relaxation techniques. Tell them: Stress is powerful. You feel stress by being in certain places. A dentist's office may be one example! Help yourself with imagery. Reduce your stress by closing your eyes and breathing deeply. Imagine you are at the beach or another fun place. Gradually open your eyes again and feel the calm and break in tension. Take deep breaths and tackle the stressful situation.

Beyond the Classroom

Home Parents and other trusted adults are always the recommended resource for teens who want to discuss the effects of stress on their lives or who need help with problem solving. Many teens may not feel comfortable turning to their parents to discuss issues they consider personal. For this reason, it is important to help students identify other people who may meet the definition of a "trusted adult." Remind them that parents of friends, adult neighbors, and other family members can be helpful. Another way of dealing with stress is to write in a private journal. Putting the problem into words helps define the problem. After writing about the problem, list healthful ways to take care of it.

Lesson 3

Cross-Curriculum Activity

VISUAL ARTS Have a volunteer summarize the techniques for managing stress and anxiety listed on pages 44 and 45. Divide the class into small groups, and have each group brainstorm a slogan that might be directed to teens under stress, informing them of ways to combat stress. Ask groups to create posters illustrating their slogans and enumerating the kinds of techniques listed in the text. **L2** **INCL** *Behavior Problems, Special Learning Needs, Different Learning Styles (Visual)*

Hands-On Health

BEING A RESILIENT TEEN

Time: 40 minutes

TEACHING THE ACTIVITY

- Gather the necessary materials. With students, read and discuss the introduction and the directions for completing the activity.
- Divide the class into small groups and have them complete Steps 1 through 3.
- Allow time for each group to present its flyer to the class.
- Lead a class discussion on the In Conclusion questions.

ASSESSMENT

Ask students:

- What did this activity teach you about building resiliency?
- How might you help friends and peers build resiliency?

- **Recognize stress.** A funny feeling in your stomach, fast breathing, and a pounding heart are all signs of stress.
- **Manage your time.** Set aside regular times to do homework and chores. That way you won't have to rush to get them done at the last minute.
- **Set your priorities.** Make a list of things you want to accomplish. Decide how important each task is. Focus on one thing at a time. Too many activities—such as practices, club meetings, or after-school work—can lead to stress.
- **Redirect your energy.** Stress increases your energy. Use that energy to do something positive. You could enjoy a hobby or offer to help a family member with a project.

Hands-On Health

BEING A RESILIENT TEEN

Everyone experiences stress and difficulties in life. Being resilient can help you cope with stress and other problems. One way to build resiliency is to develop *protective factors*. Protective factors include positive relationships and behaviors. They can protect you from the harmful effects of risky situations. In this activity, you will create a flyer with tips to promote resiliency.

WHAT YOU WILL NEED
- Plain sheets of paper
- Markers, crayons, or colored pencils

WHAT YOU WILL DO

1. In small groups, identify and list people who might be part of a teen's support system, such as adult family members, teachers, and coaches. Then, write down how teens can strengthen their relationships with others.

2. Next, brainstorm and list actions that teens can take to boost mental/emotional health. Examples include getting involved in school activities and taking up a new hobby.

3. Now, create a colorful flyer featuring the items you listed in Steps 1 and 2. Title your flyer "Building Resiliency." As a group, explain to the class how the tips in your flyer can help a teen build resiliency.

IN CONCLUSION

After all groups have presented their flyers, discuss these questions as a class: How might the tips in the flyers help build resiliency? How might developing protective factors help teens cope with difficulties?

Your teacher will make a copy of each group's flyer so that each student will have one. Put the tips in the flyer into practice to develop your own resiliency.

44 CHAPTER 2: MENTAL AND EMOTIONAL HEALTH

Beyond the Classroom

Community Divide the class into two research committees. One of the committees is to compile a list of people and places within the community that students can turn to when feeling stress. The list, which is to include phone numbers and, when relevant, addresses, may include outreach centers, neighborhood clubs with gym facilities that welcome young people, counselors in free clinics, and laypeople and members of the clergy. The other committee is to put together a list of original relaxation strategies that also make use of community resources, including playgrounds and interesting locations where people can hike, climb, or simply relax amid peaceful surroundings.

- **Talk to someone.** Talking about stress can relieve the pressure. A parent, friend, or school counselor may give you some good advice.
- **Relax.** Take a deep breath, and exhale slowly. Do it again. Try to calm yourself when you feel stress. Take time to be alone and fill your mind with positive thoughts. You could also relax by reading or listening to soothing music.
- **Put things in perspective.** Remember that you are not alone; everyone has stress and other problems. Do not make your problems seem bigger than they really are.
- **Increase your activity.** Becoming more active releases the physical energy that builds up when you feel stress. Physical activity naturally calms the body.

Redirecting your energy by being physically active is a good way to manage stress. *Describe some other strategies for managing stress and anxiety that work for you.*

Lesson 3 Review

Using complete sentences, answer the following questions on a sheet of paper.

Reviewing Terms and Facts

1. **Vocabulary** Define the terms *stress*, *eustress*, and *distress*.
2. **Explain** Define the effects of stress on individual health and relationships.
3. **List** Name two ways your body responds to stress.
4. **Identify** What is *fatigue*?

Thinking Critically

5. **Synthesize** Why is adrenaline sometimes called "the emergency hormone"?
6. **Analyze** Identify two stressors and their impact on the health of the individual and family.

Applying Health Skills

7. **Stress Management** Harley feels stressed and anxious because he has a lot of homework. What are some ways that Harley could manage his stress and anxiety?

LESSON 3: MANAGING STRESS **45**

3 Assess

Evaluating

Assign the Lesson 3 Review; then assign the Lesson 3 Quiz in the TCR.

Reteaching

- Assign Concept Map 7 and Reteaching Activity 7 in the TCR.
- Ask students to name the characteristics of eustress and distress and to give examples of each. Record their ideas in two lists on the board.

Enrichment

- Assign Enrichment Activity 7 in the TCR.
- Have students work in small groups to plan, write, and illustrate brochures that will help teens deal with common stressors.

4 Close

Ask students to write poems or songs or draw pictures that express what they do when they feel overwhelmed.

Lesson 3 Review

1. Stress is your body's response to changes around it. Eustress is positive stress. Distress is negative stress.
2. Possible response: Stress can cause a person to feel irritable and be disrespectful to others. This can have a negative effect on individual health and relationships.
3. Any two: dry mouth, shaky stomach, pounding heart, sweaty hands, tight muscles, breathing faster. Accept other reasonable responses.
4. Fatigue is extreme tiredness.
5. Adrenaline prepares the body to respond to stress, which calls for special measures, as in an emergency.
6. Responses will vary.

The Stress Test

① Focus

Objectives

Students will be able to

- identify common sources of teen stress.
- describe common symptoms of stress.
- list healthy ways to manage stress.
- locate resources for stress management.

Motivator

Quick Write

Write the phrase, "When I feel stressed, I…" on the board. Ask students to complete this sentence two times. First, they should describe one symptom of stress. ("*When I feel stressed, my palms sweat.*") Then, they should explain one way to handle stress. ("*When I feel stressed, I talk to my friends.*") List their answers on the board. Discuss the many different ways that teens experience and respond to stress.

② Teach

Brainstorming

Explain that there are healthy and unhealthy responses to stress. A healthy response is a good short- and long-term solution. An unhealthy response may feel good at the time, but creates additional problems.

Divide the class into groups. Assign each group one of the "Common Sources of Teen Stress." Direct each group to list three healthy responses to the situation and one unhealthy response. Have groups present their work to the class, explaining the potential long- and short-term outcomes of each response.

TIME HEALTH

The Stress Test

Take this quick quiz to find out more about keeping your cool when the heat is on!

Quiz

1. Symptoms of stress may include
 a. a racing heart.
 b. a flushed face.
 c. an inability to sit still.
 d. All of the above

2. The cold you have may have been brought on by stress.
 a. True   b. False

3. Which of the following study-break snacks can help ease stress?
 a. A banana
 b. A whole-wheat bagel
 c. A cup of yogurt
 d. All of the above

4. What's the best way to minimize stress during exams?
 a. Start studying well before an exam.
 b. Get regular physical activity and cut down on drinking beverages that contain caffeine.
 c. Be sure to get a good night's sleep.
 d. All of the above

Answers: 1. d. 2. a. 3. d. 4. d.

Check out the explanations on the next page!

Common Sources Of Teen Stress

- Schoolwork and tests
- Peer pressure
- Family arguments
- Parents' divorce or remarriage
- Moving to a new neighborhood or school

46 CHAPTER 2: MENTAL AND EMOTIONAL HEALTH

Health Literacy

Alcohol and Other Drugs Lead a class discussion on why using alcohol or other drugs is definitely an *unhealthy* way to cope with stress. Ask: What additional short- and long-term problems will alcohol or drug use create? List student responses on the board. Then ask: Do these seem like problems that will reduce or increase an individual's overall level of stress? Conclude the discussion with a strong message against substance use.

Explanations

1. **Stress brings about a "fight-or-flight" response**—changes in the body that occur when you feel threatened, scared, or nervous. The brain triggers a release of chemicals that cause your heart rate to speed up, your blood pressure to rise (which explains a flushed face), and your metabolism to increase, says Marianne Felice, M.D., of the University of Massachusetts Memorial Health Center. "This response is normal," she says.

2. **During times of stress, all body functions that aren't absolutely necessary for survival slow down**—and that includes the immune system. Thus, you become more vulnerable to colds and other illnesses.

3. Foods rich in complex carbohydrates (like whole-wheat bagels) can increase levels of serotonin. This brain chemical promotes a feeling of well-being. Foods high in protein (like yogurt) and vitamin B6 (such as bananas) can also ease stress. Try to avoid overeating when you feel stressed; **moderation is the best policy.**

4. **You can reduce anxiety during exam time by planning ahead.** Being prepared means you won't have to cram the night before a big test. Practicing healthful behaviors also helps. Engage in regular physical activity, limit intake of caffeine and empty-calorie foods, and get at least nine hours of sleep each night.

TIME TO THINK...

About Managing Stress
Read the "Common Sources of Teen Stress" list. Think of three other possible sources of stress for teens, and write them down on a sheet of paper. What can teens do to deal with stress in healthy ways? List your ideas on the same sheet of paper and have your teacher review them. Then create a colorful collage to illustrate some of these stress-busting techniques. Share your ideas with the class.

③ Apply

Time to Think

Have volunteers present their collages to the class and evaluate the stress-busting techniques in each. Point out to the class similar sources of teen stress and ways to manage this stress.

Journal Writing

Ask students to keep a stress management journal for the next few days. Instruct them to record any stressful situations. (Where were they? Who were they with? What were they doing?) Challenge students to try at least one new method for easing stress. How did it turn out? What have they learned?

VISUAL LEARNING

Ask students to describe the photograph on this spread. Ask: What is the teen in this photo doing? Why does he appear to be stressed? Would you be stressed in a similar situation? Why or why not? What would you do to reduce stress in this situation?

COOPERATIVE LEARNING ACTIVITY

Community Resources Explain to students that while a certain level of stress is normal, too much can lead to serious health problems. If they experience ongoing symptoms such as sleeplessness, lack of appetite, or depression, it may be time to seek help. Divide the class into small groups. Have each group compile a list of community resources that can help people manage stress. Direct groups to include contact information for resources at school, public and private health clinics, religious groups, neighborhood organizations, and so on. Have the class compile the information into a resource guide to share with fellow students.

STRESS MANAGEMENT

Objective

After completing the lesson, students will be able to manage stress effectively with better time management.

Time: 30 minutes on separate days

Materials: notebook paper, pencil, newsprint, crayons or markers

Teacher Classroom Resources

📁 Building Health Skills Activities

• Transparency Master 3, "Stress Management"

• Reproducible Master 2, "Managing Your Time"

---

1. Model

• Have students discuss how Grady manages his time wisely to reduce stress. (*He does his homework regularly. He sets aside time for homework. He manages his study time and, as a result, makes the Honor Roll.*)

• Have students brainstorm a list of techniques that they use to help them manage their time.

• Help students recognize time management techniques that Grady used. (*Examples include: avoid procrastination, set priorities, focus on one thing at a time.*)

BUILDING HEALTH SKILLS

MANAGING YOUR TIME

Model

Some teens feel like there are never enough hours in the day for all they want to do. As a result, they often feel stressed. One way to handle this stress is to learn how to use time wisely. Read how one teen manages his time to avoid stress.

Grady tells his parents that he will make the Honor Roll this semester. To accomplish that goal, Grady takes home his textbooks regularly. He sets aside time every evening for homework. When exams come, he knows his subjects well. He needs only a short review to get a good grade. He makes the Honor Roll. Grady feels stress-free and proud of his accomplishment.

48 CHAPTER 2: MENTAL AND EMOTIONAL HEALTH

Teaching Tips

Teaching Health Skills Skills such as stress management must be specifically taught. The *Teen Health* program will give you the tools you need to teach students skills, and the modeling and practice necessary for students to apply these skills. With this approach you will see improvements in student performance and behaviors—in and out of the classroom.

Building Self-Esteem Emphasize that if a student was unsuccessful the first time he or she attempted to accomplish a goal, this does not mean that he or she failed. Stress how important it is to learn from each experience and how to use that experience to be successful next time.

Practice

Write a story about a teen who is having a stressful day. In the story, show how a shortage of time contributes to the teen's stress. At the end, suggest ways the teen could better manage his or her time. Explain how those changes would help reduce the teen's stress.

Apply/Assess

The first step in learning how to use your time wisely is to see how you currently spend your time. On a sheet of notebook paper, draw a day planner for weekdays like the one shown below. Fill in each of the sections with a short phrase describing how you usually spend that hour of the day. Include items like school, sleep, meals, TV, social activities, homework, family activities, chores, and personal hobbies.

On the back of your page, draw a day planner for Saturday or Sunday. Fill it in with short phrases that show how you spend your time on a typical day during the weekend.

Look at your day planner. Are you surprised by anything you see? Now, think about some of the sources of stress in your life. Could managing your time better help you avoid these stressors? At the bottom of the page, list two or three ways you could manage your time more effectively. Then briefly explain how managing your time could help you reduce stress and improve your health.

Coach's Box

Stress Management

Stress management strategies include:
- Identify sources of stress.
- Set priorities.
- Manage your time wisely.

Self-Check
- Did I show ways to manage my time better?
- Can I explain how managing my time reduces stress?

2. Practice

- Challenge students to write about a teen who is having a stressful day. Included in the story should be some suggestions of ways the teen could better manage his or her time.
- Ask students to exchange papers and identify the positive factors that helped the teen manage his or her time.
- Distribute Transparency Master 3 and review.

3. Apply/Assess

- You may wish to distribute Building Health Skills Reproducible Master 2 in the TCR to guide students in completing this activity.
- Remind students that the more accurate their typical planner, the more benefit they will get from this activity.

BUILDING HEALTH SKILLS: MANAGING YOUR TIME **49**

Assessment Scoring

Using a rubric, student work should provide evidence of all criteria to achieve the highest score.

Skills
Student work identifies
- at least two ways to use time more wisely.
- situations where time management would be effective.

Concept
Student work explains
- why time management helps reduce stress.
- how stress affects health.

Checking Comprehension

Use the Chapter 2 Assessment to examine the most important ideas presented in the chapter.

Answers to Reviewing Vocabulary and Concepts

Lesson 1
1. self-concept
2. parents/guardians
3. reinforce
4. realistic
5. self-esteem
6. decisions

Lesson 2
7. emotions
8. hormone
9. emotional shifts
10. express
11. abstinence
12. refusal skills

Lesson 3
13. true
14. false; distress
15. false; stressor
16. true
17. true

Thinking Critically

18. Possible answer: Positive messages from parents and friends support, or reinforce, your self-concept.
19. Any three of the ways identified on page 34.
20. Responses should demonstrate an understanding that healthy ways of expressing emotions do not harm others.
21. Accept all reasonable responses.
22. Possible response: Physical activity releases pent-up energy and calms the body and mind, which can help reduce stress-related fatigue.

After You Read

Use your completed Foldable to review the information on having a positive self-concept and high self-esteem.

FOLDABLES Study Organizer

Reviewing Vocabulary and Concepts

On a sheet of paper, write the numbers 1–12. After each number, write the term from the list that best completes each statement.

- abstinence
- decisions
- emotional shifts
- emotions
- express
- hormone
- parents/ guardians
- realistic
- refusal skills
- reinforce
- self-concept
- self-esteem

Lesson 1

1. The view you have of yourself is your _____.
2. The first and greatest influence on your self-concept when you are young is your _____.
3. Positive messages will _____ your self-concept.
4. One way to help yourself develop a positive self-concept is to have _____ expectations.
5. The ability to like and respect yourself is called _____.
6. A positive self-concept helps you make confident _____.

Lesson 2

7. Happiness, sadness, and anger are examples of _____.
8. A _____ is a powerful chemical, produced by glands, that regulates many body functions.
9. Mood swings, or _____, are common for young people.
10. Talking to others, physical activity, and creating something are all ways to _____ your emotions.
11. _____ means not participating in health-risk behaviors.
12. Dealing with peer pressure is easier if you practice _____.

Lesson 3

On a sheet of paper, write the numbers 13–17. Write *True* or *False* for each statement below. If the statement is false, change the underlined word or phrase to make it true.

13. Your body's response to changes around you is <u>stress</u>.
14. Negative stress, the kind that gets in your way and holds you back, is called <u>stressor</u>.
15. A <u>distress</u> is an object, person, place, or event that triggers stress.
16. The hormone that prepares the body to respond to a stressor is called <u>adrenaline</u>.
17. <u>Fatigue</u> is extreme tiredness.

Thinking Critically

Using complete sentences, answer the following questions on a sheet of paper.

18. **Interpret** Explain how messages from parents and friends affect your self-concept.
19. **Suggest** Identify three ways to improve your self-concept.
20. **Analyze** Describe some healthy ways of expressing emotions that you have found to be effective.

50 CHAPTER 2: MENTAL AND EMOTIONAL HEALTH

INCLUSION STRATEGIES

Special Learning Needs, Behavior Problems, English Language Learners The following suggestions are helpful for students with special learning needs, students with behavior problems, and ELL students:

- Pair these students with more proficient learners who can help summarize the main concepts of the chapter.

- Direct these students to listen to the Teen Health Audio Summaries. This component provides an audio and written summary of the chapter in both English and Spanish.

- Use photographs, drawings, or magazine clippings whenever possible to help students visualize the important concepts of the chapter.

21. **Explain** List three objects, people, places, or events that are stressors for you. Identify the effect that these stressors have on your individual health and the health of your family.

22. **Apply** How might physical activity help reduce stress-related fatigue?

23. **Suggest** List some effective coping strategies that you could develop and use to manage stress. How can using these strategies help you maintain your health and well being?

Career Corner

School Counselor Would you like to help young people discover their talents and plan their futures? If so, consider a career as a school counselor. These professionals work in a school setting to help students solve problems and set career goals.

School counselors need a four-year college degree and two years of graduate training. Read more about this and other health careers by visiting Career Corner at health.glencoe.com.

CHAPTER ASSESSMENT 2

Test Practice
1. A
2. C
3. $(1,717 \div 3) - (1,579 \div 3) = 46$ more students

Reteaching
Assign Study Guide 2 in the Student Activities Workbook.

Evaluate
- Use the reproducible Chapter 2 Test in the TCR, or construct your own test using the **Exam View®** Pro Testmaker.
- Use Performance Assessment 2 in the TCR.

Enrichment
Have students form small cooperative groups. Ask each group to select one important concept presented in the chapter. Have the members of each group work together to plan, practice, and present a short skit focusing on their chosen concept.

Standardized Test Practice

Math

Read the paragraphs below and then answer the questions.

Stress is the body's response to change. While stress is a normal part of life, experiencing too much negative stress over a long period of time can harm a person's health. Here are some statistics on teens and stress.

Researchers at the University of Michigan conducted a study on levels of stress in teens and young adults in the United States. The results of this study showed that one-third of U.S. teens and young adults felt stressed out on a daily basis. Two-thirds felt stressed out at least once a week.

1. There are 1,579 students at U.S. High. Based on the statistics above, estimate how many teens at this school feel stressed out on a daily basis.
   (A) 526 students
   (B) 579 students
   (C) 1,053 students
   (D) 1,579 students

2. Estimate how many students at U.S. High feel stressed out at least once a week.
   (A) 989 students
   (B) 1,026 students
   (C) 1,053 students
   (D) 1,276 students

3. Lotus Valley High has 1,717 students. Estimate how many more students at Lotus Valley High feel stressed out on a daily basis than at U.S. High. Show your work.

TH05_C1.glencoe.com/quiz

Assessment

Self-Assessment Direct students to review the activities that are provided throughout the chapter. Encourage each student to select one finished product or activity that demonstrates his or her best work for the chapter. Have students explain what they learned and how the examples they selected show their progress.

Career Corner

School Counselor School counselors must have strong communication skills and enjoy working with young people. Invite the school counselor to your class. Have him or her discuss the responsibilities of the job. Encourage students to ask questions about how one prepares for this career.

Planning Guide

Chapter 3	Skills/ Activities	Reproducible Resources	Assessment
Lesson 1 **Your Family** pages 54–59	HEALTH SKILLS ACTIVITY ▲ Juggling Responsibilities (*Decision Making*), page 57	*Student Activities Workbook available for use with each chapter* 📁 Parent Letter & Activities 3 📁 Concept Map 8 📁 Cross-Curriculum Activity 5 📁 Decision-Making Activity 5 📁 Enrichment Activity 8 📁 Lesson Plan 1 📁 Reading Tutor Activity 8 📁 Reteaching Activity 8	📁 Lesson 1 Quiz
Lesson 2 **Your Friends and Peers** pages 60–65	HEALTH SKILLS ACTIVITY ▲ S.T.O.P. the Pressure (*Refusal Skills*), page 64	📁 Concept Map 9 📁 Decision-Making Activity 6 📁 Enrichment Activity 9 📁 Lesson Plan 2 📁 Reading Tutor Activity 9 📁 Reteaching Activity 9	📁 Lesson 2 Quiz
Lesson 3 **Communication: More Than Words** pages 66–69	Hands-On Health ▲ Reading Body Language, page 68	📁 Concept Map 10 📁 Cross-Curriculum Activity 6 📁 Enrichment Activity 10 📁 Health Lab 3 📁 Lesson Plan 3 📁 Reading Tutor Activity 10 📁 Reteaching Activity 10	📁 Lesson 3 Quiz
Lesson 4 **Resolving Conflicts** pages 70–75	HEALTH SKILLS ACTIVITY ▲ "You" and "I" (*Communication Skills*), page 72	📁 Concept Map 11 📁 Enrichment Activity 11 📁 Lesson Plan 4 📁 Reading Tutor Activity 11 📁 Reteaching Activity 11	📁 Lesson 4 Quiz 📁 Chapter 3 Test 📁 Performance Assessment 3

TIME HEALTH **Bullies: Beware!** *pages 76–77*

BUILDING HEALTH SKILLS

Working Things Out
(*Conflict Resolution*)
pages 78–79

📁 Building Health Skills Reproducible Master 3

Standards		Technology
National	State/Local	
National Health Education Standard **1.4, 2.6, 3.4, 5.3, 5.4, 6.1, 6.2, 6.3**		🖳 Transparency 9 💿 TeacherWorks™
National Health Education Standard **1.4, 3.4, 5.2, 5.4, 5.5, 5.6, 6.2**		🖳 Transparency 10 📼 💿 Tape/DVD 1, Segment 1, "Healthy Friendships" 💿 TeacherWorks™
National Health Education Standard **3.4, 5.1, 5.3, 5.5**		🖳 Transparency 11 📼 💿 Tape/DVD 3, Segment 1, "Improving Your Communication" 💿 TeacherWorks™
National Health Education Standard **3.4, 3.6, 5.4, 5.6, 5.7, 5.8**		🖳 Transparencies 12 & 13 📼 💿 Tape/DVD 1, Segment 4, "Resolving Conflicts Through Healthy Communication;" 📼 💿 Tape/DVD 2, Segment 3, "Dealing with Bullies" 💿 TeacherWorks™ 📼 💿 MindJogger Videoquiz 💿 **Exam**View® Pro Testmaker
National Health Education Standard **5.6, 5.7, 5.8**		📁 Building Health Skills Transparency Master 6

TeacherWorks™

Glencoe's new and exclusive TeacherWorks™ is an all-in-one planner and resource center. Access the complete Teacher Wraparound Edition electronically. Find all your classroom resources with just a few easy clicks, and print them right from your computer. Connect directly to Glencoe's customized Health Web site. Access the National Health Education Standards correlations, or insert your own state standards and match them directly to the electronic Teacher Wraparound Edition.

Language Diversity

- 🎧 English Audio Summaries
- 🎧 Spanish Audio Summaries
- 📁 English Summaries, Quizzes, and Activities
- 📁 Spanish Summaries, Quizzes, and Activities
- 📁 Spanish Parent Letters and Activities

KEY TO ABILITY LEVELS

Teaching Strategies that appear throughout the chapters have been identified by one of four codes to give you an idea of their suitability for students of varying learning styles and abilities.

L1 **Level 1** strategies should be within the ability range of all students. Often full class participation is required.

L2 **Level 2** strategies are for average to above-average students or for small groups. Some teacher direction is necessary.

L3 **Level 3** strategies are designed for students able and willing to work independently. Minimal teacher direction is necessary.

INCL Strategies are appropriate for students with particular special needs in a general classroom setting.

Social Health

Chapter at a Glance

Lesson 1 describes the different types of families in society and explores the kinds of problems that can occur within the family setting.

Lesson 2 discusses friends and the qualities that define a good friend. The lesson also touches on the effects of both positive and negative peer pressure.

Lesson 3 discusses the importance of good communication in healthy relationships and introduces communication skills.

Lesson 4 discusses conflict and presents ways to prevent and resolve conflicts without violence.

Health Skills

- Juggling Responsibilities (*Decision Making*), p. 57
- S.T.O.P. the Pressure (*Refusal Skills*), p. 64
- "You" and "I" (*Communication Skills*), p. 72
- Working Things Out (*Conflict Resolution*), pp. 78–79

52

HANDS-ON ACTIVITY

Brilliant Conversationalists Making conversation can be tricky. This skill is particularly difficult for students with special learning needs and students with behavior problems. These students may be impulsive and often lack the social skills necessary to communicate effectively. They will need guided practice and positive reinforcement for appropriate behaviors. Students need practice starting conversations, joining existing conversations, and practicing introductions. Working in small groups, have students write dialogue for social situations such as the cafeteria, a school bus, a party, or other scenes. They should include introductions appropriate for both teens and adults. Then have students role-play the dialogues and provide feedback. **INCL** *Behavior Problems, Special Learning Needs*

Social Health

HEALTH *Online*

Rate your ability to communicate effectively. Take the Health Inventory for Chapter 3 at health.glencoe.com.

FOLDABLES™
Study Organizer

Before You Read

Make this Foldable to help you organize what you learn about different types of families. Begin with four plain sheets of 8½" × 11" paper.

Step 1

Collect four sheets of paper and place them ½" apart.

Step 2

Roll up the bottom edges, stopping them ½" from the top edges. This makes all tabs the same size.

Step 3

Crease the paper to hold the tabs in place. Staple along the fold.

Step 4

Label the tabs as shown.

Types of Families
Nuclear Family
Extended Family
Couple Family
Single-Parent Family
Blended Family
Grandparent/Grandchild
Foster Family

As You Read

Use your Foldable to describe each type of family detailed in Lesson 1 and to list ways that family members care for one another.

53

Chapter Introduction

Use the options below to motivate students and preview chapter content.

HEALTH *Online*

Encourage students to take Health Inventory 3 at **health.glencoe.com**. Then brush up on health education by reading Professional Articles for health teachers. These articles can help keep you informed of national and state trends.

GLENCOE TECHNOLOGY

Teen Health Video and DVD Series
(Each format available in both English and Spanish)

You may wish to use:

- Tape/DVD 1, Segment 4, "Resolving Conflicts Through Healthy Communication"
- Tape/DVD 2, Segment 3, "Dealing with Bullies"

MindJogger Videoquiz

Use MindJogger to preview or review Chapter 3 content.

TIME HEALTH

Bullies: Beware!
pages 76–77

FOLDABLES™
Study Organizer

Dinah Zike Study Fold

Descriptive Writing and Interviewing Use this Foldable study guide for student writing about families. Direct students to use their completed Foldable to describe each type of family and take notes and record what they learn about how family members care for each other. Have them interview members of several different types of families. Ask students to write down under the appropriate tab what they learned from their interviews about different types of families and what roles the individuals they interviewed play in each type of family.

Lesson

Your Family

❶ Focus

Lesson Objectives

Students will be able to

- describe how family members care for each other.
- identify the types of families.
- explain their role within their family.
- describe types of family problems and where to turn for help.

Health Skills
- Decision Making, p. 57

Motivators

Quick Write

Ask volunteers to describe their family activities. Discuss how such activities can bring family members closer together.

Bellringer Activity

Ask students to list television shows or novels that depict families. Discuss the makeup of each family that is depicted. Ask what the variety of examples suggests about the definition of family in America. (*The definition of family has evolved in recent decades away from the traditional two-parents-with-children formula.*)

VOCABULARY

Using short paraphrases of definitions as clues, have students create crossword puzzles containing the vocabulary terms. Students can exchange their puzzles with partners and solve the puzzles they are given.

Quick Write

Write a short letter to a new pen pal describing some activities you do regularly with your family. Explain how these activities bring you closer together as a family.

LEARN ABOUT...

- how family members care for each other.
- different kinds of families.
- your role within your family.
- ways to handle problems in families.

VOCABULARY

- family
- nurture
- abuse
- sexual abuse
- neglect

Belonging to a Family

Ever since you were a baby, you have been connecting and bonding with your parents and other members of your family. The **family** is *the basic unit of society.* As a group, it provides for the needs of its members. **Figure 3.1** shows some basic ways people in families care for, support, and value one another.

FIGURE 3.1

HOW FAMILIES CARE FOR THEIR MEMBERS

The family provides for the needs of its members in many ways. *How can you show that you support and value all members of your family?*

Families provide for members' emotional needs

Family members keep each other safe.

Terry always laughs and giggles when he gets a hug.

Mom is really careful when it comes to safety belts.

Grandma really likes to make sure we're warm and protected.

Dad always encourages us to do our best in everything.

Basic needs for food, clothing, and shelter are met within the family.

Giving guidance and support is an important family function.

Lesson 1 Resources

Teacher Classroom Resources

- 📁 Parent Letter & Activities 3
- 📁 Concept Map 8
- 📁 Cross-Curriculum Activity 5
- 📁 Decision-Making Activity 5
- 📁 Enrichment Activity 8
- 📁 Lesson Plan 1
- 📁 Lesson 1 Quiz

- 📁 Reading Tutor Activity 8
- 📁 Reteaching Activity 8
- Transparency 9

Student Activities Workbook

- 📁 Chapter 3 Study Guide
- 📁 Applying Health Skills 8

FIGURE 3.2

Building Strong Families

Love, caring for one another, and respecting one another's needs make up the foundation of a healthy family. *How can you develop strategies for supporting and respecting all family members?*

Communicate
Family members build trust by talking openly and honestly and by respecting one another.

Spend time together
Family members share work and play.

Keep traditions
Ethnic and religious traditions may be handed down for generations. Families may also start their own traditions.

Be flexible
Families adjust to changes when they are needed.

Types of Families

There are many kinds of family structures. A nuclear family is made up of two parents and one child or two or more children. An extended family is a nuclear family plus other relatives such as grandparents. Couples are families with no children. A child or children living with only one parent make up a single-parent family.

Blended families are formed when two people who marry each other bring children from earlier marriages into their new family. Children living with grandparents make up yet another type of family. Sometimes, a child who has lost his or her parents is raised by another person or couple, who are known as foster parents.

Recognizing Healthy Families

All healthy families share the same goal. They seek to **nurture**, or *provide for the physical, mental/emotional, and social needs* of their members. They encourage positive relationships and good health behaviors among their members. **Figure 3.2** shows some ways to help build healthy families.

② Teach

Discussing

Ask students to discuss unconventional uses of the word *family*, such as a metaphorical usage meant to indicate a class of people or things rather than blood relatives. They may note that certain product lines are advertised as a "family" of products. Ask students why they believe this term receives the kind of exposure it does. **L1**

VISUAL LEARNING

FIGURE 3.1 As students look at the picture in Figure 3.1, have volunteers read the captions aloud. Ask students to suggest other specific ways family members meet one another's physical and emotional needs. Ask students to develop strategies for supporting and respecting all family members. Have students share their strategies with the class. **INCL** *Behavior Problems, Special Learning Needs, English Language Learners*

Interviewing

Have students interview a grandparent or another older adult relative. Students should attempt to determine how family life was different when that person was the student's age. Have students write the relative's "memoirs" in a composition of at least two pages. **L3**

COOPERATIVE LEARNING ACTIVITY

Family Bulletin Board Let students work together, either as a class or in several groups, to create a family bulletin board. Encourage students to begin by discussing the various groupings that make up families. Be sure they at least note all the kinds of family groups to which class members belong. Then have group members plan and make a bulletin board display that shows the diversity of families. They may want to use a collage technique, gathering magazine photographs and headlines or even using their own family pictures; or they may want to use drawings, cartoons, or a combination of family depictions.

Analyzing Influences

Make a "family" poster using pictures showing activities, traditions, and customs. Have students present them to the class. (Pictures can be cut from magazines, actual photos, or student drawings.) **L1**

Discussing

Guide students in discussing their responses to these questions:

• What situations can make it difficult to talk with your parents about daily events?

• What can you do to make it easier to talk with your parents?

• What are the benefits of discussing daily events with your parents? **L1**

In a healthy family, each member participates in daily activities that help maintain the family unit. For example, one or both parents may work to support the family. Teens may help with household tasks such as preparing meals or washing the dishes. Younger children may help by picking up their toys.

Your Role in the Family

Your relationship with your family positively affects your health in many ways. When you were a baby, your family provided you with everything you needed, including food, clothing, and shelter. Your family also gave you love and attention. They were the first system of support in your life.

Now, as you grow older, your family is helping you develop the skills you need to become an independent adult. Within your family, you are starting to learn who you are. Your family members help you develop your personality, attitudes, and values. They teach you how to make responsible choices and get along with others. They also help you learn to accept the consequences of your actions.

During your teen years, you will begin developing your own set of values and beliefs. Sometimes, you will not agree with your parents. When this happens, use effective communication skills. Talk with parents calmly, and remain respectful.

A simple thing like sharing the events of your day with a parent can help build good family relationships. *Describe how you communicate important issues with parents or guardians.*

56 CHAPTER 3: SOCIAL HEALTH

INCLUSION STRATEGIES

Physically Disabled, Special Learning Needs If any student in the class has a hearing impairment, arrange any measures necessary to ensure his or her grasp of lesson materials. This may entail having an individual on site who can sign to the student, or the teacher may learn some fundamentals of American Sign Language to better communicate directly with the student.

Students with special learning needs often have difficulty with peer relationships because their disabilities are not apparent. By pairing these students with positive peer tutors and supporting them through positive reinforcement, teachers can help promote social acceptance among peers as well.

Dealing with Changes

Every family goes through changes. Some changes, like the birth of a new baby, are generally happy events. They also require family members to take on new roles and responsibilities. Other changes, like a family member's illness, can be difficult. When someone in the family is ill, try to help care for him or her and show your concern. When appropriate, discuss home care with parents.

Separation and divorce can bring on negative stress or feelings of anger, sadness, or guilt. Calmly expressing these feelings to your parents or another person who is part of your support system may help. Let both parents know that you care for them. Try to help younger siblings understand and cope.

One of the most difficult changes of all is a death in the family. When this happens, people may feel many emotions, including sadness, grief, fear, and even anger. It is important to express these feelings in healthful ways. One way to manage grief is to remember the good times you had with the person. Talking with parents and other trusted adults about your loss can also help. If your family members are grieving over a loss, you can develop strategies for supporting and respecting them. You can do this by listening and being considerate.

✔ Reading Check

Identifying synonyms will help you build a larger vocabulary. List synonyms for these words: _help, calmly, generally, unhappy._

Lesson 1

Discussing

Display a world map, and using pushpins, have students identify where they were born. Then have students put in pins to represent everywhere they have lived. Ask volunteers to share their own experiences with moving. Encourage them to tell:

- what kinds of changes they had expected from the move;
- what unexpected changes the move involved; and
- what actions and attitudes they found most useful in coping with the changes. **L1** **INCL** *English Language Learners*

HEALTH SKILLS ACTIVITY

DECISION MAKING

Use these suggestions to help students discuss Hunter's decision:

1. Hunter has to decide whether to help his sister by baby-sitting or to attend play rehearsal.

2. He could babysit, find someone else to babysit, attend rehearsal, or ask for an excuse from rehearsal.

3. He risks feeling that he has let others (and himself) down with nearly all choices.

4. Hunter values both his family and his activities.

5. Have students explain their choices.

6. Remind students to evaluate both short- and long-term consequences.

HEALTH SKILLS ACTIVITY

DECISION MAKING

Juggling Responsibilities

Last night, Hunter's older sister called. She explained that she had to go to the dentist one afternoon this week. She wanted to know whether Hunter could babysit for her son while she was at the dentist.

Hunter was about to say yes, but then he remembered that he had a play rehearsal that day after school. He wants to help his sister, but he doesn't want to miss rehearsal. What should he do?

WHAT WOULD YOU DO?

Apply the six steps of the decision-making process to Hunter's situation.

1. STATE THE SITUATION.
2. LIST THE OPTIONS.
3. WEIGH THE POSSIBLE OUTCOMES.
4. CONSIDER VALUES.
5. MAKE A DECISION AND ACT ON IT.
6. EVALUATE THE DECISION.

LESSON 1: YOUR FAMILY 57

✔ Reading Check

Synonyms Identifying synonyms improves both reading comprehension and writing skills.

Have students work together to think of synonyms for the following words from pages 56 and 57: *help* (assist, aid, facilitate, advance), *calmly* (peacefully, quietly, tranquilly, steadily), *generally* (usually, mostly, routinely), *sadness* (unhappiness, sorrow). Let students use a dictionary or thesaurus. Write students' suggestions on the board. Discuss differences among the various synonyms. Urge students to look out for synonyms as they read and to use synonyms to make their own writing more interesting.

Cross-Curriculum Activity

VISUAL ARTS Have students create brochures on the theme of abuse. The brochures should focus on information about the types of abuse, identify strategies for coping with unhealthy behaviors in the family, and indicate community resources where families in trouble may turn for help. Display the finished works, if possible, around the school. **L1**

Critical Thinking

Ask students to consider how abuse may affect all members of a family. Pose discussion questions such as these:

• How are children affected if a parent, grandparent, or other adult family member is abused? Why?

• What is the effect on teens when younger children in the family are abused? Why? **L1**

Guest Speaker

Invite a school or family counselor to speak to the class about the kinds of problems he or she is trained to counsel, such as abuse, neglect, and alcoholism. Discuss suggestions counselors often make to help families get back on track. With the counselor, have students develop and share strategies for supporting and respecting family members. **L1**

Dealing with Family Problems

All families have problems. You have learned about some ways families can deal with changes on their own. However, some problems are far too serious to solve by sharing feelings and helping one another. In these situations, the family should seek outside help. Many types of counseling are available.

One of the most serious family problems is **abuse** (uh·BYOOS), or *a pattern of mistreatment of another person.* An adult or a child might be a target of abuse. A family with an abuse problem is not a healthy family. Mistreatment and unhealthy behaviors can occur in a number of different forms.

• **Physical abuse.** This form involves excessive use of force. The abused person often shows signs of physical abuse, such as bruises, burns, bite marks, or broken bones.

• **Emotional abuse.** This form can be harder to spot. It often involves yelling and putting down another family member. Although there may not be physical marks, the emotional scars run deep. The abused person often feels worthless and ashamed.

• **Sexual abuse.** Examples of **sexual abuse** involve *an adult displaying sexual material to a child, touching a child's private body parts, or engaging in any kind of sexual activity with a child or teen.* It is often difficult to see that a child is being sexually abused.

• **Neglect.** *The failure of parents to provide basic physical and emotional care for their children* is called **neglect.** Physical neglect occurs when parents do not provide adequate food, clothing, shelter, or medical care for their child. Emotional neglect involves not giving love, affection, and other forms of emotional support.

Another serious family problem is alcoholism, the addiction to alcohol. You will learn about strategies for coping with alcoholism in Chapter 9, Lesson 4.

Victims of abuse may be afraid to tell others about it. However, overcoming this fear and telling a trusted adult about threats or abuse is the only way to get help. *What resources are available in your school and community for people dealing with abuse, alcoholism, and neglect?*

Beyond the Classroom

Community Have students begin a family abuse awareness campaign in their community. The campaign may make use of the brochures students developed in this lesson but should extend beyond that activity. (See Cross-Curriculum Activity at top of page 58.) The campaign should include creating a flyer that lists the numbers of crisis hot lines and describes the nature of abuse crimes, obtaining information from library resources. Students might make copies of their flyers and distribute them throughout the community.

Where Families Can Find Help

The best strategy for coping with abuse or other unhealthy behaviors within the family is to get outside help right away. The first step in getting help is to tell a trusted adult. A teacher or school counselor can be a good first person to talk with. Whenever there is immediate danger, the police should be called. The abuser also needs help. Professionals can help the abuser understand the reason for the behavior and why it must change. It is never acceptable to abuse others.

Troubled families can find help from a number of sources. Religious leaders, social service agencies, and hospital social workers provide professional counseling. Crisis center volunteers are also available. You can call them at the numbers listed under "crisis intervention" in your telephone book. School counselors and doctors can suggest support and self-help groups. Some support groups are for the targets of abuse. Others are for the abusers. Both types try to help the people involved.

Sometimes, people may need to see a professional family counselor about their problems. *What are some situations in which counseling could be helpful?*

Lesson 1 Review

Using complete sentences, answer the following questions on a sheet of paper.

Reviewing Terms and Facts
1. **Recall** What are the four ways in which families care for their members?
2. **Explain** Describe two ways a family relationship can positively affect health.
3. **List** What are two ways to manage grief?
4. **Vocabulary** Define *abuse* and *neglect*. How are they related?

Thinking Critically
5. **Apply** Suppose you and your parents are having a disagreement over what time your curfew should be. Name two ways that will help you as you work out the conflict with them.
6. **Synthesize** List ways a person might interact positively with family members.

Applying Health Skills
7. **Accessing Information** Use the phone book to find names of organizations where families dealing with abuse, alcoholism, and neglect can get help. Make a wallet card showing how to contact these places.

LESSON 1: YOUR FAMILY **59**

Lesson 1 Review

1. Any four from Figure 3.1 on page 54.
2. See Your Role in the Family on page 56.
3. Remembering the good times you had with the person; talking with trusted adults about the loss.
4. Abuse is a pattern of mistreatment. Neglect is a kind of abuse involving the failure of parents to meet the physical and emotional needs of children.
5. Talk about the problem calmly and remain respectful.
6. Possible response: Make time to listen, help members with household tasks, participate in fun activities as a family.

Lesson 1

➌ Assess

Evaluating
Assign the Lesson 1 Review; then assign the Lesson 1 Quiz in the TCR.

Reteaching
- Assign Concept Map 8 or Reteaching Activity 8 in the TCR.
- Have students work with partners to list what family members can do to help build a stronger family.

Enrichment
- Assign and distribute Enrichment Activity 8 in the TCR.
- Ask students to write essays about fictitious families that adjusted to crises in positive ways.

➍ Close

In a short class discussion, ask students to identify the most important facts they have learned about family life. Help them recognize that not all families have healthy relationships. Have each student write a personal journal page that identifies a list of healthy family characteristics and a separate list of family problems. Have them also list people and resources they could contact or recommend to others to deal with family problems.

Lesson 2

Your Friends and Peers

① Focus

Lesson Objectives

Students should be able to

- explain why friendships are important to social health.
- describe the qualities of a good friend.
- explain how to use refusal skills to deal with negative peer pressure.

Health Skills
- Refusal Skills, p. 64

Motivators

Quick Write

Allow students to display their poems and stories on a bulletin board.

Bellringer Activity

Have students work individually to make an ad for a friend. Set aside time for students to come to the front of the class to share their ads. As students read their ads, list some of the characteristics they share.

VOCABULARY

On the board write the word *friend* in a large circle. Have students do the same on a sheet of paper and then create a word web using the vocabulary terms and their definitions as they appear throughout the lesson.

Your Friends and Peers

Quick Write

Write a short poem or story about the qualities you look for in a good friend.

LEARN ABOUT...

- why having friends is important.
- the qualities of good friends.
- how to use refusal skills to resist negative peer pressure.

VOCABULARY

- relationship
- friendship
- reliable
- empathy
- peer
- peer pressure
- refusal skills
- assertive

Why We Need Other People

Imagine that you are having a party with a large guest list. You would probably invite relatives, close friends, and people in your neighborhood. You also might invite classmates, teammates, and others in the community. You would invite these people because you have a relationship (ri·LAY·shuhn·ship) with them. **Relationships** are *the connections you have with other people.*

The relationships you have with family members are some of your most important. You also have relationships with friends, teachers, coaches, and people from clubs you belong to. All of these relationships help meet your need to feel loved and wanted, safe and secure. Your relationships give you a sense of belonging and support.

Friends offer one another support and encouragement. *What can you do to support your friends?*

Lesson 2 Resources

Teacher Classroom Resources

- Concept Map 9
- Decision-Making Activity 6
- Enrichment Activity 9
- Lesson Plan 2
- Lesson 2 Quiz
- Reading Tutor Activity 9

- Reteaching Activity 9
- Transparency 10

Student Activities Workbook

- Chapter 3 Study Guide
- Applying Health Skills 9

The Value of Friends

Forming ties with friends is one of the most important things you do during your teens. A **friendship** is *a special type of relationship between people who enjoy being together.* Right now, most of your friends are probably the same age and gender as you. However, some of your friends might be the same age as your parents or grandparents.

You form friendships for many reasons. **Figure 3.3** shows some of the reasons that friendships develop. These are also good ways to make new friends. For example, you may join a sports team and become friends with some of the other team members. You may befriend a new student who has just moved in to the house next door to you.

FIGURE 3.3

DIFFERENT FRIENDS FOR DIFFERENT REASONS

You make and keep friends for different reasons. *Which of these reasons apply to you and your friends?*

You have similar interests. Teens become friends because they enjoy the same hobbies, sports, and other activities.

You have similar values. Teens choose people as friends because their beliefs and standards of behavior are similar.

You like one another's personal qualities. Sometimes, you choose friends because they have a personal quality that you like, such as a good sense of humor.

You go to the same school or live in the same neighborhood. Sometimes, just being near someone helps you form a friendship.

LESSON 2: YOUR FRIENDS AND PEERS **61**

✓ **Reading Check**

Find compound words on pages 60 and 61. Which two words form each of these compound words?

Lesson 2

② Teach

Discussing

Ask students what they think is required to change a relationship into a friendship. Help them discuss their ideas on these topics:

• how much time it takes to develop a friendship;

• what kinds of activities and exchanges are most important for helping friendships grow; and

• how and why some friendships fade away or break off. **L1**

VISUAL LEARNING

FIGURE 3.3 Ask students to examine Figure 3.3, which identifies reasons teens make and keep friends. Have students

• copy the reasons onto a sheet of paper, leaving several blank lines after each entry;

• think of a friend and fill in his or her traits and qualities after each reason.

Afterward, ask students to discuss which of the reasons seems to play the greatest role among people their age. Which do they suppose plays a more critical role as a person gets older? **INCL** *Behavior Problems, Special Learning Needs, English Language Learners*

✓ **Reading Check**

Compound Words Examining the meaning and spelling of the smaller words that form compound words can help students notice and understand the meaning of related words. Studying compound words lets students explore common word origins, spellings, and meanings. Learning compound words formed from words they already know is an easy way for students to expand their vocabularies.

Have students divide each of the following compound words from pages 60 and 61 into two smaller words (*class/mates, team/mates, grand/parents*). Then have them think of other compound words that are related to these.

Lesson 2

Developing Good Character

Consideration

Encourage students to brainstorm a variety of ways they could be friendly and helpful to new students in school. Then, lead a class discussion on what it feels like to be new to a school or group and not to feel included.

Journal Writing

Have students write private journal entries analyzing their own abilities to be good friends. Suggest that they answer these questions:

• What are my best qualities as a friend?

• Which friendship qualities should I try to improve? Why? **L1**

Comprehending

Have students draw concentric circles (a series of circles inside one another) to represent the various communities they belong to. The first circle in the center will be themselves, the next, family, and then friends. Continue outward until the student has thought of as many communities as possible. Some examples of other communities include school, neighborhood, religious (church, temple), nature, city, state, country, and so on. Have students explain ways of maintaining healthy relationships within these different communities. **L1**

Developing Good Character

Consideration

The next time a new student joins your class, be sure to introduce yourself. Offer to answer any questions he or she may have. With a group, role-play how you would act positively toward a new student at school. In your role-play, demonstrate acceptable and unacceptable ways of gaining attention.

What Makes a Good Friend?

Good friends share a number of special qualities. For example, good friends are loyal and faithful. They will not allow others to say untrue or mean things about you. You also expect them to be **reliable**, or *dependable*. You can count on them to do what they say.

Good friends understand how you feel if you are sad or disappointed. They listen carefully when you talk about your problems. In short, they display **empathy**, or *the ability to identify and share another person's feelings*. They show consideration by caring about you. They may even care enough to risk the friendship by trying to stop you from doing something that is harmful to you or others. Good friends have a positive relationship that improves their quality of life.

Some of your friendships are more casual. You may sit with schoolmates in the cafeteria, but that may be the only time you spend with them. Some of your relationships may be somewhere between casual and close friendships. All your different friendships are an important part of your life.

CARNATION DYEING PROJECT

PURPOSE: TO DEMONSTRATE HOW DIFFERENT COLORS ARE ABSORBED BY FLOWERS.

Your hobbies or interests become even more enjoyable when you share them with a friend. *What hobbies or interests do you have in common with your friends?*

62 CHAPTER 3: SOCIAL HEALTH

INCLUSION STRATEGIES

Students with Physical Disabilities Discuss with students—or ask a student with a physical disability in the class to moderate a discussion on—the special needs of people with physical disabilities in the area of making and maintaining friendships. (They may be—or may feel—rejected by other students. They may have limitations that prevent participation in some of the activities common among members of their age group, or they may spend part of their after-school time undergoing physical therapy or medical treatments.) Have volunteers investigate and report to the class on efforts to ensure that physically disabled individuals enjoy the same rights and benefits as individuals without a physical disability.

What Is Peer Pressure?

If you named all the people you know who are your age, you'd end up with a very long list. All of *your friends and other people in your age group* are your peers. They support you and give you confidence as you move from depending on your family to being on your own. Your peers also have expectations of you. They may pressure you to act and think like everyone else in a group. Peer pressure is *the influence you feel to go along with the behavior and beliefs of your peer group.* Because it can influence the decisions you make, peer pressure can affect your health in many ways.

Types of Peer Pressure

Peer pressure can be either positive or negative, subtle or obvious. Positive peer pressure can be a good influence. It can inspire you to improve yourself or do something worthwhile. These positive relationships can improve your health. Peers can be a positive influence, for example, when they

- challenge you to perform well as a member of a team.
- expect you to behave responsibly.
- inspire you to improve your health and your appearance.
- encourage you to do your best in school.
- get you to work with others to improve your school and community or join a club in which you are interested.
- expect you to be fair and caring.

You feel negative peer pressure when others want you to do something that is harmful or goes against your beliefs and values. These negative relationships can be harmful to your health. They may influence you to engage in self-destructive behaviors. Your peers put negative pressure on you when they

- urge you to use tobacco, alcohol, or other drugs.
- dare you to do something dangerous or unsafe.
- talk you into being unkind to someone who is different from you and your friends.
- persuade you to do something that goes against your values or something illegal such as shoplifting.
- encourage you to be disrespectful to parents or other adults.
- urge you to fight or get involved in conflicts or gangs.

When others see you trying to help people, it might motivate them to do the same. *How do your friends motivate you?*

LESSON 2: YOUR FRIENDS AND PEERS **63**

Comparing

Have two volunteers read aloud the categories and examples of positive and negative peer pressure listed in the student text. Then divide the class into small groups, and ask them to brainstorm other examples of positive and negative peer pressure. If possible, students should draw on current events and practices in their own town or community. Have students match the examples they have cited with the categories appearing in the student text. **L2**

Demonstrating

Ask volunteers to work with partners or in small groups to plan and present short skits about peer pressure. After each skit, ask the other students:

- Who was exerting peer pressure? How?
- Was it positive peer pressure or negative peer pressure? How could you tell?
- If the pressure was negative, how did the teen try to resist the pressure?
- What other suggestions can you make for resisting that specific kind of peer pressure?

When all the skits are finished, have students explain how resisting peer pressure and refusing to engage in unsafe behavior maintains healthy relationships. **L1**

Beyond the Classroom

Community Invite students to work as a team to create and promote a local holiday called Friendship Day. Similar to that of other "personal" holidays, such as Mother's Day and Father's Day, the purpose of Friendship Day is to let those who fit the description know how important they are. Working with art materials, students can design cards to give to friends.

The cards, which may be either humorous or heartfelt, should express some of the traits and ideals expressed in the lesson. Encourage students to think of actions they can perform on behalf of friends as a way of letting the friends know their value. Encourage them to include members of the family as well.

Lesson 2

HEALTH Online

By visiting the Web Links for this chapter at health.glencoe.com, students will discover how to resist negative peer pressure. Encourage them to read the article and then complete the activity.

Guest Speaker

Invite the school guidance counselor to class to speak with students about some of the sessions he or she has had with teens who have been pressured by peers to engage in high-risk behaviors.

Beforehand, have students write down questions for the speaker, noting the concerns some teens feel when it comes to resisting negative pressure, such as rejection by their peers.

In small groups, students are to brainstorm other possible concerns they have felt when placed in similar difficult situations. **L1**

HEALTH SKILLS ACTIVITY

REFUSAL SKILLS

Guide students in reading about and discussing the S.T.O.P. formula. Let several volunteers demonstrate its use. Then have groups plan and present their scenes. Encourage other students to discuss each scene and suggest other ways of refusing.

HEALTH Online

Topic: Peer pressure

For a link to more information on resisting negative peer pressure, go to health.glencoe.com.

Activity: Using the information provided at this link, write a short story in which a teen resists pressure to do something unsafe.

Dealing with Negative Peer Pressure

Standing up to negative peer pressure can be difficult. You worry about what will happen if you don't go along with the group. Will your friends still like you? Will they leave you out in the future? No matter how difficult, it is important that you develop your own identity apart from the crowd. Part of growing up is learning to avoid self-destructive behaviors by resisting negative peer pressure.

Refusal skills, or *methods for saying no,* help you resist negative peer pressure. **Figure 3.4** shows how to handle negative peer pressure using the handy S.T.O.P. formula. Saying no in a firm voice is a way of being **assertive**, or *willing to stand up for yourself in a positive way*. Practicing assertiveness can help you cope with negative peer pressure.

Remember that you can always get help from a trusted adult. A parent, older brother or sister, or a counselor will listen to your problem and can help you decide what is the best thing for you to do. They may suggest some options that you haven't considered.

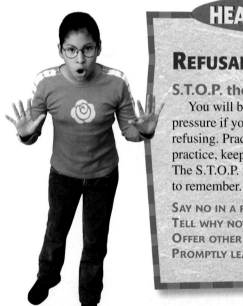

HEALTH SKILLS ACTIVITY

REFUSAL SKILLS

S.T.O.P. the Pressure

You will be more successful at resisting negative peer pressure if you are well prepared. Think of reasons for refusing. Practice what you would say and do. As you practice, keep these points in mind. The S.T.O.P. formula makes it easy to remember.

SAY NO IN A FIRM VOICE.
TELL WHY NOT.
OFFER OTHER IDEAS.
PROMPTLY LEAVE.

WITH A GROUP
Role-play a situation in which a teen faces peer pressure to engage in unsafe behavior. The teen should demonstrate the use of refusal skills in unsafe situations. After each role-play, review the responses of the teen under pressure.

COOPERATIVE LEARNING ACTIVITY

Positive Peer Pressure Divide the class into two groups. One group is to develop a project to enlist the support of peers. Through positive pressure they are to perform an act that will benefit the community at large. Possibilities include recycling and policing the school cafeteria or campus to make it a cleaner place.

The other group is to develop a grade- or class-wide campaign to combat negative peer pressure. Both groups may structure their projects around posters; a school Web site; or if the school has one, the public address system to reach out to as many peers as possible.

FIGURE 3.4

Ways to Resist Negative Peer Pressure

If your peers put negative pressure on you, you could use these methods to say no.
Which approach do you think would work best with the people you know?

Say No in a Firm Voice.
Sometimes, saying no is enough. Friends who respect you will take no for an answer. People are more likely to believe you if you speak firmly and confidently yet without being insulting to others.

Tell Why Not.
Explain your reasons for saying no. Show your peers that you value your health. It's also a chance to show your good character traits.

Offer Other Ideas.
Change the subject by coming up with something else to do instead.

Promptly Leave.
If people continue to put pressure on you, walk away. If certain people always put pressure on you whenever you see them, avoid them.

STOP

Lesson 2 Review

Using complete sentences, answer the following questions on a sheet of paper.

Reviewing Terms and Facts

1. **Vocabulary** Define the terms *relationship* and *friendship*.
2. **List** Name four different reasons why teens become friends.
3. **Identify** What are four personal qualities good friends share?

Thinking Critically

4. **Apply** Write down two ways to communicate empathy and show consideration for a friend who has just lost a grandparent.

5. **Distinguish** What types of relationships might positively affect your health? What types of relationships might negatively affect your health? Differentiate between these relationships.
6. **Explain** How can resisting negative peer pressure to engage in unsafe behavior help you maintain healthy relationships?

Applying Health Skills

7. **Communication Skills** With a partner, write a skit in which a teen demonstrates a specific positive action toward a peer. Perform your skit for the class.

LESSON 2: YOUR FRIENDS AND PEERS **65**

Lesson 2

VISUAL LEARNING

FIGURE 3.4 Have students read and discuss each approach to saying no. Then, to provide practice for all students, ask them to use each approach in sequence as you say the following:

- "Come on, just try a cigarette. Who's going to know?" (Students say no.)
- "Oh, don't be a baby. One cigarette isn't going to hurt you." (Students tell why not.)
- "Look, it's fun. Everyone else is smoking." (Students suggest other activities.)
- "That's dumb. Stick around and smoke with us." (Students turn away to leave.)

③ Assess

Evaluating
📁 Assign the Lesson 2 Review; then assign the Lesson 2 Quiz in the TCR.

Reteaching
📁 Assign Concept Map 9 or Reteaching Activity 9 in the TCR.

Enrichment
📁 Assign Enrichment Activity 9 in the TCR.

④ Close

Ask students to summarize the main concepts in this lesson.

Lesson 2 Review

1. A relationship refers to any connections you have with others, while a friendship refers to a special type of relationship among people who enjoy being together.
2. Any four from Figure 3.3 on page 61.
3. Good friends are loyal and faithful, reliable, empathetic, and caring.
4. Responses may include inviting the friend to talk about the loss.
5. Responses should include the idea that positive relationships improve health and negative relationships endanger health.
6. Responses will vary, but should include the idea that resisting negative peer pressure promotes mutual respect.

① Focus

Lesson Objectives

Students will be able to

• describe ways people communicate.

• identify the best way to communicate thoughts and feelings.

• describe ways to be a better speaker and listener.

Motivators

Quick Write

Ask students to share why they prefer talking with certain individuals.

Bellringer Activity

Write the word *communication* on the board. Ask students to work in small groups to brainstorm their own definitions for this term. Add that after reading this lesson, students will have a better idea of how to communicate.

VOCABULARY

Write the vocabulary terms on the board. Instruct students to skim the lesson for the definitions of the words. Then have them record these important terms and definitions in their notebooks, where they can be referred to as needed.

Communication: More Than Words

Quick Write

Think of someone you like to talk with. Explain why you like to talk to that person.

LEARN ABOUT...

• how people communicate.

• the best way to communicate your thoughts and feelings.

• ways to communicate important issues with parents and peers.

• how you can be a better speaker and listener.

VOCABULARY

• communication

• gesture

• body language

How Do We Communicate?

You get on the school bus and sit next to your friend, who tells you about something funny that happened in the hallway. You respond by sharing your friend's good feelings and maybe telling a story of your own. In short, you and your friend are communicating.

The sharing of thoughts and feelings between two or more people is **communication**. As **Figure 3.5** shows, communication requires a message, a sender, and a receiver. It is a two-way process that involves both sending and receiving messages.

FIGURE 3.5

THE COMMUNICATION PROCESS

When someone sends a message and another person receives it, communication has occurred.

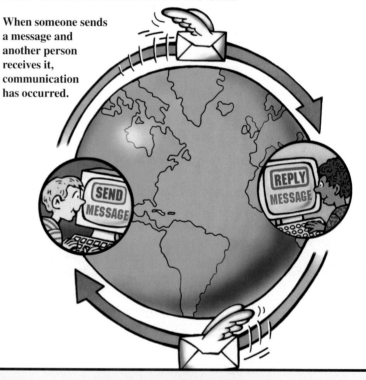

Lesson 3 Resources

Teacher Classroom Resources

📁 Concept Map 10

📁 Cross-Curriculum Activity 6

📁 Enrichment Activity 10

📁 Health Lab 3

📁 Lesson Plan 3

📁 Lesson 3 Quiz

📁 Reading Tutor Activity 10

📁 Reteaching Activity 10

 Transparency 11

Student Activities Workbook

📁 Chapter 3 Study Guide

📁 Applying Health Skills 10

Ways of Communicating

People communicate by speaking and listening to one another. However, people often say more about their feelings with their faces or the way they move their bodies. There are many ways to communicate important issues with parents, peers, and others. Messages can involve all of the following:

- **Words.** The words you use help you communicate. How you say the words gives others clues about your feelings.
- **Facial expressions.** The look on your face says a lot about how you feel. A smile suggests a person is happy. A raised eyebrow can mean someone is doubtful or suspicious.
- **Gestures.** People often use gestures—*movements of the hands, arms, and legs*—when they communicate. A clenched fist suggests that a person is angry. People sometimes tap their fingers or feet when they are nervous.
- **Posture.** The way people hold their bodies can also communicate feelings. Standing or sitting straight with the head held high suggests that a person feels good. People who are sad might slouch or walk with their heads down.

Sometimes, people send mixed messages—their words don't match their expression, gesture, posture, or tone of voice. For example, a friend might say, "I'm fine," but sound like she really wants to cry. Mixed messages are confusing for listeners.

Good Communication

Being a good communicator will help you build healthy relationships. The following skills will help you as a speaker.

1. **Use "I" messages.** Express your concerns in terms of yourself. You'll be less likely to make others angry or feel defensive.
2. **Make clear, simple statements.** Be specific and accurate. Stick to the subject. Give the other person a chance to do the same.
3. **Be honest with thoughts and feelings.** Say what you really think and feel, but be polite. Respect the feelings of your listener.
4. **Use appropriate body language.** The term body language refers to *facial expressions, gestures, and posture.* Make eye contact. Show that you are involved as a speaker.

Reading Check
The prefix *com-* means "with." *Communicating* means "sharing thoughts or feelings with others." What other words can you find with the prefix *com-*?

Lesson 3

❷ Teach

Discussing

Have students look at their definitions of the word *communication* in the Bellringer Activity. Ask:

- In what ways does the definition in the text complement their definitions?
- In what ways does it differ from their definitions? **L1**

VISUAL LEARNING

FIGURE 3.5 Have volunteers read the caption aloud and describe the scene in the picture. Ask: Which of these teens is participating in the communication process? (Be sure students recognize that both are part of the communication process.) **INCL** *Behavior Problems, Special Learning Needs, English Language Learners*

Analyzing

Have students silently read the section of the student text titled "Ways of Communicating." Divide the class into pairs, and have partners alternate, stressing different words in the same sentence: (For example, "I *said* you could go," "I said *you* could go.")

Ask partners to share what they have learned about the role the tone of a speaker's voice plays in communication. How could this knowledge be applied to communication skills? **L2** **INCL** *Behavior Problems, Special Learning Needs*

Reading Check

Prefixes and Suffixes Knowing the meanings of prefixes and suffixes helps students figure out the meanings of complex words. Draw students' attention to the word *communication* in the title. Explain that the prefix com- means "with." The suffix *-tion* means "state or quality of." *Communication* means "the act of sharing thoughts or feelings with a person or people." Have students find other words on pages 66 and 67 that are related to *communication* (*communicating, communicator*). Tell students that the suffix *-or* means "one who." Then ask a volunteer to define *communicator*.

Lesson 3

Time: 45 minutes

TEACHING THE ACTIVITY

- Ask students to describe the body language of the two teens in the photograph. What message is each communicating? Which teen do you think is more likely to get a part in the play? Why?
- Let students work with partners to look through old magazines, selecting and captioning pictures in which body language is demonstrated.
- Have students work with the same partners to develop a collage or role-play to demonstrate the use of body language.
- With students, discuss categories into which their examples can be sorted. List these categories on the board.

ASSESSMENT

In a brief class discussion, have students describe what this activity helped them learn about body language.

The following skills will help you as a listener.

1. **Use appropriate body language.** Even if you disagree, listen to what the other person has to say. Make eye contact, and don't turn away.
2. **Use conversation encouragers.** Say things like "No kidding!" or "Really?" to show you are paying attention.
3. **Mirror thoughts and feelings.** Pay attention to what is being said. Repeat what someone says to show that you understand.
4. **Ask questions.** Show that you are listening by asking the speaker questions.

Hands-On Health

READING BODY LANGUAGE

As the photograph below shows, body language can tell you a lot about how a person feels. This activity will help you practice reading body language.

WHAT YOU WILL NEED
- newspapers, magazines
- scissors, tape, tacks
- paper, pen, sketch pad

WHAT YOU WILL DO
1. Find pictures or cartoons from newspapers and magazines that demonstrate various forms of body language.
2. Write a caption for each picture describing the body language you observe and what it is communicating. Attach your caption to the back of the picture.
3. Make a sketch, or select a picture showing an effective example of body language that you have used or observed others using in the past week. Write a descriptive caption on the back of the sketch.
4. Share your pictures and sketches with your classmates. Ask them what caption they would choose for each picture. Compare their choices to yours.

IN CONCLUSION
1. How often did your interpretation of body language in a picture agree with your classmates' views?
2. How does understanding body language improve your communication with others?

Health Literacy

Interpersonal Skills Effective communication skills can be the basis of good social health and good emotional health. Research shows that the ability to communicate also contributes to good physical health. Emotional excitement raises blood pressure, but for physical health and safety, the pressure should return to normal as soon as possible. Researchers found that individuals who were able to identify and express their feelings experienced a return to normal blood pressure more quickly than people who had trouble labeling and talking about their emotions.

Developing Good Communication Skills

Whether you are sending or receiving messages, your speech and body language represent who you are to others. Like everyone else, you want others to see you in your best light. Improving your communication skills will help you reach that goal. It will also help you meet your need for healthy relationships.

You use your communication skills in all kinds of situations. *What special methods do you use to communicate plays or strategies in a team sport?*

Discussing

Demonstrate examples of negative body language, such as slouching and avoiding eye contact, crossing your arms, and looking hostile. Ask students to identify the message such body language communicates, and have them suggest other forms of body language that can hinder effective communication. Then ask: Why is it important to avoid these kinds of negative body language? **L1 INCL** *English Language Learners*

❸ Assess

Evaluating

📂 Assign the Lesson 3 Review; then assign the Lesson 3 Quiz in the TCR.

Reteaching

📂 Assign Concept Map 10 and Reteaching Activity 10 in the TCR.

Enrichment

• 📂 Assign Enrichment Activity 10 in the TCR.

• Encourage students to learn more about various forms of communication, such as American Sign Language, pictographs, and semaphore signals.

❹ Close

Ask students to identify, in their own words, the skills of good communication.

Lesson 3 Review

Using complete sentences, answer the following questions on a sheet of paper.

Reviewing Terms and Facts

1. **Vocabulary** Define the term *communication*. Use it in an original sentence.
2. **Recall** Name three ways in which people communicate with one another.
3. **Identify** List four speaking skills a good communicator uses.

Thinking Critically

4. **Apply** Write a paragraph describing a situation in which you or someone you know expressed his or her feelings in a healthy, thoughtful way.

5. **Predict** How might developing good communication skills help you in the future?

Applying Health Skills

6. **Communication Skills** Write a short essay describing how to communicate an important issue with parents and peers. Which communication methods would you use when talking with your parents? Which would you use when talking with your peers? Explain.

LESSON 3: COMMUNICATION: MORE THAN WORDS **69**

Lesson 3 Review

1. Communication is the sharing of thoughts and feelings between two or more persons. Students' sentences will vary.
2. Any three: words, facial expressions, gestures, and posture.
3. Using "I" messages, making clear and simple statements, being honest with thoughts and feelings, and using appropriate body language.
4. Responses should apply lesson principles established as tools for good communication and perhaps appropriate body language.
5. Responses may include points such as help in making new friends and getting a job.

Lesson 4

Resolving Conflicts

① Focus

Lesson Objectives

Students will be able to

- explain what conflicts are and how they begin.
- explain how to prevent and resolve conflicts, including the mediation process.
- describe ways to protect themselves from violence.

Health Skills
- Communication Skills, p. 72

Motivators

Quick Write
Allow students to briefly debate the issue. Have a volunteer list the main points on the board.

Bellringer Activity

Ask students why some conflicts result in violence. List their explanations on the board.

VOCABULARY

Have a volunteer write each of the vocabulary terms on a separate index card. Write the six definitions on the board. Ask students to take one of the cards and attach it to the board with transparent tape above or below the definition it matches.

Lesson 4

Resolving Conflicts

Quick Write

Do you think schools with violence problems should install video cameras? Why or why not? Explain in a brief paragraph.

LEARN ABOUT...

- why conflicts occur.
- what to do if you are not getting along with someone.
- how you can protect yourself from violence.

VOCABULARY

- conflict
- tolerance
- compromise
- negotiation
- peer mediation
- violence
- gang

Why Does Conflict Occur?

Have you ever argued with a friend or family member? An argument is an example of **conflict**, or *a problem in a relationship.* Conflict is a normal part of life. However, when people do not deal with their conflicts, they might end up shouting at or not speaking to one another. Conflict can even result in deliberate injuries, such as cuts and broken bones. **Figure 3.6** shows how some conflicts develop.

FIGURE 3.6

HOW CONFLICTS DEVELOP

Different situations can lead to conflict. *What situations in your life have led to conflict?*

A Differing Expectations
Mark and his sister can't agree on when each of them should get to use the home computer.

B Differing Values
Sita wants to be paid for babysitting her sister. Her mom thinks this is Sita's responsibility as a family member.

C Hurt Feelings
Jake never invites Manuel over to his house after school.

D Changing Roles
Now that Rachel's sister Gina is away at college, Rachel has to do more chores.

E Jealousy
Beth did not make the pep squad, but her friend Shira did.

F Possessions
Sam's friend Don borrowed his book two weeks ago and still hasn't returned it.

G Struggle for Power
Colleen's group of friends has always seen her as their leader. Now, Keiko, a new girl, is challenging that role.

Lesson 4 Resources

Teacher Classroom Resources

- 📁 Concept Map 11
- 📁 Enrichment Activity 11
- 📁 Lesson Plan 4
- 📁 Lesson 4 Quiz
- 📁 Reading Tutor Activity 11
- 📁 Reteaching Activity 11

🎥 Transparencies 12 & 13

Student Activities Workbook

- 📁 Chapter 3 Study Guide
- 📁 Applying Health Skills 11
- 📁 Health Inventory 3

Some conflicts can be avoided by showing common courtesy. *What are other ways you can avoid conflict?*

How to Prevent Conflict

How do you handle conflict? One way is to prevent it from happening in the first place. There are a number of strategies for avoiding conflict.

Practicing tolerance can prevent many conflicts. **Tolerance** (TAHL·er·ence) is *the ability to accept other people as they are.* People may not always behave the way you like. Use your communication skills. They can clear up a misunderstanding before it builds up and causes further trouble.

If you sense a conflict in the making, try to make the situation less tense. Try telling a joke or changing the subject.

To keep conflict from getting out of hand, respond to disrespectful behaviors in a healthy way. Practice self-control by walking away and cooling off. Angry words and insults will only make matters worse. You might say something that you will regret later. Also, ask yourself whether the issue is worth the conflict. You may not want to waste your energy on something that's not so important to you.

LESSON 4: RESOLVING CONFLICTS 71

❷ Teach

VISUAL LEARNING

FIGURE 3.6 Have students examine Figure 3.6 along with the caption. Ask students to explain how each situation might set off a conflict. Encourage them to offer ways to avoid conflict in each situation. **INCL** *Behavior Problems, Special Learning Needs, English Language Learners*

Examining the Issue

Have a volunteer read aloud the section "How to Prevent Conflict" on this page. Challenge students to think about examples from history or today's newspaper that illustrate each point. Ask: What lessons can we learn from these leaders? (*At any level, the best course of action is attempting to diffuse conflict.*) **L3**

Discussing

Help students discuss the concept of tolerance and the importance of practicing tolerance. Ask questions such as these:

• Why is it important to understand that individuals are all different?

• What are some differences that are easy to accept?

• What kinds of differences do some people find hard to accept?

• How can accepting people the way they are make life better for everyone? **L1**

 Reading Check

Main Idea Explain to students that a paragraph may contain a main idea. Have students reread the last paragraph on page 71. Ask them to identify the sentence that tells the main idea and explain why they chose that sentence. (*The main idea is expressed in the first sentence, "To keep conflicts from getting out of hand, respond to disrespectful behaviors in a healthy way." That sentence gives the most important idea about the topic: conflict. The other sentences give reasons that support the main idea.*)

Developing Good Character

Respect

Break the class up into groups of four. Have each group create a "respect" report card that lists at least five different ways to show respect in the classroom. How might they monitor their own progress in practicing these behaviors? Discuss why respect and responsibility form the basis for a good classroom community. Ask students to develop classroom guidelines listing healthy ways to respond to disrespectful behaviors. Post the guidelines in your classroom.

Respect is an abstract concept for at-risk students. Have volunteers share what respect means to them and how it's demonstrated. **INCL** *At-Risk*

Discussing

Have students think of conflicts they have been involved in when it was difficult to follow the T.A.L.K. strategy. Ask:

• Which of these points was hardest to follow? Why?

• What are some steps for making positive goals easier to achieve during conflict resolution? **L1**

HEALTH SKILLS ACTIVITY

COMMUNICATION SKILLS

Guide students in reading and discussing the activity introduction. Let several volunteers read the example "you" and "I" messages aloud, and ask students how these messages make them feel.

Then have students work in small groups to complete the activity.

Developing Good Character

Respect

All people want respect and are likely to respond well when they receive it. Everyday courtesy and good manners are a show of respect. Practicing them can help you avoid conflicts. *With your classmates, discuss how common gestures of courtesy might help prevent conflict.*

How to Resolve Conflicts

Resolving conflicts may require each side to give a little. **Compromise** means that *each person gives up something in order to reach a solution that satisfies everyone.*

Conflict-Resolution Skills

The best way to resolve conflicts is through **negotiation,** *the process of talking over problems to reach a solution.* The T.A.L.K. strategy can help you resolve a conflict through negotiation. It can even help prevent the types of deliberate injuries that can occur during physical fighting.

• **Take a time-out.** Wait at least 30 minutes before you talk over the situation. This will give both of you a chance to calm down.
• **Allow each person to tell his or her side uninterrupted.** Each person should have the chance to explain his or her feelings without the other person breaking in. Choose a time and place to talk where you won't be interrupted. Always listen carefully and show respect for the other person.
• **Let each person ask questions.** Both people should have the chance to question each other. Stay calm and respectful. Also, stick to the issue. Don't bring up other problems at this time.
• **Keep brainstorming.** Try to see the situation from the other person's point of view. It will help you find a solution that will satisfy you both.

HEALTH SKILLS ACTIVITY

COMMUNICATION SKILLS

"You" and "I"

When resolving conflicts, be careful how you use the words "you" and "I." Sentences centered on "you" tend to place blame on the other person. Sentences stressing "I" show a willingness to work things out.

• **"YOU" MESSAGE:** "Why do you always get to pick where we'll hang out?"

• **"I" MESSAGE:** "I feel frustrated that I never get to choose where we hang out."

WITH A GROUP

Write three sentences that use "you" messages to express anger or frustration. Then exchange lists with another student. Rewrite your partner's "you" messages as "I" messages. Compare your messages with your partner's.

72 CHAPTER 3: SOCIAL HEALTH

COOPERATIVE LEARNING ACTIVITY

Role-Play Have a group of students collaborate on a skit in which communication plays a central role in resolving conflict. Some of the students in the group can function as writers, some as actors, and some as consultants. Point out that the job of consultants is to take the information in the student text and apply it to the plot line. The skit should focus on a problem or conflict that is to be resolved. The rest of the students are to serve as critics and to note where the players demonstrated—and where they failed to demonstrate—the key points of the lesson.

Resolving Conflict Through Peer Mediation

A mediator can help people resolve conflicts and respond to disrespectful behaviors in healthy ways. Mediators are people who are not involved in the dispute. Counselors, parents, or other adults can be mediators. Many schools have peer mediation programs. **Peer mediation** (mee·dee·AY·shuhn) is *a process in which a specially trained student listens to both sides of an argument and then helps the opposing sides reach a solution.* **Figure 3.7** shows the steps a peer mediator might follow to help settle a conflict.

FIGURE 3.7

THE MEDIATION PROCESS

To help students resolve conflicts, peer mediators go through hours of training. Practice these mediation skills. They are the basic steps you take in any mediation situation:

Step 1 **Establish neutrality.** Tell the opposing sides you will remain neutral. You will not take sides or decide who is right or wrong.

Step 2 **Set the ground rules.** Get the opposite sides to agree on rules for keeping the discussion fair and orderly. For example, you would want to prohibit name-calling and interrupting.

Step 3 **Listen to each side.** Allow each person to tell his or her view of the situation without interruption. Then allow each person to ask questions.

Step 4 **Search for possible solutions.** Brainstorm solutions together, or ask each person to suggest a solution. Think of as many solutions as possible. Continue until you reach a solution that satisfies both sides.

Step 5 **Don't give up.** If the opposing sides can't reach an agreeable solution, ask for help from an adult trusted by both sides.

Cross-Curriculum Activity

LANGUAGE ARTS Allow students to work in pairs or small groups to create their own versions of confrontations typical of teens their age. These confrontations may be among peers, teens and adults, or teens and younger siblings. Ask that students clearly show in their dramatizations how a potential conflict is avoided through compromise, communication, and mediation. In their skits, students should demonstrate strategies for the prevention of and response to deliberate injuries. **L2**

VISUAL LEARNING

FIGURE 3.7 Have students describe each photograph and explain the differences between the two situations. Then have volunteers read aloud the steps in the mediation process. Ask:

• Which step do you think is most important? Why?

• Which do you think is most difficult? Why?

INCL *Behavior Problems, Special Learning Needs, English Language Learners*

HEALTH SKILLS PRACTICE

Conflict Resolution Invite students to practice their mediation skills by reading aloud the following: Do your family members disagree about friends, makeup, music, or something else? Agree to be the mediator. Name the problem. Listen to both sides. Write down a summary of comments from both sides, and suggest a compromise for your family to try.

INCLUSION STRATEGIES

English Language Learners, Behavior Problems, Special Learning Needs If you have students who experience language difficulties or take an inordinately long time to complete a lesson, you might use one or both of the following strategies:

• Allow students' individual strengths to complement each other by having students work in pairs and trios.

• Have such students focus on the section headings. These headings are designed to "telegraph" information to the student about the topic. Such information may prove invaluable to students with limited grasp of the language.

• Have them focus on photographs and illustrations for further comprehension.

Evaluating

Ask students to identify and describe strategies for avoiding drugs, violence, gangs, weapons, and other harmful situations. Have them write their ideas on a sheet of paper and ask volunteers to share examples with the class. **L1**

Discussing

Guide students in a discussion assessing healthy ways of responding to disrespectful behaviors. Have students write a paragraph summarizing the class discussion.

VISUAL LEARNING

FIGURE 3.8 Have students briefly discuss their own impressions of violence within their community:

- Does violence seem to be an increasing problem?
- How does the threat of violence affect the everyday lives of teens?

Divide the class into five groups and assign each group one of the common factors that contribute to violent acts. Have group members discuss their assigned factor and then explain it to the class. **INCL** *Behavior Problems, Special Learning Needs, English Language Learners*

When Conflicts Get Out of Hand

Conflicts that get out of hand can lead to violence. **Violence**, or *the use of physical force to harm someone or something*, is a serious problem in the United States. It can lead to deliberate injury and even death. **Figure 3.8** shows some causes of violence.

Some communities have problems with gang violence. A **gang** is *a group of people who associate with one another to take part in criminal activity*. Some teens join gangs because they do not have a sense of belonging to other groups such as their families. Another source of violence in communities is weapons. The presence of a weapon may increase the chance that violent behavior will occur.

FIGURE 3.8

WHY VIOLENCE ERUPTS

There are some common factors that contribute to violent acts. *Using this illustration as a guide, identify and describe strategies for avoiding violence.*

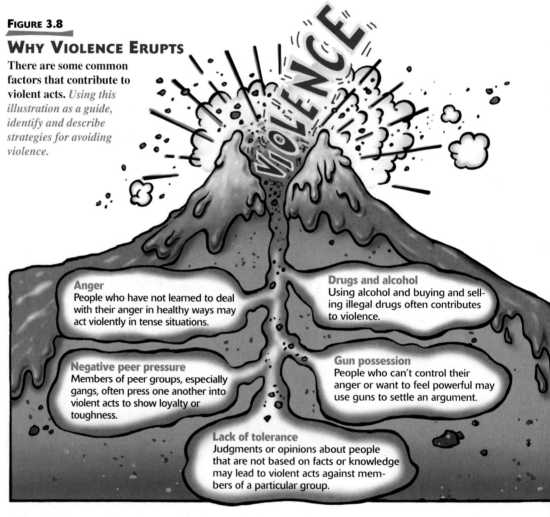

Anger
People who have not learned to deal with their anger in healthy ways may act violently in tense situations.

Drugs and alcohol
Using alcohol and buying and selling illegal drugs often contributes to violence.

Negative peer pressure
Members of peer groups, especially gangs, often press one another into violent acts to show loyalty or toughness.

Gun possession
People who can't control their anger or want to feel powerful may use guns to settle an argument.

Lack of tolerance
Judgments or opinions about people that are not based on facts or knowledge may lead to violent acts against members of a particular group.

74 CHAPTER 3: SOCIAL HEALTH

WHAT TEENS WANT TO KNOW

How do I avoid gangs? Gangs tend to recruit, confront, and harass teens who are alone and unoccupied. If possible, when you are leaving school, leave with a group of friends. Limit the opportunities for gang members to approach you by practicing a sport, rehearsing for a play, or studying in an organized group. If your school doesn't offer programs, the local YMCA or community center may have activities you can join. Never confront a gang member. Gang members may be involved with drugs, and they may be armed with weapons or violent. If you are threatened or you see gang activity, report it to your school, parents, and local law enforcement. Guide students in a discussion of these tips.

What You Can Do

Here are some strategies for avoiding violence.

- **Commit to nonviolence.** Practice self-control. Do not fight or threaten others. Don't watch fights or encourage others to fight.
- **Dress for safety.** Do not wear anything that could be mistaken for gang clothing. Avoid wearing expensive items like gold jewelry. If you use a purse, carry it with the strap across your chest.
- **Avoid weapons, gangs, and drugs.** Any contact with weapons, gangs, or drugs is likely to lead to trouble. If you know, or suspect, that someone has a weapon, immediately tell a parent or another trusted adult.
- **Avoid harmful situations.** For example, if you know that there will be gang members, alcohol, or drugs at a party, do not go. If a situation seems unsafe, leave immediately.
- **Use conflict resolution.** Recall the skills you've learned for settling disputes, and practice them whenever possible.
- **Use good manners.** Being polite can help ease tensions that can lead to violence.
- **Accept differences.** Recognize that individuals and groups are entitled to have different ideas, beliefs, and values.
- **Advocate for peace.** Serve as a positive example. Become a peer mediator or volunteer with an anticrime group.

Some schools require students to wear uniforms. This eliminates gang colors and clothes. *Do you think school uniforms are a good idea?*

Lesson 4 Review

Using complete sentences, answer the following questions on a sheet of paper.

Reviewing Terms and Facts

1. **Vocabulary** Use *conflict* and *compromise* in two original sentences that show the meanings of the terms.
2. **Identify** List two ways you can help prevent conflict from occurring.
3. **Recall** Name a healthy way of responding to disrespectful behaviors. How does this help you practice self-control?

Thinking Critically

4. **Restate** In your own words, identify the steps in the mediation process.
5. **Analyze** Write a brief paragraph that demonstrates strategies for the prevention of deliberate injuries that may result from violence.

Applying Health Skills

6. **Analyzing Influences** Create a booklet in which you explain how ads for movies or TV programs that depict violence affect viewers.

LESSON 4: RESOLVING CONFLICTS **75**

Lesson 4

Critical Thinking

Have students review their "student handbook" regarding the school's dress policy. Ask:

- Should students at our school be forced to conform to a school dress code? Why or why not?
- How does a dress code help create an atmosphere of respect within a school?
- What else could be done here in our school to encourage an atmosphere of respect? **L1**

❸ Assess

Evaluating

📁 Assign the Lesson 4 Review; then assign the Lesson 4 Quiz in the TCR.

Reteaching

- 📁 Assign Concept Map 11 and Reteaching Activity 11 in the TCR.
- Have students generate their own rules of good communication and a definition of *compromise*.

Enrichment

- 📁 Assign Enrichment Activity 11 in the TCR.
- Ask students to research professional mediators: What do they do? How are they trained? Have students write about their findings.

❹ Close

Ask students to conduct a discussion on the importance of tolerance and self-control. Have students describe ways to practice self-control and tolerance.

Lesson 4 Review

1. Sentences should demonstrate an understanding of *conflict* as a problem in a relationship and *compromise* as a give-and-take solution.
2. Any two: practice tolerance, use good communication skills to clear up misunderstandings, tell a joke, change the subject.
3. Possible response: Walk away and cool off; don't allow emotions to get the best of you.
4. Students should explain the steps in Figure 3.7 on page 73.
5. Students may choose any two: anger, drugs and alcohol, peer pressure, prejudice, or gun possession. Accept all realistic suggestions for preventing violence and deliberate injuries.

Bullies: Beware!

1 Focus

Objectives

Students will be able to

- understand the serious nature of bullying.
- recognize the three roles in a bullying situation.
- identify positive steps to handle bullying.

Motivator

Bellringer Activity

Write the following words on the board: *bully*, *victim*, and *bystander*. Ask students to list adjectives that describe each of these roles. Write these adjectives on the board. Ask the class: "Are these adjectives always true? Can you think of any situations where these adjectives might actually be misleading?" Leave the lists on the board while you complete the rest of this lesson.

2 Teach

Critical Thinking

Use the statistics in the text to reinforce that bullying is a serious issue in schools. Emphasize *that every student has the right to a safe* and *secure learning environment*. Ask students, "What do you think the term 'bullying' means? Does it just include fights or physical intimidation? What about spreading gossip or name-calling?" Ask volunteers to give examples of bullying situations and discuss them as a class. Do all students agree about what constitutes bullying? Do boys and girls differ in the way that they bully one another? Are there stereotypes at work in the way students, teachers, and administrators handle these gender differences in bullying situations?

TIME HEALTH

Bullies: BEWARE!

Are mean kids making you miserable? Take action!

The 450 freshmen and sophomores in the auditorium of Stephenson High School in Stone Mountain, Georgia, are staring at a poster with a drawing of a large, angry face and the word BULLY. That poster and two others, marked VICTIM and BYSTANDER, are backdrops to a play that is taking place onstage. One student, acting as a bully, insults the "victim" and then steals his hat. The audience laughs at the victim. However, when the play is over, its lessons begin to sink in on the audience. "It was really good," says Shina, a sophomore. "It helps teenagers not to resolve problems on their own but to get help."

People don't like to be pushed or teased for getting good or bad grades or to be made fun of for how they look. Sadly, about one in seven schoolchildren is a bully or a victim of one. Five million elementary and middle-school students in the United States are bullied

DEALING WITH SENSITIVE ISSUES

Demystifying the Bully The adjectives students generated at the beginning of class probably support the myth that bullies are powerful and secure. You can help to dispel this myth by having students analyze the motivation of bullies. Ask students, "Why do you think bullies behave the way they do? What do they gain by their actions? Are there more positive ways to achieve these same results? Why don't bullies use these more positive methods?" Guide students to the realization that bullies are often lonely, scared, or unhappy themselves. They may act out of a misguided attempt to gain friends, followers, or adult attention. Emphasize that this in no way excuses their behavior. However, it removes the aura of invincibility that often surrounds bullies.

WHAT SHOULD YOU DO IF A BULLY BOTHERS YOU?

Tips from Allan L. Beane, director of the Center for School Safety at Murray State University in Kentucky.

- **Tell a parent or a teacher about the bullying. You are not being a tattletale by letting them know what's going on.**

- **If the bullying happened at school, have a parent discuss it with your teacher. Parents should not call the parents of a bully directly.**

- **Don't be an easy target. Look the bully in the eye and walk away confidently. Don't get involved in a fight.**

- **Bullies want to hurt your feelings. Even if they're being mean, act as if they're not succeeding.**

- **Stand up for other students who are being bullied and ask them to stand up for you.**

each year, according to the National Association of School Psychologists. Each day, some 160,000 kids skip school because they're afraid of being bullied.

Taking the Bully by the Horns

Schools across the United States are fighting back against bullying. Many states observe a Safe Community = Safe Schools Awareness Week. During this week, communities hold antibullying and antiviolence activities for kids. The special week was established by Safe Schools, Safe Students, an Arizona-based group founded by Rod Beaumont. He says the purpose of the awareness week is to make people realize that bullying and other types of school violence can't be ignored.

Suffern Middle School, located north of New York City, is among the many schools that have antibullying programs all year long. At Central York Middle School in Pennsylvania, the number of fights in the school year decreased drastically after students in grades six through eight signed

anti-teasing pledges. Bullies had to offer apologies, saying how they would change their behavior.

Since bullies have been around since school was invented, can bully-busting programs really stop them? There may be hope. Spencer, a middle-school student from Colorado, says bullies can change. "I teased people all the time," he says, "but I got my act together. I didn't like making other people feel bad." ◼

TIME TO THINK...

About Stopping Bullies

Which of the tips in the box seem the most practical to you? Do you think they would work if you were confronted by a bully? Why or why not? What other tips would you add to the list? With a group, write a skit that demonstrates a specific strategy for dealing with a bully. Perform your skit for the rest of the class.

3 Apply

Time to Think

Explain to students that there are usually *three* roles in a bullying situation: the bully, the victim, and the bystander. The bystander may actively participate in the bullying by laughing at the victim or egging on the bully. Bystanders may also simply watch the violence, but do nothing to help.

Have students include one or more bystanders in their skits and perform it two ways. In the first skit, have the bystanders encourage the bully, laugh, or simply watch the event. In the second skit, have the bystanders intervene or offer assistance. Ask the class: "How do the actions of the bystanders change the behavior of the bully or the victim? How does this change the outcome of the situation?"

VISUAL LEARNING

Have students describe each photograph on the spread. Ask: "Is this a typical bullying situation? Why or why not? Can you identify which of the teens is playing each role: bully, victim, and bystander? What might the victim do in this situation?"

WHAT TEENS WANT TO KNOW

How can I respond to bullying *while* it's happening?

- Show confident body language. Stand up straight. Look the bully in the eye. Try not to look intimidated.

- Attract the attention of nearby students or teachers. Yell or wave your arms.

- Be firm. Yell, "Stop!" and put your hand out in front of you.

- Use humor. Say, "You must be really bored if you've got nothing better to do than pick on me."

- Give an excuse. Say, "If I'm not in class in 30 seconds, you're going to be in big trouble."

- Just walk away. Go into the nearest classroom or office, or toward a large group of students.

CONFLICT RESOLUTION

Objective

After completing the lesson, students will be able to demonstrate the steps for conflict resolution.

Time: 45 minutes

Materials: paper, pen or pencil

Teacher Classroom Resources

📁 Building Health Skills Activities

• Transparency Master 6, "Conflict Resolution"

• Reproducible Master 3, "Working Things Out"

---

1. Model

• Reassure students that conflicts are common in relationships. Emphasize that they can resolve conflicts in healthy ways by learning conflict resolution skills.

• Direct students to read about Kari and Samantha. Have students point out the skills that each girl used in the situation.

WORKING THINGS OUT

Model

Conflicts are common in relationships. A healthy way to resolve these conflicts is to communicate about the problem. Read about how two sisters, Kari and Samantha, resolved a conflict.

> "Samantha, I noticed something a while ago, and I'd like to talk about it."
> **T—TAKE A TIME-OUT.**

> "Sure, what's going on?"
> **L—LET EACH PERSON ASK QUESTIONS.**

> "I feel upset when you borrow my clothes without asking. I didn't get to wear that sweater yet. Why did you borrow it?"
> **A—ALLOW EACH PERSON TO TELL HIS OR HER SIDE UNINTERRUPTED; L—LET EACH PERSON ASK QUESTIONS.**

> "I guess I wasn't thinking. I just opened your drawer and saw this great sweater. Do you want it back right now?"
> **A—ALLOW EACH PERSON TO TELL HIS OR HER SIDE UNINTERRUPTED.**

> "No, but I would like to have an agreement about this. What if we always ask before we borrow each other's stuff?"
> **K—KEEP BRAINSTORMING TO FIND A GOOD SOLUTION.**

> "Sure, I will if you will."

78 CHAPTER 3: SOCIAL HEALTH

Teaching Tips

Conflict Resolution Role-Play Some students may need a model before they are able to complete an assignment. Ask for volunteers who understand the conflict-resolution process clearly to demonstrate a scene. Follow these guidelines:

• Have students role-play without words.

• Make sure all students understand the conflict and what happened.

• Role-play again without words to show the conflict being resolved.

• Make sure all students understand how the conflict was resolved.

Practice

See what you have learned about resolving conflict. Read the following conversation between Carlos and Lee. This afternoon, Lee found a CD that Carlos had lost. When Carlos asked for it back, Lee said, "Finders keepers." Can you identify the steps that the boys take to resolve their conflict? Write the conversation on your own paper, and label the steps T.A.L.K. Complete the conversation by writing an ending in which Carlos and Lee agree on a solution.

CARLOS: Lee, I'd like to talk about what happened this afternoon.
LEE: I'll listen, but I did find the CD. If I hadn't found it, someone else would have picked it up and taken it.
CARLOS: I know, and I'm glad you found it. But it's my favorite CD, and I would like to have it back.
LEE: So what should we do?

Apply/Assess

Adolescence is a good time to learn how to resolve conflicts. This ability helps keep relationships healthy. On your own paper, list several situations that lead to conflict for teens. Choose one of these situations and use it to practice your conflict-resolution skills. Write a script showing how the conflict can be resolved. Remember to use the T.A.L.K. steps for conflict resolution, and show a respectful tone.

COACH'S BOX

Conflict Resolution

T Take a time-out, at least 30 minutes.

A Allow each person to tell his or her side uninterrupted.

L Let each person ask questions.

K Keep brainstorming to find a good solution.

Self-Check

- Did my script show how to use the T.A.L.K. steps for conflict resolution?
- Did my script show both sides and use a respectful tone?

2. Practice

- Display Transparency Master 6, and review the steps.
- Direct students to read about Carlos and Lee. Have each student complete the conversation by writing an ending in which both parties agree on a solution.
- Give students a chance to share their stories with classmates. Discuss the solutions that seem most appropriate, and identify the steps that were used to reach an agreement between the two parties.

3. Apply/Assess

- You may wish to distribute Building Health Skills Reproducible Master 3 in the TCR to guide students in completing this activity.
- Have students brainstorm situations that may cause conflict for teens, such as *hurt feelings, differing expectations, differing values, changing roles, jealousy,* and so on. Have them choose one of these situations and write a script showing how the conflict can be resolved.
- Give students the opportunity to exchange their scripts with a classmate so he or she can label them with the T.A.L.K. steps. Have students choose a partner and role-play the scripts. Have observers identify the steps for conflict resolution that were included in the scripts.

BUILDING HEALTH SKILLS: WORKING THINGS OUT **79**

Assessment Scoring

Using a rubric, student work should provide evidence of all criteria to achieve the highest score.

Skills

Student work demonstrates

- a time-out from the situation.
- both persons' point of view.
- questions to clarify the conflict.
- brainstorming to find a solution.

Concept

Student work provides

- accurate information about issues that commonly cause conflict among teens.

Checking Comprehension

Use the Chapter 3 Assessment to examine the most important ideas presented in Chapter 3.

Answers to Reviewing Vocabulary and Concepts

Lesson 1
1. family
2. nuclear
3. nurture
4. emotional
5. sexual

Lesson 2
6. reliable
7. empathy
8. peers
9. peer pressure
10. refusal skills

Lesson 3
11. d
12. c
13. d

Lesson 4
14. true
15. true
16. false; compromise
17. false; peer mediation
18. true

Thinking Critically

19. Responses will vary, but should include seeking outside help.
20. Responses should include specific examples of how peers may positively or negatively influence the decision-making process.
21. Responses will vary, but may include not attending parties where gang members, weapons, alcohol, or drugs might be present.

CHAPTER ASSESSMENT 3

After You Read

Use your completed Foldable to review the information on different types of families.

FOLDABLES™
Study Organizer

Reviewing Vocabulary and Concepts

On a sheet of paper, write the numbers 1–10. After each number, write the term from the list that best completes each sentence.

- emotional
- empathy
- family
- nuclear
- nurture
- peer pressure
- peers
- refusal skills
- reliable
- sexual

Lesson 1

1. The _____ is the basic unit of society.
2. A(n) _____ family is made up of two parents and one child or two or more children.
3. Healthy families _____ their members, or provide for their physical, mental/emotional, and social needs.
4. Yelling at and putting down a family member is an example of _____ abuse.
5. _____ abuse occurs when an adult engages in sexual activity with a child or teen.

Lesson 2

6. A(n) _____ person is dependable.
7. The ability to identify and share people's feelings is called _____ .
8. Your _____ are your friends and other people in your age group.
9. When your friends urge you to do something dangerous, you are experiencing negative _____ .

---

10. Methods for saying no are called _____ .

Lesson 3

On a sheet of paper, write the numbers 11–13. After each number, write the letter of the answer that best completes each statement.

11. The sharing of thoughts and feelings between two or more people is
    a. empathy.
    b. body language.
    c. mediation.
    d. communication.
12. Movements of the hands, arms, and legs, often used in communication, are called
    a. speaking skills.
    b. mixed messages.
    c. gestures.
    d. posture.
13. Body language involves
    a. facial expressions.
    b. gestures.
    c. postures.
    d. all of the above.

Lesson 4

On a sheet of paper, write the numbers 14–18. Write *True* or *False* for each statement below. If the statement is false, change the underlined word or phrase to make it true.

14. <u>Conflict</u> is a problem in a relationship.
15. Exercising <u>tolerance</u>, the ability to accept other people as they are, is a good way to prevent conflict.
16. <u>Mediation</u> occurs when each person in a conflict gives up something in order to reach a solution that satisfies everyone.
17. <u>Peer pressure</u> is a process in which a specially trained student listens to both sides of an argument and then helps the opposing sides reach a solution.
18. The use of physical force to harm someone is known as <u>violence</u>.

INCLUSION STRATEGIES

Special Learning Needs, Behavior Problems, English Language Learners The following suggestions are helpful for students with special learning needs, students with behavior problems, and ELL students:

- Pair these students with more proficient learners who can help summarize the main concepts of the chapter.

- 🎧 Direct these students to listen to the Teen Health Audio Summaries. This component provides an audio and written summary of the chapter in both English and Spanish.

- Use photographs, drawings, or magazine clippings whenever possible to help students visualize the important concepts of the chapter.

Thinking Critically

Using complete sentences, answer the following questions on a sheet of paper.

19. Identify What are some strategies for coping with unhealthy behavior in the family, such as abuse and neglect?

20. Explain How can peer pressure affect decision making?

21. Describe What are some strategies for avoiding violence, gangs, weapons, and other harmful situations?

22. Analyze Describe a conflict you have experienced. How might the mediation steps listed in Figure 3.7 have been useful in this situation?

Career Corner

Family Counselor A family that is having problems can find help from a family counselor. These professionals teach family members how to listen to one another. They help families work together to find solutions. A family counselor needs a four-year college degree plus two years of graduate work in counseling. To learn more, click on Career Corner at health.glencoe.com.

Standardized Test Practice

Math

Read the paragraphs below and then answer the questions.

Many young people experience pressure from their peers to use alcohol and tobacco. The National Institute of Child Health and Human Development conducted a study on this topic, and found that girls are much more likely to be affected by peer pressure to drink alcohol and smoke than are boys.

The study also found that students in sixth, seventh, and eighth grades were nine times more likely to smoke and five times more likely to drink if two or more of their friends either smoke or drink. Teens who thought their parents would be upset if they found out that they drank or smoked were less likely to do so.

1. The chance that a student at Middle School A smokes if his friends don't smoke or drink is 1 in 45. Estimate the probability that a student at this school will smoke if two or more of his friends smoke or drink.

- **A** 1 in 4
- **B** 1 in 5
- **C** 1 in 9
- **D** 5 in 9

2. The chance that a student at Middle School B drinks if her friends don't smoke or drink is 1 in 30. Estimate the probability that a student at this school will drink if two or more of her friends smoke or drink.

- **A** 1 in 3
- **B** 1 in 5
- **C** 1 in 6
- **D** 1 in 15

3. From the passage, can you assume that more girls than boys smoke?

TH05_C1.glencoe.com/quiz

22. Responses will vary, but should address each of the five steps in Figure 3.7 on page 73.

Test Practice

1. B

2. C

3. Possible answer: No; girls are more likely to be affected by peer pressure to smoke or drink, but no information is given about the actual number of students who do smoke or drink.

Reteaching

- Assign Study Guide 3 in the Student Activities Workbook.

Evaluate

- Use the reproducible Chapter 3 Test in the TCR, or construct your own test using the **Exam**View® Pro Testmaker.

- Use Performance Assessment 3 in the TCR.

Enrichment

Help students plan and implement a school-wide No TV Week. As part of advertising the week, students should suggest alternate activities that teens can enjoy with family members and friends.

Assessment

Self-Assessment Direct students to review the activities that are provided throughout the chapter. Encourage each student to select one finished product or activity that demonstrates his or her best work for the chapter. Have students explain what they learned and how the examples they selected show their progress.

Career Corner

Family Counselor There are many different fields of study open to counselors, such as school counseling, family counseling, career counseling, and mental health counseling. Have students scan the help-wanted ads in the local paper for counseling positions. Discuss the different areas of counseling listed, and compare the skill requirements for each.

Promoting Physical Health

Unit Objectives

Students will study the factors that contribute to good physical health, including personal care, consumer choices, nutrition, physical activity, and issues related to growth and development. Students will also learn about the distinction between communicable and noncommunicable diseases and the impact of these diseases on health.

Unit Overview

82

DEALING WITH SENSITIVE ISSUES

The Bigger Picture When you deal with sensitive issues in the classroom, don't forget that parents, the school board, and the community may be concerned about what you teach and how you teach it. You can minimize their concerns by following these guidelines: Familiarize yourself with the regulations and guidelines in your school district about course content, parental permissions, and related issues. In your classes, emphasize abstinence from tobacco, alcohol, illegal drugs, and sexual activity. Avoid preaching to students about sensitive issues. Avoid classroom activities and behaviors that may be misinterpreted. Always thank parents for their concern.

Promoting Physical Health

Every aspect of your being—from your heartbeat to the tiniest speck of genetic material—works together to keep you healthy and contribute to who you are. All your body systems do their part so you can look and feel your best, even when you don't know how hard they're working. Add good nutrition and defense against diseases to the mix, and you have a team that just can't lose!

How are your body systems like a basketball team?

UNIT 2

Chapter 6
Growth and Development

Lesson
1 From Cells to Body Systems
2 Bones, Muscles, Blood, and Lungs
3 Nerves and Digestion
4 Adolescence: A Time of Change
5 Heredity and Growth

Chapter 7
Preventing Diseases

Lesson
1 Causes of Diseases
2 Communicable Diseases
3 Understanding STDs
4 Noncommunicable Diseases

Unit Introduction

Ask students to write menus for breakfast, lunch, and dinner that include foods that would be their first choice for each meal. Then ask them why they would choose these particular foods. Ask them to think about where and how they developed a fondness for the foods on their lists.

After students have completed their lists, ask for a show of hands of those students who think they make healthy food choices. Ask them to explain why. Ask all students to indicate whether they know how each food they eat is contributing positively to their health. Ask whether they are aware of any foods they like that may be harmful to their health. What short- or long-term benefits are the result of healthy food choices? What do they think they can do, as teens, to improve their immediate and future health?

HEALTH in Action

Read the class the question on page 83. Discuss how personal health care, proper nutrition, and regular physical activity can affect body systems. Give examples of how body systems work together. Then lead the class in the following physical group activity:

Have students jog in place for two minutes. Afterward, ask them to list the things they noticed happening to their bodies, such as "faster heartbeat." Then ask students to name the body systems involved in that brief act of jogging. Prompt as necessary to remind them of the use of food as fuel, the messages sent to and from the brain, and the roles of the heart and lungs.

Planning Guide

Chapter 4	Skills/ Activities	Reproducible Resources	Assessment
Lesson 1 **Your Teeth, Skin, and Hair** *pages 86–93*	**HEALTH SKILLS ACTIVITY** ▲ Skin Care Strategies (*Practicing Healthful Behaviors*), page 91	*Student Activities Workbook available for use with each chapter* 📁 Parent Letter & Activities 4 📁 Concept Maps 12, 13 📁 Cross-Curriculum Activity 7 📁 Enrichment Activity 12 📁 Health Lab 4 📁 Lesson Plan 1 📁 Reading Tutor Activity 12 📁 Reteaching Activity 12	📁 Lesson 1 Quiz
Lesson 2 **Protecting Your Eyes and Ears** *pages 94–99*	**Hands-On Health** ▲ Observing the Eye, page 96	📁 Concept Maps 14, 15 📁 Cross-Curriculum Activity 8 📁 Decision-Making Activity 7 📁 Enrichment Activity 13 📁 Lesson Plan 2 📁 Reading Tutor Activity 13 📁 Reteaching Activity 13	📁 Lesson 2 Quiz
Lesson 3 **Choosing Health Products** *pages 100–103*	**HEALTH SKILLS ACTIVITY** ▲ Understanding Unit Pricing (*Accessing Information*), page 102	📁 Concept Map 16 📁 Decision-Making Activity 8 📁 Enrichment Activity 14 📁 Lesson Plan 3 📁 Reading Tutor Activity 14 📁 Reteaching Activity 14	📁 Lesson 3 Quiz
Lesson 4 **Health Care in Your Community** *pages 104–107*		📁 Concept Map 17 📁 Enrichment Activity 15 📁 Lesson Plan 4 📁 Reading Tutor Activity 15 📁 Reteaching Activity 15	📁 Lesson 4 Quiz 📁 Chapter 4 Test 📁 Performance Assessment 4
TIME HEALTH **The Smile File** *pages 108–109*			
BUILDING HEALTH SKILLS **Think Before You Buy** (*Accessing Information*) *pages 110–111*		📁 Building Health Skills Reproducible Master 4	

Standards		Technology
National	**State/Local**	
National Health Education Standard **1.1, 1.3, 1.6, 2.6, 3.1, 3.4**		Transparency 14 TeacherWorks™
National Health Education Standard **1.1, 1.3, 1.6, 2.6, 3.1, 3.4**		Transparencies 15 & 16 TeacherWorks™
National Health Education Standard **2.1, 2.2, 2.3, 2.4, 2.5, 3.4**		Transparencies 17 & 18 TeacherWorks™
National Health Education Standard **1.1, 2.6, 3.1, 3.4, 5.4**		Transparency 19 TeacherWorks™ **Exam**_View_® Pro Testmaker
National Health Education Standard **2.1, 2.2, 2.3, 2.4**		Building Health Skills Transparency Master 1

TeacherWorks™

Glencoe's new and exclusive TeacherWorks™ is an all-in-one planner and resource center. Access the complete Teacher Wraparound Edition electronically. Find all your classroom resources with just a few easy clicks, and print them right from your computer. Connect directly to Glencoe's customized Health Web site. Access the National Health Education Standards correlations, or insert your own state standards and match them directly to the electronic Teacher Wraparound Edition.

Language Diversity

- English Audio Summaries
- Spanish Audio Summaries
- English Summaries, Quizzes, and Activities
- Spanish Summaries, Quizzes, and Activities
- Spanish Parent Letters and Activities

KEY TO ABILITY LEVELS

Teaching Strategies that appear throughout the chapters have been identified by one of four codes to give you an idea of their suitability for students of varying learning styles and abilities.

L1 **Level 1** strategies should be within the ability range of all students. Often full class participation is required.

L2 **Level 2** strategies are for average to above-average students or for small groups. Some teacher direction is necessary.

L3 **Level 3** strategies are designed for students able and willing to work independently. Minimal teacher direction is necessary.

INCL Strategies are appropriate for students with particular special needs in a general classroom setting.

CHAPTER 1

Personal Health

Chapter at a Glance

Lesson 1 examines the basic structures, functions, common problems, and care of teeth, skin, and hair.

Lesson 2 examines the basic structures, functions, and care of the eyes and ears. It also provides examples of vision and hearing problems.

Lesson 3 discusses what influences consumer choices of personal products, emphasizing advertisements, and provides considerations for smart shopping. Fraud is also addressed.

Lesson 4 discusses health providers, where people receive health care, and ways they pay for health care.

Health Skills

- Skin Care Strategies
  (*Practicing Healthful Behaviors*),
  p. 91
- Understand Unit Pricing
  (*Accessing Information*), p. 102
- Think Before You Buy
  (*Accessing Information*),
  pp. 110–111

84

HANDS-ON ACTIVITY

My Health Book As students learn about personal health in this chapter, have them compile notes and pictures to write their own health book. Explain that their "book" must have a Table of Contents, Chapters, and a Glossary. Each book will have four chapters, one for each lesson presented. For example, Chapter 1 could be titled "My Teeth, Skin, and Hair." Encourage students to make a list of the daily habits they should engage in to take proper care of their teeth, skin, and hair. They may include pictures or their own drawings to illustrate their chapters. If you complete any of the activities presented in each lesson, students can add these to their books as well. Reinforce their vocabulary skills by having them add a glossary of the terms mentioned in their books.

Personal Health

HEALTH *Online*

Go to health.glencoe.com and take the Health Inventory for Chapter 4 to rate how well you take care of your teeth, skin, eyes, and ears.

FOLDABLES™
Study Organizer

Before You Read

Make this Foldable to help you organize the information in Lesson 1 on teeth, skin, hair, and personal health. Begin with a plain sheet of 11″ × 17″ paper.

Step 1

Fold a sheet of paper into fourths along the short axis. This forms four columns.

Step 2

Open the paper and refold it into fourths along the long axis. This forms four rows.

Step 3

Unfold and draw lines along the folds.

Step 4

Label the chart as shown.

Chapter 4	Form	Function	Care
Teeth			
Skin			
Hair			

As You Read

Record information about teeth, skin, and hair in the appropriate section of the chart. Then use the chart to compare different types of personal care.

85

Chapter Introduction

Use the options below to motivate students and preview chapter content.

HEALTH *Online*

Have students take Health Inventory 4 or read extra-credit articles at **health.glencoe.com**. By clicking on Health Updates, both students and teachers can discover the latest news on health topics.

GLENCOE TECHNOLOGY

MindJogger Videoquiz

Use MindJogger to preview or review Chapter 4 content.

TIME HEALTH

The Smile File
pages 108–109

FOLDABLES™
Study Organizer

Dinah Zike Study Fold

Organizing Data and Making Comparisons Use this Foldable chart for student writing about the form, function, and care of teeth, skin, and hair. Instruct students to use their completed chart to take notes and define terms. Then have them use the data recorded to make comparisons. For example, how are skin and hair similar? How are they different? Give students the following guidelines: When making comparisons, first determine what will be compared, then decide what standards will be used for comparison, and then use what is known to find similarities and

Lesson 1

Your Teeth, Skin, and Hair

① Focus

Lesson Objectives

Students will be able to

- identify the basic structures, functions, and health problems of teeth, skin, and hair.
- explain the causes and stages of tooth decay and how to prevent it.
- summarize health behaviors that promote healthy teeth, skin, and hair.

Health Skills
- Practicing Healthful Behaviors, p. 91

Motivators

Quick Write
List student responses on the board. Discuss how often each behavior is practiced.

Bellringer Activity

Ask students to identify what teeth do for them. (*enable them to chew, help them talk and smile, and give shape to their mouths*) Have students imagine what they would look like without teeth. In this lesson, they will learn how to take care of their teeth and their smiles.

VOCABULARY

Prepare the vocabulary terms for the lesson on pieces of poster board. Read the definitions of the terms one at a time, and ask students to point out the corresponding vocabulary term.

Quick Write

List the things you do to take care of your teeth, skin, and hair.

LEARN ABOUT...

- how you can keep your teeth healthy.
- ways to take care of your skin.
- how you should care for your hair and nails.

VOCABULARY

- plaque
- tartar
- fluoride
- orthodontist
- epidermis
- dermis
- acne
- dermatologist
- cuticle
- dandruff

Your Teeth, Skin, and Hair

Healthy Teeth and Gums

Your teeth and gums help you eat, smile, and even talk. For these reasons and more, it is important to take care of your teeth and gums. Developing healthy dental habits now will help prevent tooth decay and loss throughout your life.

Tooth and gum problems start when plaque stays on the teeth too long. **Plaque** (PLAK) is a *soft, colorless, sticky film containing bacteria that grows on your teeth*. It is the main cause of both tooth decay and gum disease. It can also make your breath smell bad. **Figure 4.1** shows you how plaque causes tooth decay.

FIGURE 4.1

TOOTH DECAY

Tooth decay and gum disease usually result from poor dental care. *Do you know the correct way to brush your teeth?*

Stage 1
The bacteria in plaque combine with sugars to form a harmful acid. This acid eats into the enamel, the hard outer surface of the tooth.

Stage 2
Repeated acid attacks on the enamel cause a cavity, or hole, to form.

Stage 3
If the cavity grows and reaches the sensitive inner parts of the tooth, it can cause a toothache.

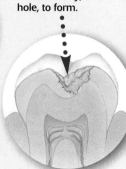

Lesson 1 Resources

Teacher Classroom Resources
- Parent Letter & Activities 4
- Concept Maps 12 & 13
- Cross-Curriculum Activity 7
- Enrichment Activity 12
- Health Lab 4
- Lesson Plan 1
- Lesson 1 Quiz

- Reading Tutor Activity 12
- Reteaching Activity 12
- Transparency 14

Student Activities Workbook
- Chapter 4 Study Guide
- Applying Health Skills 12

Preventing Tooth and Gum Problems

The best way to avoid tooth and gum problems is to clean your teeth correctly, as shown in **Figure 4.2**. If plaque is not removed by brushing, it can turn into **tartar** (TAR·ter), *a hard material that forms when plaque builds up on teeth*. Tartar threatens the health of your teeth and gums. Brushing cannot remove tartar. Only a dentist or dental hygienist can remove it with special instruments.

Reading Check

Read the paragraphs on these pages, and find the main idea and supporting details for each.

FIGURE 4.2

BRUSHING AND FLOSSING

To reduce plaque, you should brush after eating whenever possible and floss at least once a day.

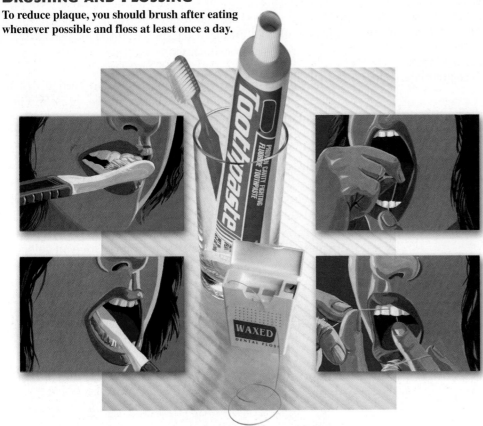

Brushing

Use a soft-bristled brush and toothpaste that contains **fluoride** (FLAWR·eyed), *a substance that fights tooth decay.* Brush the outer tooth surfaces first. Tilt the top of your toothbrush where your teeth and gum meet. Move your brush back and forth gently, using short strokes across your teeth. Then brush the inner tooth surfaces, your chewing surfaces, and your tongue.

Flossing

Take about 18 inches of dental floss, and wrap the ends around the middle finger of each hand. Hold the floss tightly between your thumbs and forefingers, and slide it gently between your teeth. Move it up or down to the gum line with a gentle sawing motion. Rub the side of the tooth, and bring the floss back out gently. Repeat the process between all of your teeth.

LESSON 1: YOUR TEETH, SKIN, AND HAIR **87**

② Teach

VISUAL LEARNING

FIGURE 4.1 As students look at Figure 4.1, have a volunteer read the caption aloud. Ask several students to share their ideas about the correct way to brush teeth. Explain that instructions will be presented later in this lesson. Have other volunteers read aloud the descriptions of the three stages of tooth decay, and ask student volunteers to tell about their own experiences with cavities and toothaches.
INCL *Behavior Problems, Special Learning Needs, English Language Learners*

VISUAL LEARNING

FIGURE 4.2 Have volunteers describe the pictures and read aloud the explanations in Figure 4.2. Then, to help students discuss the facts, ask questions such as these:

- Why is it important to replace your toothbrush every two to three months?
- Why do you think you should replace your toothbrush after an illness?
- What special brushing directions do orthodontists give their patients who wear braces?
- Why is it important to floss as well as brush?
- How can teens with braces floss their teeth? **INCL** *Behavior Problems, Special Learning Needs, English Language Learners*

Reading Check

Identifying Main Ideas and Details Being able to identify the main idea and its supporting details in a paragraph helps students understand and remember the information better. Have students read the first paragraph on page 86 and determine the main idea. (*It is important to take care of one's teeth and gums.*) Have volunteers explain how the other sentences give details that support the main idea. Ask students to work with a partner to find the main idea and details for the remainder of the text on pages 86 and 87. Remind students that the main idea of a paragraph is often stated in the first sentence.

Cross-Curriculum Activity

SOCIAL STUDIES Have volunteer students give a report about chewing gum. They should include the history of chewing gum, for example, who invented it, what it was first made of, and what it is made of now. (Note: This could be an Internet research activity.) **L3**

Discussing

Encourage students to share their own experiences, or the experiences of family members, with wearing braces.

- How was the need for braces diagnosed?
- What checkups or tests did the orthodontist do?
- How were the braces put on? How did that feel?
- What follow-up was required? How did that feel?
- How do students feel about having, or having had, braces? Why? **L1**

Researching

Ask an interested student to learn about wireless braces, finding answers to questions such as these:

- How are wireless braces different from conventional braces?
- How do they work?
- For whom are they recommended? Why?

Have the student share his or her findings with the rest of the class, either in an oral presentation or in a brief written report. **L3**

CONNECT TO
Science

SPACE-AGE BRACES
More teens than ever can wear braces comfortably, thanks to the National Aeronautics and Space Administration (NASA). NASA was the first to develop tooth-moving wires. When activated by body heat, the wires become stronger and more flexible. This makes the braces more comfortable.

Keep your teeth strong and healthy by eating right. Foods high in calcium, such as milk and yogurt, are especially good for your teeth. If you eat sugary or starchy foods, try to eat them at meals. Otherwise, brush your teeth right away.

Visiting the Dentist

To keep your teeth and gums healthy, see your dentist twice a year. The dentist or dental hygienist will clean your teeth to prevent decay and disease. Then the dentist will look for signs of tooth decay and gum disease in order to provide treatment before problems occur. Brushing and flossing regularly and seeing your dentist twice a year will benefit your dental hygiene. Immediate effects are that your teeth will be cleaner and your breath will smell fresher. Long-range effects include having fewer cavities and healthier gums.

In addition to your regular dentist, you may need to visit an orthodontist. An **orthodontist** is *a dentist who specializes in dealing with irregularities of the teeth and jaw.* Straightening crooked teeth makes them look better. It also makes them easier to clean. This reduces the chance that tooth decay or gum disease will develop.

To straighten teeth, an orthodontist will apply braces. This involves attaching a small bracket to each tooth and connecting the brackets with wires. Braces can be made of metal, ceramic, or plastic. Patients can also choose from a variety of colors.

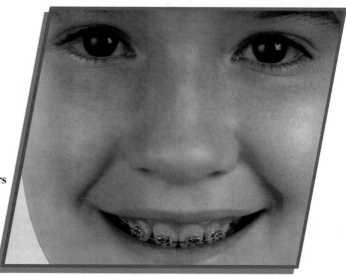

Choosing different colors makes wearing braces more fun. *Why do you think patients would choose colored braces?*

88 CHAPTER 4: PERSONAL HEALTH

WHAT TEENS WANT TO KNOW

Do I really need braces? To find out whether you really need braces, visit a dentist. If you need braces, the dentist will refer you to an orthodontist, a dentist trained to correct crooked or crowded teeth. Wearing braces to straighten your teeth is important for many reasons. For one, improper bite and the continual pressure of teeth rubbing up against one another can cause a gradual loosening of teeth, premature tooth loss, and chipping of the teeth. An improper bite can also produce temporal mandibular joint (TMJ) syndrome, a painful condition of the jaw. Today's braces make it easier and more comfortable to get a healthy, cosmetically appealing smile. Braces are now available in a wide variety of colors.

Healthy Skin

Your skin is your body's largest organ. Like your other body organs, your skin performs many important functions. It protects you from germs and helps control your body temperature. The nerve endings in your skin allow you to feel textures, temperatures, pressures, and pain.

Parts of the Skin

Your skin is a complex organ. It is made up of various tissues that work together to perform many functions. Your skin consists of two main layers. The *thinner outer layer of the skin* is called the **epidermis**. The *thicker inner layer of the skin* is known as the **dermis**. See **Figure 4.3**.

HEALTH *Online*

Topic: Tooth and skin care

For links to more information on healthy teeth and skin, go to health.glencoe.com.

Activity: Using the information provided at these links, create a pamphlet on preventing cavities and treating acne.

Lesson 1

HEALTH *Online*

Encourage students to explore the Web Links for this lesson and then complete the activity. Prompt them by asking: How does fluoride prevent cavities? Does sunlight really help clear up acne?

Discussing

Have the class imagine someone touching a hot pot. Ask students:

- How would skin protect the person? (*Nerve endings in the skin send messages to the brain that the pot is hot. The brain, in turn, tells the hand to move away from the hot object.*)
- What are other functions of the skin? (*It provides a shield against water; protects against germs; controls body temperature; and allows you to feel textures, temperatures, pressure, and pain*) **L1**

VISUAL LEARNING

FIGURE 4.3 As students look at the drawing in Figure 4.3, ask them:

- Which parts of your own skin can you see?
- Which parts can't you see? Why?
  Then have volunteers read aloud the information about the various parts of the skin. For each part, ask:
- How does knowing this affect your understanding of your own skin?
- How does this help you understand the importance of taking good care of your skin? **INCL** *Behavior Problems, Special Learning Needs, English Language Learners*

FIGURE 4.3

THE SKIN

Your skin has many more parts than just the outside surface.

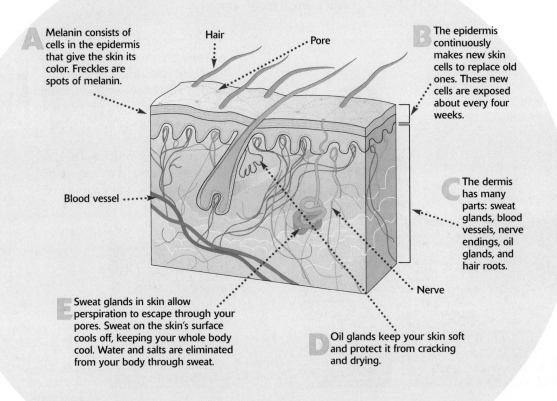

A Melanin consists of cells in the epidermis that give the skin its color. Freckles are spots of melanin.

Hair

Pore

B The epidermis continuously makes new skin cells to replace old ones. These new cells are exposed about every four weeks.

C The dermis has many parts: sweat glands, blood vessels, nerve endings, oil glands, and hair roots.

Blood vessel

Nerve

E Sweat glands in skin allow perspiration to escape through your pores. Sweat on the skin's surface cools off, keeping your whole body cool. Water and salts are eliminated from your body through sweat.

D Oil glands keep your skin soft and protect it from cracking and drying.

 Health Literacy

Health Information Athlete's foot is a fungal infection on the skin of the feet. Its medical name is *tinea pedis,* but it is called athlete's foot because it spreads easily in locker rooms and shared showers. Athlete's foot causes itching, scaly skin, and redness between the toes and on the soles of the feet. It usually takes several weeks of treatment with an antifungal cream or spray to completely clear up the infection. Once the infection disappears, using a medicated powder may help to prevent another infection. Completely drying your feet after showers and changing your socks daily can help prevent athlete's foot.

Demonstrating

Bring in a real sponge. Show the pores in the sponge; and discuss how, when the sponge was alive, water circulated through the pores to keep it alive. Ask the class to name other structures, in addition to pores, that our skin has. (*blood vessels, nerve endings, hair roots, oil glands, sweat glands*) **L1**
INCL *Special Learning Needs, English Language Learners*

Demonstrating

Bring in several kinds of sunscreens. Ask students which they use, if any. Ask students why people should use sunscreen. (*to block the harmful rays of the sun and protect against skin cancer*) Have students demonstrate where they would apply sunscreen. (*to all exposed body parts: face, arms, back, legs, tops of feet, and hands*) Discuss the SPF, or sun protection factor. Which is "better": SPF 6, SPF 15, or SPF 30? Tell students that sunscreen should be applied to dry skin one hour before going into the sun and re-applied after swimming, as directed. **L1**

Cross-Curriculum Activity

SCIENCE Have interested students report on two types of ultraviolet rays that have damaging effects on the skin. Reinforce that the shorter UVB (ultraviolet B) rays are the main cause of sunburn and that UVA (ultraviolet A) rays contribute to wrinkles and premature aging of the skin. **L1**

Caring for Your Skin

The best way to care for your skin is to keep it clean and protect it from the sun.

- **Keep your skin clean.** As your body develops, sweat glands increase their activity. When sweat mixes with bacteria that live on your body, it starts to smell. Washing sweat away keeps your skin clean and smelling fresh. To control odor, use a deodorant. This product slows the growth of bacteria.
- **Protect your skin from the sun.** Ultraviolet (UV) rays from the sun damage your skin. In the short term, they can give you a sunburn. Over time, they can cause wrinkles and contribute to skin cancer. The lighter your skin is, the more easily these rays can harm you. UV rays are strongest between 10:00 A.M. and 4:00 P.M. in the summertime and 9:00 A.M. and 3:00 P.M. in the wintertime. Try to stay out of direct sunlight during these hours. When you are in the sun, wear protective clothing such as long-sleeved shirts and wide-brimmed hats. Cover exposed skin with sun-blocking agents or sunscreens with a sun protection factor (SPF) of 15 or higher. An SPF of 15 gives your skin 15 times its natural protection from sunburn. Read the label on the bottle to find out how often to apply sunscreen.

Skin Problems

During the teen years, the oil glands in your skin start to work harder. This increased oil can clog hair follicles or pores, the tiny holes from which hairs grow. Pimples, whiteheads, and blackheads can form in blocked follicles. These are all forms of **acne** (AK·nee), a *skin condition caused by overly active oil glands.*

Protecting your skin from the sun will help you avoid skin damage in later life. *Compare the immediate and long-range effects of using sunscreen.*

MORE ABOUT...

Skin Problems Cold sores are caused by a herpes virus. The virus produces small, painful red blisters on your lips and the edge of your mouth. The herpes virus that causes cold sores becomes inactive but never completely leaves the body. Cold sores usually go away in about a week but reappear when the virus is triggered. The virus may be triggered by physical stress, such as a cold or other infection, fever, or sun exposure, or by emotional stress. Medicated lip balms can help relieve discomfort. Never share them with friends or you may spread the virus. Guide students in a discussion of other skin problems and the importance of good personal hygiene.

HEALTH SKILLS ACTIVITY

PRACTICING HEALTHFUL BEHAVIORS

Skin Care Strategies

To prevent acne, wash your skin twice a day with a mild soap or cleanser. Rinse with warm water and blot it dry gently with a clean towel. You can also help keep your skin healthy by following these tips:

- Eat sensibly.
- Drink plenty of water.
- Exercise regularly.
- Manage stress.
- Avoid greasy, oil-based makeup and creams.
- Get enough sleep.
- Wash bed linens and towels regularly.
- Keep your hair clean to prevent oil from spreading to your face.
- Keep your hands away from your face. Your fingers can spread bacteria.
- Resist the urge to pop, pick, or squeeze pimples. You could cause more skin irritation, leaving tiny pits and scars.

ON YOUR OWN
Create a personal routine for skin and face care. Follow your routine for a week. Do you notice any change in the appearance of your skin?

Most teens—about 90 percent—have some form of acne. Stress can make acne worse. Mild acne can usually be treated at home. For serious acne, see your regular doctor or a **dermatologist** (DER·muh·TAH·luh·jist), *a doctor who treats skin disorders.*

Skin decorations, such as tattoos and piercings, can also cause skin problems. If needles and other equipment are not perfectly clean and disinfected, they can spread serious infections. These include HIV (the virus that causes AIDS) and hepatitis, a dangerous inflammation of the liver.

Taking care of your skin can keep it smooth and healthy-looking. Protecting your skin from sunburn now can reduce the number of wrinkles you have later in life. It will also help reduce your risk of developing skin cancer.

The earlobe is the only body part generally considered safe for piercing. *Why might ear piercing be safer than other kinds of body piercing?*

LESSON 1: YOUR TEETH, SKIN, AND HAIR **91**

PROMOTING COORDINATED SCHOOL HEALTH

The Payoffs In the face of the immediate challenges to schools, a coordinated effort is necessary to ensure that today's children become tomorrow's healthy, productive adults and parents. To that end, the benefits of developing a coordinated school program are far-reaching. Consider how a coordinated school health program might impact the following areas: positive self-image; interpersonal skills; coping skills to reduce tension and frustration; self-responsibility; and the potential for students becoming secure, knowledgeable adults. For more information, consult *Planning a Coordinated School Health Program* in the TCR.

Demonstrating

Bring to class the nail-care products mentioned in the text: cuticle stick, cuticle remover, nail clipper or small scissors, and emery board or nail file. Show and describe the products and, if appropriate, briefly demonstrate their uses. **L2**

Discussing

You may want to let students describe and explain special hair-care procedures they use, such as flat-ironing, braiding, or weaving. Help students discuss the healthiest approaches to these procedures. **L1**

Cross-Curriculum Activity

MATH Explain to students that the average person's scalp has about 100,000 hairs growing from it. It is normal to lose about 100 hairs from your scalp each day. Fortunately, new hairs grow to replace those that fall out. Ask students to calculate, at this rate, how many years it takes for an entire head of hair to be replaced. (*It takes about 1,000 days or 2 years 9 months to lose a head of hair.*) **L2**

FYI

Melanin gives color not only to an individual's skin but also to hair and the iris of the eyes.

You can keep your cuticles looking neat by pushing them back with a cuticle stick. *What else can you do to improve the appearance of your nails?*

Healthy Nails

Fingernails and toenails are dead cells that grow out of living tissue located in the dermis. A *nonliving band of epidermis* called the **cuticle** (KYOO·ti·kuhl) surrounds the nails. Well-kept nails make your hands look attractive and healthy. Follow these steps to care for your nails.

- Soften your hands with warm water, and use a cuticle stick to push back the cuticle.
- Use a nail clipper or small scissors to trim your nails. Round the ends of your fingernails slightly. Cut your toenails straight across, with the nail at or slightly beyond skin level.
- Use an emery board or nail file to round out the ends of your fingernails. An emery board also smoothes out rough edges.

Healthy Hair

No part of your body grows faster than your hair. Hair shafts, the part of the hair you can see, consist of dead protein cells that overlap each other like shingles on a roof. The shape of these hair shafts determines the overall appearance of your hair: wavy, straight, or curly. Your hair color comes from melanin, the same substance that gives your skin its color.

What Causes Hair and Scalp Problems?

If the scalp produces too much oil, hair may become flat, stringy, and greasy. If it produces too little oil, hair may be coarse and brittle. That's why you should always use the right shampoo for your hair type—dry, oily, or normal.

Sun exposure and excessive heat from hair dryers can make hair dry, brittle, and faded. Curling irons also can overdry hair and increase breakage. Dyeing or bleaching hair at home can cause disastrous results. Chlorine in pool water can damage and dry your hair shafts. Special shampoos can remove chlorine from your hair to prevent damage.

A common scalp problem is **dandruff**, *flaking of the outer layer of dead skin cells.* A dry scalp usually causes dandruff. Washing your hair regularly controls dandruff. If this does not work, use a dandruff shampoo. Sometimes, head lice cause an itchy scalp. These tiny, wingless insects that live in the hair are very common and easy to catch from someone else. To

92 CHAPTER 4: PERSONAL HEALTH

COOPERATIVE LEARNING ACTIVITY

Personal and Dental Hygiene Divide students into groups. Assign each group to research personal and dental hygiene. Students should learn why taking care of their bodies, including teeth and gums, is important, why having semiannual check-ups is recommended, what is involved in a semiannual dental check-up, and other essentials of personal and dental hygiene. When students

have finished their research, have each group prepare a chart or poster that compares the immediate and long-range effects of personal health care choices involving personal and dental hygiene. Ask groups to present their findings to the entire class. You may wish to prepare a bulletin board to display student work.

prevent lice from spreading, avoid sharing hats, combs, and brushes with other people. If you get lice, you can kill them with a medicated shampoo. You will also need to wash all your bedding, towels, combs, brushes, and clothing. Everyone else in your house will need to take these steps too.

Caring for Your Hair

To keep your hair healthy and looking good, wash it regularly, and comb or brush it carefully.

- **Washing.** Use a gentle shampoo and rinse completely with warm water to remove excess shampoo or conditioner. Oily hair may require a deep cleaning shampoo. If possible, let your hair dry by itself. If you use a blow dryer, use low heat. Avoid washing your hair too often, which can dry it out.
- **Brushing and combing.** Brushing or combing once a day helps spread natural scalp oils down the hair shaft. Too much brushing, though, can break the hair shaft or pull hair out. If you use a brush, choose one with rounded or balled tips so you do not scratch your scalp. Getting into the habit of properly brushing or combing your hair will help keep your hair healthy throughout your life.

No matter what type of hair you have, taking good care of it is a healthful habit. *List three things you can do to take care of your hair.*

Round shaft, straight hair

Oval shaft, wavy hair

Flat shaft, curly hair

Applying Information

Have students create charts that compare the immediate and long-range effects of personal health care choices including dental hygiene, personal hygiene, and skin care. Remind students that the choices they make now, especially taking care of their teeth, skin, muscles, and bones, will impact their health throughout their lives. **L2**

❸ Assess

Evaluating

📁 Assign the Lesson 1 Review; then assign the Lesson 1 Quiz in the TCR.

Reteaching

📁 Assign Concept Maps 12 and 13, and Reteaching Activity 12 in the TCR.

Enrichment

📁 Assign and distribute Enrichment Activity 12 in the TCR.

❹ Close

Divide students into groups. Have them design a graphic slogan for a commercial that begins "Your (skin, teeth, or hair) will be healthy when you _____." Display the slogans around the classroom.

Lesson 1 Review

Using complete sentences, answer the following questions on a sheet of paper.

Reviewing Terms and Facts

1. **Vocabulary** Define *plaque* and *tartar*. How are they related?
2. **Vocabulary** Define the words *epidermis* and *dermis.*
3. **Recall** What is dandruff, and how can you get rid of it?

Thinking Critically

4. **Explain** What can you do to keep the sun from damaging your skin?
5. **Apply** What can teens do to prevent acne?

Applying Health Skills

6. **Advocacy** Create a pamphlet that compares the immediate and long-range effects of dental hygiene choices. Distribute the pamphlet to a younger class.

LESSON 1: YOUR TEETH, SKIN, AND HAIR **93**

Lesson 1 Review

1. Plaque is a soft, colorless, sticky film of bacteria that grows on your teeth. Tartar is plaque that hardens and cannot be removed by brushing and flossing.
2. The epidermis is the thinner outer layer of skin. The dermis is the thicker inner layer.
3. Dandruff is the flaking of the outer layer of dead skin cells on the scalp. You can control it by washing hair regularly or using a special dandruff shampoo.
4. Avoid being outdoors when sunlight is strongest. When you go outside, protect your skin with clothing and sunscreen.
5. Teens could wash their skin daily and avoid greasy creams and makeup that could clog pores and hair follicles.

1 Focus

Lesson Objectives

Students should be able to

- label and define the parts of the eye and ear.
- summarize ways to care for their eyes and ears.
- describe vision and hearing problems and how they may be corrected.

Motivators

Quick Write

Have students identify their preference with a raise of hands. Ask volunteers from each group to share their paragraphs.

Bellringer Activity

Have students list activities that might require protection for the eyes or ears. Then ask them to identify what they can do or products they can use to provide protection.

VOCABULARY

Write the vocabulary words for the lesson on index cards. On the board, arrange two columns. Above one column, draw an eye; above the other column, draw an ear. Have students attach the index cards in the correct column on the board. Define each word. Call on students to point to the index card bearing the correct word.

Lesson 2

Protecting Your Eyes and Ears

Quick Write

Do you like studying with music on? Do you prefer quiet when you read or talk with friends? Write a paragraph about what level of sound feels most comfortable for you.

LEARN ABOUT...

- how to care for your eyes and vision.
- how to protect your ears and hearing.

VOCABULARY

- farsightedness
- nearsightedness
- astigmatism
- decibels
- sound waves

Healthy Eyes

Your eyes allow you to see your friends, read your favorite books, and do much more. Taking care of your eyes will help you look and feel good throughout your life. First, find out how the eye works by looking at **Figure 4.4**.

Caring for Your Eyes

The following habits will keep your eyes healthy.

- **Protect your eyes from eyestrain.** Reading, watching television, and using a computer for too long can strain your eyes. To avoid this, read and watch television in a well-lighted room. Place your reading lamp so it shines on your reading material. When you use a computer, keep the screen about two feet from your face and tilted slightly away from you. Take breaks whenever you watch TV, work on the computer, or do other close-up work.

Protecting your eyes is a good health habit that will help you maintain good vision throughout your life. *List some of the ways you can keep your eyes healthy.*

Lesson 2 Resources

Teacher Classroom Resources

- Concept Maps 14 & 15
- Cross-Curriculum Activity 8
- Decision-Making Activity 7
- Enrichment Activity 13
- Lesson Plan 2
- Lesson 2 Quiz

- Reading Tutor Activity 13
- Reteaching Activity 13
- Transparencies 15 & 16

Student Activities Workbook

- Chapter 4 Study Guide
- Applying Health Skills 13

FIGURE 4.4

THE EYE

The many parts of the eye work together to tell you about the world around you. *How do your eyelids and eyelashes help protect your eyes?*

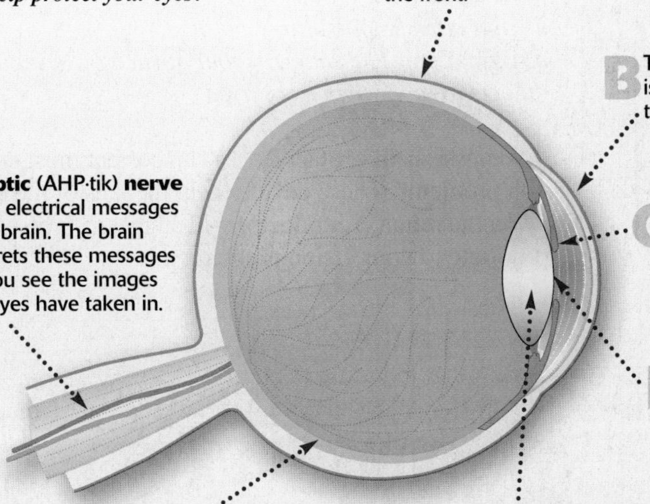

A The **sclera** (SKLEHR·uh) is a tough, white outer coat that protects the eye. It covers all of the eye except the front.

B The **cornea** (KOR·nee·uh) is the clear outer layer of the eyeball that lets in light.

G The **optic** (AHP·tik) **nerve** carries electrical messages to the brain. The brain interprets these messages and you see the images your eyes have taken in.

C The round, colored part of the eye is the **iris** (EYE·ris). The iris controls the size of the pupil.

D Light enters the interior of the eye through the **pupil** (PYOO·puhl), the dark opening in the center of the iris. In dim light, the pupil lets in more light by becoming larger. In bright light, the pupils keep out some light by becoming smaller.

F The **retina** (RE·tin·uh), a complex layer of nerve cells, absorbs light rays from the lens. It changes light rays into electrical images and sends them to the optic nerve.

E Light rays pass through the **lens** (LENZ). The lens adjusts to focus the light on the retina like the lens of a camera.

- **Protect your eyes from injury.** Use safety eyewear when using power tools or playing certain sports. If you get something in your eye, do not rub it. Try to blink, and let tears wash the object out. If this does not work, rinse the eye with water or an eyewash.
- **Protect your eyes from infection.** If your eyes hurt or itch, do not rub them. The discomfort could be caused by an infection. See your doctor for treatment. To avoid spreading infections, don't share eye makeup or eye care products.
- **Protect your eyes from the sun.** When in strong sunlight, wear a hat or visor and sunglasses. Make sure that your sunglasses protect your eyes from both kinds of ultraviolet light: UVA rays and UVB rays.
- **Get regular vision screenings.** If you wear glasses or contact lenses, get your vision checked every year. Otherwise, get a checkup every two years.

LESSON 2: PROTECTING YOUR EYES AND EARS **95**

Lesson 2

2 Teach

Demonstrating

Bring a small reading lamp to class and set it up on a desk or table. Let students take turns adjusting the lamp so it provides the best source of light for their reading. In addition, if your classroom has a computer, let students take turns showing the proper posture and position for working at a computer. **L1**

VISUAL LEARNING

FIGURE 4.4 Tell students that people with full vision gather 80 percent of their knowledge through their eyes. Have students look at Figure 4.4 to find out how their eyes work. Ask them to look at the model of the eye shown and read and discuss the captions. **INCL** *Behavior Problems, Special Learning Needs, English Language Learners*

Health Literacy

Health Information Ask students what 20/20 vision means. (*A person with 20/20 vision, which is considered normal vision, can read a designated line of letters on the Snellen chart from a distance of 20 feet.*) Borrow a Snellen chart from the school nurse for demonstration. Have students speculate what 20/40 vision means. (*At a distance of 20 feet, a person with 20/40 vision can read a designated line of letters on the Snellen chart that a person with normal vision can read from a distance of 40 feet.*) Ask students whether a person with 20/40 or 20/20 vision has better vision. (*the person with 20/20 vision*) Discuss the importance of students getting their vision checked annually if they wear glasses or contacts and every two years if they don't.

Hands-On Health

OBSERVING THE EYE

Time: 20 minutes (Additional class time or out-of-class time required for research.)

TEACHING THE ACTIVITY

- In a brief discussion, let students share what they already know about the eyes' means of adjusting to various light sources and about problems with color vision.
- Have a volunteer read aloud the What You Will Do steps, and distribute small mirrors.
- You may want to have students work with partners to complete the three steps of the activity. Provide two periods of darkness so both partners can watch their own pupils and check their own color vision.
- Ask students to complete the In Conclusion research independently, or have several volunteers do the research and share their findings with the rest of the class.

As an alternative, you can also find interactive color blindness checks on the Internet.

ASSESSMENT

Guide students in discussing the activity. Ask what they learned about their own eyes and about problems with color vision.

Vision Problems

A complete eye exam by a doctor can uncover these problems:

- **Farsightedness.** *You can see objects at a distance, but close objects look blurry.*
- **Nearsightedness.** *You can see objects close to you, but distant objects look blurry.*
- **Astigmatism.** *The shape of your cornea or lens causes objects to look wavy or blurred.*

Eyeglasses and contact lenses can correct most common vision problems. These devices help the lens of the eye focus light on the retina. Your doctor will suggest a type of lens appropriate to your vision problem.

Hands-On Health

OBSERVING THE EYE

Your eyes can adjust very quickly to different light levels. The muscles in the iris change so that the pupils let in more or less light. The eyes of most people can also distinguish the colors of different objects. However, about 1 in 12 men and 1 in 250 women have some problems with color vision. Try this activity to observe your eyes' reactions to light and color.

WHAT YOU WILL NEED
- a mirror

WHAT YOU WILL DO
1. Turn off the lights, and sit in the dark for two to three minutes.
2. Turn the lights back on, and quickly look in the mirror. Watch what your pupils do. You should be able to see them shrinking to block out some of the light.
3. After your eyes have adjusted to the light, do the color vision test. Look at the circle shown here. Can you see a number in the circle? If not, you may have trouble

distinguishing the colors red and green. This condition is not dangerous, but you should let an adult know about it.

IN CONCLUSION
As a class, make a chart or graph that compares the results for all students. What do your findings show?

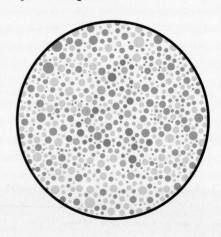

MORE ABOUT...

Correcting Vision Laser in-situ keratomileusis (LASIK) is an increasingly popular surgical procedure that uses the excimer laser, a cold beam of ultraviolet light, to improve vision. LASIK has been performed in the United States since 1995 and is considered safe and effective.

Using the excimer laser, controlled by a computer, the ophthalmologist reshapes the cornea, enabling it to better focus images onto the retina. The procedure takes about 15 minutes per eye. LASIK is not recommended for children and teens, since their vision is still changing.

Most people find glasses easy to wear. They come in many attractive styles and colors. By law, prescription glasses must resist impact, but they are not shatterproof.

Some people prefer to wear contact lenses. These tiny lenses cling to the cornea, are nearly invisible, and often offer better sight than glasses. Compared to glasses, they take more time to properly clean and store. Also, users must follow wearing schedules and have more follow-up visits to maintain eye health.

Healthy Ears

Your ears do not just enable you to hear. They also help keep your balance so you can stand upright or walk. Protecting your ears will help you hear better throughout your life. **Figure 4.5** shows the parts of the ear.

FIGURE 4.5

THE EAR

Your ears transmit sound to your brain and help you keep your balance. *Why is it important to protect your ears?*

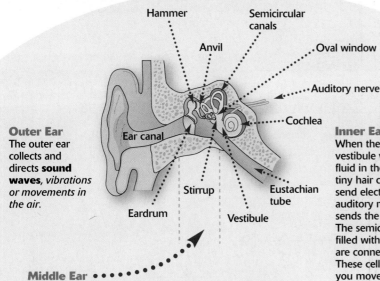

Outer Ear
The outer ear collects and directs **sound waves**, *vibrations or movements in the air*.

Middle Ear
Sound waves strike the eardrum, causing it to vibrate. As it vibrates, the eardrum moves three tiny bones called the hammer, anvil, and stirrup. Sound vibrations are carried to the oval window, which leads to the inner ear. The eustachian tube goes from behind the eardrum to the throat. This tube helps keep air pressure on either side of the eardrum equal. Without it, the eardrum would tear with sudden pressure changes.

Inner Ear
When the oval window in the vestibule vibrates, it moves the fluid in the cochlea. Thousands of tiny hair cells inside the cochlea send electrical messages to the auditory nerve. This nerve then sends the messages to the brain. The semicircular canals are also filled with fluid and hair cells that are connected to nerve endings. These cells tell your brain when you move, which helps you keep your balance.

Labels in figure: Hammer, Anvil, Semicircular canals, Oval window, Auditory nerve, Cochlea, Ear canal, Stirrup, Eustachian tube, Eardrum, Vestibule

Discussing

Ask students to discuss in a group their own experiences with glasses or contact lenses. Which do they prefer? Why? **L1**

Critical Thinking

Stretch an elastic band, and then release it. Repeat the procedure several times. Ask students why the rubber band makes a noise when twanged in this fashion. (*The elastic band is vibrating. Sound happens when something moves back and forth or vibrates very quickly. The band's vibrations are within the range of human hearing and also mimic how the eardrum vibrates with sound.*) **L1**

VISUAL LEARNING

FIGURE 4.5 Have students read the captions in Figure 4.5 to find out how they can hear sound. Write the labels *Step 1: Outer Ear, Step 2: Middle Ear,* and *Step 3: Inner Ear* on the board. Have students discuss what happens with sound at each step. Ask students to read the paragraph on this page that explains how we keep our balance. (*The hair- and fluid-filled semicircular canals send messages to the brain.*) **INCL** *Behavior Problems, Special Learning Needs, English Language Learners*

✔ **Reading Check**
Create a Venn diagram. Use information from these pages and facts you already know to describe both eyeglasses and contact lenses. Write each fact in the diagram.

✔ **Reading Check**

Venn Diagrams Creating a Venn diagram can help students compare and contrast descriptions more easily. Have students list facts about both eyeglasses and contact lenses. Point out that although some information is given only about one type of eyewear, they may already know how it compares. One example could be that glasses are breakable. Guide students in using the information in the first two paragraphs in the section of their diagram labeled *Both*. To complete the lesson, have students compare and contrast the two types of eyewear using their Venn diagrams. **INCL** *Behavior Problems, Special Learning Needs, English Language Learners*

Lesson 2

Demonstrating

Bring to class a personal stereo with earphones, and let several students demonstrate its safe use. Emphasize that turning the volume up so that others can hear the music makes the use of headphones dangerous. **L1**

VISUAL LEARNING

FIGURE 4.6 As students look at Figure 4.6, provide the following:

- Noise from firecrackers is about 120 decibels.
- Heavy city traffic is about 90 decibels.
- Normal conversation is 60 decibels.
- Breathing that is barely heard is 10 decibels.

Have students read the illustration on this page to find the decibel value of noise from selected machines. **INCL** *Behavior Problems, Special Learning Needs, English Language Learners*

Discussing

Point out that, although too much wax in the ear canal can cause hearing problems, individuals should never try to remove wax themselves. Ask: What is the safe way to keep your ears clean? Emphasize that while washing the outer ear is safe and effective, cotton swabs and other small objects should not be placed in the ear. **L1**

CONNECT TO
Performing Arts

PLUG IT IN
Concerts are fun, but loud music can damage your hearing. Wearing ear plugs is the easiest way to protect your ears. Some bands make earplugs available at concerts. Many rock musicians use them during their own concerts.

Caring for Your Ears

What's the best way to care for your ears? Protect them from loud sounds. *Loudness of sound* is measured in **decibels**. Normal conversation measures about 60 decibels. **Figure 4.6** shows how louder noises can affect your hearing.

Sudden loud noises can injure the tiny hair cells in your inner ear. So can repeated exposure to sounds higher than 85 decibels. This can cause temporary or even permanent hearing loss. It can also cause a ringing in the ears called tinnitus (tin·EYE·tus). Many people hurt their ears by wearing earphones with the volume turned up too high.

Cold weather can also harm your ears. When cold air enters your ear canal, it can irritate your middle ear, causing pain. In cold weather, wear earmuffs or a hat that covers your ears.

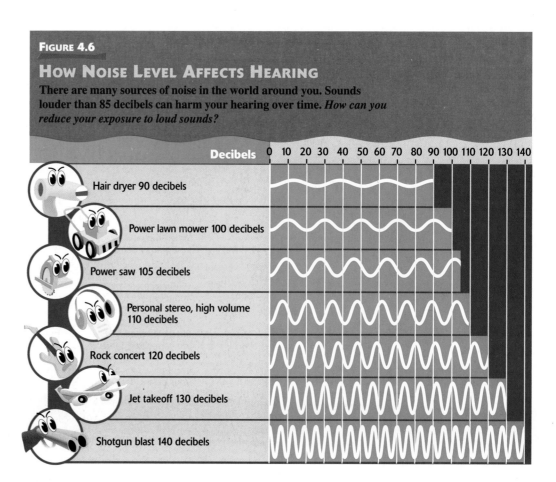

FIGURE 4.6

HOW NOISE LEVEL AFFECTS HEARING

There are many sources of noise in the world around you. Sounds louder than 85 decibels can harm your hearing over time. *How can you reduce your exposure to loud sounds?*

Decibels 0 10 20 30 40 50 60 70 80 90 100 110 120 130 140

Hair dryer 90 decibels
Power lawn mower 100 decibels
Power saw 105 decibels
Personal stereo, high volume 110 decibels
Rock concert 120 decibels
Jet takeoff 130 decibels
Shotgun blast 140 decibels

98 CHAPTER 4: PERSONAL HEALTH

COOPERATIVE LEARNING ACTIVITY

Investigating Hearing in Animals Allow students to form groups of four or five to research the normal range of hearing for animals. Stimulate the students' critical thinking by asking them to brainstorm what they know about the sounds made by animals such as bats or dolphins. (*They make sounds that are higher pitched than humans can hear and locate objects by reflection of those sounds.*) Encourage students to investigate other animals whose normal pitch is too low for humans to hear, such as whales and elephants.

Ear Problems

Infections of the middle ear are the most common ear problems. A nose or throat infection can also lead to pain in the ear. Sometimes, infections move from the throat up the eustachian tube to the ear. A doctor can treat these infections.

Hearing loss and deafness are the most serious ear problems. Too much wax in the ear canal, an ear infection, and nerve damage can cause partial hearing loss or ringing in the ears. A total hearing loss can result from ear injury, disease, and birth defects.

People with hearing problems often communicate using lipreading and sign language. Some may wear hearing aids that increase the loudness of sound waves. *What other ways can people communicate?*

Lesson 2 Review

Using complete sentences, answer the following questions on a sheet of paper.

Reviewing Terms and Facts

1. **Vocabulary** Define the words *farsightedness* and *nearsightedness.*
2. **Explain** What do glasses and contact lenses do?
3. **Recall** What part of the ear helps you maintain your balance?

Thinking Critically

4. **Analyze** How do loud noises harm hearing?

5. **Summarize** What changes could you make in your life that would give greater protection to your eyes and your ears?

Applying Health Skills

6. **Accessing Information** Survey at least six people who wear glasses or contact lenses. First, find out why they need the glasses or lenses. Then find out how long they have worn them and what they think the advantages and disadvantages of each are. Prepare a chart of your findings.

Lesson 2 Review

1. See definitions on page 96.
2. They correct common vision problems by helping the lens of the eye focus light on the retina.
3. The semicircular canals affect balance.
4. Loud noises can damage the tiny hair cells in the inner ear that send sound messages to the brain.

5. Protect eyes by working and reading in adequate light, wearing special eyewear when playing certain sports or working with power tools, not rubbing eyes when they itch, wearing sunglasses, and having regular checkups. Protect ears by avoiding loud noises and covering them in cold weather.

③ Assess

Evaluating

📁 Assign the Lesson 2 Review; then assign the Lesson 2 Quiz in the TCR.

Reteaching

• 📁 Assign Concept Maps 14 and 15 and Reteaching Activity 13 in the TCR.

• Have students prepare a demonstration for a younger class to tell them how to take care of their vision and hearing.

Enrichment

• 📁 Assign and distribute Enrichment Activity 13 in the TCR.

• Have a group of students look at basic first-aid books to find out what they should do if they ever get an object or a chemical in their eyes. Ask them to share this information with the class.

④ Close

Have students listen to a television program at home or a video in class with their eyes closed. After five to ten minutes, have them watch the program or video with the sound turned off. Ask each student to describe his or her feelings during the experience.

Lesson 3

Choosing Health Products

1 Focus

Lesson Objectives

Students will be able to

- identify what influences their decisions about health products.
- explain how to decide which health products are best for them.
- describe how to choose health products wisely.

Health Skills

- Accessing Information, p. 102

Motivators

Quick Write

Allow students time to discuss how they made their health product choices.

Bellringer Activity

Ask students to brainstorm influences that help them decide on purchasing a specific product. Then have them rank the influences from most to least influential.

VOCABULARY

Write the vocabulary terms on the board. Instruct students to skim the lesson for the definitions of the words. Then have them record these important terms and definitions in their notebooks, where they can be referred to as needed.

Lesson 3

Choosing Health Products

Quick Write

Think about the health products you used last week for your hair, skin, nails, eyes, and ears. Make a list of all of these products. How did you decide which products to use?

LEARN ABOUT...

- what influences your decisions about health products.
- how to decide which health products are best for you.
- how to choose health products wisely.

VOCABULARY

- consumer
- advertisement
- warranty
- discount store
- coupon
- generic
- fraud

Recognizing Influences

You are a **consumer**, *someone who buys products or services.* For example, you use health products such as toothpaste, sunscreen, and deodorant. You also use health services—the work of doctors, dentists, and other health professionals.

Sometimes, choosing health products and services can be confusing. **Figure 4.7** shows the many thoughts a person might have before deciding to buy a product. Building consumer skills will help you choose wisely and be aware of what influences your choices.

FIGURE 4.7

MAKING AN INFORMED CHOICE

Many factors affect consumers' decisions. *Identify the influences that this teen is considering. How might each of these influences affect her buying decisions?*

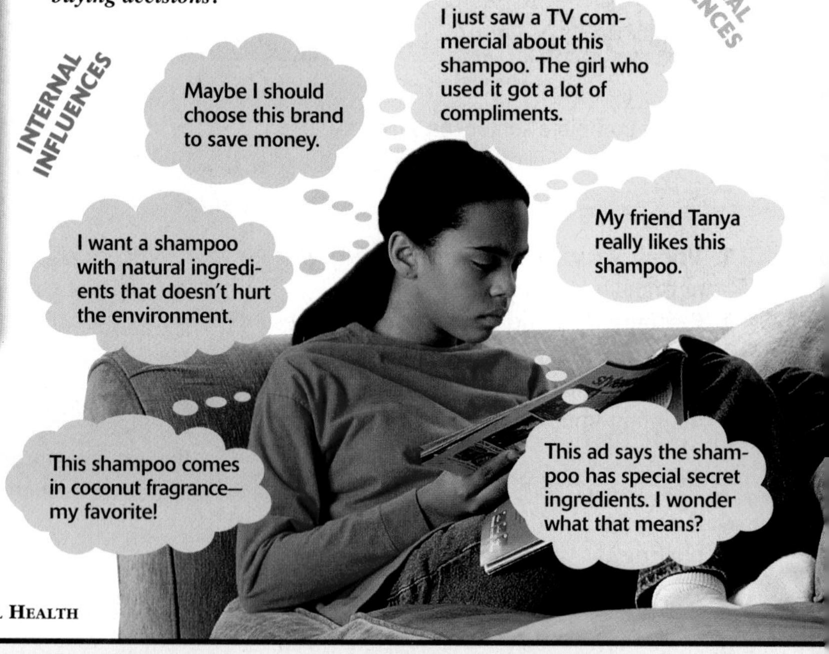

EXTERNAL INFLUENCES
INTERNAL INFLUENCES
Maybe I should choose this brand to save money.
I just saw a TV commercial about this shampoo. The girl who used it got a lot of compliments.
I want a shampoo with natural ingredients that doesn't hurt the environment.
My friend Tanya really likes this shampoo.
This shampoo comes in coconut fragrance—my favorite!
This ad says the shampoo has special secret ingredients. I wonder what that means?

Lesson 3 Resources

Teacher Classroom Resources

- Concept Map 16
- Decision-Making Activity 8
- Enrichment Activity 14
- Lesson Plan 3
- Lesson 3 Quiz
- Reading Tutor Activity 14
- Reteaching Activity 14
- Transparencies 17 & 18

Student Activities Workbook

- Chapter 4 Study Guide
- Applying Health Skills 14

Making Good Consumer Choices

A major influence on your consumer choices is advertising. **Advertisements** are *messages used to persuade consumers to buy goods or services.* Ads may claim that products and services will make you happier, healthier, and more attractive.

If an advertising claim sounds too good to be true, it probably is. Ads are meant to sell products and services. Be critical of any health information used to sell a health product or service. Seek advice from trusted adults.

Be cautious about buying products from an unfamiliar source. You may not be able to get your money back if the product does not work.

Smart Shopping

Smart shopping can help you save money. One way to be a smart shopper is to compare products and prices before buying. Reading and understanding product labels, like the one shown in **Figure 4.8**, can help you determine whether a product is worth the price.

FIGURE 4.8

WHAT LABELS CAN TELL YOU

Product labels give you important information. *How does the information on a product label help you make a wise choice?*

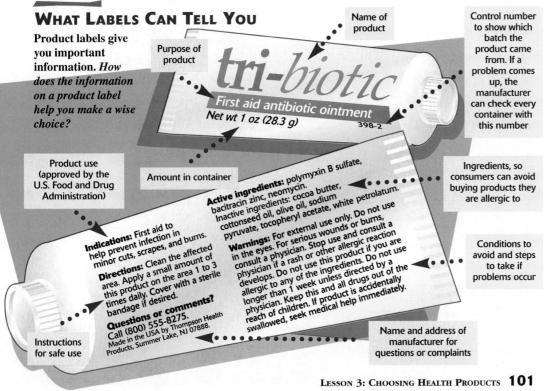

Name of product

Control number to show which batch the product came from. If a problem comes up, the manufacturer can check every container with this number

Purpose of product

tri-biotic
First aid antibiotic ointment
Net wt 1 oz (28.3 g)
398-2

Product use (approved by the U.S. Food and Drug Administration)

Amount in container

Ingredients, so consumers can avoid buying products they are allergic to

Active ingredients: polymyxin B sulfate, bacitracin zinc, neomycin. **Inactive ingredients:** cocoa butter, cottonseed oil, olive oil, sodium pyruvate, tocopheryl acetate, white petrolatum.

Indications: First aid to help prevent infection in minor cuts, scrapes, and burns. **Directions:** Clean the affected area. Apply a small amount of this product on the area 1 to 3 times daily. Cover with a sterile bandage if desired.

Warnings: For external use only. Do not use in the eyes. For serious wounds or burns, consult a physician. Stop use and consult a physician if a rash or other allergic reaction develops. Do not use this product if you are allergic to any of the ingredients. Do not use longer than 1 week unless directed by a physician. Keep this and all drugs out of the reach of children. If product is accidentally swallowed, seek medical help immediately.

Conditions to avoid and steps to take if problems occur

Instructions for safe use

Questions or comments? Call (800) 555-8275. Made in the USA by Thompson Health Products, Summer Lake, NJ 07888.

Name and address of manufacturer for questions or complaints

② Teach

VISUAL LEARNING

FIGURE 4.7 Ask students to describe what the teen in the picture is doing, and then have volunteers read aloud each of her "thoughts." Have students explain the difference between the internal influences and the external influences. Then have students list ways to evaluate health care products such as sunblocks, dietary aids, and over-the-counter medication. Have them differentiate which evaluation factors are external and which are internal. **INCL** *Behavior Problems, Special Learning Needs, English Language Learners*

Cross-Curriculum Activity

RESEARCHING Give each student an index card with a specific health topic on it. Direct students to use critical thinking skills to research and evaluate their topics. Tell them that critical thinking skills include analyzing, applying, and predicting. Have students present their findings to the class and to identify the critical thinking skills they used for this project. **L2**

VISUAL LEARNING

FIGURE 4.8 Have students work in groups to evaluate and discuss health care product labels. Then pass out empty product containers, and have groups identify and discuss the information on the labels.

Health Literacy

Influencing Factors Advertising can help consumers learn about products, but it can also unduly influence consumers' decisions about buying these products. Tell students that, as smart consumers, they need to watch television advertising with a critical eye. Explain three common methods of advertising found on television: the bandwagon appeal, which proclaims that everyone is using the product; the image appeal, which claims that the product will make people attractive; and the trust appeal, which says that you should use the product because trustworthy people use or endorse it. Have students give examples they have seen on television.

Cross-Curriculum Activity

MATH Have students go to a supermarket and copy the price per unit, as listed on the supermarket shelves, of several personal products. Have these students report their findings and explain what price per unit means. Encourage students to tell how knowing a price per unit helps consumers decide what quantity, size, and product to purchase. **L3**

HEALTH SKILLS ACTIVITY

ACCESSING INFORMATION

Let volunteers describe the two containers of liquid soap pictured here. Ask students which they would like to buy. Why?

Help students read and discuss the activity introduction. Have students work independently to write their answers to the On Your Own questions; then have students compare and discuss their responses.

Note: This skill is introduced in Chapter 1 on page 9.

Analyzing

Bring beauty and bodybuilding magazines to class. Have students note how men and women are portrayed. In addition, have students analyze how products are advertised and marketed. Ask students if they believe that advertising can lead to poor body image in individuals. Have students identify the effects associated with poor body image such as eating disorders. List their responses on the board.

✓ Reading Check

Investigate word origin. Determine what the following words have in common: *warranty, cover, garage, guarantee.*

Comparison Shopping

When evaluating health products, consider these factors.

- **Price.** How much can you afford to spend on the product?
- **Unit Price.** How much does the product cost per ounce or per gram? (See the Health Skills Activity for details.)
- **Benefits.** Does one brand offer more features than another?
- **Reputation.** Do people you know use and like this brand?
- **Warranty.** Does this brand come with a warranty? A **warranty** is *a promise to make repairs or refund money if the product does not work as claimed.*

Saving Money

Smart shoppers know how to save money. For example, they may buy personal products at **discount stores**. These are *stores that offer lower prices but have fewer salespeople and services.* They may also clip and use **coupons**, *slips of paper that save you money on certain brands.* You can often save money by buying store brands or **generic** (juh·NEHR·ik) products, which are *products that imitate name-brand products, and are sold in plain packages.* These cost less because the packaging is cheaper and little money is spent on advertising. However, some generic drugs may not contain all of the same ingredients as name brands; so check with your pharmacist before using them.

HEALTH SKILLS ACTIVITY

ACCESSING INFORMATION

Understand Unit Pricing

To compare the value of two products, you need to compare their unit price, or cost per unit of weight or volume. To do this, follow these steps.

- Find the weight or volume given on each product container. Make sure that both products are measured in the same type of units.
- Divide the price of the product by its weight or volume. The result is the unit price.
- Compare the unit prices.

ON YOUR OWN
Find the unit prices of the two bottles of soap shown here. Which costs less per fluid ounce? Which is the most economical purchase?

Silky Soap Antibacterial Soap $2.⁸⁹ 15 fl.oz

ULTRA $1.⁶⁹ *Silky Soap* Antibacterial Soap with Vitamin E NEW! Decorative Pump Bottle 7.5 fl. oz

102 CHAPTER 4: PERSONAL HEALTH

COOPERATIVE LEARNING ACTIVITY

Cost Versus Effectiveness Divide the class into small groups. Have each group examine the concept of cost versus effectiveness of health care products. Have each group make a list of the health care products teens use on a regular basis. Have them address the following: Does cost influence effectiveness? When? How? Under what circumstances would a more expensive product be the best choice? Under what circumstances would a less expensive product be the best choice?

FIGURE 4.9

False or Misleading Claims

These product labels make false or misleading claims. *What other false claims have you seen in ads?*

Slimmo: Lose Weight Without Dieting or Exercising!

Glisten: Make Your Smile Shine!

X-treme Tan: Tan Fast with No Sun!

Zitex: Makes Pimples Disappear Overnight!

Super Silk: For the Hair You've Always Wanted!

Mint Mouth: Keeps Breath Fresh All Day!

Spotting False Claims

Consumers need to beware of **fraud**, *deliberate deceit or trickery*. People who practice fraud make false claims about a product or service. **Figure 4.9** shows some examples of false and misleading claims. Health fraud can be especially dangerous. Some products and services falsely claim to cure serious diseases. Use critical thinking skills to research and evaluate health information about products and services. It is unsafe to use any treatment that has not been approved by the U.S. Food and Drug Administration (FDA).

Lesson 3 Review

Using complete sentences, answer the following questions on a sheet of paper.

Reviewing Terms and Facts

1. **Vocabulary** Define the word *consumer.*
2. **Recall** What is the purpose of an advertisement?
3. **List** Give examples of three ways to save money when shopping.

Thinking Critically

4. **Apply** List ways to evaluate health products such as sunblocks, dietary aids, and over-the-counter medications.

5. **Synthesize** Give an example of why a less expensive medicine may not be the best purchase. Write a paragraph that examines the concept of cost versus effectiveness of health care products.

Applying Health Skills

6. **Analyzing Influences** Select a personal product that you would recommend to others. Explain to the class why it is worth its cost.

LESSON 3: CHOOSING HEALTH PRODUCTS **103**

Lesson 4

Health Care in Your Community

① Focus

Lesson Objectives

Students will be able to

- list health care professionals who prevent and/or treat health problems.
- explain the importance of getting regular checkups.
- identify groups that provide health care.

Motivators

Quick Write

Ask volunteers to share their ideas with the class. Lead a class discussion on the importance of regular health screenings.

Bellringer Activity

Ask students why it is recommended that everyone have regular medical checkups. Ask: What are possible consequences of not getting regular checkups?

VOCABULARY

Write the word *specialist* on the board. Have students discuss the specialists listed on page 105 of the student text. Write *health insurance* and *managed care* on the board. Have volunteers read the definitions of these terms on pages 106 and 107.

Health Care in Your Community

Quick Write

Why do you think it's important to have regular medical and dental screenings? Jot down your ideas in a brief paragraph.

LEARN ABOUT...

- which health care professionals to see when you are sick.
- the importance of regular checkups for your health.
- groups that provide health care.

VOCABULARY

- specialist
- voluntary health group
- health insurance
- managed care

Goals of Health Care

Health care focuses on two areas: preventing health problems and treating problems when they arise. Many health professionals are involved in preventing problems. They include dietitians, dental hygienists, health teachers, nurses, and counselors. An important part of their job is to help you develop healthy habits. Practicing good health habits is easier and less costly than treating problems. When problems do arise, various health professionals identify and treat them. These people include doctors, dentists, nurses, pharmacists, and others.

When you feel ill, you probably go to see your family doctor. Sometimes, your family doctor will send you to see a **specialist** (SPEH·shuh·list), *a doctor trained to handle particular health problems.* Some specialists treat specific types of people. For example, pediatricians treat children and teens. Other specialists treat specific conditions or body systems. **Figure 4.10** shows some of these specialists.

Your local pharmacist is a reliable source of information about health products. *What questions might this teen have for the pharmacist?*

Lesson 4 Resources

Teacher Classroom Resources

- Concept Map 17
- Enrichment Activity 15
- Lesson Plan 4
- Reading Tutor Activity 15
- Reteaching Activity 15

 Transparency 19

Student Activities Workbook

- Chapter 4 Study Guide
- Applying Health Skills 15
- Health Inventory 4

Regular Health Screenings

Getting regular health screenings is one way to avoid health problems and maintain wellness. During a health screening, the doctor will measure your height and weight and check your heart and lungs. Your vision and hearing may also be tested. The doctor will give you any immunizations you need. You should get a health screening about once a year. If you have a serious medical condition, you may need to visit the doctor more often. Cooperate with the doctor and your parents or guardians. Discuss with them any concerns you have about your illness.

FIGURE 4.10

THE SPECIALISTS

Each specialist treats a different type of person or condition. *Have you ever visited a specialist?*

Pediatrician
Treats children and teens.

Urologist
Treats problems of the urinary system.

Ophthalmologist
Treats diseases of the eye.

Dermatologist
Treats skin conditions and diseases.

Allergist
Treats asthma, hay fever, and other allergies.

Cardiologist
Treats heart problems.

Orthopedist
Treats broken bones and related problems.

Otolaryngologist
Treats the ears, nose, and throat.

Orthodontist
Treats tooth and jaw irregularities.

Lesson 4

② Teach

Discussing

Ask students to share their own experiences with health care professionals:

- Which health care professionals do you see for routine checkups? Why?
- Which health care professionals are most likely to help you when you have a medical problem? How do they help?
- How might you evaluate health care practices and services? **L1**

VISUAL LEARNING

FIGURE 4.10 Write the names of the specialists from Figure 4.10 on index cards. Write the definitions on the reverse side. Have students play "Who Am I?" One student reads a definition to the class, and asks, "Who am I?" Other students volunteer the correct identification using the information provided in Figure 4.10. **INCL** *Behavior Problems, Special Learning Needs, English Language Learners*

Cross-Curriculum Activity

VISUAL ARTS Have students create the type of brochure that they might find in a doctor's office or health clinic. The brochure should describe the importance of establishing and implementing a periodic health-maintenance clinical assessment. Encourage students to create an attractive and informative brochure. You may wish to bring in samples of brochures or ask the school nurse to provide samples for students to use. **L2**

Beyond the Classroom

Community Tell students that some of the work done by state health department employees may seem unimportant or unpleasant. For example, discuss what sanitation workers do. Have students imagine their living conditions without sanitation workers. Encourage them to draw pictures of their homes and community showing the results. (*piles of garbage*) Ask students how a surplus of garbage would increase disease. (*Garbage is dirty and is a haven for germs that cause disease. Rodents and other disease-harboring animals live in garbage.*) Have students find out what is done with the garbage after sanitation workers collect it.

Lesson 4

Developing Good Character

Citizenship

As a class, brainstorm a variety of health-based service projects that would benefit your community. For example, students might sew quilts and donate them to a children's hospital. Ask:

- How would this help young patients?
- Why is it important for citizens to do these kinds of projects?

Applying Knowledge

Ask volunteers to gather information about local voluntary health groups, including addresses, phone numbers, and Web addresses; the services provided; and volunteer opportunities for teens. Have these students share the information on a classroom bulletin board. **L2**

VISUAL LEARNING

FIGURE 4.11 Have students review the information in the chart. Ask:

- What are the responsibilities of local and state government?
- What are the responsibilities of the federal government?

Then have them list a variety of health services in their community and state and suggest ways to evaluate these services. Students may wish to conduct outside research to compile a list of available health services. **INCL** *Behavior Problems, Special Learning Needs, English Language Learners*

Developing Good Character

Citizenship

One way to be a good citizen is to volunteer your time. Ask your parents and teachers about ways to volunteer. You can also contact a hospital or a local first aid and rescue squad. Some organizations seeking volunteers may post notices in public areas, such as the local library.

Sources of Health Care

You get health care from many sources such as doctors' or dentists' offices, clinics, and hospitals. Your school nurse, if you have one, gives general advice and medical care. Other sources provide care for specific health problems. For example, counselors help people with mental and emotional problems.

The government also provides health care. **Figure 4.11** describes some of the health services performed by local, state, and federal governments. In addition, government agencies create laws and set public policies that influence health. For example, laws regarding the disposal of waste help to keep drinking water safe.

Voluntary health groups are *organizations that work to treat and eliminate certain diseases.* Usually, these groups are run by volunteers. Instead of selling products, they ask people to donate money. Some of the money pays for research on disease. These groups also teach people how to prevent the disease and help those who have the disease.

Paying for Health Care

Many people use **health insurance** to help pay for health care. This means they pay *a monthly or yearly fee to an*

FIGURE 4.11

LOCAL, STATE, AND FEDERAL HEALTH SERVICES

Many government agencies work to protect the health of Americans. Look in the phone book to find out the location of your local health department.

	Preventing and Treating Disease	Information
Local and State Governments	• Make sure restaurant and hotel kitchens are clean • Collect and dispose of garbage • Make sure water is safe to drink • Help stop the spread of disease	• Teach people how to care for their health • Keep records of births, deaths, and diseases
Federal Government	• Helps support people who cannot work because of chronic illness or injury • Helps prevent and treat problems involving mental health, including alcohol and other drugs • Identifies and stops the spread of disease • Provides Medicaid (health care funds for people who cannot afford medical treatment) • Provides Medicare (health care funds for people over 65)	• Does research in areas such as cancer, heart disease, and the health of the elderly and children

Health Literacy

Influencing Factors School nurses are usually present at schools. However, to many people, school nurses are just the purveyors of bandages. Invite the school nurse to the classroom and have students interview him or her to find out how good health is promoted in the school. Possible questions are:

- How do you protect students from communicable diseases such as chicken pox, measles, and conjunctivitis?
- What kinds of health screenings do you do at school? Explain how you do them.
- What do you do for students in the case of an emergency?
- What training is necessary for your job?

RACE FOR THE CURE

People involved with voluntary health organizations give time and money to help prevent and cure certain diseases.

insurance company that agrees to pay for some or most costs of medical care. One type of health insurance is managed care, *a health insurance plan that saves money by limiting people's choice of doctors.* It often costs less than traditional insurance plans. Many employers help pay for their employees' health insurance.

Lesson 4 Review

Using complete sentences, answer the following questions on a sheet of paper.

Reviewing Terms and Facts

1. **Vocabulary** Define the term *specialist*.
2. **Recall** How do managed care plans save money over other forms of health insurance?
3. **Describe** Why is it important to have regular health screenings?

Thinking Critically

4. **Speculate** List some ways that a person might evaluate health practices and services.

5. **Explain** Why is it important to communicate and cooperate with health care providers and parents or guardians in the treatment or management of a disease?

Applying Health Skills

6. **Accessing Information** Use reliable resources to identify and analyze how computer software, the World Wide Web, and other forms of media and technology influence individual and community health. Present your findings to the class in a brief report.

LESSON 4: HEALTH CARE IN YOUR COMMUNITY **107**

Speculating

Have students speculate why having health insurance is an advantage over paying out of pocket for medical bills. Help them come to the conclusion that people may not have the money available to pay for the high cost of medical care. **L3**

③ Assess

Evaluating

📁 Assign the Lesson 4 Review; then assign the Lesson 4 Quiz in the TCR.

Reteaching

📁 Assign Concept Map 17 and Reteaching Activity 15 in the TCR.

Enrichment

• 📁 Assign and distribute Enrichment Activity 15 in the TCR.
• Invite a physician or nurse to speak to the class. Have the guest discuss what should be included in a routine checkup and how students can take an active part in the doctor visit.

④ Close

Have students summarize the main points in this lesson by asking them: What are the goals and sources of health care?

Lesson 4 Review

1. A specialist is a doctor trained to handle particular health problems.
2. Managed care plans save money by limiting people's choice of doctors.
3. Regular health screenings help you evaluate and maintain your health.
4. Possible response: Conduct research to make sure that a service is reputable.
5. Communicating and cooperating with health care providers and parents or guardians will help ensure that a disease will be treated or managed properly.

The Smile File

1 Focus

Objectives

Students will be able to
- explain basic dental care.
- identify key parts of the teeth and gums.
- locate reliable online and print resources for dental care information.

Motivator

Quick Write

Have students list five things they do to take care of their teeth. (*Brush, floss, go to the dentist, limit sugary foods, use fluoride toothpaste, and so on.*) Next to each entry, have students write down how often they do each of these things (*every day, once a week, twice a year, and so on*) and how much time each task takes. List a variety of student answers on the board.

2 Teach

Brainstorming

Much of the text in this spread addresses dental care products. Direct the class to brainstorm different types of these products: brushes, flosses, gums, tongue scrapers, pastes, whitening products, and so on and write them on the board. When the list is complete, ask students to identify products that are critical for dental *health* (fluoride toothpaste, floss). Put an "H" next to these items. Then have students identify products that merely promote better *appearance* (whitening strips) or *attraction* (mouthwash). Put an "A" next to these. Look at the list again. How many products are actually necessary to ensure dental health? What claims do the products marked with an "A" make to consumers? Ask students, "Do you think most consumers understand the difference between these two groups of products? Why or why not?"

TIME HEALTH

THE Smile FILE

Take this quiz to brush up on a few dental details!

Quiz

1. The firmer the bristles on your toothbrush are, the cleaner your teeth will be.
   a. True   b. False

2. The most important time to brush is in the morning.
   a. True   b. False

3. You should change your toothbrush at least once a month.
   a. True   b. False

4. Which of the following is the proper motion to use when brushing your teeth?
   a. Up and down
   b. Back and forth
   c. A circular motion
   d. All of the above

5. Germs on the tongue can cause bad breath.
   a. True   b. False

6. You should always floss before you brush.
   a. True   b. False

7. Over-the-counter whitening toothpastes can whiten your teeth by several shades.
   a. True   b. False

Answers: 1.b.; 2.b.; 3.b.; 4.c.; 5.a.; 6.b.; 7.b.

Check out the explanations on the next page!

108 CHAPTER 4: PERSONAL HEALTH

MORE ABOUT...

Oral Health and Eating Habits Go back to the lists students generated in the Quick Write activity. Did they include anything about eating habits? Most teens know to avoid sugary, sticky foods, such as candy and soda, which lead to cavities. They may not know that good eating habits help teeth stay healthy. Students should eat a variety of foods, including plenty of fruits and vegetables, every day. Milk and dairy products, which include calcium, help build strong teeth. Also, remind students to limit sweets between meals. Save them for after a meal and then follow immediately with brushing.

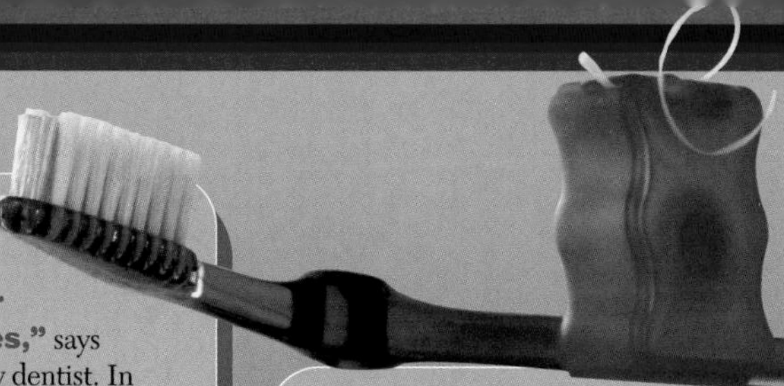

Explanations

1. **"The best bristles for brushing are soft ones,"** says Marc Lowenberg, a New York City dentist. In fact, stiff bristles can do more harm than good, since they're more likely to injure gums and wear away enamel (the teeth's protective coating).

2. **At night, when we don't swallow as often, our saliva is less able to wash away plaque,** the sticky film on teeth that can cause cavities and gum disease. That's why, Lowenberg says, "you don't want to go to sleep with any plaque buildup sitting on your teeth."

3. **You should invest in a new brush at least once every six months,** Lowenberg says, or "as soon as the bristles are not standing straight up." Scraggly bristles can't get hard-to-reach places, so they leave behind cavity-causing food and germs.

4. **Brushing in a circular motion is the best way to clean teeth, as well as the least damaging.** Other methods can cause wear and tear on gums, possibly causing them to bleed and recede. As Lowenberg explains, "Brushing in a circular motion sweeps plaque in hard-to-reach places away from teeth, while brushing back and forth, or up and down, doesn't get at hidden plaque."

5. **The main cause of bad breath is bacteria on your tongue.** The best tool for removing bacteria is a tongue scraper, but brushing your tongue with a toothbrush and toothpaste will also do the trick.

6. **Believe it or not, it doesn't matter when you floss**—as long as you do it once a day. As Lowenberg explains, it takes plaque 24 hours to form on teeth. Flossing reaches the areas in between your teeth that your toothbrush misses.

7. **Whitening toothpastes are not bleaches, so they won't turn your teeth snow white.** However, they do contain some ingredients that can lighten teeth a little by attacking surface stains. ▨

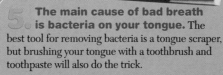

About Healthy Teeth and Gums

Use the article and the diagram to answer these questions:

- **What is another name for the gum?**
- **What is the purpose of enamel?**
- **Between the crown and the root, you will find what part of the tooth?**

Use reliable online and print resources to find out more about dental care. Then, using the information on these pages as well as the facts you obtained from your research, create a tooth-care brochure for younger students. Include tips on the proper way to brush and floss, visiting the dentist, and developing healthy eating habits. You might also want to include a note to parents reminding them of the importance of good dental hygiene for children.

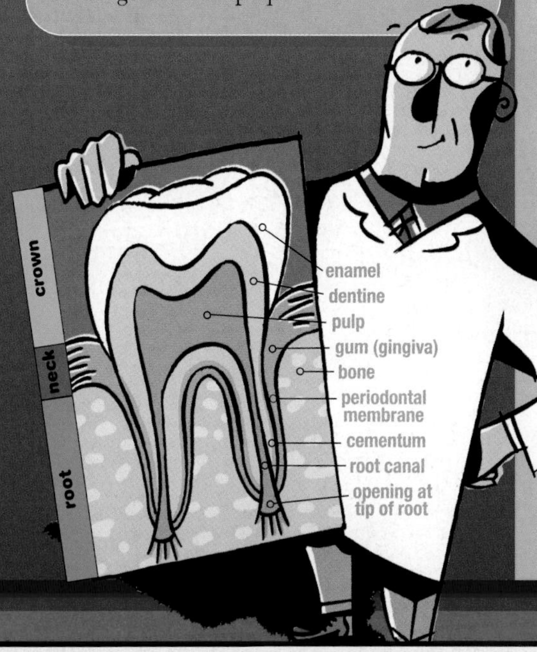

Diagram labels:
- crown
- neck
- root
- enamel
- dentine
- pulp
- gum (gingiva)
- bone
- periodontal membrane
- cementum
- root canal
- opening at tip of root

TIME HEALTH: THE SMILE FILE **109**

③ Apply

Time to Think

As students conduct their dental care research, have them analyze the validity of Web sites by asking the following questions:

- What are the qualifications and background of the Web site author or administrator?
- Is the site sponsored by a nationally known and respected health organization?
- Are visitors advised to purchase a health-related product or service?
- Is there a cost involved in visiting the site?
- How frequently is the site information updated?

Remind students that URL extensions also provide clues about a site: .edu for education sites, .gov for government sites, .org for organization sites, .com for commercial sites.

Ask, "Does a commercial site operated by a toothpaste company provide the same type of information as the American Dental Association (www.ada.org) or the American Academy of Pediatric Dentistry (www.aapd.org)? Why or why not?"

VISUAL LEARNING

Ask students to describe the photograph on page 108. Ask: "How does this teen's smile affect her appearance? Imagine her with missing, broken, or discolored teeth. How would your impression of her change?"

Health Literacy

Fluoride As students research dental health, they are sure to come across information about fluoride. Explain that fluoride is a substance that fights tooth decay. It is included in many toothpastes and mouthwashes and also comes in a tablet form (by prescription only). Many cities and states add fluoride to the public water as a dental health preventive. However, this practice has come under attack recently. Tell students that they will be debating the issue of whether or not fluoride should be added to public drinking water. Give students up to a week to do their research and prepare for the debate.

ACCESSING INFORMATION

Objectives

After completing the lesson, students will be able to

- identify sources of valid and reliable information about health care products.

- evaluate claims made in advertisements based on information from other sources.

Time: 35–40 minutes

Materials: pencil or pen, notebook paper, teen magazines

Teacher Classroom Resources

📁 Building Health Skills Activities

- Transparency Master 1, "Accessing Information"

- Reproducible Master 4, "Think Before You Buy"

1. Model

- Ask students to identify and discuss some of the health care products in their home such as pain relievers, cough medicines, and others. Then ask them: What are possible sources of information for personal care/health care products (*friends, product inserts, pharmacist, library, ads in magazines, TV, and so on.*) Which of these sources do you think is most valid or reliable?

- Direct students to read the story of Sandra. This teen accesses valid and reliable sources of information to make a responsible choice. Then ask them how many follow all of Sandra's steps when considering what health care products to purchase.

THINK BEFORE YOU BUY

Model

With so many health care products available, how do you choose the best one for you? You have many sources of information. The product label is a good place to start. A pharmacist can also answer your questions. Read about how Sandra decides which skin cleanser to buy.

Sandra is looking for a product that will clean and moisturize at the same time. She begins by reading the labels of several skin cleansers. She looks at the directions to see what the product is supposed to do and how to use it. She reads the list of ingredients in each product. If she isn't sure how the different ingredients work, she asks the pharmacist. Finally, she calculates the unit price. With all this information, she can make a confident choice.

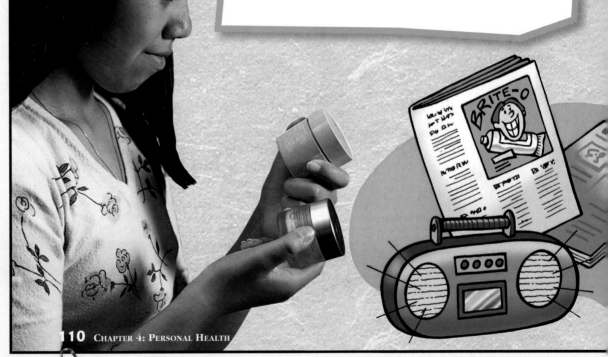

110 CHAPTER 4: PERSONAL HEALTH

Teaching Tips

Advertising Techniques Review these advertising techniques: **Bandwagon** (*Image*: Groups of teens; *Message*: Other teens use this product so you should, too); **Beautiful People** (*Image*: A glamorous person; *Message*: You'll be like this person if you use this product); **Good Times** (*Image*: Teens having fun; *Message*: You'll have fun if you use this product); **Status** (*Image*: Designer items; *Message*: You'll be "cool" if you have these items); **Symbols** (*Image*: Well-known character; *Message*: You'll be popular like this character if you use this product.)

Practice

You have learned how to find useful information about health products. You should also remember that advertisements are not good sources of information. They often exaggerate a product's effectiveness, promising "miracle" results in "no time at all." Compare the product claims below.

- *"Dynodent makes teeth whiter and brighter—instantly!"*
- *"Acnex cleanser is guaranteed to wash your pimples away."*
- *"Winter Cool mouthwash kills the germs that cause tooth decay."*
- *"Drink away ten pounds in no time with Choco-Slim!"*
- *"So-Soft conditioner contains natural oils that add moisture to your hair."*

1. Which claims appear to be genuine?
2. Which ones may be inaccurate or misleading?
3. Where could you find more reliable information to help you evaluate these product claims?

Apply/Assess

Look through teen magazines for advertisements that include product claims. Write them down on a sheet of paper. Which claims appear genuine? Which are inaccurate or misleading?

Write a statement identifying two sources where teens could find reliable information about health products. Explain why you would choose these resources.

Self-Check

- Did I identify health claims as genuine or misleading?
- Did I name two sources of reliable information about health products?
- Did I explain why these sources are reliable?

BUILDING HEALTH SKILLS: THINK BEFORE YOU BUY **111**

2. Practice

- Display Transparency Master 1, and discuss with the class.

Instruct the class to read each product claim and on a sheet of notebook paper answer the three questions at the end. **INCL** *Behavior Problems, Special Learning Needs, English Language Learners*

- After students have answered the questions, direct them to interview at least two other students in class and compare their answers. Afterward, solicit answers from the entire class.

3. Apply/Assess

- You may wish to distribute Building Health Skills Reproducible Master 4 in the TCR to guide students in completing this activity.
- Have small groups of students examine teen magazines and then write down health product claims they feel are genuine and those they feel are misleading.
- Next, have them identify two sources of reliable information about each product, and explain why they would choose these sources. Ask each group to present their ads and analysis to the class. Make sure that students examine the concept of cost versus effectiveness in their analyses.

Assessment Scoring

Using a rubric, student work should provide evidence of all criteria to achieve the highest score.

Skills

Student work provides

- two sources of reliable information about health products.
- reasons why these sources were chosen.

Concept

Student work includes

- a logical determination regarding the legitimacy of health claims.
- analysis of why the health claims are genuine or misleading.

Checking Comprehension

Use the Chapter 4 Assessment to examine the most important ideas presented in the chapter.

Answers to Reviewing Vocabulary and Concepts

Lesson 1
1. cavity
2. cuticle
3. dermatologist
4. melanin
5. orthodontist

Lesson 2
6. farsightedness
7. nearsightedness
8. sound waves
9. astigmatism
10. decibels

Lesson 3
11. true
12. false; generic
13. true
14. false; less
15. true

Lesson 4
16. false; cardiologists
17. false; year
18. true
19. true
20. false; less

Thinking Critically

21. Students may mention brushing and flossing teeth; washing skin and hair; protecting skin from the sun; avoiding eyestrain, eye injury, and loud noises; and getting regular checkups.

CHAPTER ASSESSMENT 4

After You Read

Use your completed Foldable to review the information on personal health care.

FOLDABLES Study Organizer

Reviewing Vocabulary and Concepts

On a sheet of paper, write the numbers 1–10. After each number, write the term from the list that best completes each statement.

- astigmatism
- cavity
- cuticle
- decibels
- dermatologist
- farsightedness
- melanin
- nearsightedness
- orthodontist
- sound waves

Lesson 1

1. A(n) _____ forms as a result of repeated acid attacks on the tooth enamel.
2. A nonliving band of epidermis that surrounds a fingernail is called the _____.
3. A(n) _____ is a doctor who treats skin disorders.
4. Freckles are spots of _____.
5. If you needed your teeth straightened, you would visit a(n) _____.

Lesson 2

6. If you have _____, close objects look blurry.
7. If you have _____, you have trouble seeing objects far away from you.
8. Vibrations or movements in the air are known as _____.
9. If you have _____, the shape of your cornea makes objects look blurry.
10. Sound waves are measured in _____.

112 CHAPTER 4: PERSONAL HEALTH

On a sheet of paper, write the numbers 11–20. Write *True* or *False* for each statement below. If the statement is false, change the underlined word or phrase to make it true.

Lesson 3

11. The goal of <u>advertisements</u> is to persuade you that one particular product is better than others.
12. Three ways to save money on health products are to use coupons, shop in discount stores, and buy <u>brand name</u> products.
13. A discount store has lower prices and fewer salespeople and services than other kinds of stores.
14. Generic products cost <u>more</u> than brand name products because of the difference in packaging costs.
15. People who practice <u>fraud</u> make false claims about a product or service.

Lesson 4

16. <u>Otolaryngologists</u> treat heart problems.
17. Teens need to have health screenings every <u>two years</u>.
18. Voluntary health groups are usually run by <u>volunteers</u>.
19. <u>Health insurance</u> allows people to pay a monthly or yearly fee to an insurance company, which then pays part of their medical bills.
20. People in managed care plans usually pay <u>more</u> for their medical treatment than people with traditional insurance plans.

Thinking Critically

On a sheet of paper, write the numbers 21–25. Using a complete sentences, answer the following questions.

21. **Explain** Give an example of a habit that will help you maintain the health of your teeth, skin, hair, eyes, or ears. Explain how developing this habit now will benefit your health throughout your life.

INCLUSION STRATEGIES

Special Learning Needs, Behavior Problems, English Language Learners The following suggestions are helpful for students with special learning needs, students with behavior problems, and ELL students:

- Pair these students with more proficient learners who can help summarize the main concepts of the chapter.

- 🎧 Direct these students to listen to the Teen Health Audio Summaries. This component provides an audio and written summary of the chapter in both English and Spanish.

- Use photographs, drawings, or magazine clippings whenever possible to help students visualize the important concepts of the chapter.

22. **Predict** How might allowing eye or ear problems to go untreated affect other areas of your health?
23. **Speculate** Why do you think many teens listen to loud music even though they know that it might damage their hearing?
24. **Interpret** Why should consumers evaluate claims made in advertisements before they buy health products?
25. **Hypothesize** Why do many people pay for health insurance?

Career Corner

Dental Hygienist Would you like to help improve people's smiles? With just one to two years of training at a college or vocational/technical school, you could become a dental hygienist. These professionals assist dentists. They help clean teeth and gums, insert fillings, and take X rays. Hygienists work with a variety of special tools. They also have lots of contact with people. Learn more about this and other health careers by clicking on Career Corner at health.glencoe.com.

Standardized Test Practice

Reading & Writing

Read the paragraphs below and then answer the questions.

How can you make your hair grow faster? You can't. Hair grows at a constant rate of about .44 millimeters a day. Some people think that cutting hair will make hair grow faster, but this is untrue. In addition, no special food or dietary supplement can change the amount or type of hair you have.

Ads for hair care products may claim that you can "feed your hair from the outside." However, hair is made of dead cells, which can't use nutrients. Some hair care products coat shafts of hair to make it look thicker, but the effect is only temporary. Dyeing hair will change its color, but this change won't last either. The hair will grow in with its natural color.

1. Why does the author of the passage include a question at the beginning of the first paragraph?
   - **A** to describe different ways of changing hair
   - **B** to present facts from the passage
   - **C** to give an overview of the topic
   - **D** to establish what the passage is about

2. What phrase from the passage helps readers understand the meaning of the word *dyeing*?
   - **A** make it appear thicker
   - **B** change its color
   - **C** change won't last
   - **D** hair will grow in

3. Write a paragraph explaining why you think someone might want to change the way he or she looks.

22. Possible response: Losing sight or hearing could cause depression, which could affect your mental/emotional and social health.
23. Responses will vary.
24. Consumers who do not evaluate advertising claims may pay too much for products or buy goods of poor quality.
25. Most people cannot afford to pay the full cost of medical care without insurance.

Test Practice
1. D
2. B
3. Responses should include specific reasons and details on why a person might want to alter an aspect of his or her appearance.

Reteaching
📁 Assign Study Guide 4 in the Student Activities Workbook.

Evaluate
- 📁 💿 Use the reproducible Chapter 4 Test in the TCR, or construct your own test using the **Exam***View*® Pro Testmaker.
- 📁 Use Performance Assessment 4 in the TCR.

 Assessment ✓

Self-Assessment Direct students to review the activities that are provided throughout the chapter. Encourage each student to select one finished product or activity that demonstrates his or her best work for the chapter. Have students explain what they learned and how the examples they selected show their progress.

Career Corner

Dental Hygienist After reviewing the career profile at the health Web site, students might

- describe the different tasks a dental hygienist may perform.
- research accredited dental hygiene schools in the area. (Many schools have information about their programs online.)

Planning Guide

Chapter 5	Skills/Activities	Reproducible Resources	Assessment
Lesson 1 **Why Your Body Needs Nutrients** *pages 116–120*	HEALTH SKILLS ACTIVITY ▲ Reading a Food Label (*Accessing Information*), page 119	*Student Activities Workbook available for use with each chapter* 📁 Parent Letter & Activities 5 📁 Concept Map 18 📁 Enrichment Activity 16 📁 Lesson Plan 1 📁 Reading Tutor Activity 16 📁 Reteaching Activity 16	📁 Lesson 1 Quiz
Lesson 2 **Following a Balanced Food Plan** *pages 121–125*	**Hands-On Health** ▲ Analyze Your Food Choices, page 125	📁 Concept Map 19 📁 Enrichment Activity 17 📁 Lesson Plan 2 📁 Reading Tutor Activity 17 📁 Reteaching Activity 17	📁 Lesson 2 Quiz
Lesson 3 **Making Healthful Food Choices** *pages 126–132*		📁 Concept Map 20 📁 Cross-Curriculum Activity 9 📁 Decision-Making Activity 9 📁 Enrichment Activity 18 📁 Health Lab 5 📁 Lesson Plan 3 📁 Reading Tutor Activity 18 📁 Reteaching Activity 18	📁 Lesson 3 Quiz
Lesson 4 **The Benefits of Physical Activity** *pages 133–137*	HEALTH SKILLS ACTIVITY ▲ Tension Tamers (*Stress Management*), page 136	📁 Concept Map 21 📁 Enrichment Activity 19 📁 Lesson Plan 4 📁 Reading Tutor Activity 19 📁 Reteaching Activity 19	📁 Lesson 4 Quiz
Lesson 5 **Setting Fitness Goals** *pages 138–141*	HEALTH SKILLS ACTIVITY ▲ Increasing Your Activity Level (*Goal Setting*), page 140	📁 Concept Map 22 📁 Cross-Curriculum Activity 10 📁 Decision-Making Activity 10 📁 Enrichment Activity 20 📁 Lesson Plan 5 📁 Reading Tutor Activity 20 📁 Reteaching Activity 20	📁 Lesson 5 Quiz 📁 Chapter 5 Test 📁 Performance Assessment 5

TIME HEALTH   **Food for Thought** *pages 142–143*

BUILDING HEALTH SKILLS

Fueling Your Body (*Decision Making*)
pages 144–145

📁 Building Health Skills Reproducible Master 5

Standards		Technology
National	**State/Local**	**Technology**
National Health Education Standard **1.1, 1.3, 2.2, 3.1, 3.4**		Transparency 20 TeacherWorks™ Internet Activities
National Health Education Standard **1.1, 3.1, 3.2, 3.4**		Transparency 21 Tape/DVD 1, Segment 6, "Nutrition and Physical Activity" TeacherWorks™
National Health Education Standard **1.1, 1.3, 1.6, 2.6, 3.1, 3.4**		Transparency 22 Tape/DVD 1, Segment 5, "Body Image and Media Influences" TeacherWorks™
National Health Education Standard **1.1, 1.3, 1.8, 3.1, 3.4, 3.5, 3.7**		Transparency 23 Tape/DVD 1, Segment 6, "Nutrition and Physical Activity" TeacherWorks™
National Health Education Standard **1.1, 1.6, 1.8, 3.1, 3.4, 3.5, 6.4, 6.5**		Transparency 24 TeacherWorks™ MindJogger Videoquiz *ExamView*® Pro Testmaker
National Health Education Standard **2.2, 6.1, 6.2, 6.3**		Building Health Skills Transparency Master 8

TeacherWorks™

Glencoe's new and exclusive TeacherWorks™ is an all-in-one planner and resource center. Access the complete Teacher Wraparound Edition electronically. Find all your classroom resources with just a few easy clicks, and print them right from your computer. Connect directly to Glencoe's customized Health Web site. Access the National Health Education Standards correlations, or insert your own state standards and match them directly to the electronic Teacher Wraparound Edition.

Language Diversity

- English Audio Summaries
- Spanish Audio Summaries
- English Summaries, Quizzes, and Activities
- Spanish Summaries, Quizzes, and Activities
- Spanish Parent Letters and Activities

KEY TO ABILITY LEVELS

Teaching Strategies that appear throughout the chapters have been identified by one of four codes to give you an idea of their suitability for students of varying learning styles and abilities.

L1 **Level 1** strategies should be within the ability range of all students. Often full class participation is required.

L2 **Level 2** strategies are for average to above-average students or for small groups. Some teacher direction is necessary.

L3 **Level 3** strategies are designed for students able and willing to work independently. Minimal teacher direction is necessary.

INCL Strategies are appropriate for students with particular special needs in a general classroom setting.

Nutrition and Physical Activity

Chapter at a Glance

Lesson 1 examines the nutrition requirements of teens.

Lesson 2 explains the Food Guide Pyramid and the important nutrients contained in each of the food groups.

Lesson 3 discusses the influences on teen food choices and provides guidelines for teens to stay healthy and maintain a healthy weight. Eating disorders are also addressed.

Lesson 4 examines the importance and benefits of physical activity.

Lesson 5 establishes guidelines for creating a personal fitness plan.

Health Skills

- Reading a Food Label (*Accessing Information*), p. 119
- Tension Tamers (*Stress Management*), p. 136
- Increasing Your Activity Level (*Goal Setting*), p. 140
- Fueling Your Body (*Decision Making*), pp. 144–145

CHAPTER 5

114

HANDS-ON ACTIVITY

What's for Breakfast? Not eating breakfast can adversely affect school performance. Yet 12 percent of schoolchildren routinely skip breakfast. This activity can provide ideas for a healthful breakfast. Ask students to volunteer what they usually eat for breakfast, and record their responses on poster paper. Have students use the Internet or other library resources, along with the content in this chapter, to find or come up with examples of healthful breakfasts. (The USDA publishes the Dietary Guidelines for Americans.) Students may be surprised to learn that there are many great nontraditional food choices for breakfast (e.g., peanut butter sandwiches and macaroni and cheese). Have the class review the original list and circle the healthful foods. Then list their new ideas on another sheet of poster paper.

Nutrition and Physical Activity

HEALTH *Online*

Do you practice healthful nutrition and fitness habits? Take the Health Inventory at health.glencoe.com to find out how your habits score.

FOLDABLES™ Study Organizer

Before You Read

Make this Foldable to help you organize the material in Lesson 1 on nutrients. Begin with a plain sheet of 8½" × 11" paper, or one sheet of notebook paper.

Step 1

Fold a sheet of paper along the long axis, leaving a ½" tab along the side.

Step 2

Turn the paper and fold into thirds.

Step 3

Cut the top layer along both folds. Then cut each tab in half to make six tabs.

Step 4

Turn the paper vertically and label the tabs as shown.

As You Read

Under the appropriate tab, write down major concepts, definitions, and food sources of each type of nutrient.

Carbohydrates
Proteins
Fats
Vitamins
Minerals
Water

Chapter Introduction

Use the options below to motivate students and preview chapter content.

HEALTH *Online*

Have students visit health.glencoe.com and take Health Inventory 5 to rate their knowledge of nutrition and physical activity. For new teaching ideas, click on Teaching Today to download helpful tools such as graphic organizers and Webquest activities.

GLENCOE TECHNOLOGY

Teen Health Video and DVD Series
(Each format available in both English and Spanish)

You may wish to use:

- Tape/DVD 1, Segment 5, "Body Image and Media Influences"
- Tape/DVD 1, Segment 6, "Nutrition and Physical Activity"

MindJogger Videoquiz

Use MindJogger to preview or review Chapter 5 content.

TIME HEALTH

Food for Thought
pages 142–143

FOLDABLES™ Study Organizer

Dinah Zike Study Fold

Organizing Data and Formulating Questions As students begin reading the first lesson of this chapter, have them record questions that arise about each of the six categories of nutrients on the front tabs of their Foldable. As they work through the lesson and learn more about nutrients, have them write the answers to their questions under the tabs. Self-questioning is a strategy that helps students stay focused during reading and writing. Students can also use their Foldable to take notes, define terms, and list examples of foods that contain each of the six nutrients.

Lesson 1

Why Your Body Needs Nutrients

1 Focus

Lesson Objectives

Students will be able to

- discuss why food choices are important.
- describe the kinds of foods their bodies need.
- list the six categories of nutrients and good food sources for each.
- describe how the six categories of nutrients help the body.

Health Skills
- Accessing Information, p. 119

Motivators

Quick Write
Ask volunteers to describe their favorite meal and their evaluation of whether or not it is healthy. Have those students identify the main reasons why they enjoy the meal.

Bellringer Activity

Ask students to brainstorm a list of reasons why they prefer certain foods. Then have students rank the reasons from most to least healthful.

VOCABULARY

Have students look up each vocabulary term in the Glossary at the back of the student text. Then ask them to write sentences that define the terms in their own words.

Why Your Body Needs Nutrients

Quick Write
Write a menu of your favorite meal. Then explain whether you think the foods belong in a healthful eating plan.

LEARN ABOUT...

- why your food choices are important.
- what kinds of food your body needs.
- how various kinds of foods affect your body.

VOCABULARY

- nutrition
- nutrient
- carbohydrate
- fiber
- protein
- fat
- vitamin
- mineral

Food Is Fuel

When you feel hungry, your body is sending you the message that it needs more fuel. To your body, food is fuel because it gives your body the energy it needs to operate. It also provides the building blocks that allow your body to grow and to repair itself. **Figure 5.1** illustrates the steps in fueling and refueling your body.

During your teen years, your body grows more rapidly than it has since you were an infant. This means you need to provide your body with the kinds of foods it needs. Understanding nutrition will help you do this. **Nutrition** (noo·TRI·shun) is *the science that studies the substances in food and how the body uses them.*

FIGURE 5.1

Food: The Body's Fuel

Food gives your body the energy you need to move and do your daily activities. Nutritious foods help you grow, feel your best, and perform at your peak.

1 Morning is an important time to refuel.

2 An empty stomach tells your brain you need to eat. That signal is hunger.

116 CHAPTER 5: NUTRITION AND PHYSICAL ACTIVITY

Lesson 1 Resources

Teacher Classroom Resources

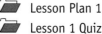 Parent Letter & Activities 5

Concept Map 18

Enrichment Activity 16

Lesson Plan 1

Lesson 1 Quiz

Reading Tutor Activity 16

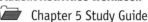 Reteaching Activity 16

Transparency 20

Student Activities Workbook

Chapter 5 Study Guide

Applying Health Skills 16

The Nutrients in Foods

Nutrients (NOO·tree·ents) are *substances in food that your body needs.* You could think of nutrients as members of a team. Each one has a special job to do, and each one is important to the team. Together, nutrients keep you healthy, help you grow, and set the foundation for lifelong health and wellness.

Altogether, there are more than 40 kinds of nutrients. They are grouped into the following six categories:

- Carbohydrates
- Proteins
- Fats
- Vitamins
- Minerals
- Water

Carbohydrates

Carbohydrates (kar·bo·HY·drayts) are *the main source of energy for your body.* Simple carbohydrates, or sugars, are found in fruits, milk, and table sugar. Starchy foods—such as bread, rice, pasta, and potatoes—contain complex carbohydrates. Your body breaks them down into simple sugars. Many starchy foods also contain fiber. **Fiber** is *the tough, stringy part of raw fruits, raw vegetables, whole wheat, and other grains, which you cannot digest.* Fiber helps carry wastes out of your body.

3 Healthful meals provide fuel to meet your body's needs.

4 Your body burns food energy to perform everyday activities, such as taking a test.

5 After spending energy, your body needs refueling again.

② Teach

Discussing

Ask students to discuss some of the normal, day-to-day activities they do. Some examples might be get up, get dressed, empty the trash, carry books, walk to school, open the door, stand, sit, and so on. Encourage students to list as many ideas as they can to emphasize that the body uses energy for even the simplest task. **L1**

Listing

Have students work in pairs to list examples of what food does besides provide energy. (*gives the body the raw materials needed for growth, provides an enjoyable activity with friends and family, and helps people feel content and secure*) Encourage a variety of specific examples. Then ask students to apply their examples to one side of the health triangle. **L2**

VISUAL LEARNING

FIGURE 5.1 Ask students to describe the pictures and tell how this teen is taking care of herself. Ask:

- How might her morning have been different if she had eaten a candy bar instead of a healthy breakfast?
- How might her morning have been different if she had skipped breakfast altogether? **INCL** *Behavior Problems, Special Learning Needs, English Language Learners*

☑ Reading Check

Learn more about the word *carbohydrate*. Use a dictionary to determine what the following words have in common: *carbohydrate, coal, water, fuel.*

☑ Reading Check

Word Study Learning about the root of a word can help students understand its meaning and function more easily. You may wish to have students find each word in a dictionary, looking especially at the roots or origins of the words. The word *carbohydrate* is formed from the root words *carbo*, meaning "coal" which, in turn, stems from "heat," and *hydrate*, meaning "to supply water." Students may make further connections about the relationships between the words as well. End the lesson by having students write their own definitions of carbohydrate.

Lesson 1

Comprehending

Reinforce information on nutrients introduced in the text. Ask students:

• Which category of nutrient supplies the main source of energy for the body? (*carbohydrates*)

• Which group of nutrients is important for the growth and repair of body cells? (*proteins*) **L1**

Analyzing

Divide the class into small groups to research and analyze one of the following dietary practices: vegetarian, low-fat, high-protein, low-calorie, high-carbohydrate, convenience food. Have each group share their analysis and explain why they think their assigned diet is healthy or unhealthy. **L2** **INCL** *English Language Learners*

Fats produce 9 calories per gram, or about 4,000 calories per pound. That's more than twice the energy provided by carbohydrates and proteins, which produce 4 calories per gram.

Researching

Ask an interested volunteer to use the Internet or library resources to learn about water-soluble and fat-soluble vitamins:

• What are they?

• How are they different?

• Why is each important?

• What are the best sources of each?

Then ask this volunteer to discuss his or her findings with the rest of the class. **L3**

Proteins

Proteins (PRO·teens) are *essential for the growth and repair of all the cells in your body.* Meat and other animal products, such as eggs and dairy products, provide "complete" proteins. This means that they contain all the building blocks your body needs to build and maintain strong muscles. However, you can also get complete proteins by combining certain plant foods, such as rice and beans. You don't need to eat these foods at the same meal; any time during the day is fine.

Fats

Fats are *another source of energy.* Fats also carry certain vitamins in your bloodstream and help keep your skin healthy. However, eating too much fat can contribute to weight gain and other health problems, such as heart disease and cancer. These conditions usually appear later in life but often result from poor health habits that began at an early age. Salad dressings and such popular fast foods as doughnuts and fries tend to be high in fat.

Vitamins

Vitamins (VI·tuh·mins) are *substances that help regulate body functions.* Vitamins help you in many ways. For example, they help your body use other nutrients and fight disease. Fruits, leafy green vegetables, whole-grain breads, and some meats are especially rich in vitamins.

Many delicious foods offer the nutrients your body needs. *Which of these foods provide complete proteins?*

COOPERATIVE LEARNING ACTIVITY

What Nutrient Am I? Divide the class into six groups. Assign a different category of nutrients to each group. Working in teams, students should write short skits that explain (without naming the nutrients) why that group of nutrients is essential for a healthy body. Make sure each person in the group has a part in the skit or in the production crew. Encourage creativity and humor along with an accurate description of the facts. Students may want to make or bring in props or simple costumes to enliven their skits. When the groups are ready, have them take turns performing their skits for another class or perhaps a younger class. The class can guess the nutrients at the end. If possible, videotape the skit to show other classes.

Some vitamins, such as vitamin C and the B-complex vitamins, dissolve in water. You must replace these water-soluble vitamins every day. Other vitamins—including vitamins A, D, E, and K—dissolve only in droplets of fat. Your body can store fat-soluble vitamins for longer periods. Because your body stores these vitamins instead of quickly releasing them, consuming very large amounts can be harmful.

ACCESSING INFORMATION

Have students compare the pictured label to the labels they have seen on other food packages. Then ask volunteers to read aloud the explanations of the information on a food label. Encourage students to discuss how they can use each item of information.

Provide several food packages for each group of students to examine and discuss.

Note: This skill is introduced in Chapter 1 on page 9.

Cross-Curriculum Activity

SCIENCE Minerals help build new cells for the body and control body processes. Ask students to consult a science text or an encyclopedia to determine the minerals the body needs and why they are necessary. Have students share their research in the form of charts or posters. **L3**

HEALTH SKILLS ACTIVITY

ACCESSING INFORMATION

Reading a Food Label

Packaged foods have labels like the one shown here. Learning to read food labels can help you choose foods that will give you enough of different nutrients.

- **SERVING SIZE** is the amount of food in one serving.
- **SERVINGS PER CONTAINER** is the number of servings the package contains.
- **CALORIES PER SERVING** is a measure of how much energy your body gets from one serving of the food.
- **DAILY VALUE** is the amount of a nutrient a typical person needs in one day. The label shows a percentage of the Daily Value for each nutrient in a serving of the food. This lets you compare nutrients in different products.
- **INGREDIENTS** in the food are listed in order. The first ingredient makes up the largest portion of the food. The last one listed makes up the smallest portion.

Nutrition Facts

Serving Size 1 cup (240 mL)
Servings Per Container   About 2

Amount Per Serving	
Calories 130	Calories from Fat 30

	% Daily Value*
	5%
Total Fat 3g	5%
Saturated Fat 1g	2%
Cholesterol 5 mg	30%
Sodium 720 mg	7%
Total Carbohydrate 21g	12%
Dietary Fiber 3g	
Sugars 11g	
Protein 4g	

Vitamin A 40%	•	Vitamin C 2%
Calcium 6%	•	Iron 8%

*Percent Daily Values are based on a 2,000 calorie diet. Your daily values may be higher or lower depending on your calorie needs:

		2,000	2,500
	Calories:	2,000	2,500
Total Fat	Less than	65g	80g
Sat Fat	Less than	20g	25g
Cholesterol	Less than	300mg	300mg
Sodium	Less than	2,400mg	2,400mg
Total Carbohydrate		300g	375g
Dietary Fiber		25g	30g

Calories per gram:
Fat 9   •   Carbohydrate 4   •   Protein 4

INGREDIENTS: TOMATO PUREE (WATER, TOMATO PASTE), CHICKEN STOCK, ZUCCHINI, CARROTS, DICED TOMATOES, CELERY, WATER, HIGH FRUCTOSE CORN SYRUP, ENRICHED MACARONI PRODUCT (WHEAT FLOUR, EGG WHITE SOLIDS, NIACIN, FERROUS SULFATE, THIAMINE MONONITRATE, RIBOFLAVIN).

WITH A GROUP

With three or four classmates, compare food labels from different products. Analyze each one for nutritional value. Which products would you consider healthy choices? Which would you consider unhealthy choices? Compare your findings with other groups of classmates.

WHAT TEENS WANT TO KNOW

Do you get fat from eating fat? You gain weight by eating more calories than you burn. It doesn't matter whether these calories are from fat, protein, or carbohydrates. However, any given amount of fat has slightly more than twice the calories as the same amount of protein or carbohydrates. So it's easier to gain weight from eating fat than from eating proteins and carbohydrates. Even if your total calorie intake is appropriate for your age, height, and activity level, it is not a good idea to consume excess fat. Eating too much saturated fat, found in animal sources such as meat, butter, and cheese, can increase the risk of heart disease. Ideally, no more than 35 percent of your diet should come from fat.

Lesson 1

Comparing

Have students discuss how the body needs and uses water in ways similar to the ways the earth does. (*It sustains growth, washes away wastes, and keeps the temperature cool.*)  **L1**

③ Assess

Evaluating

📁 Assign the Lesson 1 Review; then assign the Lesson 1 Quiz in the TCR.

Reteaching

• 📁 Assign Concept Map 18 or Reteaching Activity 16 in the TCR.

• Have students explain why water is categorized as a nutrient.

Enrichment

• 📁 Assign and distribute Enrichment Activity 16 in the TCR.

• Have students investigate the dangers of taking too many vitamin supplements.

④ Close

At the end of the lesson, have a "healthy" party. Rather than students bringing in typical party snacks, ask students to introduce foods and share each food's main nutrient content. Afterward, have students design a collage or brochure with pictures showing foods rich in each of the nutrients.

Your body needs six to eight cups of water each day to function properly. *Why do you think your body needs more water during exercise?*

Minerals

Minerals (MIN·uh·ruhls) are *elements in foods that help your body work properly.* For example, the minerals calcium and phosphorus aid many body functions. They strengthen growing bones, keep muscles healthy, and help your heart beat regularly. Several minerals allow the body to use the other types of nutrients. Most foods contain minerals, especially milk, meat, dried beans, vegetables, fruits, and whole-grain cereals. Different foods contain different minerals.

Some people take supplements, such as pills, to get extra vitamins and minerals. However, food sources are always better. Food has other nutrients that supplements don't have.

Water

Water carries nutrients around your body and so is essential to life. It also helps with digestion, removes waste, and cools you off. You need six to eight cups of water every day (plus two to four more cups in hotter weather). Your body can also get water from juices, milk, and some fruits and vegetables.

Lesson 1 Review

Using complete sentences, answer the following questions on a sheet of paper.

Reviewing Terms and Facts

1. **Vocabulary** Define the term *nutrition.* Use it in an original sentence.
2. **Identify** List three things that food does for you.
3. **List** Name the six categories of nutrients.

Thinking Critically

4. **Predict** Describe how your knowledge of nutrients might affect your choice of snack foods in the future.

5. **Analyze** Record what you eat for one day. Then analyze the nutrients you have eaten. Remember to count the cups of water you drink. What improvements, if any, could you make?

Applying Health Skills

6. **Accessing Information** Analyze the ingredients in a recipe from a magazine or newspaper. Explain which of the six nutrient categories, if any, are missing. Suggest other foods that could be served at the same meal to provide a variety of nutrients.

120 CHAPTER 5: NUTRITION AND PHYSICAL ACTIVITY

Lesson 1 Review

1. The science that studies the substances in food and how the body uses them. Sentences will vary.
2. Any three: food provides energy, helps the body to grow and repair, helps you feel your best, and helps you to perform at your peak.
3. Carbohydrates, proteins, fats, vitamins, minerals, water.
4. Students' responses may indicate an ability to make more healthful snack choices, such as fruits and vegetables.
5. Responses will vary.

Following a Balanced Food Plan

The Food Guide Pyramid

Two government departments, the U.S. Department of Agriculture (USDA) and the Department of Health and Human Services, have provided a handy tool to help you plan nutritious meals. This tool is the **Food Guide Pyramid**, which provides *a daily guideline to help you choose what and how much to eat to get the nutrients you need.*

The Food Guide Pyramid divides foods into six groups. Five of these are basic food groups. Eating foods from all five basic groups each day gives you the nutrients and energy you need to grow and stay healthy. The sixth group contains fats, oils, and sweets, which you should eat only in small amounts.

You can enjoy nutritious foods in many different settings. *What foods do you choose when you have a variety of options?*

Quick Write

List two or three reasons you think people should try to avoid eating too many fats and sugary foods.

LEARN ABOUT...

- how to use the Food Guide Pyramid.
- the names of the five food groups.
- how much of the different kinds of food you should eat.

VOCABULARY

- Food Guide Pyramid

Lesson 2

Following a Balanced Food Plan

① Focus

Lesson Objectives

Students will be able to

- explain how the Food Guide Pyramid can be used to create a balanced eating plan.
- list the five basic food groups and describe where they appear in the Food Guide Pyramid.
- list examples of servings from each of the five basic food groups.

Motivators

Quick Write
Have students share their responses. Ask: How much fat and sugar in the diet do you think is too much?

Bellringer Activity

Tell students they just won shopping sprees at a grocery store. They can buy enough food to feed a family of four for a week. Have students create a shopping list of the items they would choose. Ask volunteers to share their lists. Have the class group the items into categories and discuss them.

VOCABULARY

Ask a volunteer to draw a diagram of a pyramid on the board. Then have students write a definition of the word *pyramid*. As they encounter the Food Guide Pyramid in the text, ask students to define the term and use it correctly in a sentence.

Lesson 2 Resources

Teacher Classroom Resources

 Concept Map 19

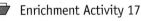 Enrichment Activity 17

Lesson Plan 2

Lesson 2 Quiz

 Reading Tutor Activity 17

Reteaching Activity 17

 Transparency 21

Student Activities Workbook

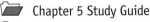 Chapter 5 Study Guide

Applying Health Skills 17

VISUAL LEARNING

FIGURE 5.2 Have students study the Food Guide Pyramid. Ask students:

- Which group of foods makes up the base of the Pyramid? (*bread, cereal, rice, and pasta*)

- How many servings a day should you have from the Milk, Yogurt, and Cheese Group? (*2 to 3 servings*)

- From which group do you need the most servings every day? (*bread, cereal, rice, and pasta*)

INCL *Behavior Problems, Special Learning Needs, English Language Learners*

Discussing

Discuss with students the importance of each food group. Reinforce the idea that each group provides nutrients that are necessary for good health, but foods from one group cannot be substituted for those in another group. Ask students to explain why fats, oils, and sweets are at the Pyramid's top. (*Very few of them are needed in a healthy eating plan.*) **L1**

You will find many of your favorite foods in **Figure 5.2**, which shows the Food Guide Pyramid. The size of each section in the Pyramid gives you a good idea of how much of each kind of food to eat every day. You should eat the most servings from the Bread, Cereal, Rice, and Pasta Group—the largest section of the Pyramid. Growing teens should get three full servings from the Milk, Yogurt, and Cheese Group. Notice that no number of servings from the smallest section—Fats, Oils, and Sweets—is recommended. Foods in this group provide energy but few nutrients.

FIGURE 5.2

THE FOOD GUIDE PYRAMID

Eating enough foods from the five basic food groups every day provides you with the nutrients you need to grow and stay healthy.

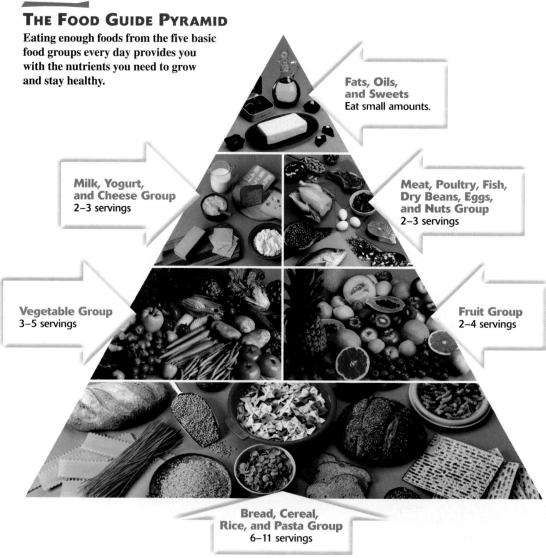

Fats, Oils, and Sweets
Eat small amounts.

Milk, Yogurt, and Cheese Group
2–3 servings

Meat, Poultry, Fish, Dry Beans, Eggs, and Nuts Group
2–3 servings

Vegetable Group
3–5 servings

Fruit Group
2–4 servings

Bread, Cereal, Rice, and Pasta Group
6–11 servings

122 CHAPTER 5: NUTRITION AND PHYSICAL ACTIVITY

 Beyond the Classroom

Community Students may justifiably ask, "If a balanced amount of nutrients is needed for a healthy body, why not just take vitamins, minerals, and other nutrients in supplement form?" Invite a registered dietitian or other qualified health professional to speak to the class about the issue. Have students prepare a short list of discussion questions, and make the questions available to the speaker well ahead of time. Also, encourage the speaker to use any appropriate visual aids—such as charts, diagrams, transparencies, and videos—to enhance his or her presentation and discussion.

The Food Groups

Which nutrients does each food group provide? Use **Figure 5.3** to find out. It shows the nutrients in each Pyramid section.

FIGURE 5.3

NUTRIENTS IN THE FOOD GROUPS

Bread, Cereal, Rice, and Pasta Group
6–11 servings

These foods are rich in complex carbohydrates, which provide energy. They supply certain vitamins and minerals. Combined with beans, or other foods such as peanut butter, they provide some protein. Whole-grain foods are also high in fiber.

Vegetable Group
3–5 servings

Fruit Group
2–4 servings

Most foods from these two groups are low in fat and high in carbohydrates. They provide many important vitamins, such as vitamins A and C, plus fiber and some minerals. Dark-green, leafy vegetables and dark-colored fruits are especially rich in nutrients. For good health, choose a variety of fruits and vegetables each day.

Milk, Yogurt, and Cheese Group
3 servings for teens

Foods in this group are a major source of calcium. They also offer protein, carbohydrates, and some vitamins. Some are high in fat. Choose mostly low-fat or fat-free milk, cheese, and yogurt.

Meat, Poultry, Fish, Dry Beans, Eggs, and Nuts Group
2–3 servings

All foods in this group are high in protein. Most also contain B vitamins and minerals such as iron. However, they can also be high in fat. Eat mostly leaner meats, poultry, and fish. Cooked dry beans, combined with grain products, are another good choice.

Fats, Oils, and Sweets
Eat small amounts.

This section contains foods that are high in fat or sugar and contain few other nutrients. Enjoy them in small amounts. They should not take the place of more nutritious foods in your meals and snacks.

LESSON 2: FOLLOWING A BALANCED FOOD PLAN **123**

Health Literacy

Influencing Factors As teens start to make their own food choices, they are often easily influenced by their peers as well as by advertising and the media. Peer pressure can be overt or subtle yet very effective in steering a teen toward, or away from, certain foods. However, advertising can have an even stronger influence. Millions of advertising dollars are spent each year on appealing techniques that often imply that people will be more successful, attractive, or popular if they eat a certain product. Encourage students to think critically about such advertising techniques in order to become more selective, literate health consumers.

FIGURE 5.4 Have a set of plastic measuring cups available when students discuss Figure 5.4. Describe the pictures and read the captions aloud, describing the various serving sizes. Ask students to select and display the relevant measuring cup. Have students discuss the relationship between these serving sizes and the servings they eat during typical meals and snacks. **INCL** *Behavior Problems, Special Learning Needs, English Language Learners*

Hands-On Health

ANALYZE YOUR FOOD CHOICES

Time: two 15-minute class sessions, two days apart

TEACHING THE ACTIVITY

• With students, read and discuss the What You Will Do instructions.

• Have students draw their charts in class, and go over the records they will need to keep in each column. Use several examples, and record them on the board.

• Have students record everything they eat, including snacks, during the next two days.

• After two days, have students meet in groups to analyze the healthy and unhealthy dietary practices revealed by the charts.

ASSESSMENT

Have students write short paragraphs describing what they learned from the activity.

Using the Food Guide Pyramid

The Food Guide Pyramid shows a range of daily servings for each food group. The number of servings recommended for you depends on your age, gender, body size, and activity level. But how much is a serving? Use **Figure 5.4** to find out. Keep in mind that many foods, such as pizza, contain servings from several different groups.

FIGURE 5.4

SERVING SIZES

These guidelines can help you eat enough of each type of food each day. List the foods you ate today. *How many servings did you eat from each food group?*

Bread, Cereal, Rice, and Pasta Group 6–11 servings
- 1 slice of bread
- ½ cup cooked pasta
- ½ cup cooked rice
- 1 cup cold cereal
- 1 tortilla
- ½ small bagel

Vegetable Group 3–5 servings
- ½ cup cooked vegetables
- ¾ cup vegetable juice
- ½ cup chopped raw vegetables
- 1 cup raw leafy vegetables

Fruit Group 2–4 servings
- ½ cup chopped, cooked, or canned fruit
- ¼ cup dried fruit
- 1 medium apple
- ¾ cup fruit juice

Milk, Yogurt, and Cheese Group 2–3 servings
- 1 cup milk
- 1½ ounces natural cheese, such as cheddar
- 2 ounces processed cheese, such as American
- 1 cup yogurt

Meat, Poultry, Fish, Dry Beans, Eggs, and Nuts Group 2–3 servings
- 2 to 3 ounces cooked lean meat, poultry, or fish
- ½ cup cooked dried beans
- 1 egg
- ½ cup tofu
- 2 tablespoons peanut butter

These count as 1 ounce of meat.

COOPERATIVE LEARNING ACTIVITY

Menu Planning Allow students to work in groups of three or four and pretend for one day they have just been put in charge of a cafeteria, where they will serve breakfast, lunch, and dinner. Each group must plan a menu that includes a balanced number of servings from all five food groups. As they chart out the menu, students should keep track of the number of recommended servings, limit the fat and sugar content, and yet strive for variety and appeal. When students are finished, encourage groups to share their menus and comment on one another's ideas. Ask the cafeteria whether one of the group's menus can be used for lunch one day.

Hands-On Health

ANALYZE YOUR FOOD CHOICES

Once you know how well your eating plan matches the Food Guide Pyramid, you will know what changes you need to make to eat more healthfully. This activity will help you make a detailed analysis of your food choices for the next two days.

WHAT YOU WILL NEED
- paper and pencil or pen
- ruler

WHAT YOU WILL DO
1. Mark off three vertical columns on your paper.
2. In the first column, list all the foods you eat in the next two days. Use a separate record for each day.
3. In the second column, write down the amount of each food you eat.

4. In the third column, list the number of servings from each food group that each food provided.
5. Add up the total number of servings you ate from each food group.

IN CONCLUSION
1. How well does your list for each day match the guidelines provided by the Food Guide Pyramid?
2. How could you improve your food choices?

Lesson 2 Review

Using complete sentences, answer the following questions on a sheet of paper.

Reviewing Terms and Facts
1. **Vocabulary** What is the *Food Guide Pyramid*?
2. **Match** For each food group, list the number of daily servings recommended for a teen.
3. **Give Examples** Give an example of one serving from each of the five basic food groups.

Thinking Critically
4. **Recommend** Working in small groups, make a list of tasty and nutritious snack foods from each of the food groups.

Compare lists with other groups to get more ideas.
5. **Synthesize** Describe a low-fat meal that has one-third of the daily servings for all five food groups.

Applying Health Skills
6. **Analyzing Influences** Collect food ads from several magazines. Make a chart categorizing the ads into the five food groups plus fats, oils, and sweets. (Some ads will fit into several groups.) Decide which group is advertised most, and explain how you think this affects the food choices of a typical teen.

LESSON 2: FOLLOWING A BALANCED FOOD PLAN **125**

Making Healthful Food Choices

Lesson Objectives

Students will be able to

- identify influences on their food choices.

- discuss the nutritional needs of teens and ways to plan for good nutrition.

- explain the three Dietary Guidelines.

- describe ways to maintain a healthy weight.

- describe the three main types of eating disorders.

Motivators

Quick Write

Have several volunteers read their paragraphs aloud. After each reading, list the influences on the board. Then ask students to think about any additional reasons people choose the foods they do.

VOCABULARY

Write each vocabulary term on an index card; then write the definition for each one on a separate card. Make several sets of the term-and-definition cards. Divide the class into small groups. Give each group a set of cards, and let students match each term with its definition.

LESSON 3

Making Healthful Food Choices

Quick Write

Think about your eating habits. Are you a snacker? Do you like to eat several small meals during the day? Write a paragraph explaining what or who influences these patterns.

LEARN ABOUT...

- making responsible food choices.
- foods that are especially nutritious.
- what foods to limit or avoid in your eating plan.
- how to maintain a healthy weight.

VOCABULARY

- calcium
- saturated fat
- cholesterol
- sodium
- calorie
- anorexia nervosa
- bulimia nervosa

Influences on Your Food Choices

Why do you choose the foods you do? It may be simply because you enjoy eating a certain food or perhaps because your friends eat it. Some foods may be family favorites or part of your cultural heritage. You may choose some foods because they are a good value or because they are convenient. You may choose other foods because they are in season or popular in your part of the country. Finally, advertisements can influence your food choices. Advertisers use marketing techniques to convince you to buy their food products. In order to select the most nutritious foods, it is important to use critical-thinking skills to analyze food ads.

Food preferences in your family can influence your food choices all your life. *What are some of your family's favorites?*

126 CHAPTER 5: NUTRITION AND PHYSICAL ACTIVITY

Lesson 3 Resources

Teacher Classroom Resources

- 📁 Concept Map 20
- 📁 Cross-Curriculum Activity 9
- 📁 Decision-Making Activity 9
- 📁 Enrichment Activity 18
- 📁 Health Lab 5
- 📁 Lesson Plan 3
- 📁 Lesson 3 Quiz

- 📁 Reading Tutor Activity 18
- 📁 Reteaching Activity 18
- 🖥 Transparency 22

Student Activities Workbook

- 📁 Chapter 5 Study Guide
- 📁 Applying Health Skills 18

Nutrition During the Teen Years

No matter what influences your choices, you want the foods you eat to help you stay healthy. During your teen years, your nutrient and energy needs are as high as they'll ever be. That's why you need to choose foods wisely and develop a personal dietary plan. Eat plenty of foods high in complex carbohydrates. These starchy foods give you most of your food energy.

Another important nutrient for teens is calcium. **Calcium** is *a mineral that helps your body build healthy teeth and bones.* It is also important for muscle function. Dairy products are excellent sources of calcium. Canned fish with soft bones (such as salmon or sardines) and dark green leafy vegetables are other good sources. Calcium is also added to some breakfast cereals.

Planning for Good Nutrition

Maybe you're so busy that it seems hard to fit healthful eating into your schedule. Try tucking some healthy snacks into your school or lunch bag. Along with the usual selection of fruit, nuts, and raisins, you can also experiment with foods from around the world, such as pita bread and hummus. Make time for breakfast; ask someone to set aside a plate of food for you if you have to miss a family dinner. When you eat at a fast-food restaurant, try having a salad instead of something high in fat, and order juice or milk to drink. When you buy foods for meals or snacks, choose foods that are nutritious and within your budget. Shop at a variety of stores to compare prices.

It is best to get your food energy from foods high in carbohydrates and low in fat. *Name some high-carbohydrate foods that are good choices for teens.*

LESSON 3: MAKING HEALTHFUL FOOD CHOICES **127**

Developing Good Character

Citizenship

Many communities maintain free food banks to help people who cannot afford the food they need. Collecting food for food banks is a way to help your fellow citizens. It shows that you care about the health of others.

② Teach

Developing Good Character

Citizenship

Have students think about ways to collect healthy foods for the local food bank. The class should develop a plan, put it into action, and reflect on the experience. Note that some at-risk students may receive free or reduced-cost meals or live at a shelter. Be sensitive to these issues during discussion.

Cooperative Learning

Have small groups of students discuss and compare the special holiday or celebration meals their families enjoy. (Note: Some students may not have these family food traditions.) Have group members identify what all the meals have in common and how they are different. **L1**

HEALTH SKILLS PRACTICE

Practicing Healthful Behaviors Have students make a T-chart with the headings "Every-Day Foods" and "Once-in-a-While Foods." "Every-Day Foods" should provide a variety of nutrients. "Once-in-a-While Foods" are the foods that are high in fat and/or sugar that should be limited. Students should list all the foods eaten in one day under the appropriate heading. Encourage them to analyze their chart and use it to design a healthy personal dietary plan.

COOPERATIVE LEARNING ACTIVITY

Comparing Cereals In this activity, students will use critical-thinking skills to research and evaluate health information. Arrange to have student or parent volunteers bring in six to eight empty cereal boxes—all different kinds, brands, and varieties. Be sure to include one or two whole-grain cereals as well as a mixture of others. Divide the class into groups of three. Have students take turns analyzing and recording information on the nutrition label of each box. After the groups have finished analyzing each kind of cereal, ask them to compare the cereals and rank them in order of nutritional value. Discuss the attributes of the cereals and the groups' conclusions and rankings.

Lesson 3

Listing

Emphasize the importance of choosing a variety of foods from the bottom sections of the Food Guide Pyramid. Then have students work together to name as many different fruits, vegetables, and whole-grain products as possible. Ask volunteers to record students' ideas in three lists on the board. You may want to bring in less-common examples of these foods for students to sample. **L1**

Researching

Ask a small group of volunteers to research the differences in grams of fat, calories, and calcium content among nonfat, low-fat, and whole milk. Encourage them to find similar information about other kinds of dairy products such as cottage cheese and yogurt. Have the volunteers create a chart or poster to share their findings with the rest of the class. **L3**

Cross-Curriculum Activity

VISUAL ARTS Ask students to draw and write advertisements for a low-fat dessert. Encourage them to address the fat, cholesterol, and sodium content of their product in their attempts to market their dessert as a healthy food product. **L2** **INCL** *Behavior Problems, Special Learning Needs, English Language Learners*

CONNECT TO
Science

KEEPING FOODS SAFE
Develop these food-preparation skills to prevent bacteria and other germs in food from causing illness:
- **Wash hands with hot, soapy water before handling food.**
- **Keep raw and cooked foods separate.**
- **Cook foods to the proper temperature.**
- **Refrigerate foods that can spoil.**

Low-fat or nonfat milk is a healthy food choice. It is an important source of calcium during your teen years, when your bones are still growing.

Guidelines for Healthy Teens

Using the Food Guide Pyramid is just one way to choose healthy foods. There are several other steps you can take to get all the nutrients you need. The USDA has summarized these steps in the Dietary Guidelines for Americans.

Following the Dietary Guidelines is as easy as A-B-C. There are three basic points to follow:
- **A**im for Fitness
- **B**uild a Healthy Base
- **C**hoose Sensibly

Aim for Fitness

The first part of the Dietary Guidelines focuses on balancing the food you eat with physical activity. Being physically active every day, throughout your life, is one of the best things you can do for your body. You will be stronger and have more energy. It will also help you maintain a healthy weight.

Build a Healthy Base

The second part of the Dietary Guidelines advises you to build your dietary plan on a healthy base. This means eating enough foods from the bottom three sections of the Food Guide Pyramid. Letting the Pyramid guide your food choices is the first step to building a healthy diet. Another important key to remember is variety. Choosing a variety of different foods will help you get all the nutrients you need. Lastly, keep food safe to eat by handling, preparing, and storing it properly. If you don't, your food may contain harmful substances that can make you sick. To protect yourself, keep hot foods hot and cold foods cold. Always wash your hands before handling food.

128 CHAPTER 5: NUTRITION AND PHYSICAL ACTIVITY

Beyond the Classroom

Community Teens and their families who frequent fast-food restaurants may find it helpful to consider the guidelines provided by the Food Guide Pyramid when selecting from a menu. For example, they might look for dishes that are made up of vegetables, lean meat or fish, and pasta or bread. Fruit dishes provide a healthful dessert. They could consider how foods are prepared and avoid fatty, salty foods, especially those that are deep fried. Serving size is another important consideration. Since most restaurants offer large portions, they might think about taking a portion of their meal home. Ask students to make suggestions for ways restaurants can help teens make healthful food choices.

Choose Sensibly

Finally, the Dietary Guidelines advise you to choose your foods sensibly. This means choosing the foods you know are healthful. It also means going easy on foods that can increase your risk of health problems. For example:

- **Moderate your intake of fats, especially saturated fats. Satu-rated** (SAT·chur·a·tuhd) **fats** are *fats found mostly in animal prod-ucts such as butter, meat, milk, and egg yolks.* Eating too much satu-rated fat can increase your body's level of cholesterol. **Cholesterol** (kuh·LES·tuh·rawl) is *a waxlike substance our bodies produce and need in small amounts.* Eating less saturated fat helps you lower your risk of heart disease, cancer, and other serious diseases.
- **Watch for added sugar.** Foods with a lot of added sugar are often low in other nutrients. A little added sugar is fine, but sugary foods should not take the place of more nutritious ones such as fruits or low-fat milk.
- **Watch your intake of salt.** Salt contains **sodium**, *a mineral that helps control the amount of fluid in your body.* Too much sodium can promote high blood pressure in some people. Read food labels to find foods with less sodium.

Smart snacking can help you meet the extra nutritional needs of your teen years. Time your snacks for two or three hours before mealtime so you won't feel like skipping a meal. Sometimes, your choices may be limited. For example, the foods available in a vending machine or convenience store are different from those at home. Try buying raisins or peanuts rather than candy bars, or buy milk instead of a soft drink.

Toast, **English muffins, and hot cereal are popu-lar breakfast foods in the United States.** *Why is it important to analyze and taste foods from different ethnic and cultural groups?*

Comparing

Ask students to compare two of their favorite foods in terms of saturated fat, sugar, cholesterol, and salt (sodium) content. Remind students to refer to the nutrition labels on foods, if possible. If a label is not available on the product, then ask them to suggest how they would learn the nutrient values. (*Check resource books, write or call the man-ufacturer, consult a dietitian.*) Have stu-dents discuss which foods contain less fat, sugar, cholesterol, and salt. **L3**

Discussing

Ask students to explain why they should limit their intake of saturated fats, cholesterol, sugar, and salt. Have them suggest ways to avoid food items that contain large amounts of saturated fats, cholesterol, sugar, and salt. **L1**

Discussing

Ask volunteers to describe their typ-ical after-school snacks. Then ask the class:

- Is eating a snack every day after school a healthful habit? Why?
- What healthful snacks do you recommend?
- What nutrients do you think are most important in a snack? Why? **L1**

MORE ABOUT...

Analyzing Sugar Content Remind students that, if a food has sugar listed as one of the first three ingredients on its label, the food has a high amount of sugar. To illustrate this point, ask stu-dents to bring in empty food item packages with nutrition labels that list sugar or an alternative name for sugar (*sucrose, brown sugar, invert sugar,* *glucose, sorbitol, lactose, honey, corn syrup, corn sweeteners, high-fructose corn syrup, molasses, maple syrup, dextrose, fructose,* and *maltose*) as one of the ingredients. Then identify the type and amount of sugar contained in each food. Finally, compare the varieties of terms used and the amounts of sugar contained in each food.

Analyzing

Have students discuss why comparing one's weight with that of a friend's may not be particularly helpful in understanding issues of personal weight. Have students identify causes associated with poor body image. Make sure students include growth patterns, and how the human body is portrayed in the entertainment and advertising industries. Then ask students to identify the effects associated with poor body image. Have students include eating disorders, cosmetic surgery, use of risky diet supplements, and use of steroids. **L1**

Cross-Curriculum Activity

LANGUAGE ARTS Ask students to look up the history of the word calorie. (*from Latin* calor *meaning "heat"*) Then ask students to guess what a calorimeter might be used for. (*an instrument for measuring the amount of heat produced by different foods when they burn*) **L1**

A survey of elementary school students in California found an awareness of body image and dieting in children as young as eight. The same survey showed that half the children considered themselves overweight.

Reading Check

Decide whether you agree or disagree with the following statements. *Everyone at the same height should weigh the same. Eating too many calories makes a person gain weight.*

Maintaining a Healthy Weight

Many growing teens fear that they weigh too much or too little. The rate at which you gain weight and grow in height is known as your *growth pattern*. Teens vary greatly in their growth patterns. Trying to gain or lose a lot of weight can interfere with your normal growth pattern. If you have serious weight concerns, however, ask your doctor for advice. He or she will assess your weight and, if necessary, suggest a plan that is just right for you.

The Role of Calories

The amount you weigh is related to how many calories you consume and how many you use. A **calorie** is *a unit of heat that measures the energy available in foods.* Your body uses this energy as you go about your daily activities. If you use up as many calories as you take in by eating, your weight will stay the same. If you consume more calories than your body uses, your body stores the extra calories as fat. About 3,500 extra calories per week adds 1 pound to your weight. Similarly, if your body needs more calories than you are taking in, it will turn its stored fat into energy. As a result, you will lose weight.

Feeling good about your body is much more important than the numbers on a scale. *Write down five things you like about your body.*

130 CHAPTER 5: NUTRITION AND PHYSICAL ACTIVITY

 Reading Check

Agree/Disagree Statements Analyzing statements helps students process information and form a personal response. Before having students discuss each statement in small groups, model group skills, such as listening and disagreeing politely. Remind students that information from the text may help them support their opinions. They should conclude that the first statement is incorrect. The second statement is typically true. Another example statement is, "There is no such thing as 'too skinny'."

You can maintain a healthy weight by eating right and being physically active. Consume as many calories as your body needs for the activities you are doing. Here are some more tips for maintaining a healthy weight.

- Choose foods wisely. Snack on healthy foods.
- Eat slowly, and take the time to enjoy your food. Stop when you feel full.
- Always eat breakfast.
- Try not to eat too many foods that are high in fat. These foods are usually high in calories and can also contribute to health problems.
- Drink plenty of water.
- Stay physically active.
- Create a personal dietary plan and a personal exercise plan. These plans will help you eat healthfully and stay fit.

Don't worry too much about what the scale says. Instead, try to be comfortable with your body. Appreciate the things it can do rather than focusing only on how it looks. This will help you develop a realistic body image. A healthy body is a wonderful thing, no matter what size it is.

Eating Disorders

Many people's self-images are closely tied to their body weight. Some people think they need to be thin to feel good about themselves. People who become overly concerned with their weight may develop eating disorders—extreme eating behaviors that can seriously damage the body. These are most common among teen girls and young women but occur in males as well. There are three main types of eating disorders.

- **Anorexia nervosa** (an·uh·REK·see·uh ner·VOH·suh) is *an eating disorder in which a person has an intense fear of weight gain and starves himself or herself.* Victims with this disorder are obsessed with the idea of controlling their bodies. They eat far fewer calories than they need to stay healthy. They often exercise excessively and become dangerously thin but still see themselves as overweight.

People with eating disorders may become obsessed with their weight. *What might cause a person to develop a poor body image?*

Discussing

Emphasize that teens often gain or lose weight in spurts. Ask students:

- What is the difference between gaining weight and having binge eating disorder?
- What is the difference between losing a few pounds and having the eating disorder anorexia nervosa? **L1**

Researching

Newspapers and magazines often have articles about eating disorders and the people who suffer from them. Have each student find and read one such article in a recent publication. Then have students meet in groups to summarize and discuss the articles. **L3**

Discussing

Emphasize that eating disorders are a mental health problem. Trained mental health counselors can help with these disorders. Then ask: What would you recommend for a friend who worried that she or he might have an eating disorder? Help students recognize that a school counselor or other guidance professional can discuss the potential problem in confidence; assure a student as appropriate; and, if necessary, make a referral. **L1**

Lesson 3

MORE ABOUT...

Weight Loss Myths regarding weight loss abound. One is that physical activity alone causes weight loss. Generally, the amount of physical activity needed to work off excessive calorie consumption is great. However, when combined with a reduction in calories consumed, regular physical activity can promote weight loss and changes in body composition. Another myth is that low-fat diets guarantee weight loss. This is true only when reducing fat in the diet also reduces the total calories consumed. Not all fat-free and low-fat foods are low in calories. Some foods add sugar to compensate for reduced fat and have as many calories as full-fat versions of the same foods.

❸ Assess

Evaluating

📁 Assign the Lesson 3 Review; then assign the Lesson 3 Quiz in the TCR.

Reteaching

- 📁 Assign Concept Map 20 or Reteaching Activity 18 in the TCR.
- Have students explain what kinds of foods they should eat in limited amounts and why.

Enrichment

- 📁 Assign and distribute Enrichment Activity 18 in the TCR.
- Ask students to evaluate the school's weekly cafeteria menu to determine whether it offers a balance of healthy food choices.

❹ Close

Have students explain the importance of a personal dietary plan.

The first step in treating an eating disorder is to seek professional help. *Name some health professionals who could help a person with an eating disorder.*

- **Bulimia nervosa** (boo·LEE·mee·uh ner·VOH·suh) is *an eating disorder in which a person repeatedly eats large amounts of food and then purges by vomiting or using laxatives.* Victims also may exercise excessively even though their weight is often normal.
- Binge eating is an eating disorder in which a person repeatedly eats large amounts of food but does not purge or exercise excessively. Victims may be overweight. Often, they "seesaw" from losing to gaining weight.

Eating disorders are a mental health problem. They are often associated with a poor body image. If you or anyone you know has symptoms of an eating disorder, talk to a trusted adult about getting professional help. The sooner a person receives treatment for an eating disorder, the likelier he or she is to recover from it.

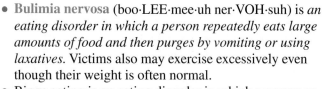

Lesson 3 Review

Using complete sentences, answer the following questions on a sheet of paper.

Reviewing Terms and Facts

1. **List** Name five factors that influence your food choices.
2. **Vocabulary** Define the word *calcium* and name one food that contains calcium.
3. **Identify** Which of the following items should you try to increase in your diet: saturated fat, fiber, cholesterol, calcium, sodium?
4. **Give Examples** Explain what an eating disorder is, and name the three main types.

Thinking Critically

5. **Apply** Use the word *calorie* in a sentence about body weight.
6. **Analyze** How is physical activity important for maintaining a healthy body weight?

Applying Health Skills

7. **Goal Setting** Create a pamphlet that analyzes healthy and unhealthy dietary practices and explains the importance of a personal dietary plan.

132 CHAPTER 5: NUTRITION AND PHYSICAL ACTIVITY

Lesson 3 Review

1. Any five from page 126.
2. Calcium is a mineral that helps your body build healthy teeth and bones. Students may list dairy products, canned fish with soft bones, dark-green leafy vegetables, or calcium-fortified breakfast cereals.
3. Fiber and calcium.
4. An eating disorder is an extreme eating behavior that can seriously damage the body.

Three main types: anorexia nervosa, bulimia nervosa, and binge eating disorder.

5. Students' sentences should show that they understand the meaning of the term *calorie* and the way net calorie intake affects weight.
6. Physical activity balances out the number of calories consumed in food.

The Benefits of Physical Activity

Physical Activity and Your Health

If you enjoy sports, you already know that exercising can make you feel good. Physical activity has many other benefits as well. **Physical activity** is *any kind of movement that causes your body to use energy.* Every kind of physical activity, vigorous or moderate, can help keep you healthy. **Figure 5.5** shows some of the health benefits of regular physical activity.

FIGURE 5.5

HOW REGULAR PHYSICAL ACTIVITY BENEFITS YOUR HEALTH

Physical activity benefits all three parts of health. *How can you include a variety of individuals in group physical activities?*

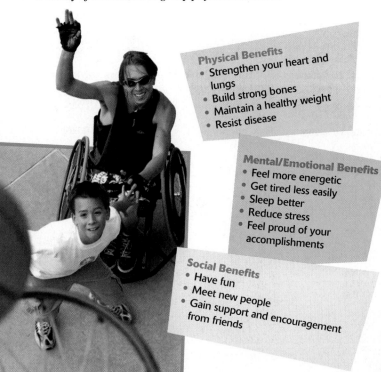

Physical Benefits
• Strengthen your heart and lungs
• Build strong bones
• Maintain a healthy weight
• Resist disease

Mental/Emotional Benefits
• Feel more energetic
• Get tired less easily
• Sleep better
• Reduce stress
• Feel proud of your accomplishments

Social Benefits
• Have fun
• Meet new people
• Gain support and encouragement from friends

Quick Write

Describe your favorite physical activity and how you think it benefits your physical, mental/emotional, and social health.

LEARN ABOUT...

• the benefits of regular physical activity.
• the different ways physical activity can improve your health.
• the importance of aerobic exercise.

VOCABULARY

○ physical activity
○ strength
○ endurance
○ aerobic exercise
○ anaerobic exercise
○ flexibility
○ physical fitness
○ exercise

LESSON 4: THE BENEFITS OF PHYSICAL ACTIVITY 133

Lesson 4

The Benefits of Physical Activity

① Focus

Lesson Objectives

Students will be able to

• identify the benefits of regular physical activity.

• describe ways to achieve and maintain strength, endurance, and flexibility.

• compare and contrast aerobic and anaerobic exercise.

• explain what fitness is.

Health Skills

• Stress Management, p. 136

Motivators

Quick Write
Ask students to share their favorite physical activities and the benefits they derive from them.

Bellringer Activity

Ask students to think about someone they know who is physically fit. Have them describe that person, explaining why they think he or she is so fit.

VOCABULARY

Have students write the definition of each vocabulary term on charts. Then next to each term and its definition, have students draw or paste pictures that relate to the meaning of the term.

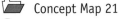
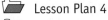

Lesson 4 Resources

Teacher Classroom Resources

📁 Concept Map 21

📁 Enrichment Activity 19

📁 Lesson Plan 4

📁 Lesson 4 Quiz

📁 Reading Tutor Activity 19

📁 Reteaching Activity 19

 Transparency 23

Student Activities Workbook

📁 Chapter 5 Study Guide

📁 Applying Health Skills 19

Lesson 4

② Teach

VISUAL LEARNING

FIGURE 5.5 Ask volunteers to describe what is happening in the photograph in Figure 5.5 on page 133. Have other volunteers read the informational lists aloud. Encourage students to share the health benefits of physical activity from their own experience. **INCL** *Behavior Problems, Special Learning Needs, English Language Learners*

FIGURE 5.6 Have volunteers describe the three pictures and read aloud the activities named in each list. **INCL** *Behavior Problems, Special Learning Needs, English Language Learners*

Analyzing

Have students think of and discuss additional forms of physical activity for endurance, and classify each of them into one of the three categories shown in Figure 5.6 (very vigorous, moderately vigorous, occasionally vigorous). **L1**

Cross-Curriculum Activity

SOCIAL STUDIES Many sports and activities that are commonly enjoyed in the United States originated in other cultures or countries. Ask interested students to investigate one of the sports listed in Figure 5.6 (or another sport of his or her choice) and write a short report describing its history and how it is played. **L3**

Citizenship

Be a good citizen. Do your part to promote health and strengthen health-related policies at your school. Support healthful activities at school. For example, if your school is organizing a fund-raising event, suggest that it be one that involves physical activity, such as a jog-a-thon. *What are some other ways you can promote school health?*

Strength, Endurance, and Flexibility

Different kinds of physical activity benefit your health in different ways. Some activities build **strength**, which is *the ability of your muscles to exert a force.* To build muscle strength, you need to push or pull against a force such as gravity. Pull-ups, for instance, build muscle strength in your arms.

Activities that build strength may also increase your endurance. **Endurance** (en·DER·uhns) means *how long you can engage in physical activity without becoming overly tired.* There are two kinds of endurance. Muscular endurance is how well your muscles can perform a task without tiring. Heart and lung endurance is how well your heart and lungs can provide your body with oxygen. See **Figure 5.6**.

Aerobic exercise—*rhythmic, nonstop, moderate to vigorous activities that work the heart*—will build endurance. **Anaerobic exercise**, by contrast, is *intense physical activity that requires short bursts of energy.* Jogging 10 miles is aerobic exercise while sprinting 50 meters at top speed is anaerobic exercise. It is a good idea to do both aerobic and anaerobic activities.

FIGURE 5.6

ACTIVITIES THAT BUILD ENDURANCE

This chart groups activities according to how well they build endurance. *Which out-of-school play activities would you like to explore?*

Vigorous Activities

(Do at least 20 minutes three times a week.)

Aerobic dancing
Cycling
Cross-country skiing
Ice hockey
In-line skating
Running
Skateboarding
Swimming

Moderately Vigorous Activities

(Do at least 30 minutes three times a week.)

Basketball
Calisthenics
Field hockey
Handball
Tennis
Walking

Occasionally Vigorous Activities

(These activities will build muscle strength and flexibility.)

Baseball
Downhill skiing
Football
Snowboarding
Softball
Volleyball

134 CHAPTER 5: NUTRITION AND PHYSICAL ACTIVITY

INCLUSION STRATEGIES

Students with Physical Disabilities For students with physical limitations or disabilities, some of the activities and exercises suggested in this lesson may not be appropriate. Ask all students to describe alternate activities that have the same sound exercise benefits as those listed. Help all students come up with a variety of ideas that fit within each category: exercises that build strong muscles (head and neck exercises or arm and hand exercises with light weights); exercises that help build endurance (walking, swimming, or wheelchair activities); and exercises that help improve flexibility (hand and finger exercises or bending, stretching, and flexing exercises). Have a local "wheelchair" or paraolympic athlete share with students his or her exercise routine.

FIGURE 5.7

CALORIES BURNED DURING VARIOUS ACTIVITIES

The graph shows how many calories a 100-pound person burns during an hour of activity. *How many hours of tennis would it take to burn 450 calories?*

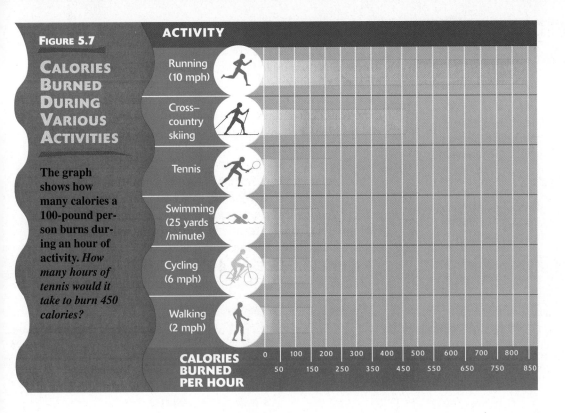

ACTIVITY																	
Running (10 mph)																	
Cross-country skiing																	
Tennis																	
Swimming (25 yards/minute)																	
Cycling (6 mph)																	
Walking (2 mph)																	

CALORIES BURNED PER HOUR

0 50 100 150 200 250 300 350 400 450 500 550 600 650 700 750 800 850

Finally, physical activity can promote flexibility. **Flexibility** is *the ability to move body joints through a full range of motion.* It helps you with everything from dancing to playing football, and it may help prevent injuries. You can improve your flexibility by stretching your muscles and joints. Ballet, yoga, swimming, and volleyball are all good ways to build flexibility.

Other Benefits

Physical activity can loosen up your muscles and help you relax. During aerobic activities, your brain releases chemicals that calm you down. Vigorous activity can also release stress. You may even find that you sleep better after an active day. These are important mental benefits of regular physical activity.

During physical activity, your body burns calories. **Figure 5.7** shows the number of calories you use doing different types of activities. Regular activity can help you maintain a healthy weight. Physical activity can also help firm up your muscles. When you are active, you look better and feel better.

Reading Check

Sort the following words into three groups: *running, basketball, swimming, stair climbing, weightlifting, soccer, karate, softball, dancing.* Label each group.

Researching

Ask a group of interested volunteers to research effective stretches for improving flexibility. Have these volunteers draw posters showing recommended stretches, or ask them to demonstrate for the rest of the class. **L1**

VISUAL LEARNING

FIGURE 5.7 Explain that calorie expenditure varies with intensity and the amount of body mass. Most calorie counters are approximate and based on a certain weight. Then have students look at Figure 5.7 and ask:

• Which activity burns the most calories per hour?

• Which activity burns the fewest calories per hour?

Then have a student read and answer the caption question. (two hours) Ask students which activity is best. Emphasize that the "best" activity varies from individual to individual, according to what each person enjoys. **INCL** *Behavior Problems, Special Learning Needs, English Language Learners*

Cross-Curriculum Activity

MATH Let students work with partners to calculate how many calories would be burned with each activity listed in Figure 5.7 during the following time periods:

• 2 hours
• 1/2 hour
• 15 minutes
• 10 minutes **L3** **INCL** *English Language Learners*

Reading Check

Word Sort Categorizing words will help students build a strong vocabulary. It also aids in retention and comprehension of content. Have students work with a partner to organize the words into categories. They may choose flexibility, strength, and endurance as their categories. Another choice could be vigorous, moderately vigorous, and occasionally vigorous activities. Point out that some words may fit into several categories. End the lesson by having volunteers share their lists. Encourage them to include their own words in each category. **INCL** *Special Learning Needs*

Lesson 4

Encourage students to explore the Web Link for this lesson and complete the activity.

Discussing

Have students describe the mental, physical, and social benefits of regular exercise and fitness. Have volunteers work at the board to illustrate the benefits. **L1**

HEALTH SKILLS ACTIVITY

STRESS MANAGEMENT

Let volunteers read aloud the descriptions of stress-relieving activities. If individuals are willing to try the activities, let them demonstrate for the rest of the class. Then have students complete the On Your Own assignment as homework, writing notes about their results. The next day, have students share and compare their responses.

Cooperative Learning

Have students meet in cooperative groups to list the lifestyle activities they engage in every day. Then have the groups share, compare, contrast, and discuss their lists with the rest of the class. **L1**

HEALTH Online

Topic: Physical fitness

For a link to more information on becoming physically fit, go to **health.glencoe.com**.

Activity: Using the information provided at this link, write down a goal for improving your fitness level.

What Is Fitness?

Staying physically active keeps you physically fit. **Physical fitness** is *the ability to handle everyday physical work and play without becoming tired.* Physical fitness gives you enough energy to carry you through the day. It makes you more confident and helps you deal with stress, which can help you get along better with others. It also helps you maintain a healthy weight level. In short, it makes your life better!

You can improve or maintain your physical fitness by exercising. **Exercise** is *planned, structured, repetitive physical activity that improves or maintains physical fitness.* An ideal exercise plan includes a variety of different activities. Types of physical activity include:

- **Lifestyle activities.** Every day, try to keep your body moving as much as possible. There are lots of ways to do this. You can

HEALTH SKILLS ACTIVITY

STRESS MANAGEMENT

Tension Tamers

Physical activity is a good strategy for managing stress. If you feel stress building up, any kind of activity, even cleaning your room, will help. Here are several activities that can help relieve tension.

- **SHOULDER LIFT.** Hunch your shoulders up to your ears for a few seconds, then release. Repeat.
- **ELASTIC JAW.** Take a few deep relaxing breaths. Open your mouth, and shift your jaw to the right as far as you can without discomfort. Hold for a count of three. Repeat on the left side. Do this exercise ten times.

- **SLEEPER.** Lie on your side, arms over your head. Stiffen your body, then relax, letting your body fall where it wants to. Repeat on the other side.
- **TENSE-RELAX.** Make a fist, and tense the muscles in your hand and forearm, then release. Repeat with the other hand. You can do the same with your abdomen, thighs, buttocks, and toes.

ON YOUR OWN

Estimate your current level of body tension or stress on a scale of one to ten. Then perform one of the exercises listed here. Write down your estimated level of body tension afterward. Repeat for each of the other exercises. How did each exercise affect your tension level? Compare your results as a class.

MORE ABOUT...

Physical Activity Increasing physical activity has many other health benefits. It improves muscle tone, strengthens bones, and reduces the risk of cardiovascular disease and selected cancers. Physical activity also produces the "fitness factor," an improved sense of well-being. The challenge is to inspire teens to watch less television, play fewer video games, and spend less time on computers in favor of physical activity. To increase their activity levels, teens may need more than the promise of risk reduction and health benefits in the distant future. Fitness programs emphasizing activities that are fun and offer improved energy, stamina, and appearance may be most appealing to teens.

walk or ride your bike to school if it's not too far. You can take a walk with your family or with a friend. Games such as tag and jump rope can also boost your activity level. Even cleaning your room is a way to get your body moving!

- **Aerobic activities.** Try to get some aerobic activity three to five times a week. Riding your bike, skateboarding, and in-line skating can give you exercise on the go. You can also try swimming, hiking, and running around the block. You will benefit most if you do these activities for at least 20 minutes at a time. You can get some of your aerobic activity from organized sports such as soccer, basketball, and skiing.

- **Strength and flexibility activities.** Two to three times a week, work on your strength and flexibility. Such exercises as push-ups and pull-ups will help you develop strength. Dancing, rope climbing, and karate will help you build flexibility.

Try to cut down on the amount of time you spend sitting still. Obviously, you have to sit still some of the time—when you're in class, doing homework, and eating meals. However, you can reduce the amount of time you spend watching television or playing video games. Replace some of these idle hours with active games and sports, and you may find you're having more fun than ever.

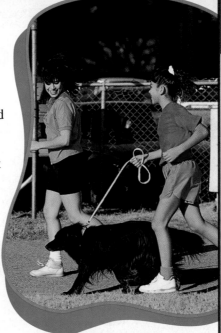

Going for a walk is an easy way to add some physical activity to your day. *What are some other ways you can be physically active every day?*

Lesson **4** Review

Using complete sentences, answer the following questions on a sheet of paper.

Reviewing Terms and Facts

1. **Vocabulary** Define the terms *strength, endurance,* and *flexibility.*
2. **Identify** What kind of exercise is best for building endurance?
3. **Describe** In a short paragraph, describe the physical, mental/emotional, and social benefits of fitness and regular exercise.

Thinking Critically

4. **Analyze** Which type of physical activity should you perform more often: lifestyle activities such as household tasks or recreational activities such as soccer? Explain why.
5. **Apply** Describe your current level of physical activity. Based on this lesson, can you use more or less activity? Explain your response.

Applying Health Skills

6. **Advocacy** Create a flyer that highlights the benefits of physical activity and encourages teens to become more physically active.

LESSON 4: THE BENEFITS OF PHYSICAL ACTIVITY **137**

Lesson 4

Brainstorming

Have students brainstorm ways they could become more physically active. You may want to have them consider alternatives to labor-saving devices such as taking the stairs instead of using the elevator. **L1**

❸ Assess

Evaluating

📁 Assign the Lesson 4 Review; then assign the Lesson 4 Quiz in the TCR.

Reteaching

- 📁 Assign Concept Map 21 or Reteaching Activity 19 in the TCR.
- Have each student list two exercises that help build each of the following: strength, endurance, and flexibility.

Enrichment

- 📂 Assign and distribute Enrichment Activity 19 in the TCR.
- Have students work in small groups to plan and create posters, skits, or dialogues that promote the benefits of physical activity and the importance of a personal exercise plan

❹ Close

Ask students to describe six reasons regular physical activity is important for their personal health.

Lesson **4** Review

1. Strength is the ability of muscles to exert a force. Endurance is how long a person can engage in physical activity without becoming overly tired. Flexibility is the ability to move body joints through a full range of motion.
2. Aerobic exercise.

3. Students' paragraphs might include increased energy and confidence, reduced stress, and opportunities for positive social interaction.
4. Responses will vary.
5. Responses will vary.

Lesson 5

Setting Fitness Goals

1 Focus

Lesson Objectives

Students will be able to

- explain how to determine their fitness goals.
- create a personal fitness plan.
- describe ways to promote safety and avoid injuries while exercising.

Motivators

Quick Write

Have students describe the physical activities and sports that they currently engage in. Discuss some of the other ideas that students listed that would help them increase their activity levels.

Bellringer Activity

Ask students to write descriptions of or sketch experiences they have had trying a sport or other physical activity for the first time. Was it hard? Confusing? Easy to do? Explain that a new skill may feel awkward, but with practice one develops muscle memory and the skill gets easier.

VOCABULARY

Ask students to write a short paragraph using each of the vocabulary words. Then have students work in pairs to read one another's paragraphs, providing peer evaluations and checking for correct usage and meaning.

Setting Fitness Goals

Quick Write

List all the ways you exercise regularly. Do you need to increase your level of activity? If so, what can you do?

LEARN ABOUT...

- how you can set goals to improve your fitness level.
- how to get the most out of exercise.
- how to avoid injuries during exercise.

VOCABULARY

- warm-up
- target pulse rate
- cool-down

Creating a Personal Fitness Plan

You can make sure that you get all the exercise and physical activity you need by creating a personal fitness or exercise plan. Having a personal exercise plan is important because it will help you achieve your goals. Before you make your plan, however, consider these questions.

- **What do you hope to accomplish?** Are you looking for muscle tone or strength, greater endurance, or increased flexibility? Maybe you have several results in mind. Determine your goals, and consider your abilities to achieve them.
- **Where should you begin?** Start small. If you've never run before, you're probably not ready to run a five-kilometer race. Begin by running short distances, for example, one city block, every other day for a week. Increase your distance gradually. You can also start by walking instead of running, then gradually increase your speed.
- **What do you enjoy?** Choose activities that you like. This will make it easier for you to meet your fitness goals.

You can reach your fitness goals if you think carefully about your exercise program before you begin. *What fitness goals are you most eager to achieve?*

138 CHAPTER 5: NUTRITION AND PHYSICAL ACTIVITY

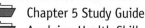

Lesson 5 Resources

Teacher Classroom Resources

- Concept Map 22
- Cross-Curriculum Activity 10
- Decision-Making Activity 10
- Enrichment Activity 20
- Lesson Plan 5
- Lesson 5 Quiz
- Reading Tutor Activity 20

- Reteaching Activity 20
- Transparency 24

Student Activities Workbook

- Chapter 5 Study Guide
- Applying Health Skills 20
- Health Inventory 5

Choosing Activities

Now that you have a clear view of your goals, you're ready to create your fitness plan. As you form your plan, you will decide which exercises to include and when you will perform them. You will also consider ways to avoid injury.

Different types of exercise will help you to meet different fitness goals. The information in **Figure 5.8** can help you choose appropriate exercises. You should also consider

- whether you want to exercise alone or with others.
- what equipment you will need.
- how much money you or your parents are willing to spend.

Discussing

Help students discuss the importance of "starting small" when creating a personal fitness or exercise plan:

- Why is it important to start small?
- Why does the definition of a small start vary from person to person? **L1**

VISUAL LEARNING

FIGURE 5.8 Direct students to study Figure 5.8. Ask:

- Which activity builds flexibility the most? (*gymnastics*)
- Which activity is rated the lowest in the two endurance categories? (*softball*)

Ask volunteers to read and answer the caption question. (Students should recognize that swimming, skating, and tennis are most effective in achieving all three goals.) Then have students discuss which activities they would choose to do and why. **INCL** *Behavior Problems, Special Learning Needs, English Language Learners*

FIGURE 5.8

Fitness Ratings for Different Activities

Different activities can promote muscular strength and endurance, heart-lung endurance, and flexibility. *Which exercises are good for achieving all three fitness goals?*

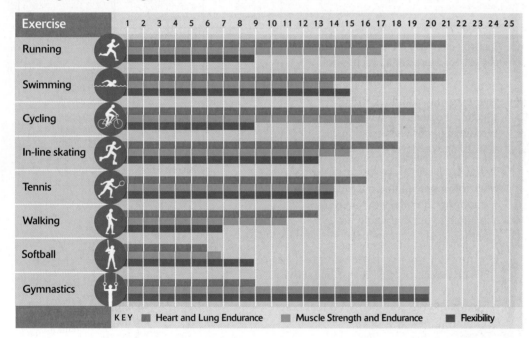

✓ Reading Check

Text Organization Have students make their own fitness plans. Have them use the headings *who, what, where, when,* and *why* to complete their fitness plans. Using "the five W's" for structure helps students organize text in a complete and concise manner. Remind the class that information from the lesson will also help them create their plans. The "who," for example, should include whether they will exercise alone, with a friend, or on a team. Also remind students that they should include several different activities for the most healthful plan and that each activity will have its own set of "the five W's." **INCL** *Special Learning Needs*

Lesson 5

Cooperative Learning

Divide students into seven groups, and assign each group one of these forms of physical activity: soccer, running, swimming, skating, baseball, basketball, and ballet. Have the members of each group work together to find out about appropriate warm-ups for the assigned activity. Then have group members demonstrate and explain the warm-ups to the rest of the class. **L2**

Demonstrating

Ask two interested volunteers to research the most effective ways for individuals to check their own pulse. Have these volunteers demonstrate the methods to the rest of the class; then help all students check their own pulse rates. **L2**

HEALTH SKILLS ACTIVITY

GOAL SETTING

Guide students in reading and discussing the ideas for increasing activity levels. Ask a volunteer to read aloud the On Your Own assignment. Draw a sample chart on the board, and let students suggest how it could be filled in.

Have students work independently to create their own charts; then let them meet with partners to compare their work and explain the importance of a personal dietary and exercise plan.

CONNECT TO
Language Arts

R.I.C.E. IS NICE
To treat a minor sports injury, remember the word *rice.* This word is an acronym (AK·roh·nim), a word formed by putting together the first letters of other words: **R**est, **I**ce, **C**ompression, and **E**levation. *How does the acronym help you remember the steps?*

Making Time for Exercise

One way to make exercise a regular part of your life is to set aside a regular time for it. For example, if you do outdoor activities, you would choose a time during the daylight hours. One time you should not exercise is right after a meal. Exercise can interfere with your digestion.

Exercising Safely

When exercising, you need to take steps to avoid injuring yourself (see **Figure 5.9**). Start with a **warm-up**, *some gentle activity that prepares your body for exercise.* Next, stretch your muscles and joints to loosen them. Then work up to your **target pulse rate**, *the level at which your heart and lungs receive the most benefit from a workout.* It is 60 to 80 percent of the heart's maximum rate, which you can estimate by subtracting your age from 220. A 12-year-old's target pulse rate is 125 to 167 beats per minute.

HEALTH SKILLS ACTIVITY

GOAL SETTING

Increasing Your Activity Level

How can busy teens find the time to get active? Here are a few possibilities.

IF YOU ARE RARELY ACTIVE, increase your everyday activities by
- taking the stairs whenever possible.
- reducing your television time.
- walking whenever you can.

IF YOU ARE ACTIVE SOME OF THE TIME, work to become more consistent by
- choosing activities you enjoy.
- planning your daily activities.
- setting goals you can meet.

IF YOU ARE ALREADY ACTIVE AT LEAST FOUR DAYS EACH WEEK, keep your activity level up by
- changing your routine if you feel bored.
- exploring new activities.

Lifestyle activity	about 1 hour every day	
Aerobic activity	about 20 minutes per week	Walk to school 2-3 times per week.
Recreational activity	soccer practice twice a week	Go skating with friends on weekend.
Flexibility and strength exercise	none	Do 10 push-ups and 10 sit-ups three days a week.
Inactivity	about 15–20 hours a week	Watch TV only 1 hour a day.

ON YOUR OWN

Draw a three-column table. In the first column, list the types of physical activity described in Lesson 4. In the second column, list the time you spend on each every week. If you fall short in any area, use the third column to list ways to improve.

140 CHAPTER 5: NUTRITION AND PHYSICAL ACTIVITY

Beyond the Classroom

Home Have students make their own long-range, personal fitness plans. Ask them to set realistic fitness goals and chart ways they plan to achieve those goals. Help students evaluate what is realistic and achievable; then ask them to take their written plans and charts home to discuss with family members. Parents and guardians should evaluate the plans with the students, asking questions like:
- Are the exercises and activities appropriate for the age and ability level?
- Are the exercises and activities practical and affordable?
- What safety equipment should be used?

Adjust for the weather. On hot, humid days, work out for a shorter time in the early morning or the evening. On cold days, wear layers of clothing to remove as you get warm. Always drink water as you exercise. Listen to your body's signals: If you feel pain, stop. End your workout with a **cool-down**—*some gentle activity to slow down after exercise*—and some more stretching.

FIGURE 5.9

TIPS FOR A SAFE WORKOUT

Following these steps will help you avoid injuries while exercising. *How many of these steps do you follow regularly?*

Exercise on soft, even surfaces.

Adjust for the weather.

Wear loose-fitting clothing.

Choose good equipment.

Drink plenty of fluids.

Lesson 5 Review

Using complete sentences, answer the following questions on a sheet of paper.

Reviewing Terms and Facts

1. **Identify** Name two good activities for building heart and lung endurance, two for building muscle strength and endurance, and two for building flexibility.
2. **Recall** Why is it unwise to exercise right after eating a meal?
3. **Vocabulary** Use the terms *warming up, target pulse rate,* and *cooling down* in an original paragraph about planning a workout. Make sure you explain the meanings of these terms in your paragraph.

Thinking Critically

4. **Explain** Why is it important to have a personal exercise plan?
5. **Describe** How can you prepare for exercise on a warm, humid day? On a cold day?

Applying Health Skills

6. **Goal Setting** Select an activity that will help meet one of your fitness goals. Write a plan that shows when and where you will do this activity. Set goals for improving your performance in this activity over a four-week period. Keep a record of your progress.

LESSON 5: SETTING FITNESS GOALS **141**

Lesson 5

VISUAL LEARNING

FIGURE 5.9 Ask volunteers to describe the picture and read the tips in Figure 5.9. Then ask them to elaborate on each tip, giving specific examples and explaining why it is important. **INCL** *Behavior Problems, Special Learning Needs, English Language Learners*

❸ Assess

Evaluating

📁 Assign the Lesson 5 Review; then assign the Lesson 5 Quiz in the TCR.

Reteaching

- 📁 Assign Concept Map 22 or Reteaching Activity 20 in the TCR.
- Ask students to identify three ways to help avoid injuries discussed in this lesson.

Enrichment

- 📁 Assign and distribute Enrichment Activity 20 in the TCR.
- Direct students to make exercise videos demonstrating various exercises with an emphasis on safety. Have them include descriptions of the mental, physical, and social benefits of regular exercise and fitness.

❹ Close

Ask students to summarize the factors to be considered in creating a personal fitness plan.

Food for Thought

① Focus

Objectives

Students will be able to

- recognize the importance of a healthy breakfast.
- interpret "healthy" words and phrases on food labels.
- analyze the nutritional value of "fortified" foods.

Motivator

Quick Write

Give students five minutes to write about the heading on this spread, "Food for Thought." What does the phrase mean? How do they think it was derived? What is the connection between food and one's ability to think? How much time do they spend each day thinking about food? Ask several students to share their work with the class.

② Teach

Discussing

Direct students' attention to quiz question #1. Ask the class: "How many of you have skipped breakfast at least once in the past month? What influenced you to skip breakfast?" Write responses on the board. Review the responses as a class, explaining that a number of factors can influence one's decision to skip breakfast: lack of time, lack of tasty breakfast options, no appetite early in the morning, and so on.

Divide the class into small groups. Direct each group to come up with a plan to combat these influences and ensure that breakfast is a pleasant and satisfying way to start the morning. (*Answers may include: set my alarm 15 minutes earlier, talk with a parent about making healthy breakfast options available, pack a healthy breakfast-to-go the night before, and so on.*)

TIME HEALTH

Food for Thought

Test your nutrition smarts by taking this quiz!

Quiz

1. Skipping breakfast can speed up metabolism and help you reduce your daily calorie intake.
   a. True   b. False

2. Which of the following can make you feel fatigued?
   a. Getting fewer than eight hours of sleep
   b. Not getting enough iron
   c. Dieting
   d. All of the above

3. Once you have reached your full height—usually between ages 14 and 18 for girls, 16 and 18 for guys—your need for bone-building calcium takes a dip.
   a. True   b. False

4. If you miss a meal, a multivitamin supplement is an acceptable substitute.
   a. True   b. False

Answers: 1. a.; 2. d.; 3. b.; 4. b.

Check out the explanations on the next page!

142 CHAPTER 5: NUTRITION AND PHYSICAL ACTIVITY

DEALING WITH SENSITIVE ISSUES

Body Image When covering the topics of nutrition and physical activity, be sure to guide students towards a healthy acceptance of their own body type and that of others.

- Do enforce all standard class rules (no put-downs, no name calling, and so on) with regard to differences in body shape and size.

- Do give students the right to pass during discussions that involve personal opinions, feelings, or experiences.

- Don't generalize about people with certain body types or eating patterns.

- Don't compare weights or other physical characteristics among students, parents, or other family members.

Label Lingo

A food product's label can be misleading. Here are explanations of some phrases that are linked to "healthy" foods.

Light or Lite These words *should* indicate one-third less calories or no more than one-half of the fat of the original product. However, both may actually refer to a product's color, sodium content, or weight—which could mean that the product is still high in fat and calories.

Low Fat Products that are low in fat usually contain 3 grams of fat or less per serving. However, they may also contain a significant amount of calories from sugar, which is used to boost the flavor that has been lost because of the lack of fat.

Reduced Fat Although these foods contain at least 25 percent less fat than the original product, the original might have contained so much fat that this reduced version still isn't healthy.

Fat-Free or Nonfat These foods have less than 0.5 grams of fat per serving. Again, however, be wary of high sugar content—consuming excess amounts of sugar can lead to unhealthful weight gain.

Explanations

1. Missing a meal can actually slow down your metabolism. Research shows that people who skip breakfast end up eating high-calorie snacks or bigger lunches and dinners. Skipping breakfast has also been linked to lower test scores. Even if you don't feel hungry in the morning, try to eat something to give your body the fuel it needs—even if it's only a cup of yogurt and a banana on the run.

2. Not getting enough sleep or food can make you weak and irritable, and so can a lack of iron. (Iron helps transport oxygen to blood cells.) Girls need 15 mg of iron daily; guys need 12 mg each day. Red meat, eggs, and dark leafy greens are your best sources of iron. You can also get this important mineral from iron-fortified cereals and breads.

3. Even when you stop growing, your bones keep strengthening through your mid-20s. They need 1,300 mg of calcium now to keep them strong in the future. Aim to get it with four servings of calcium-rich foods: Dairy products such as milk, yogurt, and cheese are your best bets. Some foods may be fortified with calcium—for example, orange juice and soy milk.

4. It's called a vitamin *supplement* for a reason: It's something to take in *addition* to—not in place of—healthy meals. Vitamins won't give you calories, carbohydrates, proteins, or fats, which you need for energy and growth. That's why it's important to eat regular meals and take a multivitamin daily to help cover any nutrients you might be missing.

TIME TO THINK...

About Nutrition

Create a class nutrition quiz. Use the information on these pages to come up with true/false statements, such as "Using the word 'light' or 'lite' always indicates that a food is good for you," or "Reduced fat means a food product must have 25 percent less fat." Have classmates choose questions at random and try to answer them.

③ Apply

Time to Think

After students have created the class nutrition quiz, gauge their reactions to the activity. Ask, "Did you enjoy working with your classmates to assess their nutrition knowledge and awareness?" Tell students that a *nutritionist* is a person who is trained in the science of nutrition. Nutritionists have a number of different job titles and work in a variety of settings such as health care, public health, food companies, colleges, health clubs, spas, schools, and government agencies. *Clinical dietitians* assess the dietary needs of patients and help them develop and maintain a healthy eating program. *Community dietitians* identify nutritional needs within a population and develop community services and programs to meet those needs. Discuss with students the types of interests, education, and experience that are required to pursue a career in nutrition.

VISUAL LEARNING

Ask students to describe the photograph on this spread. Ask, "Are these students eating a healthy meal? How many food groups do you see represented in their sandwich? What foods might they add to make this a more balanced meal?" Direct students to the issue of food handling and germs. Ask, "What might be a more hygienic way to share this sandwich?"

MORE ABOUT...

Fortified Foods What does it mean for a food to be "fortified" with a mineral? Working with a partner, have students compare and contrast a fortified food with one in which the mineral naturally occurs. For instance, is one serving of an iron-fortified cereal as nutritious as one serving of red meat or dark leafy greens? Does orange juice fortified with calcium offer as much calcium as a glass of milk? Give students several days to conduct their research and share their findings with the class.

DECISION MAKING

Objective

After completing the lesson, students will be able to demonstrate how to use the decision-making process to choose an after-school snack.

Time: 45 minutes

Materials: notebook paper, pencil or pen

Teacher Classroom Resources

📁 Building Health Skills Activities

• Transparency Master 8, "Decision Making"

• Reproducible Master 5, "Fueling Your Body"

---

1. Model

• Display Transparency Master 8, and review the six steps of the decision-making process with the class.

• Have students read how Paola uses the decision-making process to make a choice about lunch.

• Discuss reasons why the burrito was the best choice for Paola.

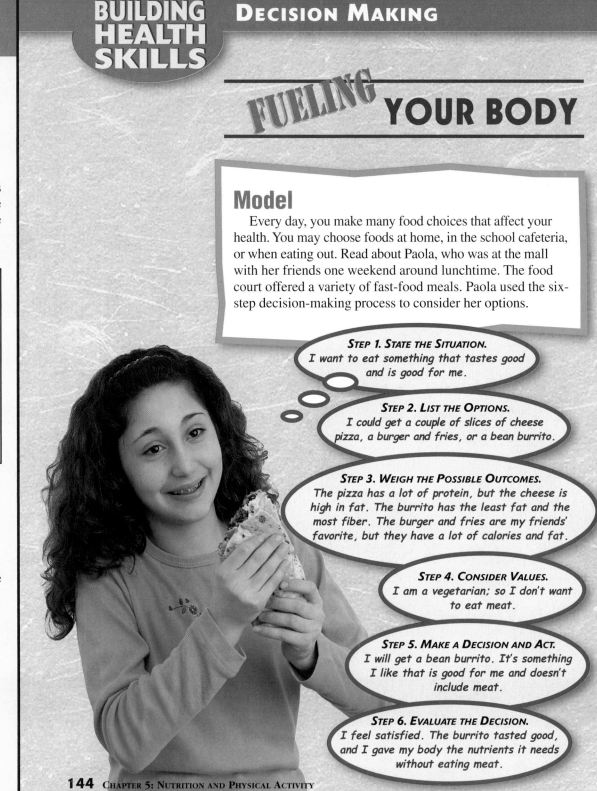

BUILDING HEALTH SKILLS — DECISION MAKING

FUELING YOUR BODY

Model

Every day, you make many food choices that affect your health. You may choose foods at home, in the school cafeteria, or when eating out. Read about Paola, who was at the mall with her friends one weekend around lunchtime. The food court offered a variety of fast-food meals. Paola used the six-step decision-making process to consider her options.

STEP 1. STATE THE SITUATION.
I want to eat something that tastes good and is good for me.

STEP 2. LIST THE OPTIONS.
I could get a couple of slices of cheese pizza, a burger and fries, or a bean burrito.

STEP 3. WEIGH THE POSSIBLE OUTCOMES.
The pizza has a lot of protein, but the cheese is high in fat. The burrito has the least fat and the most fiber. The burger and fries are my friends' favorite, but they have a lot of calories and fat.

STEP 4. CONSIDER VALUES.
I am a vegetarian; so I don't want to eat meat.

STEP 5. MAKE A DECISION AND ACT.
I will get a bean burrito. It's something I like that is good for me and doesn't include meat.

STEP 6. EVALUATE THE DECISION.
I feel satisfied. The burrito tasted good, and I gave my body the nutrients it needs without eating meat.

144 CHAPTER 5: NUTRITION AND PHYSICAL ACTIVITY

Teaching Tips

Internet Resources You may wish to direct students to use the Internet to access the nutritional value of fast foods. For example, ask students to try typing the phrase "fast-food nutrition information" into a search engine. The search should return several sites that provide this information in a simple-to-use format. Students can also search under the name of a fast-food restaurant of their choice to get more detailed information.

Practice

Antonio is late and has to eat on the run. In the kitchen he finds granola bars, peanut butter crackers, raisins, and string cheese. He wants something that is filling (contains protein) and provides energy (carbohydrates) but is low in fat. Look at the four food labels on this page. Each label provides information for one serving. Write out the decision-making steps on a sheet of paper to help Antonio choose a snack.

Apply/Assess

Imagine that you are hungry for an after-school snack. There are four snack foods that you like: granola bars, peanut butter crackers, raisins, and string cheese. Take another look at the nutrition labels on this page. Use critical-thinking skills to evaluate this health information. This time, think about what you usually eat for breakfast and at school. How many servings from each food group have you already consumed? Which of these snacks come from the food group(s) that you still need? Write your decision-making steps on a sheet of paper. Be prepared to justify your choice.

Decision Making

1. State the situation.
2. List the options.
3. Weigh the possible outcomes.
4. Consider values.
5. Make a decision and act.
6. Evaluate the decision.

Self-Check

- Did I consider each snack choice?
- Can I justify my decision?

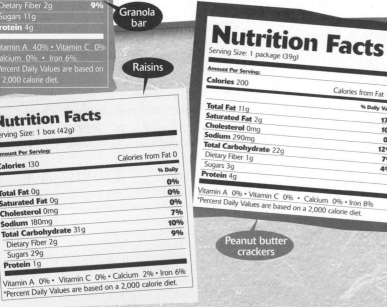

Nutrition Facts
Serving Size: 2 bars (42g)

Amount Per Serving:

Calories 180 Calories from Fat 60

	% Daily Value*
Total Fat 6g	10%
Saturated Fat 0.5g	3%
Cholesterol 0mg	0%
Sodium 160mg	7%
Total Carbohydrate 29g	10%
Dietary Fiber 2g	9%
Sugars 11g	
Protein 4g	

Vitamin A 40% • Vitamin C 0%
Calcium 0% • Iron 6%
*Percent Daily Values are based on a 2,000 calorie diet.

Granola bar

Raisins

Nutrition Facts
Serving Size: 1 box (42g)

Amount Per Serving:

Calories 130 Calories from Fat 0

	% Daily
	0%
Total Fat 0g	0%
Saturated Fat 0g	0%
Cholesterol 0mg	7%
Sodium 180mg	10%
Total Carbohydrate 31g	9%
Dietary Fiber 2g	
Sugars 29g	
Protein 1g	

Vitamin A 0% • Vitamin C 0% • Calcium 2% • Iron 6%
*Percent Daily Values are based on a 2,000 calorie diet.

Nutrition Facts
Serving Size: 1 package (39g)

Amount Per Serving:

Calories 200

Calories from Fat 100

	% Daily Value*
Total Fat 11g	17%
Saturated Fat 2g	10%
Cholesterol 0mg	0%
Sodium 290mg	12%
Total Carbohydrate 22g	7%
Dietary Fiber 1g	4%
Sugars 3g	
Protein 4g	

Vitamin A 0% • Vitamin C 0% • Calcium 0% • Iron 8%
*Percent Daily Values are based on a 2,000 calorie diet.

Peanut butter crackers

Nutrition Facts
Serving Size: 1 piece (24g)

Amount Per Serving:

Calories 70 Calories from Fat 45

	7%
Total Fat 5g	15%
Saturated Fat 3g	5%
Cholesterol 15mg	7%
Sodium 180mg	0%
Total Carbohydrate less than 1g	0%
Dietary Fiber 0g	
Sugars 0g	
Protein 6g	

Vitamin A 4% • Vitamin C 0%
Calcium 15% • Iron 0%
*Percent Daily Values are based on a 2,000 calorie diet.

String cheese

2. Practice

- Review nutrition information that is included on food labels with the class.
- Instruct students to work in small groups to choose a snack for Antonio.
- Have groups explain their snack choices to the class.

3. Apply/Assess

- You may wish to distribute Building Health Skills Reproducible Master 5 in the TCR to guide students in completing this activity.
- Have students list the foods they typically eat for breakfast and at school. Instruct them to classify these foods according to the food groups found in the Food Guide Pyramid.
- Instruct students to use the decision-making process to choose a snack item. The choice should supply the food group(s) they need most.
- Provide an opportunity for students to explain their snack choices to others in the class.

Assessment Scoring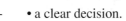

Using a rubric, student work should provide evidence of all criteria to achieve the highest score.

Skills

Student work demonstrates

- a clear statement of the situation.
- evaluation of options.
- consideration of values.
- a clear decision.
- reflection on the decision.

Concept

Student work provides

- accurate information about food groups.
- an explanation of the relationship between food groups and a healthful eating plan.

Checking Comprehension

Use the Chapter 5 Assessment to examine the most important ideas presented in the chapter.

Answers to Reviewing Vocabulary and Concepts

Lesson 1
1. nutrients
2. fat
3. vitamins
4. minerals

Lesson 2
5. vegetable
6. grains
7. calcium
8. sweets

Lesson 3
9. false; calcium
10. false; cholesterol
11. true
12. true
13. false; bulimia

Lesson 4
14. true
15. false; aerobic
16. true
17. true
18. false; decrease

Lesson 5
19. false; warm-up
20. false; after
21. true
22. true

Thinking Critically

23. Possible response: Poor body image may be caused by negative peer or media influences; effects may include the development of eating disorders.
24. Foods in the Fats, Oils, and Sweets group are low in nutrients.

146

After You Read

Use your completed Foldable to review the information on the different types of nutrients.

FOLDABLES™
Study Organizer

Reviewing Vocabulary and Concepts

On a sheet of paper, write the numbers 1–8. After each number, write the term from the list that best completes each statement.

- calcium
- fat
- grains
- minerals
- nutrients
- sweets
- vegetable
- vitamins

Lesson 1

1. Carbohydrates, proteins, and fats are all types of _____.
2. _____ is a nutrient that provides energy, carries vitamins, and helps keep your skin healthy.
3. Nutrients that help regulate body functions are called _____.
4. Elements that help your body work properly are _____.

Lesson 2

5. You need to eat 3 to 5 servings each day from the _____ Group.
6. Foods in the Bread, Cereal, Rice, and Pasta Group are made from _____.
7. Foods in the Milk, Yogurt, and Cheese Group are a good source of the mineral _____.
8. It is best to eat only small amounts of fats, oils, and _____.

On a sheet of paper, write the numbers 9–22. Write *True* or *False* for each statement below. If the statement is false, change the underlined word or phrase to make it true.

Lesson 3

9. Sodium is a mineral that helps your body build healthy teeth and bones.
10. Consuming too much saturated fat can increase your body's level of <u>calcium</u>.
11. The energy available in foods is measured in <u>calories</u>.
12. Eating less <u>saturated fat</u> is a good way to reduce the risk of heart disease.
13. People with the eating disorder <u>anorexia</u> eat large amounts of food and then purge by vomiting or using laxatives.

Lesson 4

14. Pushing or pulling against a force such as gravity builds <u>strength</u>.
15. You can build endurance by engaging in <u>anaerobic</u> exercise.
16. The ability to move body joints through a full range of motion is called <u>flexibility</u>.
17. You can become physically fit by <u>exercising</u>.
18. To stay healthy and fit, you should <u>increase</u> the amount of time you spend sitting still.

Lesson 5

19. A gentle activity that prepares the body for exercise is called a <u>cool-down</u>.
20. When exercising, you should always stretch <u>before</u> you warm up.
21. Your target pulse rate is <u>60 to 80 percent</u> of your heart's maximum rate.
22. It is best to wear <u>loose-fitting</u> clothing when exercising.

INCLUSION STRATEGIES

Special Learning Needs, Behavior Problems, English Language Learners The following suggestions are helpful for students with special learning needs, students with behavior problems, and ELL students:

- Pair these students with more proficient learners who can help summarize the main concepts of the chapter.

- 🎧 Direct these students to listen to the Teen Health Audio Summaries. This component provides an audio and written summary of the chapter in both English and Spanish.

- Use photographs, drawings, or magazine clippings whenever possible to help students visualize the important concepts of the chapter.

Thinking Critically

Using complete sentences, answer the following questions on a sheet of paper.

23. Identify What are some causes and effects associated with poor body image?

24. Explain Why does the Food Guide Pyramid recommend only small amounts from the Fats, Oils, and Sweets group?

25. Analyze If you skipped breakfast every day for a week, how might it affect your schoolwork?

26. Suggest Why does choosing activities you enjoy make it easier to meet your fitness goals?

Career Corner

Dietetic Technician Are you the one who helps plan family meals at your house? Are you concerned about people getting proper nutrition? Then you might enjoy a career as a dietetic technician. You need a two-year associate degree and internship training to become licensed. Then you could be assisting a dietitian to help people plan balanced diets. You might volunteer for a community Meals on Wheels program to prepare for this career. Visit Career Corner at health.glencoe.com to find out more about this and other health careers.

Standardized Test Practice

Reading & Writing

Read the paragraphs below and then answer the questions.

What's the difference between true hunger and a craving? When you are truly hungry, your stomach may growl, and you may have hunger pains. These are signs of your body's physical need for food. A craving is different from hunger—it's a desire for a certain type of food.

Most people have cravings for certain foods from time to time. Research has shown that commonly craved foods include chocolate and other sweets, such as cookies, cake, and ice cream. People may also crave foods that are high in fat and salt, such as potato chips, even when they are getting an adequate amount of these nutrients in their diets.

1. The first paragraph is important to the passage because it

  A compares hunger and cravings.

  B gives examples of cravings.

  C describes hunger pains.

  D contrasts types of snacks.

2. What is the second paragraph of the passage mainly about?

  A the effects of cravings

  B what to do about cravings

  C the causes of cravings

  D different types of cravings

3. Write a paragraph describing the types of foods you crave. Explain why you crave them and/or what may trigger the craving.

 TH05_C1.glencoe.com/quiz

---

25. You would probably do poorly in school because you would have difficulty concentrating.

26. When you enjoy your activities, you are more likely to stick to your personal fitness plan.

Test Practice

1. A

2. D

3. Responses will vary, but should identify specific foods and include descriptions of why the student craves them.

Reteaching

📁 Assign Study Guide 5 in the Student Activities Workbook.

Evaluate

• 📁 💿 Use the reproducible Chapter 5 Test in the TCR, or construct your own test using the **Exam***View*® Pro Testmaker.

• 📁 Use Performance Assessment 5 in the TCR.

Enrichment

Have students create a class cookbook and exercise book entitled *Food and Fitness: A Guide for Teens.* Ask each student to contribute one proven, nutritious recipe and one exercise to the book.

Assessment ✔

Self-Assessment Direct students to review the activities that are provided throughout the chapter. Encourage each student to select one finished product or activity that demonstrates his or her best work for the chapter. Have students explain what they learned and how the examples they selected show their progress.

Career Corner

Dietetic Technician After reviewing the career profile on the health Web site, students might

• describe the skills, training, and education needed.

• write a classified ad for a job in the field.

Planning Guide

Chapter 6	Skills/Activities	Reproducible Resources	Assessment
Lesson 1 **From Cells to Body Systems** *pages 150–153*	HEALTH SKILLS ACTIVITY ▲ Caring for Your Body Systems (*Practicing Healthful Behaviors*), page 152	*Student Activities Workbook available for use with each chapter* 📁 Parent Letter & Activities 6 📁 Concept Map 23 📁 Decision-Making Activity 11 📁 Enrichment Activity 21 📁 Lesson Plan 1 📁 Reading Tutor Activity 21 📁 Reteaching Activity 21	📁 Lesson 1 Quiz
Lesson 2 **Bones, Muscles, Blood, and Lungs** *pages 154–160*		📁 Concept Maps 24, 25, 26 📁 Decision-Making Activity 12 📁 Enrichment Activity 22 📁 Lesson Plan 2 📁 Reading Tutor Activity 22 📁 Reteaching Activities 22, 23	📁 Lesson 2 Quiz
Lesson 3 **Nerves and Digestion** *pages 161–164*		📁 Concept Maps 27, 28 📁 Cross-Curriculum Activity 11 📁 Enrichment Activity 23 📁 Health Lab 6 📁 Lesson Plan 3 📁 Reading Tutor Activity 23 📁 Reteaching Activity 24	📁 Lesson 3 Quiz
Lesson 4 **Adolescence: A Time of Change** *pages 165–169*	Hands-On Health ▲ Looking Ahead, page 168	📁 Concept Map 29 📁 Cross-Curriculum Activity 12 📁 Enrichment Activity 24 📁 Lesson Plan 4 📁 Reading Tutor Activity 24 📁 Reteaching Activity 25	📁 Lesson 4 Quiz
Lesson 5 **Heredity and Growth** *pages 170–173*	HEALTH SKILLS ACTIVITY ▲ The Health of Mother and Child (*Advocacy*), page 171	📁 Concept Map 30 📁 Enrichment Activity 25 📁 Lesson Plan 5 📁 Reading Tutor Activity 25 📁 Reteaching Activity 26	📁 Lesson 5 Quiz 📁 Chapter 6 Test 📁 Performance Assessment 6

TIME HEALTH   **Are You Active Enough?** *pages 174–175*

BUILDING HEALTH SKILLS

Keeping Body Systems Healthy
(*Practicing Healthful Behaviors*)
pages 176–177

📁 Building Health Skills Reproducible Master 6

Standards		Technology
National	**State/Local**	
National Health Education Standard **1.1, 1.3, 1.6, 3.1**		Transparency 25 TeacherWorks™ Internet Activities
National Health Education Standard **1.1, 1.3**		Transparency 26 TeacherWorks™
National Health Education Standard **1.3, 1.6, 3.4**		Transparencies 27 & 28 TeacherWorks™
National Health Education Standard **1.2, 1.3, 4.1, 4.2, 4.4, 5.1, 5.4**		Transparency 29 TeacherWorks™
National Health Education Standard **1.1, 1.3, 2.6, 3.1, 7.1, 7.4**		Transparency 30 TeacherWorks™ MindJogger Videoquiz **Exam***View*® Pro Testmaker
National Health Education Standard **1.1, 3.1, 3.4, 3.5**		Building Health Skills Transparency Master 2a

TeacherWorks™

Glencoe's new and exclusive TeacherWorks™ is an all-in-one planner and resource center. Access the complete Teacher Wraparound Edition electronically. Find all your classroom resources with just a few easy clicks, and print them right from your computer. Connect directly to Glencoe's customized Health Web site. Access the National Health Education Standards correlations, or insert your own state standards and match them directly to the electronic Teacher Wraparound Edition.

Language Diversity

- English Audio Summaries
- Spanish Audio Summaries
- English Summaries, Quizzes, and Activities
- Spanish Summaries, Quizzes, and Activities
- Spanish Parent Letters and Activities

KEY TO ABILITY LEVELS

Teaching Strategies that appear throughout the chapters have been identified by one of four codes to give you an idea of their suitability for students of varying learning styles and abilities.

L1 **Level 1** strategies should be within the ability range of all students. Often full class participation is required.

L2 **Level 2** strategies are for average to above-average students or for small groups. Some teacher direction is necessary.

L3 **Level 3** strategies are designed for students able and willing to work independently. Minimal teacher direction is necessary.

INCL Strategies are appropriate for students with particular special needs in a general classroom setting.

Growth and Development

Chapter at a Glance

Lesson 1 describes the building blocks of the human body, from cells to body systems, and how body systems work together.

Lesson 2 describes the function and structure of the skeletal, muscular, circulatory, and respiratory systems.

Lesson 3 describes the function and structure of the nervous, digestive, and excretory systems.

Lesson 4 describes the function and structure of the endocrine system. It also emphasizes the physical, mental/emotional, and social changes that occur during adolescence.

Lesson 5 identifies the process of heredity, how a baby develops, and stages in the life cycle.

Health Skills
- Caring for Your Body Systems (*Practicing Healthful Behaviors*), p. 152
- The Health of Mother and Child (*Advocacy*), p. 171
- Keeping Body Systems Healthy (*Practicing Healthful Behaviors*), pp. 176–177

CHAPTER

6

148

HANDS-ON ACTIVITY

Beach Ball Pass This chapter introduces many parts and functions of the human body as well as discusses growth and development. To find out how much your class already knows, pass a beach ball, or other soft object like a beanbag, to various students around the room. When a student catches the ball, ask a question related to the chapter. Have him or her answer the question while tossing the ball back to you. Possible questions include: What are some parts of your body? Can you name any body systems? What pumps your blood through your body? Which organ in your body controls your thoughts and actions? What changes occur during adolescence? (See Figure 6.11, page 167.) How are you like or different from adults? Make sure every student gets a chance to answer a question.

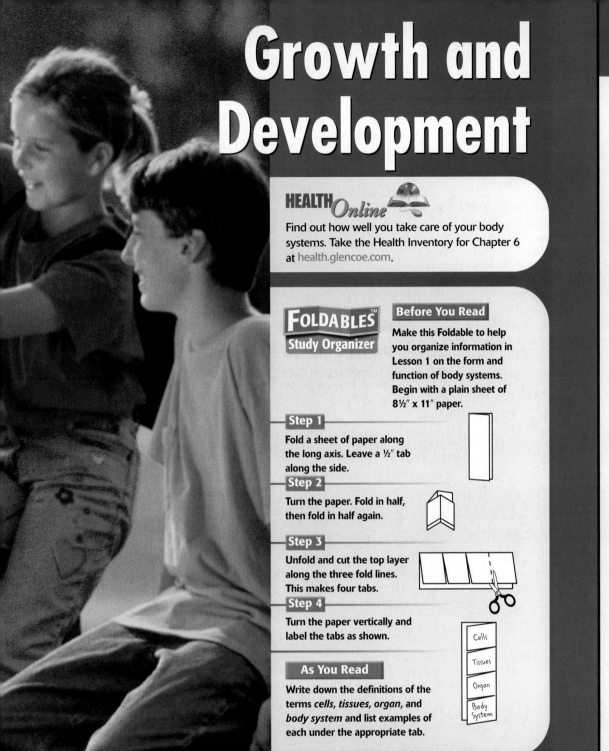

Growth and Development

HEALTH *Online*

Find out how well you take care of your body systems. Take the Health Inventory for Chapter 6 at health.glencoe.com.

FOLDABLES™ Study Organizer

Before You Read

Make this Foldable to help you organize information in Lesson 1 on the form and function of body systems. Begin with a plain sheet of 8½″ x 11″ paper.

Step 1

Fold a sheet of paper along the long axis. Leave a ½″ tab along the side.

Step 2

Turn the paper. Fold in half, then fold in half again.

Step 3

Unfold and cut the top layer along the three fold lines. This makes four tabs.

Step 4

Turn the paper vertically and label the tabs as shown.

Cells
Tissues
Organ
Body System

As You Read

Write down the definitions of the terms *cells*, *tissues*, *organ*, and *body system* and list examples of each under the appropriate tab.

149

Chapter Introduction

Use the options below to motivate students and preview chapter content.

HEALTH *Online*

Visit **health.glencoe.com**, and have students complete Health Inventory 6 to test their knowledge of the body. For other teaching strategies, explore the Lesson Plans and select from Cross-Curriculum, Reading, or Media Literacy activities

GLENCOE TECHNOLOGY

MindJogger Videoquiz

Use MindJogger to preview or review Chapter 6 content.

TIME HEALTH

Are You Active Enough?
pages 174–175

FOLDABLES™ Study Organizer

Dinah Zike Study Fold

Organizing Data and Expository Writing Direct students to use their completed Foldable to define the terms and give examples of each. At the end of the lesson, ask students to use their notes to write an exposition on body systems. The focus of this assignment should be to present information in such a manner that someone who did not know or understand body systems before will understand them after reading students' essays. Explain to students that textbooks are examples of expository writing.

Lesson 1

From Cells to Body Systems

1 Focus

Lesson Objectives

Students will be able to

- distinguish among cells, tissues, organs, and body systems.
- identify and describe the functions of the major body systems.
- describe how body systems work together.

Health Skills
- Practicing Healthful Behaviors, p. 152

Motivators

Quick Write
Allow several students to share their responses. List the identified parts on the board. Tell students they will be learning about some of the parts that cannot be seen with the naked eye.

Bellringer Activity
Ask students to identify as many body organs as they can in five minutes. Then ask: What do all organs have in common?

VOCABULARY

Write each of the vocabulary terms on the board. Have students look up each term in the Glossary at the back of the student text. Ask students to write sentences for each term, defining the term in their own words.

Lesson 1

From Cells to Body Systems

Quick Write
Look at your hand as you make a fist, then release it. What do you see? Try to name the parts you see working together.

LEARN ABOUT...

- the relationship between cells, tissues, organs, and body systems.
- the names and functions of the major body systems.
- how body systems work together.

VOCABULARY

- cells
- tissues
- organ
- body system

Cells: The Building Blocks

Your entire body is made up of tiny units called cells. Your body contains many different kinds of cells, which vary in size and shape. Each type of cell does a special job. For example, nerve cells carry messages between your brain and other parts of your body. As **Figure 6.1** shows, nerve cells are long

FIGURE 6.1

FROM CELL TO SYSTEM

The body system shown here is the nervous system. Notice how the complex system begins with cells, the body's basic units.

A Cells are *the basic building blocks of life.* Each cell in your body does a particular job. Nerve cells, like the ones shown here, carry messages to and from your brain.

B Tissues are *groups of similar cells that do the same kind of work.* The tissue shown here is made of clusters of nerve cells.

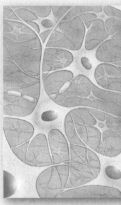

Lesson 1 Resources

Teacher Classroom Resources

- Parent Letter & Activities 6
- Concept Map 23
- Decision-Making Activity 11
- Enrichment Activity 21
- Lesson Plan 1
- Lesson 1 Quiz

- Reading Tutor Activity 21
- Reteaching Activity 21
- Transparency 25

Student Activities Workbook
- Chapter 6 Study Guide
- Applying Health Skills 21

and narrow, like electrical wires, so they can carry messages. Skin cells, on the other hand, are flat and rectangular so they can spread out to cover the surface of your body.

Systems: Parts of a Whole You

In many ways, your body is like a machine. The cells that make up your body combine to form larger structures called tissues, organs, and body systems. All of these parts work together to allow your body to function. **Figure 6.1** shows how cells combine to form the parts of a body system.

How Systems Are Organized

The parts of the body systems are organized by what they do, not by their location in your body. For example, the mouth and the small intestine are far apart, yet both are key parts of the digestive system. Some organs belong to more than one body system.

Reading Check

Make a four-column chart. List the vocabulary words in the left column. Above the empty columns, write the headings *K* (Know), *W* (Want to Know), and *L* (Learned). Fill in columns *K* and *W*. As you read, fill in column *L*.

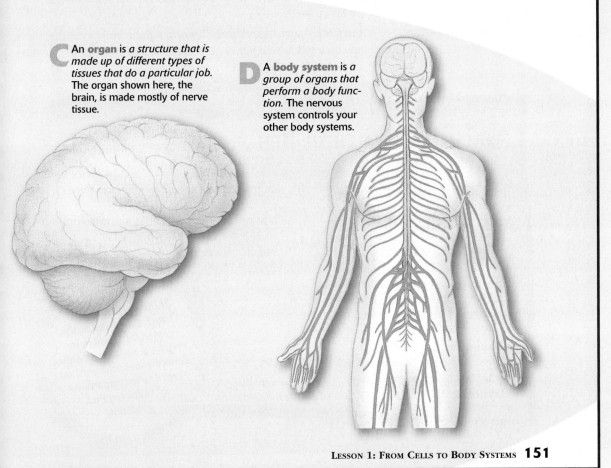

C An **organ** is *a structure that is made up of different types of tissues that do a particular job.* The organ shown here, the brain, is made mostly of nerve tissue.

D A **body system** is *a group of organs that perform a body function.* The nervous system controls your other body systems.

LESSON 1: FROM CELLS TO BODY SYSTEMS **151**

② Teach

VISUAL LEARNING

FIGURE 6.1 Have a volunteer read aloud the title and the caption for Figure 6.1. Then guide students in reading and discussing the explanation of cells, tissues, organs, and body systems. Emphasize that the nervous system shown here is an example; all body systems are composed of these same elements. **INCL** *Behavior Problems, Special Learning Needs, English Language Learners*

Discussing

To help students understand cells in the human body, ask questions such as these:

- How are the cells that make up a muscle similar to the cells in the stomach?
- How are those two kinds of cells different? **L1**

Cross-Curriculum Activity

SCIENCE Remind students that all living things, plants and animals, are composed of one or more cells. Partner with a science teacher, or borrow a few microscopes, and set up stations in the classroom. Have interested students use microscopes to examine the cells in onion skin. Ask them to sketch what they see and to share their drawings with the rest of the class. **L3**

✔ Reading Check

K-W-L Making a *K-W-L* chart activates prior knowledge. This simple technique will help students organize their preconceived ideas and new knowledge. To model the first two steps of this approach, draw a chart on the board, labeled *K* (Know), *W* (Want to Know), and *L* (Learned). Demonstrate this technique with this lesson.

Once the students have completed the *K* and *W* portions of the chart, read the lesson with them and have them complete the *L* column. Next, have the students apply this technique to the chapter. Ask them to consider the term *body systems*. Be sure to clarify that body systems are interrelated.

Lesson 1

Discussing

Lead a discussion about the relationships among the various body systems. Ask questions such as these:

- In what ways do the skeletal and muscular systems work together?
- How are the circulatory and respiratory systems interrelated? **L1**

Cross-Curriculum Activity

LANGUAGE ARTS Have students write expository paragraphs explaining why knowing how the systems of the body are interrelated is important. **L1**

HEALTH SKILLS ACTIVITY

PRACTICING HEALTHFUL BEHAVIORS

Help students read and discuss each guideline:

- How does this behavior support all three sides of the health triangle?
- What factors might make it hard for teens to practice this behavior?

Then have students work in groups to prepare, practice, and present their own public service announcements.

Note: This skill is introduced in Chapter 1 on page 10.

CONNECT TO

Language Arts

USING CORRECT TERMS
It's important to learn and use the correct terminology for body parts and systems. This not only enhances your health knowledge, it can also help you communicate effectively with health care providers. *Give another example of how using the correct terminology for parts of the body might benefit your health.*

Relationships Among Body Systems

Body systems are interrelated. This means that they work together and depend on one another to keep the body functioning well. The digestive and excretory systems work as a team to first break down food for energy (digestive), and then get rid of wastes (excretory). The circulatory system takes this energy and carries it to cells throughout the body. Some of the body systems and their functions within the body are listed below.

- **The skeletal and muscular systems** work together to support and move the body and protect organs.
- **The circulatory system** brings food and oxygen to cells and takes wastes away.
- **The respiratory system** carries oxygen to blood and removes carbon dioxide.
- **The nervous system** controls all body system; sends and receives messages; and helps you see, hear, taste, smell, and feel.
- **The digestive and excretory systems** break down food for energy and get rid of wastes.
- **The endocrine system** produces hormones that regulate body functions.

Figure 6.2 shows the relationships among the body systems and how they work together to help a runner perform well.

HEALTH SKILLS ACTIVITY

PRACTICING HEALTHFUL BEHAVIORS

Caring for Your Body Systems

For good health, follow these guidelines.

- **GET PLENTY OF REST.** Rest helps muscles recover from physical activity and reduces mental stress.
- **EAT HEALTHFUL FOODS AND DRINK PLENTY OF WATER.** Good nutrition aids digestion and helps keep muscles and bones strong. Water feeds all cells and helps eliminate wastes.
- **AVOID ALCOHOL, TOBACCO, AND OTHER DRUGS.** Chemicals in drugs can damage all of your body's systems.
- **STAY ACTIVE.** Regular physical activity helps the heart and circulation and keeps muscles strong.
- **USE GOOD POSTURE.** Sitting and standing straight helps lungs function and keeps muscles in shape.

WITH A GROUP
Choose one of the health guidelines listed here. Prepare a 30-second public service announcement that explains the importance of following this guideline.

152 CHAPTER 6: GROWTH AND DEVELOPMENT

Health Literacy

Health Information When a major organ, such as the heart or liver, stops working properly, the result can be serious, even fatal. Thanks to medical technology, however, some diseased or damaged organs can be replaced with healthy ones. Have students share what they know about organ transplants. What organs can be transplanted successfully? (e.g., *cornea, kidney, heart*) Ask volunteers to bring in magazine and newspaper articles about organ donors and transplants. Encourage a discussion of some of the issues and questions that arise concerning organ transplants. For instance, who decides who will get a heart when many may be waiting? Allow for many points of view.

FIGURE 6.2

HOW BODY SYSTEMS ARE RELATED

Each body system depends on the others to do its job effectively. ***How many body systems are active when this teen runs?***

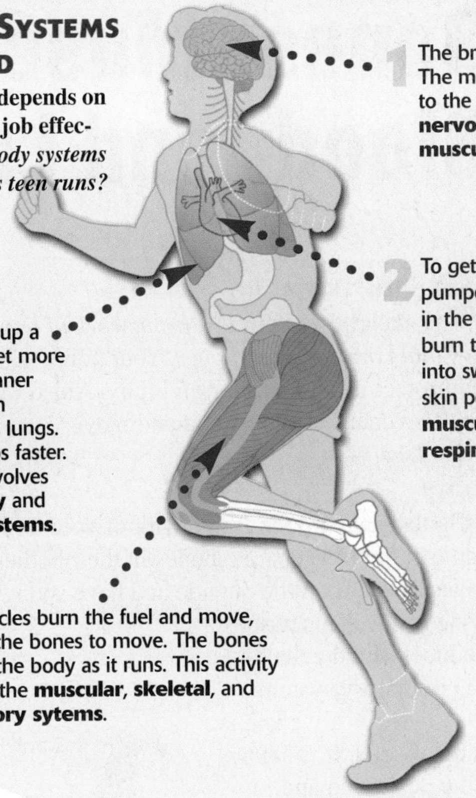

1 The brain sends out a message: Run! The message is carried through nerves to the muscles. This step involves the **nervous system** and the **muscular system**.

2 To get energy, muscles need blood that is pumped by the heart. Blood contains fuel in the form of sugar as well as oxygen to burn that fuel. As blood flows, wastes pass into sweat glands that release them through skin pores. These processes involve the **muscular, circulatory, digestive, respiratory,** and **excretory systems.**

3 The muscles burn the fuel and move, causing the bones to move. The bones support the body as it runs. This activity involves the **muscular**, **skeletal**, and **circulatory sytems**.

4 Running burns up a lot of fuel. To get more oxygen, the runner gasps for breath provided by his lungs. His heart pumps faster. This process involves the **respiratory** and **circulatory systems**.

Lesson 1 Review

Using complete sentences, answer the following questions on a sheet of paper.

Reviewing Terms and Facts

1. **Vocabulary** Define the word *tissue*.
2. **Describe** How are the parts of a body system organized?
3. **Recall** Which body system carries food and oxygen to cells?

Thinking Critically

4. **Compare** Think about the different body systems identified in this lesson. Which do you seem to have control over? Which seem to work by themselves?
5. **Analyze** Name two or three body systems, and analyze the relationships among these systems.

Applying Health Skills

6. **Goal Setting** Review the guidelines in the Health Skills Activity for keeping your body systems functioning properly. Choose one guideline you think you could follow better than you do now. List some specific steps you could take every day to follow the guideline.

Lesson 1

VISUAL LEARNING

FIGURE 6.2 Discuss the four steps explained in Figure 6.2 and have students answer the question (*nervous, muscular, circulatory, digestive, respiratory, excretory, and skeletal systems*). **INCL** *Behavior Problems, Special Learning Needs, English Language Learners*

3 Assess

Evaluating

Assign the Lesson 1 Review; then assign the Lesson 1 Quiz in the TCR.

Reteaching

Assign Concept Map 23 or Reteaching Activity 21 in the TCR.

Enrichment

- Assign Enrichment Activity 21 in the TCR.
- Have students conduct research to compare healthy and unhealthy cell growth in the disease process and the factors that affect each type of growth. Have students prepare posters or other visuals documenting their research.

4 Close

Ask students to explain the makeup of the nervous system. Then have them explain how other body systems are similarly constructed.

Lesson 1 Review

1. Cells that do similar jobs.
2. The parts of a body system are organized by what they do, not by their location in the body.
3. The circulatory system.
4. Possible responses: They have control over the skeletal and muscular systems, while the circulatory and digestive systems work by themselves. They may say that the respiratory system, the nervous system, and the excretory system are only partially controlled.
5. Responses will vary, but should correctly describe the interrelationships of two or more body systems.

Lesson 2

Bones, Muscles, Blood, and Lungs

1 Focus

Lesson Objectives

Students will be able to

• describe the structures of the skeletal and muscular systems and how the two systems support and move the body.

• describe the structure and function of the circulatory system.

• describe the structure and function of the respiratory system.

Motivators

Quick Write
Ask students to identify the body systems used to perform each action. Clarify any misconceptions.

Bellringer Activity

Ask students to think about what their bodies would look like without bones or muscles. (Note: a mound of gelatin dessert on a plate is a good visual.) Then have them identify how their body functions and actions might be affected.

VOCABULARY

Have each student write the vocabulary terms on a large sheet of paper. Next to each word, have students write its definition. Then ask students to create a rough diagram of each term or concept to illustrate each.

Lesson 2

Bones, Muscles, Blood, and Lungs

Quick Write

Take a deep breath; blow it out. Stretch your arms above your head. Shake hands with the person next to you. List the body systems you think you are using to perform these actions.

LEARN ABOUT...

• how the skeletal and muscular systems support and move your body.

• how the circulatory system moves blood throughout your body.

• how the respiratory system works to help you breathe.

VOCABULARY

• skeletal system
• joints
• muscular system
• circulatory system
• heart
• blood pressure
• respiratory system
• lungs
• diaphragm

The Skeletal System

The **skeletal system** is *a framework of bones and the tissues that connect those bones.* Your bones support your body and protect its soft parts from injury. Aided by your muscles, they also enable you to stand and move.

Bones

Bones make up the framework of your body. Adults have 206 separate bones in their bodies. Bones are hard on the outside and have spongy tissue inside. This tissue produces blood cells for the circulatory system. Bone tissue is alive and is made of cells. It is always being destroyed and re-made, especially while you are still growing.

Your skeletal system supports your body, allowing you to stand and walk. *Why might this gymnast be especially concerned about taking care of her bones and joints?*

Lesson 2 Resources

Teacher Classroom Resources

 Concept Maps 24, 25 & 26

Decision-Making Activity 12

Enrichment Activity 22

Lesson Plan 2

Lesson 2 Quiz

Reading Tutor Activity 22

Reteaching Activities 22 & 23

Transparency 26

Student Activities Workbook

Chapter 6 Study Guide

Applying Health Skills 22

Joints

Joints are *places where one bone meets another.* Different joints move in different ways. A pivot joint, like your neck, consists of the end of one bone rotating inside a ring formed by another. It can move up and down and from side to side. A hinge joint moves in only one direction, like a door hinge. Your knee is an example. A ball-and-socket joint, like your hip, consists of a round end of one bone moving inside the cup-shaped socket of another. It can move in all directions. See **Figure 6.3** for an illustration of important bones in your body and the three major types of joints.

FIGURE 6.3

THE SKELETAL SYSTEM

This skeleton shows some of the important bones found in your body and illustrates three major types of joints. *What type of joint is the hip joint?*

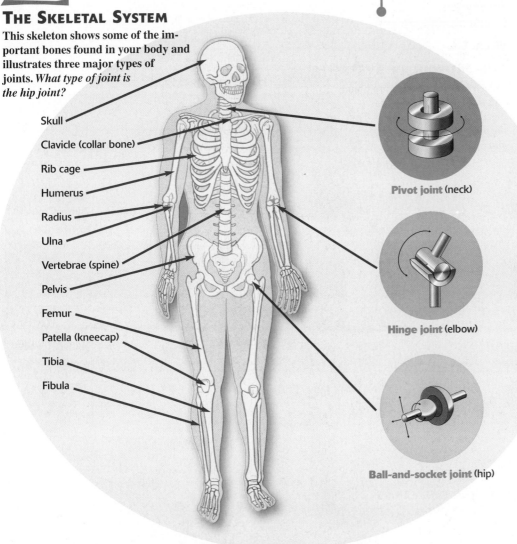

Skull
Clavicle (collar bone)
Rib cage
Humerus
Radius
Ulna
Vertebrae (spine)
Pelvis
Femur
Patella (kneecap)
Tibia
Fibula

Pivot joint (neck)

Hinge joint (elbow)

Ball-and-socket joint (hip)

Developing Good Character

Responsibility

Osteoporosis is a disease that weakens bones. To help prevent this disease, eat foods rich in calcium, such as milk, and strengthen bones with exercise.

Lesson 2

② Teach

Developing Good Character

Responsibility

Ask students: What are things you can do now to prevent osteoporosis later in life? Have them develop a plan that details ways they will be responsible for the health of their bones. Encourage them to include the best ideas they have gathered from class reading, discussion, and activities. Challenge students to find ideas from outside sources to include on their lists.

VISUAL LEARNING

FIGURE 6.3 If the classroom has a large skeleton, have volunteers use it to point out each of the bones identified in Figure 6.3. Another option might be to allow students to act out motion of joints. This strategy will help students with special learning needs understand and differentiate among the motions of the different types of joints. Encourage students to describe the position and function of those bones. Then ask the question posed in the caption; students should identify the hip joint as a ball-and-socket joint. **INCL** *Behavior Problems, Special Learning Needs, English Language Learners*

COOPERATIVE LEARNING ACTIVITY

Our Bones Have students work in groups to sketch an outline of the human body on a long piece of butcher paper or lengths of newsprint taped together, leaving plenty of room to write in all the margins. Then have students locate at least two reference books that identify the bones of the human body. Ask students to use their reference material to draw all the major bones of the human skeletal system on their outlines. (As an option, a single human outline could be a jigsaw with each group providing in-depth detail of a certain area of the body.) Students should label each bone in the margin, drawing a line from the label to the appropriate bone. When each group is finished, hang the skeletons up around the classroom or in the hall.

Lesson 2

HEALTH Online

Encourage students to explore the Web Link for this lesson and complete the activity.

VISUAL LEARNING

FIGURE 6.4 Have volunteers describe the three small boxed pictures and read the names of those muscles. Help students recall that these are examples of the three kinds of muscles. Then have other volunteers describe the larger picture and read aloud the names of the labeled muscles. Ask students to point to each muscle as it is named. **INCL** *Behavior Problems, Special Learning Needs, English Language Learners*

Discussing

Help students compare the pictured skeletal system (Figure 6.3) and the pictured muscular system (Figure 6.4): Where are the skeletal muscles in relation to the bones of the skeleton? How can you tell? **L1**

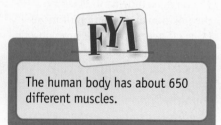

The human body has about 650 different muscles.

HEALTH Online

Topic: Body systems

For a link to more information on body systems, go to health.glencoe.com.

Activity: Using the information provided at this link, write down three facts about a body system.

The Muscular System

The **muscular system** is made of *all the muscles in your body.* Muscles move bones, pump blood, and move food through the stomach and intestines, among other jobs. The three types of muscle are skeletal, cardiac, and smooth. The skeletal muscles are called voluntary muscles because you control them. They are located in places like your arms, face, abdomen, and back. Cardiac, or heart, muscles and smooth muscles, such as those in the stomach, are involuntary muscles—they work without your controlling them. See **Figure 6.4**.

FIGURE 6.4

THE MUSCULAR SYSTEM

Muscles move bones, pump blood, and move food through the digestive system. *What are the three major types of muscles?*

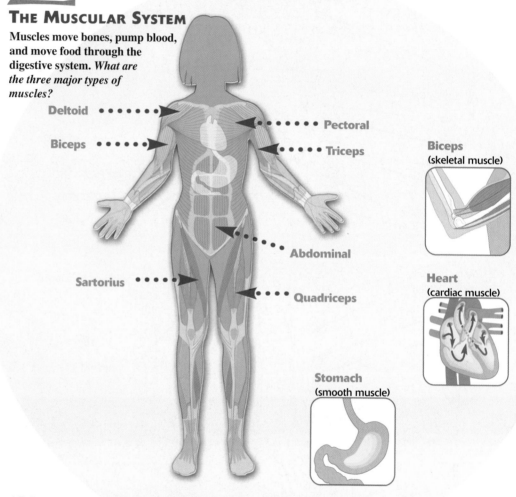

Deltoid
Biceps
Pectoral
Triceps
Abdominal
Sartorius
Quadriceps

Biceps (skeletal muscle)

Heart (cardiac muscle)

Stomach (smooth muscle)

Health Literacy

Health Information Bone tissue grows and expands from conception until early adulthood. The bones of newborns are made up primarily of cartilage as well as some spongy bone. The marrow cavities of the bones contain red marrow, which is used to manufacture red blood cells, white blood cells, and platelets. As a child grows, some of the cartilage continues to grow, while portions of the cartilage and spongy bone gradually harden into what is called true bone. By the time a person reaches late adolescence, red marrow is located in fewer bones, and the rate of new cartilage growth has begun to slow down. The growth of long bone is nearly complete by this time.

The Circulatory System

The **circulatory system** *enables the body to transport, or move, materials from one place to another.* The blood moves to and from the tissues of the body, delivering oxygen, food, and other materials to cells and removing wastes. See **Figure 6.5**.

FIGURE 6.5

THE CIRCULATORY SYSTEM

The blood vessels shown in blue carry oxygen-poor blood toward the heart and lungs. The red blood vessels carry oxygen-rich blood from the lungs to the heart and back to the rest of the body. *Why are the pulmonary arteries shown in blue?*

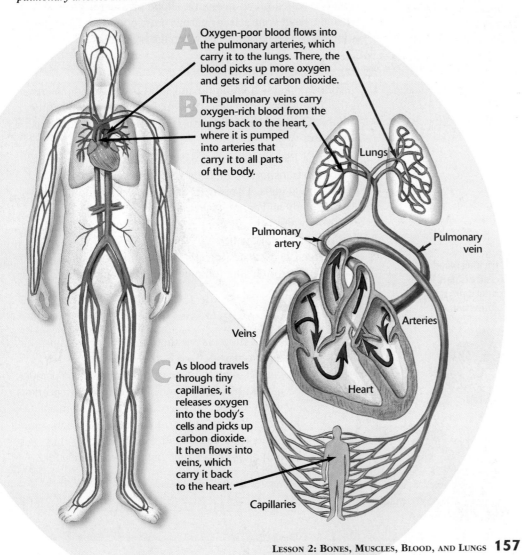

A Oxygen-poor blood flows into the pulmonary arteries, which carry it to the lungs. There, the blood picks up more oxygen and gets rid of carbon dioxide.

B The pulmonary veins carry oxygen-rich blood from the lungs back to the heart, where it is pumped into arteries that carry it to all parts of the body.

C As blood travels through tiny capillaries, it releases oxygen into the body's cells and picks up carbon dioxide. It then flows into veins, which carry it back to the heart.

Lungs

Pulmonary artery

Pulmonary vein

Veins

Arteries

Heart

Capillaries

Lesson 2

Cross-Curriculum Activity

MATH Tell students that their blood completes an entire circuit of the body in just one minute (and sometimes less than a minute). Ask them to compute the number of circuits completed in a day. (*1,440*) **L2**

VISUAL LEARNING

FIGURE 6.5 Have volunteers read aloud the caption for Figure 6.5 and the three explanations. Ask students to trace the path of blood from the heart to a foot and back again. **INCL** *Behavior Problems, Special Learning Needs, English Language Learners*

Cross-Curriculum Activity

LANGUAGE ARTS Ask students to summarize in short, written explanations how the circulatory system works. Challenge volunteers to give their explanations in oral presentations without using any visual aids. **L1**

Investigating

Have students look in the phone book to find the address and phone number of the local branch of the American Heart Association. Invite students to contact the agency to find out what services it provides the region and then share this information with the rest of the class. **L3**

WHAT TEENS WANT TO KNOW

Why do people faint? Fainting is a sudden, temporary loss of consciousness caused by decreased oxygen flow through your blood and into your brain. The medical term for fainting is *syncope*. Sometimes, people feel lightheaded, dizzy, weak, or nauseated right before they are going to faint. Fainting can happen with illnesses such as the flu, and it also may occur as a result of excessive heat or anxiety. Fainting can occur when you change position very quickly. Jumping to attention when you've been lying down can cause you to faint because the rapid change of position restricts blood flow to the brain. Other reasons people may faint include an abnormal heart rate, low blood pressure, or taking certain medications.

Cross-Curriculum Activity

SCIENCE Ask students to explain the difference between a liquid and a solid. If students have difficulty, ask a volunteer to look up the definitions in a science book or dictionary. Then have students discuss how blood could be made up of both liquid and solid parts. **L2**

Cross-Curriculum Activity

MATH Have students work with partners to solve the Connect to Math problem. (*2.4 million × 60 seconds = 144 million/minute; 144 × 60 minutes = 8.64 billion/hour; 8.64 × 24 hours = 207.36 billion/day*) **L1 INCL** *English Language Learners*

Synthesizing

Ask students to explain why blood is vital to human existence. (*The body can't receive oxygen or nutrients and can't dispose of waste without it.*) **L1**

Inferring

Ask students to discuss why they think it is important for people to know their blood type. (*If a person needs a blood transfusion, the blood must be a compatible blood type or the body will reject it.*) If students don't know their blood type, tell them they can ask a parent or guardian to contact their family doctor. **L1**

CONNECT TO
Math

SMALL BUT MIGHTY
Red blood cells, the smallest cells in the body, are continually being replaced. As you read this, your body is making red blood cells at the rate of about 2.4 million every second! *How many are made in 1 minute? In an hour? In a day?*

Checking blood pressure is part of a standard physical examination.

The Work of the Heart

The muscle that acts as the pump for the circulatory system is the **heart**. The heart pushes blood through the blood vessels, the tubes that carry blood throughout the body. The different types of blood vessels are arteries, veins, and capillaries. Arteries carry blood away from the heart. Veins return blood to the heart. The tiny blood vessels that connect arteries and veins are called capillaries. They provide blood directly to cells. **Figure 6.5** on page 157 shows how blood travels through the circulatory system.

Blood Pressure

The force of the blood pushing against the walls of the blood vessels is called **blood pressure**. Blood pressure is greatest when the heart contracts, or pushes out blood. Blood pressure is lowest between heartbeats, when the heart relaxes.

Parts of the Blood

Blood contains both liquid and solid parts. Blood plasma is the liquid part of the blood and makes up about half of its volume. Cells are the solid parts. Each element of blood has a purpose:

- **Plasma.** Plasma is made up of about 92 percent water. Its job is to transport blood cells and dissolved food.
- **Red blood cells.** These cells carry oxygen to all other cells of the body and carry away some waste products.
- **White blood cells.** These cells help destroy disease-causing germs that enter the body.
- **Platelets.** These parts of cells help your blood clot. This keeps you from losing too much blood when you have a cut.

Blood Types

All blood is not the same. There are four main types: A, B, AB, and O. The types are classified by the type of red blood cells a person has. Knowing a person's blood type is important when one person is receiving blood from another. Serious side effects can result when some of the types are mixed. Health officials mix only those types that can be combined safely.

158 CHAPTER 6: GROWTH AND DEVELOPMENT

INCLUSION STRATEGIES

Behavior Problems, Special Learning Needs, English Language Learners Construct a diagram-concept map of the respiratory system and the breathing process on the board. Begin by writing *breathing process* on the board. Then have a volunteer draw a rough diagram similar to Figure 6.6 (but without labels). Elicit from other students the names of the parts of the diagram. Have a second student write the labels on the diagram. Finally, ask volunteers to take turns describing the process of breathing in and breathing out in their own words. Challenge students to use accurate terminology to describe the breathing process.

Blood may also contain something called an Rh factor. Blood is either Rh-positive or Rh-negative. People with Rh-positive blood can receive blood from people with either Rh-positive or Rh-negative blood. People with Rh-negative blood can receive blood only from people who are also Rh-negative.

The Respiratory System

Your **respiratory system** *enables you to breathe.* When you breathe in, or inhale, you take oxygen into your lungs. The **lungs** are *the main organs of the respiratory system.* When you breathe out, or exhale, the lungs get rid of carbon dioxide. See **Figure 6.6** for a closer look at the workings of the respiratory system.

FIGURE 6.6

THE RESPIRATORY SYSTEM

The respiratory system is divided into upper and lower sections, which perform different functions. *In which section are the alveoli located?*

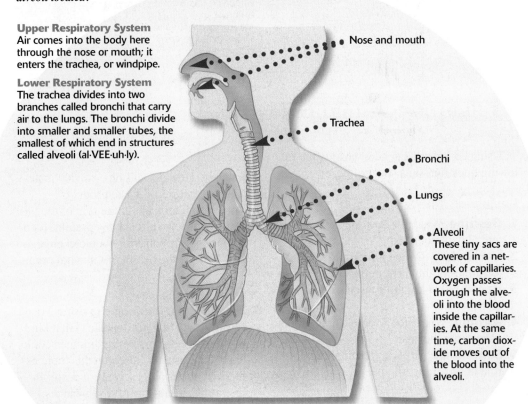

Upper Respiratory System
Air comes into the body here through the nose or mouth; it enters the trachea, or windpipe.

Lower Respiratory System
The trachea divides into two branches called bronchi that carry air to the lungs. The bronchi divide into smaller and smaller tubes, the smallest of which end in structures called alveoli (al·VEE·uh·ly).

Nose and mouth

Trachea

Bronchi

Lungs

Alveoli
These tiny sacs are covered in a network of capillaries. Oxygen passes through the alveoli into the blood inside the capillaries. At the same time, carbon dioxide moves out of the blood into the alveoli.

LESSON 2: BONES, MUSCLES, BLOOD, AND LUNGS **159**

Lesson 2

Lesson 2

VISUAL LEARNING

FIGURE 6.7 If possible, have a plastic bottle available for students to squeeze and release. Read and discuss the explanation of the lungs at work. Then have students answer the caption question; they should recognize that the hand represents the diaphragm. **INCL** *Behavior Problems, Special Learning Needs, English Language Learners*

 **Assess**

Evaluating

Assign the Lesson 2 Review; then assign the Lesson 2 Quiz in the TCR.

Reteaching

- Assign Concept Maps 24, 25, and 26 or Reteaching Activities 22 and 23 in the TCR.
- Have students sketch the major parts of each body system studied in the lesson, label the parts, and describe how the system works.

Enrichment

- Assign Enrichment Activity 22 in the TCR.
- Have each student research and report on an area of sports medicine that interests him or her.

 **Close**

Ask students to recall each of the systems discussed in the lesson and explain why each one is important.

How You Breathe

Breathing begins with the **diaphragm** (DY·uh·fram), *a large muscle at the bottom of the chest.* When you breathe in, the diaphragm contracts. When you breathe out, it expands. **Figure 6.7** shows how the breathing process works.

FIGURE 6.7

HOW YOUR LUNGS WORK

Notice what happens when you squeeze an empty plastic bottle. Your respiratory system works in a similar way. *What does the hand in this illustration represent?*

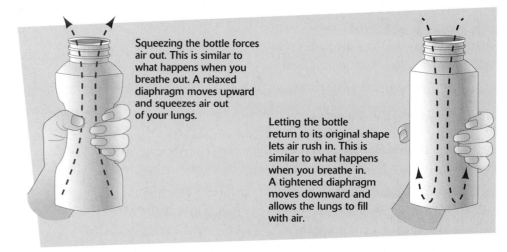

Squeezing the bottle forces air out. This is similar to what happens when you breathe out. A relaxed diaphragm moves upward and squeezes air out of your lungs.

Letting the bottle return to its original shape lets air rush in. This is similar to what happens when you breathe in. A tightened diaphragm moves downward and allows the lungs to fill with air.

Lesson 2 Review

Using complete sentences, answer the following questions on a sheet of paper.

Reviewing Terms and Facts

1. **Describe** What role does the skeletal system play in your body?
2. **Vocabulary** Define *joints*, and give examples of the three major types.
3. **Recall** What kind of muscles do you control?
4. **Identify** What blood vessels take blood away from the heart?
5. **Summarize** Explain the diaphragm's role in breathing.

Thinking Critically

6. **Explain** How do cells receive vital materials and get rid of waste products?
7. **Analyze** Think about the role of the heart within the circulatory system. Identify actions or behaviors you can engage in to protect the health of this vital organ.

Applying Health Skills

8. **Practicing Healthful Behaviors** Your respiratory system is delicate. What kind of things that a person might inhale could harm this system? Research this topic using reliable resources. Make a poster illustrating several harmful substances.

160 CHAPTER 6: GROWTH AND DEVELOPMENT

Lesson 2 Review

1. It makes up the framework of the body.
2. Joints are places where one bone meets another. Examples of the three types include the neck (pivot), the knee (hinge), and the hip (ball-and-socket).
3. Skeletal or voluntary muscles.
4. Arteries.
5. The diaphragm contracts, allowing the lungs to fill with air, when you breathe in; the diaphragm expands, forcing the air out your lungs, when you breathe out.
6. The circulatory system moves fuel, such as food and oxygen, to the cells in the blood through arteries, removing waste materials in the blood through veins.
7. Responses will vary.

160

Nerves and Digestion

The Nervous System

The **nervous system** is *the control and communication system of the body.* Its command center is the **brain**, *the organ that controls your senses, thoughts, and actions.* The brain helps the body process and respond to the information it receives from the senses. It also processes thoughts.

The brain is made up of billions of neurons. **Neurons** (NOO·rahnz) are *cells that carry electrical messages,* the language of the nervous system. There are three types of neurons. Sensory neurons, such as the ones in your eyes, receive information from the outside world. Connecting neurons transmit messages between the sensory neurons and the motor neurons, which send messages to the muscles and glands.

Structure of the Nervous System

The nervous system has two main parts. The central nervous system consists of the brain and the **spinal cord**, *a tube of neurons that runs up the spine.* The largest part of the brain, the cerebrum (suh·REE·bruhm), is where thinking takes place.

Quick Write

List all the body parts you know of that help you eat and digest food. After reading this lesson, check your list, and add any other organs that you left out.

LEARN ABOUT...

○ how your nervous system controls your body's functions.
○ how the digestive and excretory systems process food.

VOCABULARY

○ nervous system
○ brain
○ neurons
○ spinal cord
○ digestive system
○ excretory system

Your brain is one of your most vital organs. Wear the right equipment to protect it. *How is this teen protecting his brain from injury?*

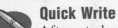 Focus

Lesson Objectives

Students will be able to

• describe how their nervous system controls their body's functions.

• describe the structures and functions of the digestive and excretory systems.

Motivators

Quick Write

After students give their responses, list the identified parts on the board. Ask: At what point do you think digestion begins?

Bellringer Activity

Ask students to think about how and why they communicate with others and identify specific examples. Then ask them why parts of the body need to communicate.

VOCABULARY

Have each student write the vocabulary words on a sheet of paper. Next to each term, students should write the word divided into syllables and then write its respelling (pronunciation). Have students use dictionaries to check respellings. Ask students to define each term and use it correctly in a sentence.

Lesson 3 Resources

Teacher Classroom Resources

📁 Concept Maps 27 & 28

📁 Cross-Curriculum Activity 11

📁 Enrichment Activity 23

📁 Health Lab 6

📁 Lesson Plan 3

📁 Lesson 3 Quiz

📁 Reading Tutor Activity 23

📁 Reteaching Activity 24

📷 Transparencies 27 & 28

Student Activities Workbook

📁 Chapter 6 Study Guide

📁 Applying Health Skills 23

② Teach

Discussing

Ask students:

- What are some examples of information neurons might receive from the outside world? (*heat sensations, light, pain, danger*)

- What kinds of messages might neurons send to muscles and organs? (*send messages to leg muscles to move or walk*) **L1**

Analyzing

Ask students to give examples of what they think would happen if some neurons failed to pass on information received from the outside. (*Example: If fingers were touching something very hot, the body would not respond and the fingers could be badly burned.*) **L1**

VISUAL LEARNING

FIGURE 6.8 Have group members point to parts of the central nervous system and parts of the peripheral nervous system in Figure 6.8 and explain the relationship between the two. Caption answer: *cerebrum.* **INCL** *Behavior Problems, Special Learning Needs, English Language Learners*

FYI

The "funny bone" in the elbow isn't a bone at all. It's the place where a nerve crosses the surface of a bone. It's referred to as the funny bone because its real name is the humerus.

The peripheral (puh·RIF·uh·ruhl) nervous system is made up of nerves that branch out from the spinal cord. It handles both your voluntary movements (the ones you control) and your involuntary movements (which you cannot control). The beating of your heart is an example of an involuntary movement. See **Figure 6.8** for a diagram of the nervous system.

Protecting Your Nervous System

The best way to keep your nervous system healthy is to protect yourself from head and spinal cord injuries. To do this, wear your safety belt whenever you ride in a car. When you skate or ride a bicycle, wear a helmet. Also, be careful when lifting heavy objects. Bend from the knees, not from the waist, and do not try to lift something that is too heavy for you.

FIGURE 6.8

DIVISIONS OF THE NERVOUS SYSTEM

The central nervous system, shown in yellow, contains the brain and spinal cord. They work together to send messages to the peripheral nervous system, shown in blue. *Which part of the brain controls your sense of smell?*

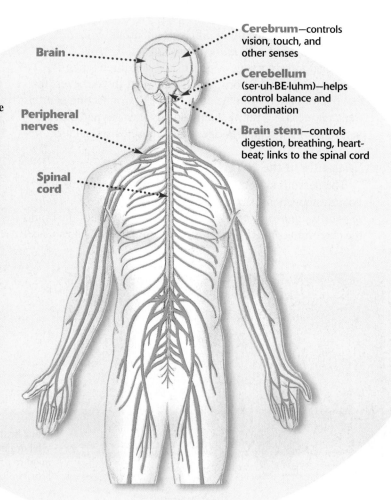

Brain

Peripheral nerves

Spinal cord

Cerebrum—controls vision, touch, and other senses

Cerebellum (ser·uh·BE·luhm)—helps control balance and coordination

Brain stem—controls digestion, breathing, heartbeat; links to the spinal cord

162 CHAPTER 6: GROWTH AND DEVELOPMENT

MORE ABOUT...

The Nervous System The human nervous system is a highly complex system that sets human development apart from that of all other life forms. Nearly all animals have some kind of nervous system, but none are as highly developed as that of humans, especially the part of the nervous system contained in the brain. Every second of its life, from birth on, the human body performs hundreds of functions. Some of the functions are voluntary, but many of the functions are automatic. Messages received by the sensory nerves are also processed automatically. The body does not decide to see, hear, taste, smell, or feel; it does so automatically.

FIGURE 6.9

THE DIGESTIVE SYSTEM

The digestive system involves many different body parts. *What other body systems work together with the digestive system?*

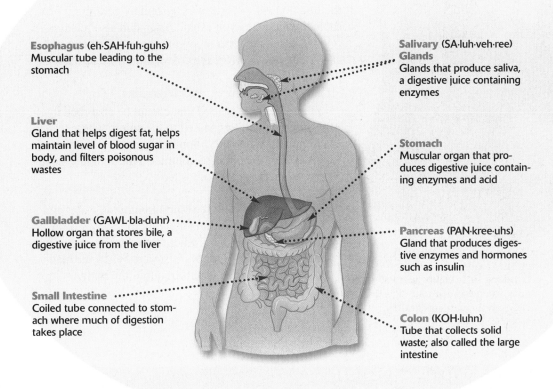

Esophagus (eh·SAH·fuh·guhs)
Muscular tube leading to the stomach

Liver
Gland that helps digest fat, helps maintain level of blood sugar in body, and filters poisonous wastes

Gallbladder (GAWL·bla·duhr)
Hollow organ that stores bile, a digestive juice from the liver

Small Intestine
Coiled tube connected to stomach where much of digestion takes place

Salivary (SA·luh·veh·ree) **Glands**
Glands that produce saliva, a digestive juice containing enzymes

Stomach
Muscular organ that produces digestive juice containing enzymes and acid

Pancreas (PAN·kree·uhs)
Gland that produces digestive enzymes and hormones such as insulin

Colon (KOH·luhn)
Tube that collects solid waste; also called the large intestine

The Digestive System

Your **digestive** (dy·JES·tiv) **system** *breaks down the food you eat into a form that your body cells can use as fuel.* This process, called digestion, turns food into nutrients.

Digestion begins with chewing, which crushes food into small pieces. Chemicals called enzymes (EN·zymz), found in your saliva (suh·LY·vuh), break down the food further. When you swallow, food enters the throat. Muscles contract and relax, pushing food along. Strong acid, enzymes, and churning muscles in your stomach break down food even further. The food particles move into the small intestine, where the nutrients are absorbed into the blood. The blood carries the nutrients to all the body cells. **Figure 6.9** illustrates the digestive system.

LESSON 3: NERVES AND DIGESTION **163**

In an average lifetime, the human digestive system handles about 50 tons of food.

❸ Assess

Evaluating

Assign the Lesson 3 Review; then assign the Lesson 3 Quiz in the TCR.

Reteaching

• Assign Concept Maps 27 and 28 or Reteaching Activity 24 in the TCR.

• Have students sketch the major parts of each body system studied in the lesson, label the parts, and describe how the system works.

Enrichment

• Assign Enrichment Activity 23 in the TCR.

• Have students research the role of the spleen in the digestive system.

❹ Close

Ask students to explain what the nervous, digestive, and excretory systems are and how they work together to process fuel for the body.

Drinking six to eight glasses of water a day will help keep your digestive and excretory systems healthy.

The Excretory System

Matter that cannot be absorbed through digestion becomes waste. Your **excretory** (EK·skruh·tohr·ee) **system** *gets rid of some of the wastes your body produces and maintains fluid balance.* The respiratory system performs some of the functions of the excretory system by getting rid of carbon dioxide when you exhale. Your skin also releases liquid wastes in the form of sweat. The major organs of this system, however, are the colon, kidneys, and bladder.

The Colon, Kidneys, and Bladder

The solid part of food that cannot be absorbed in the small intestine is passed to the colon, where water is removed. When the colon is full, a nerve sends a message for the colon to contract. This action removes solid waste from the body.

The kidneys filter the blood, removing water and waste substances and maintaining the body's fluid balance. The bladder is where liquid waste material, or urine, from the kidneys is stored. When the bladder is full, the urine is passed out of the body.

Lesson 3 Review

Using complete sentences, answer the following questions on a sheet of paper.

Reviewing Terms and Facts

1. **Vocabulary** Define *nervous system*, and use it in an original sentence.
2. **Recall** What two body parts make up the central nervous system?
3. **List** What are the major organs of the excretory system?

Thinking Critically

4. **Analyze** Why does lifting heavy objects improperly present a risk of injury to the nervous system?

5. **Hypothesize** What do you think would happen if a person's kidneys were not working properly?

Applying Health Skills

6. **Practicing Healthful Behaviors** A healthy diet keeps your digestive and excretory systems working easily and efficiently—and that helps your whole body function well. Use what you know about nutrition and digestion to write a list of several things you can do to help your digestion and stay healthy.

164 Chapter 6: Growth and Development

Lesson 3 Review

1. The nervous system is the control and communication system of the body. Sentences will vary.
2. The brain and the spinal cord.
3. The colon, kidneys, and bladder.
4. Lifting heavy objects improperly could injure the back, which could, in turn, damage the spinal cord.

5. Responses will vary, although students should recognize that without the kidneys, blood wouldn't get filtered, and the body wouldn't be able to get rid of waste.

Adolescence: A Time of Change

Changes During Adolescence

Adolescence (a·duhl·EH·suhns) is *the period between childhood and adulthood.* It is a time of rapid change in a person's life. During this period, you will develop physically, mentally, emotionally, and socially. Many of the changes of adolescence are caused by hormones (HOR·mohnz), chemicals that control body functions. Hormones also play a role in personal health, and abnormal levels can cause health problems. The glands that produce hormones are part of the endocrine system.

The Endocrine System

The endocrine (EN·duh·krin) system consists of *glands throughout the body that produce hormones.* Each hormone delivers instructions to the organs and tissues of your other body systems. **Figure 6.10** on the next page shows the glands of the endocrine system and the body functions they regulate.

During adolescence, you will grow mentally and emotionally. *How can helping others be a good way to meet your emotional needs?*

Quick Write

Think about the ways your body has changed in the past few years. Do you think your body will continue to change? List the other changes you think will take place.

LEARN ABOUT...

- how the endocrine system and hormones are related to growth and development.
- the physical, mental/emotional, and social changes of adolescence.
- what factors influence your personality.

VOCABULARY

- adolescence
- endocrine system
- puberty
- personality
- behavior

LESSON 4: ADOLESCENCE: A TIME OF CHANGE **165**

Lesson 4

Adolescence: A Time of Change

① Focus

Lesson Objectives

Students will be able to

- describe the structure and function of the endocrine system.
- describe the changes of adolescence.
- identify factors that influence personality.

Motivators

Quick Write
Discuss the students' responses. Clarify that the changes that take place during adolescence are not associated with a specific age; timing is due to the uniqueness of each individual.

Bellringer Activity

Ask students to recall the main function of the endocrine system, which was introduced in the first lesson of the chapter. Then ask: What body functions do you think need to be regulated?

VOCABULARY

Write vocabulary terms on the board. Ask volunteers to pronounce them. Have students look up each term in the Glossary and write sentences for the terms, defining each term in their own words.

 ## Lesson 4 Resources

Teacher Classroom Resources

 Concept Map 29

Cross-Curriculum Activity 12

Enrichment Activity 24

Lesson Plan 4

Lesson 4 Quiz

Reading Tutor Activity 24

Reteaching Activity 25

Transparency 29

Student Activities Workbook

Chapter 6 Study Guide

Applying Health Skills 24

② Teach

Journal Writing

Ask students to write private journal entries describing how they expect their lives to change between now and the time they finish high school. Remind them to consider physical, mental/emotional, and social changes. **L1**

Critical Thinking Activity

Draw an example of a web graphic on the board. Have students independently develop two web graphics. Have the students analyze the role of hormones in human growth, development, and health. In one graphic, students will illustrate the role of hormones as they relate to growth and development. In the other graphic, students will analyze the role of hormones as they relate to personal health. **L2**

VISUAL LEARNING

FIGURE 6.10 Divide the class into five groups, and assign each group one of the glands. Have group members read about their assigned gland and discuss it with the rest of the class. Then read the caption aloud, and have volunteers answer the question. **INCL** *Behavior Problems, Special Learning Needs, English Language Learners*

FIGURE 6.10

THE ENDOCRINE SYSTEM

The glands of the endocrine system perform many different functions in your body. *Analyze the role of hormones as they relate to growth and development.*

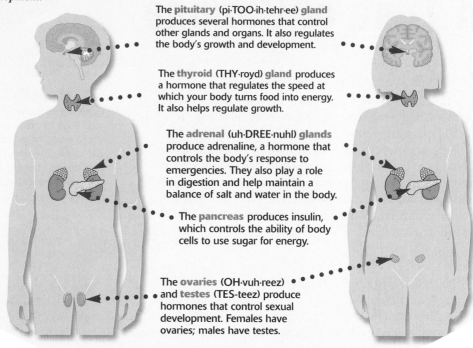

The **pituitary** (pi·TOO·ih·tehr·ee) **gland** produces several hormones that control other glands and organs. It also regulates the body's growth and development.

The **thyroid** (THY·royd) **gland** produces a hormone that regulates the speed at which your body turns food into energy. It also helps regulate growth.

The **adrenal** (uh·DREE·nuhl) **glands** produce adrenaline, a hormone that controls the body's response to emergencies. They also play a role in digestion and help maintain a balance of salt and water in the body.

The **pancreas** produces insulin, which controls the ability of body cells to use sugar for energy.

The **ovaries** (OH·vuh·reez) and **testes** (TES·teez) produce hormones that control sexual development. Females have ovaries; males have testes.

Physical Development

Adolescence begins with puberty. **Puberty** (PYOO·ber·tee) is *the time when you develop physical traits of adults of your gender and become physically able to reproduce* (see **Figure 6.11**). Hormones cause the physical changes of puberty, which typically begin between the ages of 8 and 14 and end between the ages of 16 and 20. However, puberty can occur earlier or later. Girls often enter puberty earlier than boys.

During puberty most girls will begin menstruating. This is the monthly shedding of the lining of the uterus. To learn more about menstrual health and how it affects reproduction, speak with a parent or other trusted adult.

Practicing good personal hygiene habits is especially important during adolescence and the time right before it, known as *preadolescence*.

166 CHAPTER 6: GROWTH AND DEVELOPMENT

DEALING WITH SENSITIVE ISSUES

Talking About the Issues You might want to share the following information about menstrual health with students: Most females begin menstruating between the ages of 10 and 15. The menstrual cycle may be irregular at first. Although hormones control the menstrual cycle, poor nutrition, stress, and illness can influence menstrual health and cause irregularities. These factors can in turn affect reproduction. Cleanliness, changing tampons and sanitary pads often, and regular checkups with a family doctor or gynecologist are all important for a female's menstrual health. Students should discuss these issues with their parents or guardians or a health care professional.

Mental and Emotional Development

As you get older, you begin to think about things in new ways. You learn that some problems do not have simple solutions. During adolescence, you may experience powerful emotions that you do not always understand. You may have mood swings. These kinds of emotional changes are normal during your teen years. They are related to the changing levels of hormones in your body. To manage these feelings, try to express them in healthy ways. Practice self-control—don't lash out at people when you feel angry or upset.

Social Development

During adolescence, you begin to see yourself as separate from your parents. At the same time, your parents begin to see that you are growing up. They may expect you to take on more responsibility.

FIGURE 6.11

PHYSICAL CHANGES OF ADOLESCENCE

Both boys and girls go through many physical changes during puberty. *Describe changes in male and female anatomy and physiology during puberty.*

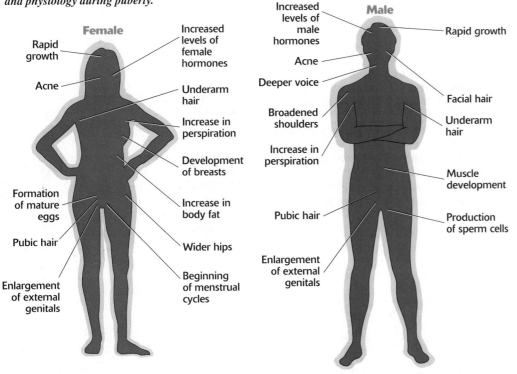

Female
- Rapid growth
- Acne
- Increased levels of female hormones
- Underarm hair
- Increase in perspiration
- Development of breasts
- Increase in body fat
- Formation of mature eggs
- Pubic hair
- Wider hips
- Enlargement of external genitals
- Beginning of menstrual cycles

Male
- Increased levels of male hormones
- Acne
- Deeper voice
- Broadened shoulders
- Increase in perspiration
- Rapid growth
- Facial hair
- Underarm hair
- Muscle development
- Pubic hair
- Production of sperm cells
- Enlargement of external genitals

LESSON 4: ADOLESCENCE: A TIME OF CHANGE **167**

Developing Good Character ★

Respect

You and your classmates will change a lot during adolescence. A considerate person understands that every individual grows and develops at a different rate. Don't tease others about their changing bodies, even in fun. *What are some specific ways individuals differ in growth and development?*

Lesson 4

VISUAL LEARNING

FIGURE 6.11 Read aloud the title and caption. Then have volunteers read aloud each of the listed changes for females and males, and guide students in discussing these changes. Ask: Which changes take place in both females and males? (You may wish to refer to page 172 of the student text to discuss the uterus and its relationship to the menstrual cycle.) To link good personal hygiene habits to some of the physical changes of adolescence, have students review Chapter 4. **INCL** *Behavior Problems, Special Learning Needs, English Language Learners*

Developing Good Character ★

Respect

Lead a class discussion on why it is important to respect individual differences in growth and development. Ask students for examples of how they can show this respect.

HEALTH SKILLS PRACTICE

Goal Setting Assign the following: During adolescence you need a plan to give your body three basics—food, physical activity, and rest. Create a table with five columns. List the seven days of the week in one column. Add the headings—food, physical activity, and rest—in the next three. Write in your goals for these three needs each day. Use the fifth column to monitor your goals.

MORE ABOUT...

Hormones and Teens The same hormone that promotes growth of body hair also stimulates oil glands in the skin. Often, the oil is produced more quickly than it can be released, and a pore becomes plugged up with oil. Then dead skin cells can no longer be pushed out through that pore, and a skin blemish develops.

What's the best way to treat acne? For most teens, simply waiting is the best solution. Eventually, the body reduces its hormone production, and problems with acne gradually subside. Surprisingly, vigorous scrubbing and lots of soap are not solutions to acne. Instead, they may actually stimulate additional oil production.

Synthesizing

Have students discuss some of the social changes of adolescence. Examples are

- taking more responsibility.
- not giving in to social pressure.
- changes in relationships. **L1**

Hands-On Health

LOOKING AHEAD

Time: 30 minutes

TEACHING THE ACTIVITY

- Have students work independently to complete the survey. Assure students that their responses can be kept confidential.
- In a class discussion, ask volunteers to discuss their answers and examples.
- Record students' ideas as they brainstorm other examples of mature behavior.

ASSESSMENT

- Have students write short paragraphs describing how they expect their behavior to change in the next few years.

Analyzing

Have students make a list identifying causes and effects associated with poor body image, such as eating disorders and growth patterns. Ask: Why do these problems seem more prevalent among teens and young adults? What resources are available at your school or in your community to help students with these issues? **L1**

Your friendships also become very important to you. In early adolescence, you may be strongly influenced by your friends. You may be part of a group that does everything together. Later on, you may break away from the group and form closer friendships with one or two individuals.

As you mature, you will worry less about your friends' approval and rely more on your own standards. By the end of your teens, you will be able to function on your own. You will have formed your own ideas about who you are and how you fit into the world. In short, you will be independent.

Hands-On Health

LOOKING AHEAD

Every day, you show in many ways how you are growing into a healthy, mature adult. This activity will help you recognize some of these changes in yourself.

WHAT YOU WILL NEED

- a pencil or pen
- a sheet of paper

WHAT YOU WILL DO

1. Number the paper 1–10.
2. Read through the list below. It describes many kinds of mature behavior. For each numbered item in the list, try to think of an example from your life.
3. Write down each of your examples on the line with the same number as the statement. Don't worry if you can't think of an example for every statement—just fill in as many as you can.

BECOMING AN ADULT

1. I think about the consequences before I act.
2. I do what I think is right even when it is hard.
3. I feel comfortable with who I am; I don't try to be something I'm not.

4. I respect other people's ideas even when they are different from mine.
5. I think about how my actions affect other people.
6. My parents and I show respect when we talk to one another.
7. I take time to listen to other people's problems.
8. I try to see situations from the viewpoint of my parents and other adults.
9. I think about how the choices I make now will affect my future.
10. I have a good idea of the kind of adult I would like to be.

IN CONCLUSION

1. Discuss your answers as a class. You do not have to share all of your answers unless you choose to.
2. With your classmates, brainstorm more examples of mature and responsible behavior.

 ## Beyond the Classroom

Community Help students identify sources outside the school environment where they can make responsible contributions appropriate to their age, talents, and interests. For example, many retirement homes, skilled-care facilities, and hospitals have programs for teen volunteers. A local youth job corps may exist to help young people find part-time jobs or volunteer work. Check local phone directories, or ask guidance counselors and social workers for additional resources to explore with students. Tell students to be sure to get permission from home before taking on any volunteer work or job.

Influences on Your Personality

Your **personality** is *the sum total of your feelings, actions, habits, and thoughts.* Like your fingerprints, your personality is unique. No one else is exactly like you.

Parts of your personality are inherited. Your personality is also shaped by your environment, the people and places that surround you. Your family is an important influence on your personality, especially early in your life. During your teen years, you may also be influenced by friends, teachers, and other role models. Finally, your personality includes your **behavior**, or *how you act in situations that occur in your life.* You cannot change your family or environment, but you do control what you do in any situation. If you act responsibly, you will grow up to be the kind of person you want to be.

Many people influence your personality during your lifetime. *Who do you think has the greatest influence on you at this time in your life?*

 Lesson **4** Review

Using complete sentences, answer the following questions on a sheet of paper.

Reviewing Terms and Facts

1. **Vocabulary** Define the term *endocrine system.*
2. **Recall** At what age does puberty usually begin?
3. **Describe** Name five physical changes that occur in both males and females during puberty.
4. **Identify** Name three factors that affect your personality.

Thinking Critically

5. **Apply** Analyze the role of hormones as they relate to personal health.
6. **Predict** In what ways do you think you will develop socially during your adolescence?

Applying Health Skills

7. **Communication Skills** Think of some skills that can help a teen communicate effectively with a parent or other trusted adult. Then, write a short story in which a teen uses these skills to talk to a parent or other trusted adult about the changes of preadolescence.

❸ Assess

Evaluating

📁 Assign the Lesson 4 Review; then assign the Lesson 4 Quiz in the TCR.

Reteaching

• 📁 Assign Concept Map 29 or Reteaching Activity 25 in the TCR.
• Ask students to write a brief essay describing the changes in male and female anatomy and physiology during puberty.

Enrichment

• 📁 Assign Enrichment Activity 24 in the TCR.
• Have students use library or online sources to collect statistics on the ages at which the changes of puberty occur. Have them draw bar graphs to summarize this information.

❹ Close

Have students attempt to summarize in writing the adolescent stage. Ask volunteers to share their summaries.

Lesson **4** Review

1. Glands throughout the body that produce hormones.
2. Between ages 8 and 14.
3. Any five: increased levels of hormones, rapid growth, acne, pubic hair, underarm hair, increase in perspiration; enlargement of external genitals.
4. Any three: inherited traits, environment, people (especially family), and places.
5. Responses should include the idea that abnormal hormone levels may lead to health problems.
6. Responses should reflect the social changes discussed in this lesson.

Heredity and Growth

❶ Focus

Lesson Objectives

Students will be able to
- explain what heredity is and how traits are passed on.
- explain how a baby develops inside a mother's body.
- identify the stages in the life cycle.

Health Skills
- Advocacy, p. 171

Motivators

Quick Write
Go around the room, and have students share examples of their inherited traits and identify which parent the trait came from.

Bellringer Activity

Ask students to share what they know about newborn babies (from personal experience or from photographs). Have them consider what a newborn baby looks like, sounds like, and feels like. Write identified characteristics on the board.

VOCABULARY

Have students look up the vocabulary terms in the Glossary. Ask them to make flash cards for each term, defining the term in their own words. As they encounter the terms in the text, have students refer to their flash cards to check the meanings.

Lesson 5

Heredity and Growth

Quick Write
List all the physical traits you share with different members of your family.

LEARN ABOUT...

- how traits are passed from parents to children.
- how a baby develops inside its mother's body.
- the stages in the life cycle.

VOCABULARY

- heredity
- chromosomes
- genes
- egg cell
- sperm cell
- fertilization
- uterus
- umbilical cord

Heredity

Heredity (huh·REHD·ih·tee) is *the process by which parents pass traits to their children.* These traits may include eye color, hair color, and body build. Children may also inherit musical or athletic ability. Sometimes, children inherit diseases from their parents.

Parents pass down their traits through their **chromosomes** (KROH·muh·sohmz). These are *pairs of tiny, threadlike pieces of matter that carry the codes for inherited traits.* Each pair of chromosomes in your body contains one chromosome from your father and one from your mother.

Each chromosome is divided into small sections called genes. **Genes** (JEENZ) are *the basic units of heredity.* Each gene is related to a particular trait such as height or eye color. Except for identical twins, who share 100 percent of their genes, each person has a unique arrangement of genes.

Parents and children often look alike because of heredity. *Do you resemble either of your parents?*

170 CHAPTER 6: GROWTH AND DEVELOPMENT

Lesson 5 Resources

Teacher Classroom Resources

 Concept Map 30

 Enrichment Activity 25

Lesson Plan 5

Lesson 5 Quiz

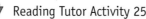 Reading Tutor Activity 25

 Reteaching Activity 26

Transparency 30

Student Activities Workbook

 Chapter 6 Study Guide

 Applying Health Skills 25

Health Inventory 6

Combining Chromosomes

Almost every cell in your body contains 46 chromosomes—23 from each parent. The only human cells that do not have 46 chromosomes are reproductive cells, which can combine to produce a new person. The *reproductive cell in the female body* is an **egg cell**. The *reproductive cell in the male body* is a **sperm cell**. Egg cells and sperm cells have 23 chromosomes each. When they combine, their chromosomes pair up to produce a cell with 46 chromosomes.

The joining together of an egg cell and a sperm cell is called **fertilization**. Each person starts as a tiny fertilized egg cell—smaller than the period at the end of this sentence. During the development process, the cell divides millions of times.

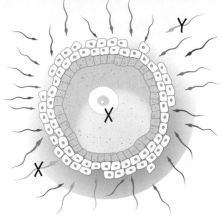

A girl has two X chromosomes. A boy has an X chromosome and a Y chromosome. *Why does every person have at least one X chromosome?*

X and Y Chromosomes

Special chromosomes in sperm cells determine whether a fertilized cell will develop into a male or a female. Each sperm cell contains either an X chromosome or a Y chromosome. Every egg cell contains only an X chromosome. If an X-carrying sperm combines with an egg, it will produce a girl. If the sperm cell has a Y chromosome, it will produce a boy.

HEALTH SKILLS ACTIVITY

ADVOCACY

The Health of Mother and Child

A mother can affect the health of her baby from the moment of fertilization. She needs to keep herself healthy to make sure the baby develops properly. Women can follow several steps to maintain good health during pregnancy.

● Have regular checkups with a health care professional who specializes in the care of pregnant women.

● Eat nutritious foods.

● Get enough rest.
● Follow an exercise plan that the health care professional recommends.
● Do not use alcohol or tobacco.
● Check with the doctor before taking any medicines.

ON YOUR OWN
Create a poster that encourages good health care during pregnancy. You can illustrate your poster with pictures showing good habits for pregnant women to practice.

Lesson 5

② Teach

Cross-Curriculum Activity

SCIENCE Mammals can be divided into three groups on the basis of the way the fertilized egg develops: placentals (such as humans); marsupials (such as kangaroos); and monotremes (such as platypuses). Ask students to research each group and share their findings. For extra credit, ask students: How are mammals different from reptiles? **L3**

HEALTH SKILLS ACTIVITY

ADVOCACY

Help students read and discuss the explanation. Ask why both males and females of all ages should be concerned about the healthy development of babies. Then have students work in cooperative groups to plan and make their posters. Remind students that caffeine should also be avoided. Encourage each group to share its completed poster

Note: This skill is introduced in Chapter 1 on page 12.

INCLUSION STRATEGIES

Different Learning Styles, Behavior Problems, Special Learning Needs Some students may benefit from a visual and/or tactile model to understand the concepts in this lesson. Invite students to create such models to share with the class. For example, students might use a large poster board to draw pictures of a sperm cell and an egg cell, each with 23 chromosomes.

In the sperm cell, students could glue 22 tiny pieces of cut-up straws or coffee stirrers. The 23rd chromosome could be a piece with a big Y (or X) drawn on it with black marker. The egg cell could be represented in a similar way but larger and with the 23rd chromosome marked with a big X. Have students take turns explaining their models.

Critical Thinking

Ask students to speculate about how a human baby's development is probably similar to that of other mammals. (*The baby begins as a fertilized cell; the baby grows inside its mother, the baby gets nourishment from its mother.*) How is a human baby different? (*Responses might include the time it takes for a human baby to develop.*) **L1**

VISUAL LEARNING

FIGURE 6.12 Read aloud the caption for Figure 6.12, and help students read the facts and figures in the table. Give students a visual or concrete aid to help them understand size. Guide them in discussing the importance of each aspect of development. Then ask volunteers to answer the caption question; they should identify a weight of seven to nine pounds. **INCL** *Behavior Problems, Special Learning Needs, English Language Learners*

Discussing

Guide students in discussing the six stages of the life cycle by asking: How can you tell which stage of life a person is in? Do you think there is a specific age at which a person leaves one stage and moves on to the next? Why or why not? **L1**

Reading Check

Understanding text organization. Look at the table and the bulleted list on these two pages. What are are the similarities and differences?

Development Before Birth

The fertilized egg cell develops inside the mother's uterus. The **uterus** (YOO·tuh·ruhs) is *a pear-shaped organ that expands as a baby grows.* The baby gets its nourishment through the **umbilical** (uhm·BIL·i·kuhl) **cord.** This is *a tube that connects the lining of the uterus to the unborn baby.* It attaches to the place where the baby's navel, or belly button, will form. Blood from the mother carries food and oxygen through the cord to the baby. The cord also carries wastes away. **Figure 6.12** shows the stages the unborn baby goes through in the mother's uterus.

FIGURE 6.12

THE DEVELOPING BABY

After fertilization, it takes about nine months of growth and development before a baby is born. *Approximately how much does a baby weigh at birth?*

Time	Size	Features	Development
Fertilization	microscopic	single cell	undeveloped
3 months after fertilization	about 3 inches long; weighs about 1 ounce	arms, legs, fingers, toes, eyes, ears	heart is beating, nervous system is forming; cannot survive outside uterus
6 months after fertilization	about 14 inches long; weighs about 2 pounds	hair, eyebrows, fingernails, toenails	can move and kick, sucks thumb, can hear sounds; might survive outside uterus
9 months after fertilization	18–20 inches long; weighs 7–9 pounds	smooth skin, fully developed organs	eyes open and close, fingers can grasp, body organs and systems can now work on their own; ready for birth

The Life Cycle

During your life, you will go through many stages of growth and development. This series of stages is sometimes called the life cycle. It begins at birth and continues through childhood, adolescence, and adulthood.

- **Infancy.** Infancy is the first year of a baby's life. Infants grow, learn, and change at an astonishing rate. This growth and development continues throughout childhood.
- **Childhood.** Young children learn to walk and talk. They also develop other physical and mental skills that they will need throughout their lives. After they enter school, children grow mentally and socially. They learn about solving problems and getting along with others.

Reading Check

Analyzing Text Thinking about how the author chose to organize information helps students retain facts and understand difficult concepts. Point out to students that the purpose of these pages is to provide information about the stages of human development before birth and after birth. The chart called The Developing Baby organizes information by time period and category. The bulleted list called The Life Cycle organizes information more simply by time period. Ask students to identify and compare the time periods used in the chart and the list and to discuss the different types of information the chart and list provide.

- **Adolescence.** Aside from infancy, adolescence is the time of most rapid change in a person's life. During this period, a person's body takes on its adult form. Adolescents also grow mentally, emotionally, and socially.
- **Early adulthood.** In early adulthood—from about age 19 to age 30—most people begin a career. They may move out of their parents' homes and begin to build their own homes and lives. Many young adults choose to marry and begin families at this stage of their lives.
- **Middle adulthood.** Adults over 30 may begin to look outward toward their families and communities. Many focus their energy on raising children. Others try to contribute something to the world through their careers or other efforts such as volunteer work or hobbies.
- **Late adulthood.** After age 60 or so, adults may begin to reflect on what they have accomplished in their lives. People who have fulfilled their goals and have lived according to their values can usually look back on their lives with satisfaction.

People go through many changes between childhood and adulthood. *What are some of the ways you have changed in the past three years?*

Lesson 5 Review

Using complete sentences, answer the following questions on a sheet of paper.

Reviewing Terms and Facts
1. **Vocabulary** Write a short paragraph explaining the meanings of *heredity, chromosomes,* and *genes.*
2. **Recall** Which cells in the human body do not have 46 chromosomes?
3. **Identify** In what part of the mother's body does a baby develop during pregnancy?

Thinking Critically
4. **Explain** What determines whether a baby will be male or female?

5. **Summarize** Describe the changes a person goes through over the course of the life cycle.

Applying Health Skills
6. **Analyzing Influences** How much does heredity influence you? Create a chart with three columns. Label them *Physical Traits, Mental/Emotional Traits,* and *Social Traits.* In each column, list characteristics that you think you have inherited from your parents or other relatives. How much of your appearance and personality appears to be inherited? How much do you think is due to other factors?

LESSON 5: HEREDITY AND GROWTH **173**

Are You Active Enough?

❶ Focus

Objectives

Students will be able to:

• list the benefits of physical activity.

• dispel common exercise myths.

• describe common barriers to physical activity and ways to overcome them.

Motivator

Quick Write

Write the words "physical activity" on the board. Have students list the first ten words or phrases that come to mind when they see these words. After a few minutes, ask students to share their lists. Write these items on the board, breaking the words up into appropriate categories such as nouns, adjectives, proper names, advertising slogans, and so on. Ask: "Do most students view physical activity as a positive or negative experience? How commercialized is our relationship to physical activity?"

❷ Teach

Investigating

Direct students' attention to quiz question #3. Ask students, "With so many benefits to working out, why are many Americans still inactive?" Tell students that they are going to conduct an informal poll among their friends and family members, asking "What barriers keep you from getting enough physical activity?" (Prompt students with several sample responses, such as *not enough time, bad weather, no money for equipment,* and so on.) Give students several days to conduct the poll. Have volunteers share their results with the class and discuss specific ways to overcome each barrier presented (e.g., *the barrier of bad weather might be overcome by joining a gym*).

174

Are You Active Enough?

Take this quiz to find out if you're on the right track when it comes to physical activity.

Quiz

1. A thin person is always more fit than a heavier person.
   a. True   b. False

2. All your muscle will quickly turn into fat if you stop working out.
   a. True   b. False

3. Regular cardiovascular workouts will
   a. make you a happier person.
   b. keep you from catching colds.
   c. help you sleep better.
   d. All of the above

4. While exercising, you should push yourself to the limit or the workout won't do you any good.
   a. True   b. False

Answers: 1. b.; 2. b.; 3. d.; 4. b.

Check out the explanations on the next page!

174 CHAPTER 6: GROWTH AND DEVELOPMENT

MORE ABOUT...

Professional Athletes Have each student write a one-page essay responding to the question, "Are professional athletes good role-models for a healthy, active lifestyle?" Ask students to consider the information they have learned in this spread (such as the "no pain, no gain" myth) in writing their responses. Student essays should include specific examples of known athletes and their activities both on and off the playing field. Ask several students to share their work with the class, and then lead a group discussion.

Explanations

1. "People equate what your body looks like to how fit you are, but **even a thin person can have too much fat and not enough muscle**," says Liz Neporent, exercise physiologist and author of *Fitness for Dummies*. Basically, the more muscle you have, the better shape you're in, no matter what your size.

2. **"When you stop exercising, muscles begin to atrophy, or shrink,"** says Nancy Yumkas of the Equinox Fitness Training Institute in New York City. As a result, the muscles become less prominent but do not turn to fat. If you continue to eat as much as you did when you were active, the excess calories that you would have burned off will now be stored as additional fat. When that happens, your muscles become harder to see. To regain muscle, you have to get back into your previous exercise routine and burn off any extra fat.

3. **Exercise helps decrease muscle tension** (especially tension caused by sedentary activities like sitting at a computer) while increasing blood circulation. Together, these two factors help make you more relaxed and calm. Regular exercise builds up the immune system and relieves frustrations. At the same time, it helps the body produce endorphins—chemicals in the brain that are believed to make you feel happier and ward off feelings of depression or anxiety.

4. **"'No pain, no gain' is such a farce,"** says Yumkas. Exercise needn't be agony to be good for you. Actually, if it hurts (especially in your joints or lower back), you may be doing something wrong and should stop immediately. Still, there's a reason it's called working out. You'll know you've had a great workout when your muscles feel tired.

Start Working Out Now!

Teens who participate in sports have a higher level of confidence, a better self-image, and lower levels of depression.

By building muscle and reducing fat, being active on a regular basis improves physical appearance.

Physical activity reduces the risk of heart disease, diabetes, and high blood pressure.

TIME TO THINK...

About Physical Activity

With the help of your physical-education instructor, create a workout that will benefit cardiovascular health—that is, one that will get the heart beating and the blood pumping. Share your class's routine with other classes.

TIME HEALTH

❸ Apply

Time to Think

Before students begin creating their workouts, help them in defining parameters. Routines should "get the heart beating and the blood pumping," but for how long and at what rate? Can they include sports equipment such as jump ropes and basketballs? Can they include music? Should the routine be done indoors or out? It is an individual or group routine? Asking students to consider these questions will help them to recognize that devising a cardiovascular workout can be fun and creative.

VISUAL LEARNING

Ask students to list the seven different ways of being active shown in this illustration. Ask, "Are these activities that almost anyone can do? Are special equipment or facilities necessary to take part in these activities? How might that affect one's ability to take part in the activity? What activities might you add to this illustration that don't require as much equipment (*dancing, walking, calisthenics*)?"

WHAT TEENS WANT TO KNOW

What if I'm just not coordinated? Remind students that there are fitness opportunities suitable for every interest, personality, and skill level. Encourage them to try a range of activities that focus on strength (weightlifting), endurance (running, swimming) or flexibility (dance), rather than hand-eye coordination. Most importantly, encourage all students to focus on fun, participation, and good sportsmanship rather than the scoreboard.

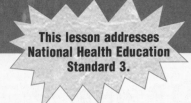

This lesson addresses National Health Education Standard 3.

PRACTICING HEALTHFUL BEHAVIORS

Objective

After completing the lesson, students will be able to describe habits that demonstrate responsibility for the body systems.

Time: 45 minutes

Materials: pen or pencil

Teacher Classroom Resources

- Building Health Skills Activities
- Transparency Master 2a, "Practicing Healthful Behaviors"
- Reproducible Master 6, "Keeping Body Systems Healthy"

---

1. Model

- Display Transparency Master 2a, and discuss its content as a class.

- Direct students to read about Terry, a teen athlete. Have them identify the strategies that Terry takes to keep his respiratory system healthy. (*Answer: He avoids areas where people are smoking, participates in outdoor activities only when the air quality is good, rests and drinks plenty of fluids when he is ill.*)

KEEPING BODY SYSTEMS HEALTHY

Model

Terry is a teen athlete. He knows that he needs to keep his body systems healthy to be able to stay in shape for his sports activities. This year, he is playing basketball and running track. Because these activities require strong lungs, he takes good care of his respiratory system. He always sits in the nonsmoking section of restaurants, and his parents do not allow guests to smoke in their house. He plans his outdoor activities for times when the air quality is good. Whenever he has a cough or cold, Terry rests and drinks plenty of fluids until he is well. These behaviors help him play better and also improve his total health.

176 CHAPTER 6: GROWTH AND DEVELOPMENT

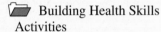

Teaching Tips

Providing Examples Before students begin working on the Apply/Assess, it may be helpful to present to the class one or two short video clips of a typical newscast, particularly one that deals with a health issue, medical breakthrough, or how to prevent or treat common health problems.

Watching how professional newscasters present information will help students formulate their reports. Having a good role model will help them get started and feel more confident in completing the assignment. Emphasize that students' news reports do not have to be perfect, but should show an understanding of the concepts of this lesson. **INCL** *Behavior Problems, Special Learning Needs*

Practice

Form small groups. Choose one of the body systems you have learned about in this chapter. Write the name of that body system at the top of a sheet of paper. Then divide the paper into two columns labeled *Healthful Habits* and *Harmful Habits*. Use the first column to identify habits that can benefit your chosen body system. Use the second column to list habits that can harm that body system. At the bottom of the page, write a statement explaining why it is important to care for this body system.

Apply/Assess

Working with your group, create a news report about how to keep your body systems healthy. Your report should be three to five minutes long and should be in a style similar to a television news broadcast. In your report, describe at least three ways to care for all of your body systems. Include an explanation of how these three behaviors can benefit specific body systems. Present your report to the class.

Coach's Box

Practicing Healthful Behaviors

Caring for your body systems includes
- staying active.
- eating nutritious foods.
- avoiding harmful substances.
- taking care of illnesses.
- managing stress.

Self-Check
- Is our report three to five minutes long?
- Did we describe at least three ways to care for body systems?
- Did we explain why these habits are healthy?

TAKE CARE OF ILLNESS

MANAGE STRESS

BUILDING HEALTH SKILLS: KEEPING BODY SYSTEMS HEALTHY **177**

2. Practice

- Divide the class into groups of three to five students, and ask each group to choose a different body system.
- Have each group identify healthful and harmful habits for their system and list these habits on a sheet of paper. Instruct them to write a summary statement at the bottom of the paper about the importance of caring for that particular body system.
- As a class, review each group's lists and summary statements. Which ones are specific to a particular body system? Which may apply to more than one system?

3. Apply/Assess

- You may wish to distribute Building Health Skills Reproducible Master 6 in the TCR to guide students in completing this activity.
- Instruct each group to create a three- to five-minute news report about maintaining the health of the body system they have chosen. Reports should discuss at least three ways to care for that body system.
- Ask students to use a news report format, with an anchor person in the studio who introduces the story and then goes to the reporter(s) who interview(s) experts on caring for body systems.

Assessment Scoring

Using a rubric, student work should provide evidence of all criteria to achieve the highest score.

Skills
Student work describes
- at least three behaviors that benefit body systems.
- how these behaviors benefit specific body systems.

Concepts
Student work provides
- accurate information about body systems.
- an explanation of the relationships among body systems.

Checking Comprehension

Use the Chapter 6 Assessment to examine the most important ideas presented in the chapter.

Answers to Reviewing Vocabulary and Concepts

Lesson 1
1. cells
2. organ
3. body system

Lesson 2
4. muscular
5. circulatory
6. blood pressure
7. lungs

Lesson 3
8. neurons
9. peripheral
10. digestive

Lesson 4
11. true
12. false; personality
13. false; behavior

Lesson 5
14. false; chromosomes
15. false; fertilization
16. true
17. true
18. false; umbilical cord

Thinking Critically

19. The alveoli are surrounded by capillaries. As blood passes through the capillaries, oxygen flows into the blood and carbon dioxide flows out to be exhaled.
20. The central nervous system (CNS) consists of the brain and spinal cord. The peripheral nervous system (PNS) is made up of nerves that branch out from the spinal cord. It carries messages from the CNS to the rest of the body.

CHAPTER ASSESSMENT 6

After You Read

Use your completed Foldable to review the information on cells, tissues, organs, and body systems.

 FOLDABLES Study Organizer

Reviewing Vocabulary and Concepts

On a sheet of paper, write the numbers 1–10. After each number, write the term from the list that best completes each sentence.

- blood pressure
- body system
- circulatory
- digestive
- cells
- lungs
- muscular
- neurons
- organ
- peripheral

Lesson 1

1. Your entire body is made up of _____, the basic building blocks of life.
2. The brain is one very important _____ in your body.
3. A(n) _____ is a group of organs that performs a specific function in your body.

Lesson 2

4. The muscles of your body make up the _____ system.
5. The heart muscle pumps blood through the _____ system.
6. _____ is lowest between heartbeats, when the heart relaxes.
7. The _____ are key organs in the respiratory system.

Lesson 3

8. The brain is made up of billions of _____, or cells that carry electrical messages.
9. The _____ nervous system is made up of nerves that branch out from the spinal cord.
10. The stomach, liver, and pancreas are all parts of the _____ system.

On a sheet of paper, write the numbers 11–18. Write *True* or *False* for each statement below. If the statement is false, change the underlined word or phrase to make it true.

Lesson 4

11. The <u>endocrine system</u> consists of glands throughout the body that produce hormones.
12. Your <u>behavior</u> is the sum total of your feelings, actions, habits, and thoughts.
13. <u>Puberty</u> is how you act in situations that occur in your life.

Lesson 5

14. <u>Genes</u> are tiny, threadlike pieces of matter that carry the codes for inherited traits.
15. An egg cell and a sperm cell join together in a process called <u>heredity</u>.
16. Aside from infancy, the period of greatest change in a person's life is <u>adolescence</u>.
17. The stages of growth and development are also known as the <u>life cycle</u>.
18. An unborn baby gets its nourishment through the <u>egg cell</u>.

Thinking Critically

Using complete sentences, answer the following questions on a sheet of paper.

19. **Analyze** Explain how the exchange of oxygen for carbon dioxide in the lungs involves both the respiratory and the circulatory systems.

INCLUSION STRATEGIES

Special Learning Needs, Behavior Problems, English Language Learners The following suggestions are helpful for students with special learning needs, students with behavior problems, and ELL students:

- Pair these students with more proficient learners who can help summarize the main concepts of the chapter.

- 🎧 Direct these students to listen to the Teen Health Audio Summaries. This component provides an audio and written summary of the chapter in both English and Spanish.

- Use photographs, drawings, or magazine clippings whenever possible to help students visualize the important concepts of the chapter.

20. **Contrast** Explain the difference between the functions of the central nervous system and those of the peripheral nervous system.
21. **Explain** In what ways do relationships between parents and children change during adolescence?
22. **Analyze** Explain why adulthood, rather than adolescence, is the best time to have children.
23. **Research** Conduct research on menstrual health. Describe menstrual health and identify its relationship to reproduction.

Career Corner

Physician Physicians are medical professionals who have completed many years of training. One of their goals is to help patients detect problems with their growth and development. If a patient has one of these problems, the physician works to find the best way of treating it. Physicians can also help prevent these problems from occurring. If you think you'd like to help people stay healthy, visit Career Corner at health.glencoe.com.

Standardized Test Practice

Reading & Writing

Read the paragraph below and then answer the questions.

As the heart pumps blood throughout the circulatory system, a pulse is produced. Here is one way to take your pulse: Place the three middle fingers of one hand on the inside of your other wrist. Press gently until you feel a regular throbbing. Look at the second hand of a clock or watch and count the number of beats you feel in your wrist for exactly thirty seconds. Multiply the number of beats you count by two. This is your pulse rate for one minute. Each beat of your pulse is equal to the two sounds your heart makes during one heartbeat.

1. The writer gives the steps for taking a pulse
   - (A) in the order that they must be done.
   - (B) in no special order.
   - (C) by comparing methods.
   - (D) by describing each step.

2. What must you do before you feel for a regular throbbing?
   - (A) multiply by two
   - (B) count the number of beats
   - (C) place three fingers on the inside of your wrist
   - (D) look for a clock

3. Write a paragraph explaining the steps you must take in order to accomplish a specific task.

 TH05_C1.glencoe.com/quiz

---

21. Possible responses: teens demonstrate more independence, understand that parents also have needs and wants, and exhibit more responsibility.
22. Adolescents may not be physically or emotionally ready to have babies because they lack the skills and resources necessary to be responsible parents. It will also be difficult for them to achieve their other goals.
23. Responses should include the concept that good menstrual health will contribute to good reproductive health as an adult.

Test Practice
   1. A
   2. C
   3. Responses should give the steps necessary for completing a specific task in the correct order.

Reteaching
📁 Assign Study Guide 6 in the Student Activities Workbook.

Evaluate
• 📁 💿 Use the reproducible Chapter 6 Test in the TCR, or construct your own test using the **Exam**View® Pro Testmaker.
• 📁 Use Performance Assessment 6 in the TCR

Enrichment
Let students work in groups to plan and present skits or pantomimes that highlight the importance or functions of one of the body systems presented in this chapter.

Assessment ✔

Self-Assessment Direct students to review the activities that are provided throughout the chapter. Encourage each student to select one finished product or activity that demonstrates his or her best work for the chapter. Have students explain what they learned and how the examples they selected show their progress.

Career Corner

Physician After reviewing the career profile on the health Web site, students might:
• Describe the skills, training, and education needed.
• Discuss what type of personal strengths would be best suited for this career (*talent to relate well with people, ability to handle emergencies*).

Planning Guide

Chapter 7	Skills/ Activities	Reproducible Resources	Assessment
Lesson 1 **Causes of Diseases** *pages 182–186*	**Hands-On Health** ▲ Learning How Germs Spread, page 186	*Student Activities Workbook available for use with each chapter* 📁 Parent Letter & Activities 7 📁 Concept Map 31 📁 Cross-Curriculum Activity 13 📁 Enrichment Activity 26 📁 Lesson Plan 1 📁 Reading Tutor Activity 26 📁 Reteaching Activity 27	📁 Lesson 1 Quiz
Lesson 2 **Communicable Diseases** *pages 187–190*		📁 Concept Maps 32, 33 📁 Cross-Curriculum Activity 14 📁 Decision-Making Activity 13 📁 Enrichment Activity 27 📁 Lesson Plan 2 📁 Reading Tutor Activity 27 📁 Reteaching Activity 28	📁 Lesson 2 Quiz
Lesson 3 **Understanding STIs** *pages 191–195*		📁 Concept Map 34 📁 Enrichment Activity 28 📁 Lesson Plan 3 📁 Reading Tutor Activity 28 📁 Reteaching Activity 29	📁 Lesson 3 Quiz
Lesson 4 **Noncommunicable Diseases** *pages 196–201*	**HEALTH SKILLS ACTIVITY** ▲ Learning More About Noncommunicable and Hereditary Diseases (*Accessing Information*), page 199	📁 Concept Map 35 📁 Decision-Making Activity 14 📁 Enrichment Activity 29 📁 Health Lab 7 📁 Lesson Plan 4 📁 Reading Tutor Activity 29 📁 Reteaching Activity 30	📁 Lesson 4 Quiz 📁 Chapter 7 Test 📁 Performance Assessment 7

TIME HEALTH | **Getting Smart About Vaccines** *pages 202–203*

BUILDING HEALTH SKILLS

Protecting Your Health
(*Goal Setting*)
pages 204–205

📁 Building Health Skills Reproducible Master 7

Standards		Technology
National	State/Local	
National Health Education Standard **1.3, 1.5, 1.8, 3.1, 3.4**		Transparency 31 TeacherWorks™
National Health Education Standard **1.1, 1.3, 1.5, 1.6, 1.7, 1.8, 2.6, 3.1, 3.4**		Transparency 32 TeacherWorks™
National Health Education Standard **1.1, 1.3, 1.5, 1.6, 1.7, 1.8, 2.6, 3.1, 3.3, 3.4**		Transparency 33 TeacherWorks™
National Health Education Standard **1.1, 1.5, 1.6, 1.7, 1.8, 2.2, 2.6, 3.1**		Transparency 34 TeacherWorks™ MindJogger Videoquiz Exam*View*® Pro Testmaker
National Health Education Standard **6.4, 6.5, 6.6**		Building Health Skills Transparency Master 9

TeacherWorks™

Glencoe's new and exclusive TeacherWorks™ is an all-in-one planner and resource center. Access the complete Teacher Wraparound Edition electronically. Find all your classroom resources with just a few easy clicks, and print them right from your computer. Connect directly to Glencoe's customized Health Web site. Access the National Health Education Standards correlations, or insert your own state standards and match them directly to the electronic Teacher Wraparound Edition.

Language Diversity

- English Audio Summaries
- Spanish Audio Summaries
- English Summaries, Quizzes, and Activities
- Spanish Summaries, Quizzes, and Activities
- Spanish Parent Letters and Activities

KEY TO ABILITY LEVELS

Teaching Strategies that appear throughout the chapters have been identified by one of four codes to give you an idea of their suitability for students of varying learning styles and abilities.

L1 **Level 1** strategies should be within the ability range of all students. Often full class participation is required.

L2 **Level 2** strategies are for average to above-average students or for small groups. Some teacher direction is necessary.

L3 **Level 3** strategies are designed for students able and willing to work independently. Minimal teacher direction is necessary.

INCL Strategies are appropriate for students with particular special needs in a general classroom setting.

Preventing Diseases

Chapter at a Glance

Lesson 1 explains the distinction between communicable and noncommunicable diseases, discusses the spread of communicable diseases, and describes the body's defenses against communicable diseases.

Lesson 2 identifies common communicable diseases and discusses how they can be prevented and treated.

Lesson 3 identifies sexually transmitted diseases (STDs) and discusses how they can be prevented and treated. Note: Be sure to obtain the permission of parents and your school administration before teaching this lesson.

Lesson 4 examines the development and treatment of noncommunicable diseases, including heart disease, cancer, allergies, asthma, and diabetes.

Health Skills

- Learning More About Noncommunicable and Hereditary Diseases (*Accessing Information*), p. 199

- Protecting Your Health (*Goal Setting*), pp. 204–205

SIGN IN

180

HANDS-ON ACTIVITY

How's Your Family's Health? Information about a family's health history is very important. Obtain a family health history form from an organization like the March of Dimes. Make up a fictitious family, consisting of a father, mother, and three children. Provide these basic facts for each family member: name, date of birth, blood with Rh factor, childhood diseases. Then add special information such as whether anyone in the family wears a medical alert bracelet. Has a chronic condition? Has a genetic condition? Create a transparency that illustrates this information for the class. Discuss with students the importance of family history, heredity, and healthful behaviors to prevent communicable and noncommunicable diseases.

Preventing Diseases

 **HEALTH** *Online*

Visit health.glencoe.com and take the Chapter 7 Health Inventory to test what you know about HIV and AIDS.

FOLDABLES™
Study Organizer

Before You Read

Make this Foldable to help you organize the information in Lesson 1 about the four types of disease-causing germs. Begin with a plain sheet of 11″ × 17″ paper.

Step 1

Fold the short sides of a sheet of paper inward so that they meet in the middle.

Step 2

Fold the top to the bottom.

Step 3

Open and cut along the inside fold lines to form four tabs.

Step 4

Label tabs as shown.

As You Read

Write down facts about viruses, bacteria, protozoa, and fungi. Give examples of each under the appropriate tab.

| Viruses | Protozoa |
| Bacteria | Fungi |

181

Chapter Introduction

Use the options below to motivate students and preview chapter content.

HEALTH *Online*

Encourage students to take Health Inventory 7 at health.glencoe.com. Then brush up on health education by reading Professional Articles for health teachers. These articles can help keep you informed of national and state trends.

GLENCOE TECHNOLOGY

MindJogger Videoquiz

Use MindJogger to preview or review Chapter 7 content.

TIME HEALTH

Getting Smart About Vaccines
pages 202–203

FOLDABLES™
Study Organizer

Dinah Zike Study Fold

Note Taking and Research
Instruct students to record information about each type of disease-causing organism under the appropriate tab of their Foldable. Explain to students that note taking is a skill that is based upon reading or listening for main ideas and then writing down those ideas for future reference. Encourage students to use reliable sources to conduct additional research on each type of pathogen.

Lesson 1

Causes of Diseases

Focus

Lesson Objectives

Students will be able to
- explain how they get sick.
- list the four most common disease-causing germs.
- explain four ways that germs are spread.
- discuss the body's defenses against disease.

Motivators

Quick Write

Allow time for students to share their responses. As responses are shared, ask students to list the symptoms, possible causes, and methods used to avoid getting sick.

Bellringer Activity

Ask students: What diseases can be passed from person to person? Give students a few minutes to list examples. Once you have identified correct examples, tell students that these types of diseases are called communicable diseases.

> **VOCABULARY**
>
> Focus students' attention on the terms *communicable disease* and *noncommunicable disease*. Point out that both words derive from the Latin word *communis*, meaning "public or common." You may also want to point out that the prefix *non-* in *noncommunicable* means "not."

Causes of Diseases

Quick Write

Think about the last time you missed school because of an illness. Can you think of anything you could have done to avoid getting sick?

LEARN ABOUT...

- what makes you sick.
- how diseases can spread.
- how your body defends itself against disease.

VOCABULARY

- disease
- communicable disease
- noncommunicable disease
- pathogen
- infection
- immune system
- lymphocyte
- antibody
- immunity

Types of Diseases

A **disease** (dih·ZEEZ) is *an unhealthy condition of the body or mind.* Some diseases, such as cancer, can be very dangerous or even deadly. Others, like colds, are far less serious.

There are two types of disease. A **communicable** (kuh·MYOO·ni·kuh·buhl) **disease** is *a disease that can be spread,* such as a cold. You can get a communicable disease from another person, an object, or an animal. A **noncommunicable disease** is *a disease that does not spread,* such as diabetes or cancer. You can't catch these diseases from another person.

With a microscope, a scientist can see disease-causing germs that are invisible to the unaided eye.

Lesson 1 Resources

Teacher Classroom Resources

 Parent Letter & Activities 7
Concept Map 31
Cross-Curriculum Activity 13
Enrichment Activity 26
Lesson Plan 1
Lesson 1 Quiz

Reading Tutor Activity 26
Reteaching Activity 27
Transparency 31

Student Activities Workbook
Chapter 7 Study Guide
Applying Health Skills 26

Germs That Cause Disease

Most communicable diseases are caused by germs, tiny organisms that can't be seen without a microscope. Lots of germs are present on your skin at all times, and most of them are harmless or even helpful. However, some germs are harmful. These *disease-causing germs* are called **pathogens**. **Figure 7.1** shows some common pathogens. *The result of pathogens invading the body, multiplying, and harming some of your body's cells* is an **infection**. If your body cannot fight off the infection, you will get sick.

FIGURE 7.1

COMMON DISEASE-CAUSING GERMS

These photos show close-ups of four common disease-causing germs. *Have you had any of the diseases caused by these germs?*

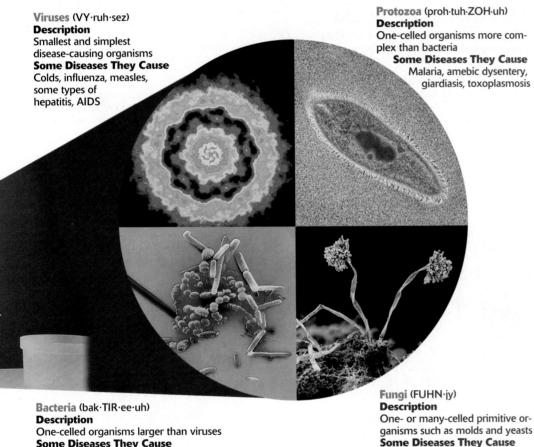

Viruses (VY·ruh·sez)
Description
Smallest and simplest disease-causing organisms
Some Diseases They Cause
Colds, influenza, measles, some types of hepatitis, AIDS

Protozoa (proh·tuh·ZOH·uh)
Description
One-celled organisms more complex than bacteria
Some Diseases They Cause
Malaria, amebic dysentery, giardiasis, toxoplasmosis

Bacteria (bak·TIR·ee·uh)
Description
One-celled organisms larger than viruses
Some Diseases They Cause
Strep throat, gonorrhea, tuberculosis, Lyme disease, whooping cough

Fungi (FUHN·jy)
Description
One- or many-celled primitive organisms such as molds and yeasts
Some Diseases They Cause
Athlete's foot, jock itch, ringworm, thrush, vaginal yeast infections

LESSON 1: CAUSES OF DISEASES **183**

How Germs Spread

There are lots of different ways germs can enter your body. You may even be spreading them without knowing it. **Figure 7.2** shows the four most common ways that disease-causing germs are transmitted to people.

Your First Line of Defense

You are exposed to millions of disease-causing germs each day. So why aren't you sick all the time? The main reason is that a healthy body is in good fighting shape. If you keep yourself healthy and strong, your body will destroy many pathogens before they can hurt you. Some pathogens are destroyed before they enter your body. Your natural defenses find and wipe out many of those that do make their way in.

FIGURE 7.2

WAYS GERMS CAN SPREAD

This picture shows some ways germs can spread. *Describe various modes of disease transmission.*

Food or Water
You can get an infection by eating or drinking impure food or water. Bacteria that cause food poisoning can be spread this way.

Indirect Contact
Some germs can spread through the air. You can also pick up germs if you share cups, utensils, or other personal items with a sick person.

Contact with Animals or Insects
You can get an infection if an infected insect or animal bites you.

Direct Contact
You can pick up germs if you touch an infected area on another person. Germs that cause skin infections are spread this way. Some diseases, such as AIDS, are spread through direct sexual contact.

184 CHAPTER 7: PREVENTING DISEASES

General Defenses

Your body has barriers to protect you from pathogens. These include your skin and mucous membranes, which line the inside of body parts such as your nose, mouth, and throat. Body fluids, such as tears and saliva, are also barriers. They contain chemicals that destroy certain germs. If germs get past these barriers, your body responds with general reactions. They are called *general* because they are the same for all pathogens.

- Special blood cells surround pathogens and destroy them.
- A chemical is released to stop viruses from reproducing.
- Fever, or a rise in body temperature, kills some pathogens and makes it hard for others to reproduce.

Your Immune System

Your **immune** (i·MYOON) **system** is *a group of cells, tissues, and organs that fight disease.* One key part of the immune system is **lymphocytes** (LIM·fuh·syts), *white blood cells that attack pathogens.* Some lymphocytes attack germs directly. Others produce **antibodies**, *chemicals produced specifically to fight a particular invading substance* (see **Figure 7.3**). If the same germ enters your body again, the existing antibodies that developed to fight this particular germ will attack and destroy it. This *resistance to infection* is called **immunity**.

FIGURE 7.3

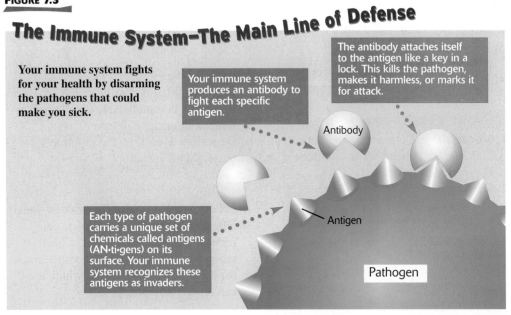

The Immune System—The Main Line of Defense

Your immune system fights for your health by disarming the pathogens that could make you sick.

Your immune system produces an antibody to fight each specific antigen.

The antibody attaches itself to the antigen like a key in a lock. This kills the pathogen, makes it harmless, or marks it for attack.

Antibody

Each type of pathogen carries a unique set of chemicals called antigens (AN·ti·gens) on its surface. Your immune system recognizes these antigens as invaders.

Antigen

Pathogen

LESSON 1: CAUSES OF DISEASES **185**

Comprehending

Guide students in discussing fevers. Have them describe how fever defends the body against illness. Ask: Do you think a fever should be treated as a symptom or as a disease? Why? Have students consider the benefits of fever-reducing medications as well as the kinds of problems they could cause. **L1**

VISUAL LEARNING

FIGURE 7.3 Ask students to meet with partners or in small groups to study and discuss Figure 7.3. Then have partners or group members work together to summarize the steps in the immune system response, using either sketches or written notes. **INCL** *Behavior Problems, Special Learning Needs, English Language Learners*

Developing Good Character ★

Responsibility

To review this lesson, have students take out a piece of paper and fold it in half. On one side have them list steps they can take when they are sick to protect others. On the other side, list steps they can take to protect themselves when others are sick.

WHAT TEENS WANT TO KNOW

What's the difference between a cold and the flu?
Typically, a cold develops gradually over the course of a day or two. You may have a runny nose, mild sore throat, headache, and body aches. Flu symptoms develop suddenly. They are similar to cold symptoms but usually more severe. When you have the flu, you generally feel more ill than you do with a cold. This is because flu viruses produce symptoms throughout the body, including muscle aches, weakness, fever, and chills. Cold viruses generally produce symptoms only in the respiratory system. Colds and the flu are very contagious. Symptoms are best treated by resting and drinking plenty of fluids.

LEARNING HOW GERMS SPREAD

Time: 30 minutes

TEACHING THE ACTIVITY

- Divide the class into four or five groups.
- To avoid later eye irritation, have students wash their hands when they have completed the activity. Also, remind them to avoid touching their faces and eyes.
- If your school has available materials, you can have students conduct the same activity using fingerprint dusting powder, which can be seen only under a black light.

ASSESSMENT

Have students discuss their responses to the In Conclusion questions.

❸ Assess

Evaluating

📁 Assign the Lesson 1 Review; then assign the Lesson 1 Quiz in the TCR.

Reteaching

📁 Assign Concept Map 31 or Reteaching Activity 27 in the TCR.

Enrichment

📁 Assign Enrichment Activity 26 in the TCR.

❹ Close

Ask students to write one or two sentences identifying habits they should adopt, or break, in order to avoid spreading germs.

Hands-On Health

LEARNING HOW GERMS SPREAD

People's hands can spread germs easily. This activity shows how.

WHAT YOU WILL NEED
- cotton balls
- peppermint or lemon extract flavoring

WHAT YOU WILL DO
1. Form groups of five or more. Place a few drops of flavoring on a cotton ball. Have one member of each group rub the cotton over the palm of his or her hand and wait for the liquid to dry.
2. Have the person who applied the food flavoring shake hands with two other people in the group. Those people, in turn, should shake hands with the rest of the people in the group.
3. Smell your hand to determine whether the flavoring was transferred to you.

IN CONCLUSION
1. If the food flavoring had been a group of cold viruses, how many people in the group would have picked up the germs on their hands?
2. What might they have done later to allow the viruses to enter their bodies?
3. How does frequent handwashing help prevent the spread of germs?

Lesson 1 Review

Using complete sentences, answer the following questions on a sheet of paper.

Reviewing Terms and Facts
1. **Vocabulary** Define the words *infection* and *immune system*. Write a sentence that includes both terms.
2. **Describe** Explain four ways that germs can spread.
3. **Identify** What barriers and general reactions help keep pathogens from infecting your body?
4. **Recall** Which in the following list are parts of the immune system: antibodies, lymphocytes, bacteria?

Thinking Critically
5. **Explain** What is the difference between a communicable disease and a noncommunicable disease?
6. **Describe** How does the immune system fight off infection?

Applying Health Skills
7. **Practicing Healthful Behaviors** Make a list of healthful behaviors that could prevent disease-causing germs from entering your body. Make sure you account for each of the four ways in which they can enter your body.

186 CHAPTER 7: PREVENTING DISEASES

Lesson 1 Review

1. See definitions on pages 183 and 185. Sentences will vary.
2. Direct contact, indirect contact, contact with animals or insects, or infected food or water.
3. Barriers are the skin, mucous membranes, tears, and saliva. General reactions are special blood cells that surround and destroy pathogens, a chemical that stops viruses from reproducing, and fever.
4. antibodies, lymphocytes
5. A communicable disease can be spread; a noncommunicable disease starts within a person's body and does not spread to other people.
6. Some lymphocytes multiply and attack the germs; other lymphocytes produce antibodies that can destroy the germ if it should reenter the body at a later time.

Communicable Diseases

Common Communicable Diseases

The most common communicable disease is the common cold. It is responsible for more school absences than any other illness. More than 200 different viruses can cause colds. Symptoms include mild fever, runny nose, itchy eyes, sneezing, coughing, sore throat, and headache. If you have these symptoms, talk to your parents or guardians about staying home for the first 24 hours after they appear. During this period, your cold is most **contagious** (cuhn·TA·jus). This means that it is *able to spread to others by direct or indirect contact.*

It is important to stay home and rest when you have a cold. Also, drink plenty of water.

Quick Write

What do you usually do when you catch a cold? Describe your favorite cold treatment, and explain why you think it is effective.

LEARN ABOUT...

- the most common communicable diseases.
- how you can keep from getting sick so often.
- what vaccines you need.

VOCABULARY

- contagious
- vaccine

Lesson 2

Communicable Diseases

1 Focus

Lesson Objectives

Students will be able to

- identify the most common communicable diseases.
- discuss healthy behaviors that can help stop the spread of communicable diseases.
- list and discuss the vaccines that can prevent diseases.

Motivators

Quick Write

Have students briefly write their responses on a half sheet of paper. Collect the student responses and share them with the class.

Bellringer Activity

Ask students to suggest the differences in treating colds for children and adults (*types and dosages of medications*).

VOCABULARY

Have students work with partners to look up and discuss the definition of each vocabulary term. Then let partners work together to write original sentences using each term in context.

Lesson 2 Resources

Teacher Classroom Resources

 Concept Map 32 & 33

 Cross-Curriculum Activity 14

 Decision-Making Activity 13

Enrichment Activity 27

Health Lab 1

Lesson Plan 2

 Lesson 2 Quiz

Reading Tutor Activity 27

Reteaching Activity 28

 Transparency 32

Student Activities Workbook

 Chapter 7 Study Guide

Applying Health Skills 27

Lesson 2

② Teach

Discussing

Guide students in describing various modes of disease transmission. Then, discuss behaviors that people can use to protect their own health and the health of others. Have students identify the health behaviors that seem most important and explain their choices. Then ask them to identify those health behaviors that are already habits and those they want to work toward developing as habits. **L1**

Scientists estimate that, in the course of one year, Americans suffer from 1 billion colds.

VISUAL LEARNING

FIGURE 7.4 Have students work in small groups to study and discuss the information presented in Figure 7.4. Ask students: How are most of these diseases transmitted? Help students conclude that most of these diseases are transmitted through infected droplets in the air. Then have the members of each group plan and present a short skit about one of the common communicable diseases. Skits may highlight symptoms, prevention, and/or treatment. **INCL** *Behavior Problems, Special Learning Needs, English Language Learners*

Other communicable diseases include influenza (known as "the flu"), mononucleosis, hepatitis (types A, B, and C), strep throat, and tuberculosis. **Figure 7.4** describes these five diseases. Some of these diseases can be prevented with **vaccines** (vak·SEENZ), *preparations of killed or weakened germs.* Vaccines cause your immune system to produce antibodies, protecting you against the disease.

FIGURE 7.4

COMMON COMMUNICABLE DISEASES

Disease	Common Symptoms	How It's Transmitted	Treatment	Prevention/ Reducing Risk
Common cold	Congestion, sore throat, cough	Infected droplets in the air from coughs/sneezes; direct or indirect contact with infected people	Rest, liquids, over-the-counter medicines	Handwashing; avoiding contact with infected people and objects they have touched
Influenza (in·floo·EN·zuh), or flu	High fever, fatigue, muscle and joint aches, cough	Infected droplets in the air from coughs/sneezes; direct contact with infected people	Rest, liquids, steam inhalations, pain relievers, antiviral medicine for serious cases	Handwashing; avoiding contact with infected people and objects they have touched; annual vaccine for adults
Mononucleosis (MAH·noh·noo· klee·OH·sis), or mono	Swollen glands (in neck, underarms, groin), headaches, sore muscles, sore throat, fever, fatigue	Infected droplets in the air from coughs/sneezes; direct contact with an infected person's saliva (kissing, sharing utensils)	Pain relievers, rest, liquids	Avoiding contact with infected person
Hepatitis (he·puh·TY·tis)	Weakness, fatigue, nausea, vomiting, fever, yellowing of eyes, abdominal pain, dark urine	Type A: Consuming food or water containing viruses Types B & C: Usually through direct contact with infected person's blood or other body fluids	Rest, healthful food choices Types B & C: medication	Type A: cleaning food carefully; vaccination for those at high risk Type B: vaccination Type C: avoiding sexual contact and drug use
Tuberculosis (tuh·ber·kyoo·LOH· sis), or TB	Cough, fatigue, persistent fever, night sweats, weight loss	Infected droplets in the air from coughs/sneezes	Antibiotics taken over a long period of time	Antibiotics for those in close contact with infected person; vaccine
Strep throat	Sore throat, fever, chills, body aches, loss of appetite, nausea, vomiting, swollen tonsils or glands	Infected droplets in the air from coughs/sneezes	Antibiotics, soft food, liquids, gargling with salt water	Handwashing; avoiding contact with infected person

MORE ABOUT...

Strep Throat Group A streptococcal infections account for about one-fourth of the sore throats in children ages 5 to 15. These bacterial infections cause a severe sore throat, fever, and difficulty swallowing because the tonsils are coated with a thick mucus. Strep throat may also produce a rash and swollen glands. Generally, if a sore throat is accompanied by nasal congestion, runny nose, and cough, it is probably a viral infection rather than a bacterial infection. Still, health professionals should evaluate all severe sore throats. The diagnosis of strep is made after the throat is swabbed. Then the sample is sent to the laboratory for culture. Strep throat is successfully treated with antibiotics.

Preventing Communicable Diseases

You can avoid germs by staying away from people who are sick. You can also remove germs by washing your hands properly, as shown in **Figure 7.5**. Finally, you can increase your body's ability to fight germs by practicing healthful behaviors, such as eating right and staying active. If you do catch a cold, take care of yourself. Rest and drink lots of liquids. Medicine can help you feel better, but time is the best cure for a cold.

Vaccines

Vaccines can protect you from many communicable diseases. When you receive a vaccine, you don't get sick because the disease-causing germs are dead or weakened. The antibodies you produce, however, make you immune to the disease. **Figure 7.6** on page 190 lists some common vaccines.

FIGURE 7.5

HANDWASHING FOR HEALTH

Washing your hands removes germs that can cause colds, flu, and more serious diseases.

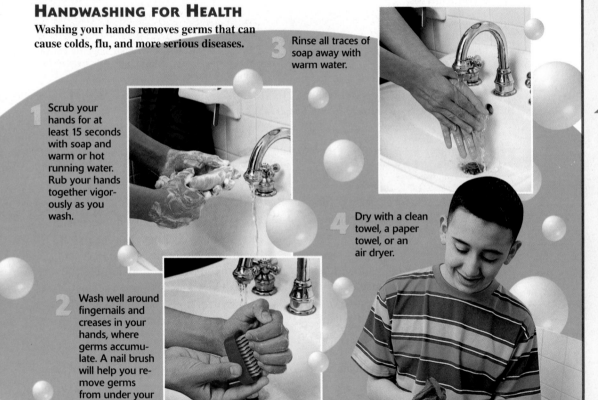

3 Rinse all traces of soap away with warm water.

1 Scrub your hands for at least 15 seconds with soap and warm or hot running water. Rub your hands together vigorously as you wash.

4 Dry with a clean towel, a paper towel, or an air dryer.

2 Wash well around fingernails and creases in your hands, where germs accumulate. A nail brush will help you remove germs from under your fingernails.

Interviewing

Ask students to work with a partner to interview a health care provider about the importance of establishing and implementing a periodic health-maintenance clinical assessment. **L3**

Researching

Ask students to use critical-thinking skills to research and evaluate the effectiveness of vitamin C in preventing and/or treating colds. What other claims have been made for vitamin C? Remind them to evaluate their sources of information. Have them share their findings with the rest of the class. **L3**

VISUAL LEARNING

FIGURE 7.5 Have students read and discuss the handwashing steps. Then ask the class to name situations in which people should wash their hands (*e.g., before preparing food, after using the bathroom*). Encourage students to practice their handwashing techniques. Point out that by turning off the faucet with a paper towel after they're finished, they can further prevent contamination. **INCL** *Behavior Problems, Special Learning Needs, English Language Learners*

Health Literacy

Health Information In the United States, babies and young children are routinely immunized against polio, diphtheria, chicken pox, pertussis (whooping cough), tetanus, measles, mumps, and rubella (German measles).

In addition, the hepatitis B vaccine is recommended for all children and adolescents. (See Figure 7.6 on page 190.) The vaccine protects against the hepatitis B virus, which can cause serious liver diseases including acute hepatitis, cirrhosis of the liver, and cancer of the liver. The virus is spread through sexual contact, intravenous drug use, contact with infected blood, and from mother to unborn child.

❸ Assess

Evaluating

📁 Assign the Lesson 2 Review; then assign the Lesson 2 Quiz in the TCR.

Reteaching

- 📁 Assign Concept Maps 32 and 33 or Reteaching Activity 28 in the TCR.
- Have students work with partners to plan and make posters promoting one or more habits teens can adopt to protect their own health and the health of others.

Enrichment

- 📁 Assign Enrichment Activity 27 in the TCR.
- Ask students to gather information about free or low-cost vaccination programs in the community.

❹ Close

Ask each student to list at least two new facts or skills she or he has learned about preventing the spread of communicable diseases.

FIGURE 7.6

VACCINES GIVEN AT DIFFERENT AGES

Vaccine and the Diseases It Protects Against	Typical Vaccination Schedule
Hep B: hepatitis B	Birth–2 months, 1–4 months, 6–18 months
DTaP: diphtheria, tetanus, pertussis (whooping cough)	2, 4, 6, and 15–18 months; 4–6 years; Td (tetanus and diphtheria toxoid) boosters at 11–12 years; and every 10 years thereafter
Hib: diseases caused by *Hemophilus influenza* type B (Hib) bacteria	2, 4, 6, and 12–15 months
IPV: poliomyelitis	2, 4, and 6–18 months; 4-6 years
PCV: diseases caused by *Streptococcus pneumoniae* bacteria	2, 4, 6, and 12–15 months
MMR: measles, mumps, rubella (German measles)	12–15 months; 4–6 years, or anytime before 12 years
Varicella: chicken pox	12–18 months
Hep A: hepatitis A	2 doses at least 6 months apart, anytime between 2 and 18 years; used only in high-risk areas or for high-risk groups

Source: Table based on immunization schedule recommended by the Centers for Disease Control and Prevention, the American Academy of Pediatrics, and the American Academy of Family Physicians

---

 **Lesson 2 Review**

Using complete sentences, answer the following questions on a sheet of paper.

Reviewing Terms and Facts

1. **Vocabulary** Define the word *contagious* and use it in a sentence.
2. **Describe** List the symptoms of a common communicable disease. Explain what a person with that disease could do to get rid of it or feel better.
3. **List** Name five diseases that can be prevented with vaccines.

Thinking Critically

4. **Compare** How might a hygiene habit like washing your hands protect your health in the short term? How might it protect you over the long term?
5. **Infer** How does getting a vaccination help protect both your health and the health of people around you?

Applying Health Skills

6. **Practicing Healthful Behaviors** Create a poster explaining what people can do to keep themselves and others healthy during the "cold season," or winter months. Display your poster in the school hallway.

190 CHAPTER 7: PREVENTING DISEASES

Lesson 2 Review

1. Able to spread to others by direct or indirect contact. Sentences will vary.
2. See Figure 7.4 on page 188 for possible responses.
3. Any five from Figure 7.6 on page 190.
4. Responses will vary, but should include the concept that handwashing can remove pathogens that cause both short- and long-term illnesses.
5. Being vaccinated against a disease protects you from that disease and, therefore, prevents you from spreading it to others.

Understanding STDs

Sexually Transmitted Diseases

Sexually transmitted diseases (STDs) are *communicable diseases that are passed from one person to another through sexual contact.* STDs are also known as sexually transmitted infections (STIs). Anyone who is sexually active can become infected with an STD. Here are some facts about STDs:

- STDs can damage the reproductive system and cause sterility.
- Most STDs are spread only through sexual contact.
- There are no vaccines for STDs.
- Someone who has an STD may have no visible symptoms, or have symptoms that come and go, but he or she can still be contagious.
- Having an STD once doesn't make you immune.
- Many STDs can cause death if left untreated.
- To get rid of an STD, a person *must* see a doctor.

Some other communicable diseases, such as hepatitis, can also spread through sexual contact. **Figure 7.7** on page 192 lists the symptoms of five common STDs.

Quick Write

You probably know that HIV, the virus that causes AIDS, sickens and kills many people. Make a list of the ways you think HIV is spread.

LEARN ABOUT...

- what sexually transmitted infections are.
- how HIV and other STDs are spread.
- what you can do to protect yourself from STDs.
- why it is important to seek help in dealing with STDs.

VOCABULARY

- sexually transmitted diseases (STDs)
- HIV
- AIDS

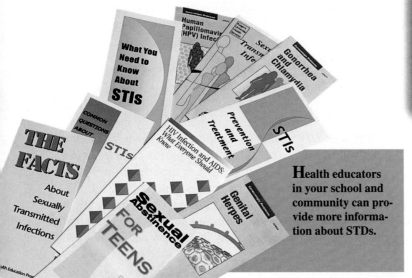

Health educators in your school and community can provide more information about STDs.

Lesson 3

Understanding STDs

① Focus

Lesson Objectives

Students should be able to

- explain what sexually transmitted diseases are and how people can protect themselves against them.
- explain how HIV and other STDs are spread.
- explain why it is important to seek help in dealing with STDs.

Motivators

Quick Write

Allow students to keep their responses confidential. Encourage them to check their responses, and correct any misconceptions after studying the lesson.

Bellringer Activity

Write *STD* on the board, and explain that the initials are a shortened form of the term *sexually transmitted disease.* Explain that in this lesson they will learn about the various types of sexually transmitted diseases.

VOCABULARY

Have students skim the lesson to find the definition provided for each vocabulary term. Then have them write a sentence using each term.

Lesson 3 Resources

Teacher Classroom Resources

📁 Concept Map 34

📁 Enrichment Activity 28

📁 Lesson Plan 3

📁 Lesson 3 Quiz

📁 Reading Tutor Activity 28

📁 Reteaching Activity 29

🕹 Transparency 33

Student Activities Workbook

📁 Chapter 7 Study Guide

📁 Applying Health Skills 28

② Teach

Critical Thinking

Have students share their responses to this question: Why is it important for everyone, even teens and adults who are not sexually active, to know the facts about STDs? **L1**

Analyzing

Abstinence from sexual activity before marriage should be encouraged. Have students explain the benefits of abstinence from sexual activity. Have them suggest values, activities, and habits that can encourage teens to practice abstinence. **L1**

VISUAL LEARNING

FIGURE 7.7 Have volunteers read aloud the information about each STD presented in Figure 7.7 Read aloud the caption question, and help students recognize that there is no cure for genital herpes or for genital warts. **INCL** *Behavior Problems, Special Learning Needs, English Language Learners*

Critical Thinking

As students consider the definition of AIDS, ask:
• What does it mean that there is no cure for AIDS?
• What are the implications for teens who risk contracting AIDS? **L2**

FIGURE 7.7

COMMON STDs

People under 24 are in the age group that is most likely to get STDs. *Which of these five common STDs cannot be cured?*

STD	Causes	Common Symptoms	Treatment
Chlamydia (kluh·MIH·dee·uh)	Bacteria	Pain or burning feeling during urination; unusual discharge from penis or vagina; often has no symptoms (especially in females) but can still be spread	Cured with antibiotics
Gonorrhea (gah·nuh·REE·uh)	Bacteria	Pain or burning during urination; unusual discharge from penis or vagina; abdominal pain; sometimes has no symptoms (especially in females) but can still be spread	Cured with antibiotics
Genital herpes (HER·peez)	Herpes simplex virus (HSV)	Itching or pain followed by painful, itchy sores in genital area; symptoms come and go, but virus is still present and able to be spread	Antiviral medication relieves symptoms when sores appear; no cure
Syphilis (SI·fuh·lis)	Bacteria	Red, wet, painless sores at place where virus enters body, followed by rash and flulike symptoms; can lead to brain damage and other serious health problems, especially in infants	Cured with antibiotics
Genital warts	Human papilloma virus (HPV)	Small pink or red bumps in genital area; can increase risk of certain cancers in women	Warts can be removed by a doctor but may return because virus remains in the body

HIV and AIDS

HIV, or human immunodeficiency virus, is *the virus that causes AIDS*. HIV attacks a person's immune system, decreasing its ability to fight infection. **Figure 7.8** shows how HIV attacks the immune system.

People can be infected with HIV for ten years or longer before any symptoms appear. However, eventually, they will develop AIDS, or acquired immunodeficiency syndrome. **AIDS** is *an HIV infection combined with severe immune system problems*. When AIDS weakens the immune system, other infections set in. Symptoms can include fatigue, frequent long-lasting fevers, sweating heavily at night, and a chronic cough. Drugs can delay the onset of AIDS and help fight the symptoms, but there is no cure. People with AIDS eventually die from diseases that a healthy immune system could easily have resisted.

192 CHAPTER 7: PREVENTING DISEASES

Health Literacy

Health and Technology Assign students to investigate recent health problems and epidemics, especially those diseases that have spread quickly from one country to another and for which there seems to be no cure or effective treatment. Then guide students in a discussion about health needs and technology development, especially the creation of new vaccines and medical treatment for new diseases. Have students write brief essays in which they explain the relationship between health needs and technology development, including the development of a vaccine for the Human Immunodeficiency Virus (HIV).

How HIV Spreads

HIV is carried in the body fluids of people infected with the disease. Significant amounts of the virus—enough to transmit HIV to other people—may be found in

- semen.
- vaginal fluid.
- blood.
- breast milk.

When these infected fluids enter another person's body, HIV infection may occur. HIV is transmitted mostly through sexual contact and sharing needles. A drug user can become infected with HIV by using a needle that was previously used by a person with HIV. A woman with HIV can also pass the virus to her baby during pregnancy or while breast-feeding. Before 1985, HIV was sometimes spread when people infected with HIV donated blood. Today, all donated blood in the United States is tested for HIV, and infected blood is discarded. It is safe to donate and receive blood in this country.

FIGURE 7.8

HOW HIV ATTACKS THE IMMUNE SYSTEM

HIV keeps the immune system from doing its job. A person with AIDS will have trouble resisting certain infections.

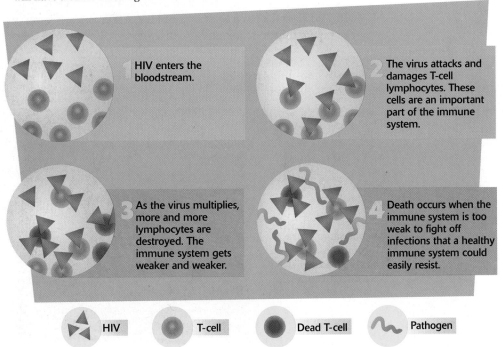

1. HIV enters the bloodstream.

2. The virus attacks and damages T-cell lymphocytes. These cells are an important part of the immune system.

3. As the virus multiplies, more and more lymphocytes are destroyed. The immune system gets weaker and weaker.

4. Death occurs when the immune system is too weak to fight off infections that a healthy immune system could easily resist.

HIV   T-cell   Dead T-cell   Pathogen

Lesson 3

VISUAL LEARNING

FIGURE 7.8 Have students work with partners to study and discuss the information presented in Figure 7.8. Then with their books closed, have partners work together to sketch or describe the process through which HIV attacks the immune system. Students could create sketches in a storyboard format. **INCL** *Behavior Problems, Special Learning Needs, English Language Learners*

Comprehending

Go over the information in Figure 7.8 with the class. Let students explain, in their own words, what they can do to prevent the spread of HIV. **L1**

Critical Thinking

Ask students to consider the fact that there is currently no vaccine available for HIV or for AIDS. Have students explain the relationship between health needs and technology development, including the development of a vaccine for the Human Immunodeficiency Virus (HIV).

 ✓ **Reading Check**

Reading Comprehension Summarizing information can help students remember facts. This activity uses the headings in Figure 7.7 to help focus students on the most important details for effective summaries. Have the class point out the writing conventions used in the chart in Figure 7.7, such as sentence fragments, phonetic spellings, and beginning capitalization. Remind students that the text provides all the information needed to complete the chart. Copy the chart onto an overhead or the board, leaving room for another row. Have volunteers add information about AIDS to the chart. **INCL** *Special Learning Needs*

Lesson 3

Listing

Have students meet in small groups to describe and discuss the photograph on this page. Then have group members work together to list specific forms of contact that pose no danger of HIV infection. **L1**

Discussing

Emphasize the importance of getting medical treatment for any STD. Ask: Why must anyone who has, or who might have, an STD see a doctor? **L1**

Researching

Have each student find and read a recent news article about advancements in the treatment of AIDS or about research into an HIV vaccine. Have students meet in groups to summarize their articles and discuss the importance of each reported development. **L3**

Guest Speaker

You may want to invite to your class a doctor, nurse, hospice worker who has worked with HIV/AIDS patients, or leader of an HIV/AIDS support group. Ask the speaker to share with students some of his or her experiences with AIDS patients and to emphasize the importance of preventing the spread of HIV. **L1**

CONNECT TO

Social Studies

THE AIDS QUILT
The AIDS Memorial Quilt contains more than 44,000 panels contributed by people all over the world. Each panel is a tribute to one or more people who have died from AIDS. The money people pay to view the quilt goes to help people living with the disease. So far, the quilt has raised over $3 million.

It is important to realize that HIV spreads only through contact with infected body fluids. You *cannot* get HIV from

- the air.
- sweat and tears.
- mosquito bites.
- donating blood.
- touching, such as shaking hands or hugging.
- contact with objects, such as eating utensils or toilet seats.

Detecting HIV

Many people infected with HIV show no symptoms for a long time. They can still pass on the virus, however. Laboratories perform tests to find out whether a person is infected with HIV. These tests show whether antibodies to the virus are present. If a blood test is negative, it should be repeated in six months. A person recently infected with the virus may not have had time to develop antibodies.

Technology, HIV, and AIDS

The need to prevent HIV infection and the development of AIDS has led to advances in technology. Doctors and scientists are trying to create an effective HIV vaccine. New medicines to treat HIV infection and AIDS are also being developed. Technology such as the World Wide Web has allowed scientists to track cases of HIV/AIDS and has kept the public informed about these diseases.

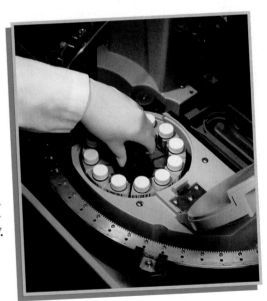

Blood samples are carefully tested to determine whether they are infected with HIV.

MORE ABOUT...

Symptomless STDs Students should understand that a person who has an STD may not have any symptoms. Gonorrhea, for example, initially produces no noticeable symptoms in more than half the women and in a small percentage of the men who contract the infection. In addition, chlamydia often has no symptoms, especially in females. There are two important implications of these facts: (1) People who do not practice abstinence from sexual activity cannot assume they do not have an STD simply because they are symptom free. (2) It is possible not to see physical symptoms of an STD on a potential sexual partner.

Preventing STDs and HIV

STDs can cause serious health problems and even death. To avoid these risks, you must avoid contact with other people's body fluids, including blood, semen, and vaginal fluid. Specifically, you should avoid

- having sexual contact. Abstinence from sexual activity is the only sure way to prevent STDs. Go out with groups of friends to avoid being pressured to be sexually active.
- sharing needles or other objects that break the skin. Sharing a needle with an HIV-infected person exposes you to HIV-infected blood. If you get your ears pierced, have it done professionally by someone who uses sterilized equipment.
- using alcohol or drugs. People are more likely to engage in risky behaviors when under the influence of alcohol or drugs.

Getting Help

Many people, especially teens, do not seek help when they think they have an STD. This is the worst thing a person can do. If left untreated, STDs can cause serious damage.

Teens who suspect that they have an STD should talk to a parent or trusted adult. At first, it may feel uncomfortable. However, it is the first step toward getting the needed treatment. It is also a necessary step in preventing permanent damage to the reproductive system.

Lesson 3 Review

Using complete sentences, answer the following questions on a sheet of paper.

Reviewing Terms and Facts

1. **Vocabulary** Define the term *sexually transmitted disease*.
2. **List** Name five common STDs.
3. **Recall** Explain the relationship between HIV and AIDS. Describe two ways that HIV can be transmitted.

Thinking Critically

4. **Apply** Why is it important for a person who thinks that he or she has an STD to see a health care provider?

5. **Hypothesize** Why might teens be reluctant to seek help for STDs?

Applying Health Skills

6. **Practicing Healthful Behaviors** Write a letter to a teen explaining the role alcohol, drugs, and other substances play in unsafe situations that could result in the transmission of HIV and other STDs. Explain the consequences of sexual activity and the benefits of abstinence from sexual activity.

LESSON 3: UNDERSTANDING STDS **195**

Lesson 3

Journal Writing

Help students identify the adults with whom they might feel comfortable talking to if they suspected they had an STD. (To preserve student/family privacy, remind students not to name specific individuals.) Ask:

- What would make you feel comfortable talking with these adults?
- What other difficult subjects do you think you could bring up with them? Why?

Then have students write private journal entries about adults with whom they could talk about STDs or other sensitive topics. L1

❸ Assess

Evaluating

Assign the Lesson 3 Review; then assign the Lesson 3 Quiz in the TCR.

Reteaching

Assign Concept Map 34 or Reteaching Activity 29 in the TCR.

Enrichment

Assign Enrichment Activity 28 in the TCR.

❹ Close

Have students review their Quick Write responses and correct any misconceptions they might have had.

Lesson 3 Review

1. A communicable disease that is passed from one person to another through sexual contact.
2. Chlamydia, gonorrhea, herpes/HSV, syphilis, genital warts/HPV.
3. HIV, or human immunodeficiency virus, is the virus that causes AIDS. AIDS, acquired immunodeficiency syndrome, is an HIV infection combined with severe immune-system problems. HIV is transmitted through exposure to contaminated blood sexual contact, sharing needles, pregnancy, and breast-feeding.
4. A person with an STD should see a health care provider right away so that he or she can be treated before serious complications occur.
5. Responses may include embarrassment or worry about reputation. Accept all reasonable responses.

195

Lesson 4

Noncommunicable Diseases

① Focus

Lesson Objectives

Students should be able to

• explain what noncommunicable and hereditary diseases are.

• list the three causes of noncommunicable diseases.

• explain what heart disease, cancer, allergies, asthma, and diabetes are.

• describe ways to avoid or control specific noncommunicable diseases.

Health Skills

• Accessing Information, p. 199

Motivators

Quick Write
List the students' answers on the board as they are shared. Then ask students to identify some reasons a disease might start in someone's body. Have students list noncommunicable and hereditary diseases and prevention techniques.

Bellringer Activity
Have students list as many risk factors for heart disease as they can think of in one minute.

VOCABULARY

Have students work with partners to write, in their own words, definitions of the vocabulary terms. Then have students compare and discuss their definitions.

Lesson 4

Noncommunicable Diseases

Quick Write

Some diseases are not spread from person to person. Name some diseases you know about that you don't catch from someone else. List some reasons why these diseases might develop.

LEARN ABOUT...

• diseases that are not spread by germs.
• what you can do to keep your heart healthy.
• how you can avoid diseases such as cancer and diabetes.

VOCABULARY

• chronic
• cancer
• tumor
• allergy
• allergen
• asthma
• diabetes
• insulin

What Are Noncommunicable Diseases?

Heart disease, cancer, diabetes, allergies, and asthma are noncommunicable diseases. Some people are born with these diseases, while others develop them later in life (see **Figure 7.9**). If a noncommunicable disease has been passed on to you from a parent, it is called a hereditary disease. Some communicable diseases can damage your body in ways that put you at risk for developing a noncommunicable disease. Many noncommunicable diseases are **chronic** (KRAH·nik), or *long-lasting*.

FIGURE 7.9

CAUSES OF NONCOMMUNICABLE AND HEREDITARY DISEASES

People can get noncommunicable and hereditary diseases in any of these three ways. Sometimes, more than one factor is present. *What can you do to protect yourself from lifestyle diseases?*

Diseases Present at Birth
Some people are born with noncommunicable diseases. Problems may occur during the development or birth of a baby. Other times, heredity is the cause. Examples of hereditary diseases include allergies, muscular dystrophy, and sickle cell anemia. Many people inherit a tendency to develop certain types of diseases such as heart disease and some cancers.

Lifestyle Diseases
Some noncommunicable diseases are caused by unhealthy habits. For example, having an unhealthy weight and being physically inactive may contribute to heart disease and diabetes. Tobacco use may lead to heart disease or cancer.

Environmental Diseases
Poisons in the enviroment may contribute to lung cancer, asthma, and other noncommunicable diseases. Pollution is a factor that can cause disease.

196 CHAPTER 7: PREVENTING DISEASES

Lesson 4 Resources

Teacher Classroom Resources
- Concept Map 35
- Decision-Making Activity 14
- Enrichment Activity 29
- Health Lab 7
- Lesson Plan 4
- Lesson 4 Quiz
- Reading Tutor Activity 29

 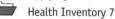
- Reteaching Activity 30
- Transparency 34

Student Activities Workbook
- Chapter 7 Study Guide
- Applying Health Skills 29
- Health Inventory 7

Heart Disease

Heart disease includes several problems of the heart and blood vessels. **Figure 7.10** describes the major types of heart disease and shows how each type can lead to others.

Heart disease is the number one cause of death in the United States. Many people inherit a tendency to develop heart disease. You can lessen your chances of developing heart disease later in life by adopting healthy habits now.

- **Stay active.** Aerobic activity can strengthen your heart and blood vessels and lower blood pressure.
- **Maintain a healthy weight.** Having less body fat reduces the strain on the heart and blood vessels.
- **Eat nutritious foods.** Choose foods that are high in fiber and low in salt, fat, and cholesterol.
- **Learn to manage stress.** Reducing or managing stress can help lower blood pressure and decrease the risk of heart disease.
- **Avoid tobacco products.** Avoiding tobacco can lower your risk of stroke and heart attack (and other diseases too).

FIGURE 7.10

TYPES OF HEART DISEASE

There are several types of heart disease. The arrows in this illustration show how one type of disorder can lead to another. *Can you explain why arteriosclerosis might lead to high blood pressure?*

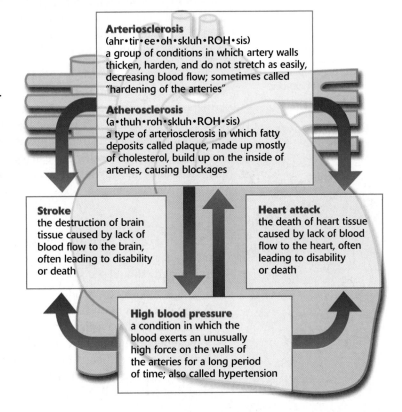

Arteriosclerosis
(ahr•tir•ee•oh•skluh•ROH•sis)
a group of conditions in which artery walls thicken, harden, and do not stretch as easily, decreasing blood flow; sometimes called "hardening of the arteries"

Atherosclerosis
(a•thuh•roh•skluh•ROH•sis)
a type of arteriosclerosis in which fatty deposits called plaque, made up mostly of cholesterol, build up on the inside of arteries, causing blockages

Stroke
the destruction of brain tissue caused by lack of blood flow to the brain, often leading to disability or death

Heart attack
the death of heart tissue caused by lack of blood flow to the heart, often leading to disability or death

High blood pressure
a condition in which the blood exerts an unusually high force on the walls of the arteries for a long period of time; also called hypertension

HEALTH Online

Topic: Heart disease

For a link to more information on reducing the risk of heart disease, go to **health.glencoe.com**.

Activity: Using the information provided at this link, create a booklet that lists ways to prevent heart disease.

Lesson 4

② Teach

HEALTH Online

Have students to explore the Web Links for this chapter and then complete the activity.

VISUAL LEARNING

FIGURE 7.9 Have students read and discuss Figure 7.9. Help students recognize that they can protect themselves from lifestyle diseases by eating nutritious foods, being physically active, and avoiding tobacco, alcohol, and other drugs. **INCL** *Behavior Problems, Special Learning Needs, English Language Learners*

VISUAL LEARNING

FIGURE 7.10 Have students read and discuss the explanation of each type of heart disease. Help students understand that thickened artery walls leave a narrower passage for the same amount of blood, which might cause high blood pressure. Demonstrate this concept with a concrete example to help students with special learning needs comprehend the concept. **INCL** *Behavior Problems, Special Learning Needs, English Language Learners*

Beyond the Classroom

Community Arrange for a local paramedic or other health professional to visit the class and discuss symptoms and treatments of heart attacks. Ask the paramedic to demonstrate how CPR is administered and to explain how CPR can be effective in saving the lives of heart attack victims. Also, make sure students understand that only carefully trained individuals should administer CPR. Ask the guest speaker to share information about local CPR training courses, if appropriate.

Lesson 4

Applying Knowledge

Have students work in small groups to brainstorm a list of reasons for avoiding smoking and smoke-related environments. Direct them to list not only the health benefits but also the social and psychological benefits of not smoking. **L2**

Discussing

Guide students in discussing the importance of preventing heart disease. Ask them to explain why establishing habits that prevent heart disease is easier than dealing with heart disease that has already developed. **L1**

Discussing

Help students discuss the three most common methods of treating heart disease. Lead students to an understanding of how the treatment options underscore the importance of preventing heart disease. **L1**

Comparing

Ask students to compare healthy cell growth to cell growth in the disease process. Ask students to use a Venn diagram to show the differences and similarities. **L1**

Cross-Curriculum Activity

SCIENCE Ask interested students to do further reading on food plan programs intended to reduce the risks of heart disease and cancer. Then have students plan a complete menu for a full day of heart-healthy meals and snacks that will appeal to teens. **L3**

Reading Check

Sort the following words into categories: *sunscreen, chewing tobacco, oatmeal, doctors, sunburns, cigarettes, radiation.* Label each category and add more words that would fit in each group.

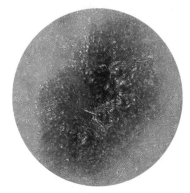

Skin cancer is the most common type of cancer. Over 1 million new cases are diagnosed each year. *What habits help you lower your risk of skin cancer?*

Treating Heart Disease

It is better to prevent heart disease now than to treat it later. However, there are many treatments available.

- Medication can dissolve blood clots, enlarge blood vessels, lower blood pressure, and control a person's heartbeat.
- Surgical procedures can open up blocked arteries or insert devices to regulate the heartbeat. Advanced surgical techniques even allow a new heart to be transplanted into a person's body.
- Changes in lifestyle can help lower blood pressure and prevent more heart damage. These changes include regular physical activity, healthy eating, and avoiding tobacco.

Cancer

Healthy cells in the body are produced at a steady rate as older cells die. In some disease processes, abnormal cells are produced at a very fast rate and destroy the healthy tissue around them. **Cancer** is *a disease caused by abnormal cells that grow out of control.* It is the second most common cause of death in the United States. Many cancers start out as **tumors**, or *masses of abnormal cells,* in one tissue or organ. Some tumors are noncancerous, or benign (bih·NYN). This means they do not spread. Tumors that are cancerous, or malignant (muh·LIG·nuhnt), invade surrounding tissue. Eventually, cancerous cells from the tumor may spread throughout the body.

What causes cancer? Many people inherit an increased risk of getting cancer. The most important factor, however, seems to be exposure to cancer-causing substances. For skin cancer, sun exposure is the main risk. However, the single biggest cancer threat is tobacco use. Cigarette smoking accounts for at least 30 percent of all cancer deaths. You can lower your cancer risk by making healthy choices such as avoiding tobacco and protecting yourself from the sun.

Treating Cancer

Detecting cancer early improves the chances that it will be treated successfully. People who notice one of these seven warning signs should see a doctor right away:

- **C** hange in bowel or bladder habits
- **A** sore that does not heal
- **U** nusual bleeding or discharge
- **T** hickening or lump in the breast or elsewhere
- **I** ndigestion or difficulty swallowing
- **O** bvious change in a wart or mole
- **N** agging cough or hoarseness

Reading Check

Categorizing Organizing words in categories can help students understand the terms in the context of the categories and the text as a whole. Have students work in groups to sort, label, and add to the word list. Have students volunteer different categories to use, if needed. Conclude the lesson by having students discuss each group's completed list. Point out differences, such as the word *radiation*, which can be interpreted and categorized in different ways. Exposure to radiation can be a cancer risk, but it can also be used as a treatment for cancer. **INCL** *Special Learning Needs*

Thanks to advances in treatment, more than half of all cancers can be completely cured. Three common treatments for cancer are surgery, radiation, and chemotherapy. Surgery is used to remove tumors and repair damaged organs. Radiation (ray·dee·AY·shuhn) such as X rays destroys cancer cells. Surgery and radiation are more effective when the cancer has not yet spread.

Chemotherapy (kee·moh·THEHR·uh·pee) destroys cancer cells with powerful drugs. Chemotherapy can be used to fight cancers that have already spread throughout the body.

Allergies

An **allergy** is *the body's sensitivity to certain substances.* A *substance that causes an allergic reaction* is called an **allergen** (AL·er·juhn). When you have allergies, your immune system reacts to allergens as if they were germs entering your body.

If you feel sick when you are around certain things, see your doctor. He or she can perform simple tests to determine the source of your allergy. Though there is no cure for an allergy, certain medicines can relieve the symptoms. You can also try to avoid the allergen. Keeping your home clean can help, especially if you have dust allergies.

Discussing

Guide students in considering the importance of knowing the seven warning signs of cancer. Ask:

• What are the advantages of knowing these warning signs?

• In addition to checking for these signs, what else should you know and do to help protect yourself from cancer? **L1**

Cross-Curriculum Activity

MATH Have students find current statistics on the total number of cancer cases in the United States and on the number of cases of specific kinds of cancers. Then ask students to plan and draw pie graphs that summarize those statistics. **L3**

HEALTH SKILLS ACTIVITY

ACCESSING INFORMATION

Learning More About Noncommunicable and Hereditary Diseases

If you develop healthy habits now, you can reduce your risk of getting many noncommunicable diseases, including cancer, heart disease, and diabetes. Here are some examples of healthy habits that can prevent disease.

• Do not use tobacco products.
• Stay active. Get some physical activity every day.

• Eat nutritious foods, including plenty of fiber. Avoid fat, especially saturated fat, and large amounts of salt.
• Protect yourself from exposure to the sun.
• Maintain a healthy weight.
• Manage your stress.

WITH A GROUP
Form groups of three or four students. Using library resources and the Internet, each group should research a different noncommunicable or hereditary disease. List prevention and treatment techniques for these diseases. Share your results with the class.

LESSON 4: NONCOMMUNICABLE DISEASES **199**

HEALTH SKILLS ACTIVITY

ACCESSING INFORMATION

Have volunteers read aloud the activity introduction and the examples of healthy habits. Help students discuss how each habit can help prevent noncommunicable diseases.

Then have students meet in groups to complete the activity. Provide time for each group to share its findings with the rest of the class.

Note: This skill is introduced in Chapter 1 on page 9.

COOPERATIVE LEARNING ACTIVITY

Healthy Heart Diagram Have each student bring a small lunch bag of scraps or throwaway items from home (fabric, paper clips, yarn, stickers, small beads, buttons, and so on). Divide students into groups of four or more. Give each group a piece of poster board. Using the scraps, have them construct a diagram of a healthy heart.

Encourage creativity in the design of the hearts. When they have finished their diagrams, have them label the parts. Invite the groups to take turns presenting their diagram to the class. **INCL** *Behavior Problems, Special Learning Needs, English Language Learners*

Surveying

Have students work together to conduct a survey about allergies. Suggest that they follow these steps:

1. Decide what kind of information you want to gather. For example, students may want to find what percentage of the surveyed group has diagnosed allergies and what percentage takes allergy medication.

2. Write survey questions to elicit that information. For example:
   • Have you been diagnosed with a specific allergy?
   • If so, what are you allergic to?

3. Use the prepared survey questions to gather information.

4. Tally the responses to the survey questions.

5. Draw conclusions from the tallied responses. **L2**

VISUAL LEARNING

FIGURE 7.11 Ask volunteers to describe the differences between the air passages in the two drawings and to read aloud the descriptions of the two pictures. Then pose the question in the caption. Help students recognize that the narrowed airways make breathing difficult. Demonstrate this concept with a concrete example to help students with special learning needs comprehend the concept. **INCL** *Behavior Problems, Special Learning Needs, English Language Learners*

Asthma

Asthma (AZ·muh) is *a chronic breathing disease caused by allergies, physical exertion, air pollution, or other factors.* Untreated, it can lead to lung infections and permanent lung damage. Most people develop asthma during elementary school, but symptoms may also appear later in life.

People with asthma experience asthma attacks, illustrated in **Figure 7.11**. Many factors can trigger an attack, including common allergens like pollen or mold, the dander in animal fur or hair, and certain foods. Smoke, physical activity, and a cold virus can also bring on an attack. To avoid an attack, it's best to avoid any known allergens or take preventive medicine as prescribed. Medication helps people with asthma to lead normal lives. If you have asthma, ask your parents or guardians to meet with the school nurse, who can work with you to help you properly manage the condition.

FIGURE 7.11

AN ASTHMA ATTACK

This figure illustrates how the airways become narrowed during an asthma attack. *Why does a person have difficulty breathing during an asthma attack?*

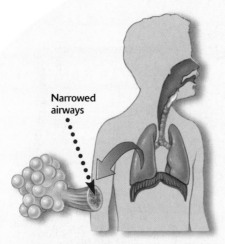
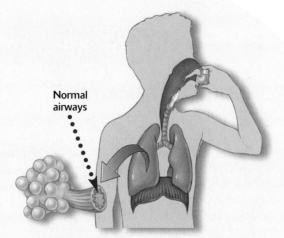

Narrowed airways

Normal airways

During an asthma attack, the airways in the lungs become swollen and clogged with mucus. Since the airways are narrower, less air can enter the lungs. Symptoms of an attack can include wheezing (a whistling sound), tightness in the chest, and a dry cough. The person may panic because breathing is so difficult. Without medication, attacks can last several hours or more.

Medication can help open up the air passages in the lungs. An inhaler is a small handheld device that dispenses the exact amount of medication needed. Some people have to take this medicine every day. All people with asthma should carry it with them at all times in case of an asthma attack.

200 CHAPTER 7: PREVENTING DISEASES

MORE ABOUT...

Insulin A person with diabetes has low levels of insulin, a hormone produced in the pancreas. Insulin regulates the levels and utilization of blood sugars. Reduced insulin results in increased levels of blood sugar; the symptoms of increased blood sugar levels are frequent urination, extreme thirst, and glucose in the urine. Some people also suffer from unusually high levels of insulin, which result in low blood sugar; the symptoms of that problem include dizziness and weakness.

Diabetes

Diabetes (dy·uh·BEE·teez) is *a disease that prevents the body from using the sugars and starches in food for energy.* It is caused by problems with **insulin**, *a hormone produced by the pancreas* that normally moves sugars into cells. In type 1 diabetes, the body does not produce insulin. Type 2 diabetes prevents the body from using insulin effectively. Being overweight or inactive can contribute to type 2 diabetes. **Figure 7.12** lists the symptoms and treatment of diabetes.

FIGURE 7.12

DIABETES SYMPTOMS AND TREATMENT

Diabetes cannot be cured, but it can be controlled. *Why might wearing a medical alert bracelet be a good idea for people with diabetes?*

Symptoms
- excess production of urine
- increased hunger and thirst
- weight loss
- lack of energy
- blurred vision

Treatment
- regular checks of blood sugar level
- regulating food choices
- controlling weight
- oral medication
- insulin injections

Lesson 4 Review

Using complete sentences, answer the following questions on a sheet of paper.

Reviewing Terms and Facts

1. **Vocabulary** What is a *chronic* disease?
2. **List** Name two noncommunicable diseases and two hereditary diseases.
3. **Identify** Which of these noncommunicable diseases can be triggered by exposure to allergens: diabetes, allergies, or heart disease?
4. **Describe** Compare healthy cell growth to cell growth that occurs in the disease process.

Thinking Critically

5. **Compose** Choose one of the noncommunicable diseases and one of the hereditary diseases discussed in this lesson. Write a paragraph about how each disease can be prevented and treated.
6. **Synthesize** Name two healthy lifestyle choices that help prevent more than one noncommunicable disease.

Applying Health Skills

7. **Goal Setting** Being overweight and inactive can increase a person's chances of getting type 2 diabetes. Name some healthy habits that can lower this risk.

LESSON 4: NONCOMMUNICABLE DISEASES **201**

Lesson 4 Review

1. A disease that lasts a long time.
2. Noncommunicable diseases (any two): heart disease, cancer, diabetes, allergies, asthma; hereditary diseases (any two): allergies, muscular dystrophy, sickle cell anemia. A tendency to develop heart disease or cancer can also be inherited.
3. Allergies.
4. Healthy cells are produced at a steady rate as older cells die. In some disease processes, abnormal cells are produced at a very fast rate and destroy the healthy tissue around them.
5. Paragraphs should accurately address prevention and treatment of different diseases.
6. Accept all reasonable responses.

Lesson 4

Guest Speakers

Invite two or three people with diabetes (if possible, both type 1 and type 2) to speak to the class about their experiences with the disease. Ask students to write a paragraph analyzing the role of the hormone insulin as it relates to personal health. **L1**

VISUAL LEARNING

FIGURE 7.12 Let students describe the pictured medical alert bracelet and share what they know about the use of such bracelets. **INCL** *Behavior Problems, Special Learning Needs, English Language Learners*

③ Assess

Evaluating

Assign the Lesson 4 Review; then assign the Lesson 4 Quiz in the TCR.

Reteaching

- Assign Concept Map 35 or Reteaching Activity 30 in the TCR.
- Have pairs of students work together to make charts of the noncommunicable and hereditary diseases highlighted in this lesson. Students should include disease symptoms, treatment, and prevention techniques.

Enrichment

Assign Enrichment Activity 29 in the TCR.

④ Close

Discuss healthy habits that can help prevent heart disease and cancer.

① Focus

Objectives

Students will be able to

- state the benefits and risks of common vaccinations.
- identify resources for free or low-cost medical care in the community.
- encourage peers to get regular health screenings and make sure their vaccinations are up to date.

Motivator

Quick Write

Give students five minutes to brainstorm answers to the question, "What is the most important reason to have regular health screenings?" Write responses on the board and leave the list in view as you teach the rest of the lesson.

② Teach

Critical Thinking

According to this article, vaccines "occasionally cause bad reactions, but the risks associated with not getting vaccinated are much greater." Divide the class into pairs and assign each pair a common vaccine (see Figure 7.6 on page 190). Guide students in researching the risks versus the benefits of their vaccine, using the Internet and library resources. Have students consider the following:

- How serious is this disease? Is it treatable? (For instance, diseases such as smallpox and polio can be deadly. Chicken pox, on the other hand, is usually mild and not life threatening.)
- What complications may arise from this disease?
- What benefits does the vaccine offer?
- What are the potential risks of the vaccine?
- What are the long-term public health implications of the vaccine?

Getting Smart About Vaccines

Shots may hurt a little, but they're the best way to fight off many diseases.

You've probably been getting shots, or vaccinations, since you were a young child. In fact, by the time you are 5 years old, you should have had about 20 vaccinations!

A vaccine helps you fight disease. Think of it as a protective wall between you and the germs that invade your body. Doctors have developed vaccines to battle 22 of the most common diseases caused by bacteria and viruses. Kids no longer get sick from many of these diseases, which include smallpox and polio. Before vaccines were invented, however, millions of children around the world died of these diseases.

Teaching Your Body To Fight

Getting a vaccine is a little like hanging a WANTED poster inside your body. The vaccine shows your body's police force—the immune system—what the bad guys look like. (Vaccines are actually made from little bits of those bad-guy germs.) Once the immune system knows what the germs look like, it can form special attack chemicals called antibodies. They aim for the invaders and mark them for destruction.

Once your body makes enough antibodies to a germ, you are "immune," or protected from it.

Since the 1950s, U.S. health officials have urged that every child be vaccinated against certain diseases. Most children—9 out of 10—get all their shots. The shots occasionally cause bad reactions, but the risks associated with not getting vaccinated are much greater. For example, there was an outbreak of measles among unvaccinated children in Korea. Some of them came to the United States and brought the measles virus with them, and a few kids here who were not vaccinated got sick. "If children are not protected," says Dr. Ben Schwartz of the Centers for Disease Control and Prevention in Atlanta, Georgia, "they risk becoming ill."

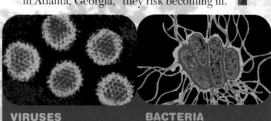

VIRUSES
Got the sniffles, a cough, and a scratchy throat? This adenovirus may be the culprit.

BACTERIA
This nasty one is salmonella. One type can give you a bad case of food poisoning.

Beyond the Classroom

Community Explain to students that many people in this country cannot afford regular health screenings. Tell students that they will be accessing information about free or low-cost medical care in the community, including vaccinations. Advise students to use the Internet, local phone book, and library resources to guide their search. Once they have found a location for free or low-cost medical care, have students do a presentation about how easily this service can be accessed by those who need it. Is it located near public transportation? Are appointments readily available? Do the clinicians speak the variety of languages represented in your community? What does their research tell us about the state of public health in the community?

Checking Up On You

What exactly is the doctor looking for during your checkup? Check it out for yourself!

BLOOD PRESSURE

A doctor measures how hard your heart is pumping blood by placing a cuff around your arm. He or she pumps air into the cuff so that it inflates like a balloon and then releases the air slowly. As the cuff deflates, the doctor reads the numbers on the meter to make sure that your blood pressure isn't dangerously high or low.

TEMPERATURE

A doctor will take your temperature to make sure it's normal (around 98.6°F). If it's not, you may have an infection and need medicine.

BLOOD TEST

The quick sting of the needle in your fingertip may hurt a bit, but it will help you a lot. Using a small sample of blood from your finger or arm, a doctor tests your sugar and iron levels. If they are too high or low, the doctor can advise you if you need to take certain vitamin supplements, improve your eating habits, or undergo more tests.

HEARTBEAT

The doctor listens to your heart by pressing a round stethoscope to your chest. The rhythmic "lub-dub" sound indicates that the blood is pumping through your heart correctly. If the doctor detects any strange noises, he or she can do more tests to find out if there's a problem.

REFLEXES

A quick tap on the knee with a small rubber hammer should make you suddenly kick up your foot. This reflex test tells your doctor that nerves carrying messages to your brain are working properly.

TIME TO THINK...

About Vaccines

Create a "call to action" flyer to remind students to make sure that their vaccinations are up to date and to get regular health screenings. Come up with a catchy slogan and make your flyer colorful. Present your completed flyer to the class.

TIME HEALTH: GETTING SMART ABOUT VACCINES **203**

❸ Apply

Time to Think

What makes for an effective "call to action" flyer? Before students begin work on their flyers, review the following development steps:

• Focus on a clear message. (Get regular health screenings.)

• Know your audience. What words, phrases, or images will appeal to middle-school students?

• Grab the audience's attention immediately with something catchy, funny, or eye-opening.

• Tell your audience how they will benefit from getting regular health screenings and vaccinations. (They'll feel better and avoid potentially serious health problems.)

• Offer advice and resources. Now that you've convinced students of the importance of regular health screenings and vaccinations, what do they do? Where do they go? How can they learn more?

VISUAL LEARNING

Have students analyze the drawing on page 203. Ask, "Is this a realistic depiction of a health screening? Why or why not? How would you revise this drawing to show a more realistic and/or encouraging image of a health screening?"

WHAT TEENS WANT TO KNOW

Is my health screening confidential? Health care confidentiality for minors is a controversial issue, hotly debated by physicians, parents, medical ethicists, and legislators. According to the American Medical Association's Code of Medical Ethics, "Where the law does not require otherwise, physicians should permit a competent minor to consent to medical care and should not notify parents without the patient's consent." However, as laws vary from state to state, a concerned minor patient should always check with a medical provider prior to treatment. Brainstorm with students a list of reasons why it is a good idea to include one's parents or other family members in all health care decisions.

GOAL SETTING

Objective

After completing the lesson, students will be able to demonstrate how to set a goal that prevents or controls diseases.

Time: 45 minutes

Materials: colored markers, glue or tape, old magazines, construction paper, notebook paper, pen or pencil

Teacher Classroom Resources

📁 Building Health Skills Activities

• Transparency Master 9, "Goal Setting"

• Reproducible Master 7, "Protecting Your Health"

1. Model

• Have the class brainstorm the possible health implications of their short-term and long-term personal goals.

• Have students read about Jenny and have them review the steps she takes to reach her goal.

• Briefly discuss how physical activity may prevent communicable and non-communicable diseases.

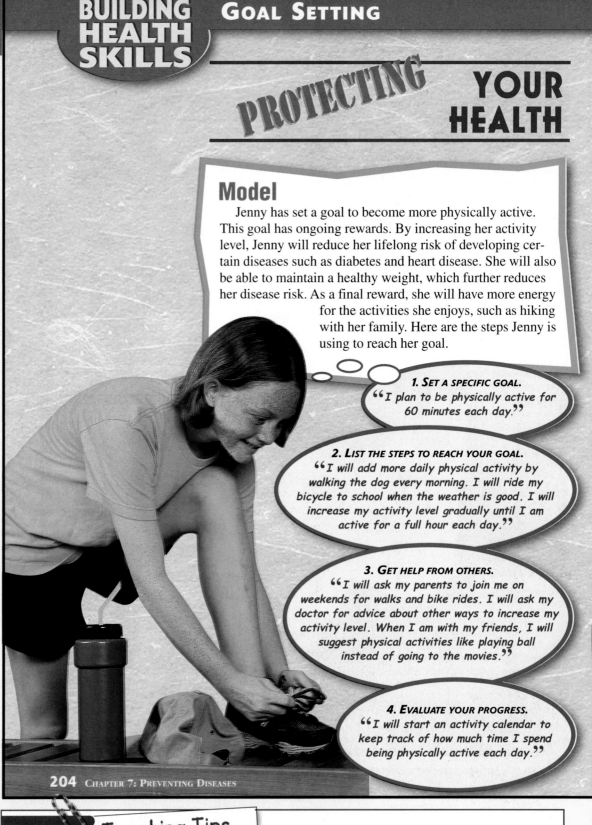

BUILDING HEALTH SKILLS — GOAL SETTING

PROTECTING YOUR HEALTH

Model

Jenny has set a goal to become more physically active. This goal has ongoing rewards. By increasing her activity level, Jenny will reduce her lifelong risk of developing certain diseases such as diabetes and heart disease. She will also be able to maintain a healthy weight, which further reduces her disease risk. As a final reward, she will have more energy for the activities she enjoys, such as hiking with her family. Here are the steps Jenny is using to reach her goal.

1. SET A SPECIFIC GOAL.
"I plan to be physically active for 60 minutes each day."

2. LIST THE STEPS TO REACH YOUR GOAL.
"I will add more daily physical activity by walking the dog every morning. I will ride my bicycle to school when the weather is good. I will increase my activity level gradually until I am active for a full hour each day."

3. GET HELP FROM OTHERS.
"I will ask my parents to join me on weekends for walks and bike rides. I will ask my doctor for advice about other ways to increase my activity level. When I am with my friends, I will suggest physical activities like playing ball instead of going to the movies."

4. EVALUATE YOUR PROGRESS.
"I will start an activity calendar to keep track of how much time I spend being physically active each day."

204 CHAPTER 7: PREVENTING DISEASES

Teaching Tips

Briefly discuss how following the goal-setting steps increases the chances of success. Link the goal-setting skill to setting both short- and long-term goals. As a working adult, share your personal experiences with setting goals and help students identify the possible health implications of setting long-term vocational goals.

Overcoming Resistance to Setting Goals
Students may initially balk at the idea of setting goals. Explain to them that they have probably been using many of the goal-setting steps in their everyday life. Emphasize that the skill of goal setting takes on even greater importance as teens' responsibilities increase.

Practice

Max and Scott are meeting at Scott's house for an after-school snack. Read their conversation, and use what you know about disease prevention to answer the questions below.

SCOTT: I'm starving! Let's make a sandwich.
MAX: Hold on a minute—time out to wash my hands.
SCOTT: But I'm starving now!
MAX: Me too, but I'm trying to avoid getting a cold this winter. Part of the plan is to wash my hands a lot more often, especially before I eat. I also want to get enough sleep— my mom is helping me with that.
SCOTT: So is your plan working?
MAX: So far, it's been two months, and I'm feeling great.
SCOTT: Hey, that makes a lot of sense. Pass the soap!

1. What is Max's goal?
2. What actions will he take to achieve his goal?
3. How does Scott's willingness to share Max's goal help Max?

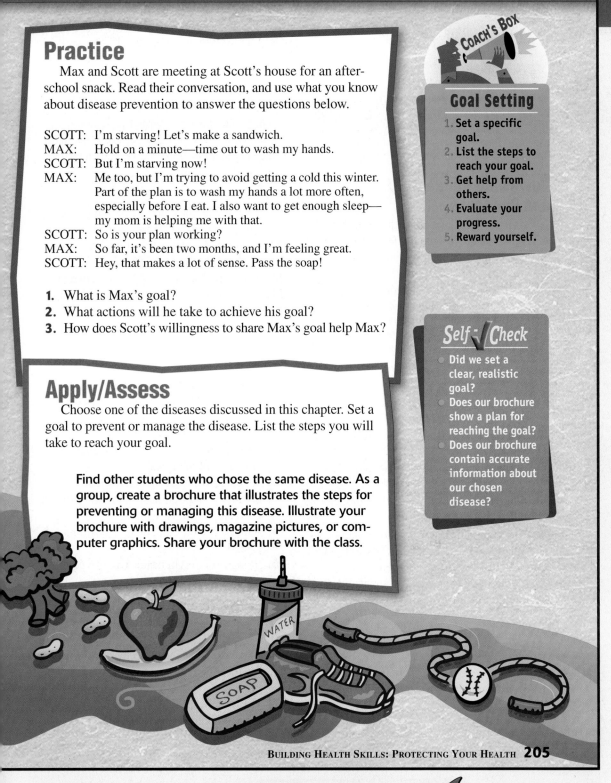

COACH'S BOX

Goal Setting

1. Set a specific goal.
2. List the steps to reach your goal.
3. Get help from others.
4. Evaluate your progress.
5. Reward yourself.

Self-✓-Check

- Did we set a clear, realistic goal?
- Does our brochure show a plan for reaching the goal?
- Does our brochure contain accurate information about our chosen disease?

Apply/Assess

Choose one of the diseases discussed in this chapter. Set a goal to prevent or manage the disease. List the steps you will take to reach your goal.

Find other students who chose the same disease. As a group, create a brochure that illustrates the steps for preventing or managing this disease. Illustrate your brochure with drawings, magazine pictures, or computer graphics. Share your brochure with the class.

BUILDING HEALTH SKILLS: PROTECTING YOUR HEALTH **205**

2. Practice

- Have two volunteers role-play the dialogue between Scott and Max.
- Instruct students to answer the questions at the end of the dialogue and compare their answers with others in the class.
- Display Transparency Master 9. Have students identify the steps Max is taking to reach his goal.

3. Apply/Assess

- You may wish to distribute Building Health Skills Reproducible Master 7 in the TCR to guide students in completing this activity.
- Instruct students to choose a disease and develop a goal to prevent, treat, or manage it. Diseases in the chapter include heart disease, cancer, allergies, asthma, arthritis, and diabetes.
- Have students develop a brochure by working with others who chose the same disease.
- Provide time for each group to present its brochure to the class.

Assessment Scoring ✓

Using a rubric, student work should provide evidence of all criteria to achieve the highest score.

Skills

Student work demonstrates

- a clear goal statement.
- steps that lead to achievement of the goal.
- resources that support achievement of the goal.
- a strategy that evaluates progress.
- a healthy reward.

Concept

Student work provides

- accurate information about how disease can be prevented or controlled.
- facts about actions that prevent or control disease.

Checking Comprehension

Use the Chapter 7 Assessment to examine the most important ideas presented in the chapter.

Answers to Reviewing Vocabulary and Concepts

Lesson 1
1. disease
2. noncommunicable diseases
3. pathogens
4. lymphocytes
5. antibodies
6. immunity

Lesson 2
7. handwashing
8. hepatitis
9. vaccine

Lesson 3
10. false; can
11. false; genital herpes/HSV, genital warts/HPV, or syphilis
12. true
13. false; cannot
14. true

Lesson 4
15. false; tumors
16. false; cancer
17. true
18. true
19. false; long-lasting
20. false; type 2

Thinking Critically

21. Responses should address the steady growth of normal cells and the fast, uncontrolled growth of cancer cells.
22. Reponses should list noncommunicable and hereditary diseases, prevention and treatment techniques, and include the concept that regular health screenings can aid in early detection.
23. The artery walls thicken, harden, and become less elastic. This decreases blood flow, which can lead to a heart attack.

After You Read

Use your completed Foldable to review the information on the four types of pathogens.

 FOLDABLES Study Organizer

Reviewing Vocabulary and Concepts

On a sheet of paper, write the numbers 1–9. After each number, write the term from the list that best completes each sentence.

> - antibodies
> - disease
> - handwashing
> - hepatitis
> - immunity
> - lymphocytes
> - noncommunicable diseases
> - pathogens
> - vaccine

Lesson 1

1. A(n) _____ is an unhealthy condition of the body or mind.
2. You can't catch _____ from another person.
3. Germs that cause disease are known as _____.
4. White blood cells that attack pathogens are called _____.
5. Your immune system produces chemicals called _____ specifically to fight a particular invading substance.
6. If your body is resistant to a particular infection, you have a(n) _____ to it.

Lesson 2

7. _____ is a good way to prevent the spread of germs.
8. Nausea, weakness, and yellowing of the eyes are common symptoms of _____.

---

9. One way to protect yourself from certain communicable diseases is to receive a(n) _____, a preparation of killed or weakened germs.

On a sheet of paper, write the numbers 10–20. Write *True* or *False* for each statement. If the statement is false, change the underlined word or phrase to make it true.

Lesson 3

10. People who have no visible symptoms <u>cannot</u> spread STDs to others.
11. Gonorrhea, chlamydia, and the <u>common cold</u> are all types of STDs.
12. The virus that causes AIDS is called <u>HIV</u>.
13. HIV <u>can</u> be spread through casual contact such as shaking hands or hugging.
14. By practicing sexual <u>abstinence</u>, you will avoid the dangers of STDs.

Lesson 4

15. Most cancers start as <u>infections</u>, or masses of abnormal cells in an organ or tissue.
16. Radiation and chemotherapy are two ways of treating <u>heart disease</u>.
17. Foods and pollen are common <u>allergens</u>, or causes of allergies.
18. A person who has sudden difficulty breathing and tightness in the chest during exercise may have <u>asthma</u>.
19. Asthma is a chronic, or <u>short-lasting</u>, disease.
20. Being overweight or inactive can contribute to <u>type 1</u> diabetes.

Thinking Critically

Using complete sentences, answer the following questions on a sheet of paper.
21. **Explain** Describe how cell growth in cancer is different from healthy cell growth.
22. **Explain** Make a list of noncommunicable and hereditary diseases. Then list

---

INCLUSION STRATEGIES

Special Learning Needs, Behavior Problems, English Language Learners The following suggestions are helpful for students with special learning needs, students with behavior problems, and ELL students:

- Pair these students with more proficient learners who can help summarize the main concepts of the chapter.

- 🎧 Direct these students to listen to the Teen Health Audio Summaries. This component provides an audio and written summary of the chapter in both English and Spanish.

- Use photographs, drawings, or magazine clippings whenever possible to help students visualize the important concepts of the chapter.

prevention and treatment techniques for those diseases. How might regular health screenings help prevent these diseases?

23. Infer Why do you think arteriosclerosis can lead to a heart attack?

24. Analyze Which warning sign of cancer could signify skin cancer? Why?

25. Suggest How can you demonstrate care and concern for someone with a serious illness at school or in the community?

26. Analyze Explain the relationship between health needs and technology development. For example, the spread of HIV has prompted research into the development of an HIV vaccine.

Career Corner

Medical Technologist Do you like looking at things under a microscope? Do you enjoy doing science experiments? If so, you might think about a career as a medical technologist. These professionals work in hospitals and laboratories. Their job is to test patients' blood and other tissues. This helps doctors diagnose and treat diseases. To do this job, you will need a four-year degree in medical technology or life sciences. Visit Career Corner at health.glencoe.com to learn more about this and other careers.

24. An obvious change in a wart or mole or a sore that doesn't heal might be signs of skin cancer; they are found on the skin.

25. Responses may include providing assistance and speaking kindly.

26. Responses should accurately link a specific health need with a technological advance.

Test Practice
1. B
2. D
3. Responses will vary, but might include that Salk did not want to accept money for preventing an illness.

Reteaching
📁 Assign Study Guide 7 in the Student Activities Workbook.

Evaluate
- 📁 💿 Use the reproducible Chapter 7 Test in the TCR, or construct your own test using the **Exam***View*® Pro Testmaker.
- 📁 Use Performance Assessment 7 in the TCR.

Enrichment
Ask students to collect at least five newspaper articles and two magazine stories about noncommunicable diseases, their symptoms, and treatment. Have students list the diseases and the different issues surrounding them, including respective prevention and treatment techniques.

Standardized Test Practice

Reading & Writing

Read the paragraphs below and then answer the questions.

Polio is a serious infection caused by a virus. Until the 1950s this infection affected people in all parts of the world. It sometimes left them paralyzed for life. In the 1950s, however, Jonas Salk developed a way to prevent the spread of polio.

Salk developed a vaccine that could prevent polio. The vaccine was first tested on Salk's family, and then on a large group of schoolchildren. Salk's vaccine kept people from catching polio. Because of Salk and his work, polio has been eliminated in most parts of the world.

Salk received many honors for his work, but refused all financial awards.

1. What is the passage mainly about?
 Ⓐ the causes and cures for polio
 Ⓑ Jonas Salk and the development of the polio vaccine
 Ⓒ how polio changed the world before 1950
 Ⓓ Jonas Salk's hard work looking for a cure for polio

2. The first paragraph is important because it
 Ⓐ describes the effects of polio on children.
 Ⓑ explains why polio had to be cured.
 Ⓒ compares polio with other diseases.
 Ⓓ explains what a serious disease polio was.

3. Write a paragraph explaining why you think Salk refused all financial awards.

TH05_C1.glencoe.com/quiz

Assessment

Self-Assessment Direct students to review the activities that are provided throughout the chapter. Encourage each student to select one finished product or activity that demonstrates his or her best work for the chapter. Have students explain what they learned and how the examples they selected show their progress.

Career Corner

Medical Technologist Medical technologists are trained to work with a variety of high-tech equipment. Discuss some of the medical and technological advances that could influence the job. Have students research the types of equipment that a medical technologist may use.

Protecting Your Health

Unit Objectives

Students will learn about the dangers of tobacco, alcohol, and drug use and ways to avoid such harmful behaviors. They will also learn safety measures they can take, the basics of first aid, and how to further protect the environment, which can impact their health.

Unit Overview

208

DEALING WITH SENSITIVE ISSUES

Enhancing Self-Esteem You can help students build self-esteem by convincing them they have potential. Urge them to maximize their potential by working to increase their skills. Convey to them that achievements, such as good grades and athletic awards, can make them feel better about themselves. Everyone has value; it is what is done to increase that value that enhances self-esteem.

Encourage students to realize that their problems are separate from who they are. Make them aware that, although they have difficult problems or have made poor choices, they themselves are not bad. Tell students that most problems can be resolved and that whatever pain they feel now will not last forever. **INCL** *Behavior Problems, Special Learning Needs*

Protecting Your Health

UNIT 3

Chapter 10
Safety and the Environment

Lesson
1 Personal Safety
2 Safety at Home and Away
3 Safety Outdoors
4 First Aid for Emergencies
5 Protecting Your Environment

HEALTH in Action

Substances in your environment and unhealthy habits alike can threaten your well-being. Thoughtful practices like recycling, finding new ways to use old items, and being prepared for emergencies help keep your environment safe and healthy—and when you protect your environment, you protect yourself.

How is recycling a form of self-defense?

Unit Introduction

Ask students to suggest factors in their lives that help to protect their health. Coach them to recognize both immediate factors, such as staying away from people who are ill and looking both ways when they cross a street, and factors that are more distant to them, such as national, state, and local laws that are designed to protect minors. Encourage them to explain how these factors are, or are not, within their control. Remind them that learning about issues related to substance abuse and personal safety will help them make wiser health choices. Tell them that the chapters in Unit 3 will help them sharpen their health skills.

209

HEALTH in Action

Read the class the question on page 209. Have students consider the things they can do to stay safe and healthy. Then lead the class in the following physical group activity:

Have students name some daily activities. List these on the board. Then ask volunteers to act out one of the activities without naming it. Have the rest of the class try to identify the activity. When a student identifies the activity, have him or her name one way to perform the activity in a safer or more environmentally friendly manner. For instance, for the activity *washing the dishes*, students might mention not keeping the faucet on. Repeat with each activity on the list.

Planning Guide

Chapter 8	Skills/ Activities	Reproducible Resources	Assessment
Lesson 1 **Why Tobacco Is Harmful** *pages 212–217*	**HEALTH SKILLS ACTIVITY** ▲ The Dangers of Smoking (*Advocacy*), page 216	*Student Activities Workbook available for use with each chapter* 📁 Parent Letter & Activities 8 📁 Concept Map 36 📁 Cross-Curriculum Activity 15 📁 Decision-Making Activity 15 📁 Enrichment Activity 30 📁 Health Lab 8 📁 Lesson Plan 1 📁 Reading Tutor Activity 30 📁 Reteaching Activity 31	📁 Lesson 1 Quiz
Lesson 2 **Staying Tobacco Free** *pages 218–221*	**Hands-On Health** ▲ Straw Breathing, page 220	📁 Concept Map 37 📁 Cross-Curriculum Activity 16 📁 Decision-Making Activity 16 📁 Enrichment Activity 31 📁 Lesson Plan 2 📁 Reading Tutor Activity 31 📁 Reteaching Activity 32	📁 Lesson 2 Quiz 📁 Chapter 8 Test 📁 Performance Assessment 8
TIME HEALTH	**Can Kids Stop Kids from Smoking?** *pages 222–223*		
BUILDING HEALTH SKILLS **Stand Firm Against Tobacco** (*Refusal Skills*) *pages 224–225*		📁 Building Health Skills Reproducible Master 8	

Standards		Technology
National	**State/Local**	
National Health Education Standard **1.1, 1.3, 1.5, 1.6, 1.8, 3.4, 7.4, 7.5**		🎙 Transparency 35 💿 TeacherWorks™ 🖱 Internet Activities
National Health Education Standard **1.1, 1.4, 3.1, 3.4, 4.1, 4.2, 4.4, 5.6**		🎙 Transparency 36 📼💿 Tape/DVD 2, Segment 1, "Teen Advocacy;" Segment 2, "Refusal Skills" 💿 TeacherWorks™ 📼💿 MindJogger Videoquiz 💿 **Exam**_View_® Pro Testmaker
National Health Education Standard **5.1, 5.3, 5.4, 5.6**		📁 Building Health Skills Transparency Master 7

TeacherWorks™

Glencoe's new and exclusive TeacherWorks™ is an all-in-one planner and resource center. Access the complete Teacher Wraparound Edition electronically. Find all your classroom resources with just a few easy clicks, and print them right from your computer. Connect directly to Glencoe's customized Health Web site. Access the National Health Education Standards correlations, or insert your own state standards and match them directly to the electronic Teacher Wraparound Edition.

Language Diversity

- 🎧 English Audio Summaries
- 🎧 Spanish Audio Summaries
- 📁 English Summaries, Quizzes, and Activities
- 📁 Spanish Summaries, Quizzes, and Activities
- 📁 Spanish Parent Letters and Activities

KEY TO ABILITY LEVELS

Teaching Strategies that appear throughout the chapters have been identified by one of four codes to give you an idea of their suitability for students of varying learning styles and abilities.

L1 **Level 1** strategies should be within the ability range of all students. Often full class participation is required.

L2 **Level 2** strategies are for average to above-average students or for small groups. Some teacher direction is necessary.

L3 **Level 3** strategies are designed for students able and willing to work independently. Minimal teacher direction is necessary.

INCL Strategies are appropriate for students with particular special needs in a general classroom setting.

Tobacco

Chapter at a Glance

Lesson 1 explores the harmful effects of cigarette smoking and using smokeless tobacco, the process of addiction, and the dangers of secondhand smoke.

Lesson 2 explains ways to stay tobacco free and helps students recognize healthy alternatives to using tobacco.

Health Skills
- The Dangers of Smoking (*Advocacy*), p. 216
- Stand Firm Against Tobacco (*Refusal Skills*), pp. 224–225

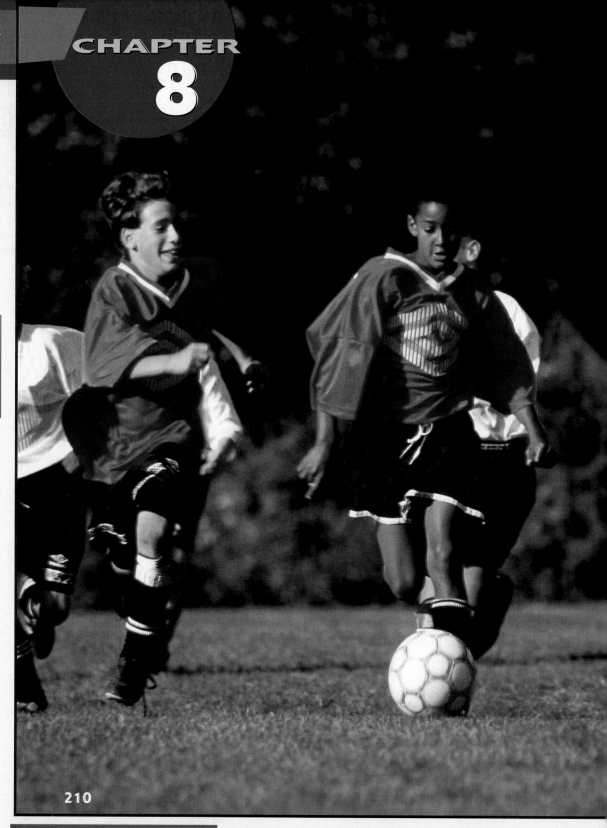

210

HANDS-ON ACTIVITY

Up in Smoke Cover a bulletin board with sky blue construction paper. Hand out sheets of gray construction paper and have students cut out cloud shapes so that each student has one cloud. Ask the class to think of something they could lose if they decided to smoke. For example, money, health, future plans, lungs, and so forth. Then have each student write at least one of the examples on a strip of paper and attach the strip to the cloud. Decorate the bulletin board with the clouds. Clouds with similar strips can be grouped into "cloud formations." At the end of the chapter, ask students whether they have any clouds to add.

Tobacco

Chapter Introduction

Use the options below to motivate students and preview chapter content.

HEALTH *Online*

Have students take Health Inventory 8 or read extra-credit articles at **health.glencoe.com**. By clicking on Health Updates, both students and teachers can discover the latest news on health topics.

HEALTH *Online*

Go to health.glencoe.com and take the Health Inventory for Chapter 8. In the activity, you will rate your commitment to staying tobacco free.

GLENCOE TECHNOLOGY

Teen Health Video and DVD Series
(Each format available in both English and Spanish)

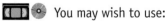 You may wish to use:

- Tape/DVD 2, Segment 1, "Teen Advocacy"
- Tape/DVD 2, Segment 2, "Refusal Skills"

MindJogger Videoquiz

Use MindJogger to preview or review Chapter 8 content.

FOLDABLES™ Study Organizer

Before You Read

Make this Foldable to take notes on the material in Lesson 1 about the causes and effects of tobacco addiction. Begin with a plain sheet of 8½" × 11" paper.

Step 1

Fold a sheet of paper in half along the short axis.

Step 2

Open and fold the bottom edge up to form a pocket. Glue the edges.

Step 3

Label the cover as shown. Label the pockets "Causes" and "Effects." Place an index card or quarter sheet of notebook paper into each pocket.

Tobacco Addiction

As You Read

List and describe the causes and effects of tobacco addiction on index cards or sheets of notebook paper cut into quarter sections. Store these cards in the appropriate pocket of your Foldable.

TIME HEALTH

Can Kids Stop Kids from Smoking?
pages 222–223

211

FOLDABLES™ Study Organizer

Dinah Zike Study Fold

Analyzing Causes and Effects
Tell students that their completed Foldable will help them organize the information they learn on tobacco addiction. Provide students with 3 × 5" index cards or sheets of notebook paper cut into quarter sections to use as study cards. As students read about and discuss the content of Lesson 1, have them list and describe the causes and effects of tobacco addiction on their cards. Direct them to store these cards in the appropriate pocket of their Foldable. Tell students that these study cards can help them analyze the causes and effects of tobacco addiction.

Lesson 1

Why Tobacco Is Harmful

1 Focus

Lesson Objectives

Students will be able to

- describe the harmful effects of using tobacco products.
- explain why tobacco use leads to addiction.
- describe the harmful effects of smokeless tobacco.
- identify the dangers of secondhand smoke.

Health Skills
- Advocacy, p. 216

Motivators

Quick Write

Allow several students to read their paragraphs aloud. Then collect all of the students' responses to create a bulletin board or pamphlet to be shared.

Bellringer Activity

Ask: What are the harmful effects of cigarette smoking? Give students several minutes in which to list their responses, including as many effects as possible.

VOCABULARY

Have each student use index cards to make a set of flash cards for the terms. Students should write each term on an index card. Then, as they come across the term in the lesson, have them write the definition on the other side of the card.

Lesson 1

Why Tobacco Is Harmful

Quick Write

Write a paragraph about the reasons many people choose to remain tobacco free.

LEARN ABOUT...

- how using tobacco products damages your health.
- why tobacco use leads to addiction.
- the harmful effects of smokeless tobacco.
- the dangers of secondhand smoke.

VOCABULARY

- nicotine
- tar
- carbon monoxide
- addiction
- emphysema
- snuff
- secondhand smoke

Tobacco Use: The Inside Story

Tobacco products include cigarettes, clove cigarettes, bidis (hand-rolled, flavored cigarettes), cigars, pipe tobacco, and smokeless tobacco. All contain dangerous substances. Tobacco smoke contains more than 4,000 chemicals, and at least 43 of them cause cancer. Harmful substances in tobacco include:

- **Nicotine** (NI·kuh·teen), *a drug that speeds up the heartbeat and affects the central nervous system.* Nicotine, which is found only in tobacco, narrows blood vessels and contributes to heart disease. People who use tobacco regularly develop a physical need for nicotine.
- **Tar**, *a thick, oily, dark liquid that forms when tobacco burns.* Tar coats the inside of the lungs. Over time, chemicals in tar can cause cancer and lung diseases.
- **Carbon monoxide** (KAR·buhn·muh·NAHK·syd), *a poisonous, odorless gas produced when tobacco burns.* When inhaled, it reduces the amount of oxygen in the blood.

Avoiding the harmful chemicals in tobacco offers lifelong benefits. *Why is avoiding tobacco smoke an important choice for this teen?*

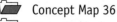

Lesson 1 Resources

Teacher Classroom Resources

- Parent Letter & Activities 8
- Concept Map 36
- Cross-Curriculum Activity 15
- Decision-Making Activity 15
- Enrichment Activity 30
- Health Lab 8
- Lesson Plan 1

- Lesson 1 Quiz
- Reading Tutor Activity 30
- Reteaching Activity 31
- Transparency 35

Student Activities Workbook

- Chapter 8 Study Guide
- Applying Health Skills 30

Tobacco: An Addictive Drug

Nicotine, which is found in all tobacco products, can cause addiction. **Addiction** is *the body's physical or mental need for a drug or other substance.* The need for a substance is also called dependency. There are two kinds of dependency.

- Psychological, or mental, dependency means that users believe they need the substance to feel good.
- Physical, or chemical, dependency means the body needs the substance to function. People who stop using the substance experience unpleasant symptoms, such as shakiness, headache, nervousness, and sleeping problems.

Nicotine is a highly addictive drug. Most tobacco users admit that it is hard to quit. **Figure 8.1** shows how people become addicted to tobacco. Addiction leads to heavier use, which can harm the whole body. **Figure 8.2** on page 214 shows how tobacco use harms many different body parts.

Reading Check
Find pairs of phrases in the following list that have a cause-and-effect relationship: *nicotine, reduced oxygen, tar, carbon monoxide, faster heartbeat, addiction, black lungs, can't quit.*

FIGURE 8.1

STAGES OF TOBACCO ADDICTION

Addiction can start with the first use, or it can be a slow process, taking many years. *When do you think most adult smokers began smoking?*

1 First Use/ Occasional Use
Users may be curious or want to be accepted socially. Some feel that using tobacco just once can't do any harm. First-time users may cough or feel dizzy, light-headed, or nauseated.

2 Regular Use
Users begin to use tobacco more often. Repeated use leads to higher tolerance. Users need more nicotine to experience the effects of the drug. Smokers may go through a pack of cigarettes or more a day.

3 Total Dependency
Users need tobacco regularly. They start early in the day, often before breakfast. At this stage, tobacco users may be unable to quit without help.

LESSON 1: WHY TOBACCO IS HARMFUL **213**

Reading Check

Cause-and-Effect Pairing Identifying cause-and-effect relationships aids in reinforcing associations for students. Remind students that each phrase is discussed in the lesson. Model the activity by writing *black lungs* and *tar* on the board. Guide students to identify *tar* as the cause and *black lungs* as the effect. Have a volunteer give a sentence identifying the relationship. For example, "The tar in cigarettes turns a person's lungs black." Have the class find other pairings and suggest a relationship sentence for each. **INCL** *Special Learning Needs*

Lesson 1

2 Teach

Discussing

Have students read the lesson's first paragraph. Then lead a discussion that focuses on why students think people still allow the air to be polluted with the chemicals from tobacco smoke. Who should be held responsible for such pollution, and what can teens do to help reduce the pollution from cigarette smoke? **L1**

Comprehending

Let volunteers read aloud the list of tobacco products and explain what they are. Emphasize that all these tobacco products pose serious health risks. Bidis (flavored unfiltered cigarettes from India), for example, have a nicotine concentration 28 percent higher than that of regular cigarettes. **L1**

VISUAL LEARNING

FIGURE 8.1 Have volunteers describe the three pictures and read aloud the explanation that goes with each. Let them explain what each picture shows about that stage of addiction. Ask: Do you think a smoker imagines becoming addicted when he or she smokes that first cigarette? Have students read the caption for Figure 8.1 and share their responses to the question. Help them recognize that most adult smokers started smoking as teens. Have students describe the mental and physical symptoms of chemical dependency and addiction to tobacco. **INCL** *Behavior Problems, Special Learning Needs, English Language Learners*

VISUAL LEARNING

FIGURE 8.2 Guide students in reading and discussing the facts about tobacco's effects; encourage students to share their ideas about each of these effects. Ask which effect they consider most unsightly and which they consider most dangerous. Read the caption question and guide students in recognizing that the blood vessels of a smoker carry less oxygen to the organs than do the blood vessels of a nonsmoker. **INCL** *Behavior Problems, Special Learning Needs, English Language Learners*

Cross-Curriculum Activity

VISUAL ARTS Discuss how smoking alters a person's looks. (Focus on the negative effects on skin, mouth, teeth, and fingers.) Then ask students to draw pictures to go with this caption: "What makes you think I smoke?" Display the pictures in a school hallway where other students can see them. **L1 INCL** *Behavior Problems, Special Learning Needs, English Language Learners*

Reviewing

Referring to Chapters 6 and 7, help students review what they have learned about the functions of the heart and about heart disease. Ask them to relate the effects of cigarette smoke on the heart and explain why those effects are so dangerous. **L1**

MEDIA WATCH

LIMITING TOBACCO ADS

Laws have placed strict limits on tobacco ads. For example, they can no longer appear outdoors, on T-shirts, or on any merchandise other than a tobacco product.

FIGURE 8.2

THE HARMFUL EFFECTS OF TOBACCO

The chemicals in tobacco harm many parts of the body. *What is the harmful effect on the blood vessels?*

Skin
Smoking ages the skin, causing it to wrinkle earlier than a nonsmoker's skin.

Mouth, Teeth, and Throat
Cigarette smoke and smokeless tobacco lead to bad breath and stained teeth. Chemicals in tobacco cause mouth and throat cancers. Smokeless tobacco can cause leukoplakia—white sores in the mouth that can lead to cancer—as well as bone loss around the teeth. It also wears away tooth enamel.

Throat

Lungs
The tar in cigarette smoke coats the inside of the lungs so they cannot work efficiently. Exposure to tar is one cause of **emphysema** (em·fuh·SEE·muh), *a disease that occurs when the tiny air sacs in the lungs lose their elasticity, or ability to stretch.* Chemicals in tobacco smoke can also contribute to lung cancer. Smoking causes nearly 87 percent of lung cancers.

Heart
Nicotine increases the heart rate and causes blood vessels to become narrower. Narrow vessels make the heart pump harder to move blood through the body. This extra effort raises blood pressure and can result in heart attack or stroke.

Fingers
Over time, tobacco use can cause fingers to yellow and stain.

Stomach, Bladder, and Colon
Harmful substances in tobacco smoke can lead to stomach ulcers and bladder and colon cancers. Compared to nonsmokers, smokers are more than twice as likely to get bladder cancer.

Health Literacy

Health Information In spite of the health dangers posed by smoking, the tobacco industry retains a powerful position in the economy of the United States. Tobacco is the seventh largest cash crop in the country, involving some 130,000 farms.

Although per capita consumption of cigarettes has decreased markedly over the past three decades in the United States, the tobacco industry continues to flourish, increasingly supported by smokers in Asia, the Middle East, and eastern Europe.

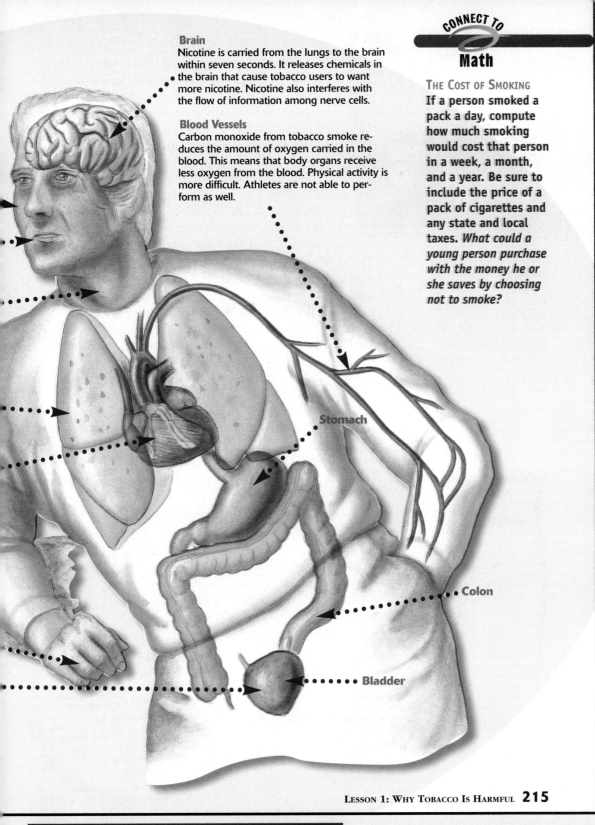

Brain
Nicotine is carried from the lungs to the brain within seven seconds. It releases chemicals in the brain that cause tobacco users to want more nicotine. Nicotine also interferes with the flow of information among nerve cells.

Blood Vessels
Carbon monoxide from tobacco smoke reduces the amount of oxygen carried in the blood. This means that body organs receive less oxygen from the blood. Physical activity is more difficult. Athletes are not able to perform as well.

Stomach

Colon

Bladder

CONNECT TO
Math

THE COST OF SMOKING
If a person smoked a pack a day, compute how much smoking would cost that person in a week, a month, and a year. Be sure to include the price of a pack of cigarettes and any state and local taxes. *What could a young person purchase with the money he or she saves by choosing not to smoke?*

Lesson 1

According to the American Cancer Society, every day more than 3,000 American teens and preteens try cigarette smoking for the first time. For many of these teens, the first symptoms of addiction appear within days of that initial tobacco use.

Discussing

Ask students how smoking does or does not affect the "first impression" a person makes on others:
- What is your reaction when you meet an adult who is smoking?
- A teen who is smoking?
- An adult or teen whose hair and clothes smell of cigarette smoke? **L1**

Critical Thinking

Ask students how tobacco use is likely to affect a teen's ability to take part in these activities:
- Running
- Swimming
- Singing
- Playing soccer
- Acting
- Surfing

Have students explain how and why tobacco can make each activity more difficult. Then ask: How do you think tobacco use affects a teen's success in school? Again, encourage students to explain their ideas. **L1**

COOPERATIVE LEARNING ACTIVITY

Cigarette Warning Labels Have groups of students brainstorm responses to this question: What are the most important reasons for young people not to smoke or use smokeless tobacco? Then have groups work together to design and write their own warning labels to be printed on cigarette packages. For reference, assign students to look through magazines to find Surgeon General warnings in tobacco ads. If students have access to a word processing or other computer program with graphic capabilities, encourage them to design flyers or posters that feature their original warning labels and call attention to the dangers of using tobacco.

Comparing

Ask students to compare the health risks of smoking cigarettes to the health risks of using smokeless tobacco. Emphasize that the only positive health choice is to avoid all forms of tobacco use. **L1**

HEALTH SKILLS ACTIVITY

ADVOCACY

Have students describe familiar cigarette ads, or have them bring ads to class. Then help students discuss the importance of balancing the images in cigarette ads with facts about smoking risks.

Have students work in small groups to list facts and plan, write, and illustrate original posters.

Note: This skill is introduced in Chapter 1 on page 12.

Applying Knowledge

Point out that even those who recognize the dangers of secondhand smoke may have trouble avoiding it. Encourage students to share ideas about when and where it is appropriate to ask friends and acquaintances not to smoke and under what conditions it is appropriate to ask strangers not to smoke. Have them role-play appropriate ways to ask someone to put out a cigarette or to smoke outside. **L1**

All major sports are taking efforts to discourage the use of tobacco products among its athletes. *How does this send a positive message about staying tobacco free?*

Smokeless Tobacco

As its name indicates, smokeless tobacco is not smoked like cigarettes. Instead, it is chewed in a coarsely ground form. It is also used as **snuff**, *finely ground tobacco that is inhaled or held in the mouth between the lower lip and gum.* Chewing tobacco and snuff are not smoked; so are they safe? No.

Harmful substances in smokeless tobacco mix with saliva. This mixture contacts the sensitive tissues of the mouth. In addition, some of this mixture is swallowed and enters the stomach. Smokeless tobacco use leads to serious health problems.

- The nicotine in smokeless tobacco is just as addictive as the nicotine in smoked tobacco.
- Tobacco juice can cause white spots to form on the gums and inside the cheeks. These spots can turn into cancer.
- Swallowed tobacco can cause sores in the stomach.
- People who use smokeless tobacco tend to lose their senses of taste and smell.
- Smokeless tobacco causes bad breath and stains the teeth.
- Grit and sugar in tobacco can cause cavities and red, inflamed gums (gingivitis). This can lead to an advanced stage of gum disease that causes tooth decay and tooth loss.

HEALTH SKILLS ACTIVITY

ADVOCACY

The Dangers of Smoking

Cigarette ads often show smokers having fun. They never show the dangers of tobacco use. By showing how tobacco harms people, you can help teens decide to stay tobacco free.

- There are at least 43 cancer-causing chemicals in tobacco and tobacco smoke.

- Smoking at an early age increases the risk of lung cancer.
- Cigarettes kill more than 400,000 Americans every year. That is more than 1,000 per day.

WITH A GROUP
Use library resources, the Internet, and your textbook to find more facts about smoking. Poll classmates to see which fact they believe to be the best reason to avoid smoking. Make a poster that uses this fact to encourage teens to avoid tobacco.

PROMOTING COORDINATED SCHOOL HEALTH

Community Support Tapping into local resources is a key to effectively working a coordinated school health plan. It is important to involve local health agencies, parents, churches, youth groups, and other organizations. By enlisting local groups and individuals, the committee establishes grassroots support. Community involvement provides the resources and support needed to reduce fragmentation of efforts or duplication of programs. Ongoing collaboration and cooperation among the team and other community members also prevents unwarranted controversy. For more information about enlisting community support, consult *Planning a Coordinated School Health Program* in the TCR.

Secondhand Smoke

Secondhand smoke is *tobacco smoke that stays in the air.* Nonsmokers who breathe secondhand smoke can develop some of the same health problems as smokers. Secondhand smoke kills more than 40,000 nonsmokers each year. About 3,000 of them die of lung cancer. The remaining deaths are from heart disease and other cancers.

Secondhand smoke causes other health problems. In children under 18 months old, it can cause pneumonia, bronchitis, and other lower respiratory tract infections. Each year, 150,000 to 300,000 children develop these diseases as a result of second-hand smoke. Between 7,500 and 15,000 of these children are hospitalized. Many children with asthma have more frequent and more severe attacks when secondhand smoke is present.

Many offices, factories, restaurants, and other places have banned smoking because of the risks to nonsmokers. Some towns and cities have even banned smoking outside, in places such as beaches, building entrances, outdoor dining areas, children's play areas, and public gardens.

Because of the health risks of secondhand smoke, smoking has been banned in many public buildings. *Name some buildings in your community that are officially smoke free.*

Lesson 1 Review

Using complete sentences, answer the following questions on a sheet of paper.

Reviewing Terms and Facts

1. **List** Name three harmful substances found in tobacco smoke, and describe each one.
2. **Recall** Identify the three stages of tobacco addiction.
3. **Identify** What are two forms of smoke-less tobacco?
4. **Vocabulary** Define the term *secondhand smoke.* Use it in an original sentence.

Thinking Critically

5. **Apply** Make healthy choices from among environmental alternatives: What would you do if you found yourself in a smoke-filled room?
6. **Analyze** In a brief paragraph, compare the risks and benefits of the positive health behavior of choosing not to smoke.

Applying Health Skills

7. **Advocacy** Create a radio advertisement against tobacco use. The ad might mention the many health problems caused by tobacco use. Be sure the ad describes chemical dependency and addiction to tobacco. You might read your ad in front of the class or over the school's public address system.

Researching

Ask volunteers to read about the risks to a developing fetus if a female smokes while pregnant. Have them summarize their findings in a report to be shared with the rest of the class. Students could expand their research to include how the negative effects can linger into childhood (*increased respiratory problems, asthma, and so on*). Also, encourage them to contact the March of Dimes or American Lung Association for information. **L3**

③ Assess

Evaluating

📂 Assign the Lesson 1 Review; then assign the Lesson 1 Quiz in the TCR.

Reteaching

📂 Assign Concept Map 36 or Reteaching Activity 31 in the TCR.

Enrichment

📂 Assign Enrichment Activity 30 in the TCR.

④ Close

Ask each student to identify what he or she considers the single most important reason for avoiding the use of tobacco.

Staying Tobacco Free

① Focus

Lesson Objectives

Students will be able to
- explain why people start using tobacco.
- discuss strategies for staying tobacco free.

Motivators

Quick Write
Ask volunteers to share their responses. If students can not come up with any examples, then ask them to think about characters in movies. Discuss how realistic the characters' reactions were.

Bellringer Activity

Ask students to share what influences them in their daily lives not to smoke. Then ask: How does self-concept affect a person's decision on whether or not to smoke?

VOCABULARY

Ask students to find the definition of the term *media* in the lesson and write an original sentence using the term.

Staying Tobacco Free

Quick Write

Think about your favorite television show. Do any of the characters smoke? Write a short paragraph describing how the other characters react to this character's smoking.

LEARN ABOUT...

- why people start using tobacco.
- how you can stay tobacco free.

VOCABULARY

- media

The Reality of Teens and Tobacco Use

Most teens don't risk their health by using tobacco. Those who do use it may be unaware of the realities of tobacco use.

- Some teens think tobacco will help them fit in. In reality, as **Figure 8.3** shows, less than 15 percent of teens ages 12 to 17 smoke.
- Teens may think that using tobacco makes them seem more grown-up. However, the number of adult smokers has dropped drastically. Many former smokers quit to improve their health and the health of their families.
- Teens may believe that tobacco won't hurt their health for many years. In fact, some of tobacco's harmful effects—such as increased heart rate—start with the first use.
- Teens may try tobacco to look "cool." However, tobacco actually harms the user's appearance. It can cause bad breath, stained teeth, and wrinkled skin.

FIGURE 8.3

NONSMOKERS IN DIFFERENT AGE GROUPS

This graph shows the percentage of nonsmokers in three different age groups. *Why do you think most teens choose not to smoke?*

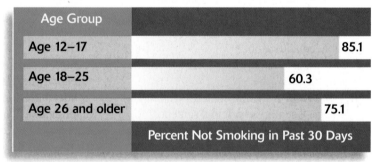

Age Group	Percent Not Smoking in Past 30 Days
Age 12–17	85.1
Age 18–25	60.3
Age 26 and older	75.1

Source: U.S. Substance Abuse and Mental Heath Services Administration, *National Household Survey on Drug Abuse,* 1999.

Lesson 2 Resources

Teacher Classroom Resources
- 📁 Concept Map 37
- 📁 Cross-Curriculum Activity 16
- 📁 Decision-Making Activity 16
- 📁 Enrichment Activity 31
- 📁 Lesson Plan 2
- 📁 Lesson 2 Quiz
- 📁 Reading Tutor Activity 31

- 📁 Reteaching Activity 32
- 📁 Transparency 36

Student Activities Workbook
- 📁 Chapter 8 Study Guide
- 📁 Applying Health Skills 31
- 📁 Health Inventory 8

Pressures You May Face

If tobacco is so harmful, why do some teens start using it? There is no one answer. They may be influenced by factors such as the media, friends, and family.

- **Pressure from the media.** Many teens use tobacco because of the images they see and hear in the media. The **media** are *the various methods of communicating information, including newspapers, magazines, radio, television, movies, and the Internet.* In some movies, for example, characters may express their personalities by smoking. In addition, tobacco companies spend billions of dollars each year on advertising. Studies have shown that tobacco companies target teens, especially through magazines.
- **Pressure from peers.** Peer pressure is a major factor in teen tobacco use. If a teen's friends use tobacco, then he or she is more likely to try it. By choosing friends who are tobacco free, teens can avoid this pressure.
- **Pressure from family.** Family influence is another large factor in teen tobacco use. Teens are more likely to use tobacco if parents or siblings use it. If parents don't use tobacco, teens are much less likely to use it.
- **Other pressures.** Teens may think that tobacco use will help them cope with stress. Others think it will help control their weight. However, tobacco use can actually add to stress because smokers experience discomfort if they do not have nicotine regularly. Tobacco users may also find it harder to participate in physical activity, a key to healthy weight control.

The key to resisting these pressures is to exercise self-control.

Compare the condition of the smoker's lung on the right with the healthy lung shown on the left. *How might these pictures influence teens who are thinking about using tobacco?*

LESSON 2: STAYING TOBACCO FREE **219**

Topic: Dangers of tobacco use

For a link to more information on tobacco's harmful effects on health, go to **health.glencoe.com**.

Activity: Using the information provided at this link, prepare a fact sheet that highlights the dangers of tobacco use.

Lesson 2

② Teach

Have students explore the Web Links for this chapter and then complete the activity.

VISUAL LEARNING

FIGURE 8.3 Help students read and discuss the information in the bar graph. Ask volunteers to read aloud the graph title and the labels for each axis; emphasize that the graph shows the percentage of people in each group who have *not* smoked in the past 30 days. **INCL** *Behavior Problems, Special Learning Needs, English Language Learners*

HEALTH SKILLS PRACTICE

Advocacy Teens generally agree that the most effective deterrent to smoking is a perception of smoking as "not cool." Have students work in pairs or groups to plan "don't start smoking" skits that present smoking as "uncool." Let students practice their skits and then present them to the rest of the class. **L2**

WHAT TEENS WANT TO KNOW

Does smoking lead to the use of other drugs? Not every teen who smokes cigarettes will use other addictive drugs, but many teens will. For this reason, alcohol, marijuana, and the nicotine in cigarettes have been called "gateway" drugs. Research shows that fifth- and sixth-graders who smoke follow a predictable pattern. They begin with the "gateway" drugs and progress to other drugs such as cocaine, narcotics, and stimulants. It seems that regular users of any addictive drug, including nicotine, are more likely to abuse other more harmful drugs. You don't have to be hooked on a drug to be in danger. Even teens who only occasionally smoke or drink alcohol are more likely to go on to use more dangerous drugs.

Researching

Encourage students to research when and how adults who used to smoke (or used smokeless tobacco) began smoking, why they chose to quit, and how difficult the process was for them. If students need guidance, help them develop an interview sheet with space to record answers. Provide time for students to share and discuss the results of their interviews. **L3**

Hands-On Health

STRAW BREATHING

Time: 20 minutes

TEACHING THE ACTIVITY

- Read the activity directions with students, and distribute materials. If possible, provide each student with a short, narrow "cocktail straw."
- Caution students with asthma to participate only as timekeepers.
- Have students work with partners or as a group to perform the exercises.
- Provide time between activity sessions for students to record their reactions.

ASSESSMENT

In a class discussion, have students share their responses to the In Conclusion questions. Then have each student write a one-sentence summary of what she or he learned.

Reasons to Say No

There are many reasons to say no to tobacco. Tobacco use damages nearly all of your body systems and increases your risk of developing cancer and other serious diseases. It exposes others to dangerous secondhand smoke. Tobacco products are also very expensive. They make your breath, clothing, skin, and hair smell bad. **Figure 8.4** gives more reasons to say no.

Here is one more reason. In many states, it is illegal to possess tobacco if you are younger than 18. In some states, teens can go to jail for possessing tobacco.

Hands-On Health

STRAW BREATHING

Smoking can damage the lungs and cause emphysema, a disease that damages the tiny sacs in the lungs called alveoli. People with emphysema struggle to get air into and out of their lungs. How do you think this disease would affect your ability to do physical activities? Find out by performing this simple experiment.

WHAT YOU WILL NEED
- a small drinking straw
- paper and pencil or pen
- a stopwatch, clock with a second hand, or other timer

WHAT YOU WILL DO
1. Stand up and do an exercise, such as running in place or jumping jacks, for one minute. Have someone time you.
2. After doing a minute of exercise, write down how you feel. How tired are you? How easily can you breathe?
3. Put a small straw in your mouth. Then hold your nose closed and breathe only through the straw. Do this for one minute.
4. Continue to breathe through the straw as you stand up and perform a minute of exercise. Have someone time you.
5. After you finish your exercise, write down how it felt this time. Was it much harder than the first time?

IN CONCLUSION
1. How did you feel when your breathing was constricted?
2. How do you think it would affect your life if you felt that way all the time?
3. Do you think this experiment is a convincing argument against smoking?

Health Literacy

Smoking Cessation Nicotine gum and patches are available to help smokers quit. As the urge to smoke fades, smokers who use the gum chew fewer pieces each week. The patch, which looks like a bandage, is worn on the upper arm and releases constant amounts of nicotine into the bloodstream through the skin. Over time, patch users apply smaller patches, which release decreasing amounts of nicotine. Patches should never be worn by nonsmokers as they can cause very serious side effects.

To resist the temptation to resume smoking, smokers often need to learn new, healthier ways of managing stress. They can also benefit from counseling on how to avoid the weight gain that may accompany quitting.

FIGURE 8.4

SAYING NO TO TOBACCO

If someone offers you tobacco, you should be well armed with different ways to say no. *Name two other ways to refuse tobacco.*

VISUAL LEARNING

FIGURE 8.4 Have students read and discuss the responses for refusing tobacco. Then have volunteers act out scenes in which one or more friends urge another to try tobacco and a single teen uses these (or other) techniques to refuse. Note: You may want to take the role of the friend applying pressure. **INCL** *Behavior Problems, Special Learning Needs, English Language Learners*

③ Assess

Evaluating

📁 Assign the Lesson 2 Review; then assign the Lesson 2 Quiz in the TCR.

Reteaching

📁 Assign Concept Map 37 or Reteaching Activity 32 in the TCR.

Enrichment

• 📁 Assign and distribute Enrichment Activity 31 in the TCR.

④ Close

Peer pressure to smoke can be very persuasive. Have students write one refusal statement for a smoker who wants to quit. Encourage students to think of ways to prevent the use of tobacco, such as alternative activities.

Lesson 2 Review

Using complete sentences, answer the following questions on a sheet of paper.

Reviewing Terms and Facts

1. **Vocabulary** Define the term *media.* Explain how the media can influence teens' decisions about tobacco use.
2. **Recall** Identify three pressures teens face to start using tobacco.
3. **List** Give three ways to say no to tobacco.

Thinking Critically

4. **Apply** Identify at least three ways to prevent the use of tobacco among teens, including one alternative activity.

5. **Hypothesize** Why do you think many state governments have placed such strict controls on the sale of tobacco to minors and possession by minors?

Applying Health Skills

6. **Analyzing Influences** In a journal, keep track of pressures to use tobacco that you see and hear in one day. Write down whether people use tobacco around you or if you see the use of tobacco in various media such as magazines, television, or the World Wide Web. Which of these do you think affects you the most? How do you remain tobacco free around these influences?

LESSON 2: STAYING TOBACCO FREE **221**

Lesson 2 Review

1. The various methods of communicating information, including newspapers, magazines, radio, television, movies, and the Internet. Seeing people smoking in the movies, on TV, or in ads may give teens the impression that smoking is not harmful.
2. Responses may include the media, peers, stress, and body weight.
3. See Figure 8.4 for possible answers.
4. Responses will vary, but should include at least one healthful alternative activity.
5. Students might say that governments are trying to prevent the vast number of health problems caused by tobacco by preventing people from using tobacco during their teen years, when most smokers start.

Can Kids Stop Kids from Smoking?

① Focus

Objectives

Students will be able to
- understand how teens are taking on tobacco companies.
- define health advocacy.
- develop their own antismoking advocacy campaign.

Motivator

Bellringer Activity

Ask students, "What does advocacy mean to you? How are the teens you've read about in this article advocating for a tobacco-free lifestyle?" List their responses on the board.

② Teach

Discussing

According to this article, anti-tobacco student advocates have testified before committees, talked to lawmakers, and used skits and dances to spread their message to other students. Explain to students that these are examples of health advocacy. Health advocacy means "showing you feel strongly about actions that are healthy and encouraging others to make healthy choices." To advocate successfully for a health cause, one must
- believe the health message.
- understand the purpose of the message.
- give solid reasons why the message is good for health.
- include correct information.

Ask: "Are there other critical elements to creating a successful advocacy campaign?" Write answers on the board.

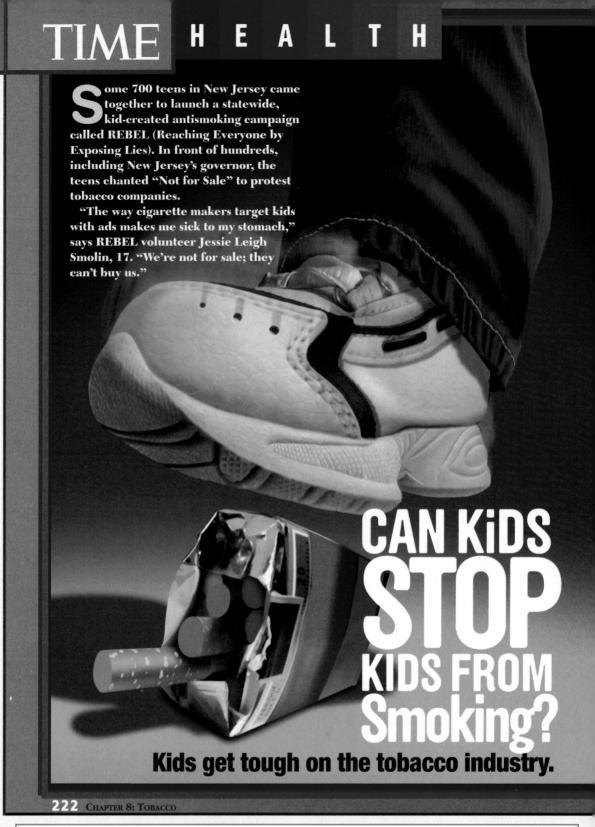

Some 700 teens in New Jersey came together to launch a statewide, kid-created antismoking campaign called REBEL (Reaching Everyone by Exposing Lies). In front of hundreds, including New Jersey's governor, the teens chanted "Not for Sale" to protest tobacco companies.

"The way cigarette makers target kids with ads makes me sick to my stomach," says REBEL volunteer Jessie Leigh Smolin, 17. "We're not for sale; they can't buy us."

CAN KiDS STOP KIDS FROM Smoking?

Kids get tough on the tobacco industry.

Health Literacy

Tobacco and Young Women Tobacco advertisers specifically target young women by using images that portray smokers as attractive, slim, and independent. In reality, more than 140,000 women die each year from smoking-related diseases. Smoking also causes unique health problems for women, including reduced fertility, increased risk of cervical cancer, and complications during pregnancy.

Have groups of students research the issue of women, smoking, and advertising. Ask: What brands specifically target women? What advertising methods do they use to appeal to young women? How can female anti-tobacco advocates counter these methods?

Taking On Tobacco Giants

The tobacco industry is being held responsible, in public and by the courts, for the negative health effects of smoking. In 1998 the industry settled a lawsuit filed by 46 states. "Big Tobacco," as the six giant cigarette makers are known,

agreed to pay the states $250 billion over the next 25 years. The money will help cover the costs of caring for people with tobacco-related illnesses.

Most of the states promised to use some of the settlement money to start smoking-prevention programs. Some states have begun tough campaigns created by kids. Their success has started a more aggressive movement against the industry. Kids are sending a message to Big Tobacco: You can't make us believe that smoking is cool.

Studies show that the earlier kids try smoking, the greater their chances of becoming regular smokers. Health experts warn that if kids continue to smoke at current rates, more than 5 million children now under age 18 will eventually die from smoking-related diseases.

Where Are Kids Fighting Back?

Mississippi, which ranks fourth nationally in the number of lives lost to tobacco-related illnesses, created a group called Frontline to help tackle the problem. The group of high-school kids got the state to pass a bill that outlaws the use of tobacco at school athletic events. The bill also made it illegal for teachers to use tobacco in public schools, even in the teachers' lounge. The students testified before committees, talked to lawmakers, and organized support around the state.

Frontline youth counselors also go into schools to warn younger students about the hazards of smoking through skits and dances. The state claims that teen smoking rates dropped 10 percent in high schools and 21 percent in middle schools in just one year after the program began!

Seth Bassett, 18, co-chair of Frontline, says, "I have a friend who quit smoking after he saw our ad. (It shows that an 18-year-old smoker has the lungs of a 50-year-old.) I've smoked before, but I know the dangers now and wouldn't touch it."

"It's all about the delivery of the message," says Leonardo Casas, 16, a REBEL volunteer. "Just like tobacco companies try to tell kids it's cool to smoke, we frame the message so that kids can see it's much cooler not to."

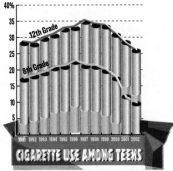

Source: Monitoring the Future

A yearly survey by the University of Michigan shows how many U.S. teens smoked a cigarette in the previous 30 days.

TIME TO THINK...

About Stopping Tobacco Use

Analyze the graph. What has been the trend in teen smoking in recent years? What year did smoking peak for 12th graders? How about for 8th graders? Use the Internet or your school's media center to research what students around the United States are doing to advocate for a tobacco-free lifestyle. Using some of the ideas you found in your research, as well as your own ideas and those of your classmates, create an antismoking campaign for your school.

3 Apply

Time to Think

Before students begin their anti-smoking campaigns, brainstorm a list of potential campaign elements. Encourage students to think beyond the standard poster/bumper sticker approach to a wide variety of activities that meet the criteria for advocacy. Examples may include

- an editorial or essay in the school paper.
- an educational brochure for younger students.
- a cartoon or photo essay.
- a skit, song, or puppet show.

Challenge students to come up with other formats for an advocacy activity.

VISUAL LEARNING

Have volunteers give their reactions to the antismoking poster on this page (RAT: Reject All Tobacco). Ask: "Who is the audience for this poster? Is it effective? Does it meet the criteria for a successful piece of anti-tobacco advocacy? Why or why not?

MORE ABOUT...

Anti-Tobacco Advocacy Direct students to the following anti-tobacco sites to find out more about student-led advocacy activities:
- Campaign for Tobacco-Free Kids (www.tobaccofreekids.org)
- American Lung Association (www.lungusa.org)
- Kick Butts Day (www.kickbuttsday.org)
- American Cancer Society (www.cancer.org)
- Centers for Disease Control and Prevention (www.cdc.gov)

REFUSAL SKILLS

Objective

After completing the lesson, students will be able to demonstrate effective refusal skills to resist peer pressure to use tobacco.

Time: 50 minutes

Materials: notebook paper, pen or pencil

Teacher Classroom Resources

📁 Building Health Skills Activities

• Transparency Master 7, "Refusal Skills"

• Reproducible Master 8, "Stand Firm Against Tobacco"

---

1. Model

• Display Transparency Master 7, and review refusal skills with the class.

• Have students read about Tasha and how she employed refusal skills to resist peer pressure to use tobacco.

• Ask the class to come up with other ways Tasha could have used refusal skills to resist the peer pressure. Write these on the board.

BUILDING HEALTH SKILLS

REFUSAL SKILLS

STAND FIRM AGAINST TOBACCO

Model

Saying no to tobacco isn't always easy, but remember—practice makes you better at it. Read about a teen named Tasha, shown below. She's at a party with her friends. Her friend Betty takes out a cigarette, lights it, and passes it to Tasha. Tasha has already decided not to smoke. Here are some ways she uses refusal skills. Would you be able to do as well?

SAY NO IN A FIRM VOICE.
"No, thanks, I don't smoke."

TELL WHY.
"I just don't want to do something that isn't good for me."

OFFER OTHER OPTIONS.
"No, I don't want one. Why don't we go to a movie instead?"

PROMPTLY LEAVE THE SITUATION.
When Betty and the other girls keep pressuring her, Tasha calls her mother and leaves the party.

224   CHAPTER 8: TOBACCO

Teaching Tips

Learning New Skills To highlight how we move past initial discomfort when learning new skills, ask students to remember what riding a bicycle, skateboarding, or in-line skating felt like when they were just starting out. (Students will probably say that it felt awkward, not smooth, and so forth.) Emphasize that learning any new skill, including refusal skills, may feel awkward at first but that with practice and repetition, performing these skills becomes "second nature."

Practice

Imagine the following scene. Then answer the questions at the end.

It's the end of the school day. Michael and Jeremy are at their lockers. Michael pulls out a can of smokeless tobacco and offers Jeremy a dip. Jeremy has already decided he doesn't want to use tobacco in any form.

JEREMY: No, thanks, I don't want any.
MICHAEL: Don't be a baby. I'll bet you've never tried it.
JEREMY: No, I've already made my decision. Besides, we could get caught and kicked out of school.
MICHAEL: Hey, a vacation would be nice. Anyway, there aren't any teachers around.
JEREMY: Look, I'm just not interested. I have to meet some friends for a basketball game. I'll see you later.

1. Which refusal skills did Jeremy use?
2. Do you think this conversation was realistic?
3. Which refusal skills would be comfortable for you?

Apply/Assess

Read the following three situations. Choose one situation and write your own conversation. Use the skills you have learned to refuse tobacco. You might role-play your conversation with another student in front of your class. Ask the class to identify the refusal skills you have used.

While Marcus is camping out in his backyard, his neighbor Tyrone enters the tent. Tyrone is a couple of years older than Marcus. After making himself comfortable, Tyrone reaches in his pocket and pulls out a pack of cigarettes. He lights one up and offers the pack to Marcus.

Marshall and Zack are best friends. They go to the same school and are on the baseball team. One day after practice, Zack surprises Marshall by reaching into his backpack and pulling out a pouch of chewing tobacco. Zack holds the pouch out to Marshall.

Anna is at the grocery store picking up some things for her mother. In the parking lot, she sees Matt, the cutest guy in her science class. Anna waves, and Matt comes over to talk. As they are talking, he offers her a cigarette.

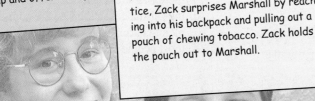

BUILDING HEALTH SKILLS: STAND FIRM AGAINST TOBACCO **225**

Checking Comprehension

Use the Chapter 8 Assessment to examine the most important ideas presented in the chapter.

Answers to Reviewing Vocabulary and Concepts

Lesson 1
1. chemicals
2. tar
3. carbon monoxide
4. nicotine
5. addiction
6. physical
7. psychological
8. emphysema
9. snuff
10. smokeless tobacco
11. secondhand smoke

Lesson 2
12. d
13. c
14. b
15. b

Thinking Critically

16. People start off using tobacco only occasionally. As the need for nicotine becomes stronger, they use tobacco regularly in more situations. They then develop a tolerance and begin a more intensified use of tobacco to experience its effects. Eventually, they become totally dependent on tobacco. If they quit, they experience withdrawal symptoms.

17. Responses should name several harmful effects of smoking on health and should state that there are no health benefits of smoking.

After You Read

Use your completed Foldable to review the information on tobacco addiction.

FOLDABLES™
Study Organizer

Reviewing Vocabulary and Concepts

On a sheet of paper, write the numbers 1–11. After each number, write the term from the list that best completes each sentence.

- addiction
- carbon monoxide
- chemicals
- emphysema
- nicotine
- psychological
- physical
- secondhand smoke
- smokeless tobacco
- snuff
- tar

Lesson 1

1. Tobacco smoke contains more than 4,000 _____.
2. A thick, oily, dark liquid that forms when tobacco burns is _____.
3. _____ is a poisonous, odorless gas that reduces the amount of oxygen in the blood when inhaled.
4. The addictive chemical found in tobacco is called _____.
5. You have formed a(n) _____ when you physically or mentally depend on a substance.
6. A person whose body cannot function without a drug has a _____ dependency.
7. A _____ dependency is a person's belief that he or she needs a particular substance to feel good.

8. Smoking can cause _____, a disease that damages the tiny air sacs in the lungs.
9. _____ is finely ground tobacco that is inhaled or held in the mouth between the lower lip and the gum.
10. Using _____ stains the teeth and causes bad breath.
11. Many children with asthma experience more severe reactions when they breathe _____.

Lesson 2

On a sheet of paper, write the numbers 12–15. After each number, write the letter of the answer that best completes each statement.

12. People may begin using tobacco because
    a. their family members use tobacco.
    b. they think it will make them look more grown-up.
    c. they think it will impress their peers.
    d. All of the above.
13. A form of media that might pressure you to use tobacco is
    a. your family.
    b. your peers.
    c. magazines.
    d. stress.
14. It is illegal in many states for people under the age of 18 to
    a. listen to tobacco advertisements.
    b. possess tobacco products.
    c. breathe tobacco smoke.
    d. advocate for a smoke-free environment.
15. Smoking is not a healthy way to manage stress because
    a. stress doesn't need to be managed.
    b. the craving for nicotine actually increases stress levels.
    c. the substances in tobacco are completely harmless.
    d. most people do not have any stress.

INCLUSION STRATEGIES

Special Learning Needs, Behavior Problems, English Language Learners The following suggestions are helpful for students with special learning needs, students with behavior problems, and ELL students:

- Pair these students with more proficient learners who can help summarize the main concepts of the chapter.

- Direct these students to listen to the Teen Health Audio Summaries. This component provides an audio and written summary of the chapter in both English and Spanish.

- Use photographs, drawings, or magazine clippings whenever possible to help students visualize the important concepts of the chapter.

Thinking Critically

Using complete sentences, answer the following questions on a sheet of paper.

16. Explain Describe how a person who begins using tobacco becomes addicted.

17. Compare What are the health risks of choosing to smoke? Are there any health benefits associated with smoking?

18. Interpret Why would an office building ban smoking at its entrances?

19. Infer Why might teens whose parents smoke be more likely to smoke themselves?

20. Suggest How would you convince a friend not to smoke?

Career Corner

Anesthesiologist People undergoing surgery or certain other medical treatments may need drugs that make them unconscious, so they don't feel pain. These drugs are called anesthetics. The physician who gives them is called an anesthesiologist. Like other doctors, anesthesiologists need at least four years of medical school. After that, they go through a residency, a period of advanced training in a medical specialty. Find out more about this and other health careers by clicking on Career Corner at health.glencoe.com.

18. So that nonsmokers do not have to enter through a cloud of smoke, so the smoke does not get in the building, or to keep the outside of the building looking neat.

19. To follow the example set by their parents, and they are more likely to try cigarettes because they have easy access to them at home.

20. Responses will vary.

Test Practice

1. B
2. A
3. Responses will vary, but might include that people started to use tobacco because it was something different.

Reteaching

Assign Study Guide 8 in the Student Activities Workbook.

Evaluate

• Use the reproducible Chapter 8 Test in the TCR, or construct your own test using the **Exam***View*® Pro Testmaker.

• Use Performance Assessment 8 in the TCR.

Enrichment

Have students work together to collect and discuss news articles about tobacco.

Standardized Test Practice

Reading & Writing

Read the paragraphs below and then answer the questions.

When explorers arrived in the New World of the Americas, they were introduced to the tobacco plant. Native Americans had been growing and using the leaves of the tobacco plant for many years. The explorers who settled in the New World began to use tobacco in the same way. They brought their new discovery back to Europe. Soon Europeans took up the habit. These people did not know that they had started a dangerous and addictive habit.

Today we know that tobacco use is unhealthy. Once a person starts using tobacco, it is difficult to stop. Using tobacco is expensive and leads to many serious health problems, including lung cancer and heart disease. Tobacco is still grown, exported, advertised, and sold in the United States and elsewhere. Now, however, it comes with a warning: Tobacco use is harmful to health.

1. The first paragraph is mostly about
   - Ⓐ how Native Americans discovered tobacco.
   - Ⓑ the discovery and spread of tobacco use.
   - Ⓒ the way Europeans used tobacco.
   - Ⓓ the reason people started to smoke.

2. The tone of the second paragraph is one of
   - Ⓐ seriousness.
   - Ⓑ sadness.
   - Ⓒ anger.
   - Ⓓ regret.

3. Write a paragraph explaining why you think people started to use tobacco when it was first introduced.

 TH05_C1.glencoe.com/quiz

Assessment

Self-Assessment Direct students to review the activities that are provided throughout the chapter. Encourage each student to select one finished product or activity that demonstrates his or her best work for the chapter. Have students explain what they learned and how the examples they selected show their progress.

Career Corner

Anesthesiologist After reviewing the career profile on the health Web site, students might:

• Calculate the average hourly rate an anesthesiologist would earn, using the annual salary range provided.

• Discuss what factors besides salary one might consider in determining whether this would be a suitable career.

Planning Guide

Chapter 9	Skills/ Activities	Reproducible Resources	Assessment
Lesson 1 **Why Alcohol is Harmful** *pages 230–233*		*Student Activities Workbook available for use with each chapter* 📁 Parent Letter & Activities 9 📁 Concept Map 38 📁 Cross-Curriculum Activity 17 📁 Enrichment Activity 32 📁 Health Lab 9 📁 Lesson Plan 1 📁 Reading Tutor Activity 32 📁 Reteaching Activity 33	📁 Lesson 1 Quiz
Lesson 2 **Using Medicines Responsibly** *pages 234–239*		📁 Concept Map 39 📁 Decision-Making Activity 17 📁 Enrichment Activity 33 📁 Lesson Plan 2 📁 Reading Tutor Activity 33 📁 Reteaching Activity 34	📁 Lesson 2 Quiz
Lesson 3 **What Are Illegal Drugs?** *pages 240–245*	**Hands-On Health** ▲ "Say No to Drugs" Skit, page 244	📁 Concept Map 40 📁 Cross-Curriculum Activity 18 📁 Enrichment Activity 34 📁 Lesson Plan 3 📁 Reading Tutor Activity 34 📁 Reteaching Activity 35	📁 Lesson 3 Quiz
Lesson 4 **Staying Drug Free** *pages 246–249*	**HEALTH SKILLS ACTIVITY** ▲ Say No and Mean It (*Refusal Skills*), page 248	📁 Concept Map 41 📁 Decision-Making Activity 18 📁 Enrichment Activity 35 📁 Lesson Plan 4 📁 Reading Tutor Activity 35 📁 Reteaching Activity 36	📁 Lesson 4 Quiz 📁 Chapter 9 Test 📁 Performance Assessment 9

TIME HEALTH **Steroids and Sports Don't Mix** *pages 250–251*

BUILDING HEALTH SKILLS			
How to Avoid Alcohol (*Decision Making*) *pages 252–253*		📁 Building Health Skills Reproducible Master 9	

Standards		Technology
National	**State/Local**	
National Health Education Standard **1.1, 1.3, 1.4, 1.8, 3.1, 3.4**		🔦 Transparency 37 💿 TeacherWorks™ 🖱 Internet Activities
National Health Education Standard **1.1, 2.2, 2.3, 2.6, 3.1, 3.4**		🔦 Transparency 38 💿 TeacherWorks™
National Health Education Standard **1.1, 1.2, 1.4, 1.8, 2.2, 5.4, 5.6**		🔦 Transparency 39 💿 TeacherWorks™
National Health Education Standard **1.1, 1.3, 1.4, 1.6, 2.6, 3.1, 3.4, 5.1, 5.6**		🔦 Transparency 40 📼💿 Tape/DVD 2, Segment 1, "Teen Advocacy;" Segment 2, "Refusal Skills" 💿 TeacherWorks™ 📼💿 MindJogger Videoquiz 💿 **Exam**View® Pro Testmaker
National Health Education Standard **6.1, 6.2, 6.3**		📁 Building Health Skills Transparency Master 8

TeacherWorks™

Glencoe's new and exclusive TeacherWorks™ is an all-in-one planner and resource center. Access the complete Teacher Wraparound Edition electronically. Find all your classroom resources with just a few easy clicks, and print them right from your computer. Connect directly to Glencoe's customized Health Web site. Access the National Health Education Standards correlations, or insert your own state standards and match them directly to the electronic Teacher Wraparound Edition.

Language Diversity

- 🎧 English Audio Summaries
- 🎧 Spanish Audio Summaries
- 📁 English Summaries, Quizzes, and Activities
- 📁 Spanish Summaries, Quizzes, and Activities
- 📁 Spanish Parent Letters and Activities

KEY TO ABILITY LEVELS

Teaching Strategies that appear throughout the chapters have been identified by one of four codes to give you an idea of their suitability for students of varying learning styles and abilities.

L1 **Level 1** strategies should be within the ability range of all students. Often full class participation is required.

L2 **Level 2** strategies are for average to above-average students or for small groups. Some teacher direction is necessary.

L3 **Level 3** strategies are designed for students able and willing to work independently. Minimal teacher direction is necessary.

INCL Strategies are appropriate for students with particular special needs in a general classroom setting.

Alcohol and Other Drugs

Chapter at a Glance

Lesson 1 helps students understand how drinking affects health and emphasizes why teens should avoid all forms of alcohol.

Lesson 2 focuses on drugs as medicines and helps students understand how prescription and over-the-counter medicines can be used safely.

Lesson 3 discusses the dangers and types of illegal drugs.

Lesson 4 explores motivations for choosing to be substance free and ways to stay substance free and helps students recognize healthy alternatives to using alcohol or other drugs.

Health Skills
- Say No and Mean It (*Refusal Skills*), p. 248
- How to Avoid Alcohol (*Decision Making*), pp. 252–253

228

HANDS-ON ACTIVITY

Counter Messages Before class, prepare index cards for half the students. Write one of these messages per card: "I'm depressed. I'm stressed out. I don't want to be left out. I'm bored. I'll be grown-up. I'll be my own person. I'll try anything once." You will probably end up with more than one card of each message. Organize students into pairs, and give each pair an index card. Tell them to imagine that a friend has just been offered alcohol or illegal drugs and that the friend is considering drinking or taking drugs for the reason or feeling written on the card. Have students provide responses to the friend that show alternative ways to deal with or think about the messages on the cards. Students can share their counter messages with the class.

Alcohol and Other Drugs

Chapter Introduction

Use the options below to motivate students and preview chapter content.

HEALTH *Online*

Rate your commitment to being alcohol and drug free. Go to health.glencoe.com and take the Chapter 9 Health Inventory.

FOLDABLES™ Study Organizer

Before You Read

Make this Foldable to record information on alcohol and its harmful effects, presented in Lesson 1. Begin with two sheets of notebook paper.

Step 1

Fold one sheet in half from top to bottom. Cut about 1" along the fold at both ends, stopping at the margin lines.

Step 2

Fold the second sheet in half from top to bottom. Cut the fold *between* the margin lines.

Step 3

Insert the first sheet through the second sheet and align folds.

Step 4

Fold the bound pages in half to make a booklet, and label the cover as shown. Then label each page as instructed by your teacher.

Chapter 9,
Lesson 1:
Why Alcohol
is Harmful

As You Read

Take notes on alcohol's harmful effects on the appropriate page of your booklet.

HEALTH *Online*

Have students visit health.glencoe.com and take Health Inventory 9 to test their knowledge of alcohol and other drugs. For new teaching ideas, click on Teaching Today to download helpful tools such as graphic organizers and Webquest activities.

GLENCOE TECHNOLOGY

Teen Health Video and DVD Series
(Each format available in both English and Spanish)

📼 💿 You may wish to use:

- Tape/DVD 2, Segment 1, "Teen Advocacy"
- Tape/DVD 2, Segment 2, "Refusal Skills"

MindJogger Videoquiz

📼 💿 Use MindJogger to preview or review Chapter 9 content.

TIME HEALTH

Steroids and Sports Don't Mix
pages 250–251

FOLDABLES™ Study Organizer

Dinah Zike Study Fold

Organizing Data Tell students that they will use their completed Foldable to organize what they learn about alcohol and its many harmful effects. As students read and study the material presented in Lesson 1, have them take notes, define terms, record statistics, and list examples on the appropriate page of their booklet. The completed booklet will serve as a useful study guide and can also be used as a motivational tool, providing students with solid reasons for avoiding alcohol.

Lesson 1

Why Alcohol Is Harmful

1 Focus

Lesson Objectives

Students will be able to

- explain how alcohol affects a person's physical and mental health.
- describe the short- and long-term risks of using alcohol.
- explain why a pregnant woman should not drink alcohol.

Motivators

Quick Write

Ask a volunteer to come up to the board. Have him or her list the ways drinking alcohol can affect behavior as they are identified by the class.

Bellringer Activity

Pose the following questions, and ask students to write brief responses: At what age is it legal to begin drinking alcohol? Is alcohol a drug? Please explain.

VOCABULARY

Guide students in reading aloud the vocabulary terms, and ask volunteers to find the definition of each term in the Glossary. Focus particular attention on the term *alcohol*. Ask students to speculate about why it is important to understand that alcohol is a drug.

Why Alcohol Is Harmful

Quick Write

Alcohol causes the brain and other parts of the body to work more slowly. List five ways in which drinking alcohol might affect a person's behavior.

LEARN ABOUT...

- how alcohol affects a person's physical and mental health.
- the short-term and long-term risks of using alcohol.
- why pregnant women should not drink alcohol.

VOCABULARY

- alcohol
- drug
- cirrhosis
- alcoholism
- fetal alcohol syndrome (FAS)

What Is Alcohol?

Alcohol (AL·kuh·hawl) is *a substance that is produced by a chemical reaction in some foods.* Alcohol is also a drug. A **drug** is *any substance that changes the structure or function of the body or mind.*

When a person drinks alcohol, it passes through the stomach and small intestine and moves into the bloodstream. When alcohol reaches the brain, it slows down the body's functions and reactions. See **Figure 9.1**.

Why Do Some Young People Drink?

In the United States, it is illegal for anyone under 21 years old to drink alcohol. Some teens break this law because they want to fit in with friends or family members who drink. They may think that drinking will make them seem more grown-up. Teens may also think drinking will help them escape their problems. However, drinking cannot solve problems—it creates new ones.

These teens are discussing the dangers of drinking. *Why is it important to stay alcohol free?*

230 CHAPTER 9: ALCOHOL AND OTHER DRUGS

Lesson 1 Resources

Teacher Classroom Resources

📁 Parent Letter & Activities 9

📁 Concept Map 38

📁 Cross-Curriculum Activity 17

📁 Enrichment Activity 32

📁 Health Lab 9

📁 Lesson Plan 1

📁 Lesson 1 Quiz

📁 Reading Tutor Activity 32

📁 Reteaching Activity 33

🎙 Transparency 37

Student Activities Workbook

📁 Chapter 9 Study Guide

📁 Applying Health Skills 32

FIGURE 9.1

HARMFUL EFFECTS OF ALCOHOL ON THE BODY

Alcohol affects many parts of the body.

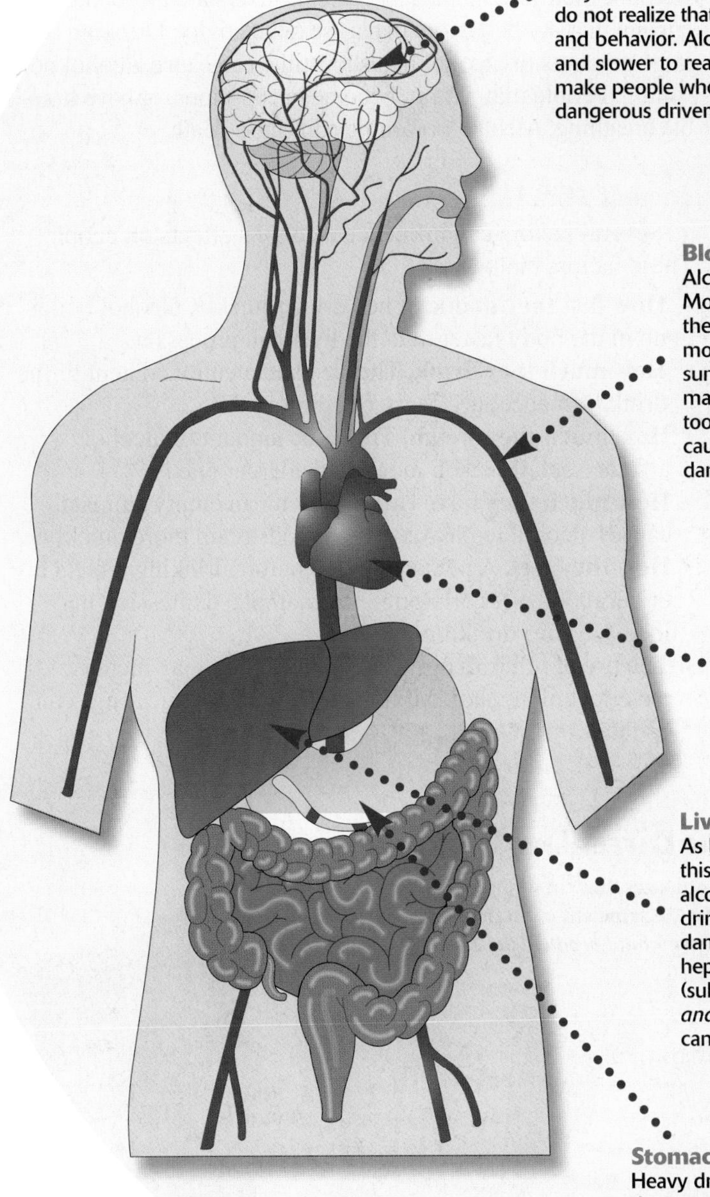

Brain
Alcohol slows down the way the brain works. When people drink, they have trouble thinking, speaking, and moving. They may say or do things they would not normally say or do. Drinkers often do not realize that alcohol has affected their thinking and behavior. Alcohol also makes a person clumsy and slower to react in an emergency. These effects make people who have been drinking very dangerous drivers.

Blood vessels
Alcohol expands the blood vessels. More blood passes through, making the drinker feel warmer. However, as more blood flows close to the body surface, the body loses heat. This may lead a person to stay outdoors too long in very cold weather, causing body temperature to fall dangerously low.

Heart
Heavy drinking can lead to high blood pressure and may damage the heart muscle.

Liver
As blood passes through the liver, this organ slowly breaks down any alcohol that is in the blood. Heavy drinking over a long period can damage the liver. It can cause hepatitis, liver cancer, or **cirrhosis** (suh·ROH·sis), which is *destruction and scarring of liver tissue*. Cirrhosis can lead to death.

Stomach
Heavy drinking can damage the lining of the stomach. Eventually, it can cause sores called ulcers.

LESSON 1: WHY ALCOHOL IS HARMFUL **231**

Lesson 1

② Teach

VISUAL LEARNING

FIGURE 9.1 Have volunteers read aloud the title and the caption for Figure 9.1. Have other volunteers identify the five labeled organs. Help students discuss the importance of these organs in maintaining good health. Then have students read and discuss the paragraph describing the effects of alcohol on each of these organs. **INCL** *Behavior Problems, Special Learning Needs, English Language Learners*

Discussing

Point out that Figure 9.1 shows some of the effects of alcohol on physical health. Guide students in discussing how alcohol can affect mental/emotional and social health. **L1**

Comprehending

Ask students:

• How do you think drinking alcohol might affect a student's school work? An athlete's performance?

• What risks does a person take by driving under the influence of alcohol?

• As a passenger, how can you tell whether a driver has drunk too much? (Emphasize that only with a driver who has not drunk alcohol at all, can you be sure the driver has not had too much.) **L1**

COOPERATIVE LEARNING ACTIVITY

Sing-Along Ask students to work in groups of four to prepare a presentation for elementary students about what alcohol does to a person's body and why it is important to choose to be alcohol free. Have groups brainstorm lists of what students in elementary school should know about alcohol. Each group should prepare an illustrated poster with a slogan and a song that they can sing—one with appropriate new words to a familiar tune such as "Happy Birthday." If a tape recorder is available, students may choose to record their song on tape. If there is an elementary school nearby, you may want to arrange for their song to be sung to a class at lunchtime.

Lesson 1

HEALTH *Online*

Have students explore the Web Links for this chapter and then complete the activity.

VISUAL LEARNING

FIGURE 9.2 Have students describe the three drinks; emphasize that the three all have the same amount of alcohol and produce the same effects. Ask: How does this help you understand the fact that drinking "just beer" is, in fact, drinking alcohol? Then pose the question in the caption for Figure 9.2. (*1½ × 12 ounces = 18 ounces of beer.*) **INCL** *Behavior Problems, Special Learning Needs, English Language Learners*

Comprehending

Discuss the list of factors that influence the effects of alcohol. Ask:

• Why should two individuals not expect the same effects from drinking the same amount of alcohol?

• Why should an individual not rely on a consistent effect from drinking the same amount of alcohol? **L1**

Cooperative Learning

Have groups of students create public service announcements (PSAs) that explain the role alcohol plays in unsafe situations such as drinking and driving. Their PSAs should deliver a strong message. For example, they could attempt to persuade other teens to refuse a ride from anyone who has been drinking. **L1**

HEALTH *Online*

Topic: Avoiding Alcohol

For a link to more information on avoiding alcohol use, go to health.glencoe.com.

Activity: Using the information provided at this link, write a dialogue in which a teen uses effective refusal skills to resist pressure to use alcohol.

Alcohol's Short-Term and Long-Term Effects

Alcohol begins to affect the body soon after it is ingested. The blood vessels expand, and the heart rate increases. The drinker's reactions, behavior, and judgment are also affected. Because their judgment is affected, drinkers are more likely to engage in risky behavior such as sexual activity. Drinking large amounts of alcohol in a short time can cause alcohol poisoning. People may vomit, become unconscious, or have trouble breathing. Alcohol poisoning can cause death.

Factors That Influence Alcohol's Effects

Several factors can influence alcohol's effects on people. These factors include:

• **How fast they drink.** When drunk quickly, alcohol builds up in the body faster than the liver can process it.

• **How much they drink.** The size and alcohol content of the drink influence its effects. See **Figure 9.2**.

• **How much they weigh.** The same amount of alcohol affects a small person more than a larger one.

• **How much they have eaten.** Having an empty stomach causes alcohol to pass into the bloodstream more quickly.

• **How they feel.** A person's mood before drinking affects his or her mood after drinking. For example, depression may increase after drinking.

• **The use of other drugs.** Certain medicines may increase the effect of alcohol. Mixing alcohol with some drugs can be fatal.

FIGURE 9.2

ALCOHOL CONTENT IN DIFFERENT DRINKS

The three drinks here are different sizes, but they contain the same amount of alcohol and have the same effect on the brain and body. *How many ounces of beer would produce the same effect as 6 ounces of wine?*

Mixed drink 1.5 ounces of liquor

Beer 12 ounces

Wine 4 ounces

232 CHAPTER 9: ALCOHOL AND OTHER DRUGS

Health Literacy

Influencing Factors Although nobody should consider himself or herself safe from alcoholism, those whose relatives have suffered from alcoholism may be at special risk. There is evidence that alcoholism frequently runs in families, and in 1990 a link was suggested between a particular gene and a susceptibility to alcoholism. It is still not certain whether the connection is hereditary; environmental; or most likely, a combination. The fact remains that nearly half of all children of alcoholics under the age of 18 will develop alcoholism, other drug problems, and/or other serious coping problems.

Addiction and Alcoholism

Alcohol use also has serious long-term effects. Not only does it damage the body, but using it can lead to addiction. *The physical and mental need for alcohol* is a disease called **alcoholism**. People who have this illness are called alcoholics. Alcoholism cannot be cured, but it can be treated. The alcoholic must go through a process to remove the effects of alcohol from his or her body. Once that has happened, the alcoholic must never drink alcohol again.

Pregnancy and Alcohol

When a pregnant woman drinks, alcohol passes from her body into the bloodstream of her developing baby. This can lead to **fetal** (FEE·tuhl) **alcohol syndrome**, or **FAS**, *a group of permanent physical and mental problems caused by alcohol.* Babies with FAS often weigh less than average. They may suffer from birth defects and mental retardation. To make sure their babies do not develop FAS, women should avoid alcohol completely during pregnancy.

GOVERNMENT WARNING: (1) ACCORDING TO THE SURGEON GENERAL, WOMEN SHOULD NOT DRINK ALCOHOLIC BEVERAGES DURING PREGNANCY BECAUSE OF THE RISK OF BIRTH DEFECTS. (2) CONSUMPTION OF ALCOHOLIC BEVERAGES IMPAIRS YOUR ABILITY TO DRIVE A CAR OR OPERATE MACHINERY, AND MAY CAUSE HEALTH PROBLEMS.

All alcoholic beverages must carry a label warning about the dangers of alcohol. *Explain the role alcohol plays in unsafe situations such as drinking and driving and HIV and STD transmission.*

Lesson 1 Review

Using complete sentences, answer the following questions on a sheet of paper.

Reviewing Terms and Facts

1. **Vocabulary** Define the word *alcohol*, and use it in an original sentence.
2. **Summarize** How does alcohol affect the brain, blood vessels, heart, liver, and stomach?
3. **List** Name four factors that influence the effect alcohol has on the body.
4. **Explain** Why is it unwise for pregnant women to drink alcohol?

Thinking Critically

5. **Explain** Why might a person who has been drinking think that the alcohol has not affected his or her ability to drive?
6. **Infer** In what ways might drinking affect a person's relationships?

Applying Health Skills

7. **Advocacy** Work with a partner to think of a slogan that would persuade young people not to drink. Put your slogan on a button or poster.

LESSON 1: WHY ALCOHOL IS HARMFUL **233**

Lesson 2

Using Medicines Responsibly

❶ Focus

Lesson Objectives

Students will be able to

- explain how medicines affect the body.
- explain why medicines have warning labels.
- discuss how to use medicines safely.
- identify and analyze the signs of drug misuse and abuse.

Motivators

Quick Write
Allow time for students to share their responses. Ask: Which ones are available only with a doctor's prescription?

Bellringer Activity

Have students work in groups to list as many drugs as they can identify and then categorize them as medicines or nonmedicines. (Nonmedicine drugs are those used for purely recreational reasons.)

VOCABULARY

Ask volunteers to read aloud the vocabulary terms. Have other volunteers suggest informal definitions of the terms and/or check the definitions in the Glossary. Then focus students' attention on the words *misuse* and *abuse*. Ask: What base word do the two words have in common? (use) How do the prefix *ab-* and *mis-* affect the meaning? (*away from correct or wrongful*)

Lesson 2

Using Medicines Responsibly

Quick Write

Write down a list of medicines you see advertised in television commercials. What symptoms or diseases do they treat?

LEARN ABOUT...

- how medicines help you when you're sick.
- why medicines have warning labels.
- how to analyze the use and abuse of prescription and nonprescription medications.

VOCABULARY

- medicine
- prescription medicine
- nonprescription medicine
- over-the-counter (OTC) medicine
- antibiotic
- side effect
- tolerance
- drug misuse
- drug abuse

How Medicines Help Your Body

Medicines are *drugs that are used to cure or prevent diseases or other conditions.* There are two types of medicines. **Prescription** (pri·SKRIP·shuhn) **medicines** can be *sold only with a written order from a doctor.* **Nonprescription** (or **over-the-counter [OTC]**) **medicines** are *medicines available without a written order from a doctor.* Prescription medicines generally require a doctor's supervision because they have more risks than nonprescription medicines. However, this does not mean that nonprescription medicines are risk free. Follow the directions on the medicine label and pay attention to any warnings about when and how to use them. Even when you are taking a prescription medicine under a doctor's care, pay attention to how it affects your body and whether it is working as expected.

Some medicines prevent disease. Others cure disease or relieve symptoms. Still others are used to manage chronic conditions such as asthma. Some of the most widely used medicines are described below.

- Vaccines are medicines that protect you from certain diseases, such as polio and measles.

Vaccines are medicines that help to prevent disease. *What immunizations did you receive in the past year?*

234 CHAPTER 9: ALCOHOL AND OTHER DRUGS

Lesson 2 Resources

Teacher Classroom Resources

- **Antibiotics** (an·ti·by·AH·tiks) are *medicines that kill or stop the growth of certain germs.* Antibiotics can treat infections caused by bacteria, such as strep throat. However, they cannot cure illnesses caused by viruses, such as colds and flu.
- Some medicines help control heartbeat, reduce high blood pressure, and open blocked blood vessels.
- Some medicines reduce pain, such as that from a headache, sore muscles, or a broken bone. Aspirin is one example.

How Medicines Affect the Body

All medicines can have powerful effects on your body and mind. Your reaction to a medicine depends on these factors:

- The type and amount of the medicine
- The way the medicine enters the body (see **Figure 9.3** on page 236)
- Your age, weight, and general health
- Other medicines you are taking
- Any allergies you have

Negative Reactions to Medicines

You may experience a reaction to some types of medicines. A **side effect** is *any reaction to a medicine other than the one intended.* Common side effects are drowsiness, dizziness, stomach upset, and a rash. Taking more than one medicine at a time can cause more dangerous side effects. It may greatly increase or decrease the effects of one or both medicines. It can also cause unexpected reactions. Always tell your doctor about all the medicines you are taking, including nonprescription medicines.

If you take a medicine for a long time, you may develop a tolerance. **Tolerance** (TAHL·er·ence) is *a condition in which the body becomes used to the effects of a medicine and needs greater amounts to get the same effect.* If a medicine seems to have stopped working for you, ask your doctor or pharmacist about your options.

Developing Good Character

Responsibility

Medicine labels tell you how to use a drug safely. For example, they tell you how much to take and how often to take it. Not following these directions can have serious consequences. Always use medicines responsibly.

Read the label carefully when taking any type of medicine. *Why is it important to check the side effects of a medicine?*

② Teach

Developing Good Character

Responsibility
Discuss the importance of being a responsible consumer when taking medicine. Ask: How do people show responsible behavior when they take prescription medicine as directed? What could happen if certain medicines are combined with other drugs or alcohol? Why is it important to follow directions carefully? Encourage students to make a personal plan for taking prescription drugs safely and responsibly.

Applying Knowledge

Ask the class to sort the medicines identified in the Bellringer Activity into prescription and OTC medicines. Then have students analyze the use and abuse of prescription and nonprescription (over-the-counter) medications. **L2**

Comprehending

Discuss the factors that help determine an individual's reaction to medicine. Have students explain why it is important to take each of the factors into account. Ask: Why is age alone not a wise way to determine dosage? Encourage students to name any drug allergies that they know they have. Ask them to describe the symptoms. **L1**

LESSON 2: USING MEDICINES RESPONSIBLY **235**

MORE ABOUT...

Side Effects Even the most familiar OTC medicines, those found in nearly every household, can have side effects. Such side effects may vary from individual to individual; they may also build up and become more severe with continued use of the medicine. Aspirin, for example, is a reliable pain-relieving medication for most people. A few people, however, find that even a single dose of aspirin upsets the stomach; and regular, frequent use of aspirin over an extended period will result in an irritated stomach lining for almost all individuals. As wise consumers, students should learn to read labels carefully.

FIGURE 9.3 Have students briefly discuss what they already know about how medicines can enter the body. Then have students read and discuss each of the five explanations. Ask a volunteer to read aloud the caption for Figure 9.3, and have students name specific medicines that are applied directly (e.g., *anti-itch cream*), swallowed (*acetaminophen*), inhaled (*asthma medication*), and injected (*insulin*).

Comprehending

You may want to encourage students to share and discuss their own experiences in taking medications via the different methods identified in Figure 9.3. Have them consider the advantages and disadvantages of each method. Are the advantages and disadvantages the same for all people? Why or why not? **L1**

Researching

Ask students to use library and online resources to learn more about the FDA:

• When and why was it formed?
• What are the most important responsibilities of the organization?
• What steps does the FDA follow in evaluating a new medicine?

Have students discuss their findings with the class. **L3**

FIGURE 9.3

HOW MEDICINES ENTER THE BODY

Common ways of taking medicines include direct application to the affected area, swallowing, inhaling, and injection. *Give examples of medicines that are used in these four ways.*

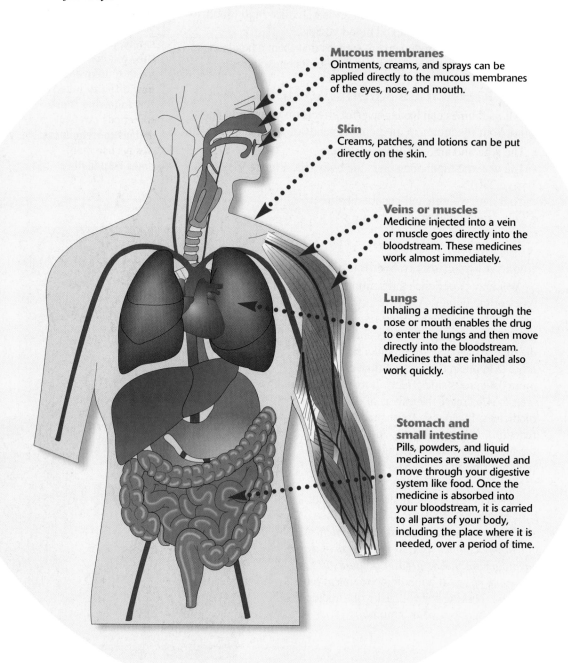

Mucous membranes
Ointments, creams, and sprays can be applied directly to the mucous membranes of the eyes, nose, and mouth.

Skin
Creams, patches, and lotions can be put directly on the skin.

Veins or muscles
Medicine injected into a vein or muscle goes directly into the bloodstream. These medicines work almost immediately.

Lungs
Inhaling a medicine through the nose or mouth enables the drug to enter the lungs and then move directly into the bloodstream. Medicines that are inhaled also work quickly.

Stomach and small intestine
Pills, powders, and liquid medicines are swallowed and move through your digestive system like food. Once the medicine is absorbed into your bloodstream, it is carried to all parts of your body, including the place where it is needed, over a period of time.

236 CHAPTER 9: ALCOHOL AND OTHER DRUGS

COOPERATIVE LEARNING ACTIVITY

Consumerism Have students work in groups to research consumer choices for pain-relieving medications. Instruct groups to select a specific kind of pain reliever for a child of a given age or for an adult and to find answers for these questions: In a large drugstore or grocery store, how many different brands of that medicine are available? What are the prices of the different brands? Other than in price, how are the brands different from one another? Which brand would you choose to purchase? Why? Have groups analyze how the medicine is used appropriately and how it might be abused. Then have each group share their results with the rest of the class.

Drug Safety

The Food and Drug Administration (FDA) is a government agency that reviews all medicines sold in the United States to make sure they are safe. It can often take several years to determine a medicine's long-term effects. The FDA then decides whether a medicine must be sold with a prescription or if it can be sold over the counter. Even medicines sold over the counter, however, are safe only when used as directed.

Reading Medicine Labels

The FDA requires drug manufacturers to put certain information on medicine labels. The label must tell how and when to take the medicine, how much to take, and special instructions for taking it. **Figure 9.4** is an example of a prescription label. **Figure 9.5** on page 238 is an example of a label on a nonprescription medicine.

FIGURE 9.4

LABEL ON A PRESCRIPTION MEDICINE

Prescription medicine labels usually show the name of the doctor who prescribed the medicine. *Why is it important to use a prescription medicine as directed on the label?*

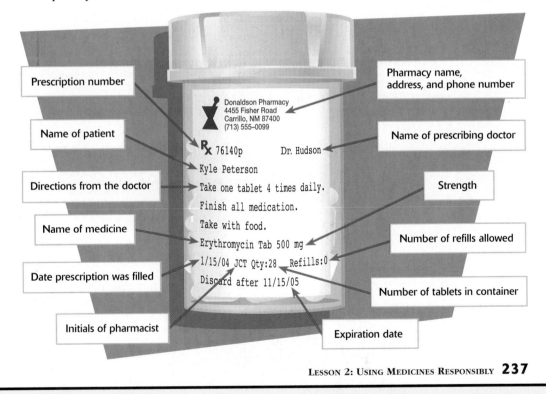

- Prescription number
- Name of patient
- Directions from the doctor
- Name of medicine
- Date prescription was filled
- Initials of pharmacist
- Pharmacy name, address, and phone number
- Name of prescribing doctor
- Strength
- Number of refills allowed
- Number of tablets in container
- Expiration date

Donaldson Pharmacy
4455 Fisher Road
Carrillo, NM 87400
(713) 555–0099

R_x 76140p   Dr. Hudson
Kyle Peterson
Take one tablet 4 times daily.
Finish all medication.
Take with food.
Erythromycin Tab 500 mg
1/15/04 JCT Qty:28 Refills:0
Discard after 11/15/05

LESSON 2: USING MEDICINES RESPONSIBLY **237**

Lesson 2

Discussing

Encourage students to share their responses to these questions:

- Who is responsible for prescribing and providing safe medicines?
- Why is it important for patients to talk with doctors about medicines?
- How does the label let you know if prescription medicine is being used appropriately? Have students briefly analyze the use and abuse of prescription medicines. **L1**

VISUAL LEARNING

FIGURE 9.4 Have students briefly describe the label and compare it to labels with which they are familiar. Students with special learning needs may need additional support to complete this task. Ask students to point to each part of the label as volunteers read the explanation aloud. Emphasize that the patient named on the label is the only person who should take the medicine. Ask the caption question, and help students recognize that the patient (or the patient's parents) might need to call the doctor if a refill is needed, the patient does not seem to be responding, or the medicine appears to have unpleasant side effects. **INCL** *Behavior Problems, Special Learning Needs, English Language Learners*

Reading Check

Inferential Thinking Making inferences about the label in Figure 9.4 will help students focus on the content and purpose of each part. As they look at each text box, tell students to decide who would need the information and how they might use it. For example, the information may be useful to the pharmacist, the doctor, or the consumer. If students have difficulty understanding the value of a piece of information, prompt them by asking questions. For example, if they can't explain why it is important to know the date the prescription was filled, ask: What would you do if you forgot when you started taking your medicine?

Discussing

Guide students in studying Figure 9.5 and discussing the sample label for OTC medicine. Have them note how that label is like the labels on OTCs they are familiar with. Ask students to share information on who usually chooses the OTCs used in their homes. Ask:

• Do you check the labels on OTCs in your home?

• When you do, what should you look for? **L1**

Using Medicines Safely

Any drug that can do some good can also do some harm. For that reason, all medicines should be used with caution. To stay safe, follow these guidelines when taking any kind of medicine.

• Ask your doctor or pharmacist if you are not sure which nonprescription medicine to buy or how to use it.
• Take medicines only as directed on the label or as instructed by your doctor or pharmacist.
• Take medicines only for their intended purpose.
• If the medicine does not help you, talk with a parent or another adult. You may need to call your doctor.
• Parents should keep medicines in child-resistant containers and place them out of the reach of young children.
• Discard any medicine that is past its expiration date.
• Finish all of the medicine prescribed by the doctor for bacterial infections.
• Do not give your medicine to anyone else.

FIGURE 9.5

LABEL ON A NONPRESCRIPTION (OTC) MEDICINE

Labels on nonprescription medicines usually include instructions on how to take the drug safely. *Name three types of people who should not take the drug shown here.*

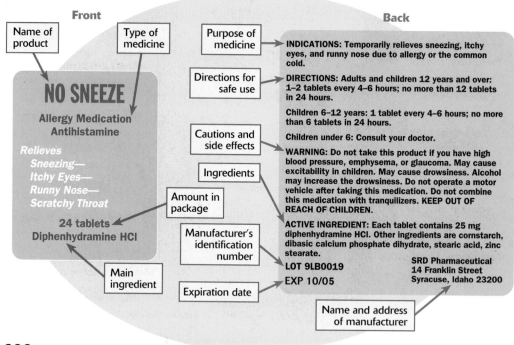

Front — Back

Name of product

Type of medicine

Purpose of medicine

Directions for safe use

Cautions and side effects

Ingredients

Amount in package

Manufacturer's identification number

Main ingredient

Expiration date

NO SNEEZE

Allergy Medication
Antihistamine

*Relieves
Sneezing—
Itchy Eyes—
Runny Nose—
Scratchy Throat*

24 tablets
Diphenhydramine HCl

INDICATIONS: Temporarily relieves sneezing, itchy eyes, and runny nose due to allergy or the common cold.

DIRECTIONS: Adults and children 12 years and over: 1–2 tablets every 4–6 hours; no more than 12 tablets in 24 hours.

Children 6–12 years: 1 tablet every 4–6 hours; no more than 6 tablets in 24 hours.

Children under 6: Consult your doctor.

WARNING: Do not take this product if you have high blood pressure, emphysema, or glaucoma. May cause excitability in children. May cause drowsiness. Alcohol may increase the drowsiness. Do not operate a motor vehicle after taking this medication. Do not combine this medication with tranquilizers. KEEP OUT OF REACH OF CHILDREN.

ACTIVE INGREDIENT: Each tablet contains 25 mg diphenhydramine HCl. Other ingredients are cornstarch, dibasic calcium phosphate dihydrate, stearic acid, zinc stearate.

LOT 9LB0019

EXP 10/05

SRD Pharmaceutical
14 Franklin Street
Syracuse, Idaho 23200

Name and address of manufacturer

238 CHAPTER 9: ALCOHOL AND OTHER DRUGS

The Misuse and Abuse of Drugs

People can harm themselves if they misuse or abuse prescription or OTC drugs. **Drug misuse** means *taking medicine in a way that is not intended.* Taking more medicine than the doctor instructed is an example of drug misuse. **Drug abuse** (uh·BYOOS) means *using drugs in ways that are unhealthy or illegal.* Taking a cold medicine to help you sleep is an example of drug abuse. See **Figure 9.6**.

FIGURE 9.6

EXAMPLES OF DRUG MISUSE AND ABUSE

All drugs can cause harm if misused or abused. *Whom should you consult if you are not sure how to use a medicine?*

Drug Misuse

- Taking a medicine for a shorter or longer time than prescribed
- Changing the amount of medicine taken without a doctor's approval
- Taking more than one medicine without approval from your doctor
- Using medicine that was prescribed for an earlier illness without a doctor's approval
- Using medicine prescribed for someone else

Drug Abuse

- Using a drug that is illegal
- Using a medicine for nonmedical purposes
- Swallowing or breathing a substance that was not meant to enter the body
- Using a drug in any way that is physically, mentally, or socially harmful

Lesson 2 Review

Using complete sentences, answer the following questions on a sheet of paper.

Reviewing Terms and Facts

1. **Vocabulary** Define *side effect.*
2. **List** What are five ways that medicines can enter the body?
3. **Recall** Which U.S. government agency helps ensure that medicines are safe?
4. **Contrast** Analyze the use and abuse of prescription and nonprescription medicines.

Thinking Critically

5. **Infer** Why might a doctor prescribe different medicines for two people with the same illness?

6. **Explain** Why might it take a long time for the FDA to approve a new medicine?

Applying Health Skills

7. **Accessing Information** Choose a nonprescription medicine to research. Analyze its use and abuse. Find out as much as you can about the medicine, including what it does, how it is taken, and what side effects it can cause. Share your information with the class, and be prepared to explain why your sources are reliable.

LESSON 2: USING MEDICINES RESPONSIBLY **239**

Lesson 2

VISUAL LEARNING

FIGURE 9.6 Guide students in reading and discussing the examples of drug misuse and drug abuse. Ask: Why is it important to read and follow directions on medicine labels? Caption answer: Help students recognize that they should consult their doctor or pharmacist if they are unsure about how to use a medicine. **INCL** *Behavior Problems, Special Learning Needs, English Language Learners*

❸ Assess

Evaluating

📁 Assign the Lesson 2 Review; then assign the Lesson 2 Quiz in the TCR.

Reteaching

📁 Assign Concept Map 39 or Reteaching Activity 34 in the TCR.

Enrichment

- 📁 Assign Enrichment Activity 33 in the TCR.
- Divide the class into small groups. Have the groups design, write, and make flyers informing other teens about the safe use of medicines.

❹ Close

Have students explain briefly the most important fact they have learned from this lesson.

Lesson 2 Review

1. Any reaction to a medicine other than the one intended.
2. Through the mucous membranes, skin, veins or muscles, lungs, or stomach and small intestine.
3. The Food and Drug Administration.
4. See Figure 9.6 above.
5. One of the people might be allergic to a particular drug or might be taking another drug that could cause a dangerous interaction.
6. It may take several years to determine whether the drug has any long-term side effects.

Lesson 3

What Are Illegal Drugs?

① Focus

Lesson Objectives

Students will be able to

- explain the dangers of illegal drugs.
- describe the main types of illegal drugs.
- identify the dangerous side effects of stimulants, depressants, narcotics, hallucinogens, inhalants, marijuana, and anabolic steroids.

Motivators

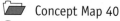

Quick Write

Allow students to list the health problems they identified under each category on the board. Correct any misconceptions.

Bellringer Activity

Ask students: What do people become addicted to? Give students several minutes to write a list of substances to which people can become addicted.

VOCABULARY

Have volunteers read aloud the vocabulary terms and find the definitions in the Glossary. Encourage students to rephrase each definition in their own words.

LESSON 3

What Are Illegal Drugs?

Quick Write

Write a list of physical, mental/emotional, and social problems that people might develop from using illegal drugs.

LEARN ABOUT...

- the dangers of illegal drugs.
- the main types of illegal drugs.

VOCABULARY

- withdrawal
- stimulant
- depressant
- narcotic
- hallucinogen
- inhalant
- marijuana
- anabolic steroids

The Dangers of Drug Abuse

Any use of illegal drugs, as well as the abuse of legal medicines, can seriously harm health and even cause death. These effects may occur the first time the drug is used. Drug abuse makes it impossible to think clearly and react quickly when driving. People who use illegal drugs may get into trouble with the law, ruining their future.

Drug abuse often leads to addiction, a psychological and physical need for a substance. Addicts who have a physical need for a particular drug have a chemical dependency. To end a chemical dependency, all traces of a drug must be removed from the user's body. This causes **withdrawal,** *a series of mental and physical symptoms that occur when a person stops using an addictive substance.* These symptoms may include vomiting, hallucinations, and severe anxiety. Withdrawal should be medically supervised. After the drug has been removed from their bodies, users must deal with their psychological dependency by learning to control their cravings.

Teens who value their health avoid tobacco, alcohol, and other drugs. *What are some healthful activities you and your friends enjoy?*

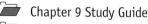

Lesson 3 Resources

Teacher Classroom Resources

📁 Concept Map 40

📁 Cross-Curriculum Activity 18

📁 Enrichment Activity 34

📁 Lesson Plan 3

📁 Lesson 3 Quiz

📁 Reading Tutor Activity 34

📁 Reteaching Activity 35

🖨 Transparency 39

Student Activities Workbook

📁 Chapter 9 Study Guide

📁 Applying Health Skills 34

Stimulants

Stimulants (STIM·yuh·luhnts) are *drugs that speed up the body's functions.* They cause blood pressure to rise, the heart to beat faster, breathing rate to increase, and the pupils of the eyes to dilate. Stimulants may be swallowed, smoked, inhaled, or injected. Amphetamines (am·FE·tuh·meenz) and cocaine (koh·KAYN) are two types of stimulants. Both are highly addictive and very dangerous.

Amphetamines

Amphetamines are sometimes called *uppers* or *speed.* Doctors may prescribe them to treat obesity, sleep disorders, or attention disorders in children. All other uses are illegal.

Any use of amphetamines can have dangerous side effects. These include

- headaches.
- restlessness.
- blurred vision.
- anxiety.
- dizziness.

At high doses, the drugs can cause more severe side effects such as

- loss of coordination.
- physical collapse.
- irregular or rapid heartbeat.
- heart failure.

Long-term use of amphetamines can lead to severe mental problems. Injecting or inhaling amphetamines can cause blood pressure to rise quickly, leading to seizure and death.

Responsible teens know that using illegal drugs is not a solution to the stress of everyday life. *How are these teens managing stress in a healthy way?*

Developing Good Character

Caring

If you suspect that a friend is using illegal drugs, you can help. Try talking to a trusted adult such as a parent or a school counselor. If no one is available, try gathering information about the harmful effects of drugs. Then share the information with your friend. You may be saving a life.

Lesson 3

② Teach

Developing Good Character

Caring

As a class, discuss why it's important to seek help from a trusted adult when you know that someone is using illegal drugs. Be a caring friend. With a partner, make a list of ways you might approach a trusted adult, and practice role-playing with each other.

Comprehending

Discuss the differences between using drugs and abusing drugs:

- Is taking an illegal drug drug use or drug abuse?
- When does taking legal drugs (or medicines) constitute drug use? When does it constitute abuse? L1

Recalling

Guide students in recalling and describing the physical and psychological aspects of chemical dependency and addiction to drugs, tobacco, and alcohol. You may want to refer them to Chapter 8, Lesson 1. L1

Discussing

Help students discuss how the use of illegal drugs or the abuse of prescription medications can affect mental/emotional and social health. Ask: How might using illegal drugs affect a teen's feelings about himself or herself? Why? L1

INCLUSION STRATEGIES

Behavior Problems, Special Learning Needs, English Language Learners It is especially important that all students understand the information about drugs in this lesson (and in all the lessons of Chapters 8 and 9). If some students have difficulty reading these chapters, you may want to provide special help by assigning reading partners. Match each student with a student who reads easily with good comprehension; have the partners read the chapter together, discussing any concepts, words, or expressions that need clarification.

Researching

Have volunteers use online sources or library sources to learn about the differences between cocaine and crack. Ask these volunteers to prepare a bulletin board display explaining the differences. **L3**

Cocaine is derived from the coca plant. Processing involves the use of dangerous solvents including kerosene, benzene, and gasoline. Traces of these solvents often remain in cocaine sold to users.

Current Events

Have students find and bring to class copies of recent news articles about incidents (including crimes and accidents) related to the use of cocaine or about the arrest or trial of individuals accused of buying or selling cocaine. **L2**

Discussing

Point out that depressants are prescribed to reduce stress or anxiety. Ask students to recall activities (e.g., physical exercise and relaxation practices) that can reduce stress. Help students discuss the responsibilities of health care professionals for urging patients to use these kinds of approaches before prescribing medicines to reduce stress. **L1**

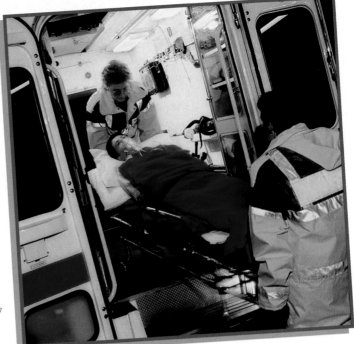

Cocaine and crack are very dangerous drugs. *Why is it risky to try these illegal drugs even once?*

Cocaine and Crack

Cocaine is an illegal stimulant drug that is highly addictive. Its effects are unpredictable and very dangerous. Even the first use of the drug can cause the user's blood pressure and heart rate to soar to levels that result in a fatal seizure or heart attack. Other dangers of cocaine use include

- sleeplessness, loss of appetite, nervousness, and suspiciousness.
- infection with HIV or hepatitis B if cocaine is injected.
- serious or fatal burns from preparing crack or freebase, a form of cocaine that is smoked.

Depressants

Depressants are *drugs that slow down the body's functions and reactions.* They cause heart rate and blood pressure to drop. Breathing and brain activity also slow down. Alcohol is an example of a depressant. The two other main types of depressants are barbiturates and tranquilizers. A doctor may prescribe them to reduce anxiety and help people sleep. However, they are highly addictive. The dangers of depressant use include lack of coordination, slurred speech, drowsiness, poor judgment, confusion, and addiction. When combined with alcohol or other drugs, they can be deadly.

242 CHAPTER 9: ALCOHOL AND OTHER DRUGS

PROMOTING COORDINATED SCHOOL HEALTH

Drug Resistance What role does the school play in helping students resist drug abuse? In recovering from addiction and other drug-related problems? In dealing with drug-related problems at home? What role can the school play in supporting teachers and other school staff deal with drug problems among students? Is there an appropriate role for the school health system in educating and helping other members of the community? These are questions to be considered and resolved in the development of a coordinated school health program. For more information about developing such a program, consult *Planning a Coordinated School Health Program* in the TCR.

Narcotics

Narcotics (nar·KAH·tics) are *certain drugs that relieve pain.* They include morphine, codeine, and heroin. Doctors may prescribe morphine to reduce severe pain. For example, it may be used after surgery or serious injury. Some prescription cough syrups and painkillers contain codeine. Legal narcotics are strongly addictive and must be used very carefully.

Heroin is very dangerous and has no legal uses. Heroin users risk unconsciousness and death. People who inject heroin also risk HIV infection from shared needles.

Hallucinogens

Hallucinogens (huh·LOO·suhn·uh·jenz) are *illegal drugs that cause the user's brain to distort images and to see and hear things that aren't real.* In other words, these drugs cause hallucinations. Users often behave strangely or violently. PCP (angel dust) and LSD (acid) are two very dangerous hallucinogens.

People who use PCP or LSD often think they have super strength. They may try dangerous acts that can lead to death. People who use these drugs sometimes have delayed effects, called flashbacks, long after they stop using the drugs. The person has no control over when a flashback could occur.

Another hallucinogen, called MDMA or Ecstasy, is also a stimulant. Users may experience confusion, depression, and nausea. Continued use can result in permanent brain damage.

This antidrug ad appeared on the back of a garbage truck.
Do you think the ad is effective?

Lesson 3

Critical Thinking

Help students discuss the medicinal uses of morphine and codeine. Have students use encyclopedias in class to determine how and why each is used. Ask:

• Do you believe their legal use and availability may lead teens to drug misuse and drug abuse? Why or why not?

• Why should these drugs be taken only under supervision by a doctor? **L2**

Examining the Issues

Teens in recovery from heroin addiction have explained that adult community members seem unaware of the availability of heroin and the problems it creates. Ask students what they think parents and other adults should know about heroin and other illegal drugs. Who should be responsible for helping parents learn about dangerous drugs? **L1**

Describing

Ask students to describe the short-term and long-term effects of chemical dependency and addiction to drugs and other substances. **L1**

✔ Reading Check

Cause-and-Effect Relationships Identifying cause-and-effect relationships will reinforce students' comprehension of the negative effects of drugs. Have students first brainstorm key words that signify a cause-and-effect relationship, such as *result in, cause, lead to,* and others. Have students work with a partner to make their lists into flow charts.
INCL *Behavior Problems, Special Learning Needs, English Language Learners*

Applying Knowledge

Help students recognize that, unlike most other illegal drugs, many inhalants are common household substances. Why does that fact make them especially dangerous for teens? What role might these substances play in unsafe situations such as being under the influence and driving, and HIV and STD transmission? **L1**

"SAY NO TO DRUGS" SKIT

Time: 2 hours (may be spread out over several class meetings)

TEACHING THE ACTIVITY

• Read the activity title and the listed directions with students.
• Have students select partners and work together to plan and practice their skits.
• Have each pair of students present their skit to the rest of the class. Encourage audience members to offer constructive criticism and to ask thoughtful questions. If the "no" was not convincing, offer encouragement to try it again.

ASSESSMENT

In a brief class discussion, have students share what they learned from this activity.

Inhalants

Inhalants (in·HAY·luhnts) are *substances whose fumes are inhaled to produce hallucinations.* Most inhalants are common household products not meant to be taken into the body. If ingested, these would commonly cause death. When inhaled, they can fill the lungs and suffocate the user. They also kill brain cells, causing permanent brain damage or coma. This can happen the *first* time inhalants are used. Using substances such as inhalants can result in psychological addiction and chemical dependency.

Marijuana

Marijuana (mar·uh·WAHN·uh) is *an illegal drug that comes from the hemp plant.* Marijuana is also known as pot or weed. It increases heart rate and may cause panic attacks. It also interferes with concentration and memory. People who use marijuana may lack energy. They often lose interest in activities they once enjoyed. Users lack coordination, injure themselves more often, and are unable to react well in emergencies. Long-term use may cause lasting damage to the brain. People who use marijuana may be more likely to try other dangerous drugs.

Hands-On Health

"SAY NO TO DRUGS" SKIT

In this activity, you and your classmates will identify and describe strategies for avoiding drugs.

WHAT YOU WILL NEED
• pencil and paper

WHAT YOU WILL DO
1. With a partner, list ways someone might try to persuade you to use a drug.
2. On a second sheet of paper, list ways to use your refusal skills in the situations you listed.
3. Review your lists. Select the three most persuasive reasons that you might encounter and your three best refusals.

4. Use these statements to create a skit to perform for your classmates. Ask them to evaluate your presentation.

IN CONCLUSION
1. Did your classmates find your refusal statements convincing?
2. If not, how could they be strengthened?

MORE ABOUT...

Huffing Dangers Huffing is another term for inhalant abuse. The inhaled fumes act like anesthesia, replacing oxygen in the blood. Users may become dizzy, vomit, hallucinate, or lose consciousness. Death can result from suffocation, dangerous behavior, aspiration (removal of liquids or gases), and sudden sniffing death syndrome. Suffocation occurs when users lose consciousness inhaling from a plastic bag that blocks the nose and mouth. Aspiration deaths occur when users choke on their vomit. Sudden sniffing death from cardiac arrest can occur with the first use or after months of abuse.

Anabolic Steroids

Anabolic steroids (a·nuh·BAH·lik STIR·oydz) are *synthetic drugs based on a male hormone.* Doctors sometimes prescribe steroids to treat certain medical conditions. Some athletes use steroids illegally to increase their body weight and strength. Steroids should never be used for this purpose. Users may become violent, aggressive, and deeply depressed. Steroids also cause severe acne, sexual underdevelopment in both males and females, liver and brain cancer, and heart attacks.

Smart teens avoid steroids and strengthen their muscles safely with strength-building exercises such as push-ups.

CONNECT TO
Social Studies

TESTING ATHLETES WORLDWIDE

To stop drug use among athletes, several countries have established independent agencies to manage the testing of athletes. The United States Anti-Doping Agency (USADA) and the Australian Sports Drug Agency (ASDA) are two such organizations. The World Anti-Doping Agency (WADA) coordinates antidrug programs on the international level. WADA's motto is "Think positive, test negative."

Lesson 3 Review

Using complete sentences, answer the following questions on a sheet of paper.

Reviewing Terms and Facts

1. **Explain** How are the terms *dependency* and *withdrawal* related?
2. **Recall** Which of the following drugs is not a stimulant: amphetamines, crack, or barbiturates?
3. **List** How can the use of inhalants cause injury or death?
4. **Explain** Analyze how prescription medications such as anabolic steroids are used and abused.

Thinking Critically

5. **Apply** How would you reply if someone told you that using cocaine only once is harmless? Explain your answer.
6. **Predict** What do you think could happen to the schoolwork of someone who uses marijuana? Give reasons for your answer.

Applying Health Skills

7. **Advocacy** Create a TV commercial that persuades teens to avoid illegal drugs. In your commercial, briefly examine the social influences on drug-taking behaviors.

LESSON 3: WHAT ARE ILLEGAL DRUGS? **245**

Lesson 3

Critical Thinking

Briefly discuss with students the varying rates at which teens grow and mature. Then ask why teens may be especially likely to be tempted to use steroids. What are the most compelling reasons to avoid steroid use? **L1**

3 Assess

Evaluating

📁 Assign the Lesson 3 Review; then assign the Lesson 3 Quiz in the TCR.

Reteaching

• 📁 Assign Concept Map 40 or Reteaching Activity 35 in the TCR.
• Have students work in groups to create charts summarizing the information about illegal drugs presented in this lesson. Be sure students include a section describing chemical dependency and addiction to drugs and other substances.

Enrichment

• 📁 Assign Enrichment Activity 34 in the TCR.
• Have students discuss the role they think drugs and other substances play in unsafe situations such as being under the influence and driving, and HIV and STD transmission.

4 Close

Have each student complete the following sentence: Even though all illegal drugs pose risks to my health, I consider _____ the most dangerous illegal drug because...

Lesson 3 Review

1. People who develop a dependency on a drug need the drug to feel good and to function. If they ever stop using the drug, they go through withdrawal, a series of mental and physical symptoms.
2. Barbiturates are not stimulants.
3. Inhalants cause death when the fumes fill the lungs and suffocate the user or when the fumes kill the user's brain cells, causing permanent brain damage or coma.
4. Responses will vary, but should include the concept that anabolic steroids are used to treat certain medical conditions, but may be abused to increase muscle mass.
5. Even one use of cocaine could result in death from heart attack or seizure.
6. Accept all reasonable responses.

Staying Drug Free

Lesson Objectives

Students will be able to

- identify why they should avoid using alcohol, drugs, and other substances.
- discuss the laws that regulate substance use.
- identify ways to stay substance free.
- explain how families of substance abusers can find help.

Health Skills
- Refusal Skills, p. 248

Motivators

Quick Write

Compile the responses by having volunteers key them into a word processing program. Print copies to be shared among the class.

Bellringer Activity

Have students discuss what they think it means to stay "substance free, healthy, and ready for life." How are the three interrelated?

VOCABULARY

Help students recognize the relationship between *alternative* and *alternate*. Then have pairs of students compose sentences using *alternative*, demonstrating that they understand its meaning.

LESSON

4

Staying Drug Free

Quick Write

What are the activities that you enjoy most? Write a paragraph explaining how the use of alcohol and other drugs could interfere with your favorite activities.

LEARN ABOUT...

- ways to avoid using alcohol and drugs.
- the laws about substance abuse.
- how families of substance abusers can find help.

VOCABULARY

- substance abuse
- alternative

Why You Should Avoid Alcohol, Drugs, and Other Substances

Staying healthy means saying no to **substance abuse**—*use of illegal or harmful drugs, including any use of alcohol while under the legal drinking age.* Being substance free shows self-control and helps keep you healthy and ready for life. **Figure 9.7** lists many reasons to avoid alcohol, drugs, and other substances.

FIGURE 9.7

REFUSAL MADE EASY

There are many good reasons to avoid alcohol and other drugs.

Reasons to Avoid Alcohol

- Any alcohol use is against the law for teens.
- Alcohol can be addictive.
- People who drink may have trouble controlling their bodies and emotions. They become clumsy and often do or say things they regret later.
- Drinking can make people feel sick to their stomachs.
- Drinking can lead to lack of judgment and loss of control, often ending in violence.
- People who drink may engage in sexual activity that they would otherwise avoid. This may lead to becoming infected with an STD such as HIV.
- Responsible adults do not want teens to use alcohol.
- Alcohol ruins your ability to think clearly and react quickly when driving.
- You can have fun without consuming alcohol.

Reasons to Avoid Drugs and Other Substances

- There are severe legal penalties for using drugs and inhalants.
- Many drugs are addictive.
- Drugs and inhalants can permanently damage health. Many can be fatal even the first time they are used.
- Drugs and inhalants can impair judgment while driving—the results could be fatal.
- Because substance use affects judgment, people who use drugs or inhalants may be more likely to engage in sexual activity. This can result in becoming infected with an STD such as HIV.
- Many illegal drugs are produced by untrained people. Harmful and untested chemicals, including rat poison, may be added to these drugs, making their effects completely unpredictable.

246 CHAPTER 9: ALCOHOL AND OTHER DRUGS

Lesson 4 Resources

Teacher Classroom Resources

 Concept Map 41

Decision-Making Activity 18

Enrichment Activity 35

Lesson Plan 4

Lesson 4 Quiz

Reading Tutor Activity 35

 Reteaching Activity 36

 Transparency 40

Student Activities Workbook

 Chapter 9 Study Guide

Applying Health Skills 35

Health Inventory 9

The Law Is on Your Side

In all states, a person must be 21 years old to legally possess or purchase alcohol. Some drugs, such as codeine, are illegal except for certain medical uses. Drugs such as heroin and crack are always illegal. Selling any of these drugs on the street or near schools is a crime with serious penalties.

Like other dangerous drugs, marijuana is illegal. The penalties for use and possession vary from state to state. Depending on where a person is caught and how much marijuana he or she has, a person can pay a large fine and serve lengthy jail time.

Ways to Stay Substance Free

Pressure to use alcohol and drugs may come from many sources. Ads and peers may try to convince you that drinking is cool. You may see drug use in movies. Pressure can also come from within. Some young people might think that they will fit in better if they drink or use drugs. Others might try alcohol or drugs to prove they are not afraid to do it.

The best way to refuse these harmful—and illegal—substances is to state your decision assertively. You can also choose friends who are substance free. If someone persists in trying to persuade you to have a drink or use a drug or other substance, use one of the strategies in **Figure 9.8**. If the pressure continues, seek help from a parent or other trusted adult.

FIGURE 9.8

Ways to Say NO TO ALCOHOL AND DRUGS

If someone offers you alcohol, drugs, or other dangerous substances, you can use one of these responses. *Describe additional strategies for saying no to unsafe behaviors.*

"Get that stuff away from me! You can be arrested just for having it."

"No way! I'd be thrown off the team."

"I'm having a better time without drinking."

"No, thanks, I like having all my brain cells working."

"Are you kidding? My parents would ground me forever."

LESSON 4: STAYING DRUG FREE **247**

CONNECT TO

Social Studies

WHAT'S YOUR ANTI-DRUG? In 2000, the National Youth Anti-Drug Media Campaign asked young people between the ages of 10 and 17 to tell what stood between them and drugs. Thousands responded with essays, poems, videos, paintings, music, and even single-word answers. From friends and family to singing and sports, these kids showed that most young people don't use drugs. *How would you respond?*

Lesson 4

② Teach

VISUAL LEARNING

FIGURE 9.7 After students have read and discussed the listed reasons to avoid alcohol, drugs, and other substances, have them suggest other reasons for living substance free. **INCL** *Behavior Problems, Special Learning Needs, English Language Learners*

Guest Speaker

Find out how drug laws are enforced in your community or at your school. Invite a local law enforcement officer or school official to speak to the class about arrests and sentences for the possession and sale of illegal drugs. Ask the speaker what social factors might influence a person to take drugs. Ask students to suggest other social influences. **L1**

Discussing

Ask: Is a person who urges you to use drugs or alcohol really a friend? **L1**

VISUAL LEARNING

FIGURE 9.8 Ask volunteers to take turns reading the different responses aloud. Encourage them to use body language and expressive voices to make their messages clear. Then have students identify ways to prevent the use of tobacco, alcohol, and other drugs and substances, including alternative activities.

Beyond the Classroom

Community As students discuss activities that they consider attractive alternatives to drug and alcohol use, encourage them to explore local centers and organizations where those activities might be available. For example, they might investigate a basketball league at the local recreation center, afternoon classes at a nearby youth organization or community college, or volunteer opportunities at a neighborhood hospital. Encourage them to find as many community resources as possible. Also, if they have an interest that is not met by community groups, they might consider starting an after-school club for that activity.

Lesson 4

Demonstrating

Teens often feel awkward trying to find out whether drugs or alcohol will be available at a get-together. Assure students that it's easier to find out in advance than to deal with the pressure at the event. Ask several volunteers to demonstrate how they might ask questions about what will be happening in a given situation. **L1**

Applying Knowledge

Guide students in discussing the choice to stay substance free. Ask:

- Do you think you have a responsibility to help keep other teens from using drugs or alcohol?

- What do you think are the most effective approaches to encouraging other teens to stay substance free? **L1**

HEALTH SKILLS ACTIVITY

REFUSAL SKILLS

Direct students to meet in groups to read about Tammy's situation and to discuss how she can use refusal skills. Have volunteers in each group role-play a dialogue before students write their own versions.

Note: This skill is introduced in Chapter 3 on page 64.

Reading Check

Explore memory aids. How does S.T.O.P. help you remember the steps to the refusal process?

Alternatives to Drug and Alcohol Use

When you refuse drugs or alcohol, you may want to suggest a positive alternative. An **alternative** (ahl·TER·nuh·tihv) is *another way of thinking or acting.* If the person you are with wants to sneak a beer, you might suggest playing video games instead. Other healthy alternatives include the following:

- **Have fun at drug-free and alcohol-free events.** Avoid environments where alcohol or other drugs are present. Use positive peer pressure to help others avoid these environments.
- **Improve your talents.** Choose an activity you like and practice it until you become an expert. Become a great skateboarder, a computer whiz, or the best artist at school.
- **Be part of a group.** Join a sports team, a club, or a community group. A network of substance-free friends with a common interest will help you feel confident and supported.
- **Start your own business.** Let friends and neighbors know that you are available for babysitting, yard work, or other odd jobs. Post a sign advertising your business at the local supermarket or community center.

HEALTH SKILLS ACTIVITY

REFUSAL SKILLS

Say No and Mean It

Tammy loves soccer. She is thrilled to be a member of the school team this year. In her first game, she is too excited to concentrate. She loses control of the ball, and the other team scores, winning the game in the last seconds of play. Tammy feels miserable and tries to hide in the locker room. Her teammate Sara sits down next to her and says, "Don't worry about it. Why don't you come over to my house tonight? We'll have something there that's guaranteed to make you feel better."

Tammy is relieved that her teammates are not angry—until she arrives at Sara's house. Sara offers her a pill, saying, "Try it—you'll feel great." Tammy wants to be part of the team, but she doesn't want to use drugs.

What Would You Do?

Apply refusal skills to Tammy's situation. Write a dialogue between Tammy and Sara in which Tammy uses refusal skills to avoid drugs.

SAY NO IN A FIRM VOICE.
TELL WHY NOT.
OFFER OTHER IDEAS.
PROMPTLY LEAVE.

248 CHAPTER 9: ALCOHOL AND OTHER DRUGS

Reading Check

Study Skills Using a mnemonic, or memory device, can aid students in both learning and remembering the topic. Refer students to the Health Skills Activity on this page. Tell students that S.T.O.P. is an acronym, a word formed from the initial letters of other words and pronounceable. Challenge students to find other examples of acronyms. Have students practice S.T.O.P. by saying to a partner what each letter represents. Encourage students to devise their own acronyms for other facts to be memorized.

Help for Families of Substance Abusers

Drug and alcohol abuse doesn't just harm users. It also affects their friends and family. Several organizations provide help and support for people whose lives are affected by a loved one's addiction to alcohol or drugs. Local phone books can help people find these organizations. They include hospitals, substance abuse treatment centers, and special groups.

- Alateen helps children of alcoholic parents learn how to cope with problems at home.
- Al-Anon helps adult family members and friends of alcoholics learn more about the disease. They also discuss how to meet their own needs.
- Nar-Anon, similar to Al-Anon, holds meetings for families of drug addicts.

Many organizations can help families and friends of substance abusers. *Identify strategies for coping with unhealthy behaviors in the family, such as alcoholism.*

Using complete sentences, answer the following questions on a sheet of paper.

Reviewing Terms and Facts

1. **Vocabulary** Define the term *substance abuse*. Use it in an original sentence.
2. **List** Name five reasons to avoid drug and alcohol use.
3. **Identify** Describe two ways to prevent the use of alcohol, drugs, and other substances such as inhalants.
4. **Give examples** Identify two organizations that help the families and friends of alcoholics and drug addicts.

Thinking Critically

5. **Apply** Why do teens who are substance free have more fun than those who use alcohol and drugs?

6. **Analyze** Explain the relationship between tobacco, alcohol, drugs, and other dangerous substances.

Applying Health Skills

7. **Stress Management** Imagine that a peer lives in an environment where alcohol, tobacco, or drug abuse exists. How can he or she overcome the negative effects of this environment? Describe your ideas in a brief paragraph.

LESSON 4: STAYING DRUG FREE **249**

Lesson 4

③ Assess

Evaluating

📁 Assign the Lesson 4 Review; then assign the Lesson 4 Quiz in the TCR.

Reteaching

- 📁 Assign Concept Map 41 or Reteaching Activity 36 in the TCR.
- Work with small groups of students to review reasons not to use alcohol or drugs and to explain the relationship between tobacco, alcohol, drugs, and other substances.

Enrichment

- 📁 Assign Enrichment Activity 35 in the TCR.
- Have students brainstorm and develop ideas for an activity group that provides a healthy alternative to using drugs or alcohol. Support student efforts to put their plans into action.

④ Close

Have each student respond to this question: What is the most important reason for you to stay substance free?

Lesson 4 Review

1. Use of illegal or harmful drugs, including any use of alcohol while under the legal drinking age. Sentences should apply the term accurately.
2. See Figure 9.7 on page 246 for possible responses.
3. Possible responses: Attend drug- and alcohol-free events, improve your talents, be part of a group, start your own business.
4. Any two: Alateen, Al-Anon, Nar-Anon.
5. Possible answer: They are able to focus on productive activities, such as schoolwork, sports, clubs, hobbies, and other activities that keep them healthy and active.
6. Responses should indicate an understanding that all these substances are dangerous, and may include that using one type increases the chances that another type will also be used.

Steroids and Sports Don't Mix

① Focus

Objectives

Students will be able to

- list the dangerous side effects of anabolic steroid use.
- demonstrate communication and refusal skills for avoiding steroid use.
- create an ad campaign advocating against steroid use.

Motivator

Bellringer

Tell students, "Imagine that you are an athlete and must compete against an opponent who is physically stronger and bigger than you are. How would that make you feel? What is the likely outcome of such a competition?" Give students several minutes to discuss these questions. Then, explain that this situation occurs every time an athlete competes against an opponent who is using steroids. Ask, "Is this fair? Who has the competitive edge?"

② Teach

Role-Plays

Divide the class into small groups. Assign each group one of the following situations involving steroids. Ask each group to prepare a scene and role-play it for the class, utilizing the information on this spread, as well as effective communication and refusal skills.

1. You find out that your best friend, a varsity athlete, is using steroids to add muscle mass.

2. You are pressured by a teammate to use steroids prior to a big competition.

3. You are devastated when a professional athlete you admire is caught using steroids.

Steroids and Sports Don't Mix

Steroid use may explain why some athletes end up on the disabled list.

250 CHAPTER 9: ALCOHOL AND OTHER DRUGS

WHAT TEENS WANT TO KNOW

What happens if an athlete is caught using steroids? Sadly, the use of performance-enhancing drugs has become so prevalent that mandatory drug testing has become common in professional sports. As a result, a number of professional athletes have tested positive for such drugs. Athletes have been banned from their sport or denied membership in organizations such as the Baseball Hall of Fame. Fines and other financial penalties have also been assessed.

Policies for school-aged athletes vary, but tend to focus on education and rehabilitation. Talk to coaches at your school to learn more about how steroid use is handled.

As more athletes build over-muscled bodies by using anabolic steroids and other drugs, they are suffering severe injuries in ever-greater numbers. "We're seeing more and more injuries you used to associate with a contact sport like football," says Lou Piniella, manager of the Tampa Bay Devil Rays. He's talking about tears of muscles, ligaments, and tendons.

James Andrews, a sports doctor from Birmingham, Alabama, says he rarely used to see these muscle-tendon injuries in baseball. "It was always the sport for the athlete with the small frame," he says. "Over the last 10 years, that's changed." Andrews says steroids and supplements are to blame for the extra bulk and the increased injuries.

Anabolic steroids are dangerous— and illegal.

Costly Injuries

According to figures from Major League Baseball, big-league players made 467 trips to the disabled list (DL) during just one season. That's about 18 trips to the DL per week. Those players stayed on the DL for an average of 59 days, 10 days longer than the average stay in 1997—an increase of 20 percent.

In one year, major league teams paid $317 million to players who couldn't play because of injuries. That cost was a 130 percent increase from only four years earlier.

"I see so many body changes. One season they're average, the next season they're massive. [Steroid use] is obvious," Andrews says. He adds that more athletes are carrying more muscle than their frames can support, and so the amount of injury is greater. Not only do overly developed muscles tear more easily, they can also cause ligaments and tendons to rupture. There's just too much mass for the body to handle, and more and more of these injuries are career-threatening.

"I'm seeing four to five times as many of these injuries as I did just 10 years ago, Andrews

continues, "and I'm seeing them in younger and younger athletes. If the pros are doing it, the college kids aren't far behind, and the high schools and junior highs are right behind them. I try to counsel some of them, but it is a secret box that they find themselves in, and they don't want to talk to me about it."

The Dark Side of Steroids

Kevin Towers, general manger of the San Diego Padres, says suspected steroid use and the cost of injuries from steroid use have become important factors in how general managers think about players. "It matters when you're doing contracts or when you're looking to acquire a player from another team," Towers says.

Given by doctors for specific problems, anabolic steroids can be helpful. However, using them to increase performance can be harmful—even deadly. Side effects of steroid use include acne, weight gain, elevated cholesterol levels, weakened tendons, liver damage, heart attacks, strokes, and death. Steroids also affect a person's behavior, causing a user's mood to swing wildly between sadness and rage. Finally, people who inject steroids increase their risk of exposure to HIV, hepatitis, and other disease-causing agents if needles are shared or contaminated.

About the Dangers of Steroid Use
Using steroids to increase muscle mass or enhance athletic performance is harmful to health. Create an ad campaign warning athletes of the dangers of steroid use. Present your campaign to the rest of the class.

❸ Apply

Time to Think

Review with students the medical dangers of steroid use highlighted in this spread (acne, weight gain, liver damage, heart attack, and so on). Then ask, "What about the mental and emotional toll of steroid use? What about the toll it takes on other competitors, sports fans, and the reputation of the sport?" Encourage students to include these ideas in their ad campaigns.

VISUAL LEARNING

Ask students to compare and contrast the two images on this spread: one of the baseball players competing, the other of dangerous anabolic steroids. Why are these two images so jarring side-by-side? How might the use of steroids among professional baseball players taint the image of "America's favorite pastime"?

Health Literacy

Females and Steroid Use According to the National Institute on Drug Abuse (NIDA), "National surveys indicate that girls account for about one-third of all high-school students who abuse steroids." According to their research, the primary reason these girls use steroids is to lose fat and gain lean muscle. Along with the many harmful side effects mentioned on these pages, steroid use in woman also promotes excess facial hair, changes in menstruation, voice deepening, and breast reduction.

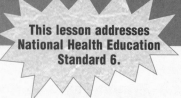
DECISION MAKING

Objective

After completing the lesson, students will be able to apply the decision-making process to a situation involving the use of alcohol.

Time: 45 minutes

Materials: pen or pencil, notebook paper

Teacher Classroom Resources

📁 Building Health Skills Activities

• Transparency Master 8, "Decision Making"

• Reproducible Master 9, "How to Avoid Alcohol"

---

1. Model

• Display Transparency Master 8, and review the six steps of the decision-making process.

• Have students read the scenario about Debra and Lisa. As a class, review and discuss each step of the girls' decision. (*Their decision was to walk down the beach to find something else to drink.*)

BUILDING HEALTH SKILLS **DECISION MAKING**

HOW TO AVOID ALCOHOL

Model

Knowing about alcohol's negative effects on physical and mental health can help you decide to say no to alcohol. Read about a teen named Debra and her cousin Lisa.

Lisa's older sister, Tanya, and Tanya's boyfriend have taken the two girls to the beach. When lunchtime comes, Tanya and her boyfriend open up the picnic basket. It contains a six-pack of beer but nothing else to drink. Debra is concerned and looks at Lisa, who also appears troubled.

1. STATE THE SITUATION. "There's nothing here to drink but beer."

2. LIST THE OPTIONS. "We could drink the beer, we could drink nothing until we get home, or we could walk down the beach and find a water fountain or a snack stand."

3. WEIGH THE POSSIBLE OUTCOMES. "I don't like the smell of beer, and it could make me sick. If we walk down the beach, we will get tired and hot, and we still might not find anything else to drink. If we don't drink anything, we will get very thirsty and maybe get sick."

4. CONSIDER VALUES. "It's not right for us to drink beer. It's against the law."

5. MAKE A DECISION AND ACT. "Let's walk down the beach."

252 CHAPTER 9: ALCOHOL AND OTHER DRUGS

📎 Teaching Tips

Practicing Health Skills Help students understand that health skills, such as decision making, are applicable to their daily lives. Encourage them to write down situations they encounter within the next two or three days that require them to put their decision-making skills to use. Emphasize that responsible decision making promotes their health and the health of others.

Brainstorming Allot a brief period of time (e.g., 2 minutes) for brainstorming. Record the decisions without discussion or criticism. When time is up, invite comments about the recorded decisions.

Practice

Read the following paragraph. What would you do in John's situation? Use your own paper to write the steps John could take to make a decision.

Nick used to be the star of the football team. This season, however, he is struggling—both on the football field and in the classroom. Last week, his friend John overheard some classmates saying that Nick had been drinking with some of the older kids in the neighborhood. When John asked Nick whether that was true, Nick became angry and said he could handle his drinking.

Apply/Assess

As a class, brainstorm a list of ways a teen might be affected by someone else's use of alcohol. With a small group, choose one of these ideas, and write a scenario about a teen who is in that situation. Explain the impact of peer pressure on decision making. In the scenario, show how the teen uses the steps of the decision-making process to handle the situation.

Decision Making

1. State the situation.
2. List the options.
3. Weigh the possible outcomes.
4. Consider values.
5. Make a decision and act.
6. Evaluate the decision.

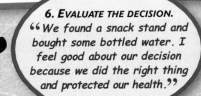

6. EVALUATE THE DECISION. "We found a snack stand and bought some bottled water. I feel good about our decision because we did the right thing and protected our health."

Self-Check

- Did we state the situation clearly?
- Did the teen in our story use the steps for decision making?

2. Practice

- Direct students to read about John and his friend Nick. Lead a class discussion about John's situation and his concerns about Nick's health and safety.
- Ask students to use the six steps of the decision-making process to demonstrate what they would do in John's situation.
- Have volunteers share their decisions with the rest of the class.

3. Apply/Assess

- You may wish to distribute Building Health Skills Reproducible Master 9 in the TCR to guide students in completing this activity.
- Ask the class to come up with a list of ways that a teen might be affected by someone else's use of alcohol. Write these on the board.
- Divide the class into groups of three or four students. Have each group choose one of the ideas from the list and write a scenario about a teen in that particular situation. Each story should show how a teen uses the first five steps of the decision-making process to make a healthful decision in this situation.
- Ask one member of each group to read the decision-making steps in their story aloud. Discuss the various decisions as a class. Have students explain the impact of peer pressure on decision making.
- Remind students to refer to the Self-Check before and after they write their scenarios.

Assessment Scoring

Using a rubric, student work should provide evidence of all criteria to achieve the highest score.

Skills

Student work demonstrates

- a clear statement of the situation.
- consideration of options.
- consideration of values.
- a clear decision.
- reflection on the decision.
- identification of an action to be taken or decision to be made.

Concept

Student work provides an understanding of the negative consequences of using alcohol.

Checking Comprehension

Use the Chapter 9 Assessment to examine the most important ideas presented in the chapter.

Answers to Reviewing Vocabulary and Concepts

Lesson 1
1. drug
2. cirrhosis
3. alcoholism
4. fetal alcohol syndrome (FAS)

Lesson 2
5. prescription
6. over-the-counter
7. antibiotics
8. tolerance

Lesson 3
9. true
10. false; stimulant
11. false; depressants
12. false; narcotics
13. true

Lesson 4
14. d
15. c
16. a

Thinking Critically

17. Responses should identify that there are no risks and many benefits of not using alcohol and other drugs.
18. Responses should focus on the concept that substance use impairs judgment, coordination, and reaction time, potentially leading to car crashes and/or HIV/STD infection.

After You Read

Use your completed Foldable to review the information on alcohol's harmful effects.

 FOLDABLES Study Organizer

Reviewing Vocabulary and Concepts

On a sheet of paper, write the numbers 1–8. After each number, write the term from the list that best completes each sentence.

- alcoholism
- antibiotics
- cirrhosis
- drug
- fetal alcohol syndrome (FAS)
- nonprescription
- prescription
- tolerance

Lesson 1

1. Alcohol is a(n) _____ that slows down the body's functions and reactions.
2. Heavy drinking can cause _____, or destruction and scarring of liver tissue.
3. _____ is a disease in which a person develops a physical and mental need for alcohol.
4. Drinking alcohol during pregnancy may cause a baby to be born with _____.

Lesson 2

5. A(n) _____ medicine can only be used with written permission from a doctor.
6. _____ medicines can be purchased without a written order from a doctor.
7. Doctors often prescribe _____ for illnesses that are caused by bacteria.
8. A person develops a(n) _____ when his or her body becomes used to the effects of a medicine.

Lesson 3

On a sheet of paper, write the numbers 9–13. Write *True* or *False* for each statement. If the statement is false, change the underlined word or phrase to make it true.

9. The sickness that occurs when a person stops using an addictive substance is called <u>withdrawal</u>.
10. Amphetamines are a type of <u>hallucinogen</u>.
11. Drugs that slow down the body's functions and reactions are called <u>stimulants</u>.
12. <u>Anabolic steroids</u> are a group of drugs that relieve pain.
13. Many <u>inhalants</u> are household products.

Lesson 4

On a sheet of paper, write the numbers 14–16. After each number, write the letter of the answer that best completes each statement.

14. An example of substance abuse would be
   a. using illegal drugs.
   b. using any drugs that are not medically necessary.
   c. using alcohol if you are under the legal drinking age.
   d. any of the above.
15. Joining a club is an example of
   a. substance abuse.
   b. addiction.
   c. an alternative to drug use.
   d. refusal skills.
16. The group that offers help to teens with alcoholic parents is called
   a. Alateen.
   b. Al-Anon.
   c. Nar-Anon.
   d. a hospital.

Thinking Critically

Using complete sentences, answer the following questions on a sheet of paper.

17. **Analyze** Compare the risks and benefits of not using alcohol and illegal drugs.

INCLUSION STRATEGIES

Special Learning Needs, Behavior Problems, English Language Learners The following suggestions are helpful for students with special learning needs, students with behavior problems, and ELL students:

- Pair these students with more proficient learners who can help summarize the main concepts of the chapter.

- Direct these students to listen to the Teen Health Audio Summaries. This component provides an audio and written summary of the chapter in both English and Spanish.

- Use photographs, drawings, or magazine clippings whenever possible to help students visualize the important concepts of the chapter.

18. **Explain** Describe the role drugs and other substances play in unsafe situations such as being under the influence while driving and HIV/STD transmission.
19. **Identify** What are some ways to prevent the use of alcohol, drugs, and other substances such as inhalants?
20. **Compare** Describe the similarities between chemical dependency and addiction to alcohol, drugs, and other substances such as inhalants.
21. **Hypothesize** Why might joining a group like Al-Anon or Nar-Anon make it easier to deal with another person's substance abuse?

Career Corner

Pharmacist Your pharmacist helps you use medicines wisely. Pharmacists work in drug-stores, clinics, and hospitals. Their job is to fill prescriptions written by doctors and dentists. They create the labels that explain how to use medicines properly. They also answer customers' questions. A person must spend at least four years in a pharmacy program to enter this career. To learn more about how pharmacists help people maintain their health, visit Career Corner at health.glencoe.com.

Standardized Test Practice

Math

Read the paragraph below and then answer the questions.

When you're ill or have a chronic health problem, you may need to take medicine. The medicine will help you only if it's taken in the proper amount, or dose.

1. Keisha takes medication for an under-active thyroid gland. She had been taking 75 micrograms each day, but today her doctor raised the dose to 88 micro-grams each day. Assuming that a month is 30 days, how much more medicine will Keisha take this next month than she took last month?

    Ⓐ 13 micrograms
    Ⓑ 163 micrograms
    Ⓒ 225 micrograms
    Ⓓ 390 micrograms

2. One adult dose of a certain medication is 15 milligrams for every 50 pounds of body weight. How many milligrams of this medication would be in one dose for an adult male weighing 200 pounds?

    Ⓐ 60 milligrams
    Ⓑ 100 milligrams
    Ⓒ 150 milligrams
    Ⓓ 200 milligrams

3. The label on a bottle of cough syrup states that children 6 to 12 years old should take 1 teaspoon of cough syrup every four hours. Each teaspoon contains 10 milligrams of cough suppressant. Explain in your own words how you would determine the number of milligrams of cough suppressant that an 11-year-old takes in one day.

 TH05_C1.glencoe.com/quiz

CHAPTER 9 ASSESSMENT **255**

19. Responses might include participating in healthful alternative activities.
20. Responses should indicate that chemical dependency on and addiction to any of these substances is harmful to health.
21. Possible response: Being part of a group of people who are facing the same problem gives members support and makes them feel less alone.

Test Practice
1. D
2. A
3. Sample answer: Because there are 24 hours in a day, 6 doses would be taken. You multiply 6 doses times 10 mg per dose for a total amount of 60 mg a day.

Reteaching
Assign Study Guide 9 in the Student Activities Workbook.

Evaluate
- Use the reproducible Chapter 9 Test in the TCR, or construct your own test using the **Exam**View® Pro Testmaker.
- Use Performance Assessment 9 in the TCR.

Enrichment
Have students work together to plan a presentation or performance that will make other teens aware of dangers, such as chemical dependency and addiction, when using alcohol and drugs.

Assessment

Self-Assessment Direct students to review the activities that are provided throughout the chapter. Encourage each student to select one finished product or activity that demonstrates his or her best work for the chapter. Have students explain what they learned and how the examples they selected show their progress.

Career Corner

Pharmacist Discuss with students the importance of knowing the outlook of an occupation before making a decision to enter that career field. Have students go to the library and research the career outlook for pharmacists. This information can also be found online at the government's Bureau of Labor Statistics Web site.

Planning Guide

Chapter 10	Skills/ Activities	Reproducible Resources	Assessment
Lesson 1 **Personal Safety** *pages 258–260*	**HEALTH SKILLS ACTIVITY** ▲ Having Fun and Staying Safe (*Goal Setting*), page 260	*Student Activities Workbook available for use with each chapter* 📁 Parent Letter & Activities 10 📁 Concept Map 42 📁 Enrichment Activity 36 📁 Lesson Plan 1 📁 Reading Tutor Activity 36 📁 Reteaching Activity 37	📁 Lesson 1 Quiz
Lesson 2 **Safety at Home and Away** *pages 261–265*	**HEALTH SKILLS ACTIVITY** ▲ Dangerous Situations (*Practicing Healthful Behaviors*), page 264	📁 Concept Map 43 📁 Decision-Making Activity 19 📁 Enrichment Activity 37 📁 Lesson Plan 2 📁 Reading Tutor Activity 37 📁 Reteaching Activity 38	📁 Lesson 2 Quiz
Lesson 3 **Safety Outdoors** *pages 266–271*	**HEALTH SKILLS ACTIVITY** ▲ Preparing an Emergency Supplies Kit (*Practicing Healthful Behaviors*), page 270	📁 Concept Maps 44, 45 📁 Cross-Curriculum Activity 19 📁 Enrichment Activity 38 📁 Lesson Plan 3 📁 Reading Tutor Activity 38 📁 Reteaching Activity 39	📁 Lesson 3 Quiz
Lesson 4 **First Aid for Emergencies** *pages 272–277*	**HEALTH SKILLS ACTIVITY** ▲ Minor Injury Lookout (*Accessing Information*), page 277	📁 Concept Map 46 📁 Enrichment Activity 39 📁 Lesson Plan 4 📁 Reading Tutor Activity 39 📁 Reteaching Activity 40	📁 Lesson 4 Quiz
Lesson 5 **Protecting Your Environment** *pages 278–283*	**Hands-On Health** ▲ Are You Earth-Friendly?, page 282	📁 Concept Maps 47, 48 📁 Cross-Curriculum Activity 20 📁 Decision-Making Activity 20 📁 Enrichment Activity 40 📁 Lesson Plan 5 📁 Reading Tutor Activity 40 📁 Health Lab 10 📁 Reteaching Activity 41	📁 Lesson 5 Quiz 📁 Chapter 10 Test 📁 Performance Assessment 10

TIME HEALTH   **Play Smart!** *pages 284–285*

BUILDING HEALTH SKILLS

Reuse to Reduce Waste (*Advocacy*) *pages 286–287*		📁 Building Health Skills Reproducible Master 10	

Standards		Technology
National	**State/Local**	
National Health Education Standard **1.1, 1.6, 3.4, 3.5, 6.4**		Transparencies 41 & 42 TeacherWorks™ Internet Activities
National Health Education Standard **1.1, 1.5, 1.6, 3.1, 3.4, 3.5, 3.6**		Transparencies 43 & 44 TeacherWorks™
National Health Education Standard **1.1, 1.5, 1.6, 3.1, 3.4, 3.5, 3.6**		Transparencies 45 & 46 TeacherWorks™
National Health Education Standard **1.1, 2.2, 2.6, 3.4, 3.5**		Transparency 47 TeacherWorks™
National Health Education Standard **1.1, 1.5, 2.6, 3.1, 3.4, 3.5, 4.3**		Transparency 48 TeacherWorks™ MindJogger Videoquiz **Exam**View® Pro Testmaker
National Health Education Standard **7.2, 7.4, 7.5**		Building Health Skills Transparency Master 10

TeacherWorks™

Glencoe's new and exclusive TeacherWorks™ is an all-in-one planner and resource center. Access the complete Teacher Wraparound Edition electronically. Find all your classroom resources with just a few easy clicks, and print them right from your computer. Connect directly to Glencoe's customized Health Web site. Access the National Health Education Standards correlations, or insert your own state standards and match them directly to the electronic Teacher Wraparound Edition.

Language Diversity

- English Audio Summaries
- Spanish Audio Summaries
- English Summaries, Quizzes, and Activities
- Spanish Summaries, Quizzes, and Activities
- Spanish Parent Letters and Activities

KEY TO ABILITY LEVELS

Teaching Strategies that appear throughout the chapters have been identified by one of four codes to give you an idea of their suitability for students of varying learning styles and abilities.

L1 **Level 1** strategies should be within the ability range of all students. Often full class participation is required.

L2 **Level 2** strategies are for average to above-average students or for small groups. Some teacher direction is necessary.

L3 **Level 3** strategies are designed for students able and willing to work independently. Minimal teacher direction is necessary.

INCL Strategies are appropriate for students with particular special needs in a general classroom setting.

CHAPTER
10

Safety and the Environment

Chapter at a Glance

Health Skills

256

HANDS-ON ACTIVITY

Recycling Club Invite your class to start a recycling club to cut down on excess waste. Start with an election of officers. Have the class vote on volunteer nominees for president, vice president, secretary, and treasurer. The president will run the club meetings with the vice president providing backup and the secretary taking notes.

Encourage the club to start a recycling project in an area where there is a lot of waste (e.g., paper in the classrooms, bottles or cans in the cafeteria, and so forth.). Any proceeds from the recycling project would be given to the treasurer for classroom or school improvement.

Safety and the Environment

HEALTH *Online*

Go to health.glencoe.com, where you can take the Health Inventory for Chapter 10 and rate how well you demonstrate safe behaviors.

FOLDABLES™ Study Organizer

Before You Read

Make this Foldable to help you organize what you learn in Lesson 1 about personal safety. Begin with a plain sheet of 8½" × 11" paper.

Step 1

Fold a sheet of paper from bottom to top, leaving a 2" tab at the top.

Step 2

Fold in half from side to side.

Step 3

Unfold and cut along the center fold line of the top layer only. This will make two tabs.

Step 4

Label as shown.

Injury:
Why did it occur?   How could it have been prevented?

As You Read

Think about an injury that you or someone else had. Briefly describe the injury on the top tab of your Foldable. Then, under the appropriate tab, explain why the injury occurred and what could have been done to prevent it.

257

Chapter Introduction

Use the options below to motivate students and preview chapter content.

HEALTH *Online*

Visit health.glencoe.com, and have students complete Health Inventory 10 to test their safety skills at home and in the environment. For other teaching strategies, explore the Lesson Plans and select from Cross-Curriculum, Reading, or Media Literacy activities.

GLENCOE TECHNOLOGY

MindJogger Videoquiz

Use MindJogger to preview or review Chapter 10 content.

TIME HEALTH

Play Smart!
pages 284–285

FOLDABLES™ Study Organizer

Dinah Zike Study Fold

Narrative Writing Ask students to think of a specific injury that they or someone they know has had. Direct them to write a brief description of the injury on the top tab of their Foldable. As students read and study the material in Lesson 1 on building safe habits, have them write narratives on why the injury occurred and what could have been done to prevent it under the appropriate tab. You may also wish to have students record main ideas, define terms, and/or give an example of an accident chain on the back of their Foldable.

Lesson 1

Personal Safety

① Focus

Lesson Objectives

Students will be able to

- explain the importance of building safe habits.

- describe the accident chain and ways to prevent accidental injuries.

Health Skills
- Goal Setting, p. 260

Motivators

 **Quick Write**

Have a volunteer read the Quick Write. Allow students to share their experiences and discuss how their injuries could have been prevented.

Bellringer Activity

Write the following statement on the board: *There's been an accident.* Give students three or four minutes to brainstorm words and phrases that come to mind when they read the statement.

VOCABULARY

Go over the vocabulary terms with students. Let volunteers share what they already know about each term, including experiences and ideas about safety. Then have students make their own study cards for the terms, with the correct spelling on one side of a card and the Glossary definition on the other side.

Personal Safety

Quick Write

Describe how an injury you had could have been prevented. Explain whether you think you could have avoided the injury by using protective behaviors.

LEARN ABOUT...

- why it is important to make safety a habit.
- what causes injuries.
- how you can prevent unintentional injuries.

VOCABULARY

- injury
- deliberate injury
- accidental injury
- accident chain

Building Safe Habits

Your health and safety depend on practicing good safety habits. This means protecting yourself from **injury**, or *physical damage or harm to the body*. **Deliberate injuries** are *injuries that result when one person intentionally harms another*. **Accidental injuries** are *injuries caused by unexpected events*. These are also called unintentional injuries.

Many common activities, such as riding a bicycle or cutting fruit with a sharp knife, carry a risk of injury. However, good safety habits can help reduce the risk of an injury. That includes being careful, thinking ahead, and taking precautions. Some strategies for preventing accidental injuries are

- **staying away from risky behaviors.** Make the decision to avoid activities that lead to injuries.

- **ignoring peer pressure.** Do not give in to friends who want to take careless chances.

FIGURE 10.1

THE ACCIDENT CHAIN

Unsafe habits can lead to accidental injury. *How could Tina have avoided this accident?*

1 **The Situation** Tina wants to get a serving dish that is stored on the top shelf of a high cabinet.

2 **The Unsafe Habit** Tina climbs on chairs or countertops to reach high shelves.

258 CHAPTER 10: SAFETY AND THE ENVIRONMENT

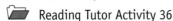

Lesson 1 Resources

Teacher Classroom Resources

📁 Parent Letter & Activities 10

📁 Concept Map 42

📁 Enrichment Activity 36

📁 Lesson Plan 1

📁 Lesson 1 Quiz

📁 Reading Tutor Activity 36

📁 Reteaching Activity 37

🎮 Transparencies 41 & 42

Student Activities Workbook

📁 Chapter 10 Study Guide

📁 Applying Health Skills 36

- **thinking before you act and taking your time.** Being upset or excited can distract you and cause you to be careless.
- **knowing your limits.** Do not attempt to do more than you can do safely. For example, do not go into deep water if you are not a good swimmer.

The Accident Chain

The unexpected events that cause accidental injuries are known as accidents. Many accidents can be prevented. They often occur because of an accident chain, *a sequence of events that often leads to an accidental injury.* **Figure 10.1** shows the accident chain in action.

Preventing Accidental Injuries

Like most accidental injuries, Tina's sprained wrist could have been prevented. She could have broken the accident chain by eliminating one of the first three links:

- **Change the situation.** If the dish had been on a lower shelf, Tina would not have had to climb up to reach it.
- **Change the unsafe habit.** Tina needs to break the unsafe habit of climbing on chairs and countertops.
- **Change the unsafe action.** Tina should always use a sturdy step stool to reach items on high shelves.

② Teach

VISUAL LEARNING

FIGURE 10.1 After students have considered each picture individually, ask them to explain what the chain itself tells about all the events in the series. Then ask a volunteer to read and answer the caption question. Students should recognize that Tina could have avoided the accident by standing on a stepladder or another secure surface. Also, someone could have stood close by as she retrieved the dish. **INCL** *Behavior Problems, Special Learning Needs, English Language Learners*

Comprehending

Have partners make their own accident chains, using five strips of construction paper and glue or tape. Have them write a specific accident element on each strip and then glue the strips into interlocking rings in the correct order. Ask each pair to show how the chain might be broken by tearing apart one of the first three links. **L1 INCL** *English Language Learners*

3 **The Unsafe Act** Tina stands on a chair with wheels to reach the dish.

4 **The Accident** Tina falls off the chair.

5 **The Results of the Accident** Tina is injured—she sprains her wrist. The dish shatters, creating a risk of unintentional injury for anyone walking there.

LESSON 1: PERSONAL SAFETY **259**

INCLUSION STRATEGIES

Special Learning Needs, Behavior Problems, Different Learning Styles (Visual, Kinesthetic), Gifted As students consider hazards and safety routines throughout this chapter, some class members may benefit from physical examples and from brief, focused role-playing activities. Whenever possible, bring in safety devices; let students handle each item, and show how it can be used. For example, when studying safety at home, you might suggest that each student select a specific room in the house (e.g., bathroom, kitchen, or garage) and become an expert on safety in that room. Alternately, students may become experts on specific types of accidents or hazards (e.g., falls, poisoning, fire, and so on.)

Lesson 1

Note: This skill is introduced in Chapter 1 on pages 20–23.

HEALTH SKILLS ACTIVITY

GOAL SETTING

Have students read Karen's situation, and guide them in a discussion about her goal. Also review the four steps in setting goals. Then have students work with partners to draw an accident chain for one of Karen's injuries, write out a goal-setting plan for Karen, and draw a new sequence in which Karen breaks the accident chain. Ask several pairs of students to share their work with the rest of the class.

Note: This skill is introduced in Chapter 1 on pages 20–23.

③ Assess

Evaluating

 Assign the Lesson 1 Review; then assign the Lesson 1 Quiz in the TCR.

Reteaching

 Assign Concept Map 42 or Reteaching Activity 37 in the TCR.

Enrichment

 Assign Enrichment Activity 36 in the TCR.

④ Close

Ask each student to identify one important habit he or she plans to develop or change as a result of studying this lesson.

HEALTH SKILLS ACTIVITY

GOAL SETTING

Having Fun and Staying Safe

Soccer is Karen's favorite sport. Last season, she was injured twice. The first injury happened when she was late to practice. She didn't have time to warm up, so she strained a muscle in her leg. The second injury occurred because Karen forgot her soccer shoes. She wore her tennis sneakers instead, which caused her to slide into another player.

Karen's mom told her that if she keeps getting hurt, she won't be allowed to stay on the team. Karen knows she has to find a way to make it through this season without injuries.

What Would You Do?

Create a drawing representing the accident chain that led to one of Karen's injuries. Then show how she could use the steps for goal setting to avoid future injuries.

Finally, draw a new sequence that shows Karen breaking one or more of the links in the accident chain.

1. **SET A SPECIFIC GOAL.**
2. **LIST THE STEPS TO REACH YOUR GOAL.**
3. **GET HELP FROM OTHERS.**
4. **EVALUATE YOUR PROGRESS.**
5. **REWARD YOURSELF.**

Lesson 1 Review

Using complete sentences, answer the following questions on a sheet of paper.

Reviewing Terms and Facts

1. **Vocabulary** Define *deliberate injuries* and *accidental injuries*.
2. **Recall** List three strategies for the prevention of and response to deliberate and accidental injuries.
3. **Describe** Define the *accident chain* and explain how it can be broken.

Thinking Critically

4. **Explain** Explain why it is wise to know your limitations.

5. **Apply** Give an example of a situation in which peer pressure could lead someone to act unsafely. Explain how you would resist peer pressure in that situation.

Applying Health Skills

6. **Practicing Healthful Behaviors** Draw your own example of an accident chain, and label each part. Exchange drawings with a classmate. Analyze your classmate's chain, and name three ways to break it.

Lesson 1 Review

1. See definitions on page 258.
2. Any three strategies from pages 258–259.
3. A sequence of events that often leads to an accidental injury. It can be broken by changing the situation, changing the unsafe habit, or changing the unsafe action.
4. Responses should indicate that knowing one's limitations can help a person avoid potentially risky situations.
5. Students should name a situation in which peers might pressure one another to take unnecessary risks and should give a realistic explanation of how to use refusal skills in that situation.

Safety at Home and Away

Safety in the Home

You probably think of your home as a comfortable, safe, and friendly place. However, most homes also have some **hazards**, or *possible sources of harm*. Following safety rules can help prevent accidental injuries from home hazards. **Figure 10.2** on the next page shows some of the ways to make your home safer.

- **Preventing falls.** One goal of home safety is to prevent falls. Keep objects off the floor, where someone might trip over them. Always be sure rugs are fastened firmly to the floor, and avoid running on wet or waxed floors. Wipe up spills in the kitchen right away. Keep a sturdy step stool around for reaching items on high shelves.

Quick Write

List two or three safety rules you follow on your way to and from school.

LEARN ABOUT...

- how to prevent accidental injuries in your home.
- safety tips for traveling to and from your home.
- how to be safe in your school and community.

VOCABULARY

- hazard
- smoke alarm
- pedestrian
- Neighborhood Watch program

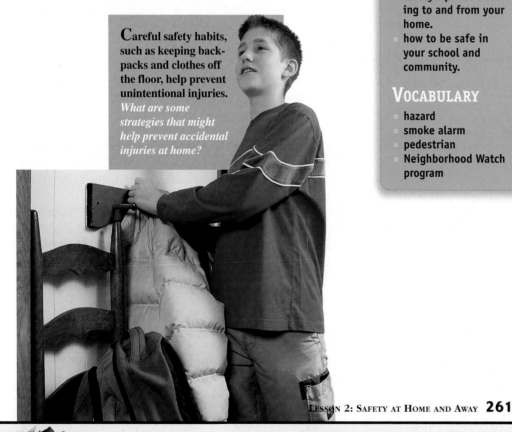

Careful safety habits, such as keeping backpacks and clothes off the floor, help prevent unintentional injuries. *What are some strategies that might help prevent accidental injuries at home?*

LESSON 2: SAFETY AT HOME AND AWAY **261**

Lesson 2

Safety at Home and Away

① FOCUS

Lesson Objectives

Students will be able to

- list ways to prevent falls as well as injuries from electricity, fire, and guns.
- list safety rules to follow as pedestrians, car passengers, and bicycle riders.
- discuss ways schools and communities protect their members from violence.

Health Skills
- Practicing Healthful Behaviors, p. 264

Motivators

Quick Write
As students respond to the Quick Write, list the safety rules on the board. Ask students to categorize the safety rules for pedestrian safety, bike safety, and so on.

VOCABULARY
Direct students to meet in groups to read and discuss the vocabulary terms. Encourage them to share what they already know and then to check the formal definition of each word in the Glossary.

Lesson 2 Resources

Teacher Classroom Resources
- Concept Map 43
- Decision-Making Activity 19
- Enrichment Activity 37
- Lesson Plan 2
- Lesson 2 Quiz
- Reading Tutor Activity 37
- Reteaching Activity 38
- Transparencies 43 & 44

Student Activities Workbook
- Chapter 10 Study Guide
- Applying Health Skills 37

261

VISUAL LEARNING

FIGURE 10.2 Help students read and discuss the safety tips in Figure 10.2. Pose questions such as these:

- What are the recommended locations for smoke alarms?
- What are some good locations for a fire extinguisher?
- What kinds of chemicals and medicines should be locked away?
- What are indications that electrical cords are damaged?
- What is clutter?

INCL *Behavior Problems, Special Learning Needs, English Language Learners*

Discussing

Help students focus on common hazards in the home. Ask them how hazards might fit in an accident chain. Have students explain why it is important first to recognize and, whenever possible, to remove hazards. **L1**

Applying Knowledge

Ask students to tour their own homes and note the safety hazards they see there. Remind them to look with a "fresh eye" because, in many cases, hazards have become an accepted part of the household routine. **L2**

FIGURE 10.2

PREVENTING ACCIDENTAL INJURIES AT HOME

A Make sure no one smokes in bed.

H Install smoke alarms near sleeping areas and on each level of the house.

G Keep a fire extinguisher within easy reach.

B Use nonskid mats in baths and showers to prevent falls.

C Keep stairways free of clutter to prevent falls.

F Keep dangerous chemicals and medicines locked up and out reach of small children.

E Check electrical cords for damage. Cover outlets with safety caps to protect children.

D To prevent fires, immediately throw away oil-soaked rags.

Reading Check

Analyze word parts. Divide the words *bicycle* and *pedestrian* into parts. What do the parts tell you about the meanings of the words?

- **Electrical safety.** To avoid electrical hazards, always pull plugs out by the plug itself, not by the cord. Don't use appliances with damaged cords. In homes with small children, cover unused outlets. Keep electrical products away from water, and never use them if your skin is wet or if you are in a bathtub.
- **Kitchen and fire safety.** When using a knife, make sure it's sharp, and handle it carefully. Don't leave food cooking on the stove unattended. Turn pot handles inward, away from the edge. Keep small children away from the stove, and always put matches and cigarette lighters out of reach. In case of fire, each level of the house should have a **smoke alarm,** *a device that makes a warning noise when it senses smoke.* Smother grease fires with a lid or baking soda, never with water. If your clothes catch fire, *stop, drop,* and *roll.* First, *stop* moving; if you run, the rush of air will fan the flames. Then *drop* to the floor and *roll* to smother the flames.
- **Gun safety.** If guns are kept in the home, they must always be stored in locked cabinets. Bullets should be stored separately. Never handle a gun without adult supervision. Never point a gun at a person.

262 CHAPTER 10: SAFETY AND THE ENVIRONMENT

Reading Check

Prefixes and Roots Identifying word parts and recognizing common meanings help students build vocabulary skills. Knowing the meaning of a prefix or root will enable readers to begin to decode unfamiliar words. Write the words *bicycle* and *pedestrian* on the board. Have a student divide the words with slashes after their initial parts. For example, *bi/cycle,* and *ped/estrian.*

Note: They should divide word parts, not syllables. Then discuss the meaning of each word part and how it affects the meaning of the word as a whole. Using a dictionary, students will find *bi-* means "two," *cycle* means "circle" or "wheel." They will also find that *ped-* means "foot."

Safety on the Road

Sometimes, you will be a pedestrian, or *a person who travels on foot*. **Figure 10.3** shows how pedestrians and other travelers can share the road with drivers. Here are some other safety tips that will help you protect your physical health:

- **Use your safety belt.** Always wear a safety belt when riding in a motor vehicle.
- **Use proper safety equipment.** Always wear a helmet. When using a skateboard, in-line skates, or a scooter, wear proper pads and gloves. Don't skate or ride a scooter after dark.
- **Dress appropriately**. Wear flat-soled shoes for riding a scooter. Wear clothes that won't catch in a bicycle chain.
- **Know where to ride.** Don't skate in traffic or in crowded pedestrian areas. Avoid wet, dirty, or uneven surfaces. On a bike, ride with traffic, single file, and obey traffic signals.
- **Be aware of others.** When cycling, check for cars before entering the traffic flow. Always watch for pedestrians.
- **Be visible to others.** Wear bright, reflective clothes. If you ride your bicycle at night, it should have lights and reflectors.
- **Ride carefully.** Keep your speed under control. Know how to stop. When skating, know how to fall properly.

FIGURE 10.3

Sharing the Road

Pedestrians, bicyclists, and drivers must share the road safely. Follow these basic safety rules.

A Always wear a safety belt when riding in a motor vehicle.

B Cross at crosswalks or intersections. Before crossing the street, look left, right, and left again.

C Watch for drivers who are turning right at a red light.

D Obey traffic signals.

E Watch for small children and animals.

F Be aware of bicyclists or pedestrians with physical disabilities.

LESSON 2: SAFETY AT HOME AND AWAY **263**

Lesson 2

Cross-Curriculum Activity

VISUAL ARTS Have students work with partners to select an important aspect of bike safety, skateboard safety, or in-line skating safety. Then have the partners plan and make an attractive poster urging other students to follow that safety guideline. **L2** **INCL** *English Language Learners*

Investigating

Ask a pair of volunteers to learn about state and local helmet laws for bicycle riders, skaters, skateboarders, and scooter riders. Direct these volunteers to share their findings with the rest of the class. **L3**

VISUAL LEARNING

FIGURE 10.3 Have students describe each aspect of the scene in Figure 10.3 and note the safety guidelines that are being followed. Ask:

- What other safety guidelines might apply at an intersection?
- On a street with no cross traffic?
- On a street with no sidewalks?
- On a highway?

INCL *Behavior Problems, Special Learning Needs, English Language Learners*

Beyond the Classroom

Community Invite the owner or manager of a local sports equipment shop to visit the class with several kinds of sports helmets. Ask the visitor to emphasize the importance of wearing safety helmets and to explain the differences among various types of helmets and among various helmet brands. In addition, ask the visitor to describe the elements of a proper fit including the correct placement on the head. It is important that helmets provide protection for the frontal lobes of the brain. Encourage a question-and-answer session.

Applying Knowledge

Guide students in discussing the school programs designed to prevent violence and the special measures used to keep weapons out of schools. Ask students to identify and describe some specific strategies in these programs and practices the school has adopted for avoiding violence and weapons. **L1**

HEALTH SKILLS ACTIVITY

PRACTICING HEALTHFUL BEHAVIORS

Help students read and discuss the listed safety rules. Remind students that if they were escaping someone who wanted to hurt them, they should try to remember that person's appearance and his or her license plate number, if any.

Have students work together to brainstorm a list of situations that could be dangerous. To help students begin, present this example: A stranger tells you she or he is lost and asks you to show the way to an address. Record students' ideas on the board. Have students meet in groups to discuss safe responses to three or four of the listed situations.

Note: This skill is introduced in Chapter 1 on page 10.

Safety in Schools

Factors that affect the physical, mental/emotional, and social health of everyone at school include safety measures and school climate. School climate involves how safe and clean the buildings and grounds are and how well students get along with one another.

Many schools are trying to prevent violence, and the deliberate injuries violence can cause, by using strategies such as:

- Peer mediation and crisis prevention programs
- Programs that teach students to respect others
- Health education classes that teach conflict resolution
- Police and security officers on campus

Preventing Violence in Schools

Schools are also taking steps to eliminate weapons and drugs, which can both contribute to violence. For example, some schools have installed metal detectors to search for weapons. You can help too. Know and follow the rules prohibiting the possession of weapons at school. Alert school officials if you know, or suspect, that someone has a weapon.

HEALTH SKILLS ACTIVITY

PRACTICING HEALTHFUL BEHAVIORS

Dangerous Situations

To avoid or cope with potentially dangerous situations, follow these safety rules:

- At home, do not open the door to anyone you don't know. Keep doors and windows locked. Never tell visitors or callers you are alone. Instead, say your parents are busy or can't come to the phone.
- If you are going out, tell your family your destination, route, and expected time of return.
- Never get into or go near a stranger's car. Never hitchhike.
- Do not enter a building with a stranger.
- Do not run errands or do other work for strangers.
- If someone tries to grab you, scream and run away. Go to the nearest place with people, and ask them to call the police, 911, or your parents.

WITH A GROUP
Identify several potentially dangerous situations. Brainstorm ways to avoid and cope with each situation.

COOPERATIVE LEARNING ACTIVITY

Safe School Report Help your students feel safe in school. Conduct a walk-through of the building, and label the safety features students find. Have groups of students gather information about the school. One group will interview students, asking how safe they feel in school. Another group will interview staff, asking how they help students feel safe in school. A third group will take pictures or draw illustrations of school safety features. A fourth group will research any school policies that refer to safety on school grounds or on the school bus. Compile students' findings into a Safe School Report to present to the principal. As a class, role-play effective responses to students who make serious or threatening comments.

Safety in Communities

To keep the streets safe, some communities have passed stricter laws against guns. They have also increased the punishments for violent crimes. In many areas, people have formed **Neighborhood Watch programs**. In these programs, *police train residents to look for and report suspicious activity in their neighborhood.* Communities may also try to protect teens by creating curfews, drug-free zones, and after-school and summer programs.

You can also help protect yourself against potentially dangerous situations. First, don't look like a target. Walk with purpose and confidence. Second, whenever possible, don't travel alone. Third, avoid unfamiliar areas and places that are known to be dangerous.

Many communities post signs to keep the violence caused by drugs and drug dealers out of their area.

Lesson 2 Review

Using complete sentences, answer the following questions on a sheet of paper.

Reviewing Terms and Facts

1. **Vocabulary** Define *hazard*.
2. **Recall** Identify two factors that affect the physical, mental/emotional, and social health of everyone at school.
3. **Describe** How does a smoke alarm protect you in case of a fire?
4. **Give examples** State four strategies communities can use to prevent violence and deliberate injuries.

Thinking Critically

5. **Hypothesize** Why is it important not to handle a gun without adult supervision?
6. **Explain** Why is obeying the rules of the road as important for bicyclists as it is for automobile drivers?
7. **Analyze** Why do you think teaching students to respect others can help prevent violence?

Applying Health Skills

8. **Advocacy** Be part of the solution to violence. Think of one way teens can help reduce violence in their schools and communities. Create a sign presenting your idea. Display the sign in the classroom or in the school hallway.

Journal Writing

Ask students to write private journal entries describing the specific changes they feel would make their school and neighborhoods safer for daily life. **L2**

❸ Assess

Evaluating

📁 Assign the Lesson 2 Review; then assign the Lesson 2 Quiz in the TCR.

Reteaching

• 📁 Assign Concept Map 43 or Reteaching Activity 38 in the TCR.
• Ask each student to review the safety guidelines for a specific area of safety. Then have students summarize and explain for the rest of the group the essential safety guidelines for that area.

Enrichment

• 📁 Assign Enrichment Activity 37 in the TCR.
• Have students work together to plan and practice a skit (or a series of skits) to teach safety rules to children. In the skit, have students demonstrate strategies for the prevention of and response to accidental injuries, such as wearing a safety belt. Try to arrange a performance for a kindergarten class.

❹ Close

Ask students: How has the information in this lesson changed your ideas about violence?

Lesson 2 Review

1. A hazard is a possible source of harm.
2. Safety measures and school climate.
3. It makes a warning noise to tell you that a fire is present so that you can escape quickly and safely.
4. Any four: stricter gun laws, increased punishments for violent crimes, Neighborhood Watch programs, curfews for teens, drug-free zones, after-school and summer programs.
5. Responses should indicate that teens are inexperienced with guns and could get hurt or hurt others.
6. Responses should reflect the idea that drivers and cyclists share the road and must follow the same laws to prevent accidents.
7. Accept any reasonable answer but expect responses to hinge on preventing arguments that could lead to violence.

Safety Outdoors

1 Focus

Lesson Objectives

Students will be able to

• list basic safety rules for outdoor activities.

• explain ways to be safe in the water while hiking or camping, and while participating in winter sports.

• describe how to be prepared for weather emergencies, such as floods, earthquakes, hurricanes, and tornadoes.

Health Skills

• Practicing Healthful Behaviors, p. 270

Motivators

Quick Write

Ask students what types of dangerous weather occur in their area; then have students discuss what they would do in each situation.

Bellringer Activity

Give students several minutes to list as many different kinds of weather emergencies around the world as possible.

VOCABULARY

Have volunteers read aloud the vocabulary terms, sharing informal definitions and using the Glossary to check exact meanings.

Quick Write

List two or three things your family should do to prepare for storms or other weather emergencies common in your area.

LEARN ABOUT...

• why you should use the buddy system.

• what you should know about water safety to prevent drowning.

• what tips you need to know for outdoor safety.

• how to be prepared for weather emergencies.

VOCABULARY

• hypothermia
• earthquake
• hurricane
• tornado

Safety Outdoors

Being Safe Outdoors

It's always fun to enjoy "the great outdoors" as long as you follow some general safety rules.

• **Plan ahead.** Always make sure you have the right equipment and enough food and water.

• **Use the buddy system.** This is an agreement you have with one or more people to stay together.

• **Know your limits.** Be aware of your skills and abilities before you start an activity.

• **Use the proper equipment.** Have the proper safety gear for each activity.

• **Check the weather forecast.** Avoid extreme temperatures and electrical storms. Carry plenty of water, and remember to wear sunscreen and other protection from the sun.

• **Warm up and cool down.** Warm up before exercising, and cool down afterward.

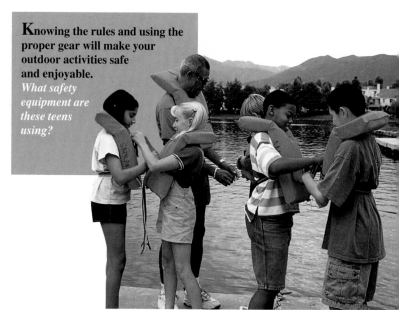

Knowing the rules and using the proper gear will make your outdoor activities safe and enjoyable. *What safety equipment are these teens using?*

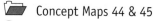

Lesson 3 Resources

Teacher Classroom Resources

📁 Concept Maps 44 & 45

📁 Cross-Curriculum Activity 19

📁 Enrichment Activity 38

📁 Lesson Plan 3

📁 Lesson 3 Quiz

📁 Reading Tutor Activity 38

📁 Reteaching Activity 39

🗂 Transparencies 45 & 46

Student Activities Workbook

📁 Chapter 10 Study Guide

📁 Applying Health Skills 38

Water and Boating Safety

Are you a fan of water activities? To avoid injury, you need to learn and follow water safety rules.

- Learn to swim well. Good swimmers are less likely to panic in an emergency.
- Never go in the water alone. Go to beaches or pools that have lifeguards, and always use the buddy system.
- If you ever feel you are in danger of drowning, stay calm. Call for help, and use the technique in **Figure 10.4**.
- Use a pole, branch, rope, or life preserver to help someone in trouble. Don't go into the water yourself.
- Check water depth before diving. Never dive into shallow water or an aboveground pool. Take diving lessons.
- Wear a life jacket when boating. Be sure the boat is in good condition and know how to operate it.
- Keep any boat steady to avoid falling in the water, which puts you at risk for **hypothermia** (hy·poh·THER·mee·uh), *a sudden and dangerous drop in body temperature.*

FIGURE 10.4

DROWNING PREVENTION

The technique shown here can help you stay afloat in warm water. In cold water, it is better to tread water slowly or float on your back to save energy.

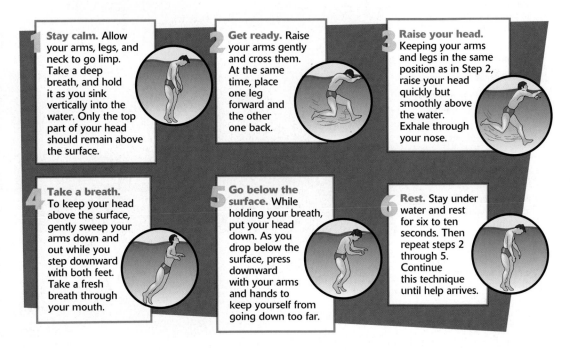

1 **Stay calm.** Allow your arms, legs, and neck to go limp. Take a deep breath, and hold it as you sink vertically into the water. Only the top part of your head should remain above the surface.

2 **Get ready.** Raise your arms gently and cross them. At the same time, place one leg forward and the other one back.

3 **Raise your head.** Keeping your arms and legs in the same position as in Step 2, raise your head quickly but smoothly above the water. Exhale through your nose.

4 **Take a breath.** To keep your head above the surface, gently sweep your arms down and out while you step downward with both feet. Take a fresh breath through your mouth.

5 **Go below the surface.** While holding your breath, put your head down. As you drop below the surface, press downward with your arms and hands to keep yourself from going down too far.

6 **Rest.** Stay under water and rest for six to ten seconds. Then repeat steps 2 through 5. Continue this technique until help arrives.

LESSON 3: SAFETY OUTDOORS **267**

COOPERATIVE LEARNING ACTIVITY

Practicing the Buddy System Have students form small groups and discuss the benefits of the buddy system. Ask group members to work together to list five different situations in which having one or more buddies would prove helpful; have a group recorder write each situation on a separate slip of paper. Then have each group select one slip of paper from another group. After a few minutes of planning, have group members present a short skit in which they demonstrate the usefulness of the buddy system in the situation suggested by the other group.

Lesson 3

② Teach

Discussing

Encourage students to discuss the benefits and limitations of the buddy system. Have them explain how having a buddy can help, but should not prevent one from following safety rules. Ask students:

- Which is safer: having no buddy or having an irresponsible buddy? Why?
- What do you do if you have an irresponsible buddy? **L1**

Comprehending

Have the class select one kind of outdoor activity such as swimming or hiking. Discuss why it is important for people to know their own limits when they participate in that activity. How can friends lead a person into trying more than he or she can handle? **L2**

Applying Knowledge

Ask students to identify local programs that teach swimming or water safety skills. Also help students to compile a list of local pools or beaches that have lifeguards on duty. **L1**

VISUAL LEARNING

FIGURE 10.4 Guide students in studying and describing the pictures that show the techniques of drowning prevention. Explain that this technique is not recommended in cold water because it can cause the body to lose body heat faster. **INCL** *Behavior Problems, Special Learning Needs, English Language Learners*

Lesson 3

Discussing

Ask volunteers to share experiences they have had while hiking or camping. If these are popular activities with students, take time to consider each safety guideline in detail. Have students explain why the guideline is important, what special preparation or consideration might be involved, and how following each guideline can help make hiking and camping more enjoyable. **L1**

Cross-Curriculum Activity

LANGUAGE ARTS Have students work with partners to brainstorm ideas for short stories about teens engaged in outdoor activities. After they have written their own stories, have them work with their partners to revise their stories. **L2**

VISUAL LEARNING

FIGURE 10.5 Ask volunteers to describe the scene in the picture and to read aloud the safety tips for hikers and campers. Have students explain the importance of each safety tip and to give specific examples of how it can be followed. **INCL** *Behavior Problems, Special Learning Needs, English Language Learners*

Reading Check

Create your own chart about outdoor safety. Include information about Who, What, When, Where, Why, and How.

Hiking and Camping

You can make a hiking or camping trip safer and more fun if you bring the right clothing and equipment. For hiking, you need sturdy, well-cushioned shoes. You should break new shoes in for a few days before wearing them on the trail. If possible, layering two pairs of socks in your shoes can help prevent blisters. You should also wear clothing appropriate for the weather and the season.

When you go camping, make sure someone knows where you are going and when you plan to return. Carrying a cellular phone or walkie-talkie can help someone find you in an emergency. A compass and a flashlight (with extra batteries) will help prevent you from losing your way. You should also bring along plenty of fresh water and a first-aid kit in case of injuries. **Figure 10.5** shows some more steps you can take to stay safe while camping and hiking.

FIGURE 10.5

HIKING AND CAMPING SAFETY

These strategies will help prevent accidental injuries while hiking or camping. *Why do you think you should not cook inside a tent?*

- Wear appropriate clothing to protect yourself from exposure to the sun and insects.
- Use proper equipment.
- Never camp alone.
- Stay in legal campsites and on marked trails.
- Learn which plants in the area are poisonous.
- Be aware of insects and animals you may encounter.
- Boil or filter stream and pond water before drinking.
- Never cook inside a tent.
- Keep all campfires in a pit, and put them out thoroughly.

Reading Check

Summarizing This activity helps students process the information in a visual manner. Ask students to fill in a chart with information from the chapter. Create a chart on the board that synthesizes the information from their individual charts:

Who: hikers, campers, ice-skaters, and others
What: drowning prevention, water and boating safety, and so on
Where: woods, lakes, pools, ski slopes, etc.
When: camping, skiing, swimming, and so on
Why: safety
How: Use the "buddy system," apply sunscreen, drink water, dress appropriately, and so on. **INCL** *Special Learning Needs, Behavior Problems*

Winter Sports

Winter sports—such as
ice-skating, skiing, and snowboarding—
require the same attention to safety as other outdoor
activities. In addition, they require protection against snow and
cold. To stay warm, dress in several layers of clothing with a
windproof jacket as the outermost layer. Layered clothing
will trap warm air next to your body. Always wear a hat and
gloves. Complete your outfit with a ski mask or scarf to protect
your face.

Before starting a winter sport, check out your location.
Be sure that ice is solid before you skate on it. There may
be a "thin ice" sign or a red flag posted if the ice is too thin.
You should have a clear path before you go downhill skiing
or sledding. Ski only in approved, supervised areas.

If the weather is extremely cold, take extra measures to
prevent frostbite (the freezing of the skin) and hypothermia.
Gloves, boots, and extra socks help protect your hands and
feet. If hypothermia or frostbite occurs, treat it at once by
taking the person indoors. For hypothermia, cover the person
with a blanket. Thaw frostbitten skin by soaking in warm, not
hot, water for at least 30 minutes. Get medical help at a ski
lodge or from a doctor as soon as possible.

Winter sports require
appropriate clothing to
protect against snow and
cold temperatures.

Lesson 3

Discussing

Guide students in discussing winter sports that are popular locally and how those sports differ from warm-weather sports. Have them discuss where and how someone can learn each sport or practice the skills safely, which locations are good, and which locations should be avoided. Emphasize that taking the time for a lesson has great benefits: safety, injury prevention, and skill development. **L1**

Presenting

Have a group of interested volunteers prepare and present a demonstration of safe dressing for winter sports. The demonstration may be done with dolls, with drawings, or with classmates as models. Suggest that the volunteers also show safe winter clothing and other covering for infants and toddlers. **L2**
INCL *English Language Learners*

Comprehending

As a review of Lessons 1, 2, and 3, ask students to identify factors that affect their physical, emotional, and social health. Summarize student responses on the board.

INCLUSION STRATEGIES

Special Learning Needs, Behavior Problems, Different Learning Styles, Gifted To help students understand the concept of hiking and camping safety, have them form groups in which students of various reading and math abilities can work together to select hiking and camping equipment.

Provide several catalogs and/or newspaper ads for each group. Then have group members describe and discuss the equipment items, choose basic equipment for a hiking or camping outing, and calculate the cost of that equipment.

Comprehending

Discuss weather emergencies most likely to occur in your area. Have students state what they already know about safety procedures before, during, and after these weather emergencies. Ask students:

- What procedures does the school follow to be sure everyone is prepared?
- What precautions do you and other family members take at home? **L1**

HEALTH SKILLS ACTIVITY

PRACTICING HEALTHFUL BEHAVIORS

Guide students in reading and discussing the activity introduction. As a class, brainstorm a list of other supplies that could go in an emergency supplies kit. Write these on the board. Discuss with the class why it is important to develop a family emergency plan, and how students might go about developing such a plan with their families.

Then have students complete the On Your Own activity.

Note: This skill is introduced in Chapter 1 on page 9.

Weather Emergencies

Being prepared will reduce risks and help you stay safe during weather emergencies. With your family, develop a plan so you know what to do in the event of a weather emergency. Make sure that you understand this plan.

Floods

Floods, the most common of all natural disasters, can occur in all areas. During heavy rains, tune in to local radio or television stations for reports of rising water levels. Never walk or ride in a car through floodwater. You risk being swept away. Downed power lines also pose a danger. Floodwaters often pollute tap water; so you should drink bottled water. After the flood, clean and disinfect everything that came in contact with the floodwater. Discard all contaminated food. Wear rubber or latex gloves during the cleanup. Make sure the water supply is safe before drinking any.

HEALTH SKILLS ACTIVITY

PRACTICING HEALTHFUL BEHAVIORS

Preparing an Emergency Supplies Kit

Being prepared for emergencies includes knowing where to find emergency supplies when you need them. Keep these supplies in a kit in case of emergencies:

- A flashlight and a battery-powered radio, both with extra batteries
- A first-aid kit
- Ready-to-eat and canned foods, and a can opener
- Gallon jugs of water (one gallon of water per person per day)
- Blankets
- A charged cell phone

If you must leave your home because of an emergency, bring your kit with you. Also take walking shoes, money, and any other necessary supplies, such as prescription medicines.

ON YOUR OWN
Create your own emergency supplies kit. Include the items listed above. Tell your parents or guardians about the kit, and talk with them about developing a family emergency plan. The plan should detail where to go during an emergency, where to meet if family members get separated, and whom to contact for help.

270 CHAPTER 10: SAFETY AND THE ENVIRONMENT

INCLUSION STRATEGIES

Special Learning Needs, Behavior Problems, English Language Learners Students may need assistance distinguishing the types of weather emergencies discussed in this lesson. Provide photographs to help them identify each. You may find good photos on weather Web sites or in an online encyclopedia.

You could also focus on the types of weather emergencies common in their countries of origin if they were not born in the United States. Then encourage students to share with the rest of the class any experiences they may have had with each type of weather emergency.

Earthquakes

An **earthquake** is *the shaking of the ground as rock below the surface moves.* If you are inside when this natural disaster strikes, stay there. Brace yourself in a doorway or crawl under a piece of sturdy furniture. Move away from objects that could fall or shatter. If you are outside during an earthquake, stand in the open. Stay away from buildings, trees, and power lines. Afterward, report any odor of gas that might indicate a leak.

Hurricanes and Tornadoes

A **hurricane** (HER·uh·kayn) is *a strong tropical windstorm with driving rain.* If a hurricane is likely in your area, board up windows, and bring in outdoor objects. Stay tuned to weather reports, and be prepared to leave the area, if necessary.

A **tornado** (tor·NAY·doh) is *a whirling, funnel-shaped windstorm that drops from the sky to the ground.* If a tornado warning is issued in your area, you should go to a storm cellar or basement. If you can't do that, go to a hallway, bathroom, or other inside area without windows. Don't stay in cars or mobile homes. If you are outdoors, try to find a ditch to lie in and cover yourself with a blanket or clothing.

Although natural disasters can strike with little warning, you can reduce your chances of injury by being prepared. *How do media and technology influence individual and community health during a weather emergency?*

Lesson 3 Review

Using complete sentences, answer the following questions on a sheet of paper.

Reviewing Terms and Facts
1. **Recall** What is the first rule of water safety?
2. **Vocabulary** What is *hypothermia?*
3. **Give Examples** List four strategies for the prevention of accidental injuries when hiking and camping.
4. **Distinguish** What is the difference between a hurricane and a tornado?

Thinking Critically
5. **Explain** What would you do if your "buddy" wanted to swim out farther than you thought you were able to swim safely?
6. **Apply** How would you protect yourself from frostbite if you wanted to go sledding with your friends?

Applying Health Skills
7. **Practicing Healthful Behaviors** Draw a layout of your home. On the sketch, indicate the best places to go for safety in the event of a tornado or an earthquake.

LESSON 3: SAFETY OUTDOORS **271**

Lesson 4

First Aid for Emergencies

❶ Focus

Lesson Objectives

Students will be able to

- define *first aid*.
- list the steps to take in an emergency.
- describe basic first-aid techniques for breathing emergencies, bleeding, choking, poisoning, and burns.

Health Skills
- Accessing Information, p. 277

Motivators

Quick Write

Ask students to identify one item that they would put in a home first-aid kit and to explain why the item is important.

Bellringer Activity

Ask students: What does first aid involve? Give students three or four minutes to write down their responses.

VOCABULARY

In pairs, have students prepare a set of game cards by writing each term on an index card and the definition of each term on another index card. Have partners lay out their game cards face down and use them to play a form of "Concentration," turning over pairs of cards and making a match each time they find a term on one card and its definition on another.

Quick Write

List three or four items you would put in a home first-aid kit, and explain why they are important.

LEARN ABOUT...

- strategies for responding to accidental and deliberate injuries.
- how you can help someone who is bleeding.
- what you can do for a person who is choking.
- what you can do to help someone who has been burned.

VOCABULARY
- first aid
- cardiopulmonary

First Aid for Emergencies

What Is First Aid?

Taking the right steps to help an injured person can prevent further injury or even death. **First aid** is *the care first given to an injured or ill person until regular medical care can be supplied.* Both accidental and deliberate injuries are cared for in the same way, but proper training is needed to give first aid. **Figure 10.6** shows the procedures to follow in an emergency.

FIGURE 10.6

WHAT TO DO IN AN EMERGENCY

In an emergency situation, follow the American Red Cross guidelines: CHECK-CALL-CARE.

1 **CHECK the scene and the victim.** To avoid further injury, move the victim only if he or she is in danger. However, do not put your own life at risk to help the victim.

2 **CALL for help.** In most areas, you can dial 911 for Emergency Medical Services (EMS). If possible, stay with the victim, and ask a passerby for help.

3 **CARE for the person until help arrives.** Use the first-aid steps discussed in this lesson to treat the victim's injuries.

Lesson 4 Resources

Teacher Classroom Resources

 Concept Map 46

 Enrichment Activity 39

 Lesson Plan 4

Lesson 4 Quiz

Reading Tutor Activity 39

 Reteaching Activity 40

 Transparency 47

Student Activities Workbook

 Chapter 10 Study Guide

 Applying Health Skills 39

Basic Techniques

Some injuries are life-threatening. For example, a victim's life is in danger if the person has stopped breathing, is bleeding severely, is choking, has swallowed poison, or has been severely burned. These victims often cannot wait for professional help to arrive. By learning a few basic techniques, you may be able to save a life.

If the victim's heart has stopped, medical professionals may perform **cardiopulmonary resuscitation (CPR)**. CPR is *a rescue measure that attempts to restore heartbeat and breathing.* Only people with special training should perform CPR.

Rescue Breathing

You can check for breathing by putting your ear and cheek close to the victim's nose and mouth. Listen and feel for air exhaled. Look to see whether the chest is rising and falling. If the victim is not breathing, call for help immediately. Then perform rescue breathing, *a substitute for normal breathing in which someone forces air into the victim's lungs.* **Figure 10.7** shows how to perform rescue breathing on an adult. The process is different for infants and younger children.

FIGURE 10.7

RESCUE BREATHING FOR ADULTS AND OLDER CHILDREN

When a victim is not breathing, immediately call 911. Then begin rescue breathing if the person has a pulse.

1 Point the victim's chin upward by gently lifting it up with your fingers and tilting the head back. The airway will now be open.

2 Pinch the victim's nostrils shut. Cover the victim's mouth with your own, forming a tight seal. Give two slow breaths each about two seconds long. Make sure the victim's chest rises during each breath.

3 Watch for the victim's chest to fall, and listen for air flowing from the lungs. If the victim begins breathing normally, stop. Otherwise, give one rescue breath every five seconds until help arrives.

LESSON 4: FIRST AID FOR EMERGENCIES **273**

② Teach

Developing Good Character

Citizenship

Emphasize to students that part of being a good citizen is being able to take care of one's fellow citizens in an emergency. Encourage students to learn CPR to protect the health of others.

VISUAL LEARNING

FIGURE 10.6 As students read about the first-aid steps in Figure 10.6, help them suggest several specific examples and identify how they would follow the steps in responding to a specific emergency situation. Examples: The victim has a deep knife cut and is at home, or the victim has fallen from a tree onto a sidewalk and cannot walk. **INCL** *Behavior Problems, Special Learning Needs, English Language Learners*

VISUAL LEARNING

FIGURE 10.7 Have students look at the pictures as volunteers read about the steps in rescue breathing. Ask students to explain each step in their own words. Explain that the American Heart Association recommends that people receive professional training before actually performing this procedure. **INCL** *Behavior Problems, Special Learning Needs, English Language Learners*

Developing Good Character

Citizenship

You have the power to save lives. Both the American Red Cross and the American Heart Association offer classes in CPR training. Contact your local chapter to find out how you can learn to perform CPR properly in emergency situations.

 Beyond the Classroom

Community Encourage students to find out where and when first-aid courses are being offered locally. Be sure students gather the following information on each class or program: who is teaching it, when and where it is being offered, what specific topics will be covered, how much it costs, when and where sign-ups are held, and a phone number people can call to get further details. Then have students work in groups to make and distribute flyers advertising the first-aid courses. As an alternate activity, contact the American Red Cross for booklets on their courses. Post the information and schedules so that students can sign up together.

Lesson 4

Discussing

Explain to students that medical professionals wear masks and gloves when performing rescue breathing. However, it may be necessary to do this without protection in an emergency. **L1**

Comprehending

Ask partners to work together to review the steps in controlling bleeding. Provide a simple outline for each pair of students. Then have the partners take turns pointing to an area of the body where a bleeding wound might occur. Have the other partner explain what he or she would do to control the bleeding while pointing to the body outline indicating where pressure should be applied. **L2**

VISUAL LEARNING

FIGURE 10.8 Guide students in identifying the pressure points in Figure 10.8. Have students speculate about why those body locations are logical pressure points. How can applying pressure there help control bleeding? **INCL** *Behavior Problems, Special Learning Needs, English Language Learners*

Discussing

Help students discuss the dangers of choking. Ask them to list the kinds of things people are most likely to choke on. Which age groups seem at special risk for choking? Why? Have students explain why it is important to act quickly when someone is choking. **L1**

FIGURE 10.8

LOCATION OF PRESSURE POINTS

The dots in this illustration are pressure points. Applying pressure to the nearest pressure point can help stop the flow of blood to a wounded area.

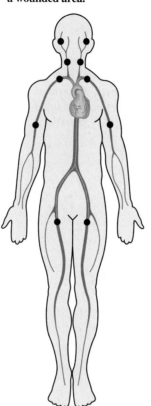

Bleeding

Nosebleeds are fairly common. Sitting upright and pinching your nostrils with your thumb and forefinger for ten minutes will usually stop a nosebleed.

A much more serious problem is severe bleeding because of injury. Treating bleeding is difficult because it can be dangerous to touch another person's blood. Take precautions by treating all blood as if it contained pathogens. Wear gloves if possible, and always wash your hands afterward. You can use the following first-aid techniques for bleeding:

- Lay the victim down, and try to elevate his or her legs to reduce the risk of fainting. If possible, carefully raise the wounded body part above the victim's heart. This technique slows the blood coming from the heart to the wound. Use it only if the body part has no broken bones.
- Apply direct, steady pressure to the wound. Press down firmly on the wound with a clean cloth. If necessary, add more cloth without removing the first cloth.
- At the same time, apply pressure to the main artery supplying blood to the wound. **Figure 10.8** shows several pressure points that can be used to stop bleeding. Push on the pressure point until you feel the bone, and hold the pressure.
- After the bleeding has stopped, cover the wound with a clean cloth to prevent infection. If the victim needs professional medical treatment, leave the bandages in place, and get him or her to the emergency room quickly.

Choking

Choking is *a condition that occurs when a person's airway becomes blocked.* A choking victim can die in minutes because air cannot get to the lungs. The universal sign for choking—grabbing the throat between the thumb and forefinger—helps you recognize a choking victim. Victims may also gasp for breath or be unable to speak. Their faces may turn red, then bluish.

If an infant is choking, position the victim on his or her abdomen along your forearm, bracing your arm against your thigh. Support the infant's head with your hand, and point the head down. Then give up to five blows with the heel of your hand between the victim's shoulder blades. Sweep your finger through the victim's mouth, and remove the dislodged object. If the object is still stuck, turn the victim on his or her back. Support the victim's shoulders and neck with one hand. With

274 CHAPTER 10: SAFETY AND THE ENVIRONMENT

PROMOTING COORDINATED SCHOOL HEALTH

Evaluating Progress Assessing the committee's progress will help identify what works, what has been successfully changed, and how the community is instrumental in the process of change. Assessment might include ongoing evaluation of each task on the action plan, a comparison of the program against a set of voluntary guidelines, review of the health statistics in the community, a comparison with statewide health objectives, or asking committee members to retake the survey that originally led to the list of prioritized problems. In addition to the program outcomes, the committee process should also be evaluated. For more information, consult *Planning a Coordinated School Health Program* in the TCR.

the other, place two fingers in the middle of the child's breastbone, and press quickly up to five times. Alternate five back blows and five chest thrusts until the object is dislodged. For more detailed instructions on helping a choking infant, consult a first-aid manual.

To help an adult or older child, ask, "Are you choking?" If the victim nods or does not respond, you can help by using **abdominal thrusts.** Apply *quick upward pulls into the diaphragm to force out the object blocking the airway.* **Figure 10.9** illustrates this technique.

If you are choking and no one is there to help you, make a fist and thrust it quickly into your upper abdomen. This will force out the object blocking your airway. You can also try shoving your abdomen against the back or arm of a chair.

FIGURE 10.9

ABDOMINAL THRUSTS

Use these steps to help a victim who is choking. If the person can talk or cough or you can hear breathing, don't do anything. *Why might it be dangerous to perform abdominal thrusts on a person who is not choking?*

1 Stand behind the victim. Wrap your arms around his or her waist, and bend victim slightly forward. Place your fist slightly above the person's navel.

2 Hold your fist with your other hand, and press it hard into the abdomen with an upward thrust. Repeat until the object is coughed up.

✓ Reading Check
Make connections. Summarize the different ways to apply pressure when helping a bleeding or choking victim.

Lesson 4

Comprehending

Have students demonstrate the universal sign for choking and tell why it is important to understand this sign. Ask them to consider how they would respond to a person who used this sign for help and then announced, "Just kidding." Why? **L1**

Researching

Explain to students that schools, hospitals, and local health centers offer courses in first aid and CPR. This training qualifies people to provide first aid in an emergency. Have interested students check with your school nurse, family doctor, or local hospital to find out about courses available in your area. **L2**

VISUAL LEARNING

FIGURE 10.9 Have students meet in groups to describe the pictures in Figure 10.9 and to read and discuss the instructions for using abdominal thrusts. Clarify that the thrusts should be directed just above the navel. Then ask the caption question; students should recognize that performing abdominal thrusts on a person who is not choking could injure that person's abdomen or inhibit her or his breathing. **INCL** *Behavior Problems, Special Learning Needs, English Language Learners*

✓ Reading Check

Summarizing Writing a concise summary of complex information will help students retain main ideas and details. Ask students to write a paragraph that reviews the different ways pressure is used as first aid for bleeding and choking victims. Suggest that they start with a topic sentence stating the essential difference in the techniques (e.g., *Direct, steady pressure is used to help bleeding victims; repeated brief blows are used with choking victims*). Then have them write a sentence or two about each technique, summarizing the key details and differences in the types of pressure used.

Discussing

Guide students in discussing symbols and words that indicate poisonous materials. Have students explain why these symbols and words are important and discuss which household members should be responsible for noticing them and responding to them. **L1**

Comprehending

Have students work in small groups or pairs to demonstrate their understanding of basic first-aid procedures for the emergencies covered in this lesson. **L2**

VISUAL LEARNING

FIGURE 10.10 Read the figure caption, and have students answer the question. Then have students form groups, and provide a set of note cards for each group. Each note card should present a short description of a burn without identifying its type. Have group members take turns drawing a card, identifying the degree of burn, and describing the kind of first aid that should be provided. **INCL** *Behavior Problems, Special Learning Needs, English Language Learners*

Poisoning

If you think someone has swallowed poison, seek professional help. Call either 911; your doctor; or a **poison control center**, *a place that helps people deal with poisons.* The inside cover of your telephone book usually gives the number of the center. Follow the directions you receive.

Keep the person warm and breathing while you wait for an ambulance. Remove extra traces of poison from around the victim's mouth with a damp, clean cloth wrapped around your finger. Be sure to save the container of poison. Show it to the ambulance team. Tell them all you know about what happened.

Burns

Burns are identified by how much they damage the skin. Use **Figure 10.10** to help you identify the three types of burns. Note the differences in first-aid treatment.

FIGURE 10.10

TYPES OF BURNS

Different kinds of burns require different treatments. *How would you treat a first-degree burn?*

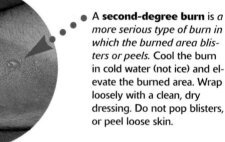

A **first-degree burn** is *a burn in which only the outer part of the skin is burned and turns red.* Cool the burned area with cold water (not ice) for at least 15 minutes, and wrap it loosely in a clean, dry dressing.

A **third-degree burn** is *a very serious burn in which deeper layers of skin and nerve endings are damaged.* Perform rescue breathing, if necessary. Cool the burn with cold water or by applying a wet cloth. Do not apply ice or ointments.

A **second-degree burn** is *a more serious type of burn in which the burned area blisters or peels.* Cool the burn in cold water (not ice) and elevate the burned area. Wrap loosely with a clean, dry dressing. Do not pop blisters, or peel loose skin.

276 CHAPTER 10: SAFETY AND THE ENVIRONMENT

MORE ABOUT...

Poisons When people think of poisoning, they most often think of a poisonous substance being swallowed. However, there are three other ways in which poisons can enter the body: poisons can be inhaled, absorbed, and injected. Poisons that can be inhaled include fumes from glues and paints. Poisons that are absorbed enter the body through the skin. Examples are weed killers and fertilizers. Injected poisons come from certain animal and insect bites and from insect stings.

ACCESSING INFORMATION

Minor Injury Lookout

Minor unintentional injuries can occur in your own home or on outings. Some can be treated at home. Here are some tips for treating minor injuries.

- **Sprains.** A sprained joint, such as a wrist or ankle, is one that has been stretched or twisted or has torn ligaments. Treatment includes the R.I.C.E. procedure: Rest, Ice, Compression, and Elevation.
- **Bites and Stings.** These injuries can cause bumps and itching on the skin. The bites of some snakes, spiders, scorpions, and flying insects, however, can affect the entire body. For these, get immediate professional help.

- **Poisonous Plants.** Plants such as poison ivy, poison oak, and poison sumac can cause redness, itching, and swelling if your skin comes in contact with them. You can treat these symptoms with soap and water, rubbing alcohol, special creams, and calamine lotion. Severe cases require a doctor's care.

WITH A GROUP
Use the Internet and library resources to research one of these types of injuries further. Suggestions include recognizing poisonous plants or dangerous snakes found in your area. Make an illustrated poster, and present it to the class.

Lesson 4 Review

Using complete sentences, answer the following questions on a sheet of paper.

Reviewing Terms and Facts

1. **Vocabulary** Define the term *first aid*. Use it in an original sentence.
2. **List** Name the three basic first-aid procedures to follow when responding to accidental or deliberate injuries.
3. **Recall** How can you check to make sure a victim is breathing?
4. **Identify** Briefly describe the techniques to control severe bleeding.
5. **Distinguish** What is the difference between a first-degree burn, a second-degree burn, and a third-degree burn?

Thinking Critically

6. **Compare and Contrast** How is the method used to help someone else who is choking similar to and different from the method used to help yourself if you are choking?
7. **Analyze** Why do you think it is important to save the container if someone has swallowed poison?

Applying Health Skills

8. **Advocacy** Work with a partner to create a first-aid handbook for baby-sitters. In the handbook, include first-aid procedures to handle the following emergencies: choking, bleeding, and swallowing poisons. Also, include local emergency phone numbers. Share your handbook with the class.

LESSON 4: FIRST AID FOR EMERGENCIES 277

Lesson 4 Review

1. The care first given to an injured or ill person until regular medical care can be supplied. Sentences will vary.
2. See Figure 10.6 on page 272.
3. See Rescue Breathing on page 273.
4. See Bleeding on page 274.
5. See Figure 10.10 on page 276.
6. When helping someone else who is choking, you wrap your arms around the victim's

waist. If you are helping yourself, you place your fist above your own navel. In both cases, you use one hand to thrust the fist quickly into the upper abdomen.

7. If professionals can identify the swallowed poison, it will help them determine the type of treatment needed.

Lesson 4

HEALTH SKILLS ACTIVITY

ACCESSING INFORMATION

Have students work as a class to read about and discuss the explanations in Minor Injury Lookout. Then have students form small cooperative groups in which to complete the research-and-presentation assignment. Check with groups to be sure all three types of injuries will be covered. If appropriate, set aside some class time for Internet and/or library research. Finally, have each group present its poster to the rest of the class.

Note: This skill is introduced in Chapter 1 on page 9.

3 Assess

Evaluating
 Assign the Lesson 4 Review; then assign the Lesson 4 Quiz in the TCR.

Reteaching
Assign Concept Map 46 or Reteaching Activity 40 in the TCR.

Enrichment
Assign Enrichment Activity 39 in the TCR.

4 Close

Go around the room asking each student to identify a type of emergency; have the next student demonstrate an understanding of the first-aid response to that emergency.

Lesson 5

Protecting Your Environment

① Focus

Lesson Objectives

Students will be able to

- explain what causes air, water, and land pollution.
- describe ways people can help protect the air, water, and land from pollution.
- explain the problems that garbage causes and list ways to reduce waste, reuse items, and recycle.

Motivators

Quick Write
Collect the students' responses to the Quick Write. Select several essays to read to the class.

Bellringer Activity
Ask: What comes to mind when you hear the word *environment*? Give students a few minutes to jot down the words and phrases that come to mind.

VOCABULARY
Ask volunteers to read aloud and share what they already understand about the vocabulary terms. Then have students check the definitions in the Glossary. Ask students to prepare a set of study cards, with a vocabulary term on one side of an index card and its formal definition on the other side.

Protecting Your Environment

Quick Write
Your school is part of your environment. How can you assume responsibility to help take care of the school?

LEARN ABOUT...

- the causes of air, water, and land pollution.
- what happens to garbage after it is thrown away.
- what you can do to protect the environment.

VOCABULARY

- environment
- pollution
- fossil fuel
- ozone
- smog
- acid rain
- recycling
- conservation
- biodegradable

Our Environment

Look around you. Everything you see, plus many other things you cannot see (such as the air), are part of your **environment** (en·VY·ruhn·ment). In fact, *you and all living and nonliving things around you* make up the environment. What types of things do you see in the environment? You see living things like people, plants, and animals. You see rivers, hills, and valleys. You also see schools, homes, and other things made by people.

Pollution

In order for you to remain healthy, you need to live in a healthy environment. Unfortunately, the way people live can damage the environment. **Pollution** (puh·LOO·shuhn) is *the changing of the air, water, and land from clean and safe to dirty and unsafe.* Pollution affects the air you breathe, the water you drink, and the land you live on.

People who care about nature want to protect it from pollution. *Describe a natural area you like to visit.*

Lesson 5 Resources

Teacher Classroom Resources

 Concept Maps 47 & 48
 Cross-Curriculum Activity 20
 Decision-Making Activity 20
 Enrichment Activity 40
 Health Lab 10
 Lesson Plan 5
Lesson 5 Quiz

 Reading Tutor Activity 40
 Reteaching Activity 41
 Transparency 48

Student Activities Workbook

Chapter 10 Study Guide
Applying Health Skills 40
Health Inventory

Air Pollution

Some natural events, such as erupting volcanoes, release gases that pollute the air. Other air pollution is caused by humans. Humans damage the air mostly by burning fossil (FAH·suhl) fuels. These are *the coal, oil, and natural gas used to power the engines of motor vehicles and factories.*

Air pollution can cause your eyes to water, give you headaches, and make you dizzy or tired. It can also damage your lungs, causing problems that make it difficult to breathe. Air pollution is responsible for a variety of environmental problems.

- Ozone (OH·zohn) is *a special form of oxygen.* A layer of ozone in the upper atmosphere helps to protect the earth from the sun's harmful rays. Certain chemicals in air pollution have begun to damage this protective layer.
- Although the ozone high above the earth protects people, ozone at ground level can be very harmful. It is a major part of smog, *a yellow-brown haze that forms when sunlight reacts with impurities in car exhaust.* Over long periods, breathing smog can cause serious damage to your lungs.
- Acid rain is *rainfall that contains air pollution from the burning of fossil fuels.* Over time, it can destroy large forests, wildlife, and plant life.

Water Pollution

All humans, animals, and plants need water to survive. Water can become polluted in many ways. For example, chemicals dumped in rivers and streams can damage the water supply. Large oil spills foul beaches and harm wildlife. Fertilizers used in farm fields can seep into the water supply. Food, human waste, detergents, and other products washed down drains end up in rivers and oceans.

Reading Check
Think about what these words have to do with safety and the environment: pollution, fossil fuel, smog, acid rain, recycling, conservation. Find other words that fit with these. Then group the words into different categories.

Local news programs will often alert residents on days when smog reaches harmful levels. *Why should you limit physical activity on smoggy days?*

LESSON 5: PROTECTING YOUR ENVIRONMENT **279**

---

② Teach

Discussing

Ask students to share their own experiences with air pollution. Have them tell whether they notice air pollution where they live and, if so, how it affects them. Ask students whether they have ever experienced air pollution in other parts of the country and, if so, to describe what it looked like and how it made them feel. **L1**

Applying Knowledge

Bring in a few bus and/or train schedules to lead students in a discussion of the public transportation available in the community. Have them look into where and when it is available and how much it costs. Ask students to explore ways to encourage more people to use the available buses, trains, and/or subways. Students should be able to explain how using public transportation can help reduce pollution. **L1**

Researching

Ask interested students to read about the alternatives to fossil fuels. Encourage them to learn about other energy sources and what benefits and problems are associated with each at this point. **L3**

Reading Check

List Group Label This activity challenges students to group words together in meaningful ways to better understand them. Discuss with students that the words in the group are all characteristics of the environment. Ask them to add as many other words or phrases to the list as possible. Challenge them to defend their choices. Accept all reasonable responses. A possible word is *biodegradable.* Next, ask students to group the terms as to whether they refer to positive effects or negative effects on the environment. For example, *recycling, conservation,* and *biodegradable* are all related to positive effects on the *environment.*

Lesson 5

Have students explore Web Links for this chapter and then complete the activity.

Cross-Curriculum Activity

SOCIAL STUDIES Have students find and bring to class news stories about recent oil spills or other pollution-causing events. **L2**

VISUAL LEARNING

FIGURE 10.11 Ask volunteers to describe the three pictures and then to read aloud the explanations of the three types of waste disposal. Guide students in discussing the need for these kinds of waste disposal and the special problems associated with each. **INCL** *Behavior Problems, Special Learning Needs, English Language Learners*

Topic: Protecting the environment

For a link to more information on what you can do to protect the environment, go to health.glencoe.com.

Activity: Using the information provided at this link, create a flyer that lists ways to protect the environment.

Water polluted in these ways threatens the life and health of plants and animals alike. People can become sick when they drink polluted water or eat fish that have absorbed these wastes and chemicals. In some parts of the world, unclean water spreads deadly diseases such as cholera (KAH·luh·ruh) and typhoid. These illnesses threaten whole communities.

Land Pollution

As a good citizen, you do your part to pick up after yourself and properly dispose of wastes. Even properly discarded wastes, however, have to go somewhere (see **Figure 10.11**). Solid wastes often go to landfills. Harmful substances from landfills can leak into the soil and the water supply. Some communities burn their trash. Burning trash can pollute the air, however; so many communities do not allow it.

Some types of waste present special problems. Hazardous wastes can cause serious illnesses and environmental damage. They include plastics, paints, acids, and chemicals used to kill insects. Nuclear wastes, the chemicals left over from nuclear power plants and factories, can be very dangerous. They sometimes take thousands or even millions of years to break down naturally.

FIGURE 10.11

HOW WE DISPOSE OF WASTE

Solid wastes are usually buried in landfills, burned in incinerators, or stored in special locations designated for hazardous materials.

Landfill. Communities build landfills to bury their wastes. Special linings are designed to prevent pollution from leaking into water under the site.

Incineration. This involves burning waste at high temperatures in a special kind of furnace. Burning waste reduces the volume of trash. It can also produce energy, reducing the need for fossil fuels. However, it can cause air pollution, and the ashes are dangerous.

Hazardous Waste Storage. Hazardous wastes are often stored in containers, tanks, or buildings. Later, they are treated and placed in special landfills.

INCLUSION STRATEGIES

Special Learning Needs, Behavior Problems, Gifted
Ask students to research scientific theories and opinions about a "hole" in the ozone layer. When was this idea first introduced? How have theories about the ozone layer changed in recent years? How dangerous is the thinning of the ozone layer?

How does it affect the occurrence of skin cancer? After they have examined several points of view, have students write essays presenting their own ideas about the ozone layer. Remind students to present specific examples and facts to support their opinions.

What You Can Do

You can do your part to dispose of trash by reducing the amount you create. The best way to do that is by reusing as many items as possible. Also, recycle whatever you can. **Recycling** means *recovering and changing items so they can be used for other purposes.*

Protecting the Air

Exhaust from motor vehicles is a major source of air pollution. Driving less, therefore, is one way to help clean up the air. You and your family might use buses, trains, or subways instead of driving. You can also walk, take your bicycle, or carpool to cut the number of cars on the road.

Another way to help is by conserving energy. **Conservation** is *the saving of resources.* If we burn less fossil fuel for energy, we create less air pollution. Your family can conserve energy by turning off electric lights and appliances when they are not in use. You can also seal off leaks around windows and doors that can let heat escape. Keep windows closed while the heat or air conditioning is on. Towel dry or air dry dishes instead of heat drying them in a dishwasher.

Protecting the Water

Do you turn the water off while you brush your teeth? If you do, you are helping to protect our water supply by using less of it. You can also save water by taking shorter showers and repairing leaky faucets.

To keep our water clean, you and your friends can remove litter from rivers and lakes. Also, try to use cleaning supplies that are **biodegradable** (by·oh·di·GRAY·duh·buhl) or *able to break down naturally without causing pollution.* Any detergents and cleaning supplies you dump down the drain end up in our rivers, lakes, and oceans.

You can help keep the air and all the other parts of our environment clean and safe. *How are these teens helping to prevent air pollution?*

Demonstrating

Ask a group of volunteers to prepare and give a presentation showing how teens can reduce waste when they pack school lunches. Volunteers might present one lunch in which all the food wrapping and the lunch container are thrown away and another lunch in which all packaging can be reused. **L2**
INCL *English Language Learners*

Listing Examples

Have each student write a list of at least eight specific things he or she can do to help protect our air and water supply. **L1**

Cross-Curriculum Activity

MATH Present the following information to students: A standard showerhead emits about 4.5 gallons of water each minute. A low-flow showerhead emits about 2.5 gallons of water each minute. Then ask: If you take a 5-minute shower every day, how many gallons of water can you save in a week by installing a low-flow showerhead? (*4.5 − 2.5 = 2 gallons saved per minute; 2 × 5 = 10 gallons saved per shower; 10 × 7 = 70 gallons saved per week*) **L1**

COOPERATIVE LEARNING ACTIVITY

School or Community Cleanup Allow students to form small groups and discuss areas of the school or community that need cleaning up. Have students work together to list several ideas. Each group should have a "recorder" to write the ideas and answers generated; a "taskmaster" to keep the group on task; and a "spokesperson" to report to the class what the group has decided.

Students may suggest other roles that would help them improve their working relationships. Then have them select one particular area. Each group will plan and carry out a clean-up project for their area. You may want to encourage students to include family members, friends, and other community members in their projects.

Applying Knowledge

Ask a small group of students to set up a classroom display of grocery items in various kinds and sizes of packaging. Then have all students participate in evaluating which items fit best into a program of reducing consumption of materials. **L2**

Hands-On Health

ARE YOU EARTH-FRIENDLY?

Time: 20 minutes

TEACHING THE ACTIVITY

- Read the activity instructions and the inventory aloud with students. Encourage them to ask questions and/or make comments about specific inventory items.
- Have students complete the inventory independently.
- Have students meet with partners to discuss their responses.

ASSESSMENT

Have students write short paragraphs explaining how they can improve their ratings.

Reducing Waste

If you want to cut down on the amount of trash you create, there are three basic steps you can take: reduce, reuse, and recycle.

- **Reduce.** Buy products that have less packaging to throw away. Also, consider whether you need an item at all. Maybe something you already have would do just as well.
- **Reuse.** Use items more than once. For example, a glass can replace several paper cups. You can also reuse items in new ways such as turning a glass bottle into a vase.
- **Recycle.** Everyday materials such as glass, paper, plastic, and aluminum can be used to manufacture new items.

To help make recycling successful, people must buy recycled products. These products are often labeled with the recycling symbol shown in **Figure 10.12**. By buying these goods, you "complete the cycle."

Hands-On Health

ARE YOU EARTH-FRIENDLY?

How do you rate as a friend of the environment? Take this conservation inventory to find out.

WHAT YOU WILL NEED
- pencil or pen
- paper

WHAT YOU WILL DO
1. Write the letters a. through j. on your paper.
2. Write *yes* or *no* for each statement:
   a. I take quick showers.
   b. I turn off lights and appliances that are not in use.
   c. I close windows at night to keep cold air out.
   d. I don't let water run when I'm brushing my teeth.
   e. I recycle products whenever possible.
   f. I bring my own bags to the store.
   g. I find new ways to use old items.
   h. I put litter in trash containers.
   i. I encourage my family to carpool.
   j. I walk or ride my bicycle whenever possible instead of asking for a ride.

IN CONCLUSION
Give yourself 1 point for each yes answer. Add up your score to see how you rate.
3 or fewer: Energy Eater
4 to 7: Average Earth Friend
8 or more: Conservation Star
List ways you can improve your rating.

Beyond the Classroom

Home Encourage students to share what they have learned about conserving resources with other family members. Have students identify what the family is already doing at home, on the road, at school, and in the workplace to save energy. For example, are they taking shorter showers, reusing old items, or walking instead of driving? What else are family members willing to do? Ask students to work with other family members in making action plans to show their commitment to saving resources and to protecting the planet.

FIGURE 10.12

REDUCE, REUSE, RECYCLE

The recycling symbol is made up of three arrows. It reminds you that one item can be used many times. Look for the recycling symbol on products you buy.

Reduce
Buy items that can be reused, refilled, or recycled. Avoid products with excess packaging. Use fewer disposable items. Choose biodegradable products whenever possible. Buy in large quantities to save on packaging.

Recycle
Learn where you can recycle different materials such as aluminum, glass, plastic, paper, batteries, motor oil, and yard waste. Help start a recycling program in your community. Take items to recycling centers. Complete the cycle by buying products made of recycled materials.

Reuse
Reuse grocery bags when you go shopping. Use empty cans for storage. Save old rags to use for cleaning. Repair broken items instead of buying new ones. Use your imagination to find new uses for items.

Lesson 5 Review

Using complete sentences, answer the following questions on a sheet of paper.

Reviewing Terms and Facts

1. **Describe** Which of the following are harmful to the environment: pollution, ozone layer, smog, acid rain, conservation?
2. **Recall** In what three ways do communities dispose of solid waste materials?
3. **Vocabulary** What are *biodegradable* products? Use this term in a statement about the environment.

Thinking Critically

4. **Compare and Contrast** Describe the similarities and differences between reducing, reusing, and recycling.
5. **Invent** Think about the kind of container your milk comes in. How could you reuse the container?

Applying Health Skills

6. **Advocacy** Research a local environmental health issue and community efforts to deal with this issue. Write a brief paragraph explaining how you could participate in this community effort.

VISUAL LEARNING

FIGURE 10.12 Divide the class into three groups, and assign each group one of the three arrows from the symbol: reduce, reuse, recycle. Have the members of each group read their assigned section of Figure 10.12, discuss its importance and practice, and then present the information to the rest of the class. **INCL** *Behavior Problems, Special Learning Needs, English Language Learners*

③ Assess

Evaluating
Assign the Lesson 5 Review; then assign the Lesson 5 Quiz in the TCR.

Reteaching
Assign Concept Maps 47 & 48 or Reteaching Activity 41 in the TCR.

Enrichment
• Assign Enrichment Activity 40 in the TCR.
• Have students identify special benefits of composting.

④ Close

Have students state what they can do to preserve and protect the environment.

Lesson 5 Review

1. Pollution, smog, and acid rain. Ozone at ground level can be harmful.
2. Landfills, burning, use storage containers for hazardous wastes.
3. Products that can break down naturally without causing pollution. Statements will vary.
4. Possible answer: Reducing wastes is different from the other two because it cuts down on waste by not creating it. Reusing and recycling both extend the life of a product or material used to make it. Reuse, however, means finding further ways to use a product in its original form while recycling involves reprocessing the material in a product to make new and different products.
5. Accept responses that are consistent with the concepts in Lesson 5.

Play Smart!

① Focus

Objectives

Students will be able to

- understand the prevalence of sports-related injuries.
- describe strategies to avoid these types of injuries.
- create their own personalized check-list for preventing sports injuries.

Motivator

Bellringer

Read students the following case study:

Sam is a high-school junior who spends his summer relaxing by the pool and eating empty-calorie foods. In the fall, he decides to try out for the football team. On the first day of practice, the weather is hot and humid, with temperatures in the 90s. Sam has a big lunch, puts on his heavy pads and helmet, and hits the field determined to prove himself to the coach.

Ask students, "What is a likely outcome of this case study?" Write their responses on the board.

② Teach

Cross-Curriculum Activity

LANGUAGE ARTS As a class, brainstorm phrases used in everyday language that are derived from athletics. (Examples may include "No pain, no gain." and "Just do it.") What do these phrases tell us about the culture of athletics in our society? Is injury prevention a focus of any of these words or phrases? Why or why not? Is injury prevention seen as incompatible with a strong athletic performance?

Injuries sideline millions of kids. Learn how to stay healthy and in the game.

PLAY

Point guard Lizzie Singer was ready to dominate the court. Her team was playing against its biggest rival, and Lizzie was pumped. But seven seconds into the game, Lizzie, 14, was limping off the court with an ankle injury. "It was bad," says Lizzie. "I sat out for the rest of the game."

Lizzie is just one of more than 30 million young people in the United States who play competitive sports. That's up from about 25 million in 1992. As the number of kid athletes rises, so does the number of sports injuries.

In 2002, more than 3.5 million young people suffered an injury related to sports or recreation, says Angela Mickalide, program director of the National SAFE KIDS Campaign in Washington, D.C. The worst offenders: basketball, football, and soccer. More than 217,000 young basketball players were treated in hospital emergency rooms in 2000.

Pain, No Gain

The good news, says Mickalide, is that "nearly half of all kids' organized-sports-related injuries can be prevented." Experts agree that there's plenty a kid can do to stay healthy and in the game.

First tip: Follow the rules. According to a poll conducted by the American Academy of Orthopedic Surgeons, 80 percent of uninjured kids know safety guidelines and use safety equipment all or most of the time.

It also helps to shape up before the season starts and to remember that even competitive sports are supposed to be fun (see "Tips from a Pro"). Michelle Klein is head of the National Youth Sports Safety Foundation in Boston, Massachusetts. Her group works with coaches, parents, and athletes to reduce kids' sports injuries. Klein cautions athletes, "Don't be afraid to say something if you get hurt. Pain means something is wrong."

Stay in shape but know your body's limits.

Health Literacy

Sports Safety The experts quoted on this page belong to organizations designed to reduce young people's sports-related injuries. Tell students that they will be doing an online search of such organizations. Working in pairs, students will research one organization and present their findings to the class. A few examples are

- National Safe Kids Campaign (www.safekids.org).
- National Youth Sports Safety Foundation (www.nyssf.org).
- American College of Sports Medicine (www.acsm.org).
- President's Council on Physical Fitness (www.fitness.gov).

SMART!

TIPS FROM A PRO

Want to jump higher, run faster, throw harder, and stay healthy? Here are some tips from Dr. Jordan D. Metzl, director of the Sports Medicine Institute for Young Athletes in New York City.

PRESEASON
Start getting in shape five to six weeks before the season starts. Try doing something new: For example, if you're a skater, play some basketball; if you're a football player, hit the pool. Choose activities that will exercise your heart and lungs. Do them for 30 to 40 minutes, four to five times a week.

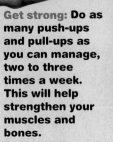

Get strong: Do as many push-ups and pull-ups as you can manage, two to three times a week. This will help strengthen your muscles and bones.

DURING THE SEASON
Warm up before play and cool down afterward. Stretch your muscles and practice with your team. Always wear the proper gear and make sure it fits correctly. Wear a mouth guard for all contact sports.

ANYTIME
Don't overdo it! Too much exercise can cause an overuse injury. Listen to your body: Tell a parent and see a doctor when activity worsens pain. Have fun: Sports should be about fun, not only about winning. Try to keep a healthy perspective. ◢

TIME TO THINK...

About Preventing Sports Injuries
Use the information from the "Tips from a Pro" box to create a personalized checklist for preventing sports injuries. Your checklist should contain three different sections: Preseason, During the Season, and Anytime. How can this checklist help you the next time you join a sports team or want to get in shape?

TIME HEALTH: PLAY SMART! **285**

---

❸ Apply

Time to Think
Before students create their personalized checklist, review "Tips from a Pro" as a class. Ask, "Are there other important ways to avoid sports injuries that are not included in this list?" (Answers may include: dress appropriately for the weather, drink plenty of water, and so on.) Advise students to include these new strategies in their checklist.

VISUAL LEARNING
Ask students to analyze the photographs on this page. Which activity is most likely to result in a sports injury? Are there things these athletes could do to decrease their risk of injury? (For instance, wear a mouth guard or safety glasses).

MORE ABOUT...

Overuse Injuries Tell students that *overuse injuries* occur when a tissue is damaged through repetitive motions with no period of rest and recovery. For instance, baseball pitchers frequently suffer overuse injuries in their throwing arm. To understand why overuse injuries have increased among young athletes, discuss the changing nature of children's athletics. How are youth sports different than they were thirty years ago? (*More competitive, athletes specialize at a young age, and so on.*) How can young athletes, their parents, and coaches decrease the risk of overuse injuries? (*Proper conditioning, gradual training progression, appropriate equipment, good technique, correct playing surface, adequate time to rest, and so on.*)

285

ADVOCACY

Objective

After completing the lesson, students will be able to advocate for reuse in creative ways.

Time: two 35-minute periods

Materials: paper, pencil or pen, poster board, drawing paper, markers, newspapers or magazines, glue or tape

Teacher Classroom Resources

📁 Building Health Skills Activities

- Transparency Master 10, "Advocacy"

- Reproducible Master 10, "Reuse to Reduce Waste"

---

1. Model

- Direct students to read about Amy. Ask volunteers to list the different ways that Amy and her family reused items instead of discarding them.

- Lead a class discussion about the importance of reuse in protecting the environment.

BUILDING HEALTH SKILLS · **ADVOCACY**

REUSE TO REDUCE WASTE

Model

When Amy looked in her family's trashcan, she saw items that she thought could still be useful. She started encouraging her family members to look carefully at every item before throwing it away. As a result, the members of Amy's family changed their habits. They gave usable items to charity instead of throwing them away. They recycled cans, bottles, and newspapers. They also found creative ways to reuse objects. Chipped mugs became pencil cups. Grocery bags were used to line wastebaskets.

When Amy saw how much they had reduced their trash, she was so excited that she started sharing her family's ideas with others. Now, all her friends are eager to start reusing too!

286 CHAPTER 10: SAFETY AND THE ENVIRONMENT

Teaching Tips

Brainstorming Brainstorming allows students to generate a list of decisions in a short time. Allot a brief period of time (about 2 minutes) for brainstorming. Record the decisions without discussion or criticism. When time is up, invite comments about the decisions that have been recorded.

Facilitating Creativity Creative expression, such as developing a collage, provides an opportunity for students to show what they have learned in an innovative way. Creative expression activities can be done individually or in groups. **INCL** *Behavior Problems, Special Learning Needs*

Practice

In groups of four, discuss some of the things your families regularly throw into the trash. On a sheet of paper, write down as many of these items as you can. Then select two or three items from your list, and brainstorm ways to reuse each item. Write the name of each item at the top of your paper, and underline it. Below, list all the ways you find to reuse it. Remember that giving away intact items is a good way to reuse them.

1. What ways did you think of to reuse different items?
2. Which of your ideas do you think would be most practical?
3. How could you persuade others to reuse items in the ways you suggested?

Apply/Assess

Work with your group to create a collage that encourages others to reuse. Each member of the group should choose one of the ideas you thought of in the Practice section. Think of a way to convince others that your idea is a good way to reuse. One way would be to draw a picture of the reused item. You could also write out a list of directions for creating it. Photos clipped from newspapers or magazines can help you illustrate your idea. Attach all your drawings and other materials to a large piece of poster board to form a group collage. Finish your collage by attaching a list of all the benefits of reusing.

2. Practice

- Divide the class into groups of four. Ask each group to come up with a list of items their families throw away that could be reused instead. Have them write these items on a sheet of paper.

- Direct each group to choose two or three items from their list and think of different ways that each item could be reused. Then have them answer the questions at the end.

3. Apply/Assess

- You may wish to distribute Building Health Skills Reproducible Master 10 in the TCR to guide students in completing this activity.

- Display Transparency Master 10, and review the skill of advocacy with the class.

- Provide each group with a piece of poster board, drawing paper, markers, newspapers or magazines, and glue or tape.

- Have groups select one of the ways to reuse a particular item that they came up with in the Practice and create a collage that convinces others why this is a good way to reuse this item.

- Provide an opportunity for each group of students to present their collage to the class.

- Remind students to refer to the Self-Check before and after they create their collages.

Assessment Scoring

Using a rubric, student work should provide evidence of all criteria to achieve the highest score.

Skills

Student work illustrates

- a clear stand.
- a persuasive message.
- a convincing message.

- an awareness of the audience.

Concepts

Student work provides

- an explanation of the importance of reusing materials.

- several creative ways to reuse common items.

Checking Comprehension

Use the Chapter 10 Assessment to examine the most important ideas presented in the chapter.

Answers to Reviewing Vocabulary and Concepts

Lesson 1
1. accidental injuries
2. injury
3. accident chain

Lesson 2
4. pedestrian
5. Neighborhood Watch program
6. falls

Lesson 3
7. drowning
8. earthquake
9. hurricane
10. tornado

Lesson 4
11. false; rescue breathing
12. true
13. true
14. true
15. false; first-degree burn

Lesson 5
16. true
17. false; pollution
18. true
19. false; conservation
20. false; can

Thinking Critically

21. Responses may include cutting yourself with a knife, breaking a glass, burning yourself, slipping on a wet floor, electrical shock, and fire. Accept other reasonable answers.
22. Possible answer: Knowing your limits will allow you to avoid situations that are unsafe.
23. Opinions will vary.

CHAPTER ASSESSMENT 10

After You Read

Use your completed Foldable to review the information on injury prevention.

FOLDABLES™
Study Organizer

Reviewing Vocabulary and Concepts

On a sheet of paper, write the numbers 1–10. After each number, write the term from the list that best completes each sentence.

- accident chain
- injury
- drowning
- accidental injuries
- pedestrian
- tornado
- Neighborhood Watch program
- hurricane
- falls
- earthquake

Lesson 1

1. Injuries caused by unexpected events are known as _____.
2. Good safety habits protect you from _____, or physical harm.
3. Changing an unsafe habit is one way to break the _____.

Lesson 2

4. A(n) _____ is a person who travels on foot.
5. In a(n) _____, police train residents to look for and report suspicious activity in their community.
6. Keeping objects off the floor is a good way to prevent _____.

Lesson 3

7. The six steps of _____ prevention are: stay calm, get ready, raise your head, take a breath, go below the surface, and rest.

---

8. A(n) _____ is the shaking of the ground as rock below the surface moves.
9. A strong windstorm with driving rain is called a(n) _____.
10. If you are warned of a(n) _____ in your area, go down to a storm cellar or basement.

On a sheet of paper, write the numbers 11–20. Write *True* or *False* for each statement below. If the statement is false, change the underlined word or phrase to make it true.

Lesson 4

11. <u>Cardiopulmonary resuscitation</u> (CPR) is a substitute for normal breathing in which someone forces air into the victim's lungs.
12. Applying pressure to a main <u>artery</u> can help stop severe bleeding.
13. You can help an adult who is choking by giving <u>abdominal thrusts</u>.
14. A <u>poison control center</u> is one place that helps people deal with poisons.
15. In a <u>third-degree burn</u>, only the outer part of the skin turns red.

Lesson 5

16. You and the living and nonliving things around you make up the <u>environment</u>.
17. When the air, water, and land change from clean and safe to dirty and unsafe, it is known as <u>conservation</u>.
18. <u>Smog</u> forms when sunlight reacts with impurities in car exhaust.
19. Turning off electric lights when they are not in use is an example of <u>recycling</u>.
20. Everyday materials such as aluminum, glass, and paper <u>cannot</u> be recycled.

Thinking Critically

Using complete sentences, answer the following questions on a sheet of paper.

21. **Suggest** Identify three possible causes of accidents in the kitchen.

INCLUSION STRATEGIES

Special Learning Needs, Behavior Problems, English Language Learners The following suggestions are helpful for students with special learning needs, students with behavior problems, and ELL students:
- Pair these students with more proficient learners who can help summarize the main concepts of the chapter.

- 🎧 Direct these students to listen to the Teen Health Audio Summaries. This component provides an audio and written summary of the chapter in both English and Spanish.
- Use photographs, drawings, or magazine clippings whenever possible to help students visualize the important concepts of the chapter.

22. Explain Why is it important to be aware of your limits before engaging in an activity such as boating?

23. Analyze What is your opinion on allowing student lockers to be searched for drugs and weapons?

24. Classify A friend has burned his arm with hot chocolate. His skin has blisters. What degree of burn is this, and what kind of first aid is needed?

25. Hypothesize Which is better for the environment: to buy individual serving packages of snacks and meals or to buy larger packages? Why?

Career Corner

Occupational Safety and Health Specialist Would you like to help keep people safe while they work? Are you good at solving problems? Then you might want to think about a career in occupational safety and health. In this career, you will look at hazards in the workplace and find ways to prevent or eliminate them. You'll need a four-year degree in occupational safety and health. Visit Career Corner at health.glencoe.com to learn more about this and other health careers.

24. He has a second-degree burn. He should apply cold water to the burn and wrap his arm in a clean, dry dressing. He should elevate the arm and not break the blisters.

25. Larger containers use less packaging.

Test Practice
1. D
2. B
3. Responses should feature safety rules for a specific game or sport.

Reteaching
📁 Assign Study Guide 10 in the Student Activities Workbook.

Evaluate
- 📁 💿 Use the reproducible Chapter 10 Test in the TCR, or construct your own test using the **Exam**View® Pro Testmaker.
- 📁 Use Performance Assessment 10 in the TCR.

Standardized Test Practice

Reading & Writing

Read the paragraphs below and then answer the questions.

Every year hundreds of people are injured or killed in bicycling accidents. Following some basic safety rules can help keep you from becoming one of these people.

The single most important rule of bicycle safety is to always wear a properly fitting helmet. According to injury-prevention experts, wearing a helmet can reduce the risk of head injury by as much as 85 percent. When bicycling, remember to look left, right, and left again before you turn onto a street or enter traffic. Always ride with traffic, staying as far to the right as possible. Remember that bicycle riders, just like everyone else on the road, must obey all traffic laws, signs, and

signals. If you must ride after dark, wear reflective tape or clothing and make sure that your bike is equipped with a light or a reflector.

1. The phrase "single most important" is used to communicate a feeling of
 (A) fun.
 (B) anger.
 (C) amusement.
 (D) seriousness.

2. The reader can tell from the passage that bicycling safety is
 (A) difficult.
 (B) important.
 (C) easy.
 (D) complicated.

3. Write a paragraph outlining the safety rules of a favorite game or sport.

Assessment

Self-Assessment Direct students to review the activities that are provided throughout the chapter. Encourage each student to select one finished product or activity that demonstrates his or her best work for the chapter. Have students explain what they learned and how the examples they selected show their progress.

Career Corner

Occupational Safety and Health Specialist
These professionals may focus on areas such as industrial hygiene or ergonomics. Have students brainstorm possible hazards or workplace practices that an occupational safety and health specialist might investigate.

Glossary

The Glossary contains all the important terms used throughout the text. It includes the boldfaced terms listed in the "Vocabulary" lists at the beginning of each lesson, which also appear in text and art.

The Glossary lists the term, the pronunciation (in the case of difficult terms), the definition, and the page on which the term is defined. The pronunciations here and in the text follow the system outlined below. The column headed "Symbol" shows the spelling used in this book to represent the appropriate method.

PRONUNCIATION KEY

Sound	As In	Symbol	Example
ă	h*a*t, m*a*p	a	abscess (AB·ses)
ā	*a*ge, f*a*ce	ay	atrium (AY·tree·uhm)
a	c*a*re, th*eir*	eh	capillaries (KAP·uh·lehr·eez)
ä, ŏ	f*a*ther, h*o*t	ah	biopsy (BY·ahp·see)
ar	f*ar*	ar	cardiac (KAR·dee·ak)
ch	*ch*ild, mu*ch*	ch	barbiturate (bar·BI·chuh·ruht)
ĕ	l*e*t, b*e*st	e	vessel (VE·suhl)
ē	b*ea*t, s*ee*, cit*y*	ee	acne (AK·nee)
er	t*er*m, st*ir*, p*urr*	er	nuclear (NOO·klee·er)
g	*g*row	g	malignant (muh·LIG·nuhnt)
ĭ	*i*t, hym*n*	i	bacteria (bak·TIR·ee·uh)
ī	*i*ce, f*i*ve	y	benign (bi·NYN)
		eye	iris (EYE·ris)
j	pa*g*e, fun*gi*	j	cartilage (KAR·tuhl·ij)
k	*c*oat, loo*k*, *ch*orus	k	defect (DEE·fekt)
ō	*o*pen, c*oa*t, gr*ow*	oh	aerobic (ehr·OH·bik)
ô	*or*der	or	organ (OR·guhn)
ȯ	fl*aw*, *a*ll	aw	palsy (PAWL·zee)
oi	v*oi*ce	oy	goiter (GOY·ter)
ou	*ou*t	ow	fountain (FOWN·tuhn)
s	*s*ay, ri*ce*	s	dermis (DER·mis)
sh	*sh*e, atten*ti*on	sh	conservation (kahn·ser·VAY·shuhn)
ŭ	c*u*p, fl*oo*d	uh	bunion (BUHN·yuhn)
u	p*u*t, w*oo*d, c*ou*ld	u	pulmonary (PUL·muh·nehr·ee)
ü	r*u*le, m*o*ve, y*ou*	oo	attitudes (AT·i·toodz)
w	*w*in	w	warranty (WAWR·uhn·tee)
y	*y*our	yu	urethra (yu·REE·thruh)
z	say*s*	z	hormones (HOR·mohnz)
zh	plea*s*ure	zh	transfusion (trans·FYOO·zhuhn)
ə	*a*bout, c*o*llide	uh	addiction (uh·DIK·shuhn)

A

Abdominal thrusts Quick upward pulls into the diaphragm to force out an object blocking the airway. (page 275)

Abstinence (AB·sti·nuhns) Not participating in health-risk behaviors. (page 39)

Abuse (uh·BYOOS) A pattern of mistreatment of another person. (page 58)

Accident chain A sequence of events that often leads to an accidental injury. (page 259)

Accidental injury An injury caused by unexpected events. (page 258)

Acid rain Rainfall that contains air pollution from the burning of fossil fuels. (page 279)

Acne (AK·nee) A skin condition caused by overly active oil glands. (page 90)

Addiction The body's physical or mental need for a drug or other substance. (page 213)

Adolescence (a·duhl·EH·suhns) The period between childhood and adulthood. (page 165)

Adrenaline (uh·DRE·nuhl·in) A hormone that prepares the body to respond to a stressor. (page 42)

Advertisement A message used to persuade consumers to buy goods or services. (page 101)

Aerobic exercise Rhythmic, nonstop, moderate to vigorous activities that work the heart. (page 134)

AIDS An HIV infection combined with severe immune system problems. (page 192)

Alcohol (AL·kuh·hawl) A substance that is produced by a chemical reaction in some foods. (page 230)

Alcoholism The physical and mental need for alcohol. (page 233)

Allergen (AL·er·juhn) A substance that causes an allergic reaction. (page 199)

Allergy The body's sensitivity to certain substances. (page 199)

Alternative Another way of thinking or acting. (page 248)

Anabolic steroids (a·nuh·BAH·lik STIR·oydz) Synthetic drugs based on a male hormone. (page 245)

Anaerobic exercise Intense physical activity that requires short bursts of energy. (page 134)

Anorexia nervosa (an·uh·REK·see·uh ner·VOH·suh) An eating disorder in which a person has an intense fear of weight gain and starves himself or herself. (page 131)

Antibiotic (an·ti·by·AH·tik) A medicine that kills or stops the growth of certain germs. (page 235)

Antibodies Chemicals produced specifically to fight a particular invading substance. (page 185)

Assertive Willing to stand up for yourself in a positive way. (page 64)

Asthma (AZ·muh) A chronic breathing disease caused by allergies, physical exertion, air pollution, or other factors. (page 200)

Astigmatism A condition in which the shape of the cornea or of the lens causes objects to look wavy or blurred. (page 96)

B

Behavior How you act in situations that occur in your life. (page 169)

Biodegradable (by·oh·di·GRAY·duh·buhl) Able to break down naturally without causing pollution. (page 281)

Blood pressure The force of the blood pushing against the walls of the blood vessels. (page 158)

Glossary

Body language Facial expressions, gestures, and posture. (page 67)

Body system A group of organs that perform a body function. (page 151)

Brain The organ that controls your senses, thoughts, and actions. (page 161)

Bulimia nervosa (boo·LEE·mee·uh ner·VOH·suh) An eating disorder in which a person repeatedly eats large amounts of food and then purges by vomiting or using laxatives. (page 132)

Calcium A mineral that helps your body build healthy teeth and bones. (page 127)

Calorie A unit of heat that measures the energy available in foods. (page 130)

Cancer A disease caused by abnormal cells that grow out of control. (page 198)

Carbohydrate (kar·bo·HY·drayt) The main source of energy for your body. (page 117)

Carbon monoxide (KAR·buhn muh·NAHK·syd) A poisonous, odorless gas produced when tobacco burns. (page 212)

Cardiopulmonary resuscitation (CPR) A rescue measure that attempts to restore heartbeat and breathing. (page 273)

Cell The basic building block of life. (page 150)

Character The way you think, feel, and act. (page 17)

Choking A condition that occurs when a person's airway becomes blocked. (page 274)

Cholesterol (kuh·LES·tuh·rawl) A waxlike substance our bodies produce and need in small amounts. (page 129)

Chromosomes (KROH·muh·sohmz) Pairs of tiny, threadlike pieces of matter that carry the codes for inherited traits. (page 170)

Chronic (KRAH·nik) Long-lasting. (page 196)

Circulatory system A body system that allows the body to transport, or move, materials from one place to another. (page 157)

Cirrhosis (suh·ROH·sis) Destruction and scarring of liver tissue. (page 231)

Communicable (kuh·MYOO·ni·kuh·buhl) **disease** A disease that can be spread. (page 182)

Communication The sharing of thoughts and feelings between two or more people. (page 66)

Compromise Each person giving up something in order to reach a solution that satisfies everyone. (page 72)

Conflict A problem in a relationship. (page 70)

Consequence A result. (page 14)

Conservation The saving of resources. (page 281)

Consumer Someone who buys products or services. (page 100)

Contagious (cuhn·TAY·jus) Able to spread to others by direct or indirect contact. (page 187)

Cool-down Some gentle activity to slow down after exercise. (page 141)

Coupon (KOO·pahn) A slip of paper that saves you money on certain brands. (page 102)

Cumulative (KYOO·myuh·luh·tiv) **risk** The addition of one risk factor to another, increasing the chance of harm or loss. (page 17)

Cuticle (KYOO·ti·kuhl) A nonliving band of epidermis, or outer layer of skin, surrounding fingernails and toenails. (page 92)

D

Dandruff Flaking of the outer layer of dead skin cells on the scalp. (page 92)

Decibel A measurement of the loudness of sound. (page 98)

Decision A choice that you make. (page 14)

Deliberate injury An injury that results when one person intentionally harms another. (page 258)

Depressant A drug that slows down the body's functions and reactions. (page 242)

Dermatologist (DER·muh·TAH·luh·jist) A doctor who treats skin disorders. (page 91)

Dermis The thicker inner layer of the skin. (page 89)

Diabetes (dy·uh·BEE·teez) A disease that prevents the body from using the sugars and starches in food for energy. (page 201)

Diaphragm (DY·uh·fram) A large muscle at the bottom of the chest. (page 160)

Digestive (dy·JEHS·tiv) **system** A body system that breaks down the food you eat into a form that your body cells can use as fuel. (page 163)

Discount store A store that offers lower prices, but has fewer salespeople and services. (page 102)

Disease (dih·ZEEZ) An unhealthy condition of the body or mind. (page 182)

Distress Negative stress. (page 42)

Drug Any substance that changes the structure or function of the body or mind. (page 230)

Drug abuse (uh·BYOOS) Using drugs in ways that are unhealthy or illegal. (page 239)

Drug misuse Taking medicine in a way that is not intended. (page 239)

E

Earthquake The shaking of the ground as rock below the surface moves. (page 271)

Egg cell The reproductive cell in the female body. (page 171)

Emotion A feeling. (page 36)

Empathy The ability to identify and share another person's feelings. (page 62)

Emphysema (em·fuh·SEE·muh) A disease that occurs when the tiny air sacs in the lungs lose their elasticity, or ability to stretch. (page 214)

Endocrine (EHN·duh·krin) **system** A body system made up of glands throughout the body that produce hormones. (page 165)

Endurance (en·DER·uhns) How long you can engage in physical activity without becoming overly tired. (page 134)

Environment (en·VY·ruhn·ment) You and all living and nonliving things around you. (page 278)

Epidermis The thinner outer layer of the skin. (page 89)

Eustress (YOO·stres) Positive stress. (page 42)

Excretory (EK·skruh·tohr·ee) **system** A body system that gets rid of some of the wastes your body produces and maintains fluid balance. (page 164)

Exercise Planned, structured, repetitive physical activity that improves or maintains physical fitness. (page 136)

F

Family The basic unit of society. (page 54)

Farsightedness The ability to see objects at a distance, while close objects look blurry. (page 96)

Glossary

Fat A source of energy found in food. (page 118)

Fatigue (fuh·TEEG) Extreme tiredness. (page 43)

Fertilization The joining together of an egg cell and a sperm cell. (page 171)

Fetal (FEE·tuhl) **alcohol syndrome (FAS)** A group of permanent physical and mental problems caused by a mother's use of alcohol while pregnant. (page 233)

Fiber The tough, stringy part of raw fruits, raw vegetables, whole wheat, and other grains, which you cannot digest. (page 117)

First aid The care first given to an injured or ill person until regular medical care can be supplied. (page 272)

First-degree burn A burn in which only the outer part of the skin is burned and turns red. (page 276)

Flexibility The ability to move body joints through a full range of motion. (page 135)

Fluoride (FLAWR·eyed) A substance that fights tooth decay. (page 87)

Food Guide Pyramid A guideline to help you choose what and how much to eat to get the nutrients you need. (page 121)

Fossil fuels The coal, oil, and natural gas used to power the engines of motor vehicles and factories. (page 279)

Fraud Deliberate deceit or trickery. (page 103)

Friendship A special type of relationship between people who enjoy being together. (page 61)

Gang A group of people who associate with one another to take part in criminal activity. (page 74)

Generic (juh·NEHR·ic) Imitates name-brand products, and sold in plain packages. (page 102)

Genes (JEENZ) The basic units of heredity. (page 170)

Gestures Movements of the hands, arms, and legs. (page 67)

Goal Something that you hope to accomplish. (page 20)

Habit A pattern of behavior that you follow almost without thinking. (page 7)

Hallucinogen (huh·LOO·suhn·uh·jen) An illegal drug that causes the user's brain to distort images and to see and hear things that aren't real. (page 243)

Hazard A possible source of harm. (page 261)

Health A combination of physical, mental, emotional, and social well-being. (page 4)

Health insurance A monthly or yearly fee to an insurance company that agrees to pay for some or most costs of medical care. (page 106)

Heart The muscle that acts as the pump for the circulatory system. (page 158)

Heredity (huh·REHD·ih·tee) The process by which parents pass traits to their children. (page 170)

HIV The virus that causes AIDS. (page 192)

Hormones (HOR·mohnz) Powerful chemicals, produced by glands, that regulate many body functions. (page 37)

Hurricane (HER·uh·kayn) A strong tropical windstorm with driving rain. (page 271)

Hypothermia (hy·poh·THER·mee·uh) A sudden and dangerous drop in body temperature. (page 267)

Immune (i·MYOON) **system** A group of cells, tissues, and organs that fight disease. (page 185)

Immunity A resistance to infection. (page 185)

Infection The result of pathogens or germs invading the body, multiplying, and harming some of your body's cells. (page 183)

Inhalant (in·HAY·luhnt) A substance whose fumes are inhaled to produce hallucinations. (page 244)

Injury Physical damage or harm to the body. (page 258)

Insulin A hormone produced by the pancreas. (page 201)

Joint A place where one bone meets another. (page 155)

Long-term goal A goal that you hope to achieve within a period of months or years. (page 20)

Lungs The main organs of the respiratory system. (page 159)

Lymphocyte (LIM·fuh·syt) A white blood cell that attacks pathogens or harmful germs. (page 185)

Managed care A health insurance plan that saves money by limiting people's choice of doctors. (page 107)

Marijuana (mar·uh·WAHN·uh) An illegal drug that comes from the hemp plant. (page 244)

Media The various methods of communicating information, including newspapers, magazines, radio, television, and the Internet. (page 219)

Medicine A drug that is used to cure or prevent diseases or other conditions. (page 234)

Mineral (MIN·uh·ruhl) An element in food that helps your body work properly. (page 120)

Muscular system All the muscles in your body. (page 156)

Narcotics (nar·KAH·tics) Certain drugs that relieve pain. (page 243)

Nearsightedness The ability to see objects close to you, while distant objects look blurry. (page 96)

Neglect The failure of adults to provide basic physical and emotional care for children. (page 58)

Negotiation The process of talking over problems to reach a solution. (page 72)

Neighborhood Watch program A program in which police train residents to look for and report suspicious activity in their neighborhood. (page 265)

Nervous system The control and communication system of the body. (page 161)

Neuron (NOO·rahn) A cell that carries electrical messages. (page 161)

Nicotine (NI·kuh·teen) A drug found in tobacco that speeds up the heartbeat and affects the central nervous system. (page 212)

Noncommunicable disease A disease that does not spread. (page 182)

Nurture To provide for someone's physical, emotional, mental, and social needs. (page 55)

Glossary

Nutrient (NOO·tree·ent) A substance in food that your body needs. (page 117)

Nutrition (noo·TRI·shun) The science that studies the substances in food and how the body uses them. (page 116)

Organ A structure that is made up of different types of tissues that do a particular job. (page 151)

Orthodontist A dentist who specializes in dealing with irregularities of the teeth and jaw. (page 88)

Over-the-counter (OTC) medicine A medicine available without a written order from a doctor. (page 234)

Ozone (OH·zohn) A special form of oxygen. (page 279)

Pathogens Disease-causing germs. (page 183)

Pedestrian A person who travels on foot. (page 263)

Peer mediation (mee·dee·AY·shuhn) A process in which a specially trained student listens to both sides of an argument and then helps the opposing sides reach a solution. (page 73)

Peer pressure The influence you feel to go along with the behavior and beliefs of your peer group. (page 63)

Peers Your friends and other people in your age group. (page 63)

Personality The sum total of your feelings, actions, habits, and thoughts. (page 169)

Physical activity Any kind of movement that causes your body to use energy. (page 133)

Physical fitness The ability to handle everyday physical work and play without becoming tired. (page 136)

Plaque (PLAK) A soft, colorless, sticky film containing bacteria that grows on your teeth. (page 86)

Poison control center A place that helps people deal with poisons. (page 276)

Pollution (puh·LOO·shuhn) The changing of the air, water, and land from clean and safe to dirty and unsafe. (page 278)

Prescription (pri·SKRIP·shuhn) **medicine** A medicine sold only with a written order from a doctor. (page 234)

Prevention Keeping something from happening. (page 8)

Protein A nutrient essential for the growth and repair of all the cells in your body. (page 118)

Puberty (PYOO·ber·tee) The time when you begin to develop certain physical traits of the adults of your gender and become physically able to reproduce. (page 166)

Recycling Recovering and changing items so they can be used for other purposes. (page 281)

Refusal skills Methods for saying no. (page 64)

Reinforce To support. (page 33)

Relationship (ri·LAY·shuhn·ship) A connection you have with another person. (page 60)

Reliable Dependable. (page 62)

Rescue breathing A substitute for normal breathing in which someone forces air into the victim's lungs. (page 273)

Resiliency The ability to bounce back from difficulties. (page 34)

Respiratory system A body system that enables you to breathe. (page 159)

Risk The chance of harm or loss. (page 14)

Role model A person whose success or behavior serves as an example for others. (page 19)

Saturated (SAT·chur·ay·tuhd) **fat** A type of fat found mostly in animal products such as butter, meat, milk, and egg yolks. (page 129)

Second-degree burn A serious type of burn in which the burned area blisters or peels. (page 276)

Secondhand smoke Tobacco smoke that stays in the air. (page 217)

Self-concept The view you have of yourself. (page 32)

Self-esteem The ability to like and respect yourself. (page 35)

Sexual abuse An adult displaying sexual material to a child, touching a child's private body parts, or engaging in any other kind of sexual activity with a child or teen. (page 58)

Sexually transmitted infections (STIs) Communicable diseases that are passed from one person to another through sexual contact. (page 191)

Short-term goal A goal that you plan to accomplish in a short time. (page 20)

Side effect Any reaction to a medicine other than the one intended. (page 235)

Skeletal system A framework of bones and the tissues that connect those bones. (page 154)

Smog A yellow-brown haze that forms when sunlight reacts with impurities in car exhaust. (page 279)

Smoke alarm A device that makes a warning noise when it senses smoke. (page 262)

Snuff Finely ground tobacco that is inhaled or held in the mouth between the lower lip and gum. (page 216)

Sodium A mineral that helps control the amount of fluid in your body. (page 129)

Sound waves Vibrations or movements in the air. (page 97)

Specialist (SPEH·shuh·list) A doctor trained to handle particular health problems. (page 104)

Sperm cell The reproductive cell in the male body. (page 171)

Spinal cord A tube of neurons that runs up the spine. (page 161)

Stimulant (STIM·yuh·luhnt) A drug that speeds up the body's functions. (page 241)

Strength The ability of your muscles to exert a force. (page 134)

Stress Your body's response to changes around you. (page 41)

Stressor An object, person, place, or event that triggers stress. (page 42)

Substance abuse Use of illegal or harmful drugs, including any use of alcohol while under the legal drinking age. (page 246)

Tar A thick, oily, dark liquid that forms when tobacco burns. (page 212)

Target pulse rate The level at which your heart and lungs receive the most benefit from a workout. (page 140)

Tartar A hard material that forms when plaque builds up on teeth. (page 87)

Third-degree burn A very serious burn in which deep layers of skin and nerve endings are damaged. (page 276)

Glossary

Tissue A group of similar cells that do the same kind of work. (page 150)

Tolerance (TAHL·er·ence) The ability to accept other people as they are. (page 71)

Tolerance (TAHL·er·ence) A condition in which the body becomes used to the effects of a substance and needs greater amounts to get the same effects. (page 235)

Tornado (tor·NAY·doh) A whirling, funnel-shaped windstorm that drops from the sky to the ground. (page 271)

Tumor A mass of abnormal cells. (page 198)

Umbilical (uhm·BIL·i·kuhl) **cord** A tube that connects the lining of the uterus to the unborn baby. (page 172)

Uterus (YOO·tuh·ruhs) A pear-shaped organ inside a woman's body that expands as a baby grows inside it. (page 172)

Vaccine (vak·SEEN) A preparation of killed or weakened germs. (page 188)

Values Beliefs you feel strongly about that help guide the way you live. (page 17)

Violence The use of physical force to harm someone or something. (page 74)

Vitamin (VI·tuh·min) A substance that helps regulate body functions. (page 118)

Voluntary health group An organization that works to treat and eliminate certain diseases. (page 106)

Warm-up Some gentle activity that prepares your body for exercise. (page 140)

Warranty A promise to make repairs or refund money if a product does not work as claimed. (page 102)

Wellness A state of well-being, or balanced health. (page 7)

Withdrawal A series of mental and physical symptoms that occur when a person stops using an addictive substance. (page 240)

Glosario

 A

Abdominal thrusts/presiones abdominales Movimientos en los que se ejerce una presión rápida hacia arriba sobre el diafragma, para desalojar un objeto que obstruye las vías respiratorias.

Abstinence/abstinencia No participar en conductas de riesgo para la salud.

Abuse/abuso Un patrón de maltrato a otra persona.

Accident chain/cadena del accidente Una secuencia de sucesos que muchas veces termina en una lesión accidental.

Accidental injury/herida accidental Una herida causada por sucesos inesperados.

Acid rain/lluvia ácida Lluvia que contiene contaminación del aire, por la combustión de combustibles fósiles.

Acne/acné Una afección de la piel causada por la actividad excesiva de las glándulas sebáceas.

Addiction/adicción La necesidad física o mental del cuerpo de consumir una droga u otra sustancia.

Adolescence/adolescencia El periodo de vida entre la niñez y la adultez.

Adrenaline/adrenalina Una hormona que facilita la reacción del cuerpo a un agente estresante.

Advertisement/anuncio publicitario Un mensaje dirigido a los consumidores para persuadirles de que compren bienes o servicios.

Aerobic exercise/ejercicio aeróbico Actividad rítmica, ininterrumpida de intensidad moderada o vigorosa que hace que el corazón trabaje.

AIDS/SIDA Una infección del virus VIH combinada con problemas graves del sistema inmunológico.

Alcohol/alcohol Una sustancia producida por una reacción química en algunos alimentos.

Alcoholism/alcoholismo La necesidad física y mental de consumir alcohol.

Allergen/alergeno Una sustancia que causa una reacción alérgica.

Allergy/alergia La sensibilidad del cuerpo a ciertas sustancias.

Alternative/alternativa Un modo distinto de pensar o actuar.

Anabolic steroids/esteroides anabólicos Drogas sintéticas basadas en una hormona masculina.

Anaerobic exercise/ejercicio anaeróbico Intensa actividad física que requiere pequeños brotes de energía.

Anorexia nervosa/anorexia nerviosa Un trastorno en la alimentación por el cual una persona sufre de un intenso temor a aumentar de peso y por consiguiente deja de comer.

Antibiotic/antibiótico Una medicina que mata o detiene el crecimiento de ciertos gérmenes.

Antibodies/anticuerpos Sustancias químicas producidas específicamente para combatir a una sustancia invasora determinada.

Glosario

Assertive/firme Dispuesto a defenderte de una manera positiva.

Asthma/asma Una enfermedad respiratoria crónica causada por alergias, fatiga física, la contaminación ambiental y otros factores.

Astigmatism/astigmatismo Una afección por la que la forma de la córnea o del cristalino del ojo causan que los objetos se vean distorsionados o borrosos.

Behavior/conducta La forma en que actúas frente a las situaciones de tu vida.

Biodegradable/biodegradable Que se descompone naturalmente, sin causar contaminación.

Blood pressure/presión arterial La fuerza que ejerce la sangre sobre las paredes de los vasos sanguíneos.

Body language/ lenguaje corporal Expresiones faciales, gestos y postura.

Body system/aparato o sistema del cuerpo Un grupo de órganos que ejecuta una función del cuerpo.

Brain/encéfalo El órgano que controla tus sentidos, pensamientos y acciones.

Bulimia nervosa/bulimia nerviosa Un trastorno en la alimentación por el que una persona ingiere grandes cantidades de comida en forma reiterada para luego purgarla por medio del vómito o del uso de laxantes.

Calcium/calcio Un mineral que contribuye a que tu cuerpo forme dientes y huesos saludables.

Calorie/caloría Una unidad de calor que mide la energía disponible en los alimentos.

Cancer/cáncer Una enfermedad causada por células anormales cuyo crecimiento está fuera de control.

Carbohydrate/hidrato de carbono La principal fuente de energía para tu cuerpo.

Carbon monoxide/monóxido de carbono Un gas tóxico e inodoro que produce el tabaco al quemarse.

Cardiopulmonary resuscitation (CPR)/resucitación cardiopulmonar Una medida de rescate que intenta restaurar la frecuencia cardiaca y la respiración.

Cell/célula Los componentes básicos de los seres vivos.

Character/carácter La manera en que piensas, sientes y actúas.

Choking/asfixia Una afección que ocurre cuando las vías respiratorias de una persona están bloquedas.

Cholesterol/colesterol Una sustancia cerosa que nuestro cuerpo produce y necesita en cantidades pequeñas.

Chromosomes/cromosomas Pares de diminutas partículas filiformes de materia que contienen los códigos genéticos de los rasgos hereditarios.

Chronic/crónico De larga duración.

Circulatory system/aparato circulatorio Un aparato corporal que permiteal cuerpo transportar o mover materiales de un lugar a otro.

Cirrhosis/cirrosis La destrucción y cicatrización del tejido del hígado.

Communicable disease/enfermedad contagiosa Una enfermedad que se puede propagar.

Communication/comunicación
Compartir pensamientos y sentimientos entre dos o más personas.

Compromise/acuerdo Cada persona cede algo para alcanzar una solución que satisfaga a todos.

Conflict/conflicto Un problema en una relación.

Consequence/consecuencia Un resultado.

Conservation/conservación La preservación de los recursos naturales.

Consumer/consumidor Una persona que compra productos o servicios.

Contagious/contagioso Capaz de propagarse a otros por contacto directo o indirecto.

Cool-down/recuperación Actividad moderada para desacelerar el ritmo del entrenamiento.

Coupon/cupón Boleta de papel que te permite ahorrar dinero en ciertas marcas.

Cumulative risk/riesgo acumulativo
La adición de un riesgo a otro aumentando la posibilidad de daño o pérdida.

Cuticle/cutícula Una franja de epidermis no viva que rodea las uñas.

Dandruff/caspa Descamado de la capa externa de las células muertas de la piel del cuero cabelludo.

Decibel/decibel Una unidad de medida del volumen del sonido.

Decision/decisión Las opciones que eliges.

Deliberate injury/lesión deliberada
Una herida causada cuando una persona intencionalmente hiere a otra.

Depressant/depresivo Una droga que disminuye las funciones y reacciones del cuerpo.

Dermatologist/dermatólogo Un médico que trata trastornos de la piel.

Dermis/dermis La capa más gruesa y profunda de la piel.

Diabetes/ diabetes Una enfermedad que le impide al cuerpo utilizar los azúcares y almidones de los alimentos para crear energía.

Diaphragm/diafragma Un músculo grande ubicado en la parte inferior del pecho.

Digestive system/aparato digestivo
Un aparato corporal que descompone los alimentos que ingieres en sustancias que las células del cuerpo pueden usar como combustible.

Discount store/tienda de descuentos Una tienda que tiene precios más bajos pero con menos vendedores y servicios.

Disease/enfermedad Una afección de la salud del cuerpo o de la mente.

Distress/angustia El estrés negativo.

Drug/droga Toda sustancia que altera la estructura o el funcionamiento del cuerpo o de la mente.

Drug abuse/abuso de drogas El uso de drogas de manera malsana o ilegal.

Drug misuse/uso indebido de las drogas El tomar medicinas sin cumplir con las indicaciones.

Glosario

Earthquake/terremoto El sacudimiento de la tierra mientras la capa de roca por debajo de la superficie terrestre se mueve.

Egg cell/óvulo La célula reproductora del cuerpo femenino.

Emotion/emoción Un sentimiento.

Empathy/empatía La habilidad de identificar y compartir los sentimientos de otra persona.

Emphysema/enfisema Una enfermedad que ocurre cuando los pequeños sacos de aire en los pulmones pierden la elasticidad o la capacidad de estirarse.

Endocrine system/sistema endocrino Un sistema del cuerpo que comprende las glándulas que producen hormonas.

Endurance/resistencia La cantidad de tiempo que puedes realizar actividad física sin cansarte demasiado.

Environment/medio ambiente Todas las cosas vivas y no vivas que te rodean.

Epidermis/epidermis La capa externa y más delgada de la piel.

Eustress/tensión positiva Estrés positivo.

Excretory system/sistema excretor Un sistema del cuerpo que elimina algunos de los desechos producidos en el cuerpo y que mantiene el equilibrio de los líquidos.

Exercise/ejercicio Actividad física planeada, estructurada y repetitiva que mejora o mantiene el buen estado físico.

Family/familia La unidad básica de la familia.

Farsightedness/hipermetropía La capacidad de ver claramente los objetos a la distancia, mientras los objetos cercanos se ven borrosos.

Fat/grasa Una fuente de energía en los alimentos.

Fatigue/fatiga Cansancio extremo.

Fertilization/fecundación La unión de un óvulo y un espermatozoide.

Fetal alcohol syndrome/síndrome de alcoholismo fetal Un conjunto de problemas físicos y mentales permanentes causados por el consumo de alcohol de la madre durante el embarazo.

Fiber/fibra La parte dura, fibrosa de las frutas y verduras crudas, el trigo integral y demás granos que no puedes digerir.

First aid/primeros auxilios Los primeros cuidados que se brindan a una persona herida o enferma, durante una emergencia hasta que se obtiene asistencia médica regular.

First-degree burn/quemadura de primer grado Una quemadura en que sólo la capa exterior de la piel se quema y enrojece.

Flexibility/flexibilidad La habilidad de mover las articulaciones del cuerpo a través del arco completo de movimiento.

Fluoride/fluoruro Una sustancia que combate las caries.

Food Guide Pyramid/Pirámide Nutricional Una guía para orientarte en la elección diaria de lo que debes comer y en qué cantidad a fin de incorporar los nutrientes necesarios.

Fossil fuels/combustibles fósiles El carbón, petróleo y gas natural que se usan para hacer funcionar los vehículos motorizados y las fábricas.

Fraud/fraude Engaño o estafa deliberada.

Friendship/amistad Un tipo especial de relación entre personas que disfrutan el estar juntas.

Gang/pandilla Un grupo de personas que se asocian para participar en actividades criminales.

Generic/genérico Imita a un producto de marca conocida y se vende en envase común.

Genes/genes Las unidades básicas de la herencia.

Gestures/gestos Movimientos de las manos, los brazos y las piernas.

Goal/meta Algo que esperas lograr.

Habit/hábito Un patrón de conducta que sigues casi sin pensarlo.

Hallucinogen/alucinógeno Una droga ilegal que afecta el cerebro de manera que la persona que la consume percibe imágenes distorsionadas y ve y oye cosas irreales.

Hazard/peligro Una posible fuente de daño.

Health/salud Una combinación de bienestar físico, mental, emocional y social.

Health insurance/seguro de salud Una cuota mensual o anual que se paga a una compañía de seguros que acuerda en cubrir parte o la mayoría de los gastos médicos.

Heart/corazón El músculo que funciona como una bomba para el aparato circulatorio.

Heredity/herencia El proceso mediante el cual los padres transfieren rasgos a sus hijos.

HIV/VIH El virus que causa el SIDA.

Hormones/hormonas Sustancias químicas potentes producidas por las glándulas que regulan muchas funciones del cuerpo.

Hurricane/huracán Una tormenta tropical fuerte con vientos y lluvia torrencial.

Hypothermia/hipotermia Un descenso repentino y peligroso de la temperatura del cuerpo.

Immune system/sistema inmunológico Un grupo de células, tejidos y órganos que combaten las enfermedades.

Immunity/inmunidad Una resistencia a un agente infeccioso.

Infection/infección El resultado de la invasión, multiplicación y daño celular de un agente patógeno en tu cuerpo.

Inhalant/inhalante Una sustancia cuyos vapores se inhalan para producir alucinaciones.

Injury/lesión Daño físico o perjuicio al cuerpo.

Insulin/insulina Una hormona producida por el páncreas.

Joint/articulación Un lugar donde un hueso se une con otro.

Long-term goal/meta a largo plazo
Una meta que esperas lograr en un periodo de meses o años.

Lungs/pulmones
Los órganos principales del aparato respiratorio.

Lymphocyte/linfocito
Un glóbulo blanco que ataca a los agentes patógenos.

Managed care/asistencia médica regulada
Un plan de seguro médico que ahorra dinero al limitar la selección de doctores de las personas.

Marijuana/marihuana
Una droga ilegal que proviene de la planta del cáñamo.

Media/medios de difusión
Los diversos métodos de comunicación de información que comprenden los periódicos, revistas, radio, televisión e Internet.

Medicine/medicina
Una droga que se usa para curar o prevenir enfermedades u otras afecciones.

Mineral/mineral
Un elemento presente en los alimentos que ayuda al buen funcionamiento del cuerpo.

Muscular system/aparato muscular
Todos los músculos de tu cuerpo.

Narcotics/narcóticos
Ciertas drogas que alivian el dolor.

Nearsightedness/miopía
La capacidad de ver claramente los objetos cercanos, mientras los objetos lejanos se ven borrosos.

Neglect/abandono
La incompetencia de los padres en proveer el cuidado básico emocional y físico para sus hijos.

Negotiation/negociación
El proceso de hablar sobre los problemas para llegar a una solución.

Neighborhood Watch Program/ Programa de Vigilancia Vecinal
Un programa en el cual la policía les enseña a los residentes a vigilar y reportar toda actividad sospechosa en su vecindario.

Nervous system/sistema nervioso
El sistema de control y comunicación del cuerpo.

Neuron/neurona
Una célula que transporta mensajes eléctricos.

Nicotine/nicotina
Una droga que acelera el ritmo cardiaco y afecta al sistema nervioso central.

Noncummunicable disease/enfermedad no contagiosa
Una enfermedad que no se propaga.

Nurture/criar
Satisfacer las necesidades físicas, emocionales, mentales y sociales de una persona.

Nutrient/nutriente
Una sustancia que tu cuerpo necesita y que está presente en los alimentos.

Nutrition/nutrición
La ciencia que estudia las sustancias presentes en los alimentos y el modo en que el cuerpo las utiliza.

Organ/órgano
Una estructura formada por diferentes clases de tejidos que ejecutan una función específica.

Orthodontist/ortodoncista Un dentista que se especializa en el tratamiento de irregularidades de los dientes y la mandíbula.

Over-the-counter medicine/medicina sin receta Una medicina que se puede adquirir sin receta de un médico.

Ozone/ozono Una forma especial del oxígeno.

Pathogens/agentes patógenos Gérmenes causantes de enfermedades.

Pedestrian/peatón Una persona que se traslada a pie.

Peer mediation/mediación entre pares. Un proceso en el cual un estudiante especialmente capacitado escucha a ambas partes de una discusión para ayudarlos a encontrar una solución.

Peer pressure/presión de pares La influencia que sientes para aceptar y seguir la conducta y las creencias de tu grupo de pares.

Peers/pares Amigos y otras personas de tu grupo de edad.

Personality/personalidad La suma total de tus sentimientos, acciones, hábitos y pensamientos.

Physical activity/actividad física Cualquier movimiento que cause que el cuerpo use energía.

Physical fitness/buen estado físico La capacidad de llevar a cabo trabajos físicos y juegos cotidianos sin sentirte cansado.

Plaque/placa bacteriana Una película blanda, incolora y pegajosa que contiene bacterias que se reproducen en los dientes.

Poison control center/centros para el control de venenos Un lugar que ayuda a las personas con información referente a venenos.

Pollution/contaminación El cambio en el aire, el agua y la tierra de estar limpios y sanos a sucios y nocivos.

Prescription medicine/medicina bajo receta Una medicina que puede venderse sólo con receta escrita por un médico.

Prevention/prevención Evitar que algo suceda.

Protein/proteína Un nutriente esencial para el crecimiento y la regeneración de todas las células de tu cuerpo.

Puberty/pubertad La etapa de la vida en la cual desarrollas ciertas características físicas adultas propias de tu sexo y te tornas físicamente apto para la reproducción.

Recycling/reciclar Recuperar y cambiar un objeto para usarlo con otro propósito.

Refusal skills/destrezas de negación Métodos para decir no.

Reinforce/reforzar Fortalecer.

Relationship/relación Una conexión que tienes con otra persona.

Reliable/confiable De fiar.

Rescue breathing/respiración de rescate. Substituto de respiración normal por la cual alguien insulfa aire a los pulmones de la víctima.

Resiliency/capacidad de recuperación La habilidad para reponerse de las dificultades.

Respiratory system/aparato respiratorio Un aparato del cuerpo que permite la respiración.

Risk/riesgo La posibilidad de daño o pérdida.

Role model/modelo de conducta Una persona cuyo éxito o conducta sirve de ejemplo para los demás.

Saturated fat/grasa saturada Un tipo de grasa que se encuentra mayormente en los productos de origen animal como la mantequilla, la carne, la leche y la yema de huevo.

Second-degree burn/quemadura de segundo grado Un tipo de quemadura grave en la que se forman ampollas o se despelleja la piel quemada.

Secondhand smoke/humo secundario El humo del tabaco que queda en el aire.

Self-concept/autoconcepto La percepción que tienes de ti mismo.

Self-esteem/autoestima La habilidad de agradarte y respetarte a ti mismo.

Sexual abuse/abuso sexual Un adulto que le muestra material sexual a un niño, toca las partes privadas de un niño, o participa en cualquier actividad sexual con un niño o adolescente.

Sexually transmitted diseases (STDs)/enfermedades de transmisión sexual (ETS) Enfermedades contagiosas que se transmiten de una persona a otra, a través del contacto sexual.

Short-term goal/meta a corto plazo Una meta que planeas lograr en un corto periodo de tiempo.

Side effect/efecto colateral Toda reacción a una medicina diferente de la que se procura.

Skeletal system/sistema osteoarticular Una estructura compuesta de huesos y los tejidos que los conectan.

Smog/smog Una neblina amarillento-café que se forma cuando la luz solar reacciona con las impurezas emanaciones de los vehículos.

Smoke alarm/alarma contra incendios Un aparato que emite un ruido de emergencia cuando detecta humo.

Snuff/rapé Tabaco finamente molido que se inhala o se mantiene en la boca entre el labio inferior y la encía.

Sodium/sodio Un mineral que ayuda a controlar la cantidad de líquido en tu cuerpo.

Sound waves/ondas sonoras Vibraciones en el aire.

Specialist/especialista Doctor entrenado para atender problemas de la salud específicos.

Sperm cell/espermatozoide La célula reproductora del cuerpo masculino.

Spinal cord/médula espinal Un conducto de neuronas que se encuentra a lo largo de la columna vertebral.

Stimulant/estimulante Una droga que acelera las funciones del cuerpo.

Strength/fortaleza La capacidad de tus músculos para ejercer una fuerza.

Stress/estrés La respuesta de tu cuerpo a los cambios que ocurren a tu alrededor.

Stressor/factor estresante Un objeto, persona, lugar o suceso que provoca el estrés.

Substance abuse/abuso de sustancias Consumo de drogas ilegales o nocivas, incluso el consumo del alcohol en cualquiera de sus formas antes de la edad legal para beber.

 T

Tar/alquitrán Un líquido espeso, aceitoso y oscuro que forma el tabaco al quemarse.

Target pulse rate/ritmo deseado del pulso El nivel en el cual tu corazón y pulmones reciben el mayor beneficio de una actividad física.

Tartar/sarro Una materia dura que se forma cuando la placa bacteriana se acumula en los dientes.

Third-degree burn/quemadura de tercer grado Una quemadura muy grave que daña las capas más profundas de la piel y las terminaciones nerviosas.

Tissue/tejido Un grupo de células similares que tienen la misma función.

Tolerance/tolerancia La capacidad de aceptar a los demás tal como son.

Tolerance/tolerancia Un estado por el cual el cuerpo se acostumbra a los efectos de una medicina y necesita mayores dosis para producir el mismo efecto.

Tornado/tornado Una tormenta en forma de torbellino que gira en grandes círculos y que cae del cielo a la tierra.

Tumor/tumor Una masa de células anormales.

 U

Umbilical cord/cordón umbilical Un conducto que conecta el revestimiento del útero con el bebé antes de nacer.

Uterus/útero Un órgano femenino en forma de pera que se expande a medida que crece un bebé en su interior.

 V

Vaccine/vacuna Un preparado de gérmenes muertos o debilitados.

Values/valores Creencias importantes para ti que te ayudan a guiar la forma en que vives.

Violence/violencia El uso de fuerza física para hacer daño a alguien o a algo.

Vitamin/vitamina Una sustancia que contribuye a regular las funciones corporales.

Voluntary health group/grupo de voluntarios de la salud Una organización que trabaja para tratar y erradicar ciertas enfermedades.

W

Warm-up/precalentamiento Una actividad moderada que prepara a tu cuerpo para hacer ejercicio.

Warranty/garantía Una promesa para reparar el producto o reembolsar el dinero en caso de que el producto no funcione como se alega.

Wellness/bienestar general Un estado de bienestar, o salud equilibrada.

Withdrawal/síndrome de abstinencia Una serie de síntomas físicos y mentales que ocurren cuando una persona deja de consumir una sustancia adictiva.

Index

Note: Page numbers in *italics* refer to art and marginal features.

A

Abdominal thrusts, 275, *275*
Abnormal cells, growth of, 198
Abstinence
  benefits of, 40
  for communicating refusal, 39
Abuse
  coping strategies for, 59
  of drugs, 239
  in families, 58
  substance, 246
Accessing information, *9, 39*
  before buying health products, 110–111
  on dealing with emotions, 39
  on family abuse, 59
  on food labels, 119
  on minor injuries, 277
  on noncommunicable and hereditary diseases, 199
  through unit pricing, 102
Accidental injuries, 258, 259
  strategies for prevention of, 258–259, 261–263
  strategies for response to, 272–276
Accident chain, 258, *258–259*
Acid (drug), 243
Acid rain, 279
Acne, 90–91
Acquired immunodeficiency syndrome (AIDS), 192. *See also* Human immunodeficiency virus (HIV)
Addiction
  to alcohol, 233
  definition of, 213
  to drugs, 240
  to inhalants, 244
  to tobacco, 213, *213*
Adolescence, 165–169, 173
  definition of, 165
  emotional changes during, 37
  endocrine system and, 165–166
  mental/emotional development during, 167
  personality influences during, 169

physical development during, 166, *167*
  social development during, 167, 168
Adrenal glands, *166*
Adrenaline, *42, 166*
Adulthood, 173
Adults
  choking rescue for, 275
  goal-setting help from, 14
  problem-solving help from, 14, 39, 57, 59, 75, 105, 187, 200, 247
  rescue breathing for, 273
Advertisements, 101
  consumer skills and, 101
  for food products, 101
  for medicine, *238*
  for tobacco, *214*
Advocacy, *9,* 12
  and dangers of smoking, 216
  for peace, 75
  for prenatal health, 171
  for waste reduction, 286–287
Aerobic exercise, 134, 137
Affection, healthy expression of, 38
AIDS. *See* Acquired immuno-deficiency syndrome
AIDS quilt, *194*
Air
  pollution of, 279
  protection of, 281
Al-Anon, 249
Alateen, 249
Alcohol, 230–233
  addiction to, 233
  alternatives to using, 248
  avoiding, 252–253
  chemical dependency on, 233
  in different drinks, *232*
  effects of, *231,* 232
  and HIV transmission, 233
  pregnancy and, 233
  reasons for drinking, 230
  reasons to avoid, *246*
  and risk behavior, 232
  and STD transmission, 233

and unsafe situations, 233
  violent acts caused by, *74*
Alcoholism, 58, 233
  coping strategies for, 249
  treatment of, 233
Alcohol poisoning, 232
Allergens, 199
Allergies, 199
Alternatives, 248
Alveoli, *159*
American Heart Association, *197, 273*
American Red Cross
  CPR training from, *273*
  emergency guidelines by, *272*
Amphetamines, 241
Anabolic steroids, 245
Anaerobic exercise, 134
Analyzing influences, *9,* 10
  on alcohol use, 230
  on community health, 271
  on drug-taking behaviors, 247
  on food choices, 126
  on health product choices, 100
  of media, *18, 199, 214,* 219, *238,* 271
  on personal health, 26–27, 271
  of relationships, 63
  of technology, 271
Anatomy, puberty and changes in, 166, *167*
Anesthesiologists, 227
Angel dust, 243
Anger, *74*
Anorexia nervosa, 131
Antibiotics, 235
Antibodies, 185, *186*
Antidrugs, *247*
Antigens, *185*
Anxiety, 41, 43
Armstrong, Lance, *199*
Arteries, 158
Arteriosclerosis, *197*
Assertiveness, 64
Asthma, 200
Astigmatism, 96
Atherosclerosis, *197*

Index

Index

Index

Index

Health Resources

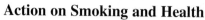

Action on Smoking and Health
2013 H Street NW
Washington, DC 20006

**Alcoholics Anonymous
Central Office**
15 E. 26th Street
New York, NY 10010-1501

**Al-Anon/Alateen Family
Group Headquarters**
1600 Corporate Landing Parkway
Virginia Beach, VA 23454-5617

**American Academy of Pediatrics
National Headquarters**
141 Northwest Point Road
Elk Grove Village, IL 60007-1098

**American Automobile Association,
Foundation for Traffic Safety
Administrative Office**
1440 New York Avenue NW
Suite 201
Washington, DC 20005

**American Cancer Society
National Headquarters**
1599 Clifton Road NE
Atlanta, GA 30329

American Counseling Association
5999 Stevenson Avenue
Alexandria, VA 22304

American Dental Association
211 East Chicago Avenue
Chicago, IL 60611

**American Heart Association
National Center**
7272 Greenville Avenue
Dallas, TX 75231-4596

American Institute of Nutrition
9650 Rockville Pike
Suite 4500
Bethesda, MD 20814

**American Insurance Association, Engineering
and Safety Service**
85 John Street
New York, NY 10038

American Lung Association
1740 Broadway
New York, NY 10019

American Medical Association
515 North State Street
Chicago, IL 60610

American Optometric Association
243 North Lindbergh Boulevard
St. Louis, MO 63141

American Society of Safety Engineers
1800 East Oakton Street
Des Plaines, IL 60018-2187

**Asthma and Allergy Foundation of America
(AAFA)**
1233 20th Street, NW
Suite 402
Washington, DC 20036

**Centers for Disease Control and Prevention
(CDC)**
1600 Clifton Road
Atlanta, GA 30333

Council on Environmental Quality
722 Jackson Place NW
Washington, DC 20503

**Department of Health and Human Services
National Clearinghouse for Alcohol and Drug
Information (a service of the Substance
Abuse and Mental Health Services
Administration)**
Information Specialist
P.O. Box 2345
Rockville, MD 20847-2345

**Juvenile Diabetes Research Foundation
International**
120 Wall Street
New York, NY 10005-4001

March of Dimes Birth Defects Foundation
1275 Mamaroneck Avenue
White Plains, NY 10605

National Institute of Arthritis and Musculoskeletal and Skin Diseases Information Clearinghouse
National Institute of Arthritis and Musculoskeletal and Skin Diseases (NIAMS)
National Institutes of Health
1 AMS Circle
Bethesda, MD 20892-3675

National Association of Sports for Cerebral Palsy
66 East 34th Street
New York, NY 10016

National Cancer Institute (NCI)— General Cancer Information
Office of Cancer Communications
31 Center Drive
Building 31, Room 10A07
Bethesda, MD 20892

National Center for Health Statistics
Centers for Disease Control and Prevention
6525 Belcrest Road
Hyattsville, MD 20782

National Council on Alcoholism and Drug Dependence
20 Exchange Place
Suite 2902
New York, NY 10005

National Dairy Council
10255 West Higgins Road
Suite 900
Rosemont, IL 60018-5606

National Fire Protection Association (NFPA)
1 Batterymarch Park
Quincy, MA 02269-9101

National Health Information Center (NHIC)
Referral Specialist
P.O. Box 1133
Washington, DC 20013-1133

The National Institute of Allergy and Infectious Diseases
NIAID Office of Communications and Public Liaison
Building 31, Room 7A-50
31 Center Drive MSC 2520
Bethesda, MD 20892-2520

National Institute of Mental Health (NIMH)
Public Inquiries
6001 Executive Boulevard
Room 8184, MSC 9663
Bethesda, MD 20892-9663

National Mental Health Association
1021 Prince Street
Alexandria, VA 22314-2971

National Parents-Teachers Association
Drug and Alcohol Abuse Prevention Project
330 North Wabash Ave., Suite 2100
Chicago, IL 60611-3690

National Safety Council
1121 Spring Lake Drive
Itasca, IL 60143-3201

National Wildlife Federation
8925 Leesburg Pike
Vienna, VA 22180

Office on Smoking and Health
Centers for Disease Control and Prevention
Publications
Mail Stop K-50
4770 Buford Highway, NE
Atlanta, GA 30341-3717

Students Against Destructive Decisions
255 Main Street
P.O. Box 800
Marlboro, MA 01752

United Cerebral Palsy, Inc.
1660 L Street, NW
Suite 700
Washington, DC 20036

USDA Food and Nutrition Information and Education Resources Center
National Agricultural Library,
U.S. Department of Agriculture
10301 Baltimore Avenue, Room 304
Beltsville, MD 20705

U.S. Food and Drug Administration
Office of Consumer Affairs
5600 Fishers Lane
Rockville, MD 20857-001

Credits

Photographs

AP Photo: Paul Sakuma, page 202 (left). Kevin Birch: pages 10, 19, 20 (left), 61 (all), 71, 132, 134 (left), 191, 204, 260. CORBIS: Paul Barton, page 3; Ed Bohon, page 239; Jim Cummings, pages 134 (center), 284; Duomo, page 154; C. Hammell, page 164; Rob Lewine, page 108; Kevin R. Morris, page 216; 95 Mugshots, page 169; Michael Neveux, page 142; F. Rossotto, page 280 (top); George Schiavone, page 158; Joseph Sohm, Visions of America, page 69; Gerhard Steiner, pages 142–143; Tom Stewart, pages 234, 285. CORBIS SYGMA: Hekimian Julien, page 251; Coulas Lourdes Inc.: Mick Coulas, page 222. Bob Daemmrich Photography, Inc.: pages 7, 36, 45, 105, 235, 241; Joel Salcido Photography/Bob Daemmrich Associates, page 35. Mary Kate Denny: pages 91, 94, 110, 128, 186. Getty Images: Bruce Ayres/Tony Stone, page 170; Chris Baker/Tony Stone, page 242; Kindra Clineff/Tony Stone, page 173; Bill Hickey/Image Bank, page 134 (right); David Madison/Tony Stone, page 161; Dick Makin, page 76; The Mooks, page 250; Ian Shaw/Tony Stone, page 165; Maria Taglienti/The Image Bank, pages 224–225; Tony Stone, pages 58, 224 (center). Richard Hutchings: pages 5 (bottom, right), 6, 8, 14, 38, 40, 48, 62, 100. The Image Works: page 133; L. Kolvoord, page 43; Larry Mulvehill, page 88; Skjold, page 269 (right). International Stock: Kirk Anderson, page 269 (left); Scott Barrow, pages 210–211; Vincent Graziani, page 280 (bottom); Victor Ramos, page 52. Ken Karp: pages xvi–1, 5 (left), 11, 13, 23, 26, 32, 41, 44, 54 (all), 56, 59, 60, 63, 64, 68, 73 (all), 75, 78, 79 (left), 87, 90, 92, 121, 122 (all), 123 (all), 125, 127, 129, 131, 136, 144, 180–181, 189 (all), 208–209, 212, 220, 228–229, 230, 244, 245, 249, 261, 264, 270, 272 (all), 275 (all), 286. James Keyser: page 285. Ken Lax: page 61 (center). David Mager: pages 104, 187, 224 (left), 282. Masterfile: Paul Eekhoff, page 109; Eliane, pages 46–47. Jordan Miller: pages 16, 118, 194. PhotoEdit: Robert Brenner, page 20 (right); Myrleen Ferguson, pages 225 (left), 114–115, 266; Tony Freeman, pages 12, 217; Richard Hutchings, pages 148–149, 256–257, 281; Felicia Martinez, page 225 (right); Michael Newman, page 224 (right); Jonathan Nourok, pages 225 (center), 271; Rudi Von Briel, page 75; David Young-Wolff, pages 93, 240. Photo Researchers Inc.: Michael Abbey, page 183 (top right); A. Glauberman/Science Source, page 219; Stevie Grand/Science Photo Library, page 276 (left); Dr. P. Marazzi/Science Photo Library, pages 198, 276 (bottom, right); Oliver Meckes/Ottawa, page 183 (bottom right); David M. Phillips, page 183 (bottom left); Tek Image/Science Photo Library, page 182; Jon Wilson/Science Photo Library, page 183 (top left). PictureQuest: Michael Newman/PhotoEdit, page 126; Frank Siteman/Stock Boston, page 265 (background). Punchstock, page 77. Michael Provost: pages 84–85, 252, 253. Science Source/PR: Bonnie Cosgrove, page 202 (middle), L. Stannard, page 202 (right). Stock Boston: Mark C. Burnett, page 280 (middle); Bob Daemmrich, pages 137, 243; John Lei, page 201. SuperStock: pages 4, 278, 279; Florian Franke, page 30; Kwame Zikomo, pages 82–83. Terry Sutherland: pages 99, 120, 130, 141. Unicorn Stock Photos: Aneal Vohra, page 265 (foreground). The Terry Wild Studio: pages 22, 34, 79 (right).

Illustrations

Tim Barnes: page 203. Ron Boisvert: pages 157, 214–215. Dan Brawner: pages 174–175. Jacques Bredy: pages 24–25. Max Crandall: page 38. Robert A. Deverell: pages 49, 98, 101, 102, 103, 135, 139, 145, 185, 193, 196, 197, 218, 232, 246, 283. Jerry Gonzalez: pages 70, 213, 262. Jim Higgins/The Mazer Corporation: page 15. David Kelley Design: pages 89, 95, 97, 153, 156, 166, 171, 200. Catherine Leery/Martha Productions: pages 33, 55, 138, 176–177, 184, 258–259. Andy Levine: pages 65, 116–117, 205. Alvalyn Lundgren: pages 87, 268, 273. Erin Mauterer/Bluewater: pages 286–287. Hilda Muinos: pages 86, 150–151, 155 (left), 159, 162, 163. Network Graphics: pages 42, 93, 96, 160, 167, 231, 233, 236, 267, 274. Parrot Graphics: pages 119, 237, 238. Mary Power: page 124. Tim Robinson: page 109. Precision Graphics: page 155 (right). Thomas Wells: page 223. Jerry Zimmerman: pages 21, 37, 66, 74, 110–111, 168, 221, 247, 263.